A DERRIDA READER

D0910966

A DERRIDA READER

BETWEEN THE BLINDS

Edited,

with an introduction and notes,

by Peggy Kamuf

Columbia University Press   New York

Columbia University Press

New York   Oxford

Copyright © 1991 Columbia University Press

All rights reserved

Library of Congress Cataloging-in-Publication Data

Derrida, Jacques.

[Selections. English. 1991]

A Derrida reader : between the blinds / edited by Peggy Kamuf.

p.   cm.

"With only one exception, all the excerpted translations
have been previously published"—Pref.

Includes bibliographical references and index.

ISBN 0-231-06658-9 (cloth).—ISBN 0-231-06659-7 (paper)

1. Philosophy. 2. Deconstruction.

I. Kamuf, Peggy, 1947– . II. Title.

B2430.D481D4713 1991

194—dc20

90-41354

CIP

Casebound editions of Columbia University Press books are Smyth-sewn
and printed on permanent and durable acid-free paper

Book design by Jennifer Dossin

Printed in the United States of America

c 10 9 8 7 6 5 4 3 2

p 10 9 8 7 6 5 4 3

Contents

Preface

In 1962, Jacques Derrida published a long critical introduction to his translation of Husserl's *The Origin of Geometry*. With that work he began what has proved to be one of the most stunning adventures of modern thought. It promised, from its first public acts, an explanation with philosophical traditions unlike any other. That promise has since been realized in more than twenty-two books and countless other uncollected essays, prefaces, interviews, and public interventions of various sorts. Many of these have been translated, integrally or in part, into English. And new texts are appearing regularly, as Derrida continues to write and to teach, in Europe and North America and indeed throughout the world.

Today, it is with the word *deconstruction* that many first associate Derrida's name. This word has had a remarkable career. Having first appeared in several texts that Derrida published in the mid-1960s, it soon became the preferred designator for the distinct approach and concerns that set his thinking apart. Derrida has confessed on several occasions that he has been somewhat surprised by the way this word came to be singled out, since he had initially proposed it in a chain with other words—for example, differance, spacing, trace—none of which can command the series or function as a master word.

No doubt the success of deconstruction as a term can be explained in part by its resonance with *structure* which was then, in the 1960s, the reigning word of structuralism. Any history of how the word deconstruction entered a certain North American vocabulary, for instance, would have to underscore its critical use in the first text by Derrida to be translated in the United States, "Structure, Sign, and Play in the Discourse of the Human Sciences." This was the text of a lecture delivered at Johns Hopkins University in 1966. In that lecture, he considered the structuralism of ethnologist Claude Lévi-Strauss whose thought, as Derrida remarked, was then exerting a strong influence on the conjuncture of contemporary theoretical activities. The word *de-construction* occurs in the following passage concerned with the inevitable, even necessary ethnocentrism of any science formed according to the concepts of the European scientific tradition. And yet, Derrida insists, there are different ways of giving in to this necessity:

> But if no one can escape this necessity, and if no one is there-
> fore responsible for giving in to it, however little he may do so,
> this does not mean that all the ways of giving in to it are of
> equal pertinence. The quality and fecundity of a discourse are
> perhaps measured by the critical rigor with which this relation
> to the history of metaphysics and to inherited concepts is
> thought. Here it is a question both of a critical relation to the
> language of the social sciences and a critical responsibility of
> the discourse itself. It is a question of explicitly and systemati-
> cally posing the problem of the status of a discourse which
> borrows from a heritage the resources necessary for the de-
> construction of that heritage itself. A problem of *economy* and
> *strategy*.*

As used here, "de-construction" marks a distance (the space of a hyphen, later dropped) from the structuring or construction of dis-courses, such as Levi-Strauss', that have uncritically taken over the legacy of Western metaphysics. If, however, it cannot be a matter of refusing this legacy—"no one can escape from it"—then the dis-tance or difference in question is in the manner of assuming respon-sibility for what cannot be avoided. Deconstruction is one name Derrida has given to this responsibility. It is not a refusal or a destruction of the terms of the legacy, but occurs through a re-marking and redeployment of these very terms, that is, the concepts of philosophy. And this raises the problem, as Derrida puts it, "of the status of a discourse which borrows from a heritage the resources necessary for the de-construction of that heritage itself." It is in the critical space of this problem, which needs to be thought through rigorously, systematically, and responsibly, that Derrida proposes to situate his discourse.

---

* *Writing and Difference* [1967], p. 289. All quotations of Derrida's works are from published translations where available. For complete reference, consult the bibliography at the end of this volume by the date given in brackets (e.g., here 1967).

Since its introduction, the work of Jacques Derrida has traced wide and diverse paths of influence both within and without the academic disciplines, wherever the relation to the heritage of Western thought has become critical. Although this influence may have been felt first among literary theorists, it quickly overran the boundaries of literary studies or of any academic discipline. Theologians, architects, film makers and critics, painters, legal scholars, musicians, dramatists, psychoanalysts, feminists, and other political and social theorists have all found indispensable support for their reflection and practice in Derrida's writing. Even philosophy in America, which began trying to purge itself of continental influences more than a century ago, has had to yield significant ground to Derrida's insistent questioning of the philosophical discipline. Thus, although one can still hear or read statements to the effect that Derridean deconstruction is the affair of a few North American literary critics, the odds are good that they are coming from a philosopher who is trying to ignore the obvious of what is going on all around him or her.

Such discursive tactics of containment or denegation have flourished in the vicinity of deconstruction, and not only among philosophers. Both academic journals and the popular press have now and then bristled with indignation when confronted with the evidence that deconstruction is taking hold in the North American cultural landscape. But this is understandable; Derrida's work *is* disconcerting and deliberately so. The present collection of essays and extracts will not conceal that fact. A reader who wants to approach this writing is therefore urged to proceed patiently, as well as carefully. Be advised that the most familiar may well begin to appear strangely different. As Derrida writes in one of the extracts from *Of Grammatology* included here, his final intention is "to make enigmatic what one thinks one understands by the words 'proximity,' 'immediacy,' 'presence'," that is, the very words with which we designate what is closest to us.

As to the choice and arrangement of texts, I have followed several principles and endeavored to make them compatible with each other. The easiest and most conventional of these is a very roughly chronological ordering that can serve to illustrate some of the ways Derrida has reshaped his thought over the last twenty or so years. Between the earliest texts included here (extracts from *Speech and Phenomena* and *Of Grammatology*) and the most recent ones, however, there is also an undeniable constancy and coherence which belie any superficial impression that Derrida has revised or moved away from some former or initial way of thinking. Indeed, one of the more extraordinary things about Derrida's thought is the way it has shaped itself along a double axis or according to a double exigency: it seems always to be moving beyond itself and yet nothing is left behind. The first writings remaining implied in the succeeding ones, they are literally folded into different shapes and yet do not lose their own particular shape in the process. Nevertheless, because the work advances by bringing its past along, it is necessary up to a point to respect its chronology.

No sooner, however, has one underscored the coherence of these writings than one must acknowledge as well their remarkable diversity in subject, theme, form, tone, procedure, occasion, and so on. Here a second principle is called for, one that does not present itself so easily. The solution I have come to for grouping texts is, needless to say, only one of the many that could have been chosen to represent this diversity. As the reader will soon see, I have applied in effect no single principle but have grouped the sets of selections according each time to a different, loosely defined criterion. Numerous other criteria suggested themselves as did so many other texts that had to be left out. What is more, almost all of the texts included here would fit in several of the categories. This is but one of many possible Derrida "readers."

As to why there are so many extracts and so few complete essays, I decided, rightly or wrongly, that only this method permitted a tolerable, though still insufficient representation of the diversity and continuity of Derrida's work. I admit, however, that I hesitated long before adopting this procedure. Derrida's writings are intricately structured and perform a delicate balancing act between recalling where they have been and forewarning where they are going. The majority of them are deployed around extensive quotation of other works and they elaborate complex patterns of *renvois*. Most often the texts juxtapose and counter one style or tone with another, shifting, for example, between the strictest form of philosophical commentary and writing of a sort that such commentary has always by definition, excluded. Needless to say, much of this intricacy, balance, and counterplay has been sacrificed by the technique of cutting out excerpts of the texts. On the one hand, I have consoled myself for this loss with the thought that, with few exceptions, all of the works excerpted here are readily available *in extenso*, and thus no reader of *A Derrida Reader* need be content with shortened versions (see the appended bibliography which also lists some suggestions for secondary reading). I made a mental note to remind readers of this fact which is what I am doing now. On the other hand, I garnered a certain courage to excerpt so ruthlessly from Derrida's own repeated insistence on the partialness of any text, a partialness that is not recuperable in some eventual whole or totality. Moreover, the notions of cutting, grafting, piecing together—extracting—are everywhere in evidence in Derrida's texts, both as themes and as practices, until they are virtually coextensive with the text he is always interrogating and performing. Indeed, the masterful work *Glas* may be read as a long reflection on cutting, which is always culpable, put into practice. This is one reason I have placed a series of brief passages from that work in the spaces between the sections. These may be thought of as blinds or jalousies lowered into place as reminders: "Look at the holes, if you can"; read between the blinds.

Ultimately, however, there is no final justification of this cutting and splicing. A desire was always obscurely in play (and desire is the very order of the unjustifiable) to offer up for another reading texts that I have returned to more than once out of love and respect, but also probably out of an unfathomable puzzlement. No doubt it is the utterly naïve desire that, by presenting these texts to be read again, I will get back some signs of my own understanding.

And that leads me to a final principle—or rather, less a principle than a wish that accompanied the editing of these pages. It is that this volume should engage each of its readers differently even as it made certain texts available to a broader general comprehension. I wanted it to be possible, in other words, for every reader to encoun ter both the same and a different book as all other readers, and for the same prepared trajectory to be nevertheless each time singular and unpredictable. How to reconcile these two aims? No answer presented itself in simple terms; instead, a reflection on that question resulted in the essay "Reading Between the Blinds" which is given here in the guise of an introduction to the selected excerpts and essays. It may be read as the record of a negotiation, or exposition, between two versions of *A Derrida Reader.*

With only one exception, all the excerpted translations have been previously published and are reproduced here most often with only minor changes, if any. It should be said that Derrida's writing actively resists translation by seeking out the most idiomatic points in the language, by reactivating lost meanings, by accumulating as far as possible the resources of undecidability which lie dormant in syntax, morphology, and semantics. The result can often seem obscure to whoever has been taught that a standard of so-called clarity of style is the first and indispensable criterion of expository prose. But Derrida never cultivates this "obscurity" for its own sake; on the contrary, the apparent density of his writing has its correlative in a relentless demand for clarity of another order, which may be called, in a seeming paradox, a clarity about the obscurity, opacity, and fundamental difference of language. Standard notions of clarity or "correct" style, when viewed from this perspective, must be seen as, themselves, obscurantist since they encourage a belief in the transparency of words to thoughts, and thus a "knowledge" constructed on this illusion. Deconstructing this knowledge will necessarily be a matter of some difficulty.

INTRODUCTION

Reading Between the Blinds

The following is not exactly a dialogue, although in places it resembles an exchange that might actually have taken place between two interlocutors. Yet, one will notice as well a certain inconstancy in this resemblance. It is perhaps a typographical rather than a dialogic form that has imposed itself here, the back and forth of more than one "voice" requiring the convention of blank intervals across the page. These, in turn, could be thought of as the slats of a venetian blind, or a jalousie, which partially obstructs the view.*

———*A Derrida Reader:* Already I see a difficulty with that title, with the concept of "reader."

———Perhaps, then, that is also the place to begin. Let me guess: you are thinking of the difficulty there would be in negotiating between the two senses of the term, between the "someone who reads" and the "something that is read." Right? It is indeed a rather unusual word in that way, and offhand I don't know of many other nominalizations that can produce a similar palindromic syntax: "A reader reads a reader." But maybe there is a reason for that. . . .

———Yes, yes. I'm listening.

———Well, imagine a somewhat peculiar dictionary entry for the word *reader*. Instead of referring one to the the verb with a phrase

---

* Titles of works included or extracted herein are printed in boldface; boldface page numbers for quotations refer to pages in this volume. All other page references are to the edition of the translation listed by date in the bibliography.

like "someone who reads," it says, "you at this moment." That's all. Such a "definition" transgresses the rules of lexicography in several ways, for example, in the use of the second-person pronoun and of the deictic *this*. Its greatest fault or idiosyncrasy, however, is that it supplies only an *example* of how the word could be correctly used (you, at this moment, are reading these words; you are thus a reader) and fails to supply the general meaning of the word abstracted from any singular moment of a particular reader's experience. The definition, that is, fails to respect the order of the *concept* as that which gives meaning to any *experience*. This "order of the concept" is not just an order of implication, of priority or anteriority; it is as well an order of command or commandment given to the reader, the order of a "thou shalt" or a "thou shalt not." It says, in effect: Thou shalt read thine own experience as commanded by the concept of reading; thou shalt read according to the law and submit thine understanding to its order; thou shalt not put the instance of thine own singular reading or idiosyncratic understanding before the law. Now, read this and obey, which is also to say, do *not* read this before submitting to its order. But to receive the order, must one not have already transgressed it by reading it?

———It's like the famous graffito, "Do not read this."

———Exactly. That negative imperative phrase enacts, in the most economical fashion, the predicament of a double bind. The reader is already at fault before the law, before the law which comes *before* or *already:* by reading the command, he or she ignores it; but ignoring the command (by not reading it) does not rectify things, does not equal obedience to a command that also demands to be read, that is, to be acknowledged as command in order to have the force of a command. Thus, the "someone who reads" is but the stage of a certain performance positioned by this double bind. That performance is always, in one way or another, to be compared to the act of reading a dictionary entry for *reader:* before one can receive the order of the concept, one has already given an example of it. The predicament is temporal (but qualifying it in this or any other manner does not resolve it; the predicament remains whole, at this very moment) because the meaning of the act (its concept) is not given in the present of its performance, it is not one with or immanent to the act, but divides that "moment" upon itself, disperses it among the non-present modes of before and after the act. The reader reads before the law that he or she comes after. Neither the singularity of an act nor the generality of a concept of reading or meaning can be thought of as absolutely prior to the other, as a cause or condition of possibility of the other. Or rather, both are at once conditions of the other. On the one hand, the order of the concept requires the very act of reading that it defines and defies; on the other hand, the reading act will have been already determined by the order of the concept. Rather than a logical order of determining priority, this relation is one of an irreducible difference, that is, a relation that cannot be comprised by one or the other of the terms. Each moment or term is only insofar as it *is related* to the other. Each moment or term is cut across, divided by the other. Each inscribes the other in itself and is inscribed by the other outside of itself.

———What you have just described sounds very much like the structure of what Derrida has called the trace or differance. Look at the essay titled **"Différance"** . . .

———Yes, of course, I was thinking of that, and it is not in the least surprising that we should encounter the problematic of the trace as soon as we begin reflecting on reading and readers. But the same problematic also requires a shift in the way we think of the reading "act": instead of centered in or originating in a subject, a consciousness, a "reader" in that sense, what we call reading would occur in the opening of the trace. Listen to this, from the first chapter of **Of Grammatology** where Derrida puts in place several of the concept-like terms, such as trace, differance, archi-writing, that form the theoretical armature of his earliest writings:

> This trace is the opening of the first exteriority in general, the enigmatic relationship of the living to its other and of an inside to an outside: spacing. The outside, "spatial" and "objective" exteriority which we believe we know as the most familiar thing in the world, as familiarity itself, would not appear without the grammē, without differance as temporalization, without the nonpresence of the other inscribed within the meaning of the present, without the relation to death as the concrete structure of the living present. . . . The presence–absence of the trace. . . ." (pp. 42–43).

Perhaps what we call a reader is precisely the impossibility of a *position* which is not already a *relation,* an ex-position to something (someone?) other. Perhaps, as well, this ex-posing of the reader explains that other common use of the term: a reader, not in the sense of someone who reads, but in the sense of a collection of sample texts, of the sort, for example, that was frequently in use in American primary education until not long ago. As pedagogical instruments of reading discipline, these primers or anthologies, which most often subordinated literacy to moral instruction (for what was the purpose of learning to read if not to read and submit to the moral law?), were called readers by means, it would seem, of a metonymical displacement from the "product" of the instructional activity— the formed or disciplined reader—to one of its instruments. The displacement, in other words, passes between what are taken to be the active and passive faces of reading—from the "someone who reads" to the "something that is read." This grammatical, syntactical convention relies on the mode of the transitive verb to space out active subject from passive object. But there is another convention at work here—call it the pedagogical convention, the convention of moral education, a whole tradition of reading (as) discipline—which reverses the transitive direction of the reading lesson. According to this latter convention, the reader is a pupil who must be submitted to the order of the moral law as given by that other reader, the text (and as translated or interpreted by the figure of the teacher who seemingly stands outside this interpretive scene, a mere animator of the voice of the law). Thus, the reader-text acts on the reader-pupil, reading his or her faults, illuminating the dark recesses of the soul, and exposing them to the light of moral reason. Yet, despite the contrary tensions of these two conventions, the grammatical-syntactic convention and the moral-pedagogical convention, they remain fundamentally conjoined in their very reversibility, a reversibility that, if all goes well, ends in the finished product of a moral subject fully formed by a reading apprenticeship. And, in any case, the teacher is there to assure, with his or her own example, the finality of the lesson and to assume as needed the position of the text's master. More important, however, these two reading conventions join together to master the relation reader–reader (pupil– text), to bring it to reason by installing a finally stable distinction between them.

Yet if the reader is not a position but an ex-posed relation, then it is only as a matter of convenience and convention that we speak of the active and passive poles of the reading "activity" (or "passivity," perhaps even passion). The grammatical distinction or division conventionally made *between* the two senses of the word (reader–reader, active–passive) would have covered over a division or difference *within* "reader(s)," within the relation designated by that word which, precisely because it is a differential relation rather than a unified point, makes for uneasy reference as soon as one steps a little outside lockstep convention. For the sake of convenient reference, we must have recourse to pronoun substitutes which, inevitably, substitute an identity for a difference. Thus do we speak of the reader, *it* or *he* or *she* or *I* or *you*. With each distinction, a decision—that is, a cut —is made that arrests the transfer (or inscription) within difference: inanimate or animate, nonhuman or human, masculine or feminine (a distinction that invariably accompanies the other distinction of active from passive), addressor or addressee.

——Are you suggesting that these discursive habits, the decisions operated by discourse, should be broken or discarded?

——No, of course not, because discourse is possible only on the condition of such decisions. I was merely attempting to recall the difference that the *convenience* of discursive reference (but what, exactly, is the value of this convenience? for whom is it convenient?) too easily relegates to oblivion: the difference between linguistic, discursive institutions of meaning and the ex-posed space of differential relations—the space opened up by the movement of differance —within which or on which such institutions come to stand. Mistaking the former for the latter, the structures of language for that which opens the very possibility of meaning, substituting the closure of constructed, instituted identities for this opening to and by difference is an essential trait of what Jacques Derrida has called *logocentrism*.

——And he has called deconstruction the work by which these institutions, which are not just linguistic institutions, are being opened to the difference or exteriority repressed—forgotten in a strong sense—within them.

In sum, then, you are saying that *A Derrida Reader* ought to remark as far as possible the ex-position you have just described. Otherwise, what is the point? Much of Derrida's work has been translated and is widely, easily available. So why collect a very small part of it in one volume? Merely for someone's convenience (that word again!)? Here, then, is the first risk or difficulty: it is the risk of occulting the eruptive movement of the trace so that it can be more conveniently presented. And with that, *A Derrida Reader* could well end up absorbed by the structures that are always at work obliterating or reducing the trace, the very structures, in other words, that these writings ought to deconstruct.

Yet isn't that also inevitable from the moment—always and already—that, as Derrida writes in the same chapter of **Of Grammatology,** "the movement of the trace is necessarily occulted; it is produced as self-occultation. When the other announces itself as such, it presents itself in the dissimulation of itself" ([1967], p. 47). So I don't see how . . .

——Yes, yes, of course, and I'm not suggesting you have to seek some pure exteriority, some extra- or counter-institutional purity. On the contrary. Derrida's thinking, as you know, is all about the necessary contamination of insides and outsides, and deconstruction always works at the margins, on the limits of this organizing opposition. I was thinking, instead, of the rather facile judgments that have been made concerning the so-called institutionalization of deconstruction. That charge, and it is indeed meant to have the force of a charge or accusation, has always seemed to me to depend on at least two fundamental misconceptions. In the first place, there is the same naïve conception of a pure exteriority that I just mentioned: according to such a notion, deconstruction can prove its "purity" only by demonstrating that it has no effect whatever within institutions, that it does not let itself be contaminated by institutional concerns. But in the second place, there is what appears to be a deliberate confusion over the word or the name *deconstruction.* You said a moment ago something like this: "Deconstruction names the movement or work which is opening institutions to the difference forgotten within them." I would only add that, as a name, deconstruction, like any other name, is replaceable; its effacement is even made necessary or predicted by the disaggregation of the traits of the "proper" (as in "proper name") which deconstruction uncovers in its wake. Deconstruction, then, does not name a theory, a method, a school, or any other such delimitable entity. Instead, deconstruction is what is going on, happening, coming to pass, or coming about, all intransitive locutions that dislocate the predicate's tie to any stable present. That the name has been taken by some to be the name of a school of thought, a method of reading, or a theory of some kind is exactly the sort of logocentric confusion that deconstruction has made apparent.

——That helps me to formulate another difficulty I foresee in bringing this reader to term. The confusion you have just indicated

well end up absorbed by the structures that are always at work obliterating or reducing the trace, the very structures, in other words, that these writings ought to deconstruct.

Yet isn't that also inevitable from the moment—always and already—that, as Derrida writes in the same chapter of **Of Grammatology,** "the movement of the trace is necessarily occulted; it is produced as self-occultation. When the other announces itself as such, it presents itself in the dissimulation of itself" ([1967], p. 47). So I don't see how . . .

——Yes, yes, of course, and I'm not suggesting you have to seek some pure exteriority, some extra- or counter-institutional purity. On the contrary. Derrida's thinking, as you know, is all about the necessary contamination of insides and outsides, and deconstruction always works at the margins, on the limits of this organizing opposition. I was thinking, instead, of the rather facile judgments that have been made concerning the so-called institutionalization of deconstruction. That charge, and it is indeed meant to have the force of a charge or accusation, has always seemed to me to depend on at least two fundamental misconceptions. In the first place, there is the same naïve conception of a pure exteriority that I just mentioned: according to such a notion, deconstruction can prove its "purity" only by demonstrating that it has no effect whatever within institutions, that it does not let itself be contaminated by institutional concerns. But in the second place, there is what appears to be a deliberate confusion over the word or the name *deconstruction*. You said a moment ago something like this: "Deconstruction names the movement or work which is opening institutions to the difference forgotten within them." I would only add that, as a name, deconstruction, like any other name, is replaceable; its effacement is even made necessary or predicted by the disagregation of the traits of the "proper" (as in "proper name") which deconstruction uncovers in its wake. Deconstruction, then, does not name a theory, a method, a school, or any other such delimitable entity. Instead, deconstruction is what is going on, happening, coming to pass, or coming about, all intransitive locutions that dislocate the predicate's tie to any stable present. That the name has been taken by some to be the name of a school of thought, a method of reading, or a theory of some kind is exactly the sort of logocentric confusion that deconstruction has made apparent.

——That helps me to formulate another difficulty I foresee in bringing this reader to term. The confusion you have just indicated

the generality of a concept of reading or meaning can be thought of as absolutely prior to the other, as a cause or condition of possibility of the other. Or rather, both are at once conditions of the other. On the one hand, the order of the concept requires the very act of reading that it defines and defies; on the other hand, the reading act will have been already determined by the order of the concept. Rather than a logical order of determining priority, this relation is one of an irreducible difference, that is, a relation that cannot be comprised by one or the other of the terms. Each moment or term is only insofar as it *is related* to the other. Each moment or term is cut across, divided by the other. Each inscribes the other in itself and is inscribed by the other outside of itself.

——What you have just described sounds very much like the structure of what Derrida has called the trace or difference. Look at the essay titled **"Différance"** . . .

——Yes, of course, I was thinking of that, and it is not in the least surprising that we should encounter the problematic of the trace as soon as we begin reflecting on reading and readers. But the same problematic also requires a shift in the way we think of the reading "act": instead of centered in or originating in a subject, a consciousness, a "reader" in that sense, what we call reading would occur in the opening of the trace. Listen to this, from the first chapter of **Of Grammatology** where Derrida puts in place several of the concept-like terms, such as trace, differance, archi-writing, that form the theoretical armature of his earliest writings:

> This trace is the opening of the first exteriority in general, the enigmatic relationship of the living to its other and of an inside to an outside: spacing. The outside, "spatial" and "objective" exteriority which we believe we know as the most familiar thing in the world, as familiarity itself, would not appear without the grammē, without differance as temporalization, without the nonpresence of the other inscribed within the meaning of the present, without the relation to death as the concrete structure of the living present. . . . The presence–absence of the trace. . . ." (pp. **42–43**).

Perhaps what we call a reader is precisely the impossibility of a *position* which is not already a *relation*, an ex-position to something (someone?) other. Perhaps, as well, this ex-posing of the reader explains that other common use of the term: a reader, not in the sense of someone who reads, but in the sense of a collection of sample texts, of the sort, for example, that was frequently in use in American primary education until not long ago. As pedagogical instruments of reading discipline, these primers or anthologies, which most often subordinated literacy to moral instruction (for what was the purpose of learning to read if not to read and submit to the moral law?), were called readers by means, it would seem, of a metonymical displacement from the "product" of the instructional activity—the formed or disciplined reader—to one of its instruments. The displacement, in other words, passes between what are taken to be the active and passive faces of reading—from the "someone who reads" to the "something that is read." This grammatical, syntactical convention relies on the mode of the transitive verb to space out active subject from passive object. But there is another convention at work here—call it the pedagogical convention, the convention of moral education, a whole tradition of reading (as) discipline—which reverses the transitive direction of the reading lesson. According to this latter convention, the reader is a pupil who must be submitted to the order of the moral law as given by that other reader, the text (and as translated or interpreted by the figure of the teacher who seemingly stands outside this interpretive scene, a mere animator of the voice of the law). Thus, the reader-text acts on the reader-pupil, reading his or her faults, illuminating the dark recesses of the soul, and exposing them to the light of moral reason. Yet, despite the contrary tensions of these two conventions, the grammatical-syntactic convention and the moral-pedagogical convention, they remain fundamentally conjoined in their very reversibility, a reversibility that, if all goes well, ends in the finished product of a moral subject fully formed by a reading apprenticeship. And, in any case, the teacher is there to assure, with his or her own example, the finality of the lesson and to assume as needed the position of the text's master. More important, however, these two reading conventions join together to master the relation reader–reader (pupil–text), to bring it to reason by installing a finally stable distinction between them.

Yet if the reader is not a position but an ex-posed relation, then it is only as a matter of convenience and convention that we speak of the active and passive poles of the reading "activity" (or "passivity," perhaps even passion). The grammatical distinction or division conventionally made *between* the two senses of the word (reader–reader, active–passive) would have covered over a division or difference

within "reader(s)," within the relation designated by that word which, precisely because it is a differential relation rather than a unified point, makes for uneasy reference as soon as one steps a little outside lockstep convention. For the sake of convenient reference, we must have recourse to pronoun substitutes which, inevitably, substitute an identity for a difference. Thus do we speak of the reader, *it* or *he* or *she* or *I* or *you*. With each distinction, a decision—that is, a cut—is made that arrests the transfer (or inscription) within difference: inanimate or animate, nonhuman or human, masculine or feminine (a distinction that invariably accompanies the other distinction of active from passive), addressor or addressee.

——Are you suggesting that these discursive habits, the decisions operated by discourse, should be broken or discarded?

——No, of course not, because discourse is possible only on the condition of such decisions. I was merely attempting to recall the difference that the *convenience* of discursive reference (but what, exactly, is the value of this convenience? for whom is it convenient?) too easily relegates to oblivion: the difference between linguistic, discursive institutions of meaning and the ex-posed space of differential relations—the space opened up by the movement of differance—within which or on which such institutions come to stand. Mistaking the former for the latter, the structures of language for that which opens the very possibility of meaning, substituting the closure of constructed, instituted identities for this opening to and by difference is an essential trait of what Jacques Derrida has called *logocentrism*.

——And he has called deconstruction the work by which these institutions, which are not just linguistic institutions, are being opened to the difference or exteriority repressed—forgotten in a strong sense—within them.

In sum, then, you are saying that *A Derrida Reader* ought to remark as far as possible the ex-position you have just described. Otherwise, what is the point? Much of Derrida's work has been translated and is widely, easily available. So why collect a very small part of it in one volume? Merely for someone's convenience (that word again!)? Here, then, is the first risk or difficulty: it is the risk of occulting the eruptive movement of the trace so that it can be more conveniently presented. And with that, *A Derrida Reader* could

has become widespread. Even experienced teachers and scholars, eminent critics, and philosophers speak of the "theory" or the "method" of deconstruction, and often in order to tax it with a theoretical inconsistency or insufficiency. This distortion has achieved a certain currency which creates an expectation. The expectation goes something like this: If, as so many say, deconstruction is a method, a theory, a school, then one ought to be able to design a manual that describes its tenets, defines its terms, and classifies its principal texts. Now, *A Derrida Reader . . .*

——. . . has to serve a certain, let's say, pedagogical function?

——Yes, but it cannot do so simply by meeting this expectation, or submitting to this virtual demand for a reassuring map of unfamiliar territory. Whereas most written material may be only too eager to find and take up its place on the map of known coordinates, so that it can be easily recognized by the largest number, some texts are writing *on* the map itself, displacing the boundaries, blotting out the cardinal reference points, thus making it more difficult to read off the coordinates. Accordingly, these texts are called "difficult." In the case of Derrida's texts, of this writing *on* writing ("but you know I never write *on* anything . . . I seek above all to produce effects (on you)" writes the signatory of "**Envois**"), one might be tempted to deal with this difficulty by extracting another set of coordinates with which to orient reading. These coordinates would take their names from the Derridean corpus and would, if possible, come together as a meta-text or a meta-language with which to discipline and order the landscape of that corpus. Such ordering would have a pedagogical aim that is entirely laudable. But the pedagogical aim has to misfire in its concern, precisely, to help wanderers find their bearings there where the street signs have been turned around or, more disturbingly, where they have been made to point off at an angle to every intersection. The problem for this or any reader is therefore how to find and show a way into these writings which does not *simply* restore the kind of order they would put in question?

——What if, however, this were not a problem to be solved, but rather a demand or a command, something like "Do not read this," which one can neither faithfully obey nor simply betray? In that case, the question would be *how not to betray* a text whose self-betrayal is the very condition of its readability—for nothing could ever become readable unless it betrayed itself, gave itself away.

——Yes, yes, I see that.

——"How not to betray?" This form of question is one Derrida has explored in a text titled "How to Avoid Speaking" [1987]. It is at once rhetorical and not rhetorical. That is, it says at once that one *cannot* avoid betrayal; it is a statement in the form of a question. But it also asks: Given this inevitability, which modes of betrayal are nevertheless to be avoided? How must one *not* betray? There thus appears, with this latter inflection of the question, the possibility of a faithfulness to the text's betrayal of itself. It is a faithfulness, however, that is now reinscribed in a general economy of (self-) betrayal.

This is the question or demand to which you must respond, to which you are already responding, although as yet rather inchoately. Shall I go on?

——Yes, I will interrupt you before long.

——You are asking how not to betray, how to respond to the text's double demand: "Read me! But, whatever you do, do not read me!" That is, read (hear, understand, translate, respond to) *me*; and do not confuse me with others, with all the other *me*'s who may use the same language, who, like me, are constricted and surpassed by this use. But, on the other hand, you also worry about meeting the expectation for a manual, a map, or a meta-language. It is there, between the demand and the expectation, that your ex-position must occur, has, in fact, already begun. On both sides, the question: "How to read—Derrida?" If you respond with a generality that would be valid for anyone and everyone (a manual), you betray the demand for a singular reading. If, however, your singular response has no general validity, then *A Derrida Reader* will be unreadable. In fact, of course, neither one of these responses is strictly possible without engaging the other, without ex-posing the other. That is the movement of the trace. Generalization is always limited, constricted by an unassimilable and singular other that is each time different; and singularities can always be generalized, which is both a misery—and a chance. So now you have to . . .

——Take a chance? You were right that I had already begun to respond, but at a kind of threshold or liminal space on the edge of what I heard you saying. When you spoke about betrayal of the other, self-betrayal, faithfulness, another word began to take shape for me, as if on the command of some silent dictation: the word *jealousy.* Not just the word, of course, not just its referent or the "thing" called jealousy, but a web of relations that all pass through jealousy. Resonating somewhere near the center of this web, a vaguely remembered phrase, almost totally detached from any context, something like "In everything I talk about, jealousy is at stake." It occurs in a polyvocal text of Derrida's, and, as I recall, it is spoken by a feminine interlocutor. And when you came to the question "How to read—Derrida?" it made contact with this web and set off a vibration that I will translate in these terms: What if, to be "faithful" to the (self-)betrayal of Derrida's writing, one must pay attention to what it has to say about jealousy? And not only to what it has to say *about* it—jealousy as a theme, a topic, or a subject—but to a certain movement *through* jealousy, in the sense of both *of* and *against:* the movement *of* jealousy, as that through which movement is given or provoked; and the movement *against* jealousy, as that through which movement passes and which offers a resistance. What if, in other words, jealousy were indeed "at stake" in *everything* Derrida talks about? And what would happen if we looked at Derrida's work through such a particular device, a device for selecting, cutting, extracting which leaves whole large areas in shadow?

——But you said you thought that phrase was spoken by a feminine voice, that is, one which, even if it is comprised by Derrida's signature on that text, cannot be simply identified as Jacques Derrida speaking in his own name, self-referentially, and so on. Doesn't that make any difference?

——Yes, it makes all the difference. Just as it makes all the difference that, as I said a moment ago, the word jealousy took shape through a kind of silent dictation. In effect, you gave me the word and the order to follow it. The hypothesis would be this: If jealousy is indeed at stake in everything he talks about, then it is not Derrida himself who says so or who authorizes that description of his writing. And yet it comes from him, but as if from another than himself. I am sure that if we look at this structure more closely, we will see that it is already caught up in a jealous movement, a movement *through* jealousy.

——And one that does not stop at the limits, the apparent limits of a printed text; it can carry over, be translated off the page, into other texts, but not only other texts. Here, for example . . .

———Of course, but first, some preliminary grounding of my hypothesis (or rather yours because you have given it to me; later, perhaps, I'll ask you whether gifts are ever exempt from jealousy, whether they are even possible without jealousy): Derrida often speaks of jealousy, but almost always in passing or on a sidetrack from the principal path of a text. He has never devoted more than a few lines, at most a paragraph, to the problem of jealousy although he has always marked it as a problem whenever he speaks of it. Yet it never comes under sustained scrutiny, never quite comes into focus. If it did not seem to be rushing things a little, one might conclude that some kind of jealous guard had been mounted around the subject.

———Yes, that would be a hasty conclusion, a short-circuit. You said yourself that "it comes from him, but as if from another than himself." If this jealousy is guarded, then that guard is not always on guard. So I advise you to take another tack. For example, can you avoid asking whose jealousy is "at stake" here?

———No, I won't avoid it, but will ask the question somewhat differently. I want to follow a double movement through jealousy, and that movement can always fold jealousy back onto itself, set it against itself, make it jealous of itself. If jealousy can always double itself, then the question of *whose* jealousy we are tracking through these texts (or simply the question "who?") has to lead us away from the double figure jealous of itself and therefore already (an)other than itself. I will even risk a second preliminary hypothesis: If jealousy were indeed a simple attribute assignable to a subject, so that the question "who?" could receive a simple answer, then it could not be provoked and would not even arise. Instead of a simple attribute, jealousy is always jealousy of the other: one has to try to hear that phrase in both of its senses at once.

But I think the tack you want me to take goes in a different sense. The question "who?" may not be so easily dismissed as we approach the heart of the subject of jealousy. It is as if that question and that subject were related, possibly even the same, as if "who?" were already a jealous question, posed on the restless edge of an answer that is both desired and feared. So let us ask it anyway: whose jealousy?

Is it the jealousy of God? What kind of answer is that? Such a figure occurs frequently in Derrida's texts. I'll show you a few of these places. First, however, there is the Scripture: "For I the Lord thy God am a jealous God, visiting the iniquity of the fathers upon the children unto the third and fourth generation of them who hate me" (Deuteronomy 5:9). The God who is said to be jealous not only demands an exclusive devotion ("Thou shalt have no other gods before me") but also refuses to manifest Himself, forbids the substitution of an image for this non-manifestation ("Thou shalt not make unto thee any graven image"), including the substitution of written symbols for His name. The uniqueness and unicity of God must forever prevent His appearance through any kind of substitute, any doubling of the eternal One and the Same. God, who is unique and uniquely the one who is, cannot tolerate a double, a replacement, a representative.

But the jealousy of God also scandalizes reason, as Derrida at one point recalls with this quotation fron Spinoza:

> However, as we should depart as little as possible from the literal sense, we must first ask whether this text, God is a fire *(Deus est ignis)*, admits of any but the literal meaning. . . . However, as we find the name fire applied to anger and jealousy (see Job 31:12), we can thus easily reconcile the words of Moses, and legitimately conclude that the two propositions of Moses, God is a fire, and God is jealous *(zelotypus)*, are in meaning identical. Further, as Moses clearly teaches that God is jealous . . . we must evidently infer that Moses held this doctrine himself, or at any rate that he wished to teach it, nor must we refrain because *such a belief seems contrary to reason.* (**Ulysses Gramophone** [1987], p. 40, n. 1; italics added.)

Spinoza's rational exegesis, in which fire and jealousy are metaphors for each other, readily admits, despite the scandal for reason, the substitutability which jealousy both forbids and commands: it forbids that Moses should see an image of God Himself, His double; and it commands that the image be presented and consumed in the burning bush. "God is a fire" is a metaphor not only *for* jealousy, but one whose very manifestation as metaphor is inscribed by the movement of jealousy. God's jealousy moves to subtract His name and face from the substitutions of metaphor, but in forbidding substitution, it commands that there must be (only) substitution.

Derrida has translated the scene of God's jealousy in several texts —and translated it, precisely, as the scene of translation. The story of the Tower of Babel in *Genesis* is a story of God's jealousy, provoked by the pretensions of men

> *to make a name for themselves,* to give themselves the name, to construct themselves their own name, to gather themselves there . . . as in the unity of a place which is at once a tongue and a tower, the one as well as the other, the one as the other. He punishes them for having thus wanted to assure themselves, by themselves a unique and universal genealogy. . . . *Can we not, then, speak of a jealousy of God?* [italics added] Out of resentment against that unique name and lip of men, he imposes his name, his name of father; and with this violent imposition, he opens the deconstruction of the tower, as of the universal language; he scatters the genealogical filiation. He breaks the lineage. He *at the same time* imposes and forbids translation. He imposes and forbids it, constrains, but as if to failure, the children who henceforth *will bear* his name. (**"Des Tours de Babel," pp. 248–49**)

Translation becomes "necessary and impossible," writes Derrida, "as the effect of a struggle for the appropriation of the name"; it is "necessary and forbidden in the interval between two absolutely proper names." Again, the double bind, which Derrida renders as, "Translate my name; but, whatever you do, do not translate my name." Because the proper name of God, Babel, which can be confused with a homonym in the language of the Shemites, a common noun meaning "confusion," is itself divided, *"God deconstructs. Himself"* (**p. 249**). The destruction of the Tower of Babel, the imposition of the multiplicity of languages, and with it the necessity and impossibility of translation—these are traits of what Derrida calls here the deconstruction of God. It is a movement through jealousy: God's jealousy against the jealousy of the Shemites. God interrupts the completion of the tower which would have erected the name of Shem as the sole name, the sole language of men. This project of gathering men together under one name, the name of a father to whom all future generations would remain bound, is made to fail when God—out of jealousy—proclaims his own name, Babel, which the Shemites cannot appropriate without confusion into their language. The clamor of God's name rends the univocality of the community, opens within it the rift of the other's name that cannot be subsumed to the same, the Shem. But at the same time as God gives his name to the sons of Shem, He loses it as a properly proper name. The Shemites are dispersed among many tongues, but so is God's name that can impose itself only by deposing or deconstructing its own unity. In order to reach men's ears and constrain them to hear

His name above all others, God must go outside Himself and risk the confusion of that name with a common noun, its generalization in the other's language, its difference from itself. Hence, the deconstruction of God will have been, from the origin, a movement of difference within which a unity of the proper tries and fails to impose itself as absolutely proper.

———I am getting caught up in your web, the subtle, just visible threads going from one text to the other. Here, for example, jealousy of the proper and the proper name is linked, at one end, to these lines which one can read in **Glas**: "What is the excess of zeal around a signature? Can one be jealous of anything other than a *seing?*" (**Glas** [1974] pp. 70–71). (The last word, an archaic term for signature, sounds like and is made to resonate throughout with *sein*, breast. Jealousy brings us back to the mother, the arch-mother who comes before, always before—even God the Father. Hence His jealousy?) And look here: these questions occur in a passage inset into a sentence about the spider's web: "The thread and the web of the spider, of the phallic or castrating mother, of the tarantula or the great spider [inset] that eats her male." The inset, about jealousy, is itself suspended in the web of the spidery phrase, of this prose that is stretched over the page like a net meant to catch and hold anything that flies into it. That makes it sound as if Derrida were the spider (and for Nietzsche the spider or tarantula is a principal figure of jealousy, for example in "On Tarantulas" in *Thus Spake Zaranthustra*, Part II), but we should beware another hasty conclusion. One would have to look, first, at the ways in which the signature, or the *seing*, "Jacques Derrida" is itself caught up in the jealous spider's web, consumed as a proper name and *already* transformed into the common word *déjà*. One would have to follow the thread that leads from this inset to another one, sixty pages further on, and that echos it closely: "So one is only jealous of a *seing* or, what comes down here to the same, of a *déjà*" (ibid., p. 152). And one would have to unpack patiently everything that is compacted in the abbreviation of that common word: here, the first letters of a proper name "Dé Ja," but also the mother's breast (Derrida recalls that Freud, in his "Lecture on Femininity," gives the mother's milk as the source of jealousy; thus we should not forget that feminine jealousy, which Freud calls penis envy, is also in the picture), an absolute already or past that has never been present. Already, *déjà*, there is jealousy: *déjà jalousie, déjalousie*. To *déjalouser* the signature, by giving away all its jealous tricks, and with it the relation to the other, might that not describe Derrida's double movement through jealousy? *Déja-louser:* This made-up word is untranslatable, of course, like any signature. De-jealousize? The movement, however, is not only negative; it allows as well an affirmation of the other, the concealed face of jealousy.

————No, don't attempt to translate. Let the word resonate between our languages.

But I am impatient to know where else you are going. You said "at one end" jealousy of the proper name has many links with **Glas.** That's clear. And at the other end?

————One of the other ends. I was thinking of that devilishly conceived text **"To Speculate—on 'Freud'."** There, it is not the jealousy of God but of the devil that one would have to follow. They resemble each other, however, which is perhaps why they are both jealous. Recall the phrase from Rousseau's *Letter to d'Alembert* which Derrida says he takes as an epigraph for his remarks: "I read, when I was young, a tragedy, which was part of the Escalade, in which the Devil was actually one of the actors. I have been told that when this play was once performed, this character, as he came on stage, appeared double, as if the original had been jealous that they had had the audacity to counterfeit him, and instantly everybody, seized by fright, took flight, thus ending the performance" (*The Post Card* [1980], pp. 270–71). Derrida is interested in, among other things, the uncanny doubling of the devil that puts an end to representation, in the double that Freud also wants to exorcise and chase off the stage. He does not, however, explicitly comment on Rousseau's speculation that the devil acted out of jealousy: "as if the original were jealous that anyone had had the audacity to counterfeit him." And yet I would say that **"To Speculate—on 'Freud' "** is *all* about jealousy, that it is "at stake" in everything Derrida is talking about there. Every step that is taken and then taken back, as Derrida follows the rhythm of Freud's inconclusive speculations in *Beyond the Pleasure Principle,* is marked, impelled, pushed along by a jealous devil who keeps interrupting the representation whenever it has the audacity to replace him with a counterfeit. Without thematizing jealousy or even naming it very often, Derrida shows it at work in a large constellation around Freud's name and signature, in its ascendant and descendant relations, its philosophical, institutional, and familial ties. The constellation is made up of other names, the rival names: Nietzsche, Socrates, Schopenhauer, Heidegger are either pushed aside or silenced altogether so Freud need not assume the debt of a philosophical inheritance; the son-in-law, Halberstadt, is eclipsed in the speculation that joins Freud to his daughter; the grandson, Ernst, is assimilated in an identification with the grandfather; the younger brother of Ernst, Heinerle, who had come along to trouble the "exclusive possession of the mother," dies at the age of four; Freud's own younger brother, Julius, died at eight months and left Freud with a sense of guilt that, as he confided to Fliess, had never left him.

Confronted with Freud's resolute irresolution, Derrida keeps asking, "But what is it that impels this writing-(un)step [*pas d'écriture*]?" (ibid., p. 269). "Which is the devil that impels Freud to write?" (p. 271) "What is it that gives the impetus to go further?" (p. 279). These are questions about the *pulsion,* the drive that drives all the speculation. Freud is trying to distinguish what might be proper to a death drive from the recognized properties of the pleasure principle, or life drives, but his effort keeps falling back on this side of the death drive proper. Derrida situates this continued hesitation, deferral, or detour in the insurmountable but impossible desire (drive) to die one's own or proper death (it is thus, notes Derrida, a theory of deferred suicide). Death drives, life drives are all subsumed or subordinated to this overdrive which Derrida designates "the drive of the proper."

> If . . . the drive of the proper is stronger than life and stronger than death, it is because, neither living nor dead, its force does not qualify it otherwise than by its own, proper drivenness, and this drivenness would be the strange relation to oneself that is called the relation to the proper: the most driven drive is the drive of the proper, in other words the one that tends to reappropriate itself. The movement of reappropriation is the most driven drive. The proper of drivenness is the movement or the force of reappropriation. The proper is the tendency to appropriate itself. Whatever the combinatory of these tautologies or analytic statements, never can they be reduced to the form S *is* P. Each time, concerning the drive, the force, or the movement, the tendency or the *telos,* a division must be maintained. This forbids the drive of the proper from being designated by a pleonastic expression defining the simple relation to itself of the inside. Heterology is involved, and this is why there is force, and this is why there is legacy and scene of writing, distancing of oneself and delegation, sending, *envoi.* The proper

> is not the proper, and if it appropriates itself it is that it disap-
> propriates itself—properly, improperly. Life death are no longer
> opposed in it. [ibid., pp. 356–57]

Because heterology is involved or in the picture, there is force, drive, movement—jealousy. If I had to risk a drastically economical description, I would say that Derrida has always been writing on this movement. The necessary failure of the proper to appropriate itself, the *écart* or spacing that must be maintained within the relation of the proper to itself are not, however, just the dominant themes of a discourse: this writing-*on* is also always a writing-*through*, a writing driven by the very movement it treats. Thus, a text like **"To Specu-late—on 'Freud' "** doubles *Beyond the Pleasure Principle*, follows it step by step from beginning to end, and espouses its movement. In this way, Derrida can isolate the moments where the "logic of the proper" must be supplemented and overridden by another, more powerful "logic," a "hetero-logic," if the writing is not to be stopped dead in its tracks. His writing remarks the mark of heterology within the proper. He is thus also always writing against or through the enclosure of the "logic of the proper," molding his writing to the movement he has called "exappropriation." The double prefix "exap-"marks the sense of "-propriation" with an irreducible discordance or dissociation between its two directions. Whereas the proper movement of the proper can only be in an *ap*propriative direction back to itself, the circle of return cannot complete itself without also tracing the contrary movement of *ex*propriation. The more it seeks to keep itself to itself—uncontaminated, purely proper —the more "propriation" loses itself in the "ex-" of an exteriority to itself. The more it seeks to remain faithful to itself, the more it betrays itself. Deconstruction occurs because there is exappropriation. Deconstructive writing, or writing on deconstruction, attempts to formalize the laws of exappropriation as far as possible without being able, of course, to do so completely. (See **The Post Card,** of which "To Speculate . . ." is the second chapter, where Derrida sustains this attempt at formalization through reference to the postal system and code, that is, the series of relays or posts, that space out any address, self-address, destination, and so forth.) Exappropriation will always override the effort to say what it is in a proper sense. And it is here, in this impossibility, that one must situate a certain affirmation. Deconstruction is carried by a force of affirmation of the other's impossible appropriation.

———Yes. But what about jealousy? If we understand it as the drive of the proper, it must always, like Freud's drive, have recourse to a supplemental path through the other that cannot finally be appropriated. Yet it is precisely because jealousy is always defeated in its aim that there is jealousy in the first place. If otherness *could* simply be appropriated, it *would* be appropriated and jealousy would never even arise. If, on the other hand, this appropriation were simply and strictly impossible, if it were altogether out of the question, as one says, then similarly it would never arise. Don't we have to conclude that jealousy can mark the relation to the other because, instead of this simple alternative, its possibility is ineluctably inscribed as its impossibility? One could even say that this is the jealous character —possible–impossible, possible because impossible—of any mark, trace, inscription, writing.

———But here I can imagine an objection that would go something like this: "If you are saying that jealousy is inevitable, so we might as well learn to live with it, even affirm it, are you not encouraging a political irresponsibility? After all, we're not just talking about a theory of drives or whatever; jealousy can also be a real plague, especially when it is considered to be a 'natural' or inevitable component of social relations, in particular sexual relations. And yet you say nothing about these political effects." In other words, what is to prevent someone (a feminist, for example) from saying that deconstructive thinking, in the end, gives comfort to machismo?

———If there is a prior determination to refuse the implications of this thinking (in particular the implications that follow on its analysis of phallogocentrism, which take in far more than the attitude identified here as "machismo"), and to get others to refuse them by issuing dire warnings about "political irresponsibility," then perhaps indeed little can be done to forestall this reaction on the part of the jealous watchdogs of "right thinking." But one might ask whether such a refusal is not itself a political effect of jealousy, and therefore whether it has much chance of leading beyond the very effects it indicates.

This is not the place to analyze a feminist reception or nonreception of deconstruction; however, since you brought up the example here, I wonder whether such an analysis, if anyone were ever to undertake it seriously, could bypass everything we have been saying about jealousy. Is there or can there be something like a feminist theory of jealousy which is not just an indictment of a masculine prerogative to "possess" or "own" women? Given the virtually unanimous rejection by feminist thinkers of *Penisneid,* of Freud's theory of penis envy, what has been thought to take its place? I believe the answer for many would be: a thinking that does not dissimulate, as Freud did, the overwhelming fact that women have a real cause for resentment given their sexual and economic oppression by men (who, for their part, would be jealous in an essential way, jealous of the very fact of women's otherness). In that case, feminine jealousy is merely contingent (unlike penis envy which would be essential and determinant), that is, based on conditions which are liable to change and which are already changing for many women. If it is only contingent, then there is no essential feminine jealousy, or women are essentially without jealousy. To put this in other terms: feminism thinks its "own" jealousy on the basis of a position without-jealousy. Now, the question one must ask about this position . . .

——Wait a minute. Before you get to that, it seems to me the "jealous watchdogs," as you called them, might also be heard, not at all in a suspicious or accusatory tone, asking a perfectly good question. The jealousy of God you are talking about is a term that Derrida would call a quasi-transcendental because it is neither simply inside nor outside a history of meaning, but inaugurates that division and that history by dividing itself. Now, what is the relation between this quasi-transcendental jealousy and jealousy in an everyday or restricted sense? Why, if the very possibility of the relation to the other, to an exteriority, is marked by jealousy, does it develop into a relational or social pathology only in certain cases and not in others? How, in other words, is your or my jealousy (or Derrida's or anyone's) articulated with quasi-transcendental jealousy, God's or no one's?

——Could there ever be a *general* answer to that question, one which would be equally valid for you, me, Derrida, and everyone else? Is there not, instead, each time a singular articulation with the general law which is, for that very reason and at the same time, a restriction—or constriction—of both singularity and generality? A double constriction and a double bind? The questions you have relayed have to be addressed to that place of double binding that Derrida calls the signature. Recall the other questions you quoted earlier from **Glas:** "What is this excess of zeal around a signature? Can one be jealous of anything other than a *seing?*" Are we, in fact, doing anything here other than trying to analyze an excess of zeal around the signature of "Jacques Derrida," to understand, as you put it, how it articulates jealousy in both a singular and general sense? That is the place of ex-position, to recall your term, which we have chosen, or which has befallen us, or which has been assigned—to me by you, or to both of us—by the demand and the expectation that we read, interpret, present Derrida's signature. Jealousy is "at stake," but can you say for certain that it is yours or mine or Derrida's—or someone else's? Perhaps indeed there is a pathology . . .

——You are being exceedingly coy with the quotation "Jealousy is at stake" which you have yet to identify fully in its context. It is as if you were trying to get me to hear it in many contexts at once, including this one, the one in which we are talking, as if you wanted constantly to remind me of the jealousy between us, or worse, to provoke a jealous scene. Or perhaps you are reluctant to give it up to someone else, out of jealousy.

——I was about to quote the passage from which the phrase is taken when you interrupted me. It has to do with the position "without-jealousy" which grounds, not only for some feminists but for many others as well, a certain thinking about jealousy, and thus about the other, which itself would not be jealous. As I was saying, one has to ask where such a position could be located other than outside the field of difference, of the trace, of contaminating differences. And if one is prepared to claim such a transcendental position, then one must also be prepared to accept certain theological consequences, because this position "without-jealousy," which has to be thought non-jealously, is fundamental to a theology. If not, then the position "without-jealousy" must be allowed to deconstruct. In fact, it already deconstructs itself. It is another version of the deconstruction of God, this time not the jealous God, but, precisely, "God-without-jealousy." (However between these two monotheisms, the old and the new, there is also jealousy.)

It is near the end of Derrida's contribution to a 1980 volume, *Textes pour Emmanuel Levinas,* that the phrase occurs. This text is, as I mentioned, polyvocal; throughout, the principal voice addresses a feminine interlocutor who, from time to time, intervenes. Well, near the end, this feminine interlocutor locates, in Levinas's thinking of the trace, "a singular relation of God (uncontaminated by being) to jealousy." Here is how she describes this singular relation:

> He, the one who has passed beyond all Being, must be exempt from any jealousy, from any desire for possession, for guarding, property, exclusivity, nonsubstitution, and so on. And the relation to Him must be pure of all jealous economy. But this without-jealousy *[sans-jalousie]* cannot not guard itself jealously; and insofar as it is a past absolutely held in reserve, it is the very possibility of all jealousy. Ellipsis of jealousy: . . . always a jalousie through which, seeing without seeing everything, and especially without being seen, before and beyond the phenomenon, the without-jealousy guards itself jealously, in other words, loses itself, keeps-itself-loses-itself. By means of a series of regular traits and re-treats *[traits et retraits]:* the figure of jealousy, beyond the face. Never more jealousy, ever, never more zeal; is it possible? (**"At This Very Moment in This Work Here I Am,"** p. 438)

The interlocutor introduces this passage with the brief and enigmatic statement, "In everything I am talking about, jealousy is at stake. *[Dans tout ce dont je parle, il y va de la jalousie]*." That statement would seem to refer in part to what this interlocutor has been saying up until this point about a certain phallocentrism in Levinas's thought: the privileging of paternity (over maternity) and of the son (over the daughter), but especially the subordination of sexual difference to the neutrality of an "il," the (masculine or neuter) "Pro-noun marking with its seal everything that can bear a name," in Levinas's phrase. She asks whether, through these kinds of moves, Levinas (who is also designated here by the initials E. L. that resonate with both the French feminine pronoun "elle" and an elliptical designation for the name of God) has not sought a mastery of the feminine, has not sought to enclose it within the home and the economy of the same. Whereupon she wonders whether "feminine difference does not thus come to stand for the wholly-other of this Saying of the wholly other . . . ? Does it not show, on the inside of the work, a surfeit of un-said alterity? . . . The other as feminine (me), far from being derived or secondary, would become the other of the Saying of the wholly-other, of this one in any case. . . . Then, the Work apparently signed by the Pro-noun He would be dictated, aspired and inspired by the desire to make She secondary, thus *by* She *[Elle]*" (ibid., p. 434). A wholly other "she" *(elle)* would have dictated—or signed—Levinas's writing on the altogether other of the "he" or "it" *(il)*, the Pro-noun that marks everything that can bear a name with its—or his—seal. It is a *pro*-noun, then, less in the sense of that which replaces a noun than of that which *precedes* every noun, every name, the nonphenomenal which disappears at the limit of the phenomenal and allows it to appear, to be named: the trace. For Levinas, *religion* consists precisely in a *ligere*, a linking or tying of a *relation* to this precedence or trace of anteriority. As the feminine interlocutor puts it: "Monotheistic humanity has a relation to this trace of a past that is absolutely anterior to any memory, to the absolute *re-trait* [both retreat or withdrawal, and retracing] of the revealed name, to its very inaccessibility" (p. **436**). When she then comments that Levinas's "thought of the trace . . . thinks a singular relation of God (uncontaminated by being) to jealousy," she is saying that the notion of God Himself is being thought in relation to "this trace of a past that is absolutely anterior to any memory." And this "relation-to" leaves open the possibility of contamination by that which must be excluded for God to be thought of as having "passed beyond being." That which must be excluded, in other words, jealousy: "any desire for possession, guarding, property, exclusivity, non-substitution." Recall Spinoza's dismay before the belief in a jealous God, a belief that goes contrary to reason because jealousy can only be the attribute of a finite being. But this belief is constructed on and partially conceals an even greater scandal: that of God in a *necessarily* contaminating relation to jealousy. She says, "This without-jealousy [an infinite God, one who is uncontaminated by being] *cannot not* guard itself jealously [ne peut pas ne pas *se garder jalousement*]." That is, in order that no desire for possession or nonsubstitution, which are marks of finitude, contaminate the beyond-being of God, it must keep itself from substituting another, finite, jealous nature for its own infinite one. Any substitution is possible except that one. Its infinite substitutability thus encounters an *internal* limit; having undergone an operation of included exclusion, the trait of jealousy, from within, puts the Infinite in *relation* to an outside. The scandal of the deconstruction of God.

Our feminine interlocutor says of this "without-jealousy," which cannot exclude without also including what it excludes, that it is a "past absolutely held in reserve" and as such "it is the very possibility of all jealousy." The phrase translated as "past absolutely held in reserve" reads in the original French "passée absolument réservée." What the English translation must efface here without a trace is the feminine inflection of the noun "passée" used in place of the stan-

dard masculine (or neuter) form, "passé." While it is not at all un-
common for French to nominalize the feminine form of past partici-
ples ("venue," "portée," "vue," for example) which then function in
a nongendered sense, the unusual inflection of "passée" cannot pass
unnoticed; it leaves a feminine trace, all the more so since the phrase
qualifies a neuter (or masculine) subject: "as a past absolutely held
in reserve, *it* is . . . [il *est, en tant que passée absolument réservée*
. . .]" The discrete, but undeniable trace of the feminine in or on that
masculine–neuter beyond-being-without-jealousy marks it with the
passage of an exteriority, a difference that has withdrawn into its
absolute reserve. Or rather, not a single difference, but differences,
which is why the absolute reserve can be called "the very possibility
of *all* jealousy." The possibility of jealousy resides in the drawing
and withdrawing of the trace.

If this notion of the trace seems difficult to grasp, it is precisely
because it concerns that which disappears as soon as one tries to
hold onto it. The figure of God-without-jealousy is an example of
this effect, one which, however, is not just any example, but the
culmination of a long tradition of thought that has aimed precisely
at reducing, sublimating, denying the trace. There, the trait "without-jealousy" withdraws before the grasp that would fix it in a figure,
a concept, a sign, a representation. One is left holding (jealously) the
shell from which the desired thing has retreated. The figure "without-jealousy" is expropriated by the gesture of appropriation: it is
exappropriated, its nonjealous face appears in the guise of jealousy.
As our feminine interlocutor says, "Ellipsis of jealousy . . . this without-jealousy guards itself jealously, in other words, loses itself, keeps-
itself-loses-itself. By means of a series of regular traits and re-treats:
the figure of jealousy, beyond the face. Never more jealousy, ever,
never more zeal, is it possible?" The final sentence reads, "Plus de
jalousie, toujours, plus de zèle, est-ce possible?" The adverbial phrase
"plus de" can, in certain contexts, allow for two absolutely contradictory readings: more and no more. This particularity of the French
idiom is being fully exploited here to show the outline of the movement of exappropriation. Because "no more jealousy" cannot secure
its borders against contamination by "more jealousy," no more is
always also more, and that calls up more zeal (jealous and zealous
were once the same word: *zelotypus*) in order to reduce the trace of
the other, to purify the figure of no (more) jealousy. Puritanical
zealotry in the name of no (more) jealousy, is that possible? But the
question should also be: how is it possible *not* to be jealous if what
arrives or comes from the other retreats from the grasp that would

hold it? If by being kept, held, grasped—in a concept, a name—the trace gets lost? If, as Derrida has written elsewhere, "la trace n'arrive qu'à s'effacer"—both it "arrives only on the condition of effacing itself," and it "succeeds only in effacing itself"?

——Since you are insisting on the movement (drawing and withdrawing) of the trace in the idiom in which Derrida writes (and can one be jealous of anything other than a signature or an idiom?), shouldn't you say something about the phrase "il y va de la jalousie" which is only approximately translated by "jealousy is at stake"? There is, however buried beneath conventional usage, some movement implied in the phrase; jealousy goes there, one could say. You have noticed, no doubt, that the same phrase has a prominent place in **Glas,** set off by itself on the page (236, left column, in the original edition [1974]). It articulates the two versions of God's relation to jealousy that you have been spinning out. Look at the pages that follow and you'll find Kant and Hegel locked in a dispute over the jealousy of God. Briefly it goes like this: Hegel reproaches Kant for his stubborn refusal to admit any knowledge of the infinite God by a finite subjectivity. Kant, on the other hand, reproaches those who believe God is knowable (Hegel would be an example) for having degraded religion, replaced it, out of excessive pride, with a fetishism. For Hegel, Kant's God is jealous, envious; he hides His manifestation, keeps it to Himself, does not reveal His face. But, says Hegel, the truth of the true religion (Christianity) is revelation, and if one is going to think this truth in its essence (and not forbid oneself to think it, as Kant does), then one must think revelation itself, the revelation of revelation: "God's infinite revelation revealing itself in its infinity . . . the un-veiling as the unveiling of the veil itself" (p. 212). Infinite, and therefore without exteriority, without any view on or of an other; instead, pure view, pure knowledge that knows itself and is present to itself without any detour through otherness —and thus without jealousy. For Hegel, jealousy will have been but a necessary negative moment (or movement) in the production of this truth. "In pure essentiality, jealousy is totally relieved" [*relevée*, which is Derrida's translation of *aufgehoben*, usually translated as "sublated"] (p. 240). But this relieving, sublation, or cancellation of jealousy will have taken place only at the end of history, which is thus a history of jealousy, of a movement through jealousy:

What he says of absolute religion and the nonjealous God is valid only at the term of the absolute's process of reappropriation by itself. Before term, prematurely, there is finitude and thus jealousy. But self-jealousy. Of whom could God be jealous, except himself and thus his very own son? The Nemesis, Judaism, Kantianism are necessary, but abstract, moments of this infinite process. In *Sa*, jealousy has no place any more. Jealousy always comes from the night of the unconsious, the unknown, the other. Pure sight relieves all jealousy. Not seeing what one sees, seeing what one cannot see and what cannot present itself, that is the jealous operation. Jealousy always has to do with some trace, never with perception. Seen from the *Sa*, thought of the trace would then be a jealous (finite, filial, servile, ignorant, lying, poetic) thought. (pp. 214–15)

Yet "pure sight" cannot be the sight of any particular figure or face, which would determine it and thus limit it in a representation. Hegel's Absolute Spirit (*Sa* in Derrida's acronym) is unrepresentable: finally it cannot show a face or figure. It thus ends up, in its invisibility, strangely resembling Kant's jealous God. Or rather, as Derrida puts it, "Jealousy is between them *[La jalousie est entre eux]*" (p. 237). Between the hidden God at the origin (Kant), and the infinite revelation of God in the end (Hegel), there is history. Jealousy goes there.

———I would say that, like the other phrase "Jealousy is at stake or goes there," which led you to the beginning of this sequence in **Glas,** the phrase "Jealousy is between them" cannot be easily settled into a certain context. "Between them," that is, between God (in Kant's version, the Jewish God) and God (in Hegel's version, the Christian God), between God and himself—after all, "of whom could God be jealous except himself?"—God and His only Son, God in a difference from himself. But what if Kant and Hegel, who are here made to stage a philosophical debate over the jealousy of God, were also implicated in this interval of jealousy "between them"? What if the jealousy in question were not just the object of their dispute, but also its force, that which puts it in motion and makes space for remarking a difference? What if, in other words, this discourse on jealousy were already a discourse of jealousy? (But whose jealousy?) This is essentially the question Derrida asks in **"To Speculate—on 'Freud',"** in the midst of what, as you already mentioned, are multiple motifs of jealousy. "What happens," he asks, "when acts or performances (discourse or writing, analysis or description, etc.) are part of the objects they designate? When they can be given as examples of precisely that which they speak or write?" The answer he proposes is not simple; indeed, it is the limit on the very possibility to answer or give an account of what happens in that situation: "A reckoning is no longer possible, nor can an account be rendered, and the borders of the set are neither closed nor open. Their trait is divided . . ." (*The Post Card* [1980], p. 391).

——Are you suggesting that the history of philosophy is a history of jealousy between philosophers?

——Would you find that a shocking suggestion? But for the moment I am merely pursuing the consequences of the divided trait for the phrase "Jealousy is between them." I am tempted now to understand that phrase before or beyond any context," indeed as the very possibility of any "context" whatever, any opening of a space of meaning. "Jealousy is between": it "is," that is, an interval, a gap, a space—difference—that joins and divides "them." The interval "between" relates them across a divide which the copulative verb "is" cannot reduce. Copulated, "they" remain apart, a part and not a whole. Desire is between them. But no desire without jealousy. Jealousy is between them. The difference between them?

Always between, jealousy is persistently figured in veils, webs, curtains—partitions of all sorts. Hence, a "jalousie" is a venetian blind or a louvered shutter (a semantic displacement which is masterfully exploited in Alain Robbe-Grillet's celebrated novel, *La Jalousie*). Such jalousies or partitions proliferate in Derrida's texts. Any list of them would be necessarily partial because their traits are always dividing, or opening and closing like the slats of a venetian blind. (All the more partial since that device is the very one through which we are looking at everything Derrida is talking about; there is always one more "jalousie" to be accounted for.) Think of the veils and sails in **Spurs: Nietzsche's Styles,** or yet again the umbrella (opening and closing) in the same text; the curtain around little Ernst's bed in **"To Speculate—on 'Freud' "**; the draperies and other frames which are unwrapped in "The Parergon" [1978]; the ear drum or tympanum stretched obliquely across **"Tympan";** the eyelid, a kind of organic jalousie, that is raised and lowered in "The Principle of Reason: The University in the Eyes of Its Pupils" [1983], and so forth. These last two examples could, in turn, initiate another partial list of body parts dissected or disassembled. Derrida writes "on the body" in an unheard-of sense, on the body jealous of its unity, its place in a hierarchy, its difference from the body either of animals or of machines—in short, its property and properness, its bodiness. The human body—itself—deconstructs, decomposes even, under pressure from this writing which is exerted typically there where a partition divides its trait between the inside and outside of the body proper. From the organs of the abstract senses—ears and eyes—which philosophy has always privileged, Derrida elsewhere turns to the baser because more organic senses of smell and taste (see for example "Economimesis" [1975]). And in this regard, **Glas** could be read as a long treatise on the jealous functioning of the mouth, that place where the other is at once symbolically ingested and named ("This is my body . . ."), where the processes of interiorization, assimilation, and appropriation, by which the proper self tries to constitute itself, are made to pass through the contrary movements of exteriorization and expropriation (exhaling or expiring, but also speaking and vomiting). The mouth—lips, teeth, tongue, palate—is also an antechamber of the throat, that is, trachea and oesophagus, double columns which, like the double columns of **Glas,** are made up of a series of sphincters or bands of constricting tissue the rhythmic opening and closing of which regulates the passage between inside and outside. The rhythm of the sphincter's constrictions punctuates the movement of jealousy across and through the body "proper," traversing all the orifices of sense, ingestion, respiration, vocalization, elimination, but also the organs that are called sexual in the strictest sense. Sexual jealousy—jealousy in a limited sense—is a particularly acute constriction of this movement that continually opens the body to an outside, even turns it inside out like a glove.

——Couldn't one extend this demonstration beyond the body's orifices in the strict sense to those parts, such as hands and feet, which have variously stood for what is most proper to humankind, what distinguishes it from the nonhuman in general? Derrida has exposed repeatedly the humanist gesture to grasp the properly human, for example with the hand (see "Heidegger's Hand" [1987]), or to stand the human subject on its own feet (see **"Restitutions . . ."**). These body parts would also be partitions, jalousies, or veils, that is, self-dividing traits between inside and outside, proper and improper. Such an extended demonstration, however, could not stop with a list of body parts; it would have to follow the movement of a certain interlacing that grafts prostheses, supplements, simulacra, or mimetic doubles onto the body "proper."

But as you were enumerating the partial list of divided body parts,

I was thinking of the one that, perhaps more than any other, concentrates all of these several motifs of jealousy in Derrida's thought: the hymen. In **"The Double Session,"** as you recall, this term imposes itself, in all its undecidability, between the two versions of mimesis that Derrida is reading side by side, Plato's and Mallarmé's. In the sense of film or membrane, *hymen* already envelops many of the parts we've named: the feet of certain birds, the eyes of others, but also the wings of certain insects, etc. It is, as Derrida writes, "the tissue on which so many bodily metaphors are written" (*Dissemination* [1972], p. 213). In its etymology, the word would indeed seem to have links with the whole network of weaving, in which one also finds the spiderweb. I would even say that one could translate jealousy in the phrase "Jealousy is between them" by this other interval of sense that Derrida calls "hymen." The hymen is between—them. The phrase retains both of the word's most common senses, that is the hymen as both the veil-like tissue across the vagina that remains intact as long as virginity does, and, in a somewhat archaic but still comprehensible sense (in English as well as French), hymen as the union or marriage which is consummated by the act that ruptures it (i.e., the hymen in the first sense). In other words, it is between them, that is, it divides them, marks their difference as a sexual difference of inside from outside; and it is between them, that is, it joins them or unites them in a symbolic union. Like all the others you have named, the partition of the hymen partitions itself, departs from itself and from any proper meaning. It does so by articulating the two senses of articulation: dividing–joining, by enfolding the one in the other undecidably. Is not, therefore, the hymen a more general name for all these jealous partitionings? And if so, can one affirm, as you just did, that so-called sexual jealousy is simply a more limited sense of the jealous movement of exappropriation? Is not that movement necessarily always marked by sexual difference, even in the case of the jealousy of God?

———Marked by sexual difference, yes; but perhaps there is still a good reason to maintain some notion of the strict or limited sense of sexual jealousy. If only in order to be able to point to the ways in which it is constantly overrun. Consider, for example, the fact that the Mallarmé text, *Mimique,* which is featured in **"The Double Session"** may be read as concerning the mime drama of a jealous husband's murderous revenge for his wife's infidelity. This would be the mime's "subject," but one that, as Derrida is concerned to show, is constantly retreating from the stage of the present behind a series of textual veils or folds. Its presence is absolutely held in reserve, which is to say, it is always already past. The classical, Platonic theory of mimesis, on the other hand, posits a model or an original that would have been fully present with a presence that can be represented in the copy or imitation. Now, the question one might ask—the question I hear you asking—is this: Is it a matter of indifference that the deconstruction of this mimetic model passes by way of a staging of sexual jealousy in the most limited sense? Or is it not rather the case that what we call sexual jealousy—the jealousy of the possessive lover—harbors, in its most acute or pointed form, the possibility of this opening onto a past that has never been present, an absolute past and an absolute other? The lover, in sum, is jealous because nothing in the present can ground his jealousy, which is how I understand Derrida's remark that the jealous operation "always has to do with some trace, never with perception." Pierrot's revenge, his remembered or imagined crime (tickling his wife to death), would serve above all to try to put a halt to the slide toward the abyss into which the other retreats from any present that could be grasped or possessed. The crime of murder can seem to be a resolution of jealousy because it fixes the other in an unshakeable grasp. However, the presence fixed thereby is, of course, the derisive, mocking figure of death. Colombine dies, comes laughing.

Yet, such a *representation* of the jealous act never simply appears here. It is enveloped in the undecidable folds of a hymen: between past and future (is Pierrot remembering or imagining his act?); between revenge and love (is Colombine convulsed in the throes of death or a paroxysm of pleasure?); between murder and suicide (is Pierrot miming Colombine's demise or submitting to it himself)? What is finally enveloped in all these folds of "pure fiction" is that last instance or final appeal—the ultimate model, signified, meaning, or referent—demanded by the "trial of truth" [*le procès de la vérité*] which is philosophy. Philosophy wants to get at the truth behind all these feminine veils. And because the philosopher behaves *like* a jealous husband, "pure fiction"—a mime drama such as *Pierrot assassin de sa femme*—can deconstruct the truth claims which have always required a reduction of feminine difference, and which accompany the substitution of a perceptible presence for the trace of a past that has never been present.

One is never jealous in front of a present scene—even the worst imaginable—nor a future one, at least insofar as it would

be pregnant with a possible theater. Zeal is lashed into fury
only by the whip of an absolute past. . . . So one is only jealous
of the mother or of death. Never of a man or a woman as such.
(**Glas** [1974], p. 134)

——Once again, I imagine an objection, which would go something like this: Is a deconstruction of this jealousy possible? Granted,
the metaphysics of presence is jealous, as you have just asserted and
as Derrida writes in the same passage from **Glas** ("That is why
metaphysics, which is jealous, will never be able to account, in its
language, the language of presence, for jealousy"). Yet, is not the
thinking of the trace always a thinking of the impossible reduction
of jealousy? And as such, does it not promise always more jealousy,
rather than no more jealousy?

——I, in turn, will imagine a reply that reapplies something you
said earlier about affirmation and that was left suspended: Do not
confuse a deconstruction of jealousy with its destruction, that is,
with a solely negative movement. There is also displacement of the
jealous structures from their human, all too human incarnations.
"The 'mother' of jealousy in question here—the trace of an absolute
past—stands beyond," writes Derrida, "the sexual opposition. This
above all is not a woman. She only lets herself, detached, be represented by sex." This displacement would not be, then, a beyond-
jealousy or without-jealousy except in the restricted sense that depends on the terms of sexual opposition. There is beyond-jealousy
only beyond this opposition. And this is where the possibility of
affirmation can arise: to *déjalouser* the relation of sexual difference,
to affirm and thus exempt the jealousy of the other.
But having let that be said, I wonder if, all the same and after all,
we have not betrayed something through an excess of zeal . . .

——Ah, my dear, are you still asking the same anxious question?
I do believe you are jealous of the web we have spun for each other
once you consider the necessity of cutting it off, detaching it, and
exposing its loose ends for *A Derrida Reader*. Come now, give me
your jealousy; it will not betray you unless you try to keep it to
yourself. You asked a moment ago whether gifts are ever exempt
from jealousy. You were puzzled, perhaps, by the double gesture this
supposes, since a jealous gift immediately takes back what it proffers. But if I ask you to take my jealousy, if I give it to you, give it to

you to read, is it not yours to take away? Who else but you can exempt this gift from retracting and betraying itself?

So here, take this, my jealousy, it is already yours to read.

——A series of jalousies, then, one laid over the next. "Let the transference float" between one jalousie and the other, between one language and the other. Read between the blinds. First of all, there is translation. Do not forget that. These texts have already passed through the filter of another language. And because Derrida's is a jealous idiom, much will have filtered out or withheld itself from view. But welcome this limitation as a chance to open the shutters and the blinders of thought to what comes from its other, beyond any one language or idiom. Let your language play in the slanting rays. Whoever said that the most serious things must always be treated gravely, somberly, behind closed doors was probably afraid of letting a certain necessary play come to light within the serious. Listen to Colombine's laughter.

A DERRIDA READER

JALOUSIE ONE

Let us space. The art of this text is the air it causes to circulate between its screens. The chainings are invisible, everything seems improvised or juxtaposed. This text induces by agglutinating rather than by demonstrating, by coupling and uncoupling, gluing and ungluing rather than by exhibiting the continuous, and analogical, instructive, suffocating necessity of a discursive rhetoric.

—*Glas,* p. 75

PART ONE

DIFFERANCE AT THE ORIGIN

IN 1980, MORE than twenty years after he had begun teaching in France (first at a provincial *lycée*, then at the Sorbonne, the Ecole Normale Supérieure, and currently at the Ecole des Hautes Etudes en Sciences Sociales), Jacques Derrida received a Doctorat d'Etat *sur travaux*, that is, on the basis of a body of published work. In the statement with which he presented this work at the formal defense or *soutenance* (subsequently published in English translation with the title "The Time of a Thesis: Punctuations" [1983]), Derrida described the itinerary he had followed since 1957, the year he elected to prepare a thesis that would have been entitled "The Ideality of the Literary Object." Although this project was abandoned then by choice, and later not revived because of the inhospitableness of the French university to his work and that of many others who were similarly working in its margins, Derrida evoked the premises of his unwritten protothesis so as to underscore a certain continuity of his preoccupation with philosophy *and* literature, in all the conjugations of their similarity and difference: the philosophy of literature, philosophy as literature, literature before or beyond philosophy, literature in excess of philosophy. "It was then for me a matter of bending, more or less violently, the techniques of transcendental phenomenology to the needs of elaborating a new theory of literature, of that very peculiar type of ideal object that is the literary object" (p. 37). Looking back at his never-abandoned interest in the "literary object," Derrida saw there his earliest formulations of questions such as What is writing? How does writing disturb the question "What is?" or "What does that mean?" When and how does an inscription become literature? And these questions would, he suggested, have their roots in another, more obscure question he asks of himself: "Why finally does inscription so fascinate me, preoccupy me, precede me? Why am I so fascinated by the literary ruse of the inscription?" (p. 38)

It was as a philosopher trained in the rigors of phenomenological discipline that Derrida approached the question of inscription. His first major publication was a critical introduction to his translation of Husserl's *The Origin of Geometry* in 1962. There followed essays —on Michel Foucault, Edmond Jabès, Emmanuel Levinas, Antonin Artaud, Freud, Georges Bataille, Claude Lévi-Strauss—that both set out Derrida's affinities and marked his distance from thinkers around him. In the same year, 1967, that these essays were collected under the title *L'Ecriture et la différence (Writing and Difference)*, Derrida also published two other books, *La Voix et le phénomène* (**Speech and Phenomena**) and *De la grammatologie* (**Of Grammatology**). The first of these analyzes Husserl's doctrine of signification; the second extends the analysis to a larger philosophical tradition which Husserl both inherited and continued, at least as concerns certain key features of his description of signification. One feature in particular, which is consistently marked in one way or another from Plato to Lévi-Strauss, attracted Derrida's most relentless attention: the privileging of voice as the medium of meaning and the consequent dismissal of writing as a derivative, inessential medium. This systematic evaluation has been preserved virtually unchanged by a history of philosophy that has undergone so many other, apparently profound revolutions. In a move that recognized the irreversible significance of Heidegger's thought, Derrida argued that, if philosophers have always failed to account for their own medium—writing—it is because material inscription is so thoroughly inconsistent with the fundamental requirement of their thinking, one that is supposed by the very notion of philosophy in the West: truth or meaning as a presence without difference from itself. Whatever else it is, writing, or in general the inscription of marks, always supposes and indicates an absence. In his initial considerations of the "question of inscription," Derrida turned to Husserl's phenomenological research into signification for both the most systematic version of meaning as self-presence and the most rigorous tools with which to deconstruct this system. Thus, the deconstruction of the philosophy of presence (which, being the philosophy of proper sense, is the only philosophy in the proper sense) undertaken by Derrida will not proceed like some frontal attack or siege from outside philosophy's walls. It begins necessarily within those walls, but this starting point is also only the place from which to unsettle the very distinction between inside and outside essential to the construction of self-presence.

Derrida's first two major works, **Speech and Phenomena** and **Of Grammatology,** are concerned with certain systematic treatments of signification and language: Husserl's, as mentioned, but also those of Ferdinand de Saussure and Jean-Jacques Rousseau, among others. Although it would be misleading to understand these earlier works as in some simple way more systematic than his later work, Derrida himself recognizes in "The Time of a Thesis" that they conform perhaps more readily to some standard expectations governing discursive exposition of a thesis. In subsequent writings, most notably **Glas** [1974], **The Truth in Painting** [1978], and **The Post Card** [1980], these constraints are greatly loosened as Derrida moves beyond thematic considerations of writing as formal spacing and attempts new, active determinations of the relation between theme and form. Later sections in this book make room for many of these "experiments." Here, however, in the initial set of selections, it is possible to follow Derrida as he sets into place a number of his key concepts—or what he calls semi- or quasi-concepts—that will remain in force wherever his thinking takes him thereafter. These semi-concepts—trace, differance, archi-writing, for example—so-called because they do not function as the name of anything that can be thought of as ever simply present, are not so much invented by Derrida as they are found inscribed in the gaps of the theory of signification, the theory of the sign. The gap, in French *l'écart* which can also mean divergence, is that opening to difference, to an outside, to an other—to absence and to death—which, in any theory based on fully present meaning, will have been covered over. Derrida's writing uncovers and remarks these gaps.

ONE

From *Speech and Phenomena*

(*La Voix et le phénomène* [1967])

"The present essay," writes Derrida in a note to his introduction, "analyzes the doctrine of signification as it is constituted already in the first of [Husserl's] *Logical Investigations*." This first investigation is titled "Expression and Meaning" and in it Husserl is principally concerned with separating sign *(Zeichen)* in the sense of expression from sign in the other sense of indication. Only the former, he will argue, can be understood as a meaningful sign since the concept of meaning *(Bedeutung)* is reserved for the intention to mean. Indicative signs, on the other hand, signify but they are not themselves the bearers of an animating intention which infuses life into the body of signs. (For example, gathering dark clouds indicate a coming storm, but not anyone's intention to rain.) From the description and elaboration of this initial distinction, Husserl proceeds to propose as the model of meaningful speech, and therefore the place wherein it can be studied in its essence, not a communicated discourse, but the silent colloquy of consciousness with itself in "solitary mental life." Derrida compares this isolation of interior conscious phenomena to what Husserl himself will later formalize as the practice of phenomenological reduction whereby the "worldly" support of conscious processes is systematically stripped away, reduced, so as to allow more precise description of those processes. Commenting on each step of this reduction, Derrida carefully follows the logic that labors to exclude any trace of indication, of absence of intention, of difference within a living present present to itself. It is a logic of presence both in the temporal sense, in that it supposes an undifferentiated present moment, and in a more spatial sense, in that it supposes a meaning altogether immanent or interior to itself, one that need never be proffered outside. Derrida demonstrates repeatedly that such a description of the sign is always finally an attempted effacement of the sign and of its essential and necessary exteriority to any living intention—an effacement of the sign, that is, of whatever can come along to interrupt the living present. Derrida writes, "Indication is the process of death at work in signs. As soon as the other appears, indicative language—another name for the relation to death—can no longer be effaced. The relation to the other as nonpresence is thus impure expression. To reduce indication in language and reach pure expression at last, the relation to the other must perforce be suspended" (p. 40). For this reason among others, Derrida will be led, in one of the extracts given here, to speak of the logic of presence as a logic of pure auto-affection, and from there to overturn the relation between expression and indication within the other "logic" he calls that of the trace, which is a logic of repeated inscription without simple origin. "This trace is unthinkable on the basis of a simple present whose life would be interior to itself; the self of the living present is primordially a trace."

Extracted here are all of chapter 4, "Meaning and Representation," and most of chapter 6, "The Voice That Keeps Silence."

[. . . .]

Let us recall the object and crux of this demonstration: the pure function of expression and meaning is not to communicate, inform, or manifest, that is, to indicate. "Solitary mental life" would prove that such an expression without indication is possible. In solitary discourse the subject learns nothing about himself, manifests nothing to himself. To support this demonstration, whose consequences for phenomenology will be limitless, Husserl invokes two kinds of argument.

1. In inward speech, I communicate nothing to myself, I indicate nothing to myself. I can at most imagine myself doing so; I can only represent myself as manifesting something to myself. This, however, is only *representation* and *imagination*.

2. In inward speech I communicate nothing to myself *because there is no need of it*; I can only pretend to do so. Such an operation, the self-communication of the self, could not take place because it would make no sense, and it would make no sense because there would be *no finality*[1] to it. The existence of mental acts does not have to be indicated (let us recall that in general only an existence can be indicated) because it is immediately present to the subject in the present moment.

Let us first read the paragraph that ties these two arguments together:

One of course *speaks*, in a certain sense, even in soliloquy, and it is certainly possible to think of oneself as speaking, and even as speaking to oneself, as, e.g., when someone says to himself: "You have gone wrong, you can't go on like that." But in the genuine sense of communication, there is no speech in such cases, nor does one tell oneself anything: one merely conceives of *(man stellt sich vor)* oneself as speaking and communicating. In a monologue words can perform no function of indicating the existence *(Dasein)* of mental acts, since such indication would there be quite purposeless *(ganz zwecklos wäre)*. For the acts in question are themselves experienced by us at that very moment *(im selben Augenblick)*.[2]

These affirmations raise some very diverse questions, all concerned with the status of *representation* in language. Representation can be understood in the general sense of *Vorstellung*, but also in the sense of re-presentation, as repetition or reproduction of presentation, as the *Vergegenwärtigung* which modifies a *Präsentation* or *Gegenwärtigung*. And it can be understood as what takes the place of, what occupies the place of, another *Vorstellung (Repräsentation, Repräsentant, Stellvertreter)*.[3]

Let us consider the first argument. In monologue, nothing is communicated; one represents oneself *(man stellt sich vor)* as a speaking and communicating subject. Husserl thus seems here to apply the fundamental distinction between reality and representation to language. Between effective communication (indication) and "represented" communication there would be a difference in essence, a simple exteriority. Moreover, in order to reach inward language (in the sense of communication) as pure representation *(Vorstellung)*, a certain fiction, that is, a particular type of representation, would have to be employed: the imaginary representation, which Husserl will later define as neutralizing representation *(Vergegenwärtigung)*.

Can this system of distinctions be applied to language? From the start we would have to suppose that representation (in every sense of the term) is neither essential to nor constitutive of communication, the "effective" practice of language, but is only an accident that may or may not be added to the practice of discourse. But there is every reason to believe that representation and reality are not merely added together here and there in language, for the simple reason that it is impossible in principle to rigorously distinguish them. And it doesn't help to say that this

happens *in* language; language in general—and language alone—
is this.

Husserl himself gives us the means to think this against what
he says. When in fact I *effectively* use words, and whether or not
I do it for communicative ends (let us consider signs in general,
prior to this distinction), I must from the outset operate (within)
a structure of repetition whose basic element can only be representative. A sign is never an event, if by event we mean an
irreplaceable and irreversible empirical particular. A sign which
would take place but "once" would not be a sign; a purely idiomatic sign would not be a sign. A signifier (in general) must be
formally recognizable in spite of, and through, the diversity of
empirical characteristics which may modify it. It must remain
the *same*, and be able to be repeated as such, despite and across
the deformations which the so-called empirical event necessarily
makes it undergo. A phoneme or grapheme is necessarily always
to some extent different each time that it is presented in an
operation or a perception. But, it can function as a sign, and in
general as language, only if a formal identity enables it to be
issued again and to be recognized. This identity is necessarily
ideal. It thus necessarily implies a representation: as *Vorstellung*,
the locus of ideality in general, as *Vergegenwärtigung*, the possibility of reproductive repetition in general, and as *Repräsentation*, insofar as each signifying event is a substitute (for the
signified as well as for the ideal form of the signifier). Since this
representative structure is signification itself, I cannot enter into
an "effective" discourse without being from the start involved in
unlimited representation.

One might object that it is precisely this exclusively representative character of expression that Husserl wants to bring out by
his hypothesis of solitary discourse, which would retain the essence of speech while dropping its communicative and indicative
shell. Moreover, one might object that we have precisely formulated our question with Husserlian concepts. We have indeed.
But according to Husserl's description, it is only expression and
not signification in general that belongs to the order of representation as *Vorstellung*. However, we have just suggested that the
latter—and its other representative modifications—is implied
by any sign whatsoever. On the other hand, and more important,

as soon as we admit that speech belongs essentially to the order of representation, the distinction between "effective" speech and the representation of speech becomes suspect, whether the speech is purely "expressive" or engaged in "communication." By reason of the originally repetitive structure of signs in general, there is every likelihood that "effective" language is just as imaginary as imaginary speech and that imaginary speech is just as effective as effective speech. In both expression and indicative communication the difference between reality and representation, between the true and the imaginary, and between simple presence and repetition has always already begun to be effaced. Does not the maintaining of this difference—in the history of metaphysics and for Husserl as well—answer to the obstinate desire to save presence and to reduce or derive the sign, and with it all powers of repetition? Which comes to living *in* the effect—the assured, consolidated, constituted effect of repetition and representation, of the difference which removes presence. To assert, as we have been doing, that within the sign *the difference does not take place* between reality and representation, etc., amounts to saying that the gesture that confirms this difference is the very effacement of the sign. But there are two ways of effacing the originality of the sign; we must be attentive to the instability of all these moves, for they pass quickly and surreptitiously into one another. Signs can be effaced in the classical manner in a philosophy of intuition and presence. Such a philosophy effaces signs by making them derivative; it annuls reproduction and representation by making signs a modification that happens to a simple presence. But because it is just such a philosophy—which is, in fact, *the* philosophy and history of the West—which has so constituted and established the very concept of signs, the sign is from its origin and to the core of its sense marked by this will to derivation or effacement. Consequently, to restore the original and nonderivative character of signs, in opposition to classical metaphysics, is, by an apparent paradox, at the same time to efface a concept of signs whose whole history and meaning belong to the adventure of the metaphysics of presence. This schema also holds for the concepts of representation, repetition, difference, etc., as well as for their whole system. For the present and for some time to come, the movement of that schema will only be capable of working over the language of metaphysics from within, in a certain *interior*. No doubt this work has always already begun. We shall have to grasp what happens in this interior when the closure of metaphysics is announced.

With the difference between real presence and presence in representation as *Vortstellung*, a whole system of differences involved in language is pulled along in the same deconstruction: the differences between the represented and the representative in general, the signified and signifier, simple presence and its repro-duction, presentation as *Vorstellung* and re-presentation as *Ver-gegenwärtigung*, for what is represented in the re-presentation is a presentation *(Präsentation)* as *Vorstellung*. We thus come—against Husserl's express intention—to make the *Vorstellung* itself, and as such, depend on the possibility of re-presentation *(Vergegenwärtigung)*. The presence-of-the-present is derived from repetition and not the reverse. While this is against Husserl's express intention, it does take into account what is implied by his description of the movement of temporalization and of the relation to the other, as will perhaps become clear later on.

The concept of *ideality* naturally has to be at the center of such a question. According to Husserl, the structure of speech can be described only in terms of ideality. There is the ideality of the sensible form of the signifier (for example, the word), which must remain *the same* and can do so only as an ideality. There is, moreover, the ideality of the signified (of the *Bedeutung*) or intended sense, which is not to be confused with the act of intending or with the object, for the latter two need not necessar-ily be ideal. Finally, in certain cases there is the ideality of the object itself, which then assures the ideal transparency and per-fect univocity of language; this is what happens in the exact sciences.[4] But this ideality, which is but another name for the permanence of the same and the possibility of its repetition, *does not exist* in the world, and it does not come from another world; it depends entirely on the possibility of acts of repetition. It is constituted by this possibility. Its "being" is proportionate to the power of repetition; absolute ideality is the correlate of a possi-bility of indefinite repetition. It could therefore be said that being is determined by Husserl as ideality, that is, as repetition. For Husserl, historical progress always has as its essential form the constitution of idealities the repetition and thus the tradition of which would be assured *ad infinitum,* where repetition and tradition are the transmission and reactivation of the origin. And this determination of being as ideality is properly a *valuation,* an ethico-theoretical act that revives the decision that founded philosophy in its Platonic form. Husserl occasionally admits this; what he always opposed was a conventional Platonism. When he affirms the nonexistence or nonreality of ideality, it is always to acknowledge that ideality *is* according to a mode of being that is irreducible to sensible existence or empirical reality and their fictional counterparts.[5] In determining the *ontōs on* as *eidos,* Plato himself was affirming the same thing.

Now (and here again the commentary must take its bearing from the interpretation) this determination of being as ideality is paradoxically caught up with the determination of being as presence. This occurs not only because pure ideality is always that of an ideal "ob-ject" which stands in front of, which is pre-sent before the act of repetition (*Vor-stellung* being the general form of presence as proximity to a gaze), but also because only a temporality determined on the basis of the living present as its source (the now as "source-point") can ensure the purity of ideality, that is, an opening up of the infinite repeatability of the same. For, in fact, what is signified by phenomenology's "principle of principles"? What does the value of originary presence to intuition as source of sense and evidence, as the *a priori* of *a prioris,* signify? First of all it signifies the certainty, itself ideal and absolute, that the universal form of all experience *(Erlebnis),* and therefore of all life, has always been and will always be the *present.* The present alone is all there is and ever will be. Being is presence or the modification of presence. The relation to the presence of the present as the ultimate form of being and of ideality is the move by which I transgress empirical existence, factuality, contingency, worldliness, etc.—first of all, *my own* empirical existence, factuality, contingency, worldliness, etc. To think of presence as the universal form of transcendental life is to open myself to the knowledge that in my absence, beyond my empirical existence, before my birth and after my death, *the present is.* I can empty all empirical content, imagine an absolute overthrow of the *content* of every possible experience, a radical transformation of the world. I have a strange and unique certitude that this universal form of presence, since it concerns no determined being, will not be affected by it. The relationship with *my death* (my disappearance in general) thus lurks in this determination of being as presence, ideality, the absolute possibility of repetition. The possibility of the sign is this relationship to death. The determination and effacement of the sign in metaphysics is the dissimulation of this relationship to death, which nevertheless produced signification.

If the possibility of my disappearance in general must somehow be experienced in order for a relationship to presence in general to be instituted, we can no longer say that the experience of the possibility of my absolute disappearance (my death) affects me, occurs to an *I am*, and modifies a subject. The *I am*, being lived only as an *I am present*, itself presupposes in itself the relationship to presence in general, to being as presence. The appearing of the *I* to itself in the *I am* is thus originally a relation to its own possible disappearance. Therefore, *I am* originally means *I am mortal. I am immortal* is an impossible proposition.[6] We can therefore go further: as a linguistic statement "I am the one who am" is the admission of a mortal. The move that leads from the *I am* to the determination of my being as *res cogitans* (thus, as an immortality) is a move by which the origin of presence and ideality is concealed in the very presence and ideality it makes possible.

The effacement (or derivation) of signs is thereby confused with the reduction of the imagination. Husserl's position with respect to tradition is here ambiguous. No doubt he profoundly renewed the question of imagination, and the role he reserves for fiction in the phenomenological method clearly shows that for him imagination is not just one faculty among others. Yet without neglecting the novelty and rigor of the phenomenological description of images, we should certainly be cognizant of their origin. Husserl continually emphasizes that, unlike a memory, an image is not "positional"; it is a "neutralizing" re-presentation. While this gives it a privilege in "phenomenological" practice, both an image and a memory are classified under the general concept "re-presentation" *(Vergegenwärtigung)*, that is, the reproduction of a presence, even if the product is a purely fictitious object. It follows that imagination is not a simple "modification of neutrality," even if it is neutralizing ("We must protect ourselves here against a very closely besetting confusion, namely, that between *neutrality-modification* and *imagination*").[7] Its neutralizing operation modifies a positional re-presentation *(Vergegenwärtigung)*, which is memory. "More closely stated, *imagination* in general is the *neutrality-modification applied to 'positional' presentification (Vergegenwärtigung)*, and therefore of remembering in the widest conceivable sense of the term" *(ibid.)*. Consequently, even if it is a good auxiliary instrument of phenomenological neutralization, the image is not a pure neutralization. It retains a primary reference to a primordial presentation, that is, to a perception and positing of existence, to a belief in general.

This is why pure ideality, reached through neutralization, is not fictitious. This theme appears very early,[8] and it will continually serve to feed the polemic against Hume. But it is no accident that Hume's thought fascinated Husserl more and more. The power of pure repetition that opens up ideality and the power that liberates the imaginative reproduction of empirical perception cannot be foreign to each other, nor can their products.

Thus, in this respect, the First Investigation remains most disconcerting in more than one way:

1. Expressive phenomena in their expressive purity are, from the start, taken to be imaginative representations *(Phantasievorstellungen)*.

2. In the inner sphere thus disengaged by this fiction, the communicative discourse that a subject may occasionally address to himself ("You have gone wrong") is called "fictitious." This leads one to think that a purely expressive and noncommunicative discourse can *effectively* take place in "solitary mental life."

3. By the same token, it is supposed that in communication, where the same words, the same expressive cores are at work, where, consequently, pure idealities are indispensable, a rigorous distinction can be drawn between the fictitious and the effective

and between the ideal and the real. It is consequently supposed that effectiveness comes like an empirical and exterior cloak to expression, like a body to a soul. And these are indeed the notions Husserl uses, even when he stresses the unity of the body and soul in intentional *animation*. This unity does not impair the essential distinction, for it always remains a unity of composition.

4. Inside the pure interior "representation," in "solitary mental life," certain kinds of speech could effectively take place, as *effectively* representative (this would be the case with expressive language and, we can already specify, language with a purely objective, theoretico-logical character), while certain others would remain purely *fictitious* (those fictions located in fiction would be the acts of indicative communication between the self and the self, between the self taken as other and the self taken as self, etc.).

However, if it is admitted that, as we have tried to show, every sign whatever is of an originally repetitive structure, the general distinction between the fictitious and effective usages of the sign is threatened. *The sign is originally wrought by fiction.* From this point on, whether with respect to indicative communication or expression, there is no sure criterion by which to distinguish an exterior language from an interior language or, in the hypothesis of an interior language, an effective language from a fictitious language. Such a distinction, however, is indispensable to Husserl for proving that indication is exterior to expression, with all that this entails. In declaring this distinction illegitimate, we anticipate a whole chain of formidable consequences for phenomenology.

What we have just said concerning the sign holds, by the same token, for the act of the speaking subject. "But," as Husserl says, "in the genuine sense of communication, there is no speech in such cases, nor does one tell oneself anything: one merely conceives of oneself *(man stellt sich vor)* as speaking and communicating" (*LI*, p. 280, § 8). This leads to the second argument proposed.

Between effective communication and the representation of the self as speaking subject, Husserl must suppose a difference such that the representation of the self can only be added on to the act of communication contingently and from the outside. Now, the originary structure of repetition that we just evoked for signs must govern all acts of signification. The subject cannot speak without giving himself a representation of his speaking, and this is no accident. We can no more imagine effective speech without there being self-representation than we can imagine a representation of speech without there being effective speech. This representation may no doubt be modified, complicated, and reflected in the originary modes that are studied by the linguist, the semiologist, the psychologist, the theoretician of literature or of art, or even the philosopher. They may be quite original, but they all suppose the originary unity of speech and the representation of speech. Speech represents itself; it *is* its representation. Even better, speech is *the* representation of itself.[9]

More generally, Husserl seems to allow that the subject as he is in his effective experience and the subject as he represents himself to be can be simply external to each other. The subject may think that he is talking to himself and communicating something; in truth he is doing nothing of the kind. Where consciousness is thus entirely overcome by the belief or illusion of speaking to itself, an entirely false consciousness, one might be tempted to conclude that the truth of experience would belong to the order of the nonconscious. Quite the contrary: consciousness is the self-presence of the living, the *Erleben,* of experience. Experience thus understood is simple and is in its essence free of illusion, since it relates only to itself in an absolute proximity. The illusion of speaking to oneself would float on the surface of experience as an empty, peripheral, and secondary consciousness. Language and its representation would be added on to a consciousness that is simple and simply present to itself, or in any event to an experience that could reflect its own presence in silence.

As Husserl will say in *Ideas I,* § 111:

Every experience generally (every really living one, so to speak) is an experience according to the mode of "being present." It belongs to its very essence that it should be able to reflect upon that same essence in which it is necessarily characterized as *being* certain and present (p. 310, modified).

Signs would be foreign to this self-presence, which is the ground of presence in general. It is because signs are foreign to the self-presence of the living present that they may be called foreign to presence in general in (what is currently styled) intuition or perception.

If the representation of indicative speech in the monologue is false, it is because it is useless; this is the ultimate basis of the argumentation in this section (§ 8) of the First Investigation. If the subject indicates nothing to himself, it is because he cannot do so, and he cannot do so because there is no need of it. Since lived experience is immediately self-present in the mode of certitude and absolute necessity, the manifestation of the self to the self through the delegation or representation of an indicative sign is impossible because it is superfluous. It would be, in every sense of the term, *without reason*—thus without cause. Without cause because without purpose: *zwecklos*, Husserl says.

This *Zwecklosigkeit* of inward communication is the nonalterity, the nondifference in the identity of presence as self-presence. Of course this concept of *presence* not only involves the enigma of a being appearing in absolute proximity to itself; it also designates the temporal essence of this proximity—which does not serve to dispel the enigma. The self-presence of experience must be produced in the present taken as a now. And this is just what Husserl says: If "mental acts" are not announced to themselves through the intermediary of a *"Kundgabe,"*[10] if they do not have to be informed about themselves through the intermediary of indications, it is because they are "lived by us in the same instant" *(im selben Augenblick)*. The present of self-presence would be as indivisible as the *blink of an eye.*

[Derrida then raises the question of Husserl's own apparent recognition of the necessity of inscription for the constitution of absolutely ideal objects, that is, of scientific truth. He refers back to his introduction to *The Origin of Geometry* where he demonstrated that this concession to inscription remains tied to everything said here about voice because Husserl supposes the concept of phonetic writing. Writing would thus, according to Husserl, serve "to fix, inscribe, record, and incarnate an already prepared utterance. To reactivate writing is always to reawaken an expression in an indication, a word in the body of a letter. . . . Already speech was playing the same role by first constituting the identity of sense in thought."]

In order really to understand where the power of the voice lies, and how metaphysics, philosophy, and the determination of being as presence constitute the epoch of the voice as *technical* mastery of objective being, to understand properly the unity of *technē* and *phōnē*, we must think through the objectivity of the object. The ideal object is the most objective of objects; independent of the here-and-now acts and events of the empirical subjectivity which intends it, it can be repeated infinitely while remaining the same. Since its presence to intuition, its being-before the gaze, has no essential dependence on any worldly or empirical synthesis, the restitution of its sense in the form of presence becomes a universal and unlimited possibility. But, being *nothing* outside the world, its ideal being must be constituted, repeated, and expressed in a medium that does not impair the presence and self-presence of the acts that aim at it, a medium that preserves both the *presence of the object* before intuition and *self-presence*, the absolute proximity of the acts to themselves. The ideality of the object, which is only its being-for a nonempirical consciousness, can only be expressed in an element the phenomenality of which does not have worldly form. *The name of this element is the voice. The voice is heard.* [11] Phonic signs ("acoustical images" in Saussure's sense, or the phenomenological voice) are heard [*entendus* = "heard" and also "understood"] by the subject who proffers them in the absolute proximity of their present. The subject does not have to pass forth beyond himself to be immediately affected by his expressive activity. My words are "alive" because they seem not to leave me: not to fall outside me, outside my breath, at a visible distance; not to cease to belong to me, to be at my disposition "without further props." In any event, the phenomenon of speech, the phenomenological voice, *gives itself out* in this manner. The objection will perhaps be raised that this interiority belongs to the phenomenological and ideal aspect of every signifier. The ideal form of a written signifier, for example, is not in the world, and the distinction between the grapheme and the empirical body of the corresponding graphic sign separates an inside from an outside, phenomenological consciousness from the world. And this is true for every visual or spatial signifier. To be sure. And yet every nonphonic signifier involves a spatial reference within its very "phenomenon," in the phenomenological (nonworldly) sphere of experience in which it is given. The sense of being "outside," "in the world," is an essential component of its phenomenon. Apparently there is nothing like this in the phenomenon of the voice. In phenomenological interiority, hearing oneself and seeing oneself are two radically different orders of self-relation. Even before a description of this difference is sketched out, we can understand why the hypothesis of the "monologue" could have sanctioned the distinction between indication and expression only by presupposing an essential tie between expression and *phōnē*. Between the phonic element (in the phenomenological sense and not that of a real sound) and expression, taken as the logical character of a signifier that is *animated* in view of the ideal presence of a *Bedeutung* (itself related to an object), there must be a necessary bond. Husserl is unable to bracket what in glossamatics is called the "substance of expression" without menacing his whole enterprise. The appeal to this substance thus plays a major philosophical role.

Let us try, then, to interrogate the phenomenological value of the voice, its transcendent dignity with regard to every other signifying substance. We think, and will try to show, that this transcendence is only apparent. But this "appearance" is the very essence of consciousness and its history, and it determines an epoch characterized by the philosophical idea of truth and the opposition between truth and appearance, as this opposition still functions in phenomenology. It can therefore not be called "appearance" or be named within the sphere of metaphysical conceptuality. One cannot attempt to deconstruct this transcendence without descending, feeling one's way across the inherited concepts, toward the unnamable.

The "apparent transcendence" of the voice thus results from the fact that the signified, which is always ideal by essence, the "expressed" *Bedeutung*, is immediately present in the act of expression. This immediate presence results from the fact that the phenomenological "body" of the signifier seems to be effaced at the very moment it is produced; it seems already to belong to the element of ideality. It performs a phenomenological reduction on itself, transforming the worldly opacity of its body into pure diaphaneity. This effacement of the sensible body and its exteriority is *for consciousness* the very form of the immediate presence of the signified.

Why is the phoneme the most "ideal" of signs? Where does this complicity between sound and ideality, or rather, between voice and ideality, come from? (Hegel was more attentive to this than any other philosopher, and, from the point of view of the history of metaphysics, this is a noteworthy fact, one we will examine elsewhere.)[12] When I speak, it belongs to the phenomenological essence of this operation that *I hear myself* [je m'entende] *at the same time* that I speak. The signifier, animated by my breath and by the meaning-intention (in Husserl's language, the expression animated by the *Bedeutungsintention*), is in absolute proximity to me. The living act, the life-giving act, the *Lebendigkeit*, which animates the body of the signifier and transforms it into a meaningful expression, the soul of language, seems not to separate itself from itself, from its own self-presence. It does not risk death in the body of a signifier that is given over to the world and the visibility of space. It can *show* the ideal object or ideal *Bedeutung* connected to it without venturing outside ideality, outside the interiority of self-present life. The system of *Zeigen*,[13] the finger and eye movements (concerning which we earlier wondered whether they were not inseparable from phenomenality) are not absent here; but they are interiorized. The phenomenon continues to be an object for the voice; indeed, insofar as the ideality of the object seems to depend on the voice and thus becomes *absolutely accessible* in it, the system which ties phenomenality to the possibility of *Zeigen* functions better than ever in the voice. *The phoneme is given as the dominated ideality of the phenomenon.*

This self-presence of the animating act in the transparent spirituality of what it animates, this inwardness of life with itself, which has always made us say that speech [parole] is alive, supposes, then, that the speaking subject hears himself [s'entende] in the present. Such is the essence or norm of speech. It is implied in the very structure of speech that the speaker *hears himself:* both that he perceives the sensible form of the pho- nemes and that he understands his own expressive intention. If accidents occur which seem to contradict this teleological neces- sity, either they will be overcome by some supplementary opera- tion or there will be no speech. Deaf and dumb go hand in hand. He who is deaf can engage in colloquy only by shaping his acts in the form of words, whose telos requires that they be heard by him who utters them.

Considered from a purely phenomenological point of view, within the reduction, the process of speech has the originality of presenting itself already as pure phenomenon, as having already suspended the natural attitude and the existential thesis of the world. The operation of "hearing oneself speak" is an auto-affec- tion of an absolutely unique kind. On the one hand, it operates within the medium of universality; what appears as signified therein must be idealities that are *idealiter* indefinitely repeata- ble or transmissible as the same. On the other hand, the subject can hear or speak to himself and be affected by the signifier he produces, without passing through an external detour, the world, the sphere of what is not properly his, the nonproper. Every other form of auto-affection must either pass through what is outside the sphere of "ownness" or forgo any claim to universality. When I see myself, either because I gaze upon a limited region of my body or because it is reflected in a mirror, the nonproper has already entered the field of this auto-affection, with the result that it is no longer pure. In the experience of touching and being touched, the same thing happens. In both cases, the surface of my body, as something external, must begin by being exposed in the world. But, we could ask, are there not forms of pure auto- affection in the inwardness of one's own body which do not require the intervention of any surface displayed in the world and yet are not of the order of the voice? But then these forms remain purely empirical, for they could not belong to a medium of universal signification. Now, to account for the phenomeno- logical power of the voice, we shall have to specify the concept of pure auto-affection more precisely and describe what in it makes it proper to universality. As pure auto-affection, the oper- ation of hearing oneself speak seems to reduce even the inward surface of one's own body; in its phenomenal being it seems capable of dispensing with this exteriority within interiority, this interior space in which our experience or image of our own body is spread forth. This is why hearing oneself speak [s'entendre parler] is experienced as an absolutely pure auto-affection, occurring in a self-proximity that would in fact be the absolute reduction of space in general. It is this purity that makes it fit for universality. Requiring the intervention of no determinate surface in the world, being produced in the world as pure auto-affection, it is a signifying substance absolutely at our disposition. For the voice meets no obstacle to its emission in the world precisely because it is produced as pure auto-affection. This auto-affection is no doubt the possibility for what is called subjectivity or the for-itself, but, without it, no world as such would appear. For at its core it supposes the unity of sound (which is in the world) and phōnē (in the phenomenological sense). An objective "worldly" science surely can teach us nothing about the essence of the voice. But the unity of sound and voice, which allows the voice to be produced in the world as pure auto-affection, is the sole case to escape the distinction between what is worldly and what is transcendental; by the same token, it makes that distinction possible.

It is this universality that dictates that, de jure and by virtue of its structure, no consciousness is possible without the voice. The voice is the being that is proximate to itself in the form of universality, as con-sciousness [con-science]; the voice is consciousness. In colloquy, the propagation of signs does not seem to meet any obstacles because it brings together two phenomenological origins of pure auto-affection. To speak to someone is doubtless to hear oneself speak, to be heard by oneself; but, at the same time, if one is heard by another, to speak is to make him repeat immediately in himself the hearing-oneself-speak in the very form in which I produced it. This immediate repetition is a reproduction of pure auto-affection without the help of anything external. This possibility of reproduction, the structure of which is absolutely unique, gives itself out as the phenomenon of a mastery or limitless power over the signifier, since the signifier itself has the form of what is not external. Ideally, in the teleological essence of speech, it would then be possible for the signifier to be in absolute proximity to the signified aimed at in intuition and governing the meaning. The signifier would become perfectly diaphanous due to the absolute proximity to the signified. This proximity is broken when, instead of hearing myself speak, I see myself write or gesture.

[....]

But if Husserl had to recognize the necessity of these "incarnations," even as beneficial threats, it is because an underlying motif was disturbing and contesting the security of these traditional distinctions from within and because the possibility of writing dwelt within speech, which was itself at work in the inwardness of thought.

And here again we find all the incidences of originary nonpresence the emergence of which we have already noted on several occasions. Even while repressing difference by assigning it to the exteriority of the signifiers, Husserl could not fail to recognize its work at the origin of sense and presence. As the operation of the voice, auto-affection supposed that a pure difference comes to divide self-presence. In this pure difference is rooted the possibility of everything we think we can exclude from auto-affection: space, the outside, the world, the body, etc. As soon as it is admitted that auto-affection is the condition for self-presence, no pure transcendental reduction is possible. But it was necessary to pass through the transcendental reduction in order to grasp this difference in what is closest to it—which cannot mean grasping it in its identity, its purity, or its origin, for it has none. We come closest to it in the movement of differance.[14]

This movement of differance is not something that happens to a transcendental subject; it produces the subject. Auto-affection is not a modality of experience that characterizes a being that would already be itself *(autos)*. It produces sameness as self-relation within self-difference; it produces sameness as the nonidentical.

Shall we say that the auto-affection we have been talking about up until now concerns only the operation of the voice? Shall we say that difference concerns only the order of the phonic "signifier" or the "secondary stratum" of expression? Can we always hold out for the possibility of a pure and purely self-present identity at the level Husserl wanted to disengage as a level of pre-expressive experience, that is, the level of sense prior to *Bedeutung* and expression?

It would be easy to show that such a possibility is excluded at the very root of transcendental experience.

Why, in fact, has the concept of auto-affection imposed itself on us? What constitutes the originality of speech, what distinguishes it from every other element of signification, is that its substance seems to be purely temporal. And this temporality does not unfold a sense that would itself be nontemporal; even before being expressed, sense is through and through temporal. According to Husserl, the omnitemporality of ideal objects is but a mode of temporality. And when Husserl describes a sense that seems to escape temporality, he hastens to make it clear that this is only a provisional step in analysis and that he is considering a constituted temporality. However, as soon as one takes the movement of temporalization into account, as it is already analyzed in *The Phenomenology of Internal Time-Consciousness*, the concept of pure auto-affection must be employed as well. This we know is what Heidegger does in *Kant and the Problem of Metaphysics*, precisely when he is concerned with the subject of time. The "source point" or "originary impression," that out of which the movement of temporalization is produced, is already pure auto-affection. First it is a pure production, since temporality is never the real predicate of a being. The intuition of time itself cannot be empirical; it is a receiving that receives nothing. The absolute novelty of each now is therefore engendered by nothing; it consists in an originary impression that engenders itself:

> The primal impression is the absolute beginning of this generation—the primal source, that from which all others are continuously generated. In itself, however, it is not generated; it does not come into existence as that which is generated but through *spontaneous generation*. It does not grow up (it has no seed): it is primal creation (*The Phenomenology of Internal Time-Consciousness*, trans. James S. Churchill [Bloomington, Ind.: Indiana University Press, 1964] Appendix I, p. 131; italics added).

This pure spontaneity is an impression; it creates nothing. The new now is not a being, it is not a produced object; and every language fails to describe this pure movement other than by metaphor, that is, by borrowing its concepts from the order of the objects of experience, an order this temporalization makes possible. Husserl continually warns us against these metaphors.[15] The process by which the living now, produced by spontaneous generation, must, in order to be a now and to be retained in another now, affect itself without recourse to anything empirical but with a new originary actuality in which it would become a non-now, a past now—this process is indeed a pure auto-affection in which the same is the same only in being affected by the other, only by becoming the other of the same. This auto-affection must be pure since the originary impression is here affected by nothing other than itself, by the absolute "novelty" of another originary impression which is another now. We speak metaphorically as soon as we introduce a determinate being into the description of this "movement"; we talk about "movement" in the very terms that movement makes possible. But we have been always already adrift in ontic metaphor; temporalization here is the root of a metaphor that can only be originary. The word *time* itself, as it has always been understood in the history of metaphysics, is a metaphor which *at the same time* both indicates and dissimulates the "movement" of this auto-affection. All the concepts of metaphysics—in particular those of activity and passivity, will and nonwill, and therefore those of affection or auto-affection, purity and impurity, etc.—*cover up* the strange "movement" of this difference.

But this pure difference, which constitutes the self-presence of the living present, introduces into self-presence from the beginning all the impurity putatively excluded from it. The living present springs forth out of its nonidentity with itself and from the possibility of a retentional trace. It is always already a trace. This trace cannot be thought out on the basis of a simple present whose life would be within itself; the self of the living present is primordially a trace. The trace is not an attribute; we cannot say that the self of the living present "primordially is" it. Originary-being must be thought on the basis of the trace, and not the reverse. This archewriting is at work at the origin of sense. Sense, being temporal in nature, as Husserl recognized, is never simply present; it is always already engaged in the "movement" of the trace, that is, in the order of "signification." It has always already issued forth from itself into the "expressive stratum" of lived experience. Since the trace is the intimate relation of the living present to its outside, the opening to exteriority in general, to the nonproper, etc., *the temporalization of sense is, from the outset, a "spacing."* As soon as we admit spacing both as "interval" or difference and as opening to the outside, there can no longer be any absolute inside, for the "outside" has insinuated itself into the movement by which the inside of the nonspatial, which is called "time," appears, is constituted, is "presented." Space is "in" time; it is time's pure leaving-itself; it is the "outside-itself" as the self-relation of time. The exteriority of space, exteriority as space, does not overtake time; rather, it opens as pure "outside" "within" the movement of temporalization. If we recall now that the pure inwardness of phonic auto-affection supposed the purely temporal nature of the "expressive" process, we see that the theme of a pure inwardness of speech, or of the "hearing oneself speak," is radically contradicted by "time" itself. The going-forth "into the world" is also originarily implied by the movement of temporalization. "Time" cannot be an "absolute subjectivity" precisely because it cannot be thought on the basis of a present and the self-presence of a present being. Like everything thought under this heading, and like all that is excluded by the most rigorous transcendental reduction, the "world" is originarily implied by the movement of temporalization. As a relation between an inside and an outside in general, an existent and a nonexistent in general, a constituting and a constituted in general, temporalization is at once the very power and limit of phenomenological reduction. Hearing oneself speak is not the interiority of an inside that is closed in upon itself; it is the irreducible openness in the inside; it is the eye and the world within speech. *Phenomenological reduction is a scene, a theater stage.*

Thus, just as expression is not added like a "stratum"[16] to the presence of a pre-expressive sense, so, in the same way, the inside of expression does not accidentally happen to be affected by the outside of indication. Their intertwining *(Verflechtung)* is originary; it is not a contingent association that could be undone by methodic attention and patient reduction. The analysis, necessary as it is, encounters an absolute limit at this point. If indication is not added to expression, which is not added to sense, we can nonetheless speak in regard to them, of an originary "supplement"[17]: their *addition* comes to *make up for* a deficiency, it comes to compensate for an originary nonself-presence. And if indication—for example, writing in the everyday sense— must necessarily be "added" to speech to complete the constitution of the ideal object, if speech must be "added" to the thought identity of the object, it is because the "presence" of sense and speech had already from the start fallen short of itself.

[. . . .]

—*Translated by David B. Allison*

NOTES

1. I.e., purpose—ED.

2. *Logical Investigations*, trans. J. N. Findlay (New York: Humanities Press, 1970), pp. 279–80. First Investigation § 8; further references to this translation, abbreviated *LI*, will be given in parentheses.

3. Cf. on this subject the note by the French translators of the *Logical Investigations* (French ed., vol. 2, pt. 1, p. 276) and that by the French translators of *The Phenomenology of Internal Time-Consciousness* (French ed., p. 26).

4. Cf. on this subject *The Origin of Geometry* and the introduction to the French translation, pp. 60–69.

5. The assertion implied by the whole of phenomenology is that the Being *(Sein)* of the *Ideal* is nonreality, nonexistence. This predetermination is the first word of phenomenology. Although it does not exist, ideality is anything but a nonbeing. "Each attempt to transform the being of what is ideal *(das Sein des Idealen)* into the possible being of what is real, must obviously suffer shipwreck on the fact that possibilities themselves are ideal objects. Possibilities can as little be found in the real world, as can numbers in general, or triangles in general" (*LI*, Second Investigation, p. 345). "It is naturally not our intention to put the *being of what is ideal* on a level with the *being-thought-of which characterizes the fictitious or the absurd (Widersinnigen)*" (ibid., p. 352, § 8).

6. If one were to employ distinctions from "pure logical grammar" and the *Formal and Transcendental Logic,* this impossibility would have to be specified as follows: this proposition certainly makes sense, it constitutes

intelligible speech, it is not *sinnlos;* but within this intelligibility and for the reason indicated, it is "absurd" (with the absurdity of contradiction—*Widersinnigkeit*) and *a fortiori* "false." But as the classical idea of truth, which guides these distinctions, has itself issued from such a concealment of the relationship to death, this "falsity" is the very truth of truth. Hence, it is in other completely different "categories" (if such thoughts can still be labeled thus) that these movements have to be interpreted.

7. *Ideas: General Introduction to Pure Phenomenology*, trans. W. R. Boyce Gibson (New York: Humanities Press, 1931), I, p. 309; section 3, § 111; translation modified; further references to this translation will be included in the text in parentheses.

8. Cf., particularly, *LI*, Second Investigation, ch. 2.

9. But if the *re-* of this re-presentation does not signify the simple—repetitive or reflexive—reduplication that *befalls* a simple presence (which is what the word *representation* has always *meant*), then what we are approaching or advancing here concerning the relation between presence and representation must be approached in other terms. What we are describing as originary representation can be provisionally designated with this term only within the closure the limits of which we are here seeking to transgress by setting down and demonstrating various contradictory or untenable propositions within it, attempting thereby to institute a kind of insecurity and to open it up to the outside. This can be done only from a certain inside.

10. Manifestation.—ED.

11. *"La voix s'entend":* the voice is heard, understood, but also it hears, understands, and intends itself.—ED.

12. See "The Pit and the Pyramid: Introduction to Hegel's Semiology" in *Margins of Philosophy* [1972] —ED.

13. Pointing, indication.—ED.

14. For this term, see below, pp. **59–79.**—ED.

15. See, e.g., the admirable § 36 of *The Phenomenology of Internal Time-Consciousness* which proves the absence of a proper noun for this strange "movement," which, furthermore, is not a movement. "For all this," concludes Husserl, "names fail us." We would still have to radicalize Husserl's intention here in a specific direction. For it is not by chance that he still designates this unnamable as an "absolute subjectivity," that is, as a being conceived on the basis of presence as substance, *ousia, hypokeimenon:* a self-identical being in self-presence which forms the substance of a subject. What is said to be unnameable in this paragraph is not exactly something we know to be a *present* being in the form of self-presence, a substance modified into a subject, into an absolute subject whose self-presence is pure and does not depend on any external affection, any outside. *All this is present, and we can name it, the proof being that its being as absolute subjectivity is not questioned.* What is unnameable, according to Husserl, are only the "absolute properties" of this subject; the subject therefore is indeed designated in terms of the classical metaphysical schema that distinguishes substance (present being) from its attributes. Another schema that keeps the incompa-

rable depth of the analysis within the closure of the metaphysics of presence is the subject–object opposition. This being whose "absolute properties" are indescribable is present as *absolute* subjectivity, is an *absolutely* present and *absolutely* self-present being, only in its opposition to the object. The object is relative; what is absolute is the subject: "We can say only that *this flux is something which we name in conformity with what is constituted*, but it is nothing temporally 'objective.' It is absolute subjectivity and has the absolute properties of something to be denoted metaphorically as 'flux,' as a point of actuality, primal source-point, that from which springs the 'now,' and so on. In the lived experience of actuality, we have the primal source-point and a continuity of moments of reverberation *(Nachhallmomenten)*. For all this, names are lacking" (*ITC*, § 36, p. 100; italics added). This determination of "absolute subjectivity" would also have to be crossed out as soon as we conceive the present on the basis of difference, and not the reverse. The concept of *subjectivity* belongs *a priori and in general* to the order of the *constituted*. This holds *a fortiori* for the analogical appresentation that constitutes intersubjectivity. Intersubjectivity is inseparable from temporalization taken as the openness of the present upon an outside of itself, upon *another* absolute present. This being outside itself proper to time is its *spacing:* it is a *protostage [archi-scène]*. This stage, as the relation of one present to another present *as such*, that is, as a nonderived re-presentation *(Vergegenwärtigung* or *Repräsentation)*, produces the structure of signs in general as "reference," as being-for-something *(für etwas sein)*, and radically precludes their reduction. There is no constituting subjectivity. The very concept of constitution itself must be deconstructed.

16. Moreover, in the important §§ 124–27 of *Ideas I*, which we shall elsewhere follow step by step, Husserl invites us—while continually speaking of an underlying stratum of pre-expressive experience—not to "hold too hard by the metaphor of stratification *(Schichtung)*; expression is not of the nature of an overlaid varnish or covering garment; it is a mental formation, which exercises new intentional influences on the intentional substratum *(Unterschicht)*" *(Ideas I*, p. 349, § 124).

17. This notion of originary supplementarity is developed at length in the second part of **Of Grammatology;** see below, pp. 32–33—ED.

TWO

From *Of Grammatology*

(De la grammatologie, [1967])

Of Grammatology, for many English-speaking readers Derrida's most well known book, opens with a chapter titled "The End of the Book and the Beginning of Writing." One should thus be forewarned that, despite a certain familiar appearance, this is perhaps not a book, or not a book like any other. But what is this "book" the end of which is announced here so as to make way for something else called writing?

It is the book dreamed up by *logocentrism*. On the first page of the *Grammatology*, Derrida proposes, in effect, to substitute the latter word for metaphysics in order to foreground that which has always determined metaphysical systems of thought: their dependance on a *logos* or speech, itself conceived on the model of the phonetic sign. As in Aristotle's famous formulation, "Spoken words are the symbols of mental experience and written words are the symbols of spoken words," speech is thought of as remaining closer to psychic interiority (that itself reflects things in the world by means of natural resemblance) than writing, which symbolizes interiority only at a second remove. And writing can be seen as deriving from speech because it is thought of as purely phonetic transcription. It mirrors speech but is less apt than speech to restore the "thing itself," the referent, idea, or signified which, in one way or another, occupies the place of a pure intelligibility that has never "fallen" into the sensible realm of the exterior sign or symbol, and that therefore always remains present to itself. Derrida quickly sketches a few of the most important revisions this logocentrism has undergone in the history of Western thought (the Scholastics, Cartesianism, Rousseauism—to which he will return at length in the second part of the book—Hegel, Heidegger) so as to underscore its persistence to a greater or lesser extent, even with Heidegger, who nevertheless so persistently challenged the metaphysics of presence. Nor has modern linguistics or semiotics, as inaugurated by Saussure and elaborated by structuralists such as Roman Jakobson, succeeded in divesting their science of its profoundly metaphysical, logocentric ties. Derrida insists that linguistics remains a metaphysics as long as it retains the distinction between signified and signifier within the concept of the sign. This distinction is always ultimately grounded in a pure intelligibility tied to an absolute logos: the face of God. The concept of the sign, whose history is coextensive with the history of logocentrism, is essentially theological.

How then to understand writing differently? To write differently? Within the same tradition that debases writing as the sensible exteriority of the sign there is also and paradoxically a privileged place reserved for it as the "writing" inscribed—by God or by Nature—in the soul. "The paradox that must be attended to is this," writes Derrida: "natural and universal writing, intelligible and nontemporal writing, is thus named by way of metaphor. . . . Of course, this metaphor remains enigmatic and refers to a 'literal' meaning of writing as the first metaphor. . . . It is not therefore a matter of inverting the literal meaning and the figurative meaning but of determining the 'literal' meaning of writing as metaphoricity itself" (p. 15). This determination would be the beginning of writing because "metaphoricity itself" cannot have an ultimate referent in some eternal presence. It cannot be totalized, as in a volume or a book. The idea of the book, observes Derrida, is always an idea of the totality of the signified pre-existing and watching over the inscription of the signifier while remaining independent in its ideality. "The idea of the book . . . is profoundly alien to the sense of writing. It is the encyclopedic protection of theology and of logocentrism against the disruption of writing . . . against difference in general" (p. 18).

Of Grammatology has two parts. "Writing Before the Letter," the first part to which we have been referring and from which all the following selections are taken, sets out a broad theoretical, historical grid within which are identified the stakes of a deconstruction of logocentrism. Part II, "Nature, Culture, Writing," proceeds to carry out a minute and stunning deconstructive reading of Rousseau's evaluation of writing, particularly in *The Essay on the Origin of*

Languages, as a *supplement* to speech. The latter notion, which floats between its two senses of that which is added on and that which substitutes for and supplants, is an example of the undecidability on which Derrida's deconstructive readings are often made to turn. Having discovered undecidable supplementarity in Rousseau, he will often refer to it as a semiconcept not unlike differance (see below).

[. . . .]

The reassuring evidence within which Western tradition had to organize itself and must continue to live would therefore be as follows: The order of the signified is never contemporary, is at best the subtly discrepant inverse or parallel—discrepant by the time of a breath—from the order of the signifier. And the sign must be the unity of a heterogeneity, since the signified (sense or thing, noeme or reality) is not in itself a signifier, a *trace:* in any case is not constituted in its sense by its relationship with a possible trace. The formal essence of the signified is *presence,* and the privilege of its proximity to the logos as *phonè* is the privilege of presence. This is the inevitable response as soon as one asks: "What is the sign?," that is to say, when one submits the sign to the question of essence, to the "ti esti."[1] The "formal essence" of the sign can only be determined in terms of presence. One cannot get around that response, except by challenging the very form of the question and beginning to think that the sign ~~is~~ that ill-named ~~thing~~, the only one, that escapes the instituting question of philosophy: "What is . . .?"[2]

Radicalizing the concepts of *interpretation, perspective, evaluation, difference,* and all the "empiricist" or nonphilosophical motifs that have constantly tormented philosophy throughout the history of the West, and besides, have had nothing but the inevitable weakness of being produced in the field of philosophy, Nietzsche, far from remaining *simply* (with Hegel and as Heidegger wished)[3] *within* metaphysics, contributed a great deal to the liberation of the signifier from its dependence or derivation with respect to the logos and the related concept of truth or the primary signified, in whatever sense that is understood. Reading, and therefore writing, the text were for Nietzsche "originary"[4] operations (I put that word within quotation marks for reasons to appear later) with regard to a sense that they do not first have to transcribe or discover, which would not therefore be a truth signified in the original element and presence of the logos, as *topos noetos,* divine understanding, or the structure of *a priori* necessity. To save Nietzsche from a reading of the Heideggerian type, it seems that we must above all not attempt to restore or make explicit a less naive "ontology," composed of profound ontological intuitions acceding to some originary truth, an entire fundamentality hidden under the appearance of an empiricist or metaphysical text. The virulence of Nietzschean thought could not be more completely misunderstood. On the contrary, one must *accentuate* the "naïveté" of a breakthrough which cannot attempt a step outside of metaphysics, which cannot *criticize* metaphysics radically without still utilizing in a certain way, in a certain type or a certain style of *text,* propositions that, read within the philosophic corpus, that is to say according to Nietzsche ill-read or unread, have always been and will always be "naive-tés," incoherent signs of an absolute appurtenance. Therefore, rather than protect Nietzsche from the Heideggerian reading, we should perhaps offer him up to it completely, underwriting that interpretation without reserve; in a *certain way* and up to the point where, the content of the Nietzschean discourse being almost lost for the question of being, its form regains its absolute strangeness, where his text finally invokes a different type of reading, more faithful to his type of writing: Nietzsche has *written what* he has written. He has written that writing—and first of all his own—is not originarily subordinate to the logos and to truth. And that this subordination has *come into being* during an epoch the meaning of which we must deconstruct. Now in this direction (but only in this direction, for read otherwise, the Nietzschean demolition remains dogmatic and, like all reversals, a captive of that metaphysical edifice which it professes to over-throw. On that point and in that *order of reading,* the conclu-sions of Heidegger and Fink are irrefutable), Heideggerian thought would reinstate rather than destroy the instance of the logos and of the truth of being as "primum signatum:" the "transcenden-

tal" signified ("transcendental" in a certain sense, as in the Middle
Ages the transcendental—*ens, unum, verum, bonum*—was said
to be the "primum cognitum") implied by all categories or all
determined significations, by all lexicons and all syntax, and
therefore by all linguistic signifiers, though not to be identified
simply with any one of those signifiers, allowing itself to be
precomprehended through each of them, remaining irreducible
to all the epochal determinations that it nonetheless makes possible, thus opening the history of the logos, yet itself being only
through the logos; that is, *being nothing* before the logos and
outside of it. The logos *of* being, "Thought obeying the Voice of
Being,"[5] is the first and the last resource of the sign, of the
difference between *signans* and *signatum*. There has to be a
transcendental signified for the difference between signifier and
signified to be somewhere absolute and irreducible. It is not by
chance that the thought of being, as the thought of this transcendental signified, is manifested above all in the voice: in a language of words *[mots]*. The voice *is heard* (understood)—that
undoubtedly is what is called conscience—closest to the self as
the absolute effacement of the signifier: pure auto-affection that
necessarily has the form of time and does not borrow from outside of itself, in the world or in "reality," any accessory signifier,
any substance of expression foreign to its own spontaneity. It is
the unique experience of the signified producing itself spontaneously, from within the self, and nevertheless, as signified concept, in the element of ideality or universality. The unwordly
character of this substance of expression is constitutive of this
ideality. This experience of the effacement of the signifier in the
voice is not merely one illusion among many—since it is the
condition of the very idea of truth—but I shall elsewhere show
in what it does delude itself. This illusion is the history of truth
and it cannot be dissipated so quickly. Within the closure of this
experience, the word *[mot]* is lived as the elementary and unde-
composable unity of the signified and the voice, of the concept
and a transparent substance of expression. This experience is
considered in its greatest purity—and at the same time in the
condition of its possibility—as the experience of "being." The
word *being*, or at any rate the word designating the sense of being
in different languages, is, with some others, an "originary word"

("Urwort"),[6] the transcendental word assuring the possibility of being-word to all other words. As such, it is precomprehended in all language and—this is the opening of *Being and Time*—only this precomprehension would permit the opening of the question of the sense of being in general, beyond all regional ontologies and all metaphysics: a question that broaches philosophy (for example, in the *Sophist*) and lets itself be taken over by philosophy, a question that Heidegger repeats by submitting the history of metaphysics to it. Heidegger reminds us constantly that the sense of being is neither the word *being* nor the concept of being. But as that sense is nothing outside of language and the language of words, it is tied, if not to a particular word or to a particular system of language *(concesso non dato)*, at least to the possibility of the word in general. And to the possibility of its irreducible simplicity. One could thus think that it remains only to choose between two possibilities. (1) Does a modern linguistics, a science of signification breaking up the unity of the word and breaking with its alleged irreducibility, still have anything to do with "language?" Heidegger would probably doubt it. (2) Conversely, is not all that is profoundly meditated as the thought or the question of being enclosed within an old linguistics of the word which one practices here unknowingly? Unknowingly because such a linguistics, whether spontaneous or systematic, has always had to share the presuppositions of metaphysics. The two operate on the same grounds.

It goes without saying that the alternatives cannot be so simple.

On the one hand, if modern linguistics remains completely enclosed within a classical conceptuality, if especially it naively uses the word *being* and all that it presupposes, that which, within this linguistics, deconstructs the unity of the word in general can no longer, according to the model of the Heideggerian question, as it functions powerfully from the very opening of *Being and Time*, be circumscribed as ontic science or regional ontology. Inasmuch as the question of being unites indissolubly with the precomprehension of the *word being*, without being reduced to it, the linguistics that works for the deconstruction of the constituted unity of that word has only, in fact or in principle, to have the question of being posed in order to define its field and the order of its dependence.

Not only is its field no longer simply ontic, but the limits of ontology that correspond to it no longer have anything regional about them. And can what I say here of linguistics, or at least of a certain work that may be undertaken within it and thanks to it, not be said of all research *inasmuch as and to the strict extent that* it would finally deconstitute the founding concept-words of ontology, of being in its privilege? Outside of linguistics, it is in psychoanalytic research that this breakthrough seems at present to have the greatest likelihood of being expanded.

Within the strictly limited space of this breakthrough, these "sciences" are no longer *dominated* by the questions of a transcendental phenomenology or a fundamental ontology. One may perhaps say, following the order of questions inaugurated by *Being and Time* and radicalizing the questions of Husserlian phenomenology, that this breakthrough does not belong to science itself, that what thus seems to be produced within an ontic field or within a regional ontology, does not belong to them by rights and leads back to the question of being itself.

Because it is indeed the *question* of being that Heidegger asks of metaphysics. And with it the question of truth, of sense, of the logos. The incessant meditation upon that question does not restore confidence. On the contrary, it dislodges the confidence at its own depth, which, being a matter of the meaning of being, is more difficult than is often believed. In examining the state just before all determinations of being, destroying the securities of onto-theology, such a meditation contributes, quite as much as the most contemporary linguistics, to the dislocation of the unity of the sense of being, that is, in the last instance, the unity of the word.

It is thus that, after evoking the "voice of being," Heidegger recalls that it is silent, mute, insonorous, wordless, originarily *a-phonic (die Gewähr der lautlosen Stimme verborgener Quellen ...).* The voice of the sources is not heard *[ne s'entend pas].* A rupture between the originary meaning of being and the word, between meaning and the voice, between "the voice of being" and the *"phonē,"* between "the call of being," and articulated sound; such a rupture, which at once confirms a fundamental metaphor, and renders it suspect by accentuating its metaphoric discrepancy, translates the ambiguity of the Heideggerian situation with respect to the metaphysics of presence and logocentrism. It is at once contained within it and transgresses it. But it is impossible to separate the two. The very movement of transgression sometimes holds it back short of the limit. In opposition to what we suggested above, it must be remembered that, for Heidegger, the sense of being is never simply and rigorously a "signified." It is not by chance that that word is not used; that means that being escapes the movement of the sign, a proposition that can equally well be understood as a repetition of the classical tradition and as a caution with respect to a technical or metaphysical theory of signification. On the other hand, the sense of being is literally neither "primary," nor "fundamental," nor "transcendental," whether understood in the scholastic, Kantian, or Husserlian sense. The extrication of being as "transcending" the categories of the entity, the opening of fundamental ontology, are nothing but necessary yet provisional moments. From *The Introduction to Metaphysics* onward, Heidegger renounces the project of and the word ontology.[7] The necessary, originary, and irreducible dissimulation of the meaning of being, its occultation within the very blossoming forth of presence, that retreat without which there would be no history of being which was completely *history* and history of *being*, Heidegger's insistence on noting that being is produced as history only through the logos and is nothing outside of it, the difference between being and the entity—all this clearly indicates that fundamentally nothing escapes the movement of the signifier and that, in the last instance, the difference between signified and signifier *is nothing*. This proposition of transgression, not yet integrated into a careful discourse, runs the risk of formulating regression itself. One must therefore *go by way of* the question of being as it is directed by Heidegger and by him alone, at and beyond onto-theology, in order to reach the rigorous thought of that strange nondifference and in order to determine it correctly. Heidegger occasionally reminds us that "being," as it is fixed in its general syntactic and lexicological forms within linguistics and Western philosophy, is not a primary and absolutely irreducible signified, that it is still rooted in a system of languages and an historically determined "significance," although strangely privileged as the virtue of disclosure and dissimulation; particularly when he invites us to meditate on the "privilege" of the "third person singular of the present indicative" and the "infinitive." Western metaphysics, as the limitation of the sense of being within the field of presence, is produced as the domination of a linguistic form.[8] To question the origin of that domination does not amount to hypostatizing a transcendental signified, but to a questioning of what constitutes our history and what produced transcendentality itself. Heidegger brings it up also when in *Zur Seinsfrage,* for the same reason, he lets the word *being* be read only if it is crossed out *(kreuzweise Durchstreichung).* That cross is not, however, a "merely negative symbol."[9] This erasure is the final writing of an epoch. Under its strokes the presence of a transcendental signified is effaced while still remaining legible. Is effaced while still remaining legible, is destroyed while making visible the very idea of the sign. Inasmuch as it de-limits onto-theology, the metaphysics of presence and logocentrism, this last writing is also the first writing.

To come to recognize, not before but on the horizon of the Heideggerian paths, and yet in them, that the sense of being is not a transcendental or trans-epochal signified (even if it was always dissimulated within the epoch) but already, in a truly *unheard of* sense, a determined signifying trace, is to affirm that within the decisive concept of ontico-ontological difference, *all is not to be thought at one go;* entity and being, ontic and ontological, "ontico-ontological," would be in an original style, *derivative* with regard to difference; and with respect to what I shall later call *differance,* an economic concept designating the production of differing/deferring. The ontico-ontological difference and its ground *(Grund)* in the "transcendence of Dasein"[10] are not absolutely originary. Differance by itself would be more "originary," but one would no longer be able to call it "origin" or "ground," those notions belonging essentially to the history of onto-theology, to the system functioning as the effacement of difference. It can, however, be thought of in the closest proximity to itself only on one condition: that one begins by determining it as the ontico-ontological difference before erasing that determination. The necessity of passing through that erased determination, the necessity of that *trick of writing* is irreducible. An unemphatic and difficult thought that, through much unperceived mediation, must carry the entire burden of our question, a question that I shall provisionally call *historial [historiale]*. It is with its help that I shall later be able to attempt to relate differance and writing.

The hesitation of these thoughts (here Nietzsche's and Heidegger's) is not an "incoherence": it is a trembling proper to all post-Hegelian attempts and to this passage between two epochs. The movements of deconstruction do not destroy structures from the outside. They are not possible and effective, nor can they take accurate aim, except by inhabiting those structures. Inhabiting them *in a certain way*, because one always inhabits, and all the more when one does not suspect it. Operating necessarily from the inside, borrowing all the strategic and economic resources of subversion from the old structure, borrowing them structurally, that is to say without being able to isolate their elements and atoms, the enterprise of deconstruction always in a certain way falls prey to its own work.

[. . . .]

The hinge *[brisure]*[11] marks the impossibility that a sign, the unity of a signifier and a signified, be produced within the plenitude of a present and an absolute presence. That is why there is no full speech, however much one might wish to restore it with or against psychoanalysis. Before thinking to reduce it or to restore the meaning of the full speech which claims to be truth, one must ask the question of meaning and of its origin in difference. Such is the place of a problematic of the *trace*.

Why of the *trace?* What led us to the choice of this word? I have begun to answer this question. But this question is such, and such the nature of my answer, that the place of the one and of the other must constantly be in movement. If words and concepts receive meaning only in sequences of differences, one can justify one's language, and one's choice of terms, only within a topic [an orientation in space] and an historical strategy. The justification can therefore never be absolute and definitive. It corresponds to a condition of forces and translates an historical calculation. Thus, over and above those that I have already defined, a certain number of givens belonging to the discourse of our time have progressively imposed this choice upon me. The word *trace* must of itself refer to a certain number of contemporary discourses the force of which I intend to take into account. Not that I accept them totally. But the word *trace* establishes the clearest connections with them and thus permits me to dispense with certain developments which have already demonstrated their effectiveness in those fields. Thus, I relate this concept of *trace* to what is at the center of the latest work of Emmanuel Levinas and his critique of ontology: [12] relationship to the illeity as to the alterity of a past that never was and can never be lived in the originary or modified form of presence. Reconciled here to a Heideggerian intention,—as it is not in Levinas's thought—this notion signifies, sometimes beyond Heideggerian discourse, the undermining of an ontology that, in its innermost course, has determined the meaning of being as presence and the meaning of language as the full continuity of speech. To make enigmatic what one thinks one understands by the words *proximity, immediacy, presence* (the proximate *[proche]*, the proper *[propre]*, and the pre- of presence), is my final intention in this book. This deconstruction of presence accomplishes itself through the deconstruction of consciousness, and therefore through the irreducible notion of the trace *(Spur)*, as it appears in both Nietzschean and Freudian discourse. And finally, in all scientific fields, notably in biology, this notion seems currently to be dominant and irreducible.

If the trace, arche-phenomenon of "memory," which must be thought before the opposition of nature and culture, animality and humanity, etc., belongs to the very movement of signification, then signification is *a priori* written, whether inscribed or not, in one form or another, in a "sensible" and "spatial" element that is called "exterior." Arche-writing, the first possibility of the spoken word, then of the *"graphie"* in the narrow sense, the birthplace of "usurpation," denounced from Plato to Saussure, [13] this trace is the opening of the first exteriority in general, the enigmatic relationship of the living to its other and of an inside to an outside: spacing. The outside, "spatial" and "objective" exteriority which we believe we know as the most familiar thing in the world, as familiarity itself, would not appear without the grammè, without differance as temporalization, without the nonpresence of the other inscribed within the sense of the pre-

sent, without the relationship to death as the concrete structure
of the living present. Metaphor would be forbidden. The presence–absence of the trace, which one should not even call its
ambiguity but rather its play (for the word *ambiguity* requires
the logic of presence, even when it begins to disobey that logic),
carries in itself the problems of the letter and the spirit, of body
and soul, and of all the problems whose primary affinity I have
recalled. All dualisms, all theories of the immortality of the soul
or of the spirit, as well as all monisms, spiritualist or materialist,
dialectical or vulgar, are the unique theme of a metaphysics
whose entire history was compelled to strive toward the reduction of the trace. The subordination of the trace to the full presence summed up in the logos, the humbling of writing beneath a
speech dreaming its plenitude, such are the gestures required by
an onto-theology determining the archeological and eschatological meaning of being as presence, as parousia, as life without
differance: another name for death, historial metonymy where
God's name holds death in check. That is why, if this movement
begins its era in the form of Platonism, it ends in infinitist
metaphysics. Only infinite being can reduce the difference in
presence. In that sense, the name of God, at least as it is pronounced within classical rationalism, is the name of indifference
itself. Only a positive infinity can lift the trace, "sublimate" it
(it has recently been proposed that the Hegelian *Aufhebung* be
translated as sublimation; this translation may be of dubious
worth as translation, but the juxtaposition is of interest here).[14]
We must not therefore speak of a "theological prejudice," functioning sporadically when it is a question of the plenitude of the
logos; the logos as the sublimation of the trace is *theological*.
Infinitist theologies are always logocentrisms, whether they are
creationisms or not. Spinoza himself said of the understanding—
or logos—that it was the *immediate* infinite mode of the divine
substance, even calling it its eternal son in the *Short Treatise*. It
is also to this epoch, "reaching completion" with Hegel, with a
theology of the absolute concept as logos, that all the noncritical
concepts accredited by linguistics belong, at least to the extent
that linguistics must confirm—and how can a *science* avoid it?
—the Saussurian decree marking out "the internal system of
language."

It is precisely these concepts that permitted the exclusion of writing: image or representation, sensible and intelligible, nature and culture, nature and technics, etc. They are solidary with all metaphysical conceptuality and particularly with a naturalist, objectivist, and derivative determination of the difference between outside and inside.

And above all with a "vulgar concept of time." I borrow this expression from Heidegger. It designates, at the end of *Being and Time*, a concept of time thought in terms of spatial movement or of the now, and dominating all philosophy from Aristotle's *Physics* to Hegel's *Logic*.[15] This concept, which determines all of classical ontology, was not born out of a philosopher's carelessness or from a theoretical lapse. It is intrinsic to the totality of the history of the Occident, of what unites its metaphysics and its technics. And we shall see it later associated with the linearization of writing, and with the linearist concept of speech. This linearism is undoubtedly inseparable from phonologism; it can raise its voice to the same extent that a linear writing can seem to submit to it. Saussure's entire theory of the "linearity of the signifier" could be interpreted from this point of view.

> Auditory signifiers have at their command only the dimension of time. Their elements are presented in succession; they form a chain. This feature becomes readily apparent when they are represented in writing. ... The signifier, being auditory, is unfolded solely in time from which it gets the following characteristics: (a) it represents a span, and (b) the span is measurable in a single dimension; it is a line.[16]

It is a point on which Jakobson disagrees with Saussure decisively by substituting for the homogeneity of the line the structure of the musical staff, "the chord in music."[17] What is here in question is not Saussure's affirmation of the temporal essence of discourse but the concept of time that guides this affirmation and analysis: time conceived as linear successivity, as "consecutivity." This model works by itself and all through the *Course*, but Saussure is seemingly less sure of it in the *Anagrams*. At any rate, its value seems problematic to him, and an interesting paragraph elaborates a question left suspended:

That the elements forming a word *follow one another* is a truth that it would be better for linguistics not to consider uninteresting because evident, but rather as the truth which gives in advance the central principle of all useful reflections on words. In a domain as infinitely special as the one I am about to enter, it is always by virtue of the fundamental law of the human word in general that a question like that of consecutiveness or nonconsecutiveness may be posed.[18]

This linearist concept of time is therefore one of the deepest adherences of the modern concept of the sign to its own history. For at the limit, it is indeed the concept of the sign itself, and the distinction, however tenuous, between the signifying and signified faces, that remain committed to the history of classical ontology. The parallelism and correspondence of the faces or the planes change nothing. That this distinction, first appearing in Stoic logic, was necessary for the coherence of a scholastic thematics dominated by infinitist theology, does not allow us to treat today's debt to it as a contingency or a convenience. I suggested this at the outset, and perhaps the reasons are clearer now. The *signatum* always referred, as to its referent, to a *res*, to an entity created or at any rate first thought and spoken, thinkable and speakable, in the eternal present of the divine logos and specifically in its breath. If it came to relate to the speech of a finite being (created or not; in any case of an intracosmic entity) through the *intermediary* of a *signans*, the *signatum* had an *immediate* relationship with the divine logos which thought it within presence and for which it was not a trace. And for modern linguistics, if the signifier is a trace, the signified is a meaning thinkable in principle within the full presence of an intuitive consciousness. The signified face, to the extent that it is still originarily distinguished from the signifying face, is not considered a trace; by rights, it has no need of the signifier to be what it is. It is at the depth of this affirmation that the problem of the relations between linguistics and semantics must be posed. This reference to the meaning of a signified thinkable and possible outside of all signifiers remains dependent upon the onto-theo-teleology that I have just evoked. It is thus the idea of the sign that must be deconstructed through a meditation upon writing which would merge, as it must, with the undoing *[sollicitation]*[19] of onto-theology, faithfully repeating it in its *totality* and *making* it *insecure* in its most assured evidences.[20] One is necessarily led to this from the moment that the trace affects the totality of the sign on both its faces. That the signified is originarily and essentially (and not only for a finite and created spirit) trace, that it is *always already in the position of the signifier*, is the apparently innocent proposition within which the metaphysics of the logos, of presence and consciousness, must reflect upon writing as its death and its resource.

[. . . .]

On what conditions is a grammatology possible? Its fundamental condition is certainly the undoing *[sollicitation]* of logocentrism. But this condition of possibility turns into a condition of impossibility. In fact it risks upsetting the concept of science as well. Graphematics or grammatography ought no longer to be presented as sciences; their goal should be exorbitant when compared to a grammato*logical knowledge*.

Without venturing up to that perilous necessity, and within the traditional norms of scientificity upon which we fall back provisionally, let us repeat the question; on what conditions is grammatology possible?

On the condition of knowing what writing is and how the plurivocity of this concept is formed. Where does writing begin? When does writing begin? Where and when does the trace, writing in general, the common root of speech and writing, narrow itself down into "writing" in the colloquial sense? Where and when does one pass from one writing to another, from writing in general to writing in the narrow sense, from the trace to the *graphie*, from one graphic system to another, and, in the field of a graphic code, from one graphic discourse to another, etc.?

Where and how does it begin . . . ? A question of origin. But a meditation upon the trace should undoubtedly teach us that there is no origin, that is to say simple origin; that the questions of origin carry with them a metaphysics of presence. Without venturing here up to that perilous necessity, continuing to ask questions of origin, we must recognize its two levels. "Where" and "when" may open empirical questions: what, within history and within the world, are the places and the determined moments of the first phenomena of writing? These questions must be answered by the investigation and research of facts, that is, history in the colloquial sense, what has hitherto been practiced by nearly all archeologists, epigraphists, and prehistorians who have interrogated the world's scripts.

But the question of origin is at first confused with the question of essence. It could just as well be said that it presupposes an onto-phenomenological question in the strict sense of that term. One must know *what* writing *is* in order to ask—knowing what one is talking about and what *the question is*—where and when writing begins. What is writing? How can it be identified? What certitude of essence must guide the empirical investigation? Guide it in principle, for it is a necessary fact that empirical investigation quickly activates reflexion upon essence.[21] It must operate through "examples," and it can be shown how this impossibility of beginning at the beginning of the straight line, as it is assigned by the logic of transcendental reflexion, refers to the originarity (under erasure) of the trace, to the root of writing. What the thought of the trace has already taught us is that it can not be simply submitted to the onto-phenomenological question of essence. The trace *is nothing*, it is not an entity, it exceeds the question *What is?* and contingently makes it possible. Here one may no longer trust even the opposition of fact and principle, which, in all its metaphysical, ontological, and transcendental forms, has always functioned within the system of *what is*. Without venturing up to the perilous necessity of the question or the arche-question "what is," let us take shelter in the field of grammatological knowledge.

Writing being thoroughly historical, it is at once natural and surprising that the scientific interest in writing has always taken the form of a history of writing. But science also required that a theory of writing should guide the pure description of facts, taking for granted that this last expression has a sense.

[. . . .]

The history of writing is erected on the base of the history of the *grammè* as an adventure of relationships between the face and

the hand. Here, by a precaution whose schema we must constantly repeat, let us specify that the history of writing is not
explained by what we believe we know of the face and the hand,
of the glance, of the spoken word, and of the gesture. We must,
on the contrary, disturb this familiar knowledge, and awaken a
meaning of hand and face in terms of that history. [André] Leroi-
Gourhan describes the slow transformation of manual motricity
which frees the audio-phonic system for speech, and the glance
and the hand for writing.[22] In all these descriptions, it is difficult
to avoid the mechanist, technicist, and teleological language at
the very moment when it is precisely a question of retrieving the
origin and the possibility of movement, of the machine, of the
technè, of orientation in general. In fact, it is not difficult; it is
essentially impossible. And this is true of all discourse. From one
discourse to another, the difference lies only in the mode of
inhabiting the interior of a conceptuality destined, or already
submitted, to decay. Within that conceptuality or already without it, we must attempt to recapture the unity of gesture and
speech, of body and language, of tool and thought, before the
originality of the one and the other is articulated and without
letting this profound unity give rise to confusion. These original
significations must not be confused *within the orbit* or the system where they are opposed. But to think the history of the
system, its meaning and value must, in an *exorbitant* way, be
somewhere exceeded.

This representation of the *anthropos* is then granted: a precarious balance linked to manual-visual script.[23] This balance is
slowly threatened. It is at least known that "no major change"
giving birth to "a man of the future" who will no longer be a
"man," "can any longer be easily produced without the loss of
the hand, the teeth, and therefore of the upright position. A
toothless humanity that would exist in a prone position using
what limbs it had left to push buttons with, is not completely
inconceivable."[24]

What always threatens this balance is confused with the very
thing that broaches the *linearity* of the symbol. We have seen
that the traditional concept of time, an entire organization of the
world and of language, was bound up with it. Writing in the
narrow sense—and phonetic writing above all—is rooted in a

past of nonlinear writing. It had to be defeated, and here one can speak, if one wishes, of technical success; it assured a greater security and greater possibilities of capitalization in a dangerous and anguishing world. But that was not done *one single time*. A war was declared, and a suppression of all that resisted linearization was installed. And first of what Leroi-Gourhan calls the "mythogram," a writing that spells its symbols pluri-dimensionally; there the meaning is not subjected to successivity, to the order of a logical time, or to the irreversible temporality of sound. This pluri-dimensionality does not paralyze history within simultaneity; it corresponds to another level of historical experience, and one may just as well consider, conversely, linear thought as a reduction of history. It is true that another word ought perhaps to be used; the word history has no doubt always been associated with a linear scheme of the unfolding of presence, where the line relates the final presence to the originary presence according to the straight line or the circle. For the same reason, the pluri-dimensional symbolic structure is not given within the category of the simultaneous. Simultaneity coordinates two absolute presents, two points or instants of presence, and it remains a linearist concept.

The concept of *linearization* is much more effective, faithful, and intrinsic than those that are habitually used for classifying scripts and describing their history (pictogram, ideogram, letter, etc.). Exposing more than one prejudice, particularly about the relationship between ideogram and pictogram, about so-called graphic "realism," Leroi-Gourhan recalls the unity, within the mythogram, of all the elements of which linear writing marks the disruption: technics (particularly graphics), art, religion, economy. To recover the access to this unity, to this other structure of unity, we must de-sediment "four thousand years of linear writing."[25]

The linear norm was never able to impose itself absolutely for the very reasons that intrinsically circumscribed graphic phoneticism. We now know them; these limits came into being at the same time as the possibility of what they limited; they opened what they finished and we have already named them: discreteness, differance, spacing. The production of the linear norm thus emphasized these limits and marked the concepts of symbol and language. The process of linearization, as Leroi-Gourhan describes it on a very vast historical scale, and the Jakobsonian critique of Saussure's linearist concept, must be thought of together. The "line" represents only a particular model, whatever might be its privilege. This model *has become* a model and, as a model, it remains inaccessible. If one allows that the linearity of language entails this vulgar and mundane concept of temporality (homogeneous, dominated by the form of the now and the ideal of continuous movement, straight or circular) which Heidegger shows to be the intrinsic determining concept of all ontology from Aristotle to Hegel, the meditation upon writing and the deconstruction of the history of philosophy become inseparable.

The enigmatic model of the *line* is thus the very thing that philosophy could not see when it had its eyes open on the interior of its own history. This night begins to lighten a little at the moment when linearity—which is not loss or absence but the repression of pluri-dimensional[26] symbolic thought—relaxes its oppression because it begins to sterilize the technical and scientific economy that it has long favored. In fact for a long time its possibility has been structurally bound up with that of economy, of technics, and of ideology. This solidarity appears in the process of thesaurization, capitalization, sedentarization, hierarchization, of the formation of ideology by the class that writes or rather commands the scribes.[27] Not that the massive reappearance of nonlinear writing interrupts this structural solidarity; quite the contrary. But it transforms its nature profoundly.

The end of linear writing is indeed the end of the book,[28] even if, even today, it is within the form of a book that new writings —literary or theoretical—allow themselves to be, for better or for worse, encased. It is less a question of confiding new writings to the envelope of a book than of finally reading what wrote itself between the lines in the volumes. That is why, beginning to write without the line, one begins also to reread past writing according to a different organization of space. If today the problem of reading occupies the forefront of science, it is because of this suspense between two ages of writing. Because we are beginning to write, to write differently, we must reread differently.

For over a century, this uneasiness has been evident in philosophy, in science, in literature. All the revolutions in these fields can be interpreted as shocks that are gradually destroying the linear model. Which is to say the *epic* model. What is thought today cannot be written according to the line and the book, except by imitating the operation implicit in teaching modern mathematics with an abacus. This inadequation is not *modern*, but it is exposed today better than ever before. The access to pluridimensionality and to a delinearized temporality is not a simple regression toward the "mythogram;" on the contrary, it makes all the rationality subjected to the linear model appear as another form and another age of mythography. The meta-rationality or the meta-scientificity which are thus announced within the meditation upon writing can therefore be no more shut up within a science of man than conform to the traditional idea of science. In one and the same gesture, they leave *man, science,* and the *line* behind.

[. . . .]

The necessary decentering cannot be a philosophic or scientific act as such, since it is a question of dislocating, through access to another system linking speech and writing, the founding categories of language and the grammar of the *epistémè.* The natural tendency of *theory*—of what unites philosophy and science in the *epistémè*—will push rather toward filling in the breach than toward forcing the closure. It was normal that the breakthrough was more secure and more penetrating on the side of literature and poetic writing: normal also that it, like Nietzsche, at first destroyed and caused to vacillate the transcendental authority and dominant category of the *epistémè:* being. This is the meaning of the work of Fenellosa[29] whose influence upon Ezra Pound and his poetics is well known: this irreducibly graphic poetics was, with that of Mallarmé, the first break in the most entrenched Western tradition. The fascination that the Chinese ideogram exercised on Pound's writing may thus be given all its historical significance.

Ever since phoneticization has allowed itself to be questioned in its origin, its history and its adventures, its movement has been seen to mingle with that of science, religion, politics, economy, technics, law, art. The origins of these movements and these historical regions dissociate themselves, as they must for the rigorous delimitation of each science, only by an abstraction that one must constantly be aware of and use with vigilance. This complicity of origins may be called arche-writing. What is lost in that complicity is therefore the myth of the simplicity of origin. This myth is linked to the very concept of origin: to speech reciting the origin, to the myth of the origin and not only to myths of origin.

The fact that access to the written sign assures the sacred power of keeping existence operative within the trace and of knowing the general structure of the universe; that all clergies, exercising political power or not, were constituted at the same time as writing and by the disposition of graphic power; that strategy, ballistics, diplomacy, agriculture, fiscality, and penal law are linked in their history and in their structure to the constitution of writing; that the origin assigned to writing had been—according to the chains and mythemes—always analogous in the most diverse cultures and that it communicated in a complex but regulated manner with the distribution of political power as with familial structure; that the possibility of capitalization and of politico-administrative organization had always passed through the hands of scribes who laid down the terms of many wars and whose function was always irreducible, whoever the contending parties might be; that through discrepancies, inequalities of development, the play of permanencies, of delays, of diffusions, etc., the solidarity among ideological, religious, scientific-technical systems, and the systems of writing which were therefore more and other than "means of communication" or vehicles of the signified, remains indestructible; that the very sense of power and effectiveness in general, which could appear as such, as meaning and mastery (by idealization), only with so-called "symbolic" power, was always linked with the disposition of writing; that economy, monetary or premonetary, and graphic calculation were co-originary, that there could be no law without the possibility of trace (if not, as H. Lévy-Bruhl shows, of notation in the narrow sense), all this refers to a common and radical possibility that no determined science, no abstract discipline, can think as such.

Indeed, one must understand this *incompetence* of science which is also the incompetence of philosophy, the *closure* of the *epistēmē.* Above all it does not invoke a return to a prescientific or infra-philosophic form of discourse. Quite the contrary. This common root, which is not a root but the concealment of the origin and which is not common because it does not amount to the same thing except with the unmonotonous insistence of difference, this unnameable movement of *difference-itself,* that I have strategically nicknamed *trace, reserve,* or *differance,* could be called writing only within the *historical* closure, that is to say within the limits of science and philosophy.

The constitution of a science or a philosophy of writing is a necessary and difficult task. But, a *thought* of the trace, of difference or of reserve, having arrived at these limits and repeating them ceaselessly, must also point beyond the field of the *epistēmē.* Outside of the economic and strategic reference to the name that Heidegger justifies himself in giving to an analogous but not identical transgression of all philosophemes, *thought* is here for me a perfectly neutral name, the blank part of the text, the necessarily indeterminate index of a future epoch of difference. *In a certain sense, "thought" means nothing.* Like all openings, this index belongs within a past epoch by the face that is open to view. This thought has no weight. It is, in the play of the system, that very thing which never has weight. Thinking is what we already know we have not yet begun, measured against the shape of writing, it *is broached* only in the *epistēmē.*

Grammato*logy,* this thought, would still be walled-in within presence.

[. . . .]

—*Translated by Gayatri Chakravorty Spivak*

NOTES

1. What is?—ED.
2. I attempt to develop this theme elsewhere *(Speech and Phenomena).*
3. Derrida is here referring to Heidegger's reading of Nietzsche which concludes that Nietzsche was the last of the metaphysicians. This conclusion is also questioned in **Spurs: Nietzsche's Styles** (see below, pp. **366–67**). —ED.
4. This does not, by simple inversion, mean that the signifier is fundamental or primary. The "primacy" or "priority" of the signifier would be an

untenable and absurd expression, formulated illogically with the very logic it would, no doubt legitimately, destroy. The signifier will never by rights precede the signified, in which case it would no longer be a signifier and the "signifying" signifier would no longer have a possible signified. The thought that is announced in this impossible formula without being successfully contained therein should therefore be stated in another way; it will clearly be impossible to do so without suspecting the very idea of the sign, the "sign-of" which will always remain attached to what is here put in question. At the limit, therefore, that thought would destroy the entire conceptuality organized around the concept of the sign (signifier and signified, expression and content, and so on).

5. Postface to *Was ist Metaphysik?* (Frankfurt am Main, 1960), p. 46. The insistence of the voice also dominates the analysis of *Gewissen* [conscience] in *Sein und Zeit* (pp. 312 ff.).

6. Cf. "Das Wesen der Sprache" [The Nature of Language] and "Das Wort" [Words] in *Unterwegs zur Sprache* (Pfüllingen: G. Neske, 1959); *On the Way to Language*, trans. Peter D. Hertz (New York, 1971).

7. Heidegger, *Einführung in die Metaphysik* (Tübingen: Max Niemeyer, 1953); translated as *An Introduction to Metaphysics* by Ralph Manheim (New Haven, 1959).

8. Ibid., p. 92. "All this points in the direction of what we encountered when we characterized the Greek experience and interpretation of being. If we retain the usual interpretation of being, the word *being* takes its meaning from the unity and determinateness of the horizon which guided our understanding. In short: we understand the verbal substantive *Sein* through the infinitive, which in turn is related to the *is* and its diversity that we have described. The definite and particular verb form *is*, the *third person singular of the present indicative*, has here a preeminent rank. We understand *being* not in regard to the *thou art, you are, I am*, or *they would be*, though all of these, just as much as *is*, represent verbal inflections of *to be*. ... And involuntarily, almost as though nothing else were possible, we explain the infinitive *to be* to ourselves through the *is*.

"Accordingly, *being* has the meaning indicated above, recalling the Greek view of the essence of being, hence a determinateness which has not just dropped on us accidentally from somewhere but has dominated our historical being-there since antiquity. At one stroke our search for the definition of the meaning of the word *being* becomes explicitly what it is, namely, a reflection on the source of our hidden history." One should, of course, cite the entire analysis that concludes with these words.

9. *The Question of Being*, trans. William Kluback and Jean T. Wilde, bilingual edition (New Haven: College and University Press, 1958), p. 83.

10. *The Essence of Reasons*, trans. Terence Malick (Evanston, Ill.: Northwestern University Press, 1969), p. 29.

11. On the word *brisure*, Derrida quotes a letter from a friend who wrote to him: "You have, I suppose, dreamt of finding a single word for designating difference and articulation. I have perhaps located it by chance in Robert['s

Dictionary] if I play on the word, or rather indicate its double meaning. This word is *brisure* [joint, break] '—broken, cracked part. Cf. breach, crack, fracture, fault, split, fragment *[brèche, cassure, fracture, faille, fente, fragment.]*—Hinged articulation of two parts of wood- or metal-work. The hinge, the *brisure* [folding-joint] of a shutter. Cf. *joint.'* " **Of Grammatology,** p. 65. —ED.

12. Cf. particularly "La Trace de l'autre," *Tidjschrift voor filosofie* (September 1963), and my essay "Violence and Metaphysics: An Essay on the Thought of Emmanuel Levinas" in *Writing and Difference* [1967].

13. On Plato's denunciation of writing, see below, **"Plato's Pharmacy."** —ED.

14. On Derrida's translation of *Aufhebung* as *relève* (lifting up, relief), see below, **"Différance,"** n. **11.**—ED.

15. I take the liberty of referring to a forthcoming essay, "Ousia and Grammè; Note on a Note from *Being and Time*" [since published in *Margins of Philosophy* (1972)].

16. Ferdinand de Saussure, *Course in General Linguistics*, trans. Wade Baskin (New York: Philosophical Library, 1959), p. 70; see also everything concerning "homogeneous time," pp. 38 ff.

17. Roman Jakobson and Morris Halle, *Fundamentals of Language* (The Hague: M. Nijhoff, 1956), p. 106; see also Jakobson, "À la recherche de l'essence du langage," *Diogène* 51.

18. *Mercure de France* (February 1964), p. 254. Presenting this text, Starobinski evokes the musical model and concludes, "This reading is developed according to another *tempo* (and in another time); at the very limit, one leaves the time of 'consecutivity' proper to habitual language." One could of course say "proper to the habitual concept" of time and language. [The text in question is a collection of posthumously published fragments in which Saussure speculates on anagrammatic patterns in Latin poetry.—ED.]

19. On Derrida's use of *sollicitation*, see below, **"Différance,"** n. **6.**—ED.

20. I have chosen to demonstrate the necessity of this "deconstruction" by privileging the Saussurian references, not only because Saussure still dominates contemporary linguistics and semiology; it is also because he seems to me to stand at the limit: at the same time within the metaphysics that must be deconstructed and beyond the concept of the sign (signifier/signified) which he still uses. But Saussure's scruples, his interminable hesitation, particularly in the matter of the difference between the two "aspects" of the sign and in the matter of "arbitrariness," are better realized through reading Robert Godel's *Les Sources manuscrites du Cours de linguistique générale* (Geneve: Droz, 1957), pp. 190 ff. Let us note in passing: it is not impossible that the literality of the *Course*, to which we have indeed had to refer, may one day appear very suspect in the light of unpublished material now being prepared for publication. I am thinking particularly of the *Anagrams* [now published in *Les mots sous les mots: les anagrammes de Ferdinand de Saussure*, J. Starobinski, ed. (Paris: Gallimard, 1971)]. Up to what point is Saussure responsible for the *Course* as it was edited and published

after his death? This is not a new question. Need we specify that, *here at least,* we cannot consider it to be pertinent? Unless my project has been fundamentally misunderstood, it should be clear by now that, caring very little about the thought *itself* of Ferdinand de Saussure *himself,* I have interested myself in a *text* the literality of which has played a well-known role since 1915, operating within a system of readings, influences, misunderstandings, borrowings, refutations, etc. What people have been able to read there—as well as what they have not been able to read there—under the title of *A Course in General Linguistics* has been given importance to the point of excluding all hidden and "true" intentions of Ferdinand de Saussure. If one were to discover that this text hid another text—and one will always be dealing with only texts—and hid it in a determined sense, the reading that I have just proposed would not be invalidated, at least not for that reason alone. Quite the contrary. This situation, moreover, was anticipated by the editors of the *Course* at the very end of their first preface.

21. On the empirical difficulties of a search for empirical origins, see M. Cohen, *La grande invention de l'écriture* (Paris: Imprimerie Nationale, 1958), vol. 1, pp. 3 ff. Along with J. G. Février's *Histoire de l'écriture* (Paris: Payot, 1948), this is the most important work in France on the general history of writing. Madeleine V. David has devoted a study to them in *Critique* 157 (June 1960).

22. André Leroi-Gourhan, *Le geste et la parole* (Paris: Albin Michel, 1965), vol. 1, pp. 119 ff.

23. Ibid., pp. 161 ff.

24. Ibid., p. 183. The reader is also referred to *L'Eloge de la main* by Henri Focillon (Paris: Gallimard, 1964) and to Jean Brun's *La main et l'esprit* (Paris: Presses Universitaires de France, 1963). In a totally different context, we have elsewhere specified the *epoch* of writing as the suspension of *being-upright* ("Force and Signification" and "La Parole soufflée," both in *Writing and Difference* [1967].

25. Ibid., vol. 1, ch. 4. In particular, the author shows there that "the emergence of writing no more develops out of a graphic nothingness than does the emergence of agriculture without the intervention of anterior states" (p. 278); and that "ideography is anterior to pictography" (p. 280).

26. Certain remarks of Leroi-Gourhan on "the loss of multidimensional symbolic thought" and on the thought "that moves away from linearized language" (vol. 1, pp. 293–99) can perhaps be interpreted in this way.

27. Cf. *L'écriture et la psychologie des peuples* (Proceedings of a Colloquium, 1963), pp. 138–39, and Leroi-Gourhan, *Le geste et la parole,* vol. 1, pp. 238–50. "The development of the first cities corresponds not only to the appearance of the technician of fire but . . . writing is born at the same time as metallurgy. Here again, this is not a coincidence . . ." (vol. 1, p. 252). "It is at the moment when agrarian capitalism began to establish itself that the means of stabilizing it in written balance accounts appears and it is also at the moment when social hierarchization is affirmed that writing constructs its first genealogists" (p. 253). "The appearance of writing is not fortuitous;

after millennia of maturation in the systems of mythographic representation, there emerges, along with metal and slavery (see ch. 4), the linear notation of thought. Its content is not fortuitous" (vol. 2, p. 67; cf. also pp. 161–62).

Although it is now much better known and described, this structural solidarity, notably between capitalization and writing, has been recognized for a long time, by, among many others, Rousseau, Court de Gebelin, and Engels.

28. Linear writing has therefore indeed "constituted, during several millennia, independently of its role as curator of the collective memory, by its unfolding in a single dimension, the instrument of analysis out of which grew philosophic and scientific thought. The conservation of thought can now be conceived otherwise than in terms of books which will only for a short time keep the advantage of their easy manageability. A vast 'tape-library' with an electronic selection system will in the near future deliver preselected and instantaneously retrieved information. Reading will still retain its importance for some centuries to come, in spite of its perceptible regression for most men, but writing [understood in the sense of linear inscription] seems likely to disappear rapidly, replaced by automatic dictaphones. Should one see in this a sort of restoration of the state anterior to the hand's subordination to phonetics? I rather think that it is here a question of an aspect of the general phenomenon of manual regression and of a new 'liberation.' As to the long-term consequences on forms of reasoning, on a return to diffuse and multidimensional thought, they cannot now be foreseen. Scientific thought is rather hampered by the necessity of passing through typographical channels and it is certain that if some procedure would permit the presentation of books in such a way that the materials of the different chapters are presented simultaneously in all their aspects, authors and their users would find a considerable advantage. What is certain is that, while scientific reasoning has clearly nothing to lose with the disappearance of writing, philosophy and literature will no doubt see their forms evolve. This is not particularly regrettable since printing will conserve the curiously archaic forms of thought that men will have used during the period of alphabetic graphism; as to the new forms, they will be to the old ones as steel to flint, no doubt not a sharper instrument but a handier one. Writing will pass into the infrastructure without altering the functioning of intelligence, as a transition which will have had some millennia of primacy" (Leroi-Gourhan, *Le geste et la parole*, vol. 2, pp. 261–62).

29. Questioning by turns the logico-grammatical structures of the West (and first Aristotle's list of categories), showing that no correct description of Chinese writing can tolerate them, Fenellosa recalled that Chinese poetry was essentially a writing or script. He remarked, for example, "Should we pass formally into the study of Chinese poetry ... we should beware of English grammar, its hard parts of speech, and its lazy satisfaction with nouns and adjectives. We should seek and at least bear in mind the verbal undertone of each noun. We should avoid the *is* and bring in a wealth of neglected English verbs. Most of the existing translations violate all of these

rules. The development of the normal transitive sentence rests upon the fact that one action in nature promotes another; thus the agent and object are secretly verbs. For example, our sentence, 'Reading promotes writing,' would be expressed in Chinese by three full verbs. Such a form is the equivalent of three expanded clauses and can be drawn out into adjectival, participial, infinitive, relative, or conditional members. One of many possible examples is, 'If one reads it teaches him how to write.' Another is, 'One who reads becomes one who writes.' But in the first condensed form a Chinese would write, 'Read promote write.' " "The Chinese Written Character as a Medium for Poetry," in Ezra Pound, *Instigations* (Freeport, New York: Books for Libraries Press, 1967), pp. 383–84.

THREE

From "Différance" in *Margins of Philosophy*

("La Différance" in *Marges de la philosophie* [1972]

The text of a lecture delivered in 1968 to the Société française de philosophie, "Différance" glosses the neologism Derrida had introduced into the language with the slight variance of an *a* in the familiar word *différence*. One must first of all understand this invention in the context of the modern French language. Unlike English, French has not developed two verbs from the Latin *differre*, but has maintained the senses of both to differ and to defer in the same verb, *différer*. Also, unlike English, in French no noun formed from this verb carries the sense of deferral or deferment. Derrida's invented word (which has since been recognized by lexicographers and included in dictionaries) welds together difference and deferral and thus refers to a configuration of spatial and temporal difference together. As for the *-ance* ending, it calls up a middle voice between the active and passive voices. In this manner it can point to an operation that is not that of a subject on an object, that is, therefore, not an operation at all. Instead, there is a certain nontransitivity which, Derrida suggests, may well be "what philosophy, at its outset, distributed into an active and passive voice, thereby constituting itself by means of this repression" (p. 9). And, so as to underscore the relation Derrida sees between *différance* and writing in the general sense he has worked out, he recalls that which for the audience at his lecture would have been self-evident: the difference between *différence* and *différance* is silent. Because it cannot be differentiated in speech, the mark of their difference is only graphic; the *a* of *différance* marks the difference of writing within and before speech.

It is, therefore, another name for writing. Derrida plays up the insufficiency of speech to comic effect in this oral presentation, inserting remarks about his spelling and punctuation that are totally redundant in the written text. One must imagine, therefore, as one reads the lecture, that its delivery was punctuated by laughter.

These remarks about the formation of the word, however, are only prefatory to an analysis (most of which is extracted below) of the conjoined movements of *différance* as temporization and as spacing. In the course of this explanation, Derrida also delineates that which in the thought of others—Nietzsche, Freud, Heidegger, and Levinas are mentioned—has traced a "delimination of the ontology of presence" (p. 74) and which has allowed the articulation of this nonconcept: *différance*.[1]

[. . . .]

Différance as temporization, *différance* as spacing. How are they to be joined?

Let us start, since we are already there, from the problematic of the sign and of writing. The sign is usually said to be put in the place of the thing itself, the present thing, "thing" here standing equally for meaning or referent. The sign represents the present in its absence. It takes the place of the present. When we cannot grasp or show the thing, state the present, the being-present, when the present cannot be presented, we signify, we go through the detour of the sign. We take or give signs. We signal. The sign, in this sense, is deferred presence. Whether we are concerned with the verbal or the written sign, with the monetary sign, or with electoral delegation and political representation, the circulation of signs defers the moment in which we can encounter the thing itself, make it ours, consume or expend it, touch it, see it, intuit its presence. What I am describing here in order to define it is the classically determined structure of the sign in all the banality of its characteristics—signification as the *différance* of temporization. And this structure presupposes that the sign, which defers presence, is conceivable only on the *basis* of the presence that it defers and *moving toward* the deferred presence that it aims to reappropriate. According to this classical semiology, the substitution of the sign for the thing itself is both *secondary* and *provisional:* secondary due to an original and lost presence from which the sign thus derives; provisional as concerns this final and missing presence toward which the sign in this sense is a movement of mediation.

In attempting to put into question these traits of the provisional secondariness of the substitute, one would come to see something like an originary *différance;* but one could no longer call it originary or final in the extent to which the values of origin, archi-, *telos, eskhaton,* etc. have always denoted presence —*ousia, parousia.*[2] To put into question the secondary and provisional characteristics of the sign, to oppose to them an "originary" *différance,* therefore would have two consequences.

1. One could no longer include *différance* in the concept of the sign, which always has meant the representation of a presence, and has been constituted in a system (thought or language) governed by and moving toward presence.

2. And thereby one puts into question the authority of presence, or of its simple symmetrical opposite, absence, or lack. Thus one questions the limit that has always constrained us, still constrains us—as inhabitants of a language and a system of thought—to formulate the meaning of Being in general as presence or absence, in the categories of being or beingness *(ousia).* Already it appears that the type of question to which we are redirected is, let us say, of the Heideggerian type, and that *différance seems* to lead back to the ontico-ontological difference. I will be permitted to hold off on this reference. I will note only that between difference as temporization-temporalization, which can no longer be conceived within the horizon of the present, and what Heidegger says in *Being and Time* about temporalization as the transcendental horizon of the question of Being, which must be liberated from its traditional, metaphysical domination by the present and the now, there is a strict communication, even though not an exhaustive and irreducibly necessary one.

But first let us remain within the semiological problematic in order to see *différance* as temporization and *différance* as spacing conjoined. Most of the semiological or linguistic researches that dominate the field of thought today, whether due to their own results or to the regulatory model that they find themselves acknowledging everywhere, refer genealogically to Saussure (correctly or incorrectly) as their common inaugurator. Now Saussure first of all is the thinker who put the *arbitrary character of the sign* and the *differential character* of the sign at the very foundation of general semiology, particularly linguistics. And, as we know, these two motifs—arbitrary and differential—are inseparable in his view. There can be arbitrariness only because the system of signs is constituted solely by the differences in terms, and not by their plenitude. The elements of signification function not through the compact force of their nuclei but rather through the network of oppositions that distinguishes them and then relates them one to another. "Arbitrary and differential," says Saussure, "are two correlative characteristics."

Now this principle of difference, as the condition for signification, affects the *totality* of the sign, that is, the sign as both signified and signifier. The signified is the concept, the ideal meaning; and the signifier is what Saussure calls the "image," the "psychical imprint" of a material, physical—for example, acoustical—phenomenon. We do not have to go into all the problems posed by these definitions here. Let us cite Saussure only at the point which interests us: "The conceptual side of value is made up solely of relations and differences with respect to the other terms of language, and the same can be said of its material side. . . . Everything that has been said up to this point boils down to this: in language there are only differences. Even more important, a difference generally implies positive terms between which the difference is set up; but in language there are only differences *without positive terms*. Whether we take the signified or the signifier, language has neither ideas nor sounds that existed before the linguistic system, but only conceptual and phonic differences that have issued from the system. The idea or phonic substance that a sign contains is of less importance than the other signs that surround it."[3]

The first consequence to be drawn from this is that the signified concept is never present in and of itself, in a sufficient presence that would refer only to itself. Essentially and lawfully, every concept is inscribed in a chain or in a system within which it refers to the other, to other concepts, by means of the systematic play of differences. Such a play, *différance*, is thus no longer simply a concept, but rather the possibility of conceptuality, of a conceptual process and system in general. For the same reason, *différance*, which is not a concept, is not simply a word, that is, what is generally represented as the calm, present, and self-referential unity of concept and phonic material. Later we will look into the word in general.

The difference of which Saussure speaks is itself, therefore, neither a concept nor a word among others. The same can be said, *a fortiori*, of *différance*. And we are thereby led to explicate the relation of one to the other.

In a language, in the *system* of language, there are only differences. Therefore a taxonomical operation can undertake the systematic, statistical, and classificatory inventory of a language. But, on the one hand, these differences *play:* in language, in speech too, and in the exchange between language and speech. On the other hand, these differences are themselves *effects.* They have not fallen from the sky fully formed, and are no more inscribed in a *topos noētos*, than they are prescribed in the gray matter of the brain. If the word *history* did not in and of itself convey the motif of a final repression of difference, one could say that only differences can be "historical" from the outset and in each of their aspects.

What is written as *différance*, then, will be the playing movement that "produces"—by means of something that is not simply an activity—these differences, these effects of difference. This does not mean that the *différance* that produces differences is somehow before them, in a simple and unmodified—in-different—present. *Différance* is the nonfull, nonsimple, structured and differentiating origin of differences. Thus, the name *origin* no longer suits it.

Since language, which Saussure says is a classification, has not fallen from the sky, its differences have been produced, are produced effects, but they are effects which do not find their cause in a subject or a substance, in a thing in general, a being that is somewhere present, thereby eluding the play of *différance*. If such a presence were implied in the concept of cause in general, in the most classical fashion, we then would have to speak of an effect without a cause, which very quickly would lead to speaking of no effect at all. I have attempted to indicate a way out of the closure of this framework via the "trace," which is no more an effect than it has a cause, but which in and of itself, outside its text, is not sufficient to operate the necessary transgression.

Since there is no presence before and outside semiological difference, what Saussure has written about language can be extended to the sign in general: "Language is necessary in order for speech to be intelligible and to produce all of its effects; but the latter is necessary in order for language to be established; historically, the fact of speech always comes first."[4]

Retaining at least the framework, if not the content, of this requirement formulated by Saussure, we will designate as *différance* the movement according to which language, or any code, any system of referral in general, is constituted "historically" as a weave of differences. "Is constituted," "is produced," "is created," "movement," "historically," etc., necessarily being understood beyond the metaphysical language in which they are retained, along with all their implications. We ought to demonstrate why concepts like *production*, constitution, and history remain in complicity with what is at issue here. But this would take me too far today—toward the theory of the representation of the "circle" in which we appear to be enclosed—and I utilize such concepts, like many others, only for their strategic convenience and in order to undertake their deconstruction at the currently most decisive point. In any event, it will be understood, by means of the circle in which we appear to be engaged, that as it is written here, *différance* is no more static than it is genetic, no more structural than historical. Or is no less so; and to object to this on the basis of the oldest of metaphysical oppositions (for example, by setting some generative point of view against a structural-taxonomical point of view, or vice versa) would be, above all, not to read what here is missing from orthographical ethics. Such oppositions have not the least pertinence to *différance*, which makes the thinking of it uneasy and uncomfortable.

Now if we consider the chain in which *différance* lends itself to a certain number of nonsynonymous substitutions, according to the necessity of the context, why have recourse to the "reserve," to "archi-writing," to the "archi-trace," to "spacing," that is, to the "supplement," or to the *pharmakon*, and soon to the hymen, to the margin-mark-march, etc.[5]

Let us go on. It is because of *différance* that the movement of signification is possible only if each so-called present element, each element appearing on the scene of presence, is related to something other than itself, thereby keeping within itself the mark of the past element, and already letting itself be vitiated by the mark of its relation to the future element, this trace being related no less to what is called the future than to what is called the past, and constituting what is called the present by means of this very relation to what it is not: what it absolutely is not, not even a past or a future as a modified present. An interval must separate the present from what it is not in order for the present to be itself, but this interval that constitutes it as present must, by the same token, divide the present in and of itself, thereby also dividing, along with the present, everything that is thought on the basis of the present, that is, in our metaphysical language, every being, and singularly substance or the subject. In constituting itself, in dividing itself dynamically, this interval is what might be called *spacing,* the becoming-space of time or the becoming-time of space *(temporization).* And it is this constitution of the present, as an "originary" and irreducibly nonsimple (and therefore, *stricto sensu* nonoriginary) synthesis of marks, or traces of retentions and protentions (to reproduce analogically and provisionally a phenomenological and transcendental language that soon will reveal itself to be inadequate), that I propose to call archi-writing, archi-trace, or *différance,* Which (is) (simultaneously) spacing (and) temporization.

[....]

Differences, thus, are "produced"—deferred—by *différance.* But *what* defers or *who* defers? In other words, *what is différance?* With this question we reach another level and another resource of our problematic.

What differs? Who differs? What is *différance?*

If we answered these questions before examining them as questions, before turning them back on themselves, and before suspecting their very form, including what seems most natural and necessary about them, we would immediately fall back into what we have just disengaged ourselves from. In effect, if we accepted the form of the question, in its meaning and its syntax ("What is?" "Who is?" "Who is it that?"), we would have to conclude that *différance* has been derived, has happened, is to be mastered and governed on the basis of the point of a present being, which itself could be some thing, a form, a state, a power in the world to which all kinds of names might be given, a *what,* or a present being as a *subject,* a *who.* And in this last case, notably, one would conclude implicitly that this present being, for example a being present to itself, as consciousness, eventually would come to defer or to differ: whether by delaying and turning away from the fulfillment of a "need" or a "desire," or by differing from itself. But in neither of these cases would such a present being be "constituted" by this *différance*.

Now if we refer, once again, to semiological difference, of what does Saussure, in particular, remind us? That "language [which only consists of differences] is not a function of the speaking subject." This implies that the subject (in its identity with itself, or eventually in its consciousness of its identity with itself, its self-consciousness) is inscribed in language, is a "function" of language, becomes a *speaking* subject only by making its speech conform—even in so-called creation, or in so-called transgression—to the system of the rules of language as a system of differences, or at very least by conforming to the general law of *différance*, or by adhering to the principle of language that Saussure says is "spoken language minus speech." "Language is necessary for the spoken word to be intelligible and so that it can produce all of its effects."[6]

It, by hypothesis, we maintain that the opposition of speech to language is absolutely rigorous, then *différance* would be not only the play of differences with language but also the relation of speech to language, the detour through which I must pass in order to speak, the silent promise I must make; and this is equally valid for semiology in general, governing all the relations of usage to schemata, of message to code, etc. (Elsewhere I have attempted to suggest that this *différance* in language, and in the relation of speech and language, forbids the essential dissociation of speech and language that Saussure, at another level of his discourse, traditionally wished to delineate. The practice of a language or of a code supposing a play of forms without a determined and invariable substance, and also supposing in the practice of this play a retention and protention of differences, a spacing and a temporization, a play of traces—all this must be a kind of writing before the letter, an archi-writing without a present origin, without archi-. Whence the regular erasure of the archi-, and the transformation of general semiology into grammatology, this latter executing a critical labor on everything within semiology, including the central concept of the sign, that maintained metaphysical presuppositions incompatible with the motif of *différance*.)

One might be tempted by an objection: certainly the subject becomes a *speaking* subject only in its commerce with the system of linguistic differences; or yet, the subject becomes a *signifying* (signifying in general, by means of speech or any other sign) subject only by inscribing itself in the system of differences. Certainly in this sense the speaking or signifying subject could not be present to itself, as speaking or signifying, without the play of linguistic or semiological *différance*. But can one not conceive of a presence, and of a presence to itself of the subject before speech or signs, a presence to itself of the subject in a silent and intuitive consciousness?

Such a question therefore supposes that, prior to the sign and outside it, excluding any trace and any *différance*, something like consciousness is possible. And that consciousness, before distributing its signs in space and in the world, can gather itself into its presence. But what is consciousness? What does *consciousness* mean? Most often, in the very form of meaning, in all its modifications, consciousness offers itself to thought only as self-presence, as the perception of self in presence. And what holds for consciousness holds here for so-called subjective existence in general. Just as the category of the subject cannot be, and never has been, thought without the reference to presence as *hupokeimenon* or as *ousia*, etc., so the subject as consciousness has never manifested itself except as self-presence. The privilege granted to consciousness therefore signifies the privilege granted to the present; and even if one describes the transcendental temporality of consciousness, and at the depth at which Husserl does so, one grants to the "living present" the power of synthesizing traces, and of incessantly reassembling them.

This privilege is the ether of metaphysics, the element of our thought that is caught in the language of metaphysics. One can delimit such a closure today only by soliciting[7] the value of presence that Heidegger has shown to be the ontotheological determination of Being; and in thus soliciting the value of presence, by means of an interrogation whose status must be completely exceptional, we are also examining the absolute privilege of this form or epoch of presence in general that is consciousness as meaning[8] in self-presence.

Thus one comes to posit presence—and specifically consciousness, the being beside itself of consciousness—no longer as the absolutely central form of Being but as a "determination" and as an "effect." A determination or an effect within a system which is no longer that of presence but of *différance,* a system that no longer tolerates the opposition of activity and passivity, nor that of cause and effect, or of indetermination and determination, etc., such that in designating consciousness as an effect or a determination, one continues—for strategic reasons that can be more or less lucidly deliberated and systematically calculated —to operate according to the lexicon of that which one is delimiting.

Before being so radically and purposely the gesture of Heidegger, this gesture was also made by Nietzsche and Freud, both of whom, as is well known, and sometimes in very similar fashion, put consciousness into question in its assured certainty of itself. Now is it not remarkable that they both did so on the basis of the motif of *différance?*

Différance appears almost by name in their texts, and in those places where everything is at stake. I cannot expand upon this here; I will only recall that for Nietzsche "the great principal activity is unconscious," and that consciousness is the effect of forces the essence, byways, and modalities of which are not proper to it. Force itself is never present; it is only a play of differences and quantities. There would be no force in general without the difference between forces; and here the difference of quantity counts more than the content of the quantity, more than absolute size itself. "Quantity itself, therefore, is not separable from the difference of quantity. The difference of quantity is the essence of force, the relation of force to force. The dream of two equal forces, even if they are granted an opposition of meaning, is an approximate and crude dream, a statistical dream, plunged into by the living but dispelled by chemistry."[9] Is not all of Nietzsche's thought a critique of philosophy as an active indifference to difference, as the system of adiaphoristic reduction or repression? Which according to the same logic, according to logic itself, does not exclude that philosophy lives *in* and *on différ-*

ance, thereby blinding itself to the *same,* which is not the identical. The same, precisely, is *différance* (with an *a*) as the displaced and equivocal passage of one different thing to another, from one term of an opposition to the other. Thus one could reconsider all the pairs of opposites on which philosophy is constructed and on which our discourse lives, not in order to see opposition erase itself but to see what indicates that each of the terms must appear as the *différance* of the other, as the other different and deferred in the economy of the same (the intelligible as differing-deferring the sensible, as the sensible different and deferred; the concept as different and deferred, differing-deferring intuition; culture as nature different and deferred, differing-deferring; all the others of *physis—tekhnē, nomos, thesis,* society, freedom, history, mind, etc.—as *physis* different and deferred, or as *physis* differing and deferring. *Physis* in *différance.* And in this we may see the site of a reinterpretation of *mimēsis* in its alleged opposition to *physis*). And on the basis of this unfolding of the same as *différance,* we see announced the sameness of *différance* and repetition in the eternal return. Themes in Nietzsche's work that are linked to the symptomatology that always diagnoses the detour or ruse of an agency disguised in its *différance;* or further, to the entire thematic of active interpretation, which substitutes incessant deciphering for the unveiling of truth as the presentation of the thing itself in its presence, etc. Figures without truth, or at least a system of figures not dominated by the value of truth, which then becomes only an included, inscribed, circumscribed function.

Thus, *différance* is the name we might give to the "active," moving discord of different forces, and of differences of forces, that Nietzsche sets up against the entire system of metaphysical grammar, wherever this system governs culture, philosophy, and science.

It is historically significant that this diaphoristics, which, as an energetics or economics of forces, commits itself to putting into question the primacy of presence as consciousness, is also the major motif of Freud's thought: another diaphoristics, which in its entirety is both a theory of the figure (or of the trace) and an energetics. The putting into question of the authority of consciousness is first and always differential.

The two apparently different values of *différance* are tied together in Freudian theory: to differ as discernibility, distinction, separation, diastema, *spacing;* and to defer as detour, relay, reserve, *temporization.*

1. The concepts of trace *(Spur)*, of breaching *(Bahnung)*,[10] and of the forces of breaching, from the *Project* on, are inseparable from the concept of difference. The origin of memory, and of the psyche as (conscious or unconscious) memory in general, can be described only by taking into account the difference between breaches. Freud says so overtly. There is no breach without difference and no difference without trace.

2. All the differences in the production of unconscious traces and in the processes of inscription *(Niederschrift)* can also be interpreted as moments of *différance*, in the sense of putting into reserve. According to a schema that never ceased to guide Freud's thought, the movement of the trace is described as an effort of life to protect itself by *deferring* the dangerous investment, by constituting a reserve *(Vorrat)*. And all the oppositions that furrow Freudian thought relate each of his concepts one to another as moments of a detour in the economy of *différance*. One is but the other different and deferred, one differing and deferring the other. One is the other in *différance*, one is the *différance* of the other. This is why every apparently rigorous and irreducible *opposition* (for example the opposition of the secondary to the primary) comes to be qualified, at one moment or another, as a "theoretical fiction." Again, it is thereby, for example (but such an example governs, and communicates with, everything), that the difference between the pleasure principle and the reality principle is only *différance* as detour. In *Beyond the Pleasure Principle* Freud writes: "Under the influence of the ego's instincts of self-preservation, the pleasure principle is replaced by the reality principle. This latter principle does not abandon the intention of ultimately obtaining pleasure, but it nevertheless demands and carries into effect the postponement of satisfaction, the abandonment of a number of possibilities of gaining satisfaction and the temporary toleration of unpleasure as a step on the long indirect road *(Aufschub)* to pleasure.[11]

Here we are touching upon the point of greatest obscurity, on the very enigma of *différance*, on precisely that which divides its very concept by means of a strange cleavage. We must not hasten to decide. How are we to think *simultaneously*, on the one hand, *différance* as the economic detour which, in the element of the same, always aims at coming back to the pleasure or the presence that has been deferred by (conscious or unconscious) calculation, and, on the other hand, *différance* as the relation to an impossible presence, as expenditure without reserve, as the irreparable loss of presence, the irreversible usage of energy, that is, as the death instinct, and as the entirely other relationship that apparently interrupts every economy? It is evident—and this is the evident itself—that the economical and the noneconomical, the same and the entirely other, etc., cannot be thought *together*. If *différance* is unthinkable in this way, perhaps we should not hasten to make it evident, in the philosophical element of evidentiality which would make short work of dissipating the mirage and illogicalness of *différance* and would do so with the infallibility of calculations that we are well acquainted with, having precisely recognized their place, necessity, and function in the structure of *différance*. Elsewhere, in a reading of Bataille, I have attempted to indicate what might come of a rigorous and, in a new sense, "scientific" *relating* of the "restricted economy" that takes no part in expenditure without reserve, death, opening itself to nonmeaning, etc., to a general economy that *takes into account* the nonreserve, that keeps in reserve the nonreserve, if it can be put thus. I am speaking of a relationship between a *différance* that can make a profit on its investment and a *différance* that misses its profit, the *investiture* of a presence that is pure and without loss here being confused with absolute loss, with death. Through such a relating of a restricted and a general economy the very project of philosophy, under the privileged heading of Hegelianism, is displaced and reinscribed. The *Aufhebung—la relève*—is constrained into writing itself otherwise. Or perhaps simply into writing itself. Or, better, into taking account of its consumption of writing.[12]

For the economic character of *différance* in no way implies that the deferred presence can always be found again, that we have here only an investment that provisionally and calculatedly delays the perception of its profit or the profit of its perception. Contrary to the metaphysical, dialectical, "Hegelian" interpretation of the economic movement of *différance*, we must conceive of a play in which whoever loses wins, and in which one loses and wins on every turn. If the displaced presentation remains definitively and implacably postponed, it is not that a certain present remains absent or hidden. Rather, *différance* maintains our relationship with that which we necessarily misconstrue, and which exceeds the alternative of presence and absence. A certain alterity—to which Freud gives the metaphysical name of the unconscious—is definitively exempt from every process of presentation by means of which we would call upon it to show itself in person. In this context, and beneath this guise, the unconscious is not, as we know, a hidden, virtual, or potential self-presence. It differs from, and defers, itself; which doubtless means that it is woven of differences, and also that it sends out delegates, representatives, proxies, but without any chance that the giver of proxies might "exist," might be present, be "itself" somewhere, and with even less chance that it might become conscious. In this sense, contrary to the terms of an old debate full of the metaphysical investments that it has always assumed, the "unconscious" is no more a "thing" than it is a virtual or masked consciousness. This radical alterity as concerns every possible mode of presence is marked by the irreducibility of the aftereffect, the delay. In order to describe traces, in order to read the traces of "unconscious" traces (there are no "conscious" traces), the language of presence and absence, the metaphysical discourse of phenomenology, is inadequate. (Although the phenomenologist is not the only one to speak this language.)

The structure of delay *(Nachträglichkeit)* in effect forbids that one make of temporalization (temporization) a simply dialectical complication of the living present as an originary and unceasing synthesis—a synthesis constantly directed back on itself, gathered in on itself and gathering—of retentional traces and protentional openings. The alterity of the "unconscious" makes us concerned not with horizons of modified—past or future—presents, but with a "past" that has never been present, and which never will be, whose future to come will never be a *production* or a reproduction in the form of presence. Therefore the concept of trace is incompatible with the concept of retention, of the becoming-past of what has been present. One cannot think the trace—and therefore, *différance*—on the basis of the present, or of the presence of the present.

A past that has never been present: this formula is the one that Emmanuel Levinas uses, although certainly in a nonpsychoanalytic way, to qualify the trace and enigma of absolute alterity: the Other.[13] Within these limits, and from this point of view at least, the thought of *différance* implies the entire critique of classical ontology undertaken by Levinas. And the concept of the trace, like that of *différance* thereby organizes, along the lines of these different traces and differences of traces, in Nietzsche's sense, in Freud's sense, in Levinas's sense—these "names of authors" here being only indices—the network which reassembles and traverses our "era" as the delimitation of the ontology of presence.

Which is to say the ontology of beings and beingness. It is the domination of beings that *différance* everywhere comes to solicit, in the sense that *sollicitare*, in old Latin, means to shake as a whole, to make tremble in entirety. Therefore, it is the determination of Being as presence or as beingness that is interrogated by the thought of *différance*. Such a question could not emerge and be understood unless the difference between Being and beings were somewhere to be broached. First consequence: *différance* is not. It is not a present being, however excellent, unique, principal, or transcendent. It governs nothing, reigns over nothing, and nowhere exercises any authority. It is not announced by any capital letter. Not only is there no kingdom of *différance*, but *différance* instigates the subversion of every kingdom. Which makes it obviously threatening and infallibly dreaded by everything within us that desires a kingdom, the past or future presence of a kingdom. And it is always in the name of a kingdom that one may reproach *différance* with wishing to reign, believing that one sees it aggrandize itself with a capital letter.

Can *différance*, for these reasons, settle down into the division of the ontico-ontological difference, such as it is thought, such as its "epoch" in particular is thought, "through," if it may still be expressed such, Heidegger's uncircumventable meditation?

There is no simple answer to such a question.

In a certain aspect of itself, *différance* is certainly but the historical and epochal *unfolding* of Being or of the ontological difference. The *a* of *différance* marks the *movement* of this unfolding.

And yet, are not the thought of the *meaning* or *truth* of Being, the determination of *différance* as the ontico-ontological difference, difference thought within the horizon of the question *of Being*, still intrametaphysical effects of *différance?* The unfolding of *différance* is perhaps not solely the truth of Being, or of the epochality of Being. Perhaps we must attempt to think this unheard-of thought, this silent tracing: that the history of Being, whose thought engages the Greco-Western *logos* such as it is produced via the ontological difference, is but an epoch of the *diapherein*. Henceforth one could no longer even call this an "epoch," the concept of epochality belonging to what is within history as the history of Being. Since Being has never had a "meaning," has never been thought or said as such, except by dissimulating itself in beings, then *différance*, in a certain and very strange way, (is) "older" than the ontological difference or than the truth of Being. When it has this age it can be called the play of the trace. The play of a trace which no longer belongs to the horizon of Being, but whose play transports and encloses the meaning of Being: the play of the trace, or the *différance*, which has no meaning and is not. Which does not belong. There is no maintaining, and no depth to, this bottomless chessboard on which Being is put into play.

[. . . .]

For us, *différance* remains a metaphysical name, and all the names that it receives in our language are still, as names, metaphysical. And this is particularly the case when these names state the determination of *différance* as the difference between presence and the present *(Anwesen/Anwesend)*, but above all, and, already in the most general fashion, when they state the determination of *différance* as the difference of Being and beings.

"Older" than Being itself, such a *différance* has no name in our language. But we "already know" that if it is unnameable, it is not provisionally so, not because our language has not yet found or received this *name*, or because we would have to seek it in another language, outside the finite system of our own. It is rather because there is no *name* for it at all, not even the name of essence or of Being, not even that of *"différance,"* which is not a name, which is not a pure nominal unity, and unceasingly dislocates itself in a chain of differing and deferring substitution.

"There is no name for it": a proposition to be read in its *platitude.* This unnameable is not an ineffable Being which no name could approach: God, for example. This unnameable is the play which makes possible nominal effects, the relatively unitary and atomic structures that are called names, the chains of substitutions of names in which, for example, the nominal effect *différance* is itself *enmeshed,* carried off, reinscribed, just as a false entry or a false exit is still part of the game, a function of the system.

What we know, or what we would know if it were simply a question here of something to know, is that there has never been, never will be, a unique word, a master-name. This is why the thought of the letter *a* in *différance* is not the primary prescription or the prophetic annunciation of an imminent and as yet unheard-of nomination. There is nothing kerygmatic about this "word," provided that one perceives its decapita(liza)tion. And that one puts into question the name of the name.

There will be no unique name, even if it were the name of Being. And we must think this without *nostalgia,* that is, outside of the myth of a purely maternal or paternal language, a lost native country of thought. On the contrary, we must *affirm* this, in the sense in which Nietzsche puts affirmation into play, in a certain laughter and a certain step of the dance.

From the vantage of this laughter and this dance, from the vantage of this affirmation foreign to all dialectics, the other side of nostalgia, what I will call Heideggerian *hope,* comes into question. I am not unaware how shocking this word might seem here. Nevertheless I am venturing it, without excluding any of its implications, and I relate it to what still seems to me to be the metaphysical part of "The Anaximander Fragment": the quest for the proper word and the unique name. Speaking of the first word of Being *(das frühe Wort des Seins: to khreon),* Heidegger writes: "The relation to what is present that rules in the essence of presencing itself is a unique one *(ist eine einzige),* altogether incomparable to any other relation. It belongs to the uniqueness of Being itself *(Sie gehört zur Einzigkeit des Seins selbst).* Therefore, in order to name the essential nature of Being *(das wesende Seins),* language would have to find a single word, the unique word *(ein einziges, das einzige Wort).* From this we can gather how daring every thoughtful word *(denkende Wort)* addressed to Being is *(das dem Sein zugesprochen wird).* Nevertheless such daring is not impossible, since Being speaks always and everywhere throughout language." (p. 52).

Such is the question: the alliance of speech and Being in the unique word, in the finally proper name. And such is the question inscribed in the simulated affirmation of *différance.* It bears (on) each member of this sentence: "Being / speaks / always and everywhere / throughout / language."

—Translated by Alan Bass

NOTES

1. In this chapter we have followed the translator in preserving the French spelling. Elsewhere, however, we assimilate the neographism to English orthography and write, *differance.* ——ED.

2. *Ousia* and *parousia* imply presence as both origin and end, the founding principle *(arkhē-)* as that toward which one moves *(telos, eskhaton).*—TRANS.

3. Ferdinand de Saussure, *Course in General Linguistics,* trans. Wade Baskin (New York: Philosophical Library, 1959), pp. 117–18, 120.—TRANS.

4. Ibid., p. 18.—TRANS.

5. All these terms refer to writing and inscribe *différance* within themselves, as Derrida says, according to the context. The supplement *(supplément)* is Rousseau's word to describe writing (analyzed in **Of Grammatology.** It means *both* the missing piece and the extra piece. The *pharmakon* is Plato's word for writing (analyzed in **"Plato's Pharmacy"** in *Dissemination,* meaning *both* remedy and poison; the hymen *(l'hymen)* comes from Derrida's analysis of Mallarmé's writing and Mallarmé's reflections on writing (**"The Double Session"** in *Dissemination)* and refers *both* to virginity and to consummation; *marge-marque-marche* is the series *en différance* that Derrida applies to Sollers' *Nombres* ("Dissemination" in *Dissemination).*—TRANS.

6. Saussure, *Course in General Linguistics,* p. 37.—TRANS.

7. The French *solliciter,* as the English *solicit,* derives from an Old Latin expression meaning to shake the whole, to make something tremble in its entirety. Derrida comments on this later, but is already using "to solicit" in this sense here.—TRANS.

8. "Meaning" here is the weak translation of *vouloir-dire,* which has a strong sense of willing *(voluntas)* to say, putting the attempt to mean in conjunction with speech, a crucial conjunction for Derrida.—TRANS.

9. Gilles Deleuze, *Nietzsche et la philosophie* (Paris: Presses Universitaies de France, 1970), p. 49.

10. Derrida is referring here to his essay "Freud and the Scene of Writing" in *Writing and Difference* [1967]. "Breaching" is the translation for *Bahnung* that I adopted there: it conveys more of the sense of breaking open (as in the German *Bahnung* and the French *frayage*) than the Standard Edition's "facilitation." The *Project* Derrida refers to here is the *Project for a Scientific Psychology* (1895), in which Freud attempted to cast his psychological thinking in a neurological framework.—TRANS.

11. *The Standard Edition of the Complete Psychological Works* (London: Hogarth Press, 1950 [hereafter cited as *SE*]), vol. 18, p. 10.—TRANS.

12. Derrida is referring here to the reading of Hegel he proposed in "From Restricted to General Economy: A Hegelianism Without Reserve," in *Writing and Difference* [1967]. In that essay Derrida began his consideration of Hegel as the great philosophical *speculator;* thus all the economic metaphors of the previous sentences. For Derrida the deconstruction of metaphysics implies an endless confrontation with Hegelian concepts, and the move from a restricted, "speculative" philosophical economy—in which there is nothing that cannot be made to make sense, in which there is nothing *other* than meaning—to a "general" economy—which affirms that which exceeds meaning, the excess of meaning from which there can be no speculative profit—involves a reinterpretation of the central Hegelian concept: the *Aufhebung. Aufhebung* literally means "lifting up"; but it also contains the double meaning of conservation and negation. For Hegel, dialectics is a process of *Aufhebung:* every concept is to be negated and lifted up to a higher sphere in which it is thereby conserved. In this way, there is nothing from which the *Aufhebung* cannot profit. However, as Derrida points out, there is always an effect of *différance* when the same word has two contradictory meanings. Indeed it is this effect of *différance*—the excess of the trace *Aufhebung* itself—that is precisely what the *Aufhebung* can never *aufheben:* lift up, conserve, and negate. This is why Derrida wishes to constrain the *Aufhebung* to write itself otherwise, or simply to write itself, to take into account its consumption of writing. Without writing, the trace, there could be no words with double, contradictory meanings.

As with *différance,* the translation of a word with a double meaning is particularly difficult and touches upon the entire problematics of writing and *différance.* The best translators of Hegel usually cite Hegel's own delight that the most speculative of languages, German, should have provided this most speculative of words as the vehicle for his supreme speculative effort. Thus *Aufhebung* is usually best annotated and left untranslated. (Jean Hyppolite, in his French translations of Hegel, carefully annotates his rendering of *Aufhebung* as both *supprimer* and *dépasser.* Baillies's rendering of *Aufhebung* as "sublation" is misleading.) Derrida, however, in his attempt to make

Aufhebung write itself otherwise, has proposed a new translation of it that *does* take into account the effect of *différance* in its double meaning. Derrida's translation is *la relève*. The word comes from the verb *relever*, which means to lift up, as does *Aufheben*. But *relever* also means to relay, to relieve, as when one soldier on duty relieves another. Thus the conserving-and-negating lift has become *la relève*, a "lift" in which is inscribed an effect of substitution and difference, the effect of substitution and difference inscribed in the double meaning of *Aufhebung*. A. V. Miller's rendering of *Aufhebung* as "supersession" in his recent translation of the *Phenomenology* comes close to *relever* in combining the senses of raising up and replacement, although without the elegance of Derrida's maintenance of the verb meaning "to lift" *(heben, lever)* and change of prefix *(auf-, re-)*.—TRANS.

13. On Levinas, and on the translation of his term *autrui* by "Other," see "Violence and Metaphysics," note 6, in *Writing and Difference* [1967].
—TRANS.

FOUR

"Signature Event Context" in *Margins of Philosophy*

("Signature Evénement Contexte" in *Marges de*

la philosophie [1972])

This essay, reprinted *in extenso*, was first delivered as a lecture to the Sociétés de philosophie de langue française at a colloquium on the topic of communication. It elaborates Derrida's thinking on the iterability or citationality of the sign, the place of intentionality in the possibility of meaning, the context as a nonsaturable element in any interpretation, and signature in the dimensions of its singularity and repeatability. All of these questions have remained central to Derrida's work and each is taken up in numerous other places. They are posed here in relation to the speech-act theory of J. L. Austin whose distinction of constative from performative utterances has had such an important influence on Anglo-American linguistic philosophy. While recognizing the significance of Austin's theory, Derrida remarks that, like other linguistic theories he has discussed elsewhere, Austin's theory remains true to the logocentric program when it attempts to set aside consideration of "non-serious" language use, particularly its use in literary or fictional texts. This exclusion of "parasitic" speech acts has, as Derrida argues, far-reaching consequences for any theory of meaning.

The necessary iterability or citationality of the sign has had an important place in Derrida's thinking since **Speech and Phenomena.** As he had shown with regard to Husserl's concept of *Bedeutung*, the fact that a sign must be repeatable, that it must begin by repeating (which is one reason Derrida prefers the word *trace* to *sign*), sets limits on intentionality as the determinable ground of signification.

Iterability conditions any intention as possible but thereby impossible as a pure presence to itself. Unlike Austin (or Saussure or Husserl), who sets out a theory of meaning based on a pure speech act, Derrida argues the necessity of reconceiving the whole field of signification according to "something like a law of undecidable contamination" between intentional acts or events and the "parasitical" citations or repetitions that can never be rigorously excluded from such acts and that can always divert an intention or cause it to go astray.

As if to illustrate this point, Derrida's delimitation of intentionality has been frequently misinterpreted despite the very clear terms within which his argument is posed, particularly in this essay. This might seem surprising since American academic literary studies, at least, have long been accustomed to New Criticism's reservations concerning what it called "the intentional fallacy." But the "law of undecidable contamination" does not accommodate New Criticism's formalism any better than "old" criticism's historicism because it brings out, precisely, the contamination between these classically opposed domains of interpretation. The very grounds of interpretive disciplines and institutions are put at stake here and in a far more fundamental way than New Criticism ever envisioned. If one may so easily encounter gross caricatures of deconstructive thought which promote the notion, for example, that it has simply abandoned altogether the category of intentionality, then perhaps the reason is that these high stakes tend to push argument onto an irrational ground in defense, paradoxically, of what passes for the rational ground of argument.

"Signature Event Context" provoked a polemic with, most notably, the philosopher of language and disciple of Austin, John Searle.[1] As others had done, Searle chose to read Derrida's essay as an all-out attack on, among other things, intentionality. The measure of this misunderstanding and the paradoxes it reveals were in turn laid out in Derrida's own, very polemical response to Searle, "Limited Inc a b c ..." [1977]. The serious stakes of the debate do not prevent Derrida, in this latter text, from displaying a highly developed sense of the comic spectacle of an academic dispute over the possibility of self-evident meaning even as misunderstanding writes itself large on every page. For a recent re-edition of these essays (1989), Derrida has also written an "Afterword," titled "Toward an Ethic of Discussion," which reflects on the ethical questions posed, not only by the debate with Professor Searle, but in general by discussion on the very grounds of reasonable discussion.

Signature Event Context

Still confining ourselves, for simplicity, to *spoken* utterance.
— Austin, *How to Do Things with Words*

Is it certain that there corresponds to the word *communication*[2] a unique, univocal concept, a concept that can be rigorously grasped and transmitted: a communicable concept? Following a strange figure of discourse, one first must ask whether the word or signifier "communication" communicates a determined content, an identifiable meaning, a describable value. But in order to articulate and to propose this question, I already had to anticipate the meaning of the word *communication:* I have had to predetermine communication as the vehicle, transport, or site of passage of a *meaning,* and of a meaning that is *one.* If *communication* had several meanings, and if this plurality could not be reduced, then from the outset it would not be justifiable to define communication *itself* as the transmission of a meaning, assuming that we are capable of understanding one another as concerns each of these words (transmission, meaning, etc.). Now, the word *communication,* which nothing initially authorizes us to overlook as a word, and to impoverish as a polysemic word, opens a semantic field which precisely is not limited to semantics, semiotics, and even less to linguistics. To the semantic field of the word *communication* belongs the fact that it also designates nonsemantic movements. Here at least provisional recourse to ordinary language and to the equivocalities of natural language teaches us that one may, for example, *communicate a movement,* or that a tremor, a shock, a displacement of *force* can be communicated—that is, propagated, transmitted. It is also said that different or distant places can communicate between each other by means of a given passageway or opening. What happens in this case, what is transmitted or communicated, are not phenomena of meaning or signification. In these cases we are dealing neither with a semantic or conceptual content, nor with a semiotic operation, and even less with a linguistic exchange.

Nevertheless, we will not say that this nonsemiotic sense of the word *communication,* such as it is at work in ordinary language, in one or several of the so-called natural languages, constitutes the *proper* or *primitive* meaning, and that consequently the semantic, semiotic, or linguistic meaning corresponds to a derivation, an extension or a reduction, a metaphoric displacement. We will not say, as one might be tempted to do, that semiolinguistic communication is *more metaphorico* entitled "communication," because by analogy with "physical" or "real" communication it gives passage, transports, transmits something, gives access to something. We will not say so:

1. because the value of literal, *proper meaning* appears more problematical than ever,

2. because the value of displacement, of transport, etc., is constitutive of the very concept of metaphor by means of which one allegedly understands the semantic displacement which is operated from communication as a nonsemiolinguistic phenomenon to communication as a semiolinguistic phenomenon.

(I note here between parentheses that in this communication the issue will be, already is, the problem of polysemia and communication, of dissemination—which I will oppose to polysemia —and communication. In a moment, a certain concept of writing is bound to intervene, in order to transform itself, and perhaps in order to transform the problematic.)

It seems to go without saying that the field of equivocality covered by the word *communication* permits itself to be reduced massively by the limits of what is called a *context* (and I announce, again between parentheses, that the issue will be, in this communication, the problem of context, and of finding out about writing as concerns context in general). For example, in a *colloquium* of *philosophy* in the *French language,* a conventional context, produced by a kind of implicit but structurally vague consensus, seems to prescribe that one propose "communications" on communication, communications in discursive form, colloquial, oral communications destined to be understood and to open or pursue dialogues within the horizon of an intelligibility and truth of meaning, such that in principle a general agreement may finally be established. These communications are to remain within the element of a determined "natural" language, which is called French, and which commands certain very particular uses of the word *communication*. Above all, the object of these communications should be organized, by priority or by privilege, around communication as *discourse*, or in any event as signification. Without exhausting all the implications and the entire structure of an "event" like this one, which would merit a very long preliminary analysis, the prerequisite I have just recalled appears evident; and for anyone who doubts this, it would suffice to consult our schedule in order to be certain of it.

But are the prerequisites of a context ever absolutely determinable? Fundamentally, this is the most general question I would like to attempt to elaborate. Is there a rigorous and scientific concept of the *context?* Does not the notion of context harbor, behind a certain confusion, very determined philosophical presuppositions? To state it now in the most summary fashion, I would like to demonstrate why a context is never absolutely determinable, or rather in what way its determination is never certain or saturated. This structural nonsaturation would have as its double effect:

1. a marking of the theoretical insufficiency of the *usual concept of* (the linguistic or nonlinguistic) *context* such as it is accepted in numerous fields of investigation, along with all the other concepts with which it is systematically associated;

2. a rendering necessary of a certain generalization and a certain displacement of the concept of writing. The latter could no longer, henceforth, be included in the category of communication, at least if communication is understood in the restricted sense of the transmission of meaning. Conversely, it is within the general field of writing thus defined that the effects of semantic communication will be able to be determined as particular, secondary, inscribed, supplementary effects.

Writing and Telecommunication

If one takes the notion of writing in its usually accepted sense—which above all does not mean an innocent, primitive, or natural sense—one indeed must see it as a *means of communication.* One must even acknowledge it as a powerful means of communication which *extends* very far, if not infinitely, the field of oral or gestural communication. This is banally self-evident, and agreement on the matter seems easy. I will not describe all the *modes* of this extension in time and in space. On the other hand I will pause over the value of *extension* to which I have just had recourse. When we say that writing *extends* the field and powers of a locutionary or gestural communication, are we not presupposing a kind of *homogenous* space of communication? The range of the voice or of gesture certainly appears to encounter a factual limit here, an empirical boundary in the form of space and time; and writing, within the same time, within the same space, manages to loosen the limits, to open the *same field* to a much greater range. Meaning, the content of the semantic message, is thus transmitted, *communicated,* by different *means,* by technically more powerful mediations, over a much greater distance, but within a milieu that is fundamentally continuous and equal to itself, within a homogeneous element across which the unity and integrity of meaning are not affected in an essential way. Here, all affection is accidental.

The system of this interpretation (which is also in a way *the* system of interpretation, or in any event of an entire interpretation of hermeneutics), although it is the usual one, or to the extent that it is as usual as common sense, has been *represented* in the entire history of philosophy. I will say that it is even, fundamentally, the properly philosophical interpretation of writing. I will take a single example, but I do not believe one could find, in the entire history of philosophy as such, a single counterexample, a single analysis that essentially contradicts the one proposed by Condillac, inspired, strictly speaking, by Warburton, in the *Essay on the Origin of Human Knowledge (Essai sur l'origine des connaissances humaines).*[3] I have chosen this example because an *explicit* reflection on the origin and function of the written (this explicitness is not encountered in all philosophy, and one should examine the conditions of its emergence or occultation) is organized within a philosophical discourse which like all philosophy presupposes the simplicity of the origin and the continuity of every derivation, every production, every analysis, the homogeneity of all orders. Analogy is a major concept in Condillac's thought. I choose this example also because the analysis which "retraces" the origin and function of writing is placed, in a kind of noncritical way, *under the authority of the category of communication.*[4] If men write, it is (1) because they have something to communicate; (2) because what they have to communicate is their "thought," their "ideas," their representations. Representative thought precedes and governs communication which transports the "idea," the signified content; (3) because men are *already* capable of communicating and of communicating their thought to each other when, in continuous fashion, they invent the means of communication that is writing. Here is a passage from chapter 13 of part 2 ("On Language and On Method"), section 1 ("On the Origin and Progress of Language"), (writing is thus a modality of language and marks a continuous progress in a communication of linguistic essence), section 13, "On Writing": "Men capable of communicating their thoughts to each other by sounds felt the necessity of imagining new signs apt to perpetuate them and to make them *known* to *absent* persons" (I italicize this value of *absence*, which, if newly reexamined, will risk introducing a certain break in the homogeneity of the system). As soon as men are capable of "communicating their thoughts," and of doing so by sounds (which is, according to Condillac, a secondary stage, articulated language coming to "supplement" the language of action, the unique and radical principle of all language), the birth and progress of writing will follow a direct, simple, and continuous line. The history of writing will conform to a law of mechanical economy: to gain the most space and time by means of the most convenient abbreviation; it will never have the least effect on the structure and content of the meaning (of ideas) that it will have to vehiculate. The same content, previously communicated by gestures and sounds, henceforth will be transmitted by writing, and successively by different modes of notation, from pictographic writing up to alphabetic writing, passing through the hieroglyphic writing of the Egyptians and the ideographic writing of the Chinese. Condillac continues: "Imagination then will represent but the *same* images that they had already expressed by actions and words, and which had, from the beginnings, made language figurative and metaphoric. *The most natural means* was therefore to draw the pictures of things. To *express the idea* of a man or a horse the form of one or the other will be represented, and the first attempt at writing was but a simple painting" (p. 252; my italics).

The representative character of written communication— writing as picture, reproduction, imitation of its content—will be the invariable trait of all the progress to come. The concept of *representation* is indissociable here from the concepts of *communication* and *expression* that I have underlined in Condillac's text. Representation, certainly, will be complicated, will be given supplementary way-stations and stages, will become the representation of representation in hieroglyphic and ideographic writing, and then in phonetic-alphabetic writing, but the representative structure which marks the first stage of expressive communication, the idea/sign relationship, will never be suppressed or transformed. Describing the history of the kinds of writing, their continuous derivation on the basis of a common radical which is never displaced and which procures a kind of community of analogical participation between all the forms of writing, Condillac concludes (and this is practically a citation of Warburton, as is almost the entire chapter): "This is the general history of writing conveyed by a *simple gradation* from the state of painting through that of the letter; for letters are *the last steps* which remain to be taken after the Chinese marks, which partake of letters precisely as hieroglyphs partake equally of Mexican paintings and of Chinese characters. These characters are so close to our writing that an alphabet *simply diminishes* the confusion of their number, and is their *succinct abbreviation*" (pp. 254–53).

Having placed in evidence the motif of the economic, *homogenous, and mechanical* reduction, let us now come back to the notion of *absence* that I noted in passing in Condillac's text. How is it determined?

1. First, it is the absence of the addressee. One writes in order to communicate something to those who are absent. The absence of the sender, the addressor, from the marks that he abandons, which are cut off from him and continue to produce effects beyond his presence and beyond the present actuality of his

meaning, that is, beyond his life itself, this absence, which however belongs to the structure of all writing—and I will add,
further on, of all language in general—this absence is never
examined by Condillac.

2. The absence of which Condillac speaks is determined in the
most classical fashion as a continuous modification, a progres-
sive extenuation of presence. Representation regularly *supplements* presence. But this operation of supplementation ("To supplement" is one of the most decisive and frequently employed
operative concepts of Condillac's *Essai*)[5] is not exhibited as a
break in presence, but rather as a reparation and a continuous,
homogenous modification of presence in representation.

Here, I cannot analyze everything that this concept of absence
as a modification of presence presupposes, in Condillac's philosophy and elsewhere. Let us note merely that it governs another
equally decisive operative concept (here I am classically, and for
convenience, opposing *operative* to *thematic*) of the *Essai: to
trace* and *to retrace*. Like the concept of supplementing, the
concept of trace could be determined otherwise than in the way
Condillac determines it. According to him, to trace means "to
express," "to represent," "to recall," "to make present" ("in all
likelihood painting owes its origin to the necessity of thus tracing our thoughts, and this necessity has doubtless contributed to
conserving the language of action, as that which could paint the
most easily," p. 253). The sign is born at the same time as
imagination and memory, at the moment when it is demanded
by the absence of the object for present perception ("Memory, as
we have seen, consists only in the power of reminding ourselves
of the signs of our ideas, or the circumstances which accompanied them; and this capacity occurs only by virtue of the *analogy
of signs* [my italics; this concept of analogy, which organizes
Condillac's entire system, in general makes certain all the con-
tinuities, particularly the continuity of presence to absence] that
we have chosen, and by virtue of the order that we have put
between our ideas, the objects that we wish to retrace have to do
with several of our present needs" (p. 129). This is true of all the
orders of signs distinguished by Condillac (arbitrary, accidental,
and even natural signs, a distinction which Condillac nuances,
and on certain points, puts back into question in his Letters to

Cramer). The philosophical operation that Condillac also calls "to retrace" consists in traveling back, by way of analysis and continuous decomposition, along the movement of genetic derivation which leads from simple sensation and present perception to the complex edifice of representation: from original presence to the most formal language of calculation.

It would be simple to show that, essentially, this kind of analysis of written signification neither begins nor ends with Condillac. If we say now that this analysis is "ideological," it is not primarily in order to contrast its notions to "scientific" concepts, or in order to refer to the often dogmatic—one could also say "ideological"—use made of the word *ideology*, which today is so rarely examined for its possibility and history. If I define notions of Condillac's kind as ideological, it is that against the background of a vast, powerful, and systematic philosophical tradition dominated by the self-evidence of the *idea (eidos, idea)*, they delineate the field of reflection of the French "ideologues" who, in Condillac's wake, elaborated a theory of the sign as a representation of the idea, which itself represents the perceived thing. Communication, hence, vehiculates a representation as an ideal content (which will be called meaning); and writing is a species of this general communication. A species: a communication having a relative specificity within a genus.

If we ask ourselves now what, in this analysis, is the essential predicate of this *specific difference*, we once again find *absence*.

Here I advance the following two propositions or hypotheses:

1. Since every sign, as much in the "language of action" as in articulated language (even before the intervention of writing in the classical sense), supposes a certain absence (to be determined), it must be because absence in the field of writing is of an original kind if any specificity whatsoever of the written sign is to be acknowledged.

2. If, perchance, the predicate thus assumed to characterize the absence proper to writing were itself found to suit every species of sign and communication, there would follow a general displacement: writing no longer would be a species of communication, and all the concepts to whose generality writing was subordinated (the concept itself as meaning, idea, or grasp of meaning and idea, the concept of communication, of sign, etc.) would

appear as noncritical, ill-formed concepts, or rather as concepts destined to ensure the authority and force of a certain historic discourse.

Let us attempt then, while continuing to take our point of departure from this classical discourse, to characterize the absence that seems to intervene in a fashion specific to the functioning of writing.

A written sign is proffered in the absence of the addressee. How is this absence to be qualified? One might say that at the moment when I write, the addressee may be absent from my field of present perception. But is not this absence only a presence that is distant, delayed, or, in one form or another, idealized in its representation? It does not seem so, or at very least this distance, division, delay, differance must be capable of being brought to a certain absolute degree of absence for the structure of writing, supposing that writing exists, to be constituted. It is here that differance as writing could no longer (be) an (ontological) modification of presence. My "written communication" must, if you will, remain legible despite the absolute disappearance of every determined addressee in general for it to function as writing, that is, for it to be legible. It must be repeatable—iterable— in the absolute absence of the addressee or of the empirically determinable set of addressees. This iterability (*iter*, once again, comes from *itara, other* in Sanskrit, and everything that follows may be read as the exploitation of the logic which links repetition to alterity) structures the mark of writing itself, and does so moreover for no matter what type of writing (pictographic, hieroglyphic, ideographic, phonetic, alphabetic, to use the old categories). A writing that was not structurally legible—iterable— beyond the death of the addressee would not be writing. Although all this appears self-evident, I do not want it to be assumed as such and will examine the ultimate objection that might be made to this proposition. Let us imagine a writing with a code idiomatic enough to have been founded and known, as a secret cipher, only by two "subjects." Can it still be said that upon the death of the addressee, that is, of the two partners, the mark left by one of them is still a writing? Yes, to the extent to which, governed by a code, even if unknown and nonlinguistic, it is constituted, in its identity as a mark, by its iterability in the absence of whomever, and therefore ultimately in the absence of every empirically determinable "subject." This implies that there is no code—an organon of iterability—that is structurally secret. The possibility of repeating, and therefore of identifying, marks is implied in every code, making of it a communicable, transmittable, decipherable grid that is iterable for a third party, and thus for any possible user in general. All writing, therefore, in order to be what it is, must be able to function in the radical absence of every empirically determined addressee in general. And this absence is not a continuous modification of presence; it is a break in presence, "death," or the possibility of the "death" of the addressee, inscribed in the structure of the mark (and it is at this point, I note in passing, that the value or effect of transcendentality is linked necessarily to the possibility of writing and of "death" analyzed in this way). A perhaps paradoxical consequence of the recourse I am taking to iteration and to the code: the disruption, in the last analysis, of the authority of the code as a finite system of rules; the radical destruction, by the same token, of every context as a protocol of a code. We will come to this in a moment.

What holds for the addressee holds also, for the same reasons, for the sender or the producer. To write is to produce a mark that will constitute a kind of machine that is in turn productive, that my future disappearance in principle will not prevent from functioning and from yielding, and yielding itself to, reading and rewriting. When I say "my future disappearance," I do so to make this proposition more immediately acceptable. I must be able simply to say my disappearance, my nonpresence in general, for example the nonpresence of my meaning, of my intention-to-signify, of my wanting-to-communicate-this, from the emission or production of the mark. For the written to be the written, it must continue to "act" and to be legible even if what is called the author of the writing no longer answers for what he has written, for what he seems to have signed, whether he is provisionally absent, or if he is dead, or if in general he does not support, with his absolutely current and present intention or attention, the plenitude of his meaning, of that very thing which seems to be written "in his name." Here, we could reelaborate the analysis sketched out above for the addressee. The situation of the scribe and of the subscriber, as concerns the written, is fundamentally the same as that of the reader. This essential drifting, due to writing as an iterative structure cut off from all absolute responsibility, from *consciousness* as the authority of the last analysis, writing orphaned, and separated at birth from the assistance of its father, is indeed what Plato condemned in the *Phaedrus*.[6] If Plato's gesture is, as I believe, the philosophical movement par excellence, one realizes what is at stake here.

Before specifying the inevitable consequences of these nuclear traits of all writing—to wit: (1) the break with the horizon of communication as the communication of consciousnesses or presences, and as the linguistic or semantic transport of meaning; (2) the subtraction of all writing from the semantic horizon or the hermeneutic horizon which, at least as a horizon of meaning, lets itself be punctured by writing; (3) the necessity of, in a way, *separating* the concept of polysemia from the concept I have elsewhere named *dissemination*, which is also the concept of writing; (4) the disqualification or the limit of the concept of the "real" or "linguistic" context, the theoretical determination or empirical saturation of which is, strictly speaking, rendered impossible or insufficient by writing—I would like to demonstrate that the recognizable traits of the classical and narrowly defined concept of writing are generalizable. They would be valid not only for all the orders of "signs" and for all languages in general, but even, beyond semiolinguistic communication, for the entire field of what philosophy would call experience, that is, the experience of Being: so-called presence.

In effect, what are the essential predicates in a minimal determination of the classical concept of writing?

1. A written sign, in the usual sense of the word, is therefore a mark which remains, which is not exhausted in the present of its inscription, and which can give rise to an iteration both in the absence of and beyond the presence of the empirically determined subject who, in a given context, has emitted or produced it. This is how, traditionally at least, "written communication" is distinguished from "spoken communication."

2. By the same token, a written sign carries with it a force of breaking with its context, that is, the set of presences which organize the moment of its inscription. This force of breaking is

not an accidental predicate, but the very structure of the written. If the issue is one of the so-called real context, what I have just proposed is too obvious. Are part of this alleged real context a certain "present" of inscription, the presence of the scriptor in what he has written, the entire environment and horizon of his experience, and above all the intention, the meaning which at a given moment would animate his inscription. By all rights, it belongs to the sign to be legible, even if the moment of its production is irremediably lost, and even if I do not know what its alleged author-scriptor meant consciously and intentionally at the moment he wrote it, that is, abandoned it to its essential drifting. Turning now to the semiotic and internal context, there is no less a force of breaking by virtue of its essential iterability; one can always lift a written syntagma from the interlocking chain in which it is caught or given without making it lose every possibility of functioning, if not every possibility of "communicating," precisely. Eventually, one may recognize other such possibilities in it by inscribing or *grafting* it into other chains. No context can enclose it. Nor can any code, the code being here both the possibility and impossibility of writing, of its essential iterability (repetition/alterity).

3. This force of rupture is due to the spacing that constitutes the written sign: the spacing that separates it from other elements of the internal contextual chain (the always open possibility of its extraction and grafting), but also from all the forms of a present referent (past or to come in the modified form of the present past or to come) that is objective or subjective. This spacing is not the simple negativity of a lack, but the emergence of the mark. However, it is not the work of the negative in the service of meaning, or of the living concept, the *telos*, which remains *relevable* and reducible in the *Aufhebung* of a dialectics.[7]

Are these three predicates, along with the entire system joined to them, reserved, as is so often believed, for "written" communication, in the narrow sense of the word? Are they not also to be found in all language, for example in spoken language, and ultimately in the totality of "experience," to the extent that it is not separated from the field of the mark, that is, the grid of erasure and of difference, of unities of iterability, of unities separable from their internal or external context, and separable from themselves, to the extent that the very iterability which constitutes their identity never permits them to be a unity of self-identity?

Let us consider any element of spoken language, a large or small unity. First condition for it to function: its situation as concerns a certain code; but I prefer not to get too involved here with the concept of code, which does not appear certain to me; let us say that a certain self-identity of this element (mark, sign, etc.) must permit its recognition and repetition. Across empirical variations of tone, of voice, etc., eventually of a certain accent, for example, one must be able to recognize the identity, shall we say, of a signifying form. Why is this identity paradoxically the division or dissociation from itself which will make of this phonic sign a grapheme? Is it because this unity of the signifying form is constituted only by its iterability, by the possibility of being repeated in the absence not only of its referent, which goes without saying, but of a determined signified or current intention of signification, as of every present intention of communication. This structural possibility of being severed from its referent or signified (and therefore from communication and its context) seems to me to make of every mark, even if oral, a grapheme in general, that is, as we have seen, the nonpresent *remaining* of a differential mark cut off from its alleged "production" or origin. And I will extend this law even to all "experience" in general, if it is granted that there is no experience of *pure* presence, but only chains of differential marks.

Let us remain at this point for a while and come back to the absence of the referent and even of the signified sense, and therefore of the correlative intention of signification. The absence of the referent is a possibility rather easily admitted today. This possibility is not only an empirical eventuality. It constructs the mark; and the eventual presence of the referent at the moment when it is designated changes nothing about the structure of a mark which implies that it can do without the referent. Husserl, in the *Logical Investigations*, had very rigorously analyzed this possibility. It is double:

1. A statement the object of which is not impossible but only possible might very well be proffered and understood without its

real object (its referent) being present, whether for the person who produces the statement, or for the one who receives it. If I say, while looking out the window, "The sky is blue," the statement will be intelligible (let us provisionally say, if you will, communicable), even if the interlocutor does not see the sky; even if I do not see it myself, if I see it poorly, if I am mistaken, or if I wish to trick my interlocutor. Not that it is always thus; but the structure of possibility of this statement includes the capability of being formed and of functioning either as an empty reference, or cut off from its referent. Without this possibility, which is also the general, generalizable, and generalizing iteration of every mark, there would be no statements.

2. The absence of the signified. Husserl analyzes this too. He considers it always possible, even if, according to the axiology and teleology that govern his analysis, he deems this possibility inferior, dangerous, or "critical": it opens the phenomenon of the *crisis* of meaning. This absence of meaning can be layered according to three forms:

a. I can manipulate symbols without in active and current fashion animating them with my attention and intention to signify (the crisis of mathematical symbolism, according to Husserl). Husserl indeed stresses the fact that this does not prevent the sign from functioning: the crisis or vacuity of mathematical meaning does not limit technical progress. (The intervention of writing is decisive here, as Husserl himself notes in *The Origin of Geometry*.)

b. Certain statements can have a meaning, although they are without *objective* signification. "The circle is square" is a proposition invested with meaning. It has enough meaning for me to be able to judge it false or contradictory (*widersinnig* and not *sinnlos*, says Husserl). I am placing this example under the category of the absence of the signified, although the tripartition signifier/signified/referent does not pertinently account for Husserl's analysis. "Square circle" marks the absence of a referent, certainly, and also the absence of a certain signified, but not the absence of meaning. In these two cases, the crisis of meaning (nonpresence in general, absence as the absence of the referent—of perception—or of meaning—of the actual intention to signify) is always linked to the essential possibility of writing; and this crisis is not an accident, a factual and empirical anomaly of spoken language, but also the positive possibility and "internal" structure of spoken language, from a certain outside.

c. Finally there is what Husserl calls *Sinnlosigkeit* or agrammaticality, for example, "green is or" or "abracadabra." In the latter cases, as far as Husserl is concerned, there is no more language, or at least no more "logical" language, no more language of knowledge as Husserl understands it in teleological fashion, no more language attuned to the possibility of the intuition of objects given in person and signified in *truth*. Here, we are confronted with a decisive difficulty. Before pausing over it, I note, as a point that touches upon our debate on communication, that the primary interest of the Husserlian analysis to which I am referring here (precisely by extracting it, up to a certain point, from its teleological and metaphysical context and horizon, an operation about which we must ask how and why it is always possible) is that it alleges, and it seems to me arrives at, a rigorous dissociation of the analysis of the sign or expression *(Ausdruck)* as a signifying sign, a sign meaning something *(bedeutsame Zeichen)*, from all phenomena of communication.[8]

Let us take once more the case of agrammatical *Sinnlosigkeit*. What interests Husserl in the *Logical Investigations* is the system of rules of a universal grammar, not from a linguistic point of view, but from a logical and epistemological point of view. In an important note from the second edition,[9] he specifies that from his point of view the issue is indeed one of a purely *logical* grammar, that is, the universal conditions of possibility for a morphology of significations in the relation of knowledge to a possible object, and not of a pure grammar in *general*, considered from a psychological or linguistic point of view. Therefore, it is only in a context determined by a will to know, by an epistemic intention, by a conscious relation to the object as an object of knowledge within a horizon of truth—it is in this oriented contextual field that "green is or" is unacceptable. But, since "green is or" and "abracadabra" do not constitute their context in themselves, nothing prevents their functioning in another context as signifying marks (or indices, as Husserl would say). Not only in the contingent case in which, by means of the translation of German into French "le vert est ou" might be endowed with grammaticality, *ou* (*oder*, or) becoming when heard *où* (where, the mark of place): "Where has the green (of the grass) gone *(le vert est où?*," "Where has the glass in which I wished to give you something to drink gone *(le verre est où)*." But even "green is or" still signifies an *example of agrammaticality*. This is the possibility on which I wish to insist: the possibility of extraction and of citational grafting which belongs to the structure of every mark, spoken or written, and which constitutes every mark as writing even before and outside every horizon of semiolinguistic communication; as writing, that is, as a possibility of functioning cut off, at a certain point, from its "original" meaning and from its belonging to a saturable and constraining context. Every sign, linguistic or nonlinguistic, spoken or written (in the usual sense of this opposition), as a small or large unity, can be *cited*, put between quotation marks; thereby it can break with every given context, and engender infinitely new contexts in an absolutely nonsaturable fashion. This does not suppose that the mark is valid outside its context, but on the contrary that there are only contexts without any center of absolute anchoring. This citationality, duplication, or duplicity, this iterability of the mark is not an accident or an anomaly, but is that (normal–abnormal) without which a mark could no longer even have a so-called normal functioning. What would a mark be that one could not cite? And whose origin could not be lost on the way?

The Parasites. Iter, of Writing: That Perhaps It Does Not Exist

I now propose to elaborate this question a little further with help from—but in order to go beyond it too—the problematic of the *performative*. It has several claims to our interest here.

   1. Austin,[10] by his emphasis on the analysis of perlocution and especially illocution, indeed seems to consider acts of discourse only as acts of communication. This is what his French translator notes, citing Austin himself: "It is by comparing the *constative* utterance (that is, the classical 'assertion,' most often conceived as a true or false 'description' of the facts) with the *performative* utterance (from the English *performative*, that is, the utterance which allows us to do something by means of speech itself) that Austin has been led to consider *every* utter-

ance worthy of the name (that is, destined to *communicate*, which would exclude, for example, reflex-exclamations) as being first and foremost a *speech act* produced in the *total* situation in which the interlocutors find themselves (*How to Do Things With Words*, p. 147).[11]

2. This category of communication is relatively original. Austin's notions of illocution and perlocution do not designate the transport or passage of a content of meaning, but in a way the communication of an original movement (to be defined in a *general theory of action*), an operation, and the production of an effect. To communicate, in the case of the performative, if in all rigor and purity some such thing exists (for the moment I am placing myself within this hypothesis and at this stage of the analysis), would be to communicate a force by the impetus of a mark.

3. Differing from the classical assertion, from the constative utterance, the performative's referent (although the word is inappropriate here, no doubt, such is the interest of Austin's finding) is not outside it, or in any case preceding it or before it. It does not describe something which exists outside and before language. It produces or transforms a situation, it operates; and if it can be said that a constative utterance also effectuates something and always transforms a situation, it cannot be said that this constitutes its internal structure, its manifest function or destination, as in the case of the performative.

4. Austin had to free the analysis of the performative from the authority of the *value of truth*, from the opposition true–false,[12] at least in its classical form, occasionally substituting for it the value of force, of difference of force (*illocutionary or perlocutionary force*.) (It is this, in a thought which is nothing less than Nietzschean, which seems to me to beckon toward Nietzsche, who often recognized in himself a certain affinity with a vein of English thought.)

For these four reasons, at least, it could appear that Austin has exploded the concept of communication as a purely semiotic, linguistic, or symbolic concept. The performative is a "communication" which does not essentially limit itself to transporting an already constituted semantic content guarded by its own aiming at truth (truth as an *unveiling* of that which is in its Being, or as an *adequation* between a judicative statement and the thing itself).

And yet—at least this is what I would like to attempt to indicate now—all the difficulties encountered by Austin in an analysis that is patient, open, aporetic, in constant transformation, often more fruitful in the recognition of its impasses than in its positions, seem to me to have a common root. It is this: Austin has not taken into account that which in the structure of *locution* (and therefore before any illocutory or perlocutory determination) already bears within itself the system of predicates that I call *graphematic in general,* which therefore confuses all the ulterior oppositions the pertinence, purity, and rigor of which Austin sought to establish in vain.

In order to show this, I must take as known and granted that Austin's analyses permanently demand a value of *context,* and even of an exhaustively determinable context, whether de jure or teleologically; and the long list of "infelicities" of variable type which might affect the event of the performative always returns to an element of what Austin calls the total context.[13] One of these essential elements—and not one among others—classically remains consciousness, the conscious presence of the intention of the speaking subject for the totality of his locutory act. Thereby, performative communication once more becomes the communication of an intentional meaning,[14] even if this meaning has no referent in the form of a prior or exterior thing or state of things. This conscious presence of the speakers or receivers who participate in the effecting of a performative, their conscious and intentional presence in the totality of the operation, implies teleologically that no *remainder* escapes the present totalization. No remainder, whether in the definition of the requisite conventions, or the internal and linguistic context, or the grammatical form or semantic determination of the words used; no irreducible polysemia, that is, no "dissemination" escaping the horizon of the unity of meaning. I cite the first two lectures of *How to Do Things with Words:* "Speaking generally, it is always necessary that the *circumstances* in which the words are uttered should be in some way, or ways, *appropriate,* and it is very commonly necessary that either the speaker himself or other persons should *also* perform certain *other* actions, whether 'physical' or 'mental' actions or even acts of uttering further words. Thus, for naming the ship, it is essential that I should be the person appointed to name her, for (Christian) marrying, it is essential that I should not be already married with a wife living, sane and undivorced, and so on; for a bet to have been made, it is generally necessary for the offer of the bet to have been accepted by a taker (who must have done something, such as to say 'Done'), and it is hardly a gift if I *say* 'I give it you' but never hand it over. So far, well and good" (pp. 8–9).

In the Second Lecture, after having in his habitual fashion set aside the grammatical criterion, Austin examines the possibility and origin of the failures or "infelicities" of the performative utterance. He then defines the six indispensable, if not sufficient, conditions for success. Through the values of "conventionality," "correctness," and "completeness" that intervene in the definition, we necessarily again find those of an exhaustively definable context, of a free consciousness present for the totality of the operation, of an absolutely full meaning that is master of itself: the teleological jurisdiction of a total field whose *intention* remains the organizing center (pp. 12–16). Austin's procedure is rather remarkable, and typical of the philosophical tradition that he prefers to have little to do with. It consists in recognizing that the possibility of the negative (here, the *infelicities*) is certainly a structural possibility, that failure is an essential risk in the operations under consideration; and then, with an almost *immediately simultaneous* gesture made in the name of a kind of ideal regulation, an exclusion of this risk as an accidental, exterior one that teaches us nothing about the language phenomenon under consideration. This is all the more curious, and actually rigorously untenable, in that Austin denounces with irony the "fetish" of opposition *value/fact*.

Thus, for example, concerning the conventionality without which there is no performative, Austin recognizes that *all* conventional acts are *exposed* to failure: "It seems clear in the first place that, although it has excited us (or failed to excite us) in connexion with certain acts which are or are in part acts of *uttering words*, infelicity is an ill to which *all* acts are heir which have the general character of ritual or ceremonial, all *conventional* acts: not indeed that *every* ritual is liable to every form of infelicity (but then nor is every performative utterance)" (pp. 18–19; Austin's italics).

Aside from all the questions posed by the very historically sedimented notion of "convention," we must notice here: (1) That in this specific place Austin seems to consider only the conventionality that forms the *circumstance* of the statement, its contextual surroundings, and not a certain intrinsic conventionality of that which constitutes locution itself, that is, everything that might quickly be summarized under the problematic heading of the "arbitrariness of the sign," which extends, aggravates, and radicalizes the difficulty. Ritual is not an eventuality, but, as iterability, is a structural characteristic of every mark. (2) That the value of risk or of being open to failure, although it might, as Austin recognizes, affect the totality of conventional acts, is not examined as an essential predicate or *law*. Austin does not ask himself what consequences derive from the fact that something possible—a possible risk—is *always* possible, is somehow a necessary possibility. And if, such a necessary possibility of failure being granted, it still constitutes an accident. What is a success when the possibility of failure continues to constitute its structure?

Therefore the opposition of the success/failure of illocution or perlocution here seems quite insufficient or derivative. It presupposes a general and systematic elaboration of the structure of locution which avoids the endless alternation of essence and accident. Now, it is very significant that Austin rejects this "general theory," defers it on two occasions, notably in the Second Lecture. I leave aside the first exclusion. ("I am not going into the general doctrine here: in many such cases we may even say the act was 'void' (or voidable for duress or undue influence) and so forth. Now I suppose that some very general high-level doctrine might embrace both what we have called infelicities *and* these other 'unhappy' features of the doing of actions—in our case actions containing a performative utterance—in a single doctrine: but we are not including this kind of unhappiness—we must just remember, though, that features of this sort can and do *constantly obtrude* into any case we are discussing. Features of this sort would normally come under the heading of 'extenuating circumstances' or of 'factors reducing or abrogating the agent's responsibility,' and so on"; p. 21; my italics). The second gesture of exclusion concerns us more directly here. In question, precisely, is the possibility that every performative utterance (and *a priori* every other utterance) may be "cited." Now, Austin excludes this eventuality (and the general doctrine that would account for it) with a kind of lateral persistence, all the more significant in its off-sidedness. He insists upon the fact that this possibility remains *abnormal, parasitical,* that it constitutes a kind of extenuation, that is, an agony of language that must firmly be kept at a distance, or from which one must resolutely turn away. And the concept of the "ordinary," and therefore of "ordinary language," to which he then has recourse is indeed marked by this exclusion. This makes it all the more problematic, and before demonstrating this, it would be better to read a paragraph from this Second Lecture:

"(ii) Secondly, as *utterances* our performatives are *also* heir to certain other kinds of ill which infect *all* utterances. And these likewise, though again they might be brought into a more general account, we are deliberately at present excluding. I mean, for example, the following: a performative utterance will, for example, be *in a peculiar way* hollow or void if said by an actor on the stage, or if introduced in a poem, or spoken in soliloquy. This applies in a similar manner to any and every utterance—a sea-change in special circumstances. Language in such circumstances is in special ways—intelligibly—used not *seriously* [I am italicizing here, J.D.], but in ways *parasitic* upon its normal use—ways that fall under the doctrine of the *etiolations* of language. All this we are *excluding* from consideration. Our performative utterances, felicitous or not, are to be understood as issued in ordinary circumstances" (pp. 21–22). Austin therefore excludes, along with what he calls the *sea-change,* the "nonserious," the "parasitic," the "etiolations," the "non-ordinary" (and with them the general theory which in accounting for these oppositions no longer would be governed by them), which he nevertheless recognizes as the possibility to which every utterance is open. It is also as a "parasite" that writing has always been treated by the philosophical tradition, and the rapprochement, here, is not at all fortuitous.

Therefore, I ask the following question: is this general possibility necessarily that of a failure or a trap into which language might *fall*, or in which language might lose itself, as if in an abyss situated outside or in front of it? What about *parasitism?* In other words, does the generality of the risk admitted by Austin *surround* language like a kind of *ditch*, a place of external perdition into which locution might never venture, that it might avoid by remaining at home, in itself, sheltered by its essence or *telos?* Or indeed is this risk, on the contrary, its internal and positive condition of possibility? this outside its inside? the very force and law of its emergence? In this last case, what would an "ordinary" language defined by the very law of language signify? Is it that in excluding the general theory of this structural parasitism, Austin, who nevertheless pretends to describe the facts and events of ordinary language, makes us accept as ordinary a teleological and ethical determination (the univocality of the statement—which he recognizes elsewhere remains a philosophical "ideal," pp. 72–73—the self-presence of a total context, the transparency of intentions, the presence of meaning for the absolutely singular oneness of a speech act, etc.)?

For, finally, is not what Austin excludes as anomalous, exceptional, "non-serious,"[15] that is, *citation* (on the stage, in a poem, or in a soliloquy), the determined modification of a general citationality—or rather, a general iterability—without which there would not even be a "successful" performative? Such that—a paradoxical, but inevitable consequence—a successful performative is necessarily an "impure" performative, to use the word that Austin will employ later or when he recognizes that there is no "pure" performative.[16]

Now I will take things from the side of positive possibility, and no longer only from the side of failure: would a performative statement be possible if a citational doubling did not eventually split, dissociate from itself the pure singularity of the event? I am asking the question in this form in order to forestall an objection. In effect, it might be said to me: you cannot allege that you account for the so-called graphematic structure of locution solely on the basis of the occurrence of failures of the performative, however real these failures might be, and however effective or general their possibility. You cannot deny that there are also performatives that succeed, and they must be accounted for: sessions are opened, as Paul Ricoeur did yesterday, one says "I ask a question," one bets, one challenges, boats are launched, and one even marries occasionally. Such events, it appears, have occurred. And were a single one of them to have taken place a single time, it would still have to be accounted for.

I will say "perhaps." Here, we must first agree upon what the "occurring" or the eventhood of an event consists in, when the event supposes in its allegedly present and singular intervention a statement which in itself can be only of a repetitive or citational structure, or rather, since these last words lead to confusion, of an iterable structure. Therefore, I come back to the point that seems fundamental to me, and which now concerns the status of the event in general, of the event of speech or by speech, of the strange logic it supposes, and which often remains unperceived.

Could a performative statement succeed if its formulation did not repeat a "coded" or iterable statement, in other words, if the expressions I use to open a meeting, launch a ship or a marriage were not identifiable as *conforming* to an iterable model, and therefore if they were not identifiable in a way as "citation"? Not that citationality here is of the same type as in a play, a philosophical reference, or the recitation of a poem. This is why there is a relative specificity, as Austin says, a "relative purity" of performatives. But this relative purity is not constructed *against* citationality or iterability, but against other kinds of iteration within a general iterability which is the effraction into the allegedly rigorous purity of every event of discourse or every speech act. Thus, one must less oppose citation or iteration to the noniteration of an event, than construct a differential typology of forms of iteration, supposing that this is a tenable project that can give rise to an exhaustive program, a question I am holding off on here. In this typology, the category of intention will not disappear; it will have its place, but from this place it will no longer be able to govern the entire scene and the entire system of utterances. Above all, one then would be concerned with different types of marks or chains of iterable marks, and not with an opposition between citational statements on the one hand, and singular and original statement-events on the other. The first consequence of this would be the following: given this structure of iteration, the intention which animates utterance will never be completely present in itself and its content. The iteration which structures it *a priori* introduces an essential dehiscence and demarcation. One will no longer be able to exclude, as Austin wishes, the "non-serious," the *oratio obliqua,* from "ordinary" language. And if it is alleged that ordinary language, or the ordinary circumstance of language, excludes citationality or general iterability, does this not signify that the "ordinariness" in question, the thing and the notion, harbors a lure, the teleological lure of consciousness the motivations, indestructible necessity, and systematic effects of which remain to be analyzed? Especially since this essential absence of intention for the actuality of the statement, this structural unconsciousness if you will, prohibits every saturation of a context. For a context to be exhaustively determinable, in the sense demanded by Austin, it at least would be necessary for the conscious intention to be totally present and actually transparent for itself and others, since it is a determining focal point of the context. The concept of or quest for the "context" therefore seems to suffer here from the same theoretical and motivated uncertainty as the concept of the "ordinary," from the same metaphysical origins: an ethical and teleological discourse of consciousness. This time, a reading of the connotations of Austin's text would confirm the reading of its descriptions; I have just indicated the principle of this reading.

Differance, the irreducible absence of intention or assistance from the performative statement, from the most "event-like" statement possible, is what authorizes me, taking into account the predicates mentioned just now, to posit the general graphematic structure of every "communication." Above all, I will not conclude from this that there is no relative specificity of the effects of consciousness, of the effects of speech (in opposition to writing in the traditional sense), that there is no effect of the performative, no effect of ordinary language, no effect of presence and of speech acts. It is simply that these effects do not exclude what is generally opposed to them term by term, but on the contrary presuppose it in dissymmetrical fashion, as the general space of their possibility.

Signatures

This general space is first of all spacing as the disruption of presence in the mark, what here I am calling writing. That all the difficulties encountered by Austin intersect at the point at which both presence and writing are in question, is indicated for me by a passage from the Fifth Lecture in which the divided agency of the legal *signature* emerges.

Is it by chance that Austin must note at this point: "I must explain again that we are floundering here. To feel the firm ground of prejudice slipping away is exhilarating, but brings its revenges" (p. 61). Only a little earlier an "impasse" had appeared, the impasse one comes to each time "any *single simple* criterion of grammar or vocabulary" is sought in order to distinguish between performative or constative statements. (I must say that this critique of linguisticism and of the authority of the code, a critique executed on the basis of an analysis of language, is what most interested me and convinced me in Austin's enterprise.) He then attempts to justify, with nonlinguistic reasons, the preference he has shown until now for the forms of the first-person present indicative in the active voice in the analysis of the performative. The justification of last appeal is that in these forms reference is made to what Austin calls the *source* (origin) of the utterance. This notion of the *source*—the stakes of which are so evident—often reappears in what follows, and it governs the entire analysis in the phase we are examining. Not only does Austin not doubt that the source of an oral statement in the first person present indicative (active voice) is *present* in the utterance and in the statement, (I have attempted to explain why we had reasons not to believe so), but he no more doubts that the equivalent of this link to the source in written utterances is simply evident and ascertained in the *signature:* "Where there is *not*, in the verbal formula of the utterance, a reference to the person doing the uttering, and so the acting, by means of the pronoun 'I' (or by his personal name), then in fact he will be 'referred to' in one of two ways:

"(a) In verbal utterances, *by his being the person who does* the uttering—what we may call the utterance-*origin* which is used generally in any system of verbal reference-co-ordinates.

"(b) In written utterances (or 'inscriptions'), *by his appending his signature* (this has to be done because, of course, written utterances are not tethered to their origin in the way spoken ones are)" (pp. 60–61). Austin acknowledges an analogous function in the expression "hereby" used in official protocols.

Let us attempt to analyze the signature from this point of view, its relation to the present and to the source. I take it as henceforth implied in this analysis that all the established predicates will hold also for the oral "signature" that is, or allegedly is, the presence of the "author" as the "person who does the uttering," as the "origin," the source, in the production of the statement.

By definition, a written signature implies the actual or empirical nonpresence of the signer. But, it will be said, it also marks and retains his having-been-present in a past now, which will remain a future now, and therefore in a now in general, in the transcendental form of nowness (*maintenance*). This general *maintenance* is somehow inscribed, stapled to present punctuality, always evident and always singular, in the form of the signature. This is the enigmatic originality of every paraph. For the attachment to the source to occur, the absolute singularity of an event of the signature and of a form of the signature must be retained: the pure reproducibility of a pure event.

Is there some such thing? Does the absolute singularity of an event of the signature ever occur? Are there signatures?

Yes, of course, every day. The effects of signature are the most ordinary thing in the world. The condition of possibility for these effects is simultaneously, once again, the condition of their impossibility, of the impossibility of their rigorous purity. In order to function, that is, in order to be legible, a signature must have a repeatable, iterable, imitable form; it must be able to detach itself from the present and singular intention of its production. It is its sameness which, in altering its identity and singularity, divides the seal. I have already indicated the principle of the analysis above.

To conclude this very *dry*[17] discourse:

1. As writing, communication, if one insists upon maintaining the word, is not the means of transport of sense, the exchange of intentions and meanings, the discourse and "communication of

consciousnesses." We are not witnessing an end of writing which, to follow McLuhan's ideological representation, would restore a transparency or immediacy of social relations; but indeed a more and more powerful historical unfolding of a general writing of which the system of speech, consciousness, meaning, presence, truth, etc., would only be an effect, to be analyzed as such. It is this questioned effect that I have elsewhere called *logocentrism*.

2. The semantic horizon which habitually governs the notion of communication is exceeded or punctured by the intervention of writing, that is, of a *dissemination* that cannot be reduced by a *polysemia*. Writing is read, and "in the last analysis" does not give rise to a hermeneutic deciphering, to the decoding of a meaning or truth.

3. Despite the general displacement of the classical, "philosophical," Western, etc., concept of writing, it appears necessary, provisionally and strategically, to conserve the *old name*. This implies an entire logic of *paleonymy* which I do not wish to elaborate here.[18] Very schematically: an opposition of metaphysical concepts (for example, speech–writing, presence–absence, etc.) is never the face-to-face of two terms, but a hierarchy and an order of subordination. Deconstruction cannot limit itself or proceed immediately to a neutralization: it must, by means of a double gesture, a double science, a double writing, practice an *overturning* of the classical opposition *and* a general *displacement* of the system. It is only on this condition that deconstruction will provide itself the means with which to *intervene* in the field of oppositions that it criticizes, which is also a field of nondiscursive forces. Each concept, moreover, belongs to a systematic chain and itself constitutes a system of predicates. There is no metaphysical concept in and of itself. There is a work— metaphysical or not—on conceptual systems. Deconstruction does not consist in passing from one concept to another, but in overturning and displacing a conceptual order, as well as the nonconceptual order with which the conceptual order is articulated. For example, writing, as a classical concept, carries with it predicates that have been subordinated, excluded, or held in reserve by forces and according to necessities to be analyzed. It is these predicates (I have mentioned some) whose force of generality, generalization, and generativity find themselves liberated,

grafted onto a "new" concept of writing which also corresponds to whatever always has *resisted* the former organization of forces, which always has constituted the *remainder* irreducible to the dominant force which organized the—to say it quickly—logocentric hierarchy. To leave to this new concept the old name of writing is to maintain the structure of the graft, the transition and indispensable adherence to an effective *intervention* in the constituted historic field. And it is also to give their chance and their force, their power of *communication*, to everything played out in the operations of deconstruction.

But what goes without saying will quickly have been understood, especially in a philosophical colloquium: as a disseminating operation *separated* from presence (of Being) according to all its modifications, writing, if there is any, perhaps communicates, but does not exist, surely. Or barely, hereby, in the form of the most improbable signature.

(*Remark:* the—written—text of this—oral—communication was to have been addressed to the *Association of French Speaking Societies of Philosophy* before the meeting. Such a missive therefore had to be signed. Which I did, and counterfeit here. Where? There. J.D.)

J. DERRIDA

—Translated by Alan Bass

NOTES

1. "Reiterating the Differences: A Reply to Derrida," *Glyph* 1 (1977).

2. The theme of the colloquium at which Derrida delivered this lecture, but also the term in French for a paper presented in such circumstances. Derrida will exploit this ambiguity below.—ED.

3. See Derrida's introductory essay, "The Archeology of the Frivolous" [1976], to the edition of Condillac's work.—ED.

4. Rousseau's theory of language and writing is also proposed under the general rubric of *communication*. ("On the Various Means of Communicating Our Thoughts" is the title of the first chapter of the *Essay on the Origin of Languages*.)

5. Language supplements action or perception, articulated language supplements the language of action, writing supplements articulated language, etc.

6. See Chapter 5 below, "**Plato's Pharmacy**."—ED.

7. On Derrida's translation of *Aufheben* as *relever*, and my maintenance of the French term, see note 12 to chapter 3, "Différance," for a system of references.—TRANS.

8. "So far we have considered expressions as used in communication, which last depends essentially on the fact that they operate indicatively. But expressions also play a great part in uncommunicated, interior mental life. This change in function plainly has nothing to do with whatever makes an expression an expression. Expressions continue to have *Bedeutungen* as they had before, and the same *Bedeutungen* as in dialogue." *Logical Investigations*, trans. J. N. Findlay (London: Routledge and Kegan Paul, 1970), p. 278. What I am asserting here implies the interpretation I proposed of Husserlian procedure on this point. Therefore, I permit myself to refer to **Speech and Phenomena**. [see above—ED.]

9. "In the First Edition I spoke of 'pure grammar,' a name conceived and expressly devised to be analogous to Kant's 'pure science of nature.' Since it cannot, however, be said that pure formal semantic theory comprehends the entire *a priori* of general grammar—there is, e.g., a peculiar *a priori* governing relations of mutual understanding among minded persons, relations very important for grammar—talk of pure logical grammar is to be preferred." *Logical Investigations*, vol. 2, p. 527. [In the paragraph that follows I have maintained Findlay's translation of the phrase Derrida plays upon, i.e. "green is or," and have given the French necessary to comprehend this passage in parentheses.—TRANS.]

10. J. L. Austin, *How to Do Things with Words* (New York: Oxford University Press, 1962). Throughout this section I have followed the standard procedure of translating *énoncé* as statement, and *énonciation* as utterance.—TRANS.

11. G. Lane, introduction to the French translation of *How to Do Things with Words*.

12. ". . . two fetishes which I admit to an inclination to play Old Harry with, viz., 1) the true/false fetish, 2) the value/fact fetish" (p. 150).

13. See e.g. pp. 52 and 147.

14. Which sometimes compels Austin to reintroduce the criterion of truth into the description of performatives. See e.g. pp. 51–52 and 89–90.

15. The very suspect value of the "non-serious" is a frequent reference (see e.g. pp. 104, 121). It has an essential link with what Austin says elsewhere about the *oratio obliqua* (pp. 70–71) and about *mime*.

16. From this point of view one might examine the fact recognized by Austin that "the *same* sentence is used on different occasions of utterance in *both* ways, performative and constative. The thing seems hopeless from the start, if we are to leave utterances *as they stand* and seek for a criterion" (p. 67). It is the graphematic root of citationality (iterability) that provokes

this confusion and makes it "not possible," as Austin says, "to lay down even a list of all possible criteria" (Ibid.).

17. Derrida's word here is *sec,* combining the initial letters of three words that form his title, signature, event, context.—TRANS.

18. See *Dissemination* [1972] and *Positions* [1972].

FIVE

From "Plato's Pharmacy" in *Dissemination*

("La Pharmacie de Platon" in *La Dissémination*

[1972])

"Plato's Pharmacy," which precedes and lays the ground for **"The Double Session,"** is undoubtedly one of Derrida's most important early texts because in it he examines the condemnation of writing as philosophy's self-inaugurating gesture and he does so at its source: in the texts of Plato. The key text is the *Phaedrus,* long considered an essentially flawed or disjointed dialogue, but which Derrida will argue is ordered by the "graphic" (rather than logic) of differance at a level of textual play that Plato could only partially control. The principal guide Derrida chooses to follow within the intricacies of this play is the family of pharmaceutical terms that, more or less explicitly, are associated by Plato with writing, but particularly the term *pharmakon.* In classical Greek, a *pharmakon* is a drug, and as such it may be taken to mean either a remedy or a poison, either the cure of illness or its cause. It is this essential undecidability of the *pharmakon* that poses the problem of translation which, as Derrida points out, is not simply the problem of translating Plato's Greek into another language, but already introduces within that single language (which happens to be the inaugural language of philosophy) the necessity of translating Greek to itself. Derrida situates this problem in the "violent difficulty of the transference of a nonphilosopheme into a philosopheme" (p. 72). That is, the philosophical determination of writing as *pharmakon* cannot be made to function as an unambiguous term available to dialectic reasoning (a philosopheme). Instead it enters the dialectic from both sides at once (remedy–poison, good–bad, positive–negative) and threatens the philosophical process from within. That is why Derrida writes, "With this problem of translation we will thus be dealing with nothing less than the problem of the very passage into philosophy." Whereas the "passage into philosophy" requires the reduction of the sign to its signified truth, translation cannot retain the meaning of an original sign except by supplanting it with another sign. In this respect, translation reveals itself always to be a writing (and a reading) which, like the movement of the *pharmakon*, spaces out the same in a difference from itself. It repeats, supplements, supplants. (For more on the problem of translation, see Part Three below.)

"Plato's Pharmacy" is divided into two major parts and subdivided into nine sections. The following excerpts, all taken from the first part, retain the major portion of Derrida's reading of the myth Socrates tells to account for the origin of writing. The fact that this origin is available only as myth or rumor complicates considerably the distinction of *mythos* from *logos*, of myth from philosophy that Plato wants to establish. We pick up the reading at the point at which it addresses Socrates's question that opens the final section of the dialogue, the question of the propriety or impropriety of writing.

[. . . .]

It is truly *morality* that is at stake, both in the sense of the opposition between good and evil, or good and bad, and in the sense of mores, public morals and social conventions. It is a question of knowing what is done and what is not done. This moral disquiet is in no way to be distinguished from questions of truth, memory, and dialectics. This latter question, which will quickly be engaged as *the* question of writing, is closely associated with the morality theme, and indeed develops it by affinity of essence and not by superimposition. But within a debate rendered very real by the political development of the city, the propagation of writing and the activity of the sophists and speechwriters, the primary accent is naturally placed upon political and social proprieties. The type of arbitration proposed by Socrates plays within the opposition between the values of seemliness and unseemliness (*euprepeia/aprepeia*): "But there remains the question of propriety and impropriety in writing, that is to say the conditions that make it proper or improper. Isn't that so?"[1]

Is writing seemly? Does the writer cut a respectable figure? Is it proper to write? Is it done?

Of course not. But the answer is not so simple, and Socrates does not immediately offer it on his own account in a rational discourse or *logos*. He lets it be heard by delegating it to an *akoē*, to a well-known rumor, to hearsay evidence, to a fable transmitted from ear to ear: "I can tell you what our forefathers have said about it, but the truth of it is only known by tradition. However, if we could discover that truth for ourselves, should we still be concerned with the fancies of mankind?" (274c).

The truth of writing, that is, as we shall see, (the) nontruth, cannot be discovered in ourselves by ourselves. And it is not the object of a science, only of a history that is recited, a fable that is repeated. The link between writing and myth becomes clearer, as does its opposition to knowledge, notably the knowledge one seeks in oneself, by oneself. And at the same time, through writing or through myth, the genealogical break and the estrangement from the origin are sounded. One should note most especially that what writing will later be accused of—repeating without knowing—here defines the very approach that leads to the statement and determination of its status. One thus begins by repeating without knowing—through a myth—the definition of writing, which is to repeat without knowing. This kinship of writing and myth, both of them distinguished from *logos* and dialectics, will only become more precise as the text concludes. Having just repeated without knowing that writing consists of repeating without knowing, Socrates goes on to base the demonstration of his indictment, of his *logos*, upon the premises of the *akoē*, upon structures that are readable through a fabulous genealogy of writing. As soon as the myth has struck the first blow, the *logos* of Socrates will demolish the accused.

The Father of Logos

The story begins like this:

Socrates: Very well. I heard, then, that at Naucratis in Egypt there lived one of the old gods of that country, the one whose sacred bird is called the ibis; and the name of the divinity was Theuth. It was he who first invented numbers and calculation, geometry and astronomy, not to speak of draughts and dice, and above all writing *(grammata)*. Now the King of all Egypt at that time was Thamus who lived in the great city of the upper region which the Greeks call the Egyptian Thebes; the god himself they call Ammon. Theuth came to him and exhibited his arts and declared that they ought to be imparted to the other Egyptians. And Thamus questioned him about the usefulness of each one; and as Theuth enumerated, the King blamed or praised what he thought were the good or bad points in the explanation. Now Thamus is said to have had a good deal to remark on both sides of the question about every single art (it would take too long to repeat it here); but when it came to writing, Theuth said, "This discipline *(to mathēma)*, my King, will make the Egyptians wiser and will improve their memories *(sophōterous kai mnēmonikōterous)*: my invention is a recipe *(pharmakon)* for both memory and wisdom." But the King said . . . etc. (274c-e).

Let us cut the King off here. He is faced with the *pharmakon*. His reply will be incisive.

Let us freeze the scene and the characters and take a look at them. Writing (or, if you will, the *pharmakon*) is thus presented to the King. Presented: like a kind of present offered up in homage by a vassal to his lord (Theuth is a demigod speaking to the king of the gods), but above all as a finished work submitted to his appreciation. And this work is itself an art, a capacity for work, a power of operation. This artefactum is an art. But the value of this gift is still uncertain. The value of writing—or of the *pharmakon*—has of course been spelled out to the King, but it is the King who will give it its value, who will set the price of what, in the act of receiving, he constitutes or institutes. The king or god (Thamus represents[2] Ammon, the king of the gods, the king of kings, the god of gods. Theuth says to him: *Ō basileu*) is thus the other name for the origin of value. The value of writing will not be itself, writing will have no value, unless and to the extent that god-the-king approves of it. But god-the-king nonetheless experiences the *pharmakon* as a product, an *ergon*, which is not his own, which comes to him from outside but also from below, and which awaits his condescending judgment in order to be consecrated in its being and value. God the king does not know how to write, but that ignorance or incapacity only testifies to his sovereign independence. He has no need to write. He speaks, he says, he dictates, and his word suffices. Whether a scribe from his secretarial staff then adds the supplement of a transcription or not, the consignment is always in essence secondary.

From this position, without rejecting the homage, the god-king will depreciate it, pointing out not only its uselessness but its menace and its mischief. Another way of not receiving the offering of writing. In so doing, god-the-king-that-speaks is acting like a father. The *pharmakon* is here presented to the father and is by him rejected, belittled, abandoned, disparaged. The father is always suspicious and watchful toward writing.

Even if we did not want to give in here to the easy passage uniting the figures of the king, the god, and the father, it would suffice to pay systematic attention—which to our knowledge has never been done—to the permanence of a Platonic schema that assigns the origin and power of speech, precisely of *logos*, to the paternal position. Not that this happens especially and exclusively in Plato. Everyone knows this or can easily imagine it. But the fact that "Platonism," which sets up the whole of Western metaphysics in its conceptuality, should not escape the generality of this structural constraint, and even illustrates it with incomparable subtlety and force, stands out as all the more significant.

Not that logos *is* the father, either. But the origin of logos is *its father*. One could say anachronously that the "speaking subject" is the *father* of his speech. And one would quickly realize that this is no metaphor, at least not in the sense of any common, conventional effect of rhetoric. *Logos* is a son, then, a son that would be destroyed in his very *presence* without the present *attendance* of his father. His father who answers. His father who speaks for him and answers for him. Without his father, he would be nothing but, in fact, writing. At least that is what is said by the one who says: it is the father's thesis. The specificity of writing would thus be intimately bound to the absence of the father. Such an absence can of course exist along very diverse modalities, distinctly or confusedly, successively or simultaneously: to have lost one's father, through natural or violent death, through random violence or patricide; and then to solicit the aid and attendance, possible or impossible, of the paternal presence, to solicit it directly or to claim to be getting along without it, etc. The reader will have noted Socrates's insistence on the misery, whether pitiful or arrogant, of a *logos* committed to writing: "It always needs its father to attend to it, being quite unable to defend itself or attend to its own needs" (275e).

This misery is ambiguous: it is the distress of the orphan, of course, who needs not only an attending presence but also a presence that will attend to its needs; but in pitying the orphan, one also makes an accusation against him, along with writing, for claiming to do away with the father, for achieving emancipation with complacent self-sufficiency. From the position of the holder of the scepter, the desire of writing is indicated, designated, and denounced as a desire for orphanhood and patricidal subversion. Isn't this *pharmakon* then a criminal thing, a poisoned present?

The status of this orphan, whose welfare cannot be assured by any attendance or assistance, coincides with that of a *graphein* which, being nobody's son at the instant it reaches inscription, scarcely remains a son at all and no longer *recognizes* its origins, whether legally or morally. In contrast to writing, living *logos* is alive in that it has a living father (whereas the orphan is already half dead), a father that is *present, standing* near it, behind it, within it, sustaining it with his rectitude, attending it in person in his own name. Living *logos*, for its part, recognizes its debt, lives off that recognition, and forbids itself, thinks it can forbid itself patricide. But prohibition and patricide, like the relations between speech and writing, are structures surprising enough to require us later on to articulate Plato's text between a patricide prohibited and a patricide proclaimed. The deferred murder of the father and rector.

The *Phaedrus* would already be sufficient to prove that the responsibility for *logos*, for its meaning and effects, goes to those who attend it, to those who are present with the presence of a father. These "metaphors" must be tirelessly questioned. Witness Socrates, addressing Eros: "If in our former speech Phaedrus or I said anything harsh against you, blame Lysias, the father of the subject *(ton tou logou patera)*" (275b). *Logos*—"discourse"— has the meaning here of argument, line of reasoning, guiding thread animating the spoken discussion (the *logos*). To translate it by "subject" [*sujet*], as Robin does, is not merely anachronistic. The whole intention and the organic unity of signification is destroyed. For only the "living" discourse, only a spoken word (and not a speech's theme, object, or subject) can have a father; and, according to a necessity that will not cease to become clearer to us from now on, the *logoi* are the children. Alive enough to protest on occasion and to let themselves be questioned; capable, too, in contrast to written things, of responding when their father is there. They are their father's responsible presence.

[. . . .]

But what is a father?

Should we consider this known, and with this term—the known—classify the other term within what one would hasten to classify as a metaphor? One would then say that the origin or cause of *logos* is being compared to what we know to be the cause of a living son, his father. One would understand or imagine the birth and development of *logos* from the standpoint of a domain foreign to it, the transmission of life or the generative relation. But the father is not the generator or procreator in any "real" sense prior to or outside all relation to language. In what way, indeed, is the father–son relation distinguishable from a mere cause–effect or generator–engendered relation, if not by the instance of *logos*? Only a power of speech can have a father. The father is always father to a speaking-living being. In other words, it is precisely *logos* that enables us to perceive and investigate something like paternity. If there were a simple metaphor in the expression "father of logos," the first word, which seemed the more *familiar*, would nevertheless receive more meaning *from* the second than it would transmit *to* it. The first familiarity is always involved in a relation of cohabitation with *logos*. Living-beings, father and son, are announced to us and related to each other within the household of *logos*. From which one does not escape, in spite of appearances, when one is transported, by "metaphor," to a foreign territory where one meets fathers, sons, living creatures, all sorts of beings that come in handy for explaining to anyone who does not know, by comparison, what *logos*, that strange thing, is all about. Even though this hearth is the heart of all metaphoricity, "father of logos" is not a simple metaphor. To have simple metaphoricity, one would have to make the statement that some living creature incapable of language, if anyone still wished to believe in such a thing, has a father. One must thus proceed to undertake a general reversal of all metaphorical directions, no longer asking whether *logos* can have a father but understanding that what the father claims to be the father of cannot go without the essential possibility of *logos*.

A *logos indebted* to a father, what does that mean? At least how can it be read within the stratum of the Platonic text that interests us here?

The figure of the father, of course, is also that of the good *(agathon)*. *Logos represents* what it is indebted to: the father who is also chief, capital, and good(s). Or rather *the* chief, *the* capital, *the* good(s). *Patēr* in Greek means all that at once. Neither translators nor commentators of Plato seem to have accounted for the play of these schemas. It is extremely difficult, we must recognize, to respect this play in a translation, and the fact can at least be explained in that no one has ever raised the question. Thus, at the point in the *Republic* where Socrates backs away from speaking of the good in itself (VI, 506e), he immediately suggests replacing it with its *ekgonos*, its son, its offspring:

> Let us dismiss for the time being the nature of the good in itself, for to attain to my present surmise of that seems a pitch above the impulse that wings my flight today. But about what seems to be the offspring *(ekgonos)* of the good and most nearly made in its likeness I am willing to speak if you too wish it, and otherwise to let the matter drop.
>
> Well, speak on, he said, for you will duly pay me the tale of the parent another time.
>
> I could wish, I said, that I were able to make and you to receive the payment, and not merely as now the interest *(tokous)*. But at any rate receive this interest and the offspring of the good *(tokon te kai ekgonon autou tou agathou)*.

Tokos, which is here associated with *ekgonos*, signifies production and the product, birth and the child, etc. This word functions with this meaning in the domains of agriculture, of kinship relations, and of fiduciary operations. None of these domains, as we shall see, lies outside the investment and possibility of a *logos*.

As product, the *tokos* is the child, the human or animal brood, as well as the fruits of the seed sown in the field, and the interest on a capital investment: it is a *return* or *revenue*. The distribution of all these meanings can be followed in Plato's text. The meaning of *patēr* is sometimes even inflected in the exclusive sense of financial capital. In the *Republic* itself, and not far from the passage we have just quoted. One of the drawbacks of democracy lies in the role that capital is often allowed to play in it: "But these money-makers with down-bent heads, pretending not even to see the poor, but inserting the sting of their money into any of the remainder who do not resist, and harvesting from them in interest as it were a manifold progeny of the parent sum (*tou patros ekgonous tokous pollaplasious*), foster the drone and pauper element in the state" (555e).

Now, about this father, this capital, this good, this origin of value and of appearing beings, it is not possible to speak simply or directly. First of all because it is no more possible to look them in the face than to stare at the sun. On the subject of this bedazzlement before the face of the sun, a rereading of the famous passage of the *Republic* (VII, 515c ff) is strongly recommended here.

[....]

[In the third section titled "The Filial Inscription: Theuth, Hermes, Thoth, Nabû, Nebo," Derrida fits the Platonic myth of Theuth into a pattern of traits common to gods of writing from other mythic traditions. His purpose is to demonstrate that Plato's story was not simply a spontaneous invention, as commentators have always seen it, but was also "supervised and limited by rigorous necessities" (p. 85). These necessities or structural laws consist in a series of oppositions clustered around the opposition speech and writing (e.g., life and death, father and son, legitimate and bastard, soul and body, good and evil, inside and outside, son and moon, and so forth). For instance, the Egyptian god Thoth, who seems to be Theuth's nearest forebear, is a secondary god, the son of the sun god. But his subordinate position is the position also of the supplement, that which is both added to and substituted for the father term. He represents thus a danger for the sun's supremacy. His speech is likewise never absolutely original; instead it introduces difference into language, which is why he is associated with the origin of the plurality of languages. He has power over the calculation of time and thus is associated with death. To bring out these and other traits which are repeated in Plato's myth is not merely an exercise in comparative mythology or culture. Instead, that demonstration opens "onto the general problematic of the relations between the mythemes and the philosophemes that lies at the origin of western *logos*" (p. 86). It is to this general problematic that Derrida turns his attention by considering Theuth as a repetition of Thoth who is, in turn, a figure of pure repetition without proper identity or substance.]

The system of these traits brings into play an original kind of logic: the figure of Thoth is opposed to its other (father, sun, life, speech, origin or orient, etc.), but as that which at once supplements and supplants it. Thoth extends or opposes by repeating or replacing. By the same token, the figure of Thoth takes shape and takes its shape from the very thing it resists and substitutes for. But it thereby opposes *itself*, passes into its other, and this messenger-god is truly a god of the absolute passage between opposites. If he had any identity—but he is precisely the god of nonidentity—he would be that *coincidentia oppositorum* to which we will soon have recourse again. In distinguishing himself from his opposite, Thoth also imitates it, becomes its sign and representative, obeys it and *conforms* to it, replaces it, by violence if need be. He is thus the father's other, the father, and the subversive movement of replacement. The god of writing is thus at once his father, his son, and himself. He cannot be assigned a fixed spot in the play of differences. Sly, slippery, and masked, an intriguer and a card, like Hermes, he is neither king nor jack, but rather a sort of *joker*, a floating signifier, a wild card, one who puts play into play.

This god of resurrection is less interested in life or death than in death as a repetition of life and life as a rehearsal of death, in the awakening of life and in the recommencement of death. This is what *numbers*, of which he is also the inventor and patron, mean. Thoth repeats everything in the addition of the supplement: in adding to and doubling as the sun, he is other than the sun and the same as it; other than the good and the same, etc. Always taking a place not his own, a place one could call that of the dead or the dummy, he has neither a proper place nor a proper name. His propriety or property is impropriety or inappropriateness, the floating indetermination that allows for substitution and play. *Play*, of which he is also the inventor, as Plato himself reminds us. It is to him that we owe the games of dice *(kubeia)* and draughts *(petteia)* (274d). He would be the mediating movement of dialectics if he did not also mimic it, indefinitely preventing it, through this ironic doubling, from reaching some final fulfillment or eschatological reappropriation. Thoth is never present. Nowhere does he appear in person. No being-there can properly be *his own*.

Every act of his is marked by this unstable ambivalence. This god of calculation, arithmetic, and rational science[3] also presides over the occult sciences, astrology and alchemy. He is the god of magic formulas that calm the sea, of secret accounts, of hidden texts: an archetype of Hermes, god of cryptography no less than of every other -graphy.

Science and magic, the passage between life and death, the supplement to evil and to lack: the privileged domain of Thoth had, finally, to be medicine. All his powers are summed up and find employment there. The god of writing, who knows how to put an end to life, can also heal the sick. And even the dead.[4] The steles of Horus on the Crocodiles tell of how the king of the gods sends Thoth down to heal Harsiesis, who has been bitten by a snake in his mother's absence.[5]

The god of writing is thus also a god of medicine. Of "medicine": both a science and an occult drug. Of the remedy and the poison. The god of writing is the god of the *pharmakon*. And it is writing as a *pharmakon* that he presents to the king in the *Phaedrus*, with a humility as unsettling as a dare.

The Pharmakon

This is the malady in them all for which law must find a *pharmakon*. Now it is a sound old adage that it is hard to fight against two enemies at once—even when they are enemies from opposite quarters. We see the truth of this in medicine and elsewhere. (*Laws*, 919b)

Let us return to the text of Plato, assuming we have ever really left it. The word *pharmakon* is caught in a chain of significations. The play of that chain seems systematic. But the system here is not, simply, that of the intentions of an author who goes by the name of Plato. The system is not primarily that of what someone *meant-to-say* [*un vouloir-dire*]. Finely regulated communications are established, through the play of language, among diverse functions of the word and, within it, among diverse strata or regions of culture. These communications or corridors of meaning can sometimes be declared or clarified by Plato when he plays upon them "voluntarily," a word we put in quotation marks because what it designates, to content ourselves with remaining within the closure of these oppositions, is only a mode of "submission" to the necessities of a given "language." None of these concepts can translate the relation we are aiming at here. Then again, in other cases, Plato can *not* see the links, can leave them in the shadow or break them up. And yet these links go on working of themselves. In spite of him? thanks to him? in *his* text? *outside* his text? but then where? between his text and the language? for what reader? at what moment? To answer such questions in principle and in general will seem impossible; and that will give us the suspicion that there is some malformation in the question itself, in each of its concepts, in each of the oppositions it thus accredits. One can always choose to believe that if Plato did not put certain possibilities of passage into practice, or even interrupted them, it is because he perceived them but left them in the impracticable. This formulation is possible only if one avoids all recourse to the difference between conscious and unconscious, voluntary and involuntary, a very crude tool for dealing with relations in and to language. The same would be true of the opposition between speech—or writing—

and language if that opposition, as is often the case, harked back to the above categories.

This reason alone should already suffice to prevent us from reconstituting the entire chain of significations of the *pharmakon*. No absolute privilege allows us absolutely to master its textual system. This limitation can and should nevertheless be displaced to a certain extent. The possibilities and powers of displacement are extremely diverse in nature, and, rather than enumerating here all their titles, let us attempt to produce some of their effects as we go along, as we continue our march through the Platonic problematic of writing.[6]

We have just sketched out the correspondence between the figure of Thoth in Egyptian mythology and a certain organization of concepts, philosophemes, metaphors, and mythemes picked up from what is called the Platonic text. The word *pharmakon* has seemed to us extremely apt for the task of tying all the threads of this correspondence together. Let us now reread, in a rendering derived from Robin, this sentence from the *Phaedrus*: "Here, O King, says Theuth, is a discipline *(mathēma)* that will make the Egyptians wiser *(sophōterous)* and will improve their memories *(mnemonikōterous)*: both memory *(mnēmē)* and instruction *(sophia)* have found their remedy *(pharmakon)*."

The common translation of *pharmakon* by *remedy* [*remède*] —a beneficent drug—is not, of course, inaccurate. Not only can *pharmakon* really mean *remedy* and thus erase, on a certain surface of its functioning, the ambiguity of its meaning. But it is even quite obvious here, the stated intention of Theuth being precisely to stress the worth of his product, that he *turns* the word on its strange and invisible pivot, presenting it from a single one, and most reassuring, of its *poles*. This medicine is beneficial; it repairs and produces, accumulates and remedies, increases knowledge and reduces forgetfulness. Its translation by "remedy" nonetheless erases, in going outside the Greek language, the other pole reserved in the word *pharmakon*. It cancels out the resources of ambiguity and makes more difficult, if not impossible, an understanding of the context. As opposed to "drug" or even "medicine," *remedy* says the transparent rationality of science, technique, and therapeutic causality, thus excluding from the text any leaning toward the magic virtues of a force the effects of which are hard to master, a dynamics that constantly surprises the one who tries to manipulate it as master and as subject.

Now, *on the one hand,* Plato is bent on presenting writing as an occult, and therefore suspect, power. Just like painting, to which he will later compare it, and like optical illusions and the techniques of *mimēsis* in general. His mistrust of the mantic and magic, of sorcerers and casters of spells, is well attested.[7] In the *Laws,* in particular, he reserves them terrible punishments. According to an operation we will have cause to remember later, he recommends that they be excluded—expelled or cut off—from the social arena. Expulsion and ostracism can even be accomplished at the same time, by keeping them in prison, where they would no longer be visited by free men but only by the slave that would bring them their food; then by depriving them of burial: "At death he shall be cast out beyond the borders without burial, and if any free citizen has a hand in his burial, he shall be liable to a prosecution for impiety at the suit of any who cares to take proceedings" (X, 909*b-c*).

On the other hand, the King's reply presupposes that the effectiveness of the *pharmakon* can be reversed: it can worsen the ill instead of remedy it. Or rather, the royal answer suggests that Theuth, by ruse and/or naïveté, has exhibited the reverse of the true effects of writing. In order to vaunt the worth of his invention, Theuth would thus have denatured the *pharmakon,* said the opposite *(tounantion)* of what writing is capable of. He has passed a poison off as a remedy. So that in translating *pharmakon* by *remedy,* what one respects is not what Theuth intended, nor even what Plato intended, but rather what the King says Theuth has said, effectively deluding either the King or himself. If Plato's text then goes on to give the King's pronouncement as the truth of Theuth's production and his speech as the truth of writing, then the translation *remedy* makes Theuth into a simpleton or a flimflam artist, *from the sun's point of view.* From that viewpoint, Theuth has no doubt played on the word, interrupting, for his own purposes, the communication between the two opposing values. But the King restores that communication, and the translation takes no account of this. And all the while the two interlocutors, whatever they do and whether or not they choose, remain within the unity of the same signifier. Their discourse plays within it, which is no longer the case in translation. *Remedy* is the rendition that, more than "medicine" or "drug" would have done, obliterates the virtual, dynamic references to the other uses of the same word in Greek. The effect of such a translation is most importantly to destroy what we will later call Plato's anagrammatic writing, to destroy it by interrupting the relations interwoven among different functions of the same word in different places, relations that are virtually but necessarily "citational." When a word inscribes itself as the citation of another sense of the same word, when the textual center-stage of the word *pharmakon*, even while it means *remedy*, cites, re-cites, and makes legible that which *in the same word* signifies, in another spot and on a different level of the stage, *poison* (for example, since that is not the only thing *pharmakon* means), the choice of only one of these renditions by the translator has as its first effect the neutralization of the citational play, of the "anagram," and, in the end, quite simply of the very textuality of the translated text. It could no doubt be shown, and we will try to do so when the time comes, that this blockage of the passage among opposing values is itself already an effect of "Platonism," the consequence of something already at work in the translated text, in the relation between "Plato" and his "language." There is no contradiction between this proposition and the preceding one. Textuality being constituted by differences and by differences from differences, it is by nature absolutely heterogeneous and is constantly composing with the forces that tend to annihilate it.

One must therefore accept, follow, and analyze the composition of these two forces or of these two gestures. That composition is even, in a certain sense, the single theme of this essay. On the one hand Plato decides in favor of a logic that does not tolerate such passages between opposing senses of the same word, all the more so since such a passage would reveal itself to be something quite different from simple confusion, alternation, or the dialectic of opposites. And yet, on the other hand, the *pharmakon*, if our reading confirms itself, constitutes the original medium of that decision, the element that precedes it, comprehends it, goes beyond it, can never be reduced to it, and is not separated from it by a single word (or signifying apparatus), operating within the Greek and Platonic text. All translations into languages that are the heirs and depositaries of Western metaphysics thus produce on the *pharmakon* an *effect of analysis* that violently destroys it, reduces it to one of its simple elements by interpreting it, paradoxically enough, in the light of the ulterior developments it itself has made possible. Such an interpretative translation is thus as violent as it is impotent: it destroys the *pharmakon* but at the same time forbids itself access to it, leaving it untouched in its reserve.

The translation by "remedy" can thus be neither accepted nor simply rejected. Even if one intended thereby to save the "rational" pole and the laudatory intention, the idea of the *correct* use of the *science* or *art* of medicine, one would still run every risk of being deceived by language. Writing is no more valuable, says Plato, as a remedy than as a poison. Even before Thamus has let fall his pejorative sentence, the remedy is disturbing in itself. One must indeed be aware of the fact that Plato is suspicious of the *pharmakon* in general, even in the case of drugs used exclusively for therapeutic ends, even when they are wielded with good intentions, and even when they are as such effective. There is no such thing as a harmless remedy. The *pharmakon* can never be simply beneficial.

[. . . .]

Perhaps we can now read the King's response:

> But the king said, "Theuth, my master of arts *(Ō tekhnikō-tate Theuth)*, to one man it is given to create the elements of an art, to another to judge the extent of harm and usefulness it will have for those who are going to employ it. And now, since you are father of written letters *(patēr ōn grammatōn)*, your paternal goodwill has led you to pronounce the very opposite *(tounantion)* of what is their real power. The fact is that this invention will produce forgetfulness in the souls of those who have learned it because they will not need to exercise their memories *(lēthēn men en psuchais parexei mnēmēs aneletēsiai)*, being able to rely on what is written, using the stimulus of external marks that are alien

to themselves *(dia pistin graphēs exōthen hup' allotriōn tupōn)* rather than, from within, their own unaided powers to call things to mind *(ouk endothen autous huph' hautōn anamimnēskomenous)*. So it's not a remedy for memory, but for reminding, that you have discovered *(oukoun mnēmēs, alla hupomnēseōs, pharmakon hēures)*. And as for wisdom *(sophias de)*, you're equipping your pupils with only a semblance *(doxan)* of it, not with truth *(alētheian)*. Thanks to you and your invention, your pupils will be widely read without benefit of a teacher's instruction; in consequence, they'll entertain the delusion that they have wide knowledge, while they are, in fact, for the most part incapable of real judgment. They will also be difficult to get on with since they will be men filled with the conceit of wisdom *(doxosophoi)*, not men of wisdom *(anti sophōn)*." (274e – 275b)

The king, the father of speech, has thus asserted his authority over the father of writing. And he has done so with severity, without showing the one who occupies the place of his son any of that paternal good will exhibited by Theuth toward his own children, his "letters." Thamus presses on, multiplies his reservations, and visibly wants to leave Theuth no hope.

In order for writing to produce, as he says, the "opposite" effect from what one might expect, in order for this *pharmakon* to show itself, with use, to be injurious, its effectiveness, its power, its *dunamis* must, of course, be ambiguous. As is said of the *pharmakon* in the *Protagoras*, the *Philebus*, the *Timaeus*. It is precisely this ambiguity that Plato, through the mouth of the King, attempts to master, to dominate by inserting its definition into simple, clear-cut oppositions: good and evil, inside and outside, true and false, essence and appearance. If one rereads the reasons adduced by the royal sentence, one will find this series of oppositions there. And set in place in such a way that the *pharmakon*, or, if you will, writing, can only go around in circles: writing is only apparently good for memory, seemingly able to help it from within, through its own motion, to know what is true. But in truth, writing is essentially bad, external to memory, productive not of science but of belief, not of truth but of appearances. The *pharmakon* produces a play of appearances which enable it to pass for truth, etc.

But while, in the *Philebus* and the *Protagoras*, the *pharmakon*, because it is painful, seems bad whereas it is beneficial, here, in the *Phaedrus* as in the *Timaeus*, it is passed off as a helpful remedy whereas it is in truth harmful. Bad ambiguity is thus opposed to good ambiguity, a deceitful intention to a mere appearance. Writing's case is grave.

It is not enough to say that writing is conceived out of this or that series of oppositions. Plato thinks of writing, and tries to comprehend it, to dominate it, on the basis of *opposition* as such. In order for these contrary values (good/evil, true/false, essence/appearance, inside/outside, etc.) to be in opposition, each of the terms must be simply *external* to the other, which means that one of these oppositions (the opposition between inside and outside) must already be accredited as the matrix of all possible opposition. And one of the elements of the system (or of the series) must also stand as the very possibility of systematicity or seriality in general. And if one got to thinking that something like the *pharmakon*—or writing—far from being governed by these oppositions, opens up their very possibility without letting itself be comprehended by them; if one got to thinking that it can only be out of something like writing—or the *pharmakon*—that the strange difference between inside and outside can spring; if, consequently, one got to thinking that writing as a *pharmakon* cannot simply be assigned a site within what it situates, cannot be subsumed under concepts whose contours it draws, leaves only its ghost to a logic that can only seek to govern it insofar as logic arises from it—one would then have to *bend* [*plier*] into strange contortions what could no longer even simply be called logic or discourse. All the more so if what we have just imprudently called a *ghost* can no longer be distinguished, with the same assurance, from truth, reality, living flesh, etc. One must accept the fact that here, for once, to leave a ghost behind will in a sense be to salvage nothing.

This little exercise will no doubt have sufficed to warn the reader: to come to an understanding with Plato, as it is sketched out in this text, is already to slip away from the recognized

models of commentary, from the genealogical or structural reconstitution of a system, whether this reconstitution tries to
corroborate or refute, confirm, or "overturn," mark a return-to-
Plato or give him a "send-off" in the quite Platonic manner of
the *khairein*. What is going on here is something altogether
different. That too, of course, but still completely other. If the
reader has any doubt, he is invited to reread the preceding paragraph. Every model of classical reading is exceeded there at some
point, precisely at the point where it attaches to the inside of the
series—it being understood that this excess is not a *simple* exit
out of the series, since that would obviously fall under one of the
categories of the series. The excess—but can we still call it that?
—is only a *certain* displacement of the series. And a certain
folding back [*repli*]—which will later be called a *re-mark*—of
opposition within the series, or even within its dialectic. We
cannot qualify it, name it, comprehend it under a simple concept
without immediately being off the mark. Such a functional displacement, which concerns differences (and, as we shall see,
"simulacra") more than any conceptual identities signified, is a
real and necessary challenge. It writes itself. One must therefore
begin by reading it.

If writing, according to the king and under the sun, produces
the opposite effect from what is expected, if the *pharmakon* is
pernicious, it is so because it doesn't come from around here. It
comes from afar, it is external or alien: to the living, which is the
right-here of the inside, to *logos* as the *zōon* it claims to assist or
relieve. The imprints *(tupoi)* of writing do not inscribe themselves this time, as they do in the hypothesis of the *Theaetetus*,
in the wax of the soul *in intaglio,* thus corresponding to the
spontaneous, autochthonous motions of psychic life. Knowing
that he can always leave his thoughts outside or check them
with an external agency, with the physical, spatial, superficial
marks that one lays flat on a tablet, he who has the *tekhnē* of
writing at his disposal will come to rely on it. He will know that
he himself can leave without the *tupoi's* going away, that he can
forget all about them without their leaving his service. They will
represent him even if he forgets them; they will transmit his
word even if he is not there to animate them. Even if he is dead,
and only a *pharmakon* can be the wielder of such power, *over*

death but also in cahoots with it. The *pharmakon* and writing are thus always involved in questions of life and death.

Can it be said without conceptual anachronism—and thus without serious interpretive error—that the *tupoi* are the representatives, the *physical surrogates of the psychic* that is absent? It would be better to assert that the written traces no longer even belong to the order of the *phusis*, since they are not alive. They do not grow; they grow no more than what could be sown, as Socrates will say in a minute, with a reed *(kalamos)*. They do violence to the natural, autonomous organization of the *mnēmē*, in which *phusis* and *psuchē* are not opposed. If writing does belong to the *phusis*, wouldn't it be to that moment of the *phusis*, to that necessary movement through which its truth, the production of its appearing, tends, says Heraclitus, to take shelter in its crypt? "Cryptogram" thus condenses in a single word a pleonastic proposition.

If one takes the king's word for it, then, it is this life of the memory that the *pharmakon* of writing would come to hypnotize: fascinating it, taking it out of itself by putting it to sleep in a monument. Confident of the permanence and independence of its *types (tupoi)*, memory will fall asleep, will not keep itself up, will no longer keep to keeping itself alert, present, as close as possible to the truth of what is. Letting itself get stoned *[médusée]* by its own signs, its own guardians, by the types committed to the keeping and surveillance of knowledge, it will sink down into *lēthē*, overcome by nonknowledge and forgetfulness.[8] Memory and truth cannot be separated. The movement of *alētheia* is a deployment of *mnēmē* through and through. A deployment of living memory, of memory as psychic life in its self-presentation to itself. The powers of *lēthē* simultaneously increase the domains of death, of nontruth, of nonknowledge. This is why writing, at least insofar as it sows "forgetfulness in the soul," turns us toward the inanimate and toward nonknowledge. But it cannot be said that its essence simply and *presently* confounds it with death or nontruth. For writing *has* no essence or value of its own, whether positive or negative. It plays within the simulacrum. It is in its type the mime of memory, of knowledge, of truth, etc. That is why men of writing appear before the eye of

God not as wise men *(sophoi)* but in truth as fake or self-proclaimed wise men *(doxosophoi).*

[Is not the diatribe against writing a continuation of Plato's ongoing battle with the sophists? Yes and no, replies Derrida: yes, to the extent that the sophist relies on writing as an aid to memory and thus substitutes for living memory its dead monument, mnemotechnics; no, to the extent that the sophist also argues that "one should exercise one's memory rather than entrust traces to an outside agency." The condemnation of writing thus crosses the border supposed to divide philosophy from sophistics.]

Thus, in both cases, on both sides, writing is considered suspicious and the alert exercise of memory prescribed. What Plato is attacking in sophistics, therefore, is not simply recourse to memory but, within such recourse, the substitution of the mnemonic device for live memory, of the prosthesis for the organ; the perversion that consists of replacing a limb by a thing, here, substituting the passive, mechanical "by-heart" for the active reanimation of knowledge, for its reproduction in the present. The boundary (between inside and outside, living and nonliving) separates not only speech from writing but also memory as an unveiling (re-)producing a presence from re-memoration as the mere repetition of a monument; truth as distinct from its sign, being as distinct from types. The "outside" does not begin at the point where what we now call the psychic and the physical meet, but at the point where the *mnēmē*, instead of being present to itself in its life as a movement of truth, is supplanted by the archive, evicted by a sign of re-memoration or of com-memoration. The space of writing, space *as* writing, is opened up in the violent movement of this surrogation, in the difference between *mnēmē* and *hypomnēsis*. The outside is already *within* the work of memory. The evil slips in within the relation of memory to itself, in the general organization of the mnesic activity. Memory is finite by nature. Plato recognizes this in attributing life to it. As in the case of all living organisms, he assigns it, as we have seen, certain limits. A limitless memory would in any event be not memory but infinite self-presence. Memory always therefore already needs signs in order to recall the nonpresent, with which it is necessarily in relation. The movement of dialectics bears witness to this. Memory is thus contaminated by its first substitute: *hypomnēsis*. But what Plato *dreams* of is a memory with no sign. That is, with no supplement. A *mnēmē* with no *hypomnēsis*, no *pharmakon*. And this at the very moment and for the very reason that he calls *dream* the confusion between the hypothetical and the anhypothetical in the realm of mathematical intelligibility *(Republic, 533b).*

Why is the surrogate or supplement dangerous? It is not, so to speak, dangerous in itself, in that aspect of it that can present itself as a thing, as a being-present. In that case it would be reassuring. But here, the supplement *is* not, is not a being *(on).* It is nevertheless not a simple nonbeing *(mē on),* either. Its slidings slip it out of the simple alternative presence—absence. *That* is the danger. And that is what enables the type always to pass for the original. As soon as the supplementary outside is opened, its structure implies that the supplement itself can be "typed," replaced by its double, and that a supplement to the supplement, a surrogate for the surrogate, is possible and necessary. Necessary because this movement is not a sensible, "empirical" accident: it is linked to the ideality of the *eidos* as the possibility of the repetition of the same. And writing appears to Plato (and after him to all of philosophy, which is as such constituted in this gesture) as that process of redoubling in which we are fatally (en)trained: the supplement of a supplement, the signifier, the representative of a representative. (A series the first term or rather the first structure of which does not yet—but we will do it later—have to be *kicked up [faire sauter]* and its irreducibility made apparent.) The structure and history of *phonetic* writing have of course played a decisive role in the determination of writing as the doubling of a sign, the sign of a sign. The signifier of a phonic signifier. While the phonic signifier would remain in animate proximity, in the living presence of *mnēmē* or *psuchē,* the graphic signifier, which reproduces it or imitates it, goes one degree further away, falls outside of life, entrains life out of itself and puts it to sleep in the type of its double. Whence the *pharmakon's* two misdeeds: it dulls the memory, and if it is of any assistance at all, it is not for the *mnēmē* but for *hypomnēsis.* Instead of quickening life in the original, "in person," the *phar-*

makon can at best only restore its monuments. It is a debilitating poison for memory, but a remedy or tonic for its external signs, its *symptoms*, with everything that this word can connote in Greek: an empirical, contingent, superficial event, generally a fall or collapse, distinguishing itself like an index from whatever it is pointing to. Your writing cures only the symptom, the King has already said, and it is from him that we know the unbridgable difference between the essence of the symptom and the essence of the signified; and that writings belongs to the order and exteriority of the symptom.

Thus, even though writing is external to (internal) memory, even though hypomnesia is not in itself memory, it affects memory and hypnotizes it in its very inside. That is the effect of this *pharmakon.* If it were purely external, writing would leave the intimacy or integrity of psychic memory untouched. And yet, just as Rousseau and Saussure will do in response to the same necessity, yet without discovering *other* relations between the intimate and the alien, Plato maintains *both* the exteriority of writing *and* its power of maleficent penetration, its ability to affect or infect what lies deepest inside. The *pharmakon* is that dangerous supplement[9] that breaks into the very thing that would have liked to do without it yet lets itself *at once* be breached, roughed up, fulfilled, and replaced, completed by the very trace through which the present increases itself in the act of disappearing.

If, instead of meditating on the structure that makes such supplementarity possible, if above all instead of meditating on the reduction by which "Plato–Rousseau–Saussure" try in vain to master it with an odd kind of "reasoning," one were to content oneself with pointing to the "logical contradiction," one would have to recognize here an instance of that kind of "kettle-logic" to which Freud turns in the *Traumdeutung* in order to illustrate the logic of dreams. In his attempt to arrange everything in his favor, the defendant piles up contradictory arguments: 1. The kettle I am returning to you is brand new; 2. The holes were already in it when you lent it to me; 3. You never lent me a kettle, anyway. Analogously: 1. Writing is rigorously exterior and inferior to living memory and speech, which are therefore undamaged by it. 2. Writing is harmful to them because it puts them to sleep and infects their very life which would otherwise remain intact. 3. Anyway, if one has resorted to hypomnesia and writing at all, it is not for their intrinsic value, but because living memory is finite, it already has holes in it before writing ever comes to leave its traces. Writing has no effect on memory.

The opposition between *mnēmē* and *hypomnēsis* would thus preside over the meaning of writing. This opposition will appear to us to form a system with all the great structural oppositions of Platonism. What is played out at the boundary line between these two concepts is consequently something like the major decision of philosophy, the one through which it institutes itself, maintains itself, and contains its adverse deeps.

Nevertheless, between *mnēmē* and *hypomnēsis*, between memory and its supplement, the line is more than subtle; it is hardly perceptible. On both sides of that line, it is a question of *repetition*. Live memory repeats the presence of the *eidos*, and truth is also the possibility of repetition through recall. Truth unveils the *eidos* or the *ontōs on*, in other words, that which can be imitated, reproduced, repeated in its identity. But in the anamnesic movement of truth, what is repeated must present itself as such, as what it is, in repetition. The true is repeated; it is what is repeated in the repetition, what is represented and present in the representation. It is not the repeater in the repetition, nor the signifier in the signification. The true is the presence of the *eidos* signified.

Sophistics—the deployment of hypomnesia—as well as dialectics—the deployment of anamnesia—both presuppose the possibility of repetition. But sophistics this time keeps to the other side, to the other face, as it were, of repetition. And of signification. What is repeated is the repeater, the imitator, the signifier, the representative, in the absence, as it happens, of *the thing itself*, which these appear to reedit, and without psychic or mnesic animation, without the living tension of dialectics. Writing would indeed be the signifier's capacity to repeat itself by itself, mechanically, without a living soul to sustain or attend it in its repetition, that is to say, without truth's *presenting itself* anywhere. Sophistics, hypomnesia, and writing would thus only be separated from philosophy, dialectics, anamnesis, and living speech by the invisible, almost nonexistent, thickness of that

leaf between the signifier and the signified. The "leaf": a significant metaphor, we should note, or rather one taken from the
signifier face of things, since the leaf with its recto and verso first
appears as a surface and support for writing. But by the same
token, doesn't the unity of this leaf, of the system of this difference between signified and signifier, also point to the inseparabil-
ity of sophistics and philosophy? The difference between signifier
and signified is no doubt the governing pattern within which
Platonism institutes itself and determines its opposition to sophistics. In being inaugurated in this manner, philosophy and
dialectics are determined in the act of determining their other.

[. . . .]

— *Translated by Barbara Johnson*

NOTES

1. *Phaedrus*, trans. by R. Hackforth, in *The Collected Dialogues of Plato*,
Edith Hamilton and Huntington Cairns, eds., Bollingen Series LXXI N.J.:
(Princeton, University Press, 1961), 274b. References in parentheses will be
to this edition.—Ed.

2. For Plato, Thamus is doubtless another name for Ammon, whose
figure (that of the sun king and of the father of the gods) we shall sketch out
later for its own sake. On this question and the debate to which it has given
rise, see P. Frutiger, *Les Mythes de Platon* (Paris: Alcan, 1930), p. 233, n. 2,
and notably B. Eisler, "Platon und das ägyptische Alphabet, *Archiv für Geschichte der Philosophie,* 1922; A. F. von Pauly-Wissowa, *Real-Encyclopä
die der classischen Altertumswissenschaft* (Stuttgart: J. B. Metzler, 1837–
1852 (art. Ammon); W. H. Roscher, *Ausfurliches Lexikon der griechischen
und römischen Mythologie* (Leipzig: B. G. Teubner, 1884–1937) (art. Thamus).

3. S. Morenz, *La Religion égyptienne* (Paris: Payot, 1962), p. 95. Another
of Thoth's companions is Maat, goddess of truth. She is also "daughter of Ra,
mistress of the sky, she who governs the double country, the eye of Ra which
has no match." Erman, in the page devoted to Maat, notes: "one of her
insignia, God knows why, was a vulture feather" (p. 82).

4. Jacques Vandier, *La Religion égyptienne* (Paris: Presses Universitaires
de France 1949), pp. 71 ff. Cf. especially A. J. Festugière, *La Révélation
d'Hermès Trismégiste* (Paris: Les Belles Lettres, 1981), pp. 287 ff., where a
number of texts on Thoth as the inventor of magic are assembled. One of
them, which particularly interests us, begins: "A formula to be recited *before
the sun:* 'I am Thoth, inventor and creator of philters and letters, etc.' "
(292).

5. Vandier, p. 230. Cryptography, medicinal magic, and the figure of the serpent are in fact intertwined in an astonishing folk tale transcribed by G. Maspéro in *Les Contes populaires de l'Egypte ancienne* (Paris: E. Guilmoro, 1911). It is the tale of Satni-Khamois and the mummies. Satni-Khamois, the son of a king, "spent his days running about the metropolis of Memphis so as to read the books written in sacred script and the books of the *Double House of Life*. One day a nobleman came along and made fun of him.—'Why are you laughing at me?' The nobleman said:—'I am not laughing at you; but can I help laughing when you spend your time here deciphering writings that have no powers? If you really wish to read effective writing, come with me; I will send you to the place where you will find the book which Thoth himself has written with his own hand and which will place you just below the gods. There are two formulas written in it: if you recite the first, you will charm the sky, the earth, the world of night, the mountains, the waters; you will understand what the birds of the sky and the reptiles are all saying, as they are; you will see the fish, for a divine force will make them rise to the surface of the water. If you read the second formula, even if you are in the grave you will reassume the form you had on earth; even shall you see the sun rising in the sky, and its cycle, and the moon in the form it has when it appears.' Satni cried; 'By my life! let me know what you wish and I will have it granted you; but take me to the place where I can find the book!' The nobleman said to Satni: 'The book in question is not mine. It is in the heart of the necropolis, in the tomb of Nenoferkeptah, son of king Minebptah. . . . Take great heed not to take this book away from him, for he would have you bring it back, a pitchfork and a rod in his hand, a lighted brazier on his head. . . .' Deep inside the tomb, light was shining out of the book. The doubles of the king and of his family were beside him, 'through the virtues of the book of Thoth.' . . . All this was repeating itself. Nenoferkeptah had already himself lived Satni's story. The priest had told him: 'The book in question is in the middle of the sea of Coptos, in an iron casket. The iron casket is inside a bronze casket; the bronze casket is inside a casket of cinnamon wood; the casket of cinnamon wood is inside a casket of ivory and ebony. The casket of ivory and ebony is inside a silver casket. The silver casket is inside a golden casket, and the book is found therein. [Scribe's error? the first version I consulted had consigned or reproduced it; a later edition of Maspéro's book pointed it out in a note: "The scribe has made a mistake here in his enumeration. He should have said: *inside* the iron casket is . . . etc." (Item left as evidence for a logic of inclusion).] And there is a schoene [in Ptolemy's day, equal to about 12,000 royal cubits of 0.52m] of serpents, scorpions of all kinds, and reptiles around the casket in which the book lies, and there is an immortal serpent coiled around the casket in question.' " After three tries, the imprudent hero kills the serpent, drinks the book dissolved in beer, and thus acquires limitless knowledge. Thoth goes to Ra to complain, and provokes the worst of punishments.

Let us note, finally, before leaving the Egyptian figure of Thoth, that he possesses, in addition to Hermes of Greece, a remarkable counterpart in the figure of Nabu, son of Marduk. In Babylonian and Assyrian mythology, "Nabu is essentially the son-god and, just as Markduk eclipses his father, Ea, we will see Nabu usurping Marduk's place." (E. Dhorme, *Les Religions de Babylonie et d'Assyrie* [Paris: Presses Universitaires de France], pp. 150 ff.) Marduk, the father of Nabu, is the sun-god. Nabu, "lord of the reed," "creator of writing," "bearer of the tables of the fates of the gods," sometimes goes ahead of his father from whom he borrows the symbolic instument, the *marru*. "A votive object made of copper, uncovered in Susa, representing 'a snake holding in its mouth a sort of pall,' was marked with the inscription 'the marru of the god Nabu' "(Dhorme, p. 155). Cf. also M. David, *Les Dieux et le Destin en Babylonie* (Paris: Presses Universitaires de France, 1949), pp. 86 ff.

One could spell out one by one the points of resemblance between Thoth and the biblical Nabu (Nebo).

6. I take the liberty of referring the reader, in order to give him a preliminary, indicative direction, to the "Question of Method" propossed in *Of Grammatology* [1967]. With a few precautions, one could say that *pharmakon* plays a role *analogous*, in this reading of Plato, to that of *supplément* in the reading of Rousseau.

7. Cf. in particular *Republic* II, 364 ff; Letter VII, 333e. The problem is raised with copious and useful references in E. Moutsopoulos, *La Musique dans l'œuvre de Platon* (Paris: Presses Universitaires de France, 1959), pp. 13 ff.

8. We would here like to refer the reader in particular to the extremely rich text by Jean-Pierre Vernant (who deals with these questions with quite different intentions): "Aspects mythiques de la mémoire et du temps," in *Mythe et pensée chez les Grecs* (Paris: Maspéro, 1965). On the word *tupos*, its relations with *perigraphē* and *paradeigma*, cf. A. von Blumenthal, *Tupos und Paradeigma*, quoted by P. M. Schuhl, in *Platon et l'art de son temps* (Paris: Presses Universitaires de France, 1952), p. 18, n. 4.

9. The expression "that dangerous supplement," used by Rousseau in his *Confessions* to describe masturbation, is the title of that chapter in *Of Grammatology* in which Derrida follows the consequences of the way in which the word *supplément*'s two meanings in French—'"addition" and "replacement"—complicate the logic of Rousseau's treatment of sex, education, and writing. Writing, pedagogy, masturbation, and the *pharmakon* share the property of being—with respect to speech, nature, intercourse, and living memory—at once something secondary, external, and compensatory, and something that substitutes, violates, and usurps.—TRANS.

JALOUSIE TWO

To guard against the scaffolding going up here
—it is the healthiest, the most natural reflex—
one will protest: sometimes against these too-
long citations that should have been cut; sometimes on the contrary (indeed at the same time)
against these deductions, selections, sections,
suspension points, suture points—detachments. Detachments of the sign, of course. . . .
That the sign is detached signifies that it is cut
off from its place of emission or natural belonging; but the separation is never perfect. The
bleeding detachment is also—repetition—delegation, mandate, delay, relay. Adherence. The
detached remains glued thereby, by the glue of
differance, by the a. The a of gl agglutinates the
different detached pieces. The scaffolding of
the A is gluey.
So one will protest: you cut too much, you glue
too much, you cite too much and too little.

—*Glas*, p. 167

PART TWO

BESIDE PHILOSOPHY — "LITERATURE"

O NCE, IN answer to the questions: "What is the place of a manifestly poetic performance in your writing? Do you consider
poetry to be subordinated finally to philosophical discourse?" Derrida replied: "I do not read the genre of this body as either philosophic or poetic. This means that if your questions were addressed
to the philosopher, I would have to say no. As for me, I talk about
the philosopher, but I am not simply a philosopher."[1] If we would
ask the question of genre of Derrida's writing, we must be prepared
for a response that itself poses a question to our confident distinctions among kinds of writing. Derrida repeatedly reminds us that the
concepts ordering these distinctions, and principally the concept of
a representable truth, are already determined from *within* philosophy rather than determining philosophy from some place outside it.
As such, they can distinguish philosophical from nonphilosophical
discourses only in terms that are already themselves philosophical.
And by these means, philosophy has always managed to *comprehend*
its outside, that is, to include the other-than-philosophy within philosophy. The poetic or the literary has been not so much distinguished from the discourse of philosophy as subordinated to it. By
its own terms and thus by definition, there is no outside-philosophy.

Derrida's *concern* with literature is not that of the philosopher.
This means, to begin with, that he does not ask the philosopher's
question: "What is (literature)?" which subjects the literary, the
poetic to a concept. His concern, rather, is precisely with how the
philosopher's question is dislocated, thrown off balance by a writing
practice that does not claim to represent some truth outside itself
and thus does not attempt to hide its own inscription. It is, then,
this practice that is allowed to interrogate—indirectly, discreetly—

the very distinctions supposed by philosophy to divide one kind of writing from another. Derrida stages or provokes interventions of the literary into the philosopher's domain. Some of these interventions take place almost in the wings, for example the epigraph to **Speech and Phenomena** from a Poe story where the spoken phrase "I am dead" analyzes or exposes the sense implied by the Husserlian or Cartesian subject of "I am" (see above, p. **14**).[2] In this way, we are discreetly asked why it is that, as Derrida has said in commenting on this epigraph, only the fantastic fiction "can render an account— in a philosophical or quasi-philosophical manner, both with and without philosophy—of certain utterances that control everything."[3] In later texts, however, he provokes the literary analysis or effraction of philosophy far more overtly. The text titled **"Tympan"** (reprinted below in extenso) gives perhaps the most explicit form to this strategy of intervention.

As to the place of poetic performance in Derrida's writing, one must acknowledge another consequence of the dislocation of philosophy's privilege to determine "its" other. The order of commentary or criticism, which is the order of a nonimplication with the poetic performance, can no longer pretend to be sustained. Writing *on* or *of* poetry must not remain deaf to poetry's demand to be received poetically and to learn what that demand might mean from the poem itself. Thus, for example, the short essay included here, **"Che cos'è la poesia,"** answers the question of its title with a performance of its theoretical propositions, thereby attempting to do what it says or to say what it does.

The ways in which these texts transgress the separation of critical commentary (called "secondary") from literary writing (called "primary"), and which are anything but mere formal innovations, has prompted some critics to attempt to dismiss them as "presumptuous," by which is understood that they presume to claim a poetic, primary role for criticism. Such a "reproach," which appears to exalt the literary condition, often in fact conceals a relegation of literature to a kind of empty aestheticism, and in that way it joins forces with the gesture that has always subordinated literature to philosophical truth. Derrida's gesture is altogether other. It presumes to assert, to retrieve, to reinvent that which the philosophical, aesthetic tradition has attempted to forget or suppress: the invention of truth by what the Greeks called *poiesis,* its invention, that is, as a *simulacrum.* The most far-reaching presumption here, the one that most profoundly upsets the order within which literature has always been contained, is not that a "critic" dares to measure his writing with that of the poets, but that he reads the poets—Poe, Mallarmé, Leiris, Blanchot, Ponge, but also many others[4]—as having already taken the measure of philosophy.

NOTES

1. *The Ear of the Other* [1982], p. 141.

2. The epigraph in full reads: "I have spoken both of 'sound' and 'voice.' I mean to say that the sound was one of distinct, of even wonderfully, thrillingly distinct, syllabification. M. Valdemar *spoke*, obviously in reply to the question. . . . He now said: 'Yes;—no;—I have been sleeping—and now—now—*I am dead.*' " For a more extensive treatment of Poe, see below **"Le Facteur de la vérité."** Poe's poem "The Bells" is also considered at length in *Glas.*

3. "Entre crochets" [1976], R. 108.

4. On Paul Celan, see *Schibboleth, pour Paul Celan* [1986]; on James Joyce, see below, **"Ulysses Gramophone"**; on Hölderlin, see *Mémoires for Paul de Man* [1986]; on Georg Trakl, see "Heidegger's Hand: Geschlecht II" in *Psyché* [1987]; on "Romeo and Juliet," see "L'Aphorisme à contretemps," also in *Psyché.*

"Tympan" in *Margins of Philosophy*

("Tympan" in *Marges de la philosophie* [1972])

"Tympan" is the title of the introduction to *Margins of Philosophy*, the collection of ten essays (including **"Différance"** and **"Signature Event Context"**) that Derrida published in 1972. Like **Glas** that will be published two years later, "Tympan" deploys two columns side by side on the page. On the left, an interrogation of the closed philosophical structure that comprehends or includes its own out-side and a reflection on the strategies for breaking into or out of this closure; on the right, a long quotation from the first volume of Michel Leiris's autobiographical memoirs, *Biffures* (1948). There are as well three epigraphs from Hegel and sometimes elaborate notes running across the bottom of most of the pages. By means of these typographics, Derrida contrives to proliferate the margins on which and in which he is writing. In its much narrower column, the Leiris quotation appears to be written in the margin of Derrida's column on the left, whereas the space between the two is a thin blank column running down the right third of the page. Although Derrida never explicitly refers to the quotation, it incessantly crosses over the minimal barrier set up to its left and intrudes on the space reserved for the introductory discourse. These silent crossings are effected by means of the name Leiris gives to this chapter of his work, the name Persephone, with which he associates all sorts of spirals and corkscrew figures, but particularly the French name of the insect known as an earwig: *perce-oreille*, literally, ear-piercer. The two names, as he notes, "both end with an appeal to the sense of hearing" [-*phone* and -*oreille*]. It is this appeal to the sense of hearing that is obliquely answered (obliqueness is as well one of the principal themes here) and echoed in Derrida's text, where philosophy is configured as the apparatus of an ear, one that has learned to tune out everything but the sound of its own name. This ear is x-rayed, diagrammed, analyzed, dissected so as to lay bare the mechanism of hearing-oneself-speak that Derrida first described in **Speech and Phenomena.** In the process, the question is repeatedly addressed of how to pierce this ear from outside without rendering it simply useless. This is fundamentally the question of deconstruction, and the answers Derrida brings to it provide, not a program, but an opening for the deconstructive work that does not name itself philosophy. Leiris's apparently marginalized text thus displaces the center of hearing while its spiralling words, its feminine names and sinuosities figure no longer the empty margin of philosophy, "no longer a secondary virginity but an inexhaustible reserve, the stereographic activity of an entirely other ear." (Derrida has written elsewhere on the ear; see in particular *The Ear of the Other* [1982] and, most recently, "Heidegger's Ear" [forthcoming].)

"Tympan" is reprinted here *in extenso.*

The thesis and antithesis and their proofs therefore represent nothing but the opposite assertions, that a *limit is (eine Grenze ist)*, and that the limit equally is only a *sublated (aufgehobene [relevé])* one; that the limit has a beyond with which however it stands in relation *(in Beziehung steht)*, and beyond which it must pass, but that in doing so there arises another such limit, which is no limit. The *solution* of these antinomies, as of those previously mentioned, is transcendental, that is.

—Hegel, *Science of Logic*

The essence of philosophy provides no ground *(bodenlos)* precisely for peculiarities, and in order to attain philosophy, it is necessary, if its body expresses the sum of its peculiarities, that it cast itself into the abyss *à corps perdu (sich à corps perdu hineinzustürzen)*.

—Hegel, *The Difference between the Fichtean and Schellingian Systems of Philosophy*

The need for philosophy can be expressed as its presupposition if a sort of vestibule *(eine Art von Vorhof)* is supposed to be made for philosophy, which begins with itself.

—Ibid.

To tympanize[1]—philosophy.

Being at the limit: these words do not yet form a proposition, and even less a discourse. But there is enough in them, provided that one plays upon it, to engender almost all the sentences in this book.

Does philosophy answer a need? How is it to be understood? Philosophy? The need?

Ample to the point of believing itself interminable, a discourse that has *called itself* philosophy—doubtless the only discourse that has ever intended to receive its name only from itself, and has never ceased murmuring its initial letter to itself from as close as possible— has always, including its own, meant to say its limit. In the familiarity of the languages called (instituted as) natural by philosophy, the languages elementary to it, this discourse has always insisted upon assuring itself mastery over the limit *(peras, limes, Grenze).* It has recognized, conceived, posited, declined the limit according to all possible modes; and therefore by the same token, in order better to dispose of the limit, has transgressed it. *Its own limit* had not to remain foreign to it. Therefore it has appropriated the concept for itself; it has believed that it controls the margin of its volume and that it thinks its other.

Philosophy has always insisted upon this: thinking its other. Its other: that which limits it, and from which it derives its essence, its definition, its production. To think its other: does this amount solely to *relever*[2] *(aufheben)* that from which it derives, to head the proces-

And I have chosen, as the sign beneath which to place them, the entirely floral and subterranean name of *Persephone,* which is thus extracted from its dark terrestrial depths and lifted to the heavens of a chapter heading.

The acanthus leaf copied in school when, for better or for worse, one learns to use the fusain, the stem of a morning glory or other climbing plant, the helix inscribed on the shell of a snail, the meanders of the small and the large intestine, the sandy serpentine excreted by an earth worm, the curl of childish hair encased in a medallion, the putrid simulacrum drawn

---

1. In French, *tympaniser* is an archaic verb meaning to criticize, to ridicule publicly. I have transliterated it here.—TRANS.

2. On Derrida's translation of the Hegelian term *aufheben* as *relever,* see above, "**La différance,**" note 12, for a system of notes. There is an untranslatable play of words here: "Penser son autre: cela revient-il seulement *à relever (aufheben)* ce dont elle *relève . . . ?"*— TRANS.

sion of its method only by passing the limit? Or indeed does the limit, obliquely, by surprise, always reserve one more blow for philosophical knowledge? Limit/passage.

In propagating this question beyond the precise context from which I have just extracted it (the infinity of the *quantum* in the greater *Logic* and the critique of the Kantian antinomies), almost constantly, in this book, I shall be examining the *relevance*[3] of the limit. And therefore relaunching in every sense the reading of the Hegelian *Aufhebung,* eventually beyond what Hegel, inscribing it, understood himself to say or intended to mean, beyond that which is inscribed on the internal vestibule of his ear. This implies a vestibule in a delicate, differentiated structure whose orifices may always remain unfindable, and whose entry and exit may be barely passable; and implies that the text—Hegel's for example— functions as a writing machine in which a certain number of *typed* and systematically enmeshed propositions (one has to be able to recognize and isolate them) represent the "conscious intention" of the author as a reader of his "own" text, in the sense we speak today of a mechanical reader. Here, the lesson of the finite reader called a philosophical author is but one piece, occasionally and incidentally interesting, of the machine. *To insist* upon thinking *its other:* its proper[4] other, the proper of its other, an other proper? In thinking it *as such*, in recognizing it, one misses it. One reappropriates it for oneself, one disposes of it, by a slight pressure of the fingers from a *père-la-colique,** the marblings that bloom on the edges of certain bound books, the curved wrought iron, "modern style," of the Métro entries, the interlace of embroidered figures on sheets and pillow cases, the kiss-curl pasted with grease on the cheekbone of a prostitute in the old days of *Casque d'or,* the thin and browner braid of the steel cable, the thick and blonder one of the string cable, the cerebral convolutions exemplified by, when you eat it, mutton brains, the corkscrewing of the vine, the image of what later will be —once the juice has been bottled—

---

* A *père-la-colique* is a small porcelain toy representing an old man sitting on a toilet seat. When a certain product is put into it, it excretes.—TRANS.

3. *Relevance* is not the English "relevance" but a neologism from the translation of *aufheben* as *relever.* Like *Aufhebung,* it is a noun derived from a gerund.—TRANS.

4. In French, *propre* can mean both "proper" and "own," as here with *son propre autre,* its own other, the other proper to it. I have sometimes given simply "proper," and sometimes "own, proper" (e.g., "its own, proper other").—TRANS.

one misses it, or rather one misses (the) missing (of) it, which, as concerns the other, always amounts to the same. Between the proper of the other and the other of the proper.

If philosophy has always intended, from its point of view, to maintain its relation with the nonphilosophical, that is the antiphilosophical, with the practices and knowledge, empirical or not, that constitute its other, if it has constituted itself according to this purposive *entente* with its outside, if it has always intended to hear itself speak, in the same language, of itself and of something else, can one, strictly speaking, determine a nonphilosophical place, a place of exteriority or alterity from which one might still treat *of philosophy*? Is there any ruse not belonging to reason to prevent philosophy from still speaking of itself, from borrowing its categories from the logos of the other, by affecting itself without delay, on the domestic page of its own tympanum (still the muffled drum, the *tympanon*, the cloth stretched taut in order to take its beating, to amortize impressions, to make the *types (typoi)* resonate, to balance the striking pressure of the *typtein*, between the inside and the outside), with heterogeneous percussion? Can one violently penetrate philosophy's field of listening without its immediately—even pretending in advance, by hearing what is said of it, by decoding the statement—making the penetration resonate within itself, appropriating the emission for itself, familiarly communicating it to itself between the inner and middle ear, following the path of a tube or inner opening, be it round or oval? In other words, can one puncture the tympanum of a philosopher and still be heard and understood by him?

To philosophize with a hammer. Zarathus-

the corkscrew (itself prefiguring the endless screw of drunkenness), the circulation of the blood, the concha of the ear, the sinuous curves of a path, everything that is wreathed, coiled, flowered, garlanded, twisted, arabesque, the spur (which for my purposes here I will imagine in a spiral) of an espadon, the twists of a ram's horn, all this I believe uncovered in the name of Persephone, potentially, awaiting only an imperceptible click to set it off like the ribbon of steel tightly wound on itself in the midst of the pinions of a clockwork or the spring in the closed-cover box from which the bristly-bearded devil has not yet emerged.

Therefore, essentially, in question is a *spiraled*

tra begins by asking himself if he will have to puncture them, batter their ears *(Muss man ihnen erst die Ohren zerschlagen),* with the sound of cymbals or tympani, the instruments, always, of some Dionysianism. In order to teach them "to hear with their eyes" too.

But we will analyze the metaphysical exchange, the circular complicity of the metaphors of the eye and the ear.

But in the structure of the tympanum there is something called the "luminous triangle." It is named in *Les Chants de Maldoror* (II), very close to a "grandiose trinity."

But along with this triangle, along with the *pars tensa* of the tympanon, there is also found the handle of a *"hammer."*

In order effectively, practically to transform what one decries (tympanizes), must one still be heard and understood within it, henceforth subjecting oneself to the law of the inner hammer?[5] In relaying the inner hammer, one risks permitting the noisiest discourse to participate in the most serene, least disturbed, best served economy of philosophical irony. Which is to say, and examples of this metaphysical drumming are not lacking today, that in taking this risk, one risks nothing.

From philosophy—to separate oneself, in order to describe and decry its law, in the direction of the absolute exteriority of another name—or more broadly: a *curved* name, but whose gentleness is not to be confused with the always more or less lenitive character of that which has been dulled, since—quite to the contrary—what is piercing and penetrating about it is confirmed by the rapprochement to be made between the syllables that compose its name and the syllables forming the civil status of the insect called [in French] *perce-oreille* (earpiercer) [and in English, "earwig"]. For not only do "Persephone" and *"perce-oreille"* both begin with the same allusion to

---

5. The hammer, as is well known, belongs to the chain of small bones, along with the anvil and the stirrup. It is placed on the *internal* surface of the tympanic membrane. It always has the role of mediation and communication: it transmits sonic vibrations to the chain of small bones and then to the inner ear. Bichat recognized that it has another paradoxical function. This small bone protects the tympanum while acting upon it. "Without it, the tympanum would be affected painfully by vibrations set up by too powerful sounds." The hammer, thus, can weaken the blows, muffle them on the threshold of the inner ear. The latter—the labyrinth—includes a *vestibule,* the *semicircular canals,* a *cochlea* (with its two *spirals),* that is, two organs of balance and one organ of hearing. Perhaps we shall penetrate it more deeply later. For the moment, it suffices to mark the role of the middle ear: it tends to equalize the acoustic resistance of the air and the resistance of the labyrinthine liquids, to balance internal pressures and external pressures.

place. But exteriority and alterity are concepts which by themselves have never surprised philosophical discourse. *Philosophy by itself has always been concerned* with them. These are not the conceptual headings under which philosophy's border can be overflowed; the overflow is its object. Instead of determining some other circumscription, recognizing it, practicing it, bringing it to light, forming it, in a word *producing* it (and today this word serves as the crudest "new clothes" of the metaphysical denegation which accommodates itself very well to all these projects), in question will be, but according to a movement unheard of by philosophy, an other which is no longer *its other*.

But by relating it to something to which it has no relation, is one not immediately permitting oneself to be encoded by philosophical *logos*, to stand under its banner?[6] Certainly, except by writing this relationship following the mode of a nonrelationship about which it would be demonstrated simultaneously or *obliquely*—on the philosophical surface of the discourse—that no philosopheme will ever have been prepared to conform to it or translate it. This can only be written according to a deformation of the philosophical tympanum. My intention is not to extract from the ques-

the idea of "piercing" (less decided in Persephone, because of the *s* which imparts something undulating and grassy, chimerical and fleeting, to the name, to the extent that one might be tempted, by executing an easy metathesis, to call her the Fay Person . . .), but the one and the other end with an appeal to the sense of hearing, which is overtly in play, for the insect, due to the enunciation of the word "ear" (that is, of the organ by means of which auditory sensations penetrate into us), and

---

6. Without an inventory of all the sexual investments which, everywhere and at all times, powerfully constrain the *discourse of the ear*, I shall give an example here to indicate the topics of the material left in the margins. The horn that is called *pavillon (papillon)* is a phallus for the Dogon and Bambara of Mali, and the auditory canal a vagina. [*Pavillon* in French has multiple meanings. Here, the reference is to the end of the horn called the bell in English; it also designates the visible part of the ear. Further, both senses of *pavillon* just given derive from its older sense of "military tent," because of such tents' conic shape. Finally, *pavillon* can also mean flag or banner, as in the sentence above that ends with the phrase "stand under its banner *(pavillon)*."—TRANS.] Speech is the sperm indispensable for insemination. (Conception through the ear, all of philosophy one could say.) It descends through the woman's ear, and is rolled up in a spiral around the womb. Which is hardly very distant from Arianism (from the name Arius, of course, a priest from Alexandria, the father of Arianism, a heretical doctrine of the conception in the Trinity), from *homoousios*, and from all the records of the Nicene Council.

tion of metaphor—one of the most continuous threads of this book—the figure of the oblique. This is also, thematically, the route of *Dissemination*.[7] We know that the membrane of the tympanum, a thin and transparent partition separating the auditory canal from the middle ear (the *cavity*), is stretched obliquely *(loxōs)*. Obliquely from above to below, from outside to inside, and from the back to the front. Therefore it is not perpendicular to the axis of the canal. One of the effects of this obliqueness is to increase the surface of impression and hence the capacity of vibration. It has been observed, particularly in birds, that precision of hearing is in direct proportion to the obliqueness of the tympanum. The tympanum squints.

Consequently, to luxate the philosophical ear, to set the *loxōs* in the *logos* to work, is to avoid frontal and symmetrical protest, opposition in all the forms of *anti-*, or in any case to inscribe *antism* and overturning,[8] domestic denegation, in an entirely other form of ambush, of *lokhos*, of textual maneuvers.

Under what conditions, then, could one *mark*, for a philosopheme in general, a *limit*, a less directly in play for the goddess by means of the suffix *phone,* also found in "telephone" and "gramophone," the latter being an instrument for which is more appropriate than the former the very euphonic ending that beautifully defines it as a musical mechanism.

The insect whose principal work is to gnaw on the inside of fruit pits in order to take subsistence from them, and which occasionally, so they say, perforates human tympanums with its

7. Cf. especially **"The Double Session,"** in *Dissemination*.

8. On the problematic of overturning and displacement, see *Dissemination* and *Positions*. To luxate, to tympanize philosophical autism is never an operation *within* the concept and without some carnage of language. Thus it breaks open the roof, the closed spiral· unity of the palate. It proliferates *outside* to the point of no longer being *understood*. It is no longer *a* tongue.

> Hematographic music
> "Sexual jubilation is a choice of glottis,
> of the splinter of the cyst of a dental root,
> a choice of otic canal,
> of the bad auricular ringing,
> of a bad instillation of sound,
> of current brocaded on the bottom carpet,
> of the opaque thickness,
> the elect application of the choice of the candelabra of chiselled string,
>   in order to escape the prolific avaric obtuse music
> without ram, or age, or rapage,
> and which has neither tone nor age."
> ARTAUD *(December 1946)*

margin that it could not infinitely reappropriate, *conceive* as its own, in advance engendering and interning the process of its expropriation (Hegel again, always), proceeding to its inversion by itself? How to unbalance the pressures that correspond to each other on either side of the membrane? How to block this correspondence destined to weaken, muffle, forbid the blows from the outside, the other hammer? The "hammer that speaks" to him "who has the third ear" *(der das dritte Ohr hat)*. How to interpret—but here interpretation can no longer be a theory or discursive practice of philosophy—the strange and unique property of a discourse that organizes the *economy* of its representation, the law of its proper weave, such that *its* outside is never its *outside,* never surprises it, such that the logic of its heteronomy still reasons from within the vault of its autism?

For this is how *Being* is understood: its proper. It assures without let-up the *relevant* movement of reappropriation. Can one then *pass* this singular limit which is not a limit, which no more separates the inside from the outside than it assures their permeable and transparent continuity? What form could this play of limit/passage have, this *logos* which posits and negates itself in permitting its own voice to well up? Is this a well-put question?

The analyses that give rise to one another in this book do not answer this question, bringing to it neither an *answer* nor *an* answer. They work, rather, to transform and deplace its statement, and toward examining the presuppositions of the question, the institution of its protocol, the laws of its procedure, the headings of its alleged homogeneity, of its apparent unicity: can one treat of philosophy it-

pincers, has in common with the daughter of Demeter that it too buries itself in a subterranean kingdom. The deep country of hearing, described in terms of geology more than in those of any other natural science, not only by virtue of the cartilaginous cavern that constitutes its organ, but also by virtue of the relationship that unites it to grottoes, to chasms, to all the pockets hollowed out of the terrestrial crust whose emptiness makes them into resonating drums for the slightest sounds.

Just as one might worry about the idea of the tympanum, a fragile membrane threatened with perforations by the minute pincers of an insect—unless it had already been broken by too vio-

self (metaphysics itself, that is, ontotheology) without already permitting the dictation, along with the pretention to unity and unicity, of the ungraspable and imperial totality of an order? If there are margin*s*, is there still *a* philosophy, *the* philosophy?

No answer, then. Perhaps, in the long run, not even a question. The copulative correspondence, the opposition question–answer is already lodged in a structure, enveloped in the hollow of an ear, which we will go into to take a look. To find out how it is made, how it has been formed, how it functions. And if the tympanum is a limit, perhaps the issue would be less to displace a *given* determined limit than to work toward the concept of limit and the limit of the concept. To unhinge it on several tries.

But what is a *hinge* (signifying: to be reasoned in every sense)?

Therefore, what legal question is to be relied upon if the limit in general, and not only the limit of what is believed to be one very particular thing among others, the tympanum, is structurally oblique? If, therefore, there is no limit *in general*, that is, a straight and regular form of the limit? Like every *limus*, the *limes*, the short cut, signifies the oblique.

But indefatigably at issue is the ear, the distinct, differentiated, articulated organ that produces the effect of proximity, of absolute properness, the idealizing erasure of organic difference. It is an organ whose structure (and the suture that holds it to the throat) produces the pacifying lure of organic indifference. To forget it—and in so doing to take shelter in the most familial of dwellings—is to cry out for the end of organs, of others.

But indefatigably at issue is the ear. Not lent a noise—it is equally permissible to fear for the vocal cords, which can be broken instantaneously when, for example, one screams too loudly, subjecting them to excessive tension (in the case of anger, grief, or even a simple game dominated by the sheer pleasure of shrieking), so that one's voice gets "broken." An accident my mother sometimes warned me against, whether she actually believed that it could happen, or whether—as I tend to believe—she used the danger as a scarecrow that might make me less noisy, at least for a while. Marginal to Persephone and *perce-oreille*, soldered together by a cement of relationships hardened—in broad daylight—by their names, a du-

only the sheltered portico of the tympanum, but also the vestibular canal.[9] And the phoneme as the "phenomenon of the labyrinth" in which *Speech and Phenomena*, from its epigraph and very close to its false exit, had introduced the question of writing. One might always think, of course, in order to reassure oneself, that "labyrinthic vertigo" is the name rable suture is thus formed between the throat and the tympanum, which, the one as much as the other, are subject to a fear of being injured, be-

---

9. "Anatomical term. Irregular cavity that is part of the inner ear. Genital vestibule, the vulva and all its parts up to the membrane of the hymen exclusively. Also the name of the triangular space limited in front and laterally by the ailerons of the nymphs [small lips of the vulva], and in back by the orifice of the urethra; one enters through this space in practicing a vestibular incision. *E. Lat. vestibulum,* from the augmentative particle *ve,* and *stabulum,* place in which things are held (see *stable*), according to certain Latin etymologists. Ovid, on the contrary, more reasonably, it appears, takes it from *Vesta* because the *vestibule* held a fire lit in the honor of Vesta [goddess of the proper, of familiarity, of the domestic hearth, etc.]. Among the moderns, Mommsen says that *vestibulum* comes from *vestis,* being an entryway in which the Romans left the toga *(vestis)."* Littré. [Littré is an authoritative French dictionary.—ED.]

Lodged in the vestibule, the labyrinthic receptors of balance are named *vestibular receptors.* These are the *otolithic* organs (utricle and saccule) and the *semicircular* canals. The utricle is sensitive to the head's changes of direction, which displace the otoliths, the ear's stones, small calcified granulations modifying the stimulation of the ciliary cells of the macula (the thick part of the membranous covering of the utricle). The function of the saccule in the mechanisms of balance has not yet been definitely ascertained. The semicircular canals, inside the labyrinth, are sensitive to all the movements of the head, which create currents in the liquid (endolymph). The reflex movements which result from this are indispensable for assuring the stability of the head, the direction and balance of the body in all its movements, notably in walking upright.

Tympanum, Dionysianism, labyrinth, Ariadne's thread. We are now traveling through (upright, walking, dancing), included and enveloped within it, never to emerge, the form of an ear constructed around a barrier, going round its inner walls, a city, therefore (labyrinth, semicircular canals—warning: the spiral walkways do not hold) circling around like a stairway winding around a lock, a dike (dam) stretched out toward the sea; closed in on itself and open to the sea's path. Full and empty of its water, the anamnesis of the concha resonates alone on a beach. [There is an elaborate play on the words *limaçon* and *conque* here. *Limaçon* (aside from meaning snail) means a spiral staircase and the spiral canal that is part of the inner ear. *Conque* means both conch and concha, the largest cavity of the external ear— TRANS.] How could a breach be produced, between earth and sea?

By means of the breach of philosophical identity, a breach that amounts to addressing the truth to itself in an envelope, to hearing itself speak inside without opening its mouth or showing its teeth, the bloodiness of a disseminated writing comes to separate the lips, to violate the embouchure of philosophy, putting *its* tongue into movement, finally bringing it into contact with some other code, of an entirely other kind. A necessarily unique event, nonreproducible, hence illegible as such and, when it happens, inaudible in the conch, between earth and sea, without signature.

Bataille writes in "The Structure of the Labyrinth": "Emerging from an inconceivable void in the play of beings as a satellite wandering away from two phantoms (one bristling with beard, the other, sweeter, its head covered with a chignon), it is first of all in the father and mother who transcend it that the minuscule human being encounters the illusion of sufficiency. (. . .) Thus are produced the relatively stable gatherings whose center is a city, similar in its primitive form to a corolla enclosing like a double pistil a sovereign and a king. (. . .) The universal god destroys rather than supports the human aggregations which erect its phantom. He himself is only dead, whether a mythical delirium proposes him for adoration like a cadaver pierced with wounds, or whether by his very universality he becomes more than any other incapable of opposing to the loss of being the breached walls of *ipseity."*

of a well-known and well-determined disease, the local difficulty of a particular organ.

This is—another tympanum.

If Being is in effect a process of reappropriation, the "question of Being" of a new type can never be percussed without being measured against the absolutely coextensive question of the proper. Now this latter question does not permit itself to be separated from the idealizing value of the *very-near*, which itself receives its disconcerting powers only from the structure of hearing-oneself-speak. The *proprius* presupposed in all discourses on economy, sexuality, language, semantics, rhetoric, etc. repercusses its absolute limit only in sonorous representation. Such, at least, is the most insistent hypothesis of this book. A quasi-organizing role is granted, therefore, to the motif of sonic vibration (the Hegelian *Erzittern*) as to the motif of the proximity of the meaning of Being in speech (Heideggerian *Nähe* and *Ereignis*). The logic of the event is examined from the vantage of the structures of expropriation called *timbre (tympanum), style,* and *signature*. Timbre, style, and signature are the same obliterating division of the proper. They make every event possible, necessary, and unfindable.

What is the specific resistance of philosophical discourse to deconstruction? It is the infinite mastery that the agency of Being (and of the) proper seems to assure it; this mastery permits it to interiorize every limit as *being* and as being its own *proper*. To exceed it, by the same token, and therefore to preserve it in itself. Now, in its mastery and its discourse on mastery (for mastery is a signification that we still owe to it), philosophical power always seems to combine *two types*.

sides both belonging to the same cavernous domain. And in the final analysis caverns become the geometric place in which all are joined together: the chthonian divinity, the insect piercer of pits, the matrix in which the voice is formed, the drum that each noise comes to strike with its wand of vibrating air; caverns: obscure pipe-works reaching down into the most secret part of being in order to bring even to the totally naked cavity of our mental space the exhalations—of variable temperature, consistency, and ornamentation—that are propagated in long horizontal waves after rising straight up from the fermentations of the outside world.

On the one

On the one hand, a *hierarchy:* the particular sciences and regional ontologies are subordinated to general ontology, and then to fundamental ontology.[10] From this point of view all the questions that solicit Being and the proper upset the order that submits the determined fields of science, its formal objects or materials (logic and mathematics, or semantics, linguistics, rhetoric, science of literature, political economy, psychoanalysis, etc.), to philosophical jurisdiction. In principle, then, these questions are prior to the constitution of a rigorous, systematic, and orderly theoretical discourse in these domains (which therefore are no longer simply domains, regions circumscribed, delimited, and assigned from outside and above).

On the other hand, an *envelopment:* the whole is implied, in the speculative mode of reflection and expression, in each part. Homogenous, concentric, and circulating indefinitely, the movement of the whole is remarked in the partial determinations of the system or encyclopedia, without the status of that remark, and the partitioning of the part, giving rise to any general deformation of the space.

These two kinds of appropriating mastery, hierarchy and envelopment, communicate with each other according to complicities we shall define. If one of the two types is more powerful here (Aristotle, Descartes, Kant, Husserl, Heidegger) or there (Spinoza, Leibniz, Hegel), they both follow the movement of the same wheel, whether it is a question, finally, of Heidegger's hand, therefore, is the outside; on the other hand, the inside; between them, the cavernous.

A voice is usually described as 'cavernous' to give the idea that it is low and deep, and even a bit too much so. For example: a *basse taille,*** in relation to a *basse chantante* with a higher register and also more supple line, whereas that of the *basse taille* rather would seem more proper—in that it seems rough, as if hewn with an ax—to the stone breaker, the chiseler of funerary marbles, to the miner with his pick, to the gravedigger, the ditchdigger, and (if I can refer to a social situation which,

---

10. The putting into question of this ontological subordination was begun in **Of Grammatology.**

** The *basse-taille* is the voice called in English and Italian the *basso profundo,* while the *basse chantante* is the voice usually called "bass" (between *basso profundo* and baritone). Leiris is playing on the *taille* in *basse-taille,* from the verb *tailler* meaning to hew, to cut, to chisel, etc.—Trans.

hermeneutical circle or of Hegel's ontotheological circle. ("White Mythology" deviates according to another wheel.) For as long as this tympanum will not have been destroyed (the tympanum as also a hydraulic *wheel*, described minutely by Vitruvius),[11] which cannot be achieved by means of a simply discur-

strictly speaking, is no longer a profession) to the monk, pursued with weighty steps, down along cloistered corridors and

11. In *De Architectura* Vitruvius described not only the water clock of Ctesibius, who had conceived *aquarum expressiones automatopoetasque machinas multaque deliciarum genera* ("First he made a hollow tube of gold, or pierced a gem; for these materials are neither worn by the passage of water nor so begrimed that they become clogged. The water flows smoothly through the passage and raises an inverted bowl which the craftsmen call the cork or drum *(quod ab artificibus phellos sive tympanum dicitur)*. The bowl is connected with a bar on which a drum revolves. The drums are wrought with equal teeth" (*On Architecture*, translated and edited by Frank Granger [New York: Putnam, 1934], Book 9, ch. 8, p. 259). One ought to cite all the "corks or drums" which follow. Vitruvius also describes the axle of the *anaphorical clock, ex qua pendet ex una parte phellos (sive tympanum) qui ab aqua sublevatur* ("On one ends hangs a cork or drum raised by the water," ibid., p. 263), and the famous hydraulic wheel which bears his name: a drum or hollow cylinder is divided by wedges which are open on the surface of the drum. They fill up with water. Reaching the level of the axle, the water passes into the hub and flows out.

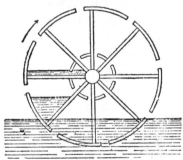

Instead of the wedges of *Vitruvius' tympanum, Lafaye's tympanum* has cylindrical partitions following the developables of a circle. The angles are economized. The water, entering into the wheel, no longer is lodged in the angles. Thus the shocks are reduced and so, by the same token, is the loss of labor. Here, I am reproducing the perhaps Hegelian figure of Lafaye's tympanum (1717).

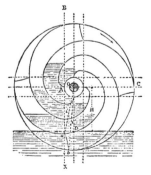

sive or theoretical gesture, for as long as these two types of mastery will not have been destroyed in their essential familiarity—which is also that of *phallocentrism* and *logocentrism*[12]—and for as long as even the philosophical concept of mastery will not have been destroyed, all the liberties one claims to take with the philosophical order will remain activated *a tergo* by misconstrued philosophical machines, according to denegation or precipitation, ignorance or stupidity. They very quickly, known or unknown to their "authors," will have been called back to order.

Certainly one will never prove *philosophically* that *one has* to transform a given situation and proceed to an effective deconstruction in order to leave irreversible marks. In the name of what and of whom in effect? And why not permit the dictation of the norm and the rule of law *a tergo* (viz. the tympanotribe)? If the displacement of forces docs not effectively transform the situation, why deprive oneself of the pleasure, and specifically of the laughter, which are never without a certain repetition? This hypothesis is not secondary. With what is one to *authorize oneself*, in the last

through the years, by the slow voyage toward an internal prey.

Of this *basse taille*, with the idea attached to it, like a stone around its neck, of steps fashioned in the ground, as if in order to go to the basement or step by step to descend a certain number of meters below sea-level (. . .) to open up a passageway through the organs by burrowing through the canal of a wound narrow but deep enough to involve the innermost muscles; whether it is that

---

12. This *écorché (Dissemination* too was to "skin the ear"), bares the *phallogocentric* system in its most sensitive philosophical articulations. [An *écorché* (from the verb *écorcher*, to skin) is a model of a human or animal without its skin used to teach the techniques of life drawing.—Trans.] Therefore, it pursues the deconstruction of the triangulocircular structure (Oedipus, Trinity, Speculative Dialectics) already long since begun, and does so explicitly in the texts of *Dissemination* and of *Positions*. This structure, the mythology of the proper and of organic indifference, is often the architectural figure of the *tympanum*, the part of a pediment included in the triangle of the three cornices, sometimes shot through with a circular opening called an *oculus*. The issue here is not one of paying it the tribute of an oracular denegation or of a thesis without a strategy of writing that the phallogocentric order manipulates at every turn in its conceptual argumentation and in its ideological, political, and literary connotations. The issue, rather, is to mark the conceptual holds and turns of writing that the order cannot turn inside out in order to get its gloves back on or to start up once more. Here, margin, march, and demarcation pass between denegation (plurality of modes) and deconstruction (systematic unity of a spiral).

Speaking of the *écorché*, there are then at least two anatomy lessons, as there are two labyrinths and two cities. In one of them, a brain dissection, the surgeon's head remains invisible. It seems to be cut off by the painter with a line. In fact, it was burned, in 1723, along with a quarter of the painting.

analysis, if not once more with philosophy, in order to disqualify naiveté, incompetence, or misconstrual, in order to be concerned with passivity or to limit pleasure? And if the value of authority remained fundamentally, like the value of the critique itself, the most naive? One can analyze or transform the desire for im-pertinence, but one cannot, within discourse, make it understand pertinence, and that one must (know how to) destroy what one destroys.

Therefore, if they appear to remain marginal to some of the great texts in the history of philosophy, these ten writings *in fact* ask the question of the margin. Gnawing away at the border which would make this question into a particular case, they are to blur the line which separates a text from its controlled margin. They interrogate philosophy beyond its meaning, treating it not only as a discourse but as a determined text inscribed in a general text, enclosed in the representation of its own margin. Which compels us not only to reckon with the entire logic of the margin, but also to take an entirely other reckoning: which is doubtless to recall that beyond the philosophical text there is not a blank, virgin, empty margin, but another text, a weave of differences of forces without any present center of reference (everything—"history," "politics," "economy," "sexuality," etc.—said not to be written in books: the worn-out expression with which we appear not to have finished stepping backward, in the most regressive argumentations and in the most apparently unforeseeable places); and also to recall that the *written* text

of an artist from the opera, cut from the heart of the rock, or fashioned in the most supple steel if it is that of a singer, emerging from the moist earth of a hothouse   or stretched out in breaking glass filament if that of one of the creatures more readily called *cantatrices* than *chanteuses* (even though *cantateur†* is an unknown species); or whether it is the most vulgar voice, issuing from the most insignificant being for the most insipid ballad or most trivial refrain, mysterious is the voice that sings, in relation to the voice that speaks.

The mystery—if we wish at any price, for the purposes of discourse, to give a figure of speech   to   that

---

† *Cantatrice* has the sense of an opera singer, a diva (a hothouse, glass-breaking voice), while *chanteuse* is simply a female singer. There is no masculine form *cantateur* corresponding to *cantatrice*. — TRANS.

of philosophy (this time in its books) overflows and cracks its meaning.

To philosophize *à corps perdu*.[13] How did Hegel understand that?

Can this text become the margin of a margin? Where has the body of the text gone when the margin is no longer a secondary virginity but an inexhaustible reserve, the stereographic activity of an entirely other ear?

Overflows and cracks: that is, on the one hand compels us to count in its margin more and less than one believes is said or read, an unfolding due to the structure of the mark (which is the same word as *marche*,[14] as limit, and as *margin*); and on the other hand, luxates the very body of statements in the pretensions to univocal rigidity or regulated polysemia. A lock opened to a double understanding no longer forming a single system.

Which does not amount to acknowledging that the margin maintains itself within *and* without. Philosophy says so too: *within* because philosophical discourse intends to know and to master its margin, to define the line, align the page, enveloping it in its volume. *Without* because the margin, *its* margin, *its* outside are empty, are outside: a negative about which there seems to be nothing to do, a negative without effect in the text *or* a negative working in the service of meaning, the margin *relevé (aufgehoben)* in the dialectics of the Book. Thus, one will have said nothing, or in any event done nothing, in declaring "against" philosophy that its margin is within or without, within and without, simultaneously the which by definition cannot have one—can be represented as a margin, a fringe surrounding the object, isolating it at the same time as it underlines its presence, masking it even as it qualifies it, inserting it into an untied harlequin of facts with no identifiable cause at the same time as the particular color that it dyes the object extracts it from the swampy depths in which ordinary facts are mixed up. Musical elocution, compared to ordinary elocution, appears to be endorsed with a similar irisation, a fairy's coat, which is the index of a connivance between that which could seem to be only a human voice and the rhythms of

---

13. See the second epigraph above for Hegel's use of the expression *à corps perdu*. It means impetuously, passionately.—TRANS.

14. Derrida often plays on the series *marque, marche, marge* (mark, step, margin).—TRANS.

inequality of its internal spacings and the regularity of its borders. Simultaneously, by means of rigorous, philosophically *intransigent* analyses, *and* by means of the inscription of marks which no longer belong to philosophical space, not even to the neighborhood of its other, one would have to displace philosophy's alignment of its own types. To write otherwise. To delimit the space of a closure no longer analogous to what philosophy can represent for itself under this name, according to a straight or circular line enclosing a homogenous space. To determine, entirely against any philosopheme, the intransigence that prevents it from calculating its margin, by means of a *limitrophic* violence imprinted according to new *types.* To eat the margin in luxating the tympanum, the relationship to itself of the double membrane. So that philosophy can no longer reassure itself that it has always *maintained* its tympanum. The issue here is the *maintenant* [maintaining, now]: it travels through the entire book. How to put one's hands *[mains]* on the tympanum and how the tympanum could escape from the hands of the philosopher in order to make of phallogocentrism an impression that he no longer recognizes, in which he no longer rediscovers himself, of which he could become conscious only *afterward* and without being able *to say to himself,* again turning on his own hinge: I will have anticipated it, with absolute knowledge.

This impression, as always, is made on some tympanum, whether resonating or still, on the double membrane that can be struck from either side.

As in the case of the *mystic writing pad,* I am asking in terms of the *manual printing press* the question of the writing machine which the fauna and flora, that is, the rhythms of the mineral domain in which every velleity of gesture is transcribed into a frozen form. And when from spoken language — which is sufficiently enigmatic itself, since it is only from the instant in which it is formulated, in external fashion or not, that thought takes on its reality — one comes to sung language, what one encounters before one is an enigma of the second degree, seeing that the closer one is in a sense to the corporal structures (of which each note emitted has the appearance of being the direct fruit) and, consequently, the more certain one is of apparently standing on firm ground, one finds oneself, in truth, in the grasp of the ineffable, the me-is to upset the entire space of the proper body in the unlimited enmeshing of machines-of-machines, hence of machines without hands.[15] The question of the machine is asked one more time, between the pit and the pyramid, in the margins (of the Hegelian text).

In terms of the printing press, therefore, the manual press, what is a tympan? We *must know this*, in order to provoke within the balance of the inner ear or the homogenous correspondence of the two ears, in the relation to itself in which philosophy understands itself to domesticate its march, some dislocation without measure. And, if the Hegelian wound *(Beleidigung, Verletzung)* always *appears* sewn up again, to give birth, from the lesion without suture, to some unheard-of partition.

In terms of the manual printing press, then, there is not one tympan[16] but several. Two frameworks, of different material, generally wood and iron, fit into one another, are lodged, if one can put it thus, in one another. One tympan in the other, one of wood the other of iron, one large and one small. Between them, the sheet of paper. Therefore, in question is an *apparatus*, and one of its essential functions will be the regular calculation of the margin. This apparatus is lowered onto the marble on which the inked form is found. A crank rolls the carriage under the platen, which is then, with the aid of the bar, lowered onto the small tympan. The carriage is rolled. The tympan and the frisket are lifted ("Frisket. Printing term. The piece of the hand-operated press that the

lodic line presenting itself as the translation, in a purely sonorous idiom, of that which could not be said by means of words. And even more so when the source of the song, rather than being a human mouth (that is, an organ with which we are more or less familiar), is a mechanical device adding to what is already strange in musical speech the surprise of being reproduced; one is then face to face with a mystery in the almost pure state. (. . .) I myself possessed a phonograph (. . .) not only were there no provisions for using it as a recording device, but it could only be used for the cylinders of small or medium

---

15. As concerns the metaphysical concept of the machine, see, for what is questioned here, "Freud and the Scene of Writing," in *Writing and Difference;* and **Of Grammatology.**

16. In French all the words on the senses of which Derrida plays throughout this essay are *tympan.* In English they are all tympanum, with the single exception of the printing term, which is tympan (as in French). I have kept the original French title—*tympan*—of this essay.—TRANS.

printer lowers onto the sheet, both to keep it on the tympan and to prevent the margins and spaces from being soiled." Littré), and the sheet is then printed on one of its sides. From a treatise on typography: "The large *tympan* is a wood chassis with a piece of silk stretched over it; the points, the margin, and successively each of the sheets to be printed are placed on the tympan. The lever to which the frisket is attached is made of iron. The large *tympan* is attached to the drum in its lower part, that is to the right-hand end of the press; it is held by a double hinge called the couplets of the *tympan*. It is ordinarily of the same width as the drum. In each of the bars that extend along its width, the large *tympan* is pierced by two holes, one in the middle, the other two-thirds up, into which the screws of the points fit. The small *tympan* is a frame formed by four bands of rather thin iron, with a sheet or parchment glued underneath, or more usually a piece of silk flattened onto the four sides of the chassis. It is fitted into the large *tympan*, to which it is attached at the top by two thin, pointed nails, which penetrate between the wood and the silk, at the bottom by a hook, and at the sides by clasps. The platen falls directly onto the small tympan when it is lowered by the bar. The sheets of cloth (satin, or merino if a less dry impression is desired), the cardboard, and the carriage are inserted between the silk of the large and the small tympans. The *tympans* require careful maintenance, and must be renewed as soon as they have begun to deteriorate."

Will the multiplicity of these tympanums permit themselves to be analyzed? Will we be led back, at the exit of the labyrinths, toward format, not for the large ones, such as those that could be heard on the other gramophone, which was fitted with bizarre accessories that tended to clutter up all the closets in the house, along with a vast series of 'rolls' (as we called the cylinders) that my father had recorded himself, and the still virgin wax rolls that had yet to be engraved.

When you wanted to listen to a roll of the medium format on the junior apparatus, which was freely available to me, you had to increase the size of the cylindrical motor; you obtained this result with the aid of a metal tube adapted to the motor, which could take only the smallest cylinders unless its diameter had been increased

some *topos* or commonplace named *tympanum?*

It may be about this multiplicity that philosophy, being situated, inscribed, and included within it, has never been able to reason. Doubtless, philosophy will have sought the reassuring and absolute rule, the norm of this polysemia. It will have asked itself if a tympanum is natural or constructed, if one does not always come back to the unity of a stretched, bordered, framed cloth that watches over its margins as virgin, homogenous, and negative space, leaving its outside outside, without mark, without opposition, without determination, and ready, like matter, the matrix, the *khōra*, to receive and repercuss type. This interpretation will have been *true*, the very history of the truth such as it is, in sum, recounted a bit in this book.

But certainly that which cannot be presented in the space of this truth, that which cannot lend itself to being heard or read, or being seen, even if in the "luminous triangle" or *oculus* of the tympanum, is that this thing, a tympanum, punctures itself or grafts itself. And *this*, however one writes it, resists the concepts of machine or of nature, of break or of body, resists the metaphysics of castration as well as its similar underside, the denegation of modern Rousseauisms, in their very academic vulgarity.

Will it be said, then, that what resists here is the unthought, the suppressed, the repressed of philosophy? In order no longer to be taken in, as one so often is today, by the confused equivalence of these three notions, a concep-

to the desired proportions by means of the addition just described. Linked to the horn‡ by a short rubber tube analogous to the joints of gas ovens and of a brick-reddish color, a diaphragm of the type ordinarily called "sapphire"—a small round box with a bottom made of a thin sheet of mica or some analogous material which bore the tiny hard appendix that was supposed to transmit the vibrations inscribed in the wax cylinder to the sensitive membrane—a diaphragm which, when taken apart, could fit in toto in the palm of your hand, did its best to transform into sound waves the oscillations communicated to it

‡I.e., the bell-shaped horn, in French *pavillon*. See above, note 6, translator's interpolation.—Trans.

tual elaboration must introduce into them a new play of opposition, of articulation, of difference. An introduction, then, to differance. If there is a *here* of this book, let it be inscribed on these steps.

It has already begun, and all of this refers, cites, repercusses, propagates its rhythm without measure. But it remains entirely unforeseen: an incision into an organ made by a hand that is blind for never having seen anything but the here-and-there of a tissue.

What is then woven does not play the game of tight succession. Rather, it plays on succession. Do not forget that to weave *(tramer, trameare)* is first to make holes, to traverse, to work one-side-and-the-other of the warp. The canal of the ear, what is called the auditory meatus, no longer closes after being struck by a simulated succession, a secondary phrase, the echo and logical articulation of a sound that has not yet been received, already an effect of that which does not take place. "Hollow time, / a kind of exhausting void between the blades of cutting / wood, / nothingness calling man's trunk / the body taken as man's trunk," such is the "tympanon" of the Tarahumaras.

This already enervated repercussion, of a kind that has not yet sounded, this timbered time between writing and speech, call for/ themselves a *coup de donc.*

As soon as it perforates, one is dying to replace it by some glorious cadaver. It suffices, in sum, barely, to wait.

by the roll, which seemed to be marked all over its surface (in a helicoid too tight to show anything other than the narrow, dense stripes) by the furrow of varying depth that the original waves had dug into it.

Michel Leiris[§]

Prinsengracht, eight-twelve May 1972

—*Translated by Alan Bass*

[§] Michel Leiris, *Biffures* (Paris: Gallimard, 1948), pp. 85ff.

SEVEN

From "The Double Session" in *Dissemination*

("La Double séance" in *La Dissémination* [1972])

Whereas **"Tympan"** functions on the principle of the oblique, un-
seen intervention of literature into philosophical discourse, in "The
Double Session" Derrida inserts the poetic text into the very "process of truth" which has always been philosophy's exclusive concern. Thus, rather than two columns running parallel, this text ini-
tiates its highly complex trajectory with a single page on which a
short prose piece by Mallarmé *(Mimique)* appears inset into a fragment from Plato's *Philebus*. By means of this typographic invention,
Derrida already announces an intention: to open up a space within
the truth process inaugurated by Plato for a consideration of the
poetic operation it has always condemned or excluded. In particular,
it is the concept of *mimesis* that *Mimique*, through Derrida's reading
of it, deconstructs. That concept, he notes, has determined "the
whole history of the interpretation of the arts of letters" (*Dissemination*, p. 187). Through its evocation of a mime drama, *Mimique*—
and beyond this single text, the whole of Mallarmé's *oeuvre*—simulates or mimics mimetic doctrine, as represented in the exemplary
extract from the Platonic dialogue. This simulation, which is no
longer comprehended by the truth process, would nevertheless be
separated from it only by the thinnest of veils, to which Derrida
assigns the name *hymen* that is found near the center of Mallarmé's
text. The term *hymen*, which designates both a joining and a separation, is made to float undecidably between not only Plato and Mallarmé (one of the alternative titles Derrida suggests for this two-part
essay is "Hymen: Between Plato and Mallarmé"), philosophy and

literature, but also all of the temporal and spatial distinctions upon which mimetic doctrine has been constructed: imitated and imitator, referent and sign, signified and signifier. (For further commentary on this essay and on the "hymen" in Derrida's thought, see above, our introduction, pp. **xxxix-x**.)

Concerning the Platonic notion of mimesis, before which or around which the Mallarmean mimicry is deployed, Derrida's analysis is succinct to the point of ellipsis. This is in part because in *Dissemination* the essay follows upon a lengthy analysis of Plato's negative evaluation of writing wherein the idea of mimesis is already heavily in question. Readers are therefore referred to extracts from that chapter, **"Plato's Pharmacy,"** which are included above.

"The Double Session" was originally presented as two long lectures in Paris in 1969. Most of Part I is excerpted or summarized here. In Part II, Derrida extends his reading of the hymen beyond *Mimique* to other prose and verse texts of Mallarmé, and in the process demonstrates how the deconstructive force of Mallarmé's writing has been ignored or recuperated by the thematic readings of its principal commentators.

The Double Session

[. . . .]

The double session, about which I don't quite have the gall to say plumb straight out that it is reserved for the question *what is literature*, this question being henceforth properly considered a quotation already, in which the place of the *what is* ought to lend itself to careful scrutiny, along with the presumed authority under which one submits anything whatever, and particularly literature, to the form of its inquisition—this double session, about which I will never have the militant innocence to announce that is is concerned with the question *what is literature*, will find its corner BETWEEN *[ENTRE]* literature and truth, between literature and that by which the question *what is? wants* answering.

[. . . .]

On the page that each of you has, a short text by Mallarmé, *Mimique*,[1] is embedded in one corner, sharing or completing it, with a segment from the *Philebus*,[2] which, without actually naming *mimēsis*, illustrates the mimetic system and even defines it, let us say in anticipation, as a system of *illustration*.

What is the purpose of placing these two texts there, and of placing them in that way, at the opening of a question about what goes (on) or doesn't go (on) *between [entre]* literature and truth? That question will remain, like these two texts and like this mimodrama, a sort of epigraph to some future development, while the thing entitled surveys (from a great height) an event, of which we will still be obliged, at the end of the coming session, to point to the absence.

SOCRATES: And if he had someone with him, he would put what he said to himself into actual speech addressed to his companion, audibly uttering those same thoughts, so that what before we called opinion (δόξαν) has now become assertion (λόγος).—PROTARCHUS: Of course.—SOCRATES: Whereas if he is alone he continues thinking the same thing by himself, going on his way maybe for a considerable time with the thought in his mind.—PROTARCHUS: Undoubtedly.— SOCRATES: Well now, I wonder whether you share my view on these matters.—PROTARCHUS: What is it?—SOCRATES: It seems to me that at such times our soul is like a book (Δοκεῖ μοι τότε ἡμῶν ἡ ψυχὴ βιβλίῳ τινὶ προσεοικέναι).—PROTARCHUS: How so?—SOCRATES: It appears to me that the conjunction of memory with sensations, together with the feelings consequent upon memory and sensation, may be said as it were to write words in our souls (γράφειν ἡμῶν ἐν ταῖς ψυχαῖς τότε λόγους). And when this experience writes what is true, the result is that true opinion and true assertions spring up in us, while when the internal scribe that I have suggested writes what is false (ψευδῆ δ ὅταν ὁ τοιοῦτος παρ ἡμῖν γραμματεὺς γράψῃ), we get the opposite sort of opinions and assertions. —PROTARCHUS: That certainly seems to me right, and I approve of the way you put it—SOCRATES: Then please give your approval to the presence of a second artist (δημιουργὸν) in our souls at such a time.—PROTARCHUS: Who is that?—SOCRA-TES: A painter (Ζωγράφον) who comes after the writer and paints in the soul pictures of these assertions that we make.—PROTARCHUS: How do we make out that he in his turn acts, and when?—SOCRA-TES: When we have got those opinions and asser-tions clear of the act of sight ('ὄψεως) or other sense, and as it were see in ourselves pictures or images (εἰκόνας) of what we previously opined or asserted. That does happen with us, doesn't it?—PROTAR-CHUS: Indeed it does.—SOCRATES: Then are the pictures of true opinions and assertions true, and the pictures of false ones false?—PROTARCHUS: Unquestionably.—SOCRATES: Well, if we are right so far, here is one more point in this connection for us to consider.—PROTARCHUS: What is that?— SOCRATES: Does all this necessarily befall us in respect of the present (τῶν ὄντων) and the past (τῶν γεγονότων), but not in respect of the future (τῶν μελλόντων)?—PROTARCHUS: On the contrary, it applies equally to them all.—SOCRATES: We said previously, did we not, that pleasures and pains felt in the soul alone might precede those that come through the body? That must mean that we have anticipatory pleasures and anticipatory pains in re-gard to the future.—PROTARCHUS: Very true.— SOCRATES: Now do those writings and paintings (γράμματά τε καὶ ξωγραφήματα), which a while ago we assumed to occur within ourselves, apply to past and present only, and not to the future?—PROTAR-CHUS: Indeed they do.—SOCRATES: When you say 'indeed they do', do you mean that the last sort are all expectations concerned with what is to come, and that we are full of expectations all our life long? —PROTARCHUS: Undoubtedly.—SOCRATES: Well now, as a supplement to all we have said, here is a further question for you to answer.

MIMIQUE

Silence, sole luxury after rhymes, an or-chestra only marking with its gold, its brushes with thought and dusk, the detail of its signification on a par with a stilled ode and which it is up to the poet, roused by a dare, to translate! the silence of an after-noon of music; I find it, with contentment, also, before the ever original reappearance of Pierrot or of the poignant and elegant mime Paul Margueritte.

Such is this PIERROT MURDERER OF HIS WIFE composed and set down by him-self, a mute soliloquy that the phantom, white as a yet unwritten page, holds in both face and gesture at full length to his soul. A whirlwind of naive or new reasons ema-nates, which it would be pleasing to seize upon with security: the esthetics of the genre situated closer to principles than any! (no)thing in this region of caprice foiling the direct simplifying instinct... This—"The scene illustrates but the idea, not any actual action, in a hymen (out of which flows Dream), trained with vice yet sacred, be-tween desire and fulfillment, perpetration and remembrance: here anticipating, there recalling, in the future, in the past, *under the false appearance of a present*. That is how the Mime operates, whose act is con-fined to a perpetual allusion without break-ing the ice or the mirror: he thus sets up a medium, a pure medium, of fiction." Less than a thousand lines, the role, the one that reads, will instantly comprehend the rules as if placed before the stageboards, their humble depository. Surprise, accompanying the artifice of a notation of sentiments by unproffered sentences—that, in the sole case, perhaps, with authenticity, between the sheets and the eye there reigns a silence still, the condition and delight of reading.

Because of a certain fold that we shall outline, these texts, and their commerce, definitively escape any exhaustive treatment. We can nevertheless begin to mark out, in a few rough strokes, a certain number of motifs. These strokes might be seen to form a sort of frame, the enclosure or borders of a history that would precisely be that of a certain play between literature and truth. The history of this relationship would be organized by—I won't say by *mimēsis*, a notion one should not hasten to translate (especially by imitation), but by a certain interpretation of *mimēsis*. Such an interpretation has never been the act or the speculative decision of any one author at a given moment, but rather, if one reconstitutes the system, the whole of a history. *Inter Platonem et Mallarmatum*, between Plato and Mallarmé—whose proper names, it should be understood, are not real references but indications for the sake of convenience and initial analysis—a whole history has taken place. This history was also a history of literature if one accepts the idea that literature was born of it and died of it, the certificate of its birth as such, the declaration of its name, having coincided with its disappearance, according to a logic that the hymen will help us define. And this history, if it has any meaning, is governed in its entirety by the value of truth and by a certain relation, inscribed in the hymen in question, *between* literature and truth. In saying "this history, it is has any meaning," one seems to be admitting that it might not. But if we were to go to the end of this analysis, we would see it confirmed not only that this history has a meaning, but that the very concept of history has lived only upon the possibility of meaning, upon the past, present, or promised presence of meaning and of truth. Outside this system, it is impossible to resort to the concept of history without reinscribing it elsewhere, according to some specific systematic strategy.

True history, the history of meaning, is told in the *Philebus*. In rereading the scene you have before your eyes, you will have remarked four facets.

[Derrida then isolates four traits of the excerpt from the *Philebus*: (1) "The book is a dialogue or a dialectic." The metaphor of the book, to represent silent discourse of the soul with itself when no interlocutor is at hand, indicates that the object of writing is to reconstitute the presence of the other, and therefore its model is dialogue. (2)

"The truth of the book is decidable." This psychic writing is either true or false, its only worth is its truth value. (3) "The value of the book (true or false) is not intrinsic to it." Since writing in general is understood as an imitation of the living *logos,* its value (truth or falsity) is dependent on this extrinsic source. (4) Writing's element is the image in general. The soul and the book can be compared because each is the likeness of the other, and both are thought to be in the image of the *logos.* Thus, the comparison with painting naturally follows.]

As of this point, the appearance of the painter is prescribed and becomes absolutely ineluctable. The way is paved for it in the scene from the *Philebus.* This other "demiurge," the *zōgraphos,* comes *after* the *grammateus:* "a painter, who comes after the writer and paints in the soul pictures of these assertions that we make." This collusion between painting *(zōgraphia)* and writing is, of course, constant. Both in Plato and after him. But painting and writing can only be images of each other to the extent that they are both interpreted as images, reproductions, representations, or repetitions of something alive, of living speech in the one case, and of animal figures in the other *(zōgraphia).* Any discourse about the relationship between literature and truth always bumps up against the enigmatic possibility of repetition, within the framework of the *portrait.*

What, in fact, is the painter doing here? He too is painting metaphorically, of course, and in the soul, just like the *grammateus.* But he comes along after the latter, retraces his steps, follows his traces and his trail. And he *illustrates* a book that is already written when he appears on the scene. He "paints in the soul pictures of these assertions." Sketching, painting, the art of space, the practice of spacing, the inscription written inside the outside (the outwork *[hors-livre]*), all these are only things that are added, for the sake of illustration, representation, or decoration, to the book of the discourse of the thinking of the innermost man. The painting that shapes the images is a portrait of the discourse; it is worth only as much as the discourse it fixes and freezes along its surface. And consequently, it is also worth only as much as the *logos* capable of interpreting it, of reading it, of saying what it is-trying-to-say and what in truth it is being made to say through the reanimation that makes it speak.

But painting, that degenerate and somewhat superfluous expression, that supplementary frill of discursive thought, that ornament of *dianoia* and *logos*, also plays a role that seems to be just the opposite of this. It functions as a pure indicator of the essence of a thought or discourse defined as image, representation, repetition. If *logos* is first and foremost a faithful image of the *eidos* (the figure of intelligible visibility) of what is, then it arises as a sort of primary painting, profound and invisible. In that case painting in its usual sense, a painter's painting, is really only the painting of a painting. Hence it can reveal the essential picturality, the representativity, of *logos*. That is indeed the task assigned by Socrates to the *zōgraphos-dēmiourgos* in the *Philebus:* "How do we make out that he in his turn acts, and when?" asks Protarchus, and Socrates replies, "When we have got those opinions and assertions clear of the act of sight *(opseōs)*, or other sense, and as it were see in ourselves pictures or images of what we previously opined or asserted." The painter who works after the writer, the worker who shapes his work after opinion and assertion, the artisan who follows the artist, is able, through an exercise of analysis, separation, and impoverishment, precisely to purify the pictorial, imitative, imaginal essence of thought. The painter, then, knows how to restore the naked image of the thing, the image as it presents itself to simple intuition, as it shows itself in its intelligible *eidos* or sensible *horaton*. He strips it of all that superadded language, of that legend that now has the status of a commentary, of an envelope around a kernel, of an epidermic canvas.

So that in psychic writing, between the *zōgraphia* and the *logos* (or *dianoia*) there exists a very strange relation: one is always the supplement of the other. In the first part of the scene, the thought that directly fixed the essence of things did not essentially need the illustrative ornament that writing and painting constituted. The soul's thinking was only intimately linked to *logos* (and to the proffered or held-back voice). Inversely, a bit further on, painting (in the metaphorical sense of psychic painting, of course, just as a moment ago it was a question of psychic writing) is what gives us the image of the thing itself, what communicates to us the direct intuition, the immediate vision of the thing, freed from the discourse that accompanied it, or even encumbered it. Naturally, I would like to stress once more, it is always the *metaphors* of painting and writing that are linked in this way back and forth: we recall that, on another plane, outside these metaphors, Plato always asserts that in their literal sense painting and writing are totally incapable of any intuition of the thing itself, since they only deal in copies, and in copies of copies.

If discourse and inscription (writing-painting) thus appear alternately as useful complements or as useless supplements to each other, now useful, now useless, now in one sense, now in another, this is because they are forever intertwined together within the tissue of the following complicities or reversibilities:

1. They are both measured against the truth they are capable of.

2. They are images of each other and that is why one can replace *[suppléer]* the other when the other is lacking.

3. Their common structure makes them both partake of *mnēmē* and *mimēsis*, of *mnēmē* precisely by dint of participating in *mimēsis*. Within the movement of the *mimeisthai*, the relation of the mime to the mimed, of the reproducer to the reproduced, is always a relation to a *past present*. The imitated comes before the imitator. Whence the problem of time, which indeed does not fail to come up: Socrates wonders whether it would be out of the question to think that *grammata* and *zōgraphēmata* might have a relation to the future. The difficulty lies in conceiving that what is imitated could be still to come with respect to what imitates, that the image can precede the model, that the double can come before the simple. The overtures of "hope" *(elpis)*, anamnesis (the future as a past present due to return), the preface, the anterior future (future perfect), all come to arrange things.[3]

It is here that the value of *mimēsis* is most difficult to master. A certain movement effectively takes place in the Platonic text, a movement one should not be too quick to call contradictory. On the one hand, as we have just verified, it is hard to separate *mnēmē* from *mimēsis*. But on the other hand, while Plato often discredits *mimēsis* and almost always disqualifies the mimetic arts, he never separates the unveiling of truth, *alētheia*, from the movement of *anamnēsia* (which is, as we have seen, to be distinguished from *hypomnēsia*).

What announces itself here is an internal division within *mi-*

mēsis, a self-duplication of repetition itself, *ad infinitum,* since this movement feeds its own proliferation. Perhaps, then, there is always more than one kind of *mimēsis;* and perhaps it is in the strange mirror that reflects but also displaces and distorts one *mimēsis* into the other, as though it were itself destined to mime or mask *itself,* that history—the history of literature—is lodged, along with the whole of its interpretation. Everything would then be played out in the paradoxes of the supplementary double: the paradoxes of something that, added to the simple and the single, replaces and mimes them, both like and unlike, unlike because it is—in that it is—like, the same as and different from what it duplicates. Faced with all this, what does "Platonism" decide and maintain? (Platonism here standing more or less immediately for the whole history of Western philosophy, including the anti-Platonisms that regularly feed into it.) What is it that is decided and maintained in ontology or dialectics throughout all the mutations or revolutions that are entailed? It is precisely the *ontological:* the presumed possibility of a discourse about what is, the deciding and decidable *logos* of or about the *on* (being-present). That which is, the being-present (the matrix-form of substance, of reality, of the oppositions between matter and form, essence and existence, objectivity and subjectivity, etc.) is distinguished from the appearance, the image, the phenomenon, etc., that is, from anything that, presenting it *as* being-present, doubles it, re-presents it, and can therefore replace and de-present it. There is thus the 1 and the 2, the simple and the double. The double comes *after* the simple; it multiplies it as a *follow-up.* It follows, I apologize for repeating this, that the image *supervenes* upon reality, the representation upon the present in presentation, the imitation upon the thing, the imitator upon the imitated. First there is what is, "reality," the thing itself, in flesh and blood as the phenomenologists say; then there is, imitating these, the painting, the portrait, the zographeme, the inscription or transcription of the thing itself. Discernability, at least numerical discernability, between the imitator and the imitated is what constitutes order. And obviously, according to "logic" itself, according to a profound synonymy, what is imitated is more real, more essential, more true, etc., than what imitates. It is anterior and superior to it. One should constantly bear in mind, henceforth, the clinical paradigm of *mimēsis*, the order of the three beds in the *Republic* X (596a ff): the painter's, the carpenter's, and God's.

Doubtless this order will appear to be contested, even inverted, in the course of history, and on several occasions. But never have the absolute distinguishability between imitated and imitator, and the anteriority of the first over the second, been displaced by any metaphysical system. In the domain of "criticism" or poetics, it has been strongly stressed that art, as imitation (representation, description, expression, imagination, etc.), should not be "slavish" (this proposition scans twenty centuries of poetics) and that consequently, through the liberties it takes with nature, art can create or produce works that are more valuable than what they imitate. But all these derivative oppositions send us back to the same root. The extra-value or the extra-being makes art a richer kind of nature, freer, more pleasant, more creative: more natural. At the time of the great systematization of the classical doctrine of imitation, Desmaret, in his *Art of Poetry*, translates a then rather common notion:

> And Art enchants us more than nature does. . . .
> Not liking what is imitated, we yet love what imitates.

Whether one or the other is preferred (but it could easily be shown that because of the nature of the imitated–imitator relation, the *preference*, whatever one might say, can only go to the imitated), it is at bottom this order of appearance, the precedence [pré-séance] of the imitated, that governs the philosophical or critical interpretation of "literature," if not the operation of literary writing. This order of appearance is *the order of all appearance*, the very process of appearing in general. It is the order of truth. "Truth" has always meant two different things, the history of the essence of truth—the truth of truth—being only the gap and the articulation between the two interpretations or processes. To simplify the analyses made by Heidegger but without necessarily adopting the order of succession that he seems to recognize, one can retain the fact that the process of truth is *on the one hand* the unveiling of what lies concealed in oblivion (*alētheia*), the veil lifted or raised [relevé] from the thing itself, from that which *is* insofar as it is, presents itself, produces itself, and can even exist in the form of a determinable hole in Being; *on the other hand* (but this other process is prescribed in the first, in the ambiguity or duplicity of the presence of the present, of its *appearance*—that which appears *and* its appearing—in the *fold* of the present participle),[5] truth is agreement *(homoiōsis* or *adaequatio),* a relation of resemblance or equality between a re-presentation and a thing (unveiled, present), even in the eventuality of a statement of judgment.

Now, mimesis, all through the history of its interpretation, is always commanded by the process of truth:

1. either, even before it can be translated as imitation, *mimēsis* signifies the presentation of the thing itself, of nature, of the physis that produces itself, engenders itself, and appears (to itself) as it really is, in the presence of its image, its visible aspect, its face: the theatrical mask, as one of the essential references of the *mimeisthai,* reveals as much as it hides. *Mimēsis* is then the movement of the *phusis,* a movement that is somehow natural (in the nonderivative sense of this word), through which the *phusis,* having no outside, no other, must be doubled in order to make its appearance, to appear (to itself), to produce (itself), to unveil (itself); in order to emerge from the crypt where it prefers itself; in order to shine in its *alētheia.* In this sense, *mnēmē* and *mimēsis* are on a par, since *mnēmē* too is an unveiling (an un-forgetting), *alētheia.*

2. or else *mimēsis* sets up a relation of *homoiōsis* or *adaequatio* between two (terms). In that case it can more readily be translated as imitation. This translation seeks to express (or rather historically produces) the thought about this relation. The two faces are separated and set face to face: the imitator and the imitated, the latter being none other than the thing or the meaning of the thing itself, its manifest presence. A good imitation will be one that is true, faithful, like or likely, adequate, in conformity with the *phusis* (essence or life) of what is imitated; it effaces itself of its own accord in the process of restoring freely, and hence in a living manner, the freedom of true presence.

In each case, *mimēsis* has to follow the process of truth. The presence of the present is its norm, its order, its law. It is in the name of truth, its only reference—*reference* itself—that *mimē-sis* is judged, proscribed or prescribed according to a regular alternation.

The invariable feature of this reference sketches out the closure of metaphysics: not as a border enclosing some homogeneous space but according to a noncircular, entirely other, figure. Now, this reference is discreetly but absolutely displaced in the workings of a certain syntax, whenever any writing both marks and goes back over its mark with an undecidable stroke. This double mark escapes the pertinence or authority of truth: it does not overturn it but rather inscribes it within its play as one of its functions or parts. This displacement does not take place, has not taken place once, as an *event*. It does not occupy a simple place. It does not take place *in* writing. This dis-location (is what) writes/is written. The redoubling of the mark, which is at once a formal break and a formal generalization, *is exemplified by the text of Mallarmé, and singularly by the "sheet" you have before your eyes* (but obviously every word of this last proposition must by the same token be displaced or placed under suspicion).

[Derrida proceeds then to rule out an interpretation of Mallarmé's text that would see in it an " 'idealist' reversal of traditional mimetology" based on the phrase, "The scene illustrates but the idea, not any actual action. . . ." On the contrary, says Derrida, there is "no imitation. The Mime imitates nothing. . . . There is nothing prior to the writing of his gestures. . . . His movements form a figure that no speech anticipates or accompanies" (pp. 193–94). There is no book prescribing the Mime's writing; he writes "upon the page he is." He is both passive and active, the page and the pen, "the author, the means, and the raw material of his mimodrama" (198). But what of the book that Mallarmé says he is reading and which contains the printed version of the silent scene? Here at least would seem to be a preexisting referent which reestablishes the order of limitation. First of all, however, the booklet referred to was written only after the performance of the mime; second, the drama itself is suspended in a "false appearance of a present" which dismantles the time frame of reference to a past event; third, the relation between the performance and the booklet is not a stable system of reference, closed on itself, because each form of writing refers also only to itself; their relation is not that of imitation but of a grafting of one onto the other (at this point Derrida suggests that one ought to explore systematically the link, indicated by etymology, between graft and writing [graph]); fourth, the mimodrama *Pierrot Murderer of His Wife* has to be reinserted in a long textual tradition—indeed "an interminable network"—of similar mime dramas (in which Pierrot tickles Colombine to death) as indicated by an epigraph to one such predecessor in a Gautier poem. In all of these ways, *Mimique* resists the mimetic tradition which subordinates writing to a truth adequately represented. If, then, the mime imitates nothing, reproduces nothing, "he must be the very movement of truth," not in the sense of *adequatio* but of *aletheia:* unveiling of the present, manifestation. Derrida contests this conclusion as well by pointing to the fact that, although there is no imitation, there is mimicry or simulation, "reference without a referent." "Mallarmé thus preserves the differential structure of mimicry or mimesis, but without its Platonic or metaphysical interpretation" (p. 206). This difference of the simulacrum, which runs unnoticed throughout the tradition of mimesis, is that "barely perceptible veil" to which Derrida assigns the undecidable name "hymen."]

What interests us here is less these propositions of a philosophical type than the mode of their reinscription in the text of *Mimique.* What is marked there is the fact that, this imitator having in the last instance no imitated, this signifier having in the last instance no signified, this sign having in the last instance no referent, their operation is no longer comprehended within the process of truth but on the contrary comprehends *it,* the motif of the last instance being inseparable from metaphysics as the search for the *arkhē,* the *eskhaton,* and the *telos.*[6]

If all this leaves its mark upon *Mimique,* it is not only in the chiseled precision of the writing, its extraordinary formal or syntactical felicity; it is also in what seems to be described as the thematic content or mimed event, and which in the final analysis, despite its effect of content, is nothing other than the space of writing: in this "event"—hymen, crime, suicide, spasm (of laughter or pleasure)—in which nothing happens, in which the simulacrum is a transgression and the transgression a simulacrum, everything describes the very structure of the text and effectuates its possibility. That, at least, is what we now must demonstrate.

The operation, which no longer belongs to the system of truth, does not manifest, produce, or unveil any presence; nor does it constitute any conformity, resemblance, or adequation between a presence and a representation. And yet this operation is not a unified entity but the manifold play of a scene that, illustrating nothing—neither word nor deed—beyond itself, illustrates nothing. Nothing but the many-faceted multiplicity of a lustre which itself is nothing beyond its own fragmented light. Nothing but the idea which is nothing. The ideality of the idea is here for Mallarmé the still metaphysical name that is still necessary in order to mark nonbeing, the nonreal, the nonpresent. This mark points, alludes without breaking the glass, to the beyond of beingness, toward the *epekeina tēs ousias:*[7] a hymen (a closeness and a veil) between Plato's sun and Mallarmé's lustre. This "materialism of the idea" is nothing other than the staging, the theater, the visibility of nothing or of the self. It is a dramatization which *illustrates nothing,* which illustrates *the nothing,* lights up a space, re-marks a spacing as a nothing, a blank: white as a yet unwritten page, blank as a difference between two lines. "I am for—no illustration. . . ."[8]

[. . . .]

The stage [*scène*] thus illustrates but the stage, the scene only the scene; there is only the equivalence between *theater* and *idea,* that is (as these two names indicate), the visibility (which remains outside) of the visible that is being effectuated. The scene illustrates, in the text of a hymen—which is more than an anagram of "hymn" [*hymne*]—*"in a hymen (out of which flows Dream), tainted with vice yet sacred, between desire and fulfillment, perpetration and remembrance: here anticipating, there recalling, in the future, in the past, under the false appearance of a present."*

"Hymen" (a word, indeed the only word, that reminds us that what is in question is a "supreme spasm") is first of all a sign of fusion, the consummation of a marriage, the identification of two beings, the confusion between two. *Between* the two, there is no longer difference but identity. Within this fusion, there is no longer any distance between desire (the awaiting of a full presence designed to fulfill it, to carry it out) and the fulfillment of presence, between distance and nondistance; there is no longer any difference between desire and satisfaction. It is not only the difference (between desire and fulfillment) that is abolished, but also the difference between difference and nondifference. Nonpresence, the gaping void of desire, and presence, the fullness of enjoyment, amount to the same. By the same token [*du même coup*], there is no longer any textual difference between the image and the thing, the empty signifier and the full signified, the imitator and the imitated, etc. But it does not follow, by virtue of this hymen of confusion, that there is now only one term, a single one of the differends. It does not follow that what remains is thus the fullness of the signified, the imitated, or the thing itself, simply present in person. It is the difference between the two terms that is no longer functional. The confusion or consummation of this hymen eliminates the spatial heterogeneity of the two poles in the "supreme spasm," the moment of dying laughing. By the same token, it eliminates the exteriority or anteriority, the independence, of the imitated, the signified, or the thing. Fulfillment is summed up within desire; desire is (ahead of) fulfillment, which, still mimed, remains desire, *"without breaking the mirror."*

What is lifted, then, is not difference but the different, the differends, the decidable exteriority of differing terms. Thanks to the confusion and continuity of the hymen, and not in spite of it, a (pure and impure) difference inscribes itself without any decidable poles, without any independent, irreversible terms. Such difference without presence appears, or rather baffles the process of appearing, by dislocating any orderly time at the center of the present. The present is no longer a mother-form around which are gathered and differentiated the future (present) and the past (present). What is marked in this hymen between the future (desire) and the present (fulfillment), between the past (remembrance) and the present (perpetration), between the capacity and the act, etc., is only a series of temporal differences without any central present, without a present of which the past and future would be but modifications. Can we then go on speaking about *time*, *tenses*, and *temporal* differences?

The center of presence is supposed to offer itself to what is called perception or, generally, intuition. In *Mimique*, however, there is no perception, no reality offering itself up, in the present, to be perceived. The plays of facial expression and the gestural tracings are not present in themselves since they always refer, perpetually allude or represent. But they don't represent anything that has ever been or can ever become present: nothing that comes before or after the mimodrama, and, within the mimodrama, an orgasm-crime that has never been committed and yet nevertheless turns into a suicide without striking or suffering a blow, etc. The signifying allusion does not go through the looking-glass: *"a perpetual allusion without breaking the ice or the mirror,"* the cold, transparent, reflective window ("without breaking the ice or the mirror" is added in the third version of the text), without piercing the veil or the canvas, without tearing the moire. The antre of Mallarmé, the theater of his glossary: it lies in this suspension, the *"center of vibratory suspense,"* the repercussions of words between the walls of the grotto, or of the glottis, sounded among others by the rhymes *"hoir"* [heir], *"soir"* [evening], *"noire"* [black], *"miroir"* [mirror], *"grimoire"* [wizard's black book], *"ivoire"* [ivory], *"armoire"* [wardrobe], etc.

What does the hymen that illustrates the suspension of differends remain, other than Dream? The capital letter marks what is new in a concept no longer enclosed in the old opposition: Dream, being at once perception, remembrance, and anticipation (desire), each within the others, is really none of these. It declares the "fiction," the "medium, the pure medium, of fiction" (the commas in *"milieu, pur, de fiction"* also appear in the third version), a presence both perceived and not perceived, at once image and model, and hence image without model, neither image nor model, a medium (medium in the sense of middle, neither/nor, what is between extremes, and medium in the sense of element, ether, matrix, means). When we have rounded a certain corner in our reading, we will place ourselves on that side of the lustre where the "medium" is shining. The referent is lifted, but reference remains: what is left is only the writing of dreams, a fiction that is not imaginary, mimicry without imitation, without verisimilitude, without truth or falsity, a miming of appearance without concealed reality, without any world behind it, and hence without appearance: *"false appearance . . ."* There remain only traces, announcements and souvenirs, foreplays and aftereffects [*avant-coups et après-coups*] which no present will have preceded or followed and which cannot be arranged on a line around a point, traces "here anticipating, there recalling, in the future, in the past, *under the false appearance of a present.*" It is Mallarmé who underlines (as of the second version, in *Pages*) and thus marks the richochet of the moment of mimed deliberation from Margueritte's *Pierrot:* at that point—in the past—where the question is raised of what to do in the future ("But how shall I go about it?"), the author of the booklet speaks to *you* in parentheses, in the "present": ("For Pierrot, like a sleepwalker, reproduces his crime, and in his hallucination, the *past* becomes *present.*") (Underlined by the author.) The historial ambiguity of the word *appearance* (at once the appearing or apparition of the being-present *and* the masking of the being-present behind its appearance) impresses its indefinite fold on this sequence, which is neither synthetic nor redundant: *"under the false appearance of a present."* What is to be re-marked in the underlining of this circumstantial complement is the displacement without reversal of Platonism and its heritage. This displacement is always an effect of language or writing, of syntax, and never simply the dialectical overturning of a concept (signified). The very motif of dialectics, which marks the beginning and end of philosophy, however that motif might be determined and despite the resources it entertains within philosophy against philosophy, is doubtless what Mallarmé has marked with his syntax at the point of its sterility, or rather, at the point that will soon, provisionally, analogically, be called the undecidable.

Or *hymen.*

The virginity of the *"yet unwritten page"* opens up that space. There are still a few words that have not been illustrated: the opposition *vicious–sacred* ("hymen (out of which flows Dream), tainted with vice yet sacred"; the parentheses intervene in the second version to make it clear that the adjectives modify "hymen"), the opposition *desire–perpetration*, and most importantly the syncategorem *"between"* [*entre*].

To repeat: the hymen, the confusion between the present and the nonpresent, along with all the indifferences it entails within the whole series of opposites (perception and nonperception, memory and image, memory and desire, etc.), produces the effect of a medium (a medium as element enveloping both terms at once; a medium located between the two terms). It is an operation that *both* sows confusion *between* opposites *and* stands *between* the opposites "at once." What counts here is the *between*, the in-between-ness of the hymen. The hymen "takes place" in the "inter-," in the spacing between desire and fulfillment, between perpetration and its recollection. But this medium of the *entre* has nothing to do with a center.

The hymen enters into the antre. *Entre* can just as easily be written with an *a*. Indeed, are these two *(e) (a)ntres* not really the same? Littré: "ANTRE, s.m. 1. Cave, natural grotto, deep dark cavern. 'These antres, these braziers that offer us oracles,' *Voltaire, Oedipe* II, 5. 2. Fig. The antres of the police, of the Inquisition. 3. *Anatomy:* name given to certain bone cavities.—*Syn: Antre, cave, grotto. Cave,* an empty, hollow, concave space in the form of a vault, is the generic term; *antre* is a deep, dark, black cave; *grotto* is a picturesque cave created by nature or by man. *Etym.* Antrum, 'άγντρον; Sanscrit, *antara,* cleft, cave. *Antara* properly signifies 'interval' and is thus related to the Latin preposition *inter* (see *entre*). Provenc. *antre;* Span. and Ital. *antro.*" And the entry for ENTRER ["to enter"] ends with the same etymological reference. The *interval* of the *entre*, the in-between of the hymen: one might be tempted to visualize these as the hollow or bed of a valley *(vallis)* without which there would be no mountains, like the sacred vale between the two flanks of the Parnassus, the dwelling place of the Muses and the site of Poetry; but *intervallum* is composed of *inter* (between) and *vallus* (pole), which gives us not the pole in between, but the space between two palisades. According to Littré.

We are thus moving from the logic of the palisade, which is always, in a sense, "full," to the logic of the hymen. The hymen, the consummation of differends, the continuity and confusion of the coitus, merges with what it seems to be derived from: the hymen as protective screen, the jewel box of virginity, the vaginal partition, the fine, invisible veil which, in front of the hystera, stands *between* the inside and the outside of a woman, and consequently between desire and fulfillment. It is neither desire nor pleasure but in between the two. Neither future nor present, but between the two. It is the hymen that desire dreams of piercing, of bursting, in an act of violence that is (at the same time or somewhere between) love and murder. If either one *did* take place, there would be no hymen. But neither would there simply be a hymen in (case events go) *no* place. With all the undecidability of its meaning, the hymen only takes place when it doesn't take place, when nothing *really* happens, when there is an all-consuming consummation without violence, or a violence without blows, or a blow without marks, a mark without a mark (a margin), etc., when the veil is, *without being*, torn, for example when one is made to die or come laughing.

A masked gap, impalpable and insubstantial, interposed, slipped between, the *entre* of the hymen is reflected in the screen without penetrating it.[9] The hymen remains in the hymen. The one —the veil of virginity where nothing has yet taken place—remains in the other—consummation, release, and penetration of the antre.

And vice versa.

The mirror is never passed through and the ice never broken. At the edge of being.

At the edge of being, the medium of the hymen never becomes a mere mediation or work of the negative; it outwits and undoes all ontologies, all philosophemes, all manner of dialectics. It outwits them and—as a cloth, a tissue, a medium again—it envelops them, turns them over, and inscribes them. This nonpenetration, this nonperpetration (which is not simply negative but stands between the two), this suspense in the antre of perpenetration, is, says Mallarmé, *"perpetual"*: *"This is how the Mime operates, whose act is confined to a perpetual allusion without breaking the ice or the mirror: he thus sets up a medium, a pure medium, of fiction."* (The play of the commas, *virgulae*, only appears, in all its multiplicity, in the last version, inserting a series of cuts marking pauses and cadence, spacing and shortness of breath, within the continuum of the sequence).[10] Hymen in perpetual motion: one can't get out of Mallarmé's antre as one can out of Plato's cave. Never min(e)d [*mine de rien*],[11] it requires an entirely different kind of speleology which no longer searches behind the lustrous appearance, outside the "beyond," "agent," "motor," "principal part or nothing" of the "literary mechanism" (*Music and Letters*, p. 647).

". . . as much as it takes to illustrate one of the aspects and this lode of language" (p. 406).

"That is how the Mime operates": every time Mallarmé uses the word *"operation,"* nothing happens that could be grasped as a present event, a reality, an activity, etc. The Mime doesn't *do* anything; there is no act (neither murderous nor sexual), no acting agent and hence no patient. Nothing *is.* The word *is* does not appear in *Mimique,* which is nevertheless conjugated in the *present,* within and upon the *"false appearance of a present,"* with one exception, and even then in a form that is not that of a declaration of existence and barely that of a predicative copula *("It is up to the poet, roused by a dare, to translate!").* Indeed, the constant ellipsis of the verb "to be" by Mallarmé has already been noted[12] This ellipsis is complementary to the frequency of the word *jeu* [play, game, act]; the practice of "play" in Mallarmé's writing is in collusion with the casting aside of "being." The *casting aside* [*mise à l'écart*] of being defines itself and literally (im)prints itself in dissemination, *as* dissemination.

[. . . .]

The Mime is *acting* from the moment he is ruled by no actual action and aims toward no form of verisimilitude. The act always plays out a difference without reference, or rather without a referent, without any absolute exteriority, and hence, without any inside. The Mime mimes reference. He is not an imitator; he mimes imitation. The hymen interposes itself between mimicry and *mimēsis* or rather between *mimēsis* and *mimēsis.* A copy of a copy, a simulacrum that simulates the Platonic simulacrum— the Platonic copy of a copy as well as the Hegelian curtain[13] have lost here the lure of the present referent and thus find themselves lost for dialectics and ontology, lost for absolute knowledge. Which is also, as Bataille would literally have it, "mimed." In this perpetual allusion being performed in the background of the *entre* that has no ground, one can never know what the allusion alludes to, unless it is to itself in the process of alluding, weaving its hymen and manufacturing its text. Wherein allusion becomes a game conforming only to its own formal rules. As its name indicates, allusion *plays.* But that this play should in the last instance be independent of truth does not mean that it is false, an error, appearance, or illusion. Mallarmé writes "allusion," not "illusion." Allusion, or "suggestion" as Mallarmé says elsewhere, is indeed that operation we are here *by analogy* calling undecidable. An undecidable proposition, as Gödel demonstrated in 1931, is a proposition which, given a system of axioms governing a multiplicity, is neither an analytical nor deductive consequence of those axioms, nor in contradiction with them, neither true nor false with respect to those axioms. *Tertium datur*, without synthesis.

"Undecidability" is not caused here by some enigmatic equivocality, some inexhaustible ambivalence of a word in a "natural" language, and still less by some *"Gegensinn der Urworte"* (Abel).[14] In dealing here with *hymen*, it is not a matter of repeating what Hegel undertook to do with German words like *Aufhebung, Urteil, Meinen, Beispiel*, etc., marveling over that lucky accident that installs a natural language within the element of speculative dialectics[15] What counts here is not the lexical richness, the semantic infiniteness of a word or concept, its depth or breadth, the sedimentation that has produced inside it two contradictory layers of signification (continuity and discontinuity, inside and outside, identity and difference, etc.). What counts here is the formal or syntactical *praxis* that composes and decomposes it. We have indeed been making believe that everything could be traced to the word *hymen*. But the irreplaceable character of this signifier, which everything seemed to grant it, was laid out like a trap. This word, this syllepsis,[16] is not indispensable; philology and etymology interest us only secondarily, and the loss of the "hymen" would not be irreparable for *Mimique*. It produces its effect first and foremost through the syntax, which disposes the *"entre"* in such a way that the suspense is due only to the placement and not to the content of words. Through the "hymen" one can remark only what the place of the word *entre* already marks and would mark even if the word "hymen" were not there. If we replaced "hymen" by "marriage" or "crime," "identity" or "difference," etc., the effect would be the same, the only loss being a certain economic condensation or accumulation, which has not gone unnoticed. It is the "between," whether it names fusion or separation, that thus carries all the force of the operation. The hymen must be determined through the *entre* and not the other way around. The hymen in the text (crime, sexual act, incest, suicide, simulacrum) is inscribed at the very tip of this indecision. This tip advances according to the irreducible excess of the syntactic over the semantic. The word "between" has no full meaning of its own. *Inter* acting forms a syntactical plug; not a categorem, but a syncategorem: what philosophers from the Middle Ages to Husserl's *Logical Investigations* have called an incomplete signification. What holds for "hymen" also holds, *mutatis mutandis,* for all other signs which, like *pharmakon, supplement, differance,* and others, have a double, contradictory, undecidable value that always derives from their syntax, whether the latter is in a sense "internal," articulating and combining under the same yoke, *huph' hen,* two incompatible meanings, or "external," dependent on the code in which the word is made to function. But the syntactical composition and decomposition of a sign renders this alternative between internal and external inoperative. One is simply dealing with greater or lesser syntactical units at work, and with economic differences in condensation. Without reducing all these to the same, quite the contrary, it is possible to recognize a certain serial law in these points of indefinite pivoting: they mark the spots of what can never be mediated, mastered, sublated, or dialecticized through any *Erinnerung* or *Aufhebung.*[17] Is it by chance that all these play effects, these "words" that escape philosophical mastery, should have, in widely differing historical contexts, a very singular relation to writing? These "words" admit into their games both contradiction and noncontradiction (and the contradiction and noncontradiction *between* contradiction and noncontradiction). Without any dialectical *Aufhebung,* without any time off, they belong in a sense both to consciousness and to the unconscious, which Freud tells us can tolerate or remain insensitive to contradiction. Insofar as the text depends upon them, *bends* to them [*s'y plie*], it thus plays a *double scene* upon a double stage. It operates in two absolutely different places at once, even if these are only separated by a veil, which is both traversed and not traversed, *inter*sected [*entr'ouvert*]. Because of this indecision and instability, Plato would have conferred upon the double science arising from these two theaters the name *doxa* rather than *epistēmē. Pierrot Murderer of His Wife* would have reminded him of the riddle of the bat struck by the eunuch.[18]

Everything is played out, everything and all the rest—that is to say, the game—is played out in the *entre*, about which the author of the *Essai sur la connaissance approchée*, who also knew all about caves,[19] says that it is "a mathematical concept" (p. 32). When this undecidability is marked and re-marked in *writing*, it has a greater power of formalization, even if it is "literary" in appearance, or appears to be attributable to a natural language, than when it occurs as a proposition in logicomathe- matical form, which would not go as far as the former type of mark. If one supposes that the distinction, still a metaphysical one, between natural language and artificial language be rigorous (and we no doubt here reach the limit of its pertinence), one can say that there are texts in so-called natural languages wherein the power of formalization would be superior to that attributed to certain apparently formal notations.

One no longer even has the authority to say that "between" is a purely syntactic function. Through the re-marking of its se- mantic void, it in fact begins to signify.[20] Its semantic void *sig- nifies*, but it signifies spacing and articulation; it has as its mean- ing the possibility of syntax; it orders the play of meaning. *Neither purely syntactic nor purely semantic*, it marks the articulated opening of that opposition.

The whole of this dehiscence, finally, is repeated and partially opened up in a certain *"lit"* ["bed," "reads"], which *Mimique* has painstakingly set up. Toward the end of the text, the syntagm *"le lit"* reproduces the strategem of the hymen.

Before we come to that, I would like to recall the fact that in this *Mimique*, which is cannily interposed between two silences that are breached or broached thereby *("Silence, sole luxury after rimes . . . there reigns a silence still, the condition and delight of reading.")*, as a "gambol" or "debate" of "language," it has never been a question of anything other than reading and writing. This text could be read as a sort of handbook of literature. Not only because the metaphor of writing comes up so often *("a phantom . . . white as a yet unwritten page")*—which is also the case in the *Philebus*—but because the necessity of that metaphor, which *nothing* escapes, makes it something other than a particular fig- ure among others. What is produced is an absolute extension of the concepts of writing and reading, of text, of hymen, to the point where nothing of what *is* can lie beyond them. *Mimique* describes a scene of writing within a scene of writing and so on without end, through a structural necessity that is marked in the text. The mime, as "corporeal writing" *(Ballets)*, mimes a kind of writing (hymen) and is himself written in a kind of writing. Everything is reflected in the medium or speculum of reading-writing, *"without breaking the mirror."* There is writing without a book, in which, each time, at every moment, the marking tip proceeds without a past upon the virgin sheet; but there is also, *simultaneously*, an infinite number of booklets enclosing and fitting inside other booklets, which are only able to issue forth by grafting, sampling, quotations, epigraphs, references, etc. Literature voids itself in its limitlessness. If this handbook of literature meant to *say* something, which we now have some reason to doubt, it would proclaim first of all that there is no—or hardly any, ever so little—literature; that in any event there is no essence of literature, no truth of literature, no literary-being or being-literary of literature. And that the fascination exerted by the *is*, or the *what is* in the question *what is literature?* is worth what the hymen is worth—that is, not exactly nothing—when for example it causes one to die laughing. All this, of course, should not prevent us—on the contrary—from attempting to find out what has been represented and determined under that name—"literature"—and why.

Mallarmé *reads*. He writes while reading; while reading the text written by the Mime, who himself reads in order to write. He reads, for example, the *Pierrot posthume* so as to write with his gestures a mimic that owes that book nothing, since he reads the mimic he thus creates in order to write after the fact the booklet that Mallarmé is reading.

But does the Mime read his role in order to write his mimic or his booklet? Is the initiative of reading his? Is he the acting subject who knows how to read what he has to write? One could indeed believe that although he is passive in reading, he at least has the active freedom to choose to begin to read, and that the same is true of Mallarmé; or even that you, dear everyreader, retain the initiative of reading all these texts, including Mallarmé's, and hence, to that extent, in that place, you are indeed attending it, deciding on it, mastering it.

Nothing could be less certain. The syntax of *Mimique* imprints a movement of (non-Platonic) simulacrum in which the function of *"le lit"* ["the bed," "reads it," "reads him"] complicates itself to the point of admitting a multitude of subjects among whom you yourself are not necessarily included. Plato's clinical paradigm is no longer operative.

The question of the test is—(for whom are) / (for whoever reads) these sheets.[21]

Among diverse possibilities, let us take this: the Mime does not read his role; he is also read *by* it. Or at least he is both read and reading, written and writing, between the two, in the suspense of the hymen, at once screen and mirror. As soon as a mirror is interposed in some way, the simple opposition between activity and passivity, between production and the product, or between all concepts in *-er* and all concepts in *-ed* (signifier–signified, imitator–imitated, structure–structured, etc.), becomes impracticable and too formally weak to encompass the graphics of the hymen, its spider web, and the play of its eyelids.

This impossibility of identifying the path *proper* to the letter of a text, of assigning a unique place to the subject, of locating a simple origin, is here consigned, plotted by the machinations of the one who calls himself "profoundly and scrupulously a syntaxer." In the sentence that follows, the syntax—and the carefully calculated punctuation—prevent us from ever deciding whether the subject of "reads" is the role *("less than a thousand lines, the role, the one that reads . . .")* or some anonymous reader *("the role, the one that reads, will instantly comprehend the rules as if placed before the stageboards . . .")* Who is "the one?" *"The one"* [*"qui"*] may of course be the indefinite pronoun meaning "whoever," here in its function as a subject. This is the easiest reading; the role—whoever reads it will instantly understand its rules. Empirical statistics would show that the so-called "linguistic sense" would most often give this reading.

But nothing in the grammatical code would render the sentence incorrect if, without changing a thing, one were to read "the one" (subject of "reads") as a pronoun the antecedent of which was *"role."* Out of this reading would spring a series of syntactic and semantic transformations in the function of the words "role," *"le* [it or him]," "placed," and in the meaning of the word "comprehend." Thus: *"Less than a thousand lines, the role* (subject, not object), *the one* (referring back to "role") *that reads* [the one that reads *"him,"* not *"it"*] (referring to the Mime, the subject of the preceding sentence), *will instantly comprehend* (embrace, contain, rule, organize: read) *the rules as if placed before the stageboards* (the role is placed facing the stage, either as the author-composer, or as the spectator-reader, in the position of the "whoever" in the first hypothesis), *their humble depository."*

This reading is possible. It is "normal" both from the syntactic and from the semantic points, of views. But what a laborious artifice! Do you really believe, goes the objection, that Mallarmé consciously parceled out his sentence so that it could be read two different ways, with each object capable of changing into a subject and vice versa, without our being able to arrest this movement? Without our being able, faced with this *"alternative sail,"* to decide whether the text is *"listing to one side or the other" (A Throw of Dice).*[22] The two poles of the reading are not equally obvious: but the syntax at any rate has produced an effect of indefinite fluctuation between two possibilities.

Whatever might have been going on in Mallarmé's head, in his consciousness or in his unconscious, does not matter to us here; the reader should now know why. That, in any event, does not hold the least interest for a reading of the text. Everything in the text is interwoven, as we have seen, so as to do without references, so as to cut them short. Nevertheless, for those who are interested in Stéphane Mallarmé and would like to know what he was thinking and meant to do by writing in this way, we shall merely ask the following question. But we are asking it on the basis of texts, and published texts at that: how is one to explain the fact that the syntactic alternative frees itself only in the third version of the text? How is one to explain the fact that, some words being moved, others left out, a tense transformed, a comma added, then and only then does the one-way reading, the only reading possible in the first two versions, come to shift, to waver, henceforth without rest? and without identifiable reference? Why is it that, when one has written, without any possible ambiguity, this: "This marvelous bit of nothing, less than a thousand lines, whoever will read it as I have just done, will comprehend the eternal rules, just as though facing the stageboards, their humble depository" (1886),

and then this: "This role, less than a thousand lines, whoever reads it will comprehend the rules as if placed before the stageboards, their humble depository" (1891),

one should finally write this, with all possible ambiguity: *"Less than a thousand lines, the role, the one that reads, will instantly comprehend the rules as if placed before the stageboards, their humble depository"* (1897)?

Perhaps he didn't know what he was doing? Perhaps he wasn't conscious of it? Perhaps, then, he wasn't completely the author of what was being written? The burst of laughter that echoes deep inside the antre, in *Mimique,* is a reply to all these questions. They can only have been formulated through recourse to certain oppositions, by presupposing possibilities of decision whose pertinence was rigorously swept away by the very text they were supposed to question. Swept away by that hymen, the text always calculates and suspends some supplementary *"surprise"* and *"delight." "Surprise, accompanying the artiface of a notation of sentiments by unproffered sentences—that, in the sole case, perhaps, with authenticity, between the sheets and the eye there reigns a silence still, the condition and delight of reading."* Supplement, principle, and bounty. The baffling economy of seduction.

enter . . . between . . . a silence

> *"Each session or play being a game, a fragmentary show, but sufficient at that unto itself . . ."*
> [Le "Livre," 93 (A)]

[. . . .]

—*Translated by Barbara Johnson*

NOTES

1. *Mimique:* "1. Adj. (a) Mimic. *Langage mimique.,* (i) sign language; (ii) dumb show. (b) Z[oology]: Mimetic. 2. Subst. fem. (a) Mimic art; mimicry.

(b) F[amiliar]: Dumb show." (Mansion's Shorter French and English Dictionary.)—TRANS.

2. *Philebus*, trans. R. Hackforth, in *The Collected Dialogues of Plato*, Edith Hamilton and Huntington Cairns, eds., Bollingen Series LXXI (Princeton, N.J.: Princeton University Press, 1961), pp. 1118–19.—TRANS.

3. Nothing in the above-mentioned logical program was to change when, following Aristotle, and particularly during the "age of classicism," the models for imitation were to be found not simply in nature but in the works and writers of Antiquity that had known how to imitate nature. One could find a thousand examples up to the Romantics (including the Romantics and often those well after them). Diderot, who nevertheless so powerfully solicited the mimetological "machine," especially in *Le Paradoxe sur le Comédien*, confirms upon the analysis of what he calls the "ideal imagined model" (supposedly non-Platonic) that all manner of reversals are included in the program. And, as for the logic of the future perfect: "Antoine Coypel was certainly a man of wit when he recommended to his fellow artists: 'Let us paint, if we can, in such a way that the figures in our paintings will be the living models of the ancient statues rather than that those statues be the originals of the figures we paint.' The same advice could be given to literati" ("Pensées détachées sur la peinture," in *Oeuvres esthétiques*, ed. Paul Vernière (Paris: Garnier, 1965) p. 816).

4. See above, **"Plato's Pharmacy"**—ED.

5. Cf. Heidegger, "Moira," in *Early Greek Thinking*, trans. D. F. Krell and F. A. Capuzzi (New York: Harper & Row, 1975).

6. The simple erasing of the metaphysical concept of last instance would run the risk of defusing the necessary critique it permits in certain determinate contexts. To take this double inscription of concepts into account is to practice a *double science*, a bifid, *dissymmetrical* writing. The "general economy" of which, defined elsewhere, does indeed constitute, in a displaced sense of the words, the last instance.

7. Beyond all being, the realm of the good in Plato.—ED.

8. The context of this quotation should here be restituted and related back to what was said, at the start of this session, concerning the book, the extra-text [*hors-livre*], the image, and the illustration; then it should be related forward to what will be set in motion, in the following session, between the book and the movement of the stage. Mallarmé is responding to a survey: "I am for—no illustration; everything a book evokes should happen in the reader's mind: but, if you replace photography, why not go straight to cinematography, whose successive unrolling will replace, in both pictures and text, many a volume, advantageously" (*Oeuvres complètes* [Paris: Pléiade, 1945], p. 878).

9. The word *Hymen*, sometimes allegorized by a capital H, is of course part of the vocabulary of "Pierrots" ("Harlequin and Polichinelle both aspire to a glorious hymen with Colombine"—Gautier), just as it is included in the "symbolist" code. It nevertheless remains—and is significant—that Mallarmé with his syntactic play remarks the undecidable ambivalence. The

"event" (the historical event, if you wish) has the form of a repetition, the mark—readable because doubled—of a quasi-tearing, a *dehiscence.* "DEHISCENCE: s.f. Botanical term. The action through which the distinct parts of a closed organ open up, without tearing, along a seam. A regular predetermined splitting that, at a certain moment in the cycle, is undergone by the closed organs so that what they contain can come out . . . E. Lat. *Dehiscere,* to open slightly, from *de* and *hiscere,* the frequentative of *hiare* (see *hiatus*)." Littré.

10. "I prefer, as being more to my taste, upon a white page, a carefully spaced pattern of commas and periods and their secondary combinations, imitating, naked, the melody—over the text, advantageously suggested if, even though sublime, it were not punctuated" (p. 407).

11. In French, *mine de rien* means, in its colloquial sense, "as though it were of no importance," but literally it can mean "a mine full of nothing." —TRANS.

12. Cf. Jacques Scherer, *l'Expression littéraire dans l'oeuvre de Mallarmé,* (Paris: Droz, 1947), pp. 142 ff.

13. As for the hymen between Hegel and Mallarmé, one can analyze, for example, in the *Phenomenology of Spirit,* a certain curtain-raising observed from the singular standpoint of the *we,* the philosophic consciousness, the subject of absolute knowing: "The two extremes . . . , the one, of the pure inner world, the other, that of the inner being gazing into this pure inner world, have now coincided, and just as they, *qua* extremes, have vanished, so too the middle term, as something other than these extremes, has also vanished. This curtain [*Vorhang*] hanging before the inner world is therefore drawn away, and we have the inner being . . . gazing into the inner world— the vision of the undifferentiated selfsame being, which repels itself from itself, posits itself as an inner being containing different moments, but for which equally these moments are immediately *not* different—*self-consciousness.* It is manifest that behind the so-called curtain which is supposed to conceal the inner world, there is nothing to be seen unless *we* go behind it ourselves, as much in order that we may see, as that there may be something behind there which can be seen. But at the same time it is evident that we cannot without more ado go straightway behind appearance" [trans. Miller, p. 103]. I would like to thank A. Boutruche for recalling this text to my attention.

14. We are referring less to the text in which Freud is directly inspired by Abel (1910) than to *Das Unheimliche* (1919), of which we are here, in sum, proposing a rereading. We find ourselves constantly being brought back to that text by the paradoxes of the double and of repetition, the blurring of the boundary lines between "imagination" and "reality," between the "symbol" and the "thing it symbolizes" ("The Uncanny," trans. Alix Strachey, in *On Creativity and the Unconscious* [New York: Harper & Row, 1958], p. 152), the references to Hoffman and the literature of the fantastic, the considerations on the *double meaning* of words: "Thus *heimlich* is a word the meaning of which develops towards an ambivalence, until it finally coincides with

its opposite, *unheimlich*. *Unheimlich* is in some way or other a sub-species of *heimlich*" (p. 131) (to be continued).

15. All of these words have contradictory meanings which Hegel exploited, leading him to remark that the German language was naturally dialectical. — ED.

16. "The mixed tropes called *Syllepses* consist of taking one and the same word in two different senses, one of which is, or is supposed to be, the original, or at least the *literal*, meaning; the other, the *figurative*, or supposedly figurative, even if it is not so in reality. This can be done by *metonymy*, *synecdoche*, or *metaphor*" (P. Fontanier, *Les Figures du discours*, introduction by G. Genette, [Paris: Flammarion 1968,] p. 105.) [This figure is more commonly called a *zeugma* in English. — TRANS.]

17. Hegelian terms: *Erinnerung*, interiorizing memory (see below, "**Psyche**," p. **203**); *Aufhebung*, canceling/preserving movement of sublation (see above, "**Différance**," note **12**). — ED.

18. "And again, do the many double things appear any the less halves than doubles? — None the less. — And likewise of the great and the small things, the light and the heavy things — will they admit these predicates any more than their opposites? — No, he said, each of them will always hold of, partake of, both. — Then each *is* each of these multiples rather than it *is not* that which one affirms it to be? — They are like those jesters who palter with us in a double sense at banquets, he replied, and resemble the children's riddle about the eunuch and his hitting of the bat — with what they signify that he struck it.* For these things too equivocate, and it is impossible to conceive firmly any one of them to be or not to be both or neither. . . . But we agreed in advance that if anything of that sort should be discovered, it must be denominated opinable, not knowable, the wanderer between being caught by the faculty that is betwixt and between" (the *Republic* V, 479 *b*, *c*, *d*, trans. Paul Shorley, [Princeton: Princeton University Press, 1961], p. 719. [*Francis M. Cornford, in his edition of the *Republic* (New York: Oxford University Press, 1945), glosses the riddle as follows (p. 188): "A man who was not a man (eunuch), seeing and not seeing (seeing imperfectly) a bird that was not a bird (bat) perched on a bough that was not a bough (a reed), pelted and did not pelt it (aimed at it and missed) with a stone that was not a stone (pumice-stone)." — TRANS.]

19. The chapter of *La Terre et les rêveries du repos* [*Earth and Dreams of Rest*] which deals with *caves* does not, however, mention Mallarmé's in its rich survey of various "caves in literature." If this fact is not simply insignificant, the reason for it may perhaps appear later in the course of our discussion of Mallarmé's "imaginary." [The reference is to Gaston Bachelard. — ED.]

20. From that point on, the syncategorem "between" contains as its meaning a semantic quasi-emptiness; it signifies the spacing relation, the articulation, the interval, etc. It can be nominalized, turn into a quasi-categorem, receive a definite article, or even be made plural. We have spoken of "betweens," and this plural is in some sense primary. *One* "between"

does not exist. In Hebrew, *entre* can be made plural: "In truth this plural expresses not the relation between one individual thing and another, but rather the intervals between things *(loca aliis intermedia)*—in this connection see chapter 10, verse 2, of Ezechiel—or else, as I said before, this plural represents preposition or relation abstractly conceived." (Spinoza, *Abrégé de grammaire hébraique* [Paris: Vrin, 1968], p. 108.)

21. *La question du texte est—pour qui le lit,* literally, can mean both "The question of the text is for the one who reads it (or him)" and "The question of the text is: whom is the bed for?"—TRANS.

22. The reference is to Mallarmé's famous poem. "Jamais un coup de dés n'abolira le hasard."—ED.

EIGHT

From "Psyche: Inventions of the Other"

("Psyché: Invention de l'autre" in *Psyché:*

Inventions de l'autre [1987])

In this title essay from a recent collection, Derrida returns to the work of the French poet Francis Ponge to which he had earlier consecrated a long text, *Signsponge*, first published in 1976. The detailed reading of an eight-line poem titled "Fable" is accompanied by a reflection on the rhetorical theory of Paul de Man, in particular on the latter's analyses of irony and allegory. These reflections are expanded in the book *Mémoires: For Paul de Man* [1986] that Derrida wrote, as he did this essay, soon after his friend's death in 1983. "Psyche" as well is strongly marked as a text of mourning and remembering. It thus joins up with one of Derrida's most constant preoccupations and the one most central to the major work **Glas.**

As he had done in **"Signature Event Context,"** Derrida employs here the theory of speech acts, in particular the category of the performative, to approach the notion of the literary event. The essay from which these pages are extracted is in fact a long meditation on the conditions of the event of *invention.* It analyzes the essence of invention, the history of its concept, and the principles of its legitimation. Derrida himself describes the essay as posing the following questions: "Why is it that *invention* cannot be reduced to the discovery, the revelation, or the unveiling of truth? No more than it can be reduced to the creation, the imagination, or the production of the thing? And is the invention *of the other* the absolute initiative for which the other is responsible and which thus comes back to him or her? Or is it what I imagine of the other who is still held in my *psyche,* my soul or the self of a mirror?"[1] Derrida's questions take into account the fact that *psyche* is from the Greek word for soul, but also that a *psyché* in French is an old-fashioned kind of mirror set on a pivot. It is these questions of self and other that are reflected or refracted in the mirror of Ponge's "Fable," which is itself written on the mirror, the tain of its own language.

[. . . .]

Fables: Beyond the Speech Act

Without yet having cited it, I have been describing for a while now, with one finger pointed toward the margin of my discourse, a text by Francis Ponge. This text is quite short: six lines in *italics*, seven counting the title line—I shall come back in a moment to this figure 7—plus a two-line parenthesis in *roman* type. The roman and italic characters, although their positions are reversed from one edition to the next, may serve to highlight the Latin linguistic heritage that I have mentioned and that Ponge has never ceased to invoke.

To what genre does this text belong? Perhaps we are dealing with one of those pieces Bach called his inventions, contrapuntal pieces in two or three voices that are developed on the basis of a brief initial cell whose rhythm and melodic contour are very clear and sometimes lend themselves to an essentially didactic writing.[2] Ponge's text arranges one such initial cell, which is the following syntagm: *"Par le mot par . . . ,"* i.e., *"By the word by."* I shall designate this invention not by its genre but by its title, namely, by its proper name, *Fable*.

This text is called *Fable*.[3] This proper name embraces, so to speak, the name of a genre. A title, always unique, like a signature, is confused here with a genre name; an apt comparison would be a novel entitled *Novel*, or an invention called "Invention." And we can bet that this fable entitled *Fable*, and constructed like a fable right through to its concluding "lesson" *(moralité)*, will treat the subject of the fable. The fable, the essence of the fabulous about which it will claim to be stating the truth, will also be its general subject. *Topos:* fable.

So I am reading *Fable,* the fable *Fable.*

Fable	*Fable*
Par le mot par commence donc ce texte	*/By the word by commences then this text*
Dont la première ligne dit la vé-rité,	*/Of which the first line states the truth*
Mais ce tain sous l'une et l'autre	*/But this silvering under the one and other*
Peut-il être toléré!	*/Can it be tolerated!*
Cher lecteur déjà tu juges	*/Dear reader already you judge*
Là de nos difficultés . . .	*/There as to our difficulties . . .*
(APRÈS sept ans de malheurs	/(AFTER seven years of misfor-tune
Elle brisa son miroir.)	/She broke her mirror.)

Why did I wish to dedicate the reading of this fable to the memory of Paul de Man? First of all because it deals with a text by Francis Ponge. I am thus recalling a beginning. The first seminar that I gave at Yale, at the invitation of Paul de Man who introduced me there, was on Francis Ponge. *La Chose* was the title of this ongoing seminar; it continued for three years, touching upon a number of related subjects: the debt, the signature, the countersignature, the proper name, and death. To remember this starting point is, for me, to mime a starting over; I take consolation in calling that beginning back to life through the grace of a fable that is also a myth of impossible origins. In addition, I wish to dedicate this reading to Paul de Man because of the resemblance Ponge's fable, bespeaking a unique intersection of irony and allegory, bears to a poem of truth. It presents itself ironically as an allegory "of which the first line states the truth": truth of allegory and allegory of truth, truth as allegory. Both are fabulous inventions, by which we mean inventions of language (at the root of fable and fabulous is *fari* or *phanai:* to speak) as the invention of language as the same and the other, of oneself as (of) the other.

The allegorical is marked here both in the fable's theme and in its structure. *Fable* tells of allegory, of one word's move to cross over to the other, to the other side of the mirror. Of the desperate effort of an unhappy speech to move beyond the specularity that it constitutes itself. We might say in another code that *Fable* puts *into action* the question of reference, of the specularity of language *or* of literature, and of the possibility of stating the other or speaking *to* the other. We shall see how it does so; but already we know the issue is unmistakably that of death, of this moment of mourning when the breaking of the mirror is the most necessary and also the most difficult. The most difficult because everything we say or do or cry, however outstretched toward the other we may be, remains *within us*. A part of us is wounded and it is with ourselves that we are conversing in the travail of mourning and of *Erinnerung*.[4] Even if this metonymy of the other in ourselves already constituted the truth and the possibility of our relation to the living other, death brings it out into more abundant light. So we see why the breaking of the mirror is still more necessary, because at the instant of death, the limit of narcissistic reappropriation becomes terribly sharp, it increases and neutralizes suffering: let us weep no longer over ourselves alas when we *must* no longer be concerned with the other *in ourselves*, we *can* no longer be concerned with anyone except the other *in ourselves*. The narcissistic wound enlarges infinitely for want of being able to be narcissistic any longer, for no longer even finding appeasement in that *Erinnerung* we call the work of mourning. Beyond internalizing memory, it is then necessary to *think*, which is another way of remembering. Beyond *Erinnerung*, it is then a question of *Gedächtnis*, to use a Hegelian distinction that Paul de Man was wont to recall in his recent work for the purpose of presenting Hegelian philosophy as an allegory of a certain number of dissociations, for example, between philosophy and history, between literary experience and literary theory.[5]

Allegory, before it is a theme, before it relates to us the other, the discourse of the other or toward the other, is here, in *Fable*, the structure of an event. This stems first of all from its narrative form.[6] The "moral" or "lesson" of the fable, as one says, resembles the ending of a story. In the first line the *donc* appears merely as the conclusive seal of a beginning, as a logical and temporal scansion that sets up a singular consequentiality; the word *APRÈS* ("AFTER") in capital letters brings it into sequential order. The parenthesis that comes *after* marks the end of the story, but in a while we shall observe the inversion of these times.

This fable, this allegory of allegory, presents itself then as an invention. First of all because this fable is called *Fable*. Before venturing any other semantic analysis, let me state a hypothesis here—leaving its justification for later. Within an area of discourse that has been fairly well stabilized since the end of the seventeenth century in Europe, there are only two major types of *authorized* examples for invention. On the one hand, people invent *stories* (fictional or fabulous), and on the other hand they invent *machines*, technical devices or mechanisms, in the broadest sense of the word. Someone may invent by fabulation, by producing narratives to which there is no corresponding reality outside the narrative (an alibi, for example), or else one may invent by producing a new operational possibility (such as printing or nuclear weaponry, and I am purposely associating these two examples, since the politics of invention is always at one and the same time a politics of culture and a politics of war). Invention as *production* in both cases—and for the moment I leave to the term "production" a certain indeterminacy. *Fabula* or *fictio* on the one hand, and on the other *tekhnē, epistēmē, istoria, methodos*, i.e., art or know-how, knowledge and research, information, procedure, etc. There, I would say for the moment in a somewhat elliptical and dogmatic fashion, are the only two possible, and rigorously specific, registers of all invention today. I am indeed saying "today," stressing the relative modernity of this semantic categorization. Whatever else may resemble invention will not be recognized as such. Our aim here is to grasp the unity or invisible harmony of these two registers.

Fable, Francis Ponge's fable, is inventing itself as fable. It tells an apparently fictional story, which seems to last seven years, as the eighth line notes. But first *Fable* is the tale of an invention, it recites and describes itself, it presents itself from the start as a beginning, the inauguration of a discourse or of a textual mechanism. It does what it says, not being content with announcing, as did Valéry, I believe, "In the beginning was the fable." This latter phrase, miming but also translating the first words of John's gospel ("In the beginning was the *logos*," the word) is perhaps also a performative demonstration of the very thing it is saying. And "fable," like *logos*, does indeed say the saying, speak of speech. But Ponge's *Fable*, while locating itself ironically in this evangelical tradition, reveals and perverts, or rather brings to light by means of a slight perturbation, the strange structure of the foreword *(envoi)* or of the evangelical message, in any case of that incipit which says that in the incipit, at the inception, there is the *logos*, the word. *Fable*, owing to a turn of syntax, is a sort of poetic performative that simultaneously describes and carries out, on the same line, its own generation. Not all performatives are somehow reflexive, certainly; they do not all describe themselves, they do not designate themselves as performatives while they take place. This one does so, but its constative description is nothing other than the performative itself. *"Par le mot par commence donc ce texte."* Its beginning, its invention or its first coming does not come about before the sentence that recounts precisely this event. The narrative is nothing other than the coming of what it cites, recites, points out, or describes. It is hard to distinguish the telling and the told faces of this sentence that invents itself while inventing the tale of its invention; in truth, telling and told are undecidable here. The tale is given to be read; it is a legend since what the tale narrates does not occur before it or outside of it, of this tale producing the event it narrates; but it is a legendary fable or a fiction in a single line of verse with two versions or two versings of the same. Invention of the other in the same—in verse, the same from all sides of a mirror whose silvering could (should) not be tolerated. By its very typography, the second occurrence of the word *par* reminds us that the first *par*—the absolute incipit of the fable—is being quoted. The quote institutes a repetition or an originary reflexivity that, even as it divides the inaugural act, at once the inventive event and the relation or archive of an invention, also allows it to unfold in order to say nothing but the same, itself, the dehiscent and refolded invention of the same, at the very instant when it takes place. And already heralded here, expectantly, is the desire for the other—and to break a mirror. But the first *par*, quoted by the second, actually belongs to the same sentence as the latter one, i.e., to the sentence that points out the operation or event, which nonetheless takes place only through the descriptive quotation and neither before it nor anywhere else. Borrowing terms employed by some proponents of speech act theory, we could say that the first *par* is used, the second quoted or mentioned. This distinction seems pertinent when it is applied to the word *par*. Is it still pertinent on the scale of the sentence as a whole? The *used par* belongs to the mentioning sentence, but also the mentioned sentence; it is a moment of quotation, and it is as such that it is used. What the sentence cites integrally, from *par* to *par*, is nothing other than itself in the process of citing, and the use values within it are only subsets of the mentioned values. The inventive event is the quotation and the narrative. In the body of a single line, on the same divided line, the event of an utterance mixes up two absolutely heterogeneous functions, "use" and "mention," but also heteroreference and self-reference, allegory and tautegory. Is that not precisely the inventive force, the masterstroke of this fable? But this *vis inventiva*, this inventive power, is inseparable from a certain syntactic play with the places in language, it is also an art of *disposition*.

If *Fable* is both performative and constative from its very first line, this effect extends across the whole of the text. By a process of poetic generation we shall have to verify, the concept of invention distributes its two essential values between these two poles: the constative—discovering or unveiling, pointing out or saying what is—and the performative—producing, instituting, transforming. But the sticking point here has to do with the figure of coimplication, with the configuration, of these two values. In this regard *Fable* is exemplary from its very first line. That line's inventiveness results from the single act of enunciation that performs and describes, operates and states. Here the conjunction "and" does not link two different activities. The constative statement is the performative itself since it points out nothing that is prior or foreign to itself. Its performance consists in the "constatation" of the constative—and nothing else. A quite unique relation to itself, a reflection that produces the self of self-reflection by producing the event in the very act of recounting it. An infinitely rapid circulation—such are the *irony* and the temporality of this text—*all at once* shunts the performative into the constative, and vice versa. De Man has written of undecidability as an infinite and thus untenable acceleration. It is significant for our reading of *Fable* that he says this about the impossible distinction between fiction and autobiography:[7] the play of our fable also lies between fiction and the implicit intervention of a certain *I* that I shall bring up shortly. As for irony, Paul de Man always describes its particular temporality as a structure of the instant, of what becomes "shorter and shorter and always climaxes in the single brief moment of a final *pointe.*" "Irony is a synchronic structure,"[8] but we shall soon see how it can be merely the other face of an allegory that always seems to be unfolded in the diachronic dimension of narrative. And there again *Fable* would be exemplary. Its first line speaks only of itself, it is immediately metalingual, but its metalanguage has nothing to set it off; it is an inevitable and impossible metalanguage since *there is no language before it,* since it has no prior object beneath or outside itself. So that in this first line, which states the truth of (the) *Fable,* everything is put simultaneously in a first language and in a second metalanguage—and nothing is. There is no metalanguage, the first line repeats; there is only that, says the echo, or Narcissus. The property of language whereby it always can and cannot speak of itself is thus graphically enacted, in accord with a paradigm account de Man elaborated. Here I refer you to a passage from *Allegories of Reading* where de Man returns to the question of metaphor and the role of Narcissus in Rousseau. I shall simply extract a few propositions that will allow you to recall the thrust of his full demonstration: "To the extent that all language is conceptual, it already speaks about language and not about things. . . . All language is language about denomination, that is, a conceptual, figural, metaphorical language. . . . If all language is about language, then the paradigmatic linguistic model is that of an entity that confronts itself."[9]

The infinitely rapid oscillation between the performative and the constative, between language and metalanguage, fiction and nonfiction, autoreference and heteroreference, etc., does not just produce an essential instability. This instability constitutes that very event—let us say, the work—whose invention disturbs normally, as it were, the norms, the statutes, and the rules. It calls for a new theory and for the constitution of new statutes and conventions that, capable of recording the possibility of such events, would be able to account for them. I am not sure that speech act theory, in its present state and dominant form, is capable of this, nor, for that matter, do I think the need could be met by literary theories either of a formalist variety or of a hermeneutic inspiration (i.e., semanticist, thematicist, intentionalist, etc.).

The fabulatory economy of a very simple little sentence, perfectly normal in its grammar, spontaneously *deconstructs* the oppositional logic that relies on an untouchable distinction between the performative and the constative and so many other related distinctions; it deconstructs that logic without disabling it totally, to be sure, since it also needs it in order to detonate the speech event. Now in this case does the deconstructive effect depend on the force of a literary event? What is there of literature, and what of philosophy, here, in this fabulous staging of deconstruction? I shall not attack this enormous problem head on. I shall merely venture a few remarks that have some bearing upon it.

1. Suppose we knew what literature is, and that in accord with prevailing conventions we classified *Fable* as literature: we still could not be sure that it is integrally literary (it is hardly certain, for example, that this poem, as soon as it speaks of the truth and expressly claims to state it, is nonphilosophical). Nor could we be sure that its deconstructive structure cannot be found in other texts that we would not dream of considering as literary. I am convinced that the same structure, however paradoxical it may seem, also turns up in scientific and especially in judicial utterances, and indeed can be found in the most foundational or institutive of these utterances, thus in the most inventive ones.

2. On this subject I shall quote and comment briefly on another text by de Man that meets up in a very dense fashion with all the motifs that concern us at this point: performative and constative, literature and philosophy, possibility or impossibility of deconstruction. This is the conclusion of the essay "Rhetoric of Persuasion" (Nietzsche) in *Allegories of Reading*.

> If the critique of metaphysics is structured as an aporia between performative and constative language, this is the

same as saying that it is structured as rhetoric. And since, if one wants to conserve the term "literature," one should hesitate to assimilate it with rhetoric, then it would follow that the deconstruction of metaphysics, or "philosophy," is an impossibility to the precise extent that it is "literary." This by no means resolves the problem of the relationship between literature and philosophy in Nietzsche, but it at least establishes a somewhat more reliable point of "reference" from which to ask the question.

This paragraph shelters too many nuances, shadings, and reserves for us to be able, in the short time we have here, to lay open all the issues it raises. I hope to deal with it more patiently some other time.[10] For now I shall make do with a somewhat elliptical gloss. In the suggestion that a deconstruction of metaphysics is impossible "to the precise extent that it is 'literary,' " I suspect there may be more irony than first appears. At least for this reason, among others, the most rigorous deconstruction has never claimed to be foreign to literature, nor above all to be *possible.* And I would say that deconstruction loses nothing from admitting that it is impossible; also that those who would rush to delight in that admission lose nothing from having to wait. For a deconstructive operation *possibility* would rather be the danger, the danger of becoming an available set of rule-governed procedures, methods, accessible approaches. The interest of deconstruction, of such force and desire as it may have, is a certain experience of the impossible: that is, as I shall insist in my conclusion, of the other—the experience of the other as the invention of the impossible, in other words, as the only possible invention. Where, in relation to this, might we place that unplaceable we call "literature"? That, too, is a question I shall leave aside for the moment.

Fable gives itself then, by itself, by herself, a patent of invention. And its double strike is its invention. This singular duplication, from *par* to *par*, is destined for an infinite speculation, and the specularization first seems to seize or freeze the text. It paralyzes it, or makes it spin in place at an imperceptible or infinite speed. It captivates it in a mirror of misfortune. The breaking of a mirror, according to the superstitious saying, announces seven years of misfortune. Here, in typographically different letters and in parentheses, it is *after* seven years of misfortune that she broke the mirror. *APRÈS*—"after"—is in capital letters in the text. This strange inversion, is it also a mirror effect, a sort of reflection of time? But if the initial effect of this fall of *Fable*, which in parentheses assumes the classic role of a sort of "moral" or lesson, retains an element of forceful *reversal*, it is not only because of this paradox, not just because it inverts the meaning or direction of the superstitious proverb. In an *inversion* of the classical fable form, this "moral" is the only element that is explicitly narrative, and thus, let us say, allegorical. A fable of La Fontaine's usually does just the opposite: there is a narrative, then a moral in the form of a maxim or aphorism. But reading the narrative we get here in parentheses and in conclusion, in the place of the "moral," we do not know where to locate the inverted time to which it refers. Is it recounting what would have happened before or what happens after the "first line"? Or again, what happens throughout the whole poem, of which it would be the very temporality. The difference in the grammatical tenses (the simple past of the allegorical "moral" following a continuous present) does not allow us to answer. And there will be no way of knowing whether the "misfortune," the seven years of misfortune that we are tempted to synchronize with the seven preceding lines, are being recounted by the fable or simply get confused with the misfortune of the narrative, this distress of a fabulous discourse able only to reflect itself without ever moving out of itself. In this case, the misfortune would be the mirror itself. Far from being expressible in the breaking of a mirror, it would consist—so as to ground the infinity of reflection—in the very presence and possibility of the mirror, in the specular play for which language provides. And upon playing a bit with these misfortunes of performatives or constatives that are never quite themselves because they are parasites of one another, we might be tempted to say that this misfortune is also the essential "infelicity" of these speech acts.

In any case, through all these inversions and perversions, through this fabulous revolution, we have come to the crossroads of what Paul de Man calls allegory and irony. Although unable to undertake the analytic work here, I shall indicate three moments or motifs to be pursued, for example, in the vitally necessary rereading of "The Rhetoric of Temporality":

1. A "provisional conclusion" (p. 222) links allegory and irony in the discovery—we can say the invention—"of a truly temporal predicament." Here are some lines that seem to have been written for *Fable*:

> The act of irony, as we now understand it, reveals the existence of a temporality that is definitely *not organic*, in that it relates to its source only in terms of distance and difference and allows for *no end, for no* totality [this is indeed the mirror, a technical and nonorganic structure]. Irony divides the flow of temporal experience into a past that is pure mystification and a future that remains harassed forever by a relapse within the inauthentic. It can know this inauthenticity but can never overcome it. It can only restate and repeat it on an increasingly conscious level, but it remains endlessly caught in the impossibility of making this knowledge applicable to the empirical world. It dissolves in the narrowing spiral of a linguistic sign that becomes more and more remote from its meaning, and it can find no escape from this spiral. The temporal void that it reveals is the same void we encountered when we found *allegory always implying an unreachable anteriority. Allegory and irony are linked in their common discovery of a truly temporal predicament."* (118, my emphasis)

Suppose we let the word "predicament" (and the word *is* a predicament) keep all its connotations, including the most adventitious ones. Here the mirror is the *predicament*: a necessary or fateful situation, a quasi-nature; we can give a neutral formulation of its predicate or category, and we can state the menacing danger of such a situation, the technical machinery, the artifice that constitutes it. We are caught in the mirror's trap. Here I am fond of the French word *piège*, meaning trap: it was, a few years ago, a favorite theme in elliptical and lighthearted discussions between Paul de Man and myself.

2. A bit later, Paul de Man presents irony as the inverted specular image of allegory: "The fundamental structure of allegory reappears here [in one of Wordsworth's Lucy Gray poems] in

the tendency of the language towards narrative, the spreading out along the axis of an imaginary time in order to give duration to what is, in fact, simultaneous within the subject. *The structure of irony, however, is the reversed mirror-image of this form"* (225, my emphasis).

3. And finally, a passage bringing these two inverted mirror images together in their sameness: "Irony is a synchronic structure, while allegory appears as a successive mode capable of engendering duration as the illusion of a continuity that it knows to be illusionary. *Yet the two modes, for all their profound distinction in mood and structure, are the two faces of the same fundamental experience of time"* (226, my emphasis).

Fable, then: an allegory stating ironically the truth of allegory that it is in the present, and doing so while stating it through a play of persons and masks. The first four lines are in the third person of the present indicative (the evident mode of the constative, although the "I," about which Austin tells us that it has, in the present, the privilege of the performative, can be implicit there). In these four lines, the first two are indicative, the next two interrogative. Lines five and six could make the implicit intervention of an "I" explicit insofar as they address the reader; they dramatize the scene by means of a detour into apostrophe or parabasis. Paul de Man gives much attention to parabasis, notably as it is evoked by Schlegel in relation to irony. He brings it up again in "The Rhetoric of Temporality" (222) and elsewhere. Now the *tu juges* (you judge, line 6) is also *both* performative and constative; and *nos difficultés* (line 7) are as well the difficulties of the author, those of the implicit "I" of a signatory, those of the fable that presents itself, and those of the community fable-author-readers. For everyone gets tangled up in the same difficulties, all reflect them, and all can judge them.

But who is *elle* (the "she" of the last line)? Who "broke her mirror?" Perhaps *Fable,* the fable itself (feminine in French), which is here, really, the subject. Perhaps the allegory of truth, indeed Truth itself, and it is often, in the realm of allegory, a Woman. But the feminine can also countersign the author's irony. She would speak of the author, she would state or show the author himself in her mirror. One would then say of Ponge what Paul de Man says of Wordsworth. Reflecting upon the "she" of a

Lucy Gray poem ("She seemed a thing that could not feel"), he writes: "Wordsworth is one of the few poets who can write proleptically about their own death and speak, as it were, from beyond their own graves. The 'she' in the poem is in fact large enough to encompass Wordsworth as well" (225).

The she, in this fable, I shall call Psyche. You know that Psyche, who was loved by Cupid, disappears when she sees Eros, the rising sun. You are familiar with the fable of Psyche painted by Raphael and found in the Farnese villa. Of Psyche it is also said that she lost her husband for giving in to her wish to contemplate him when that had been forbidden to her. But in French a psyche, a homonym and common noun, is also a large double mirror installed on a rotating stand. The woman, let us say Psyche, her beauty or her truth, can be reflected there, can admire or adorn herself from head to foot. Psyche is not named by Ponge, who could well have given his fable an ironic dedication to La Fontaine, who is celebrated in French literature both for his fables and his retelling of the Psyche myth. Ponge has often expressed his admiration for La Fontaine: "If I prefer La Fontaine —the slightest fable—to Schopenhauer or Hegel, I do know why." This Ponge writes in *Proêmes* (Part II, "Pages Bis," V, 167).

As for Paul de Man, he does name Psyche, not the mirror, but the mythical character. And he does so in a passage that matters much to us since it also points up the distance between the two "selves," the subject's two selves, the impossibility of seeing oneself and touching oneself at the same time, the "permanent parabasis" and the "allegory of irony":

> This successful combination of allegory and irony also determines the thematic substance of the novel as a whole [La Chartreuse de Parme], the underlying *mythos* of the allegory. This novel tells the story of two lovers who, like Eros and Psyche, are never allowed to come into full contact with each other. When they can touch, it has to be in a darkness imposed by a total arbitrary and irrational decision, an act of the gods. The myth is that of the unovercomable distance which must always prevail between the selves, and it thematizes the ironic distance that Stendhal the writer always believed prevailed between his pseudonymous and

nominal identities. As such, it reaffirms Schlegel's definition of irony as a "permanent parabasis" and singles out
this novel as one of the few novels of novels, as the allegory
of irony.

These are the last words of "The Rhetoric of Temporality" (*BI*,
228).

Thus, in the same strike, but a double strike, a fabulous invention becomes the invention of truth: of its truth as fable, of the
fable of truth, of the truth of truth as fable. And of that which in
the fable depends on language (*fari*, fable). It is the impossible
mourning of truth in and through the word. For you have seen it
well, if the mourning is not announced by the breaking of the
mirror, but consists in the mirror, if it comes with the specularization, well then, the mirror comes to be itself solely through
the intercession of the word. It is an invention and an intervention of the word, and here even of the word meaning "word,"
mot. The word itself is reflected in the word *mot* as it is in the
name "name." The silvering *(tain)*, which excludes transparency
and authorizes the invention of the mirror, is a trace of language
(langue):

> *Par le mot* par *commence donc ce texte*
> *Dont la première ligne dit la vérité,*
> *Mais ce tain sous l'une et l'autre*
> *Peut-il être toléré?*

Between the two *par* the silvering that is deposited between
two lines is the language itself; it depends on the word, and the
word *word*; it is *le mot*, the word; it distributes, separates, on
each side of itself, the two appearances of *par*. It opposes them,
puts them opposite or vis-à-vis each other, links them indissoci-
ably yet also dissociates them forever. This process does an unbearable violence that the law should prohibit (can this silvering
be tolerated under the two lines or between the lines?); it should
prohibit it as a perversion of usage, an overturning of linguistic
convention. Yet it happens that this perversion obeys the law of
language, it is a quite normal proposition, no grammar has anything to object to this rhetoric. We have to get along without that
prohibition, such is both the observation and the command con-

veyed by the *igitur* of this fable—the simultaneously logical, narrative, and fictive *donc* of the first line: *"Par le mot par commence donc ce texte . . ."*

This *igitur* speaks for a psyche, to it (her) and before it (her), about it (her) as well, and psyche would be only the rotating speculum that has come to relate the same to the other. Of this relation of the same to the other, we could say, playfully: It is *only* an invention, a mirage, or an admirable mirror effect, its status remains that of an invention, of a simple invention, by which is meant a technical mechanism. The question remains; Is the psyche an invention?

The analysis of this fable would be endless. I abandon it here. *Fable* in speaking of the fable does not only invent insofar as it tells a story that does not take place, that has no place outside itself and is nothing other than itself in its own inaugural in(ter)vention. This invention is not only that of a poetic fiction, a work whose production becomes the occasion for a signature, for a patent, for the recognition of its status as a literary work by its author and also by its reader. The reader, the other who judges *("Cher lecteur déjà tu juges . . .")*—but who judges from the point of his inscription in the text, from the place that, although first assigned to the addressee, becomes that of a countersigning. *Fable* has this status as an invention only insofar as, from the double position of the author and the reader, of the signatory and the countersignatory, it also puts out a machine, a technical mechanism that one must be able, under certain conditions and limitations, to reproduce, repeat, reuse, transpose, set within a public tradition and heritage. It thus has the value of a procedure, model, or method, furnishing rules for exportation, for manipulation, for variations. Taking into account other linguistic variables, a syntactic invariable can, recurringly, give rise to other poems of the same type. And this *typed* construction, which presupposes a first instrumentalization of the language, is indeed a sort of *tekhnē*. Between art and the fine arts. This hybrid of the performative and the constative that, from the first line (*premier vers* or first line) at once says the truth (*"dont la première ligne dit la vérité,"* according to the description and reminder of the second line), a truth that is nothing other than its own truth producing itself, this is indeed a unique event; but it is also a machine and a general truth. While appealing to a preexistent linguistic background (syntactic rules and the fabulous treasure of language), it furnishes a rule-governed mechanism or regulator capable of generating other poetic utterances of the same type, a sort of printing matrix. So we can propose the following example: *"Avec le mot* avec *s'inaugure donc cette fable,"* i.e., with the word "with" begins then this fable; there would be other regulated variants, at greater or lesser distances from the model, that I do not have the time to note here. Then again, think of the problems of quotability, both inevitable and impossible, that are occasioned by a self-quoting invention. If, for example, I say, as I have done already, "By the word 'by' commences then this text by Ponge entitled *Fable,* for it commences as follows: 'By the word *by'* . . ." and so forth. This is a process without beginning or end that nonetheless is only beginning, but without ever being able to do so since its sentence or its initiatory phase is already secondary, already the sequel of a first one that it describes even before it has properly taken place, in a sort of exergue as impossible as it is necessary. It is always necessary to begin again in order finally to arrive at the beginning and reinvent invention. Let us try, here in the margin of the exergue, to begin.

It was understood that we would address here the status of invention. You are well aware that an element of disequilibrium is at work in that contract of ours, and that there is thus something provocative about it. We have to speak of the status of invention, but it is better to invent something on this subject. However, we are authorized to invent only within the statutory limits assigned by the contract and by the title (status of invention or inventions of the other). An invention refusing to be dictated, ordered, programmed by these conventions would be out of place, out of phase, out of order, impertinent, transgressive. And yet, some eagerly impatient listeners might be tempted to retort that indeed there will be no invention here today unless that break with convention, into impropriety, is made; in other words, that there will be invention only on condition that the invention transgress, in order to be inventive, the status and the programs with which it was supposed to comply.

As you have already suspected, things are not so simple. No matter how little we retain of the semantic load of the word "invention," no matter what indeterminacy we leave to it for the moment, we have at least the feeling that an invention ought not, as such and as it first emerges, have a status. At the moment when it erupts, the inaugural invention ought to overflow, overlook, transgress, negate, (or, at least—this is a supplementary complication—deny) the status that people would have wanted to assign to it or grant it in advance; indeed it ought to overstep the space in which that status itself takes on its meaning and its legitimacy—in short, the whole environment of *reception* that by definition ought never to be ready to welcome an authentic innovation. On this hypothesis (which is not mine, for the time being) it is here that a theory of reception should either encounter its essential limit or else complicate its claims with a theory of transgressive gaps. About the latter we can no longer tell whether it would still be theory and whether it would be a theory of something like reception. Let's stick with this commonsense hypothesis a while longer. It would add that an invention ought to produce a disordering mechanism, that when it makes its appearance it ought to open up a space of unrest or turbulence for every status assignable to it. Is it not then spontaneously destabilizing, even deconstructive? The question would then be the following: what can be the deconstructive effects of an invention? Or, conversely, in what respect can a movement of deconstruction, far from being limited to the negative or destructuring forms that are often naively attributed to it, be inventive in itself, or be the signal of an inventiveness at work in a sociohistorical field? And finally, how can a deconstruction of the very concept of invention, moving through all the complex and organized wealth of its semantic field, still invent? Invent over and beyond the concept and the very language of invention, beyond its rhetoric and its axiomatics?

I am not trying to conflate the problematics of invention with that of deconstruction. Moreover, for fundamental reasons, there could be no *problematics* of deconstruction. My question lies elsewhere: why is the word "invention," that tired, worn-out classical word, today experiencing a revival, a new fashionableness, and a new way of life? A statistical analysis of the occidental *doxa* would, I am sure, bring it to light: in vocabulary, book titles,[11] the rhetoric of advertising, literary criticism, political oratory, and even in the passwords of art, morality, and religion. A strange return of a desire for invention. "One must invent": Not so much create, imagine, produce, institute, but rather invent; and it is precisely in the interval between these meanings (invent, create; invent, imagine; invent, produce; invent, institute; etc.) that the uniqueness of this desire to invent dwells. To invent not this or that, some *tekhnē* or some fable, but to invent the world—a world, not America, the New World, but a novel world, another habitat, another person, another desire even. A closer analysis should show why it is then the word "invention" that imposes itself, more quickly and more often than other neighboring words ("discover," "create," "imagine," "produce," and so on). And why this desire for invention, which goes so far as to dream of inventing a new desire, on the one hand remains contemporary with a certain experience of fatigue, of weariness, of exhaustion, but on the other hand accompanies a desire for deconstruction, going so far as to lift the apparent contradiction that might exist between deconstruction and invention.

Deconstruction is inventive or it is nothing at all; it does not settle for methodical procedures, it opens up a passageway, it marches ahead and marks a trail; its writing is not only performative, it produces rules—other conventions—for new performativities and never installs itself in the theoretical assurance of a simple opposition between performative and constative. Its *process* involves an affirmation, this latter being linked to the coming—the *venire*—in event, advent, invention. But it can only make it by deconstructing a conceptual and institutional structure of invention that would neutralize by putting the stamp of reason on some aspect of invention, of inventive power: as if it were necessary, over and beyond a certain traditional status of invention, to reinvent the future.

[....]

—*Translated by Catherine Porter*

NOTES

1. *Psyché: Inventions de l'autre*, jacket note.
2. We may also recall Clément Jannequin's *Inventions musicales* (circa

1545). Bach's inventions were not merely didactic, even though they were also intended to teach counterpoint technique. They may be (and often are) treated as composition exercises (exposition of the theme in its principal key, reexposition in the dominant, new developments, supplementary or final exposition in the key indicated in the sigature). There are inventions in A major, in F minor, in G minor, and so on. And as soon as one gives the title "inventions" in the plural, as I am doing here, one invites thoughts of technical virtuosity, didactic exercise, instrumental variations. But is one obliged to accept the invitation to think what one is invited to think?

3. In *Proêmes*, part I, "Natare piscem doces" (Paris: Gallimard, 1948), p. 45. The term *proême*, in the didactic sense that is emphasized by the learned *doces*, says something about invention, about the inventive moment of a discourse: beginning, inauguration, incipit, introduction. Cf. the second edition of "Fable," with roman and italic type inverted, in Ponge's *Oeuvres*, vol. 1 (Paris: Gallimard, 1965), p. 114.

Fable finds and states the truth that it finds in finding it, that is, in stating it. Philosopheme, theorem, poem. A very sober *Eureka*, reduced to the greatest possible economy in its operation. In Poe's fictive preface to *Eureka* we read: "I offer this book of truths, not in its character of Truth-Teller, but for the Beauty that abounds in its Truth, constituting it true. To these I present the composition as an Art-Product alone,—let us say as a Romance; or if I be not urging too lofty a claim, as a Poem. *What I here propound is true:*—therefore it cannot die" (*The Works of Edgar Allan Poe*, vol. 9, *Eureka* and *Miscellanies* [Chicago: Stone and Kimball, 1895], p. 4). "Fable" may be called a spongism, for here truth signs its own name, if *Eureka* is a poem.

This is perhaps the place to ask, since we are speaking of *Eureka*, what happens when one translates *eurema* as *inventio*, *euremes* as *inventor*, *eu-riskô* as "I encounter, I find by looking or by chance, upon reflection or by accident, I discover or obtain it"?

4. Remembering; Hegel contrasts *Erinnerung*, interiorizing memory, to *Gedächtnis*, rote, mechanical memory. See *Mémoires* [1986] for a longer discussion of this distinction.—ED.

5. Paul de Man, "Sign and Symbol in Hegel's Aesthetics," *Critical Inquiry*, 8 (1982), pp. 761–75.

6. "Allegory is sequential and narrative" ("Pascal's Allegory of Persuasion," in Stephen Greenblatt, ed., *Allegory and Representation* [Baltimore: The Johns Hopkins University Press, 1981], p. 1). And again: "Allegory appears as a successive mode" ("The Rhetoric of Temporality," in *Blindness and Insight*, 2nd ed. [Minneapolis: University of Minnesota Press, 1983], p. 226).

7. Cf. "Autobiography as De-facement," *MLN*, 94 (1979), p. 921.

8. "The Rhetoric of Temporality," pp. 225–26.

9. *Allegories of Reading: Figural Language in Rousseau, Nietzsche, Rilke, and Proust* (New Haven, Ct.: Yale University Press, 1979), pp. 152–53. A note appended to this sentence begins as follows: "The implication that the

self-reflective moment of the *cogito*, the self-reflection of what Rilke calls 'le narcisse exhaucé,' is not an original event but itself an allegorical (or metaphorical) version of an intralinguistic structure, with all the negative epistemological consequences it entails. . . ." The equation between allegory and metaphor, in this context, poses problems to which I shall attempt to return elsewhere.

10. See *Mémoires* [1986].—ED.

11. In the space of a few weeks I received Gerald Holton's *L'Invention scientifique* (Paris: Presses Universitaires de France, 1982), Judith Schlanger's *L'Invention intellectuelle* (Paris: Fayard, 1983), and Christian Delacampagne's *L'Invention du racisme* (Paris: Fayard, 1983). I am naturally referring to these three books and to many others (such as *L'Invention d'Athènes* by Nicole Loraux and *L'Invention de la démocratie* by Claude Lefort). Delacampagne's book reminds us that there is an invention of evil. Like all inventions, that one has to do with culture, language, institutions, history, and technology. In the case of racism in the strict sense, it is doubtless a very recent invention in spite of its ancient roots. Delacampagne connects the signifier at least to *reason* and *razza*. Racism is also an invention of the other, but in order to exclude it and tighten the circle of the same. A logic of the psyche, the topic of its identifications and projections warrants a lengthy discussion.

NINE

"Che cos'è la poesia?" [1988]

The Italian poetry journal *Poesia* invited Derrida to write something for the rubric with which it opens every issue under the title "Che cos'è la poesia?" (What is poetry? or more literally, What thing is poetry?). Derrida responded with this brief text that was then published beside its Italian translation. We reproduce it here beside our own English translation, thus devising yet another kind of "double band."

As always, Derrida works to abolish the distance between what he is writing *about* (poetry, the poem, the poetic, or as he will finally call it: the poematic) and what his writing is *doing*. Reference without referent, this poem defines or describes only itself even as it points beyond itself to the poetic in general. It is, writes Derrida, a *hérisson*, in Italian *istrice*, a name which loses all its rich resonance as soon as it is translated into English: hedgehog, a European cousin of the porcupine that has similar habits of self-defense. The risk of this loss in crossing over from one language to another, or already in the transfer into any language at all, causes the *hérisson* to roll itself into a ball in the middle of the road and bristle its spines: *hérisser* means to bristle or to spike, and therefore it may be said of a text that it is spiked with difficulties or even traps (e.g., "de nombreux pièges hérissent le texte"). If indeed the poetic bristles with difficulty, this very mechanism of turning in on itself for protection from the rush of traffic is also what exposes it to being rubbed out, obliterated. Thus, the poem's appeal to the heart and to that other mechanism for remembering which is called, in many languages, learning by heart.

To increase the *hérisson*'s chances of getting across the road, we have posted a number of signs here the length of the distance to be traversed. These guideposts, in lieu of notes, are set to one side so they will not get underfoot of the creature's movements.

Che cos'è la poesia?

*Pour répondre à une telle question—en deux
mots, n'est-ce pas?—on te demande de savoir
renoncer au savoir. Et de bien le savoir, sans
jamais l'oublier: démobilise la culture mais
ce que tu sacrifies en route, en traversant la
route, ne l'oublie jamais dans ta docte ignorance.*

*Qui ose me demander cela! Même s'il n'en
paraît rien, car disparaître est sa loi, la réponse* se voit dictée.* *Je suis* une *dictée, pro-
nonce la poésie, apprends-moi par coeur, re-
copie, veille et garde-moi, regarde-moi, dictée,
sous les yeux: bande-son,* wake, *sillage de lu-
mière, photographie de la fête en deuil.*

*Elle se voit dictée, la réponse, d'être poé-
tique. Et pour cela tenue de s'adresser à
quelqu'un, singulièrement à toi mais comme
à l'être perdu dans l'anonymat, entre ville et
nature, un secret partagé, à la fois public et
privé,* absolument *l'un et l'autre, absous de
dehors et de dedans, ni l'un ni l'autre, l'animal jeté sur la route, absolu, solitaire, roulé
en boule* auprès de soi. *Il peut se faire écraser,*
justement, *pour cela même, le hérisson,* istrice.

A common pedagogical
exercise in which stu-
dents write under a teacher's dictation. The femi-
nine noun is formed from
the past participle of the
verb *dicter*.

Che cos'è la poesia?

In order to respond to such a question—*in two words, right?*—you are asked to know how to renounce knowledge. And to know it well, without ever forgetting it: demobilize culture, but never forget in your learned ignorance what you sacrifice on the road, in crossing the road.

Who dares to ask me that? Even though it remains inapparent, since disappearing is its law, the answer *sees itself (as) dictated (dictation).* I am *a* dictation, pronounces poetry, learn me by heart, copy me down, guard and keep me, look out for me, look at me, dictated dictation, right before your eyes: soundtrack, *wake,* trail of light, photograph of the feast in mourning.

It sees itself, the response, dictated to be poetic, by being poetic. And for that reason, it is obliged to address itself to someone, singularly to you but as if to the being lost in anonymity, between city and nature, an imparted secret, at once public and private, *absolutely* one and the other, absolved from within and from without, neither one nor the other, the animal thrown onto the road, absolute, solitary, rolled up in a ball, *next to (it)self.* And for that very reason, it may get itself run over, *just so,* the *hérisson, istrice** in Italian, in English, hedgehog.

Throughout the text, the *str*-sound is stressed. One may hear in it the distress of the beast caught in the strictures of this translation.

Et si tu réponds autrement selon les cas, compte tenu de l'espace et du temps qui te sont donnés *avec cette* demande *(déjà tu parles italien), par elle-même, selon* cette *économie mais aussi dans l'imminence de quelque traversée* hors de chez soi, *risquée vers la langue de l'autre en vue d'une traduction impossible ou* refusée, *nécessaire mais désirée comme une mort, qu'est-ce que tout cela, cela même où tu viens déjà de te délirer, aurait à voir, dès lors, avec la poésie¿ Avec le* poétique, *plutôt, car tu entends parler d'une* expérience, *autre mot pour voyage, ici la randonnée aléatoire d'un trajet, la strophe qui tourne mais jamais ne reconduit au discours, ni chez soi, jamais du moins ne se réduit à la poésie—écrite, parlée, même chantée.*

Voici donc, tout de suite, en deux mots, *pour ne pas oublier.*

1. L'économie de la mémoire: *un poème doit être bref, par vocation elliptique, quelle qu'en soit l'étendue objective ou apparente. Docte inconscient de la* Verdichtung * *et du retrait.*

2. Le coeur. *Non pas le coeur au milieu des phrases qui circulent sans risque sur les échangeurs et s'y laissent traduire en toutes langues. Non pas simplement le coeur des archives cardiographiques, l'objet des savoirs ou des techniques, des philosophies et des discours bio-éthico-juridiques. Peut-être pas le coeur des Ecritures ou de Pascal, ni même, c'est moins sûr, celui que leur préfère Heidegger. Non, une histoire de "coeur" poétiquement enveloppée dans l'idiome "apprendre par*

Condensation in German, to recall, perhaps, Freud's use of the term, but also because of *Dichtung*, poetry.

And if you respond otherwise depending on each case, taking into account the space and time which you are *given* with this *demand* (already you are speaking Italian)*, by the demand itself, according to *this* economy but also in the imminence of some traversal *outside* yourself, away from *home*, venturing toward the language of the other in view of an impossible or denied translation, necessary but desired like a death— what would all of this, the very thing in which you have just begun to turn deliriously, have to do, at that point, with poetry? Or rather, with the *poetic*, since you intend to speak about an *experience*, another word for voyage, here the aleatory rambling of a trek, the strophe* that turns but never leads back to discourse, or back home, at least is never reduced to poetry—written, spoken, even sung.

Here then, right away, *in two words*, so as not to forget:

1. *The economy of memory:* a poem must be brief, elliptical by vocation, whatever may be its objective or apparent expanse. Learned unconscious of *Verdichtung* and of the retreat.

2. *The heart.* Not the heart in the middle of sentences that circulate risk-free through the interchanges and let themselves be translated into any and all languages. Not simply the heart archived by cardiography, the object of sciences or technologies, of philosophies and bio-ethico-juridical discourses. Perhaps not the heart of the Scriptures or of Pascal, nor even, this is less certain, the one that Heidegger prefers to them. No, a story of "heart" poetically enveloped in the idiom *"apprendre par coeur,"* whether

---

Because in Italian, *domanda* means question.

Stanza; from the Greek: turn.

coeur," celui de ma langue ou d'une autre, l'anglaise (to learn by heart), ou d'une autre encore, l'arabe (hafiza a'n zahri kalb)—un seul trajet à plusieurs voies.

Deux en un: le second axiome s'enroule dans le premier. Le poétique, disons-le, serait ce que tu désires apprendre, mais de l'autre, grâce à l'autre et sous dictée, par coeur: imparare a memoria. N'est-ce pas déjà cela, le poéme, lorsqu'un gage est donné, la venue d'un événement, à l'instant où la traversée de la route nommée traduction reste aussi improbable qu'un accident, intensément rêvée pourtant, requise là où ce qu'elle promet toujours laisse à désirer! Une reconnaissance va vers cela même et prévient ici la connaissance: ta bénédiction avant le savoir.

Fable que tu pourrais raconter comme le don du poème,* c'est une histoire emblématique: quelqu'un t'écrit, à toi, de toi, sur toi. Non, une marque à toi adressée, laissée, confiée, s'accompagne d'une injonction, en vérité s'institue en cet ordre même qui à son tour te constitue, assignant ton origine ou te donnant lieu: détruis-moi, ou plutôt rends mon support invisible au dehors, dans le monde (voilà déjà le trait de toutes les dissociations, l'histoire des transcendances), fais en sorte en tout cas que la provenance de la marque reste désormais introuvable ou méconnaissable. Promets le: qu'elle se défigure, transfigure ou indétermine en son port, et tu entendras sous ce mot la rive du départ aussi bien que le référent

* Title of the Mallarmé sonnet.

Voies, for which a homonym would be *voix,* voices.

La venue, also "she who has come."

in my language or another, the English language (to learn by heart), or still another, the Arab language *(hafiza a'n zahri kalb)*—a single trek with several tracks. *

Two in one: the second axiom is rolled up in the first. The poetic, let us say it, would be that which you desire to learn, but from and of the other, thanks to the other and under dictation, by heart; *imparare a memoria.* Isn't that already it, the poem, once a token is given, the advent * of an event, at the moment in which the traversing of the road named translation remains as improbable as an accident, one which is all the same intensely dreamed of, required there where what it promises always leaves something to be desired? A grateful recognition goes out toward that very thing and precedes cognition here: your benediction before knowledge.

A fable that you could recount as the gift of the poem, it is an emblematic story: someone writes *you,* to you, of you, on you. No, rather a mark addressed to you, left and confided with you, is accompanied by an injunction, in truth it is instituted in this very order which, in its turn, constitutes you, assigning your origin or giving rise to you: destroy me, or rather render my support invisible to the outside, in the world (this is already the trait of all dissociations, the history of transcendences), in any case do what must be done so that the provenance of the mark remains from now on unlocatable or unrecognizable. Promise it: let it be disfigured, transfigured or rendered indeterminate in its *port*—and in this word you will hear the shore of the departure as well as the referent toward which a trans-

vers lequel une translation se porte. Mange, bois, avale ma lettre, porte-la, transporte-la en toi, comme la loi d'une écriture devenue ton corps: l'écriture en soi. *La ruse de l'injonction peut d'abord se laisser inspirer par la simple possibilité de la mort, par le danger que fait courir un véhicule à tout être fini. Tu entends venir la catastrophe. Dés lors imprimé à même le trait, venu du coeur, le désir du mortel éveille en toi le mouvement (contradictoire, tu me suis bien, double astreinte, contrainte aporé-tique) de garder de l'oubli cette chose qui du même coup s'expose à la mort et se protège— en un mot, l'adresse, le retrait du hérisson, comme sur l'autoroute un animal roulé en boule. On voudrait le prendre dans ses mains, l'apprendre et le comprendre, le garder pour soi, auprès de soi.*

Tu aimes—garder cela dans sa forme sin-gulière, on dirait dans l'irremplaçable littéra-lité du vocable *si on parlait de la poésie et non seulement du poétique en général. Mais notre poème ne tient pas en place dans des noms, ni même dans des mots. Il est d'abord jeté sur les routes et dans les champs, chose au-delà des langues, même s'il lui arrive de s'y rappe-ler lorsqu'il se rassemble, roulé en boule auprès de soi, plus menacé que jamais dans sa re-traite: il croit alors se défendre, il se perd.*

Littéralement: *tu voudrais retenir par coeur une forme absolument unique, un événement dont l'intangible singularité ne sépare plus l'i-déalité, le sens idéal, comme on dit, du corps de la lettre. Le désir de cette inséparation ab-solue, le non-absolu absolu, tu y respires l'ori-*

lation is portered. Eat, drink, swallow my letter, carry it, transport it in you, like the law of a writing become your body: *writing in (it)self.* The ruse of the injunction may first of all let itself be inspired by the simple possibility of death, by the risk that a vehicle poses to every finite being. You hear the catastrophe coming. From that moment on imprinted directly on the trait, come from the heart, the mortal's desire awakens in you the movement (which is contradictory, you follow me, a double restraint, an aporetic constraint) to guard from oblivion this thing which in the same stroke exposes itself to death and protects itself—in a word, the address, the retreat of the *hérisson,* like an animal on the autoroute rolled up in a ball. One would like to take it in one's hands, undertake to learn it and understand it, to keep it for oneself, near oneself.

Somewhere in "Envois" Derrida wonders how one can say "I love you" in English, which does not distinguish between "you" singular and "you" plural.

You love—keep that in its singular form,* we could say in the irreplaceable *literality of the vocable* if we were talking about poetry and not only about the poetic in general. But our poem does not hold still within names, nor even within words. It is first of all thrown out on the roads and in the fields, thing beyond languages, even if it sometimes happens that it recalls itself in language, when it gathers itself up, rolled up in a ball on itself, it is more threatened than ever in its retreat: it thinks it is defending itself, and it loses itself.

Literally: you would like to retain by heart an absolutely unique form, an event whose intangible singularity no longer separates the ideality, the ideal meaning as one says, from the body of the letter. In the desire of this absolute inseparation, the absolute nonab-

gine du poétique. D'où la résistance infinie au transfert de la lettre que l'animal, en son nom, réclame pourtant. C'est la détresse du hérisson. Que veut la détresse, le stress *même?* stricto sensu *mettre en garde. D'où la prophétie: traduis-moi, veille, garde-moi encore un peu, sauve-toi, quittons l'autoroute.*

*Ainsi se lève en toi le rêve d'*apprendre par coeur. *De te laisser traverser le coeur par la dictée. D'un seul trait, et c'est l'impossible et c'est l'expérience poématique. Tu ne savais pas encore le coeur, tu l'apprends ainsi. De cette expérience et de cette expression. J'appelle poème cela même qui apprend le coeur, ce qui invente le coeur, enfin ce que le mot de coeur semble vouloir dire et que dans ma langue je discerne mal du mot coeur.* Coeur, *dans le poème "apprendre par coeur" (à apprendre par coeur), ne nomme plus seulement la pure intériorité, la spontanéité indépendante, la liberté de s'affecter activement en reproduisant la trace aimée. La mémoire du "par coeur" se confie comme une prière, c'est plus sûr, à une certaine extériorité de l'automate, aux lois de la mnémotechnique, à cette liturgie qui mime en surface la mécanique, à l'automobile qui surprend ta passion et vient sur toi comme du dehors:* auswendig, *"par coeur" en allemand.*

Donc: le coeur te bat, naissance du rythme, au-delà des oppositions, du dedans et du dehors, de la représentation consciente et de l'archive abandonnée. Un coeur là-bas, entre les sentiers ou les autostrades, hors de ta présence, humble, près de la terre, tout bas. Réi-

solute, you breath the origin of the poetic. Whence the infinite resistance to the transfer of the letter which the animal, in its name, nevertheless calls out for. That is the distress of the *hérisson*. What does the distress, *stress* itself, want? *Stricto sensu*, to put on guard. Whence the prophecy: translate me, watch, keep me yet a while, get going, save yourself, let's get off the autoroute.

Thus the dream of *learning by heart* arises in you. Of letting your heart be traversed by the dictated dictation. In a single trait—and that's the impossible, that's the poematic experience. You did not yet know the heart, you learn it thus. From this experience and from this expression. I call a poem that very thing that teaches the heart, invents the heart, *that which*, finally, the word *heart* seems to mean and which, in my language, I cannot easily discern from the word itself. *Heart*, in the poem "learn by heart" (to be learned by heart), no longer names only pure interiority, independent spontaneity, the freedom to affect oneself actively by reproducing the beloved trace. The memory of the "by heart" is confided like a prayer—that's safer—to a certain exteriority of the automaton, to the laws of mnemotechnics, to that liturgy that mimes mechanics on the surface, to the automobile that surprises your passion and bears down on you as if from an

But also "outward" or "outside." outside: *auswendig*, "by heart" in German.*

So: your heart beats, gives the downbeat, the birth of rhythm, beyond oppositions, beyond outside and inside, conscious representation and the abandoned archive. A heart down there, between paths and autostradas, outside of your presence, humble, close to

*tère en murmurant: ne répète jamais... Dans
un seul chiffre, le poème (l'apprendre par coeur)
scelle ensemble le sens et la lettre, comme un
rythme espaçánt le temps.*

*Pour répondre en deux mots, ellipse, par
example, ou élection, coeur ou hérisson, il
t'aura fallu désemparer la mémoire, désarmer
la culture, savoir oublier le savoir, incendier
la bibliothèque des poétiques. L'unicité du
poème est à cette condition. Il te faut célébrer,
tu dois commémorer l'amnésie, la sauvagerie,
voire la bêtise du "par coeur": le hérisson. Il
s'aveugle. Roulé en boule, hérissé de piquants.
vulnérable et dangereux, calculateur et ina-
dapté (parce qu'il se met en boule, sentant le
danger sur l'autoroute, il s'expose à l'accident). Pas de poème sans accident, pas de
poème qui ne s'ouvre comme une blessure,
mais qui ne soit aussi blessant. Tu appelleras
poème une incantation silencieuse, la blessure aphone que de toi je désire apprendre par
coeur. Il a donc lieu, pour l'essentiel, sans qu'on
ait à le faire: il se laisse faire, sans activité,
sans travail, dans le plus sobre pathos, étran-
ger à toute production, surtout à la création.
Le poème échoit, bénédiction, venue de l'autre.
Rythme mais dissymétrie. Il n'y a jamais que
du poème, avant toute poïèse. Quand, au lieu
de "poésie", nous avons dit "poétique", nous
aurions dû préciser: "poématique". Surtout ne
laisse pas reconduire le hérisson dans le cir-
que ou dans le manège de la* poiesis: *rien à
faire* (poiein),* ni "poésie pure", ni rhétorique
pure, ni reine Sprache,* ni "mise-en-oeuvre-*

From the Greek: to make, to create.

"Pure language": from Walter Benjamin's essay, "The Task of the Trans-lator."

the earth, low down. Reiterate(s) in a murmur: never repeat . . . In a single cipher, the poem (the learning by heart, learn it by heart) seals together the meaning and the letter, like a rhythm spacing out time.

In order to respond in two words: *ellipsis,* for example, or *election, heart, hérisson,* or *istrice,* you will have had to disable memory, disarm culture, know how to forget knowledge, set fire to the library of poetics. The unicity of the poem depends on this condition. You must celebrate, you have to commemorate amnesia, savagery, even the stupidity* of the "by heart": the *hérisson.* It blinds itself. Rolled up in a ball, prickly with spines, vulnerable and dangerous, calculating and ill-adapted (because it makes itself into a ball, sensing the danger on the autoroute, it exposes itself to an accident). No poem without accident, no poem that does not open itself like a wound, but no poem that is not also just as wounding. You will call poem a silent incantation, the aphonic wound that, of you, from you, I want to learn by heart. It thus takes place, essentially, without one's having to do it or make it: it *lets itself* be done, without activity, without work, in the most sober *pathos,* a stranger to all production, especially to creation. The poem falls to me, benediction, coming of (or from) the other. Rhythm but dissymmetry. There is never anything but some poem, before any *poiesis.* When, instead of "poetry," we said "poetic," we ought to have specified: "poematic." Most of all do not let the *hérisson* be led back into the circus or the menagerie of *poiesis:* nothing to be done *(poiein),* neither "pure poetry," nor pure rhetoric, nor *reine Sprache,* nor "setting-forth-of-truth-in-

Bêtise, from *bête,* beast or animal.

de-la-vérité". Seulement une contamination, telle, et tel carrefour, cet accident-ci. Ce tour, le retournement de cette *catastrophe. Le don du poème ne cite rien, il n'a aucun titre, il n'histrionne plus, il survient sans que tu t'y attendes, coupant le souffle, coupant avec la poésie discursive, et surtout littéraire. Dans les cendres mêmes de cette généalogie. Pas le phénix, pas l'aigle, le hérisson, très bas, tout bas, près de la terre. Ni sublime, ni incorporel, angélique peut-être, et pour un temps.*

Tu appelleras désormais poème une certaine passion de la marque singulière, la signature qui répète sa dispersion, chaque fois au-delà du logos, *anhumaine, domestique à peine, ni réappropriable dans la famille du sujet: un animal converti, roulé en boule, tourné vers l'autre et vers soi, une chose en somme, et modeste, discrète, près de la terre, l'humilité que tu* surnommes, *te portant ainsi dans le nom, au-delà du nom, un hérisson catachrétique, toutes flèches dehors, quand cet aveugle sans âge entend mais ne voit pas venir la mort.*

Le poème peut se rouler en boule mais c'est encore pour tourner ses signes aigus vers le dehors. Il peut certes réfléchir la langue ou dire la poésie mais il ne se rapporte jamais à lui-même, il ne se meut jamais de lui-même comme ces engins porteurs de mort. Son événement interrompt toujours ou dévoie le savoir absolu, l'être auprès de soi dans l'auto-télie. Ce "démon du coeur" jamais ne se rassemble, il s'égare plutôt (délire ou manie), il s'expose à la chance, il se laisserait plutôt déchiqueter par ce qui vient sur lui.

See Heidegger, *The Origin of the Work of Art.*

the-work."* Just this contamination, and this crossroads, this accident here. This turn, the turning round of *this* catastrophe. The gift of the poem cites nothing, it has no title, its histrionics are over, it comes along without your expecting it, cutting short the breath, cutting all ties with discursive and especially literary poetry. In the very ashes of this genealogy. Not the phoenix, not the eagle, but the *hérisson*, very lowly, low down, close to the earth. Neither sublime, nor incorporeal, angelic, perhaps, and for a time.

You will call poem from now on a certain passion of the singular mark, the signature that repeats its dispersion, each time beyond the *logos*, ahuman, barely domestic, not reappropriable into the family of the subject: a converted animal, rolled up in a ball, turned toward the other and toward itself, in sum, a thing—modest, discreet, close to the earth, the humility that you surname, thus transporting yourself in the name beyond a name, a catachrestic *hérisson*, its arrows held at ready, when this ageless blind thing hears but does not see death coming.

The poem can roll itself up in a ball, but it is still in order to turn its pointed signs toward the outside. To be sure, it can reflect language or speak poetry, but it never relates back to itself, it never moves by itself like those machines, bringers of death. Its event always interrupts or derails absolute knowledge, autotelic being in proximity to itself. This "demon of the heart" never gathers itself together, rather it loses itself and gets off the track (delirium or mania), it exposes itself to chance, it would rather let itself be torn to pieces by what bears down upon it.

Sans sujet: il y a peut-être du poème, et qui se laisse, mais je n'en écris jamais. Un poème je ne le signe jamais. L'autre signe. Le je n'est qu'à la venue de ce dèsir: apprendre par coeur. Tendu pour se résumer à son propre support, donc sans support extérieur, sans substance, sans sujet, absolu de l'écriture en soi, le "par coeur" se laisse élire au-delà du corps, du sexe, de la bouche et des yeux, il efface les bords, il échappe aux mains, tu l'entends à peine, mais il nous apprend le coeur. Filiation, gage d'élection confié en héritage, il peut se prendre à n'importe quel mot, à la chose, vivante ou non, au nom de hérisson par exemple, entre vie et mort, à la tombée de la nuit ou au petit jour, apocalypse distraite, propre et commune, publique et secrète.

—Mais le poème dont tu parles, tu t'égares, on ne l'a jamais nommé ainsi, ni aussi arbi-trairement.

—Tu viens de le dire. Ce qu'il fallait dé-montrer. Rappelle-toi la question: "Qu'est-ce que...?" (tí estí, was ist..., istoria, episteme, philosophia). *"Qu'est-ce que...?" pleure la dis-parition du poème—une autre catastrophe. En annonçant ce qui est tel qu'il est, une ques-tion salue la naissance de la prose.*

Without a subject: poem, perhaps there is some, and perhaps it *leaves itself*, but I never write any. A poem, I never sign(s) it. The other sign(s). The *I* is only at the coming of this desire: to learn by heart. Stretched, tendered forth to the point of subsuming its own support, thus without external support, without substance, without subject, absolute of writing in (it)self, the "by heart" lets itself be elected beyond the body, sex, mouth, and eyes; it erases the borders, slips through the hands, you can barely hear it, but it teaches us the heart. Filiation, token of election confided as legacy, it can attach itself to any word at all, to the thing, living or not, to the name of *hérisson*, for example, between life and death, at nightfall or at daybreak, distracted apocalypse, proper and common, public and secret.

——But the poem you are talking about, you are getting off the track, it has never been named thus, or so arbitrarily.

——You just said it. Which had to be demonstrated. Recall the question: "What is ... ?" (*tí estí, was ist ...* , *istoria, episteme, philosophia*). "What is ... ?" laments the disappearance of the poem—another catastrophe. By announcing that which is just as it is, a question salutes the birth of prose.

—*Translated by Peggy Kamuf*

In little continuous jerks, the sequences are en-joined, induced, glide in silence. No category outside the text should allow defining the form or bearing of these passages, of these trances of writing. There are always only sections of flowers, from paragraph to paragraph, so much so that anthological excerpts inflict only the violence neces-sary to attach importance to the remain(s). Take into account the overlap-effects, and you will see that the tissue ceaselessly re-forms itself around the incision.

a paraph is the abbreviation of a para-graph: what is written on the side, in the margin

—*Glas*, p. 25

PART THREE

MORE THAN ONE LANGUAGE

AT THE BEGINNING of a series of memorial lectures for his friend Paul de Man, Derrida reflects on a phenomenon with which this eminent literary theorist was so often associated: "deconstruction in America." In explaining why he is unwilling to undertake a thorough analysis of this phenomenon, Derrida nevertheless sketches a few principles for such an analysis. He writes:

> But is there a proper place, is there a proper story for this thing [deconstruction]? I think it consists only of transference, and of a thinking through of transference, in all the senses that this word acquires in more than one language, and first of all that of the transference between languages. If I had to risk a single definition of deconstruction, one as brief, elliptical, and economical as a password, I would say simply and without overstatement: *plus d'une langue*—more than one language, no more of one language.[1]

It should already have become clear in the preceding sections that Derrida's thought is always turning, in one sense or another, around what is called "the problem of translation." The logocentrism he identified in his earliest writings, for example, may be understood as another name for the dream of a universal language. Its denial or forgetting of materiality and exteriority attempts to leap over the fact of language as such, that is, language in its material exteriority to purely inward, autoaffecting thought. The proof, so to speak, of this materiality is that language as such manifests itself in its difference—through the multiplicity of languages.

If there is only multiplicity, then there is no master language, although in the history of the West various tongues have pretended to this throne: Greek, Latin, French, German, and currently American English (the histories of imperialisms, of colonization, and of consolidation of nation-states is also always written in and through linguistic imposition.)[2] Derrida's password definition of deconstruction—more than one language/no more of one language—situates that practice always in a very specific tension with mastery as it is invested by a language. In its limited sense and within the confines of its traditional concept, translation has always implied a secondary operation coming after the original. The deconstruction of this concept displaces that order with the almost unthinkable notion (almost unthinkable because it points to the very limits of thinking) of an originary translation before the possibility of any distinction between original and translation.

But deconstruction does not only enjoin us to think translation differently, beyond the confines of its strict sense, that is, translation of thought from one language to another. It also displays the movement of the *trans*—translation, transference, transport, transformation—as the very movement of thought between points of origin and arrival that are always being deferred, differed one by the other. That is, deconstruction is deployed both as a theory of translation which challenges the limits of that philosophical concept and as a practice of translation which exhibits, rather than conceals, its own limits. The practice of more than one language has frequently been translated in Derrida's writings as a multivocality tyographically marked as in a dialogue or a polylogue. That is why we have included below excerpts from one such polyvocal text ("Restitutions of the Truth in Pointing") even though, unlike the other texts selected here, it deals less directly with questions of translation. (See, however, its commentary on Heidegger's preoccupation with the effects for philosophy of the translation of philosophical terms from Greek into Latin.)

NOTES

1. *Mémoires for Paul de Man* [1986], pp. 14–15.
2. For a discussion of some aspects of the imposition of French as a national language, see Derrida's essay "Languages and Institutions of Philosophy" [1984].

TEN

From "Des Tours de Babel" [1985]

The title of this essay on translation, and written for translation, is itself untranslatable. "Des Tours de Babel," notes the American translator, "can be read in various ways. *Des* means 'some'; but it also means 'of the,' 'from the,' or 'about the.' *Tours* could be towers, twists, tricks, turns, or tropes, as in a 'turn' of phrase. Taken together, *des* and *tours* have the same sound as *détour*, the word for detour."[1] As for the word 'Babel' in the title, it is taken to be a proper name and as such is not translated. But Babel is the name which, according to the biblical tradition, also installs the *necessity* of translation. Babel must not be translated and yet it also must be translated. This essay, which contains one of Derrida's most sustained reflections on the problem of translation, sets out from this double-bind condition as framed by the terms of the story in Genesis, a story we must read in translation. Derrida's reading of the Babel text forms a kind of prologue (presented below in full) to an extended analysis of the influential essay by the German thinker Walter Benjamin, "The Task of the Translator." There, the relations between translation and the proper name, indebtedness, the sacred text, the law are explored through Benjamin's language. Derrida asserts that what he is doing thereby is translating "in my own way the translation of another text on translation" (p. 175). This description not only recalls that reading and writing are first of all versions of translation, but it signals as well the limits on any theory of translation. "No theorization," writes Derrida, "inasmuch as it is produced in a language, will be able to dominate the Babelian performance."

"Babel": first a proper name, granted. But when we say "Babel" today, do we know what we are naming? Do we know whom? If we consider the sur-vival of a text that is a legacy, the *récit*,[2] or the myth of the tower of Babel, it does not constitute just one *figure* among others. Telling at least of the inadequation of one tongue to another, of one place in the encyclopedia to another, of language to itself and to meaning, and so forth, it also tells of the need for figuration, for myth, for tropes, for twists and turns, for translation inadequate to compensate for that which multiplicity denies us. In this sense it would be the myth of the origin of myth, the metaphor of metaphor, the narrative of narrative, the translation of translation, and so on. It would not be the only structure hollowing itself out like that, but it would do so in its own way (itself *almost* untranslatable, like a proper name), and its idiom would have to be saved.

The "tower of Babel" does not figure merely the irreducible multiplicity of tongues; it exhibits an incompletion, the impossibility of finishing, of totalizing, of saturating, of completing something on the order of edification, architectural construction, system and architectonics. What the multiplicity of idioms actually limits is not only a "true" translation, a transparent and adequate interexpression; it is also a structural order, a coherence of construct. There is then (let us translate) something like an internal limit to formalization, an incompleteness of the constructure. It would be easy and up to a certain point justified to see there the translation of a system in deconstruction.

One should never pass over in silence the question of the

tongue in which the question of the tongue is raised and into which a discourse on translation is translated.

First: in what tongue was the tower of Babel constructed and deconstructed? In a tongue within which the proper name of Babel could also, by confusion, be translated by "confusion." The proper name Babel, as a proper name, should remain untranslatable, but, by a kind of associative confusion that a unique tongue rendered possible, one could think to translate in that very tongue, by a common noun signifying what *we* translate as confusion. Voltaire showed his astonishment in his *Dictionnaire philosophique*, at the *Babel* article:

> I do not know why it is said in *Genesis* that Babel signifies confusion, for *Ba* signifies father in the Oriental tongues, and *Bel* signifies God; Babel signifies the city of God, the holy city. The Ancients gave this name to all their capitals. But it is incontestable that Babel means confusion, either because the architects were confounded after having raised their work up to eighty-one thousand Jewish feet, or because the tongues were then confounded; and it is obviously from that time on that the Germans no longer understand the Chinese; for it is clear, according to the scholar Bochart, that Chinese is originally the same tongue as High German.

The calm irony of Voltaire means that Babel means: it is not only a proper name, the reference of a pure signifier to a single being—and for this reason untranslatable—but a common noun related to the generality of a meaning. This common noun *means*, and means not only confusion, even though "confusion" has at least two meanings, as Voltaire is aware, the confusion of tongues, but also the state of confusion in which the architects find themselves with the structure interrupted, so that a certain confusion has already begun to affect the two meanings of the word *confusion*. The signification of "confusion" is confused, at least double. But Voltaire suggests something else again: Babel means not only confusion in the double sense of the word, but also the name of the father, more precisely and more commonly, the name of God as name of father. The city would bear the name of

God the father and of the father of the city that is called confusion. God, the God, would have marked with his patronym a communal space, that city where understanding is no longer possible. And understanding is no longer possible when there are only proper names, and understanding is no longer possible when there are no longer proper names. In giving his name, a name of his choice, in giving all names, the father would be at the origin of language, and that power would belong by right to God the father. And the name of God the father would be the name of that origin of tongues. But it is also that God who, in the action of his anger (like the God of Böhme or of Hegel, he who goes out of himself, determines himself in his finitude and thus produces history), annuls the gift of tongues, or at least embroils it, sows confusion among his sons, and poisons the present *(Gift-gift).*[3] This is also the origin of tongues, of the multiplicity of idioms, of what in other words are usually called mother tongues. For this entire history deploys filiations, generations and genealogies: all Semitic. Before the deconstruction of Babel, the great Semitic family was establishing its empire, which it wanted to be universal, and its tongue, which it also attempts to impose on the universe. The moment of this project immediately precedes the deconstruction of the tower. I cite two French translations.[4] The first translator stays away from what one would want to call "literality," in other words, from the Hebrew figure of speech for "tongue," there where the second, more concerned about literality (metaphoric, or rather metonymic), says "lip," since in Hebrew "lip" designates what we call, in another metonymy, "tongue." One will have to say multiplicity of lips and not of tongues to name the Babelian confusion. The first translator, then, Louis Segond, author of the Segond Bible, published in 1910, writes this:

> Those are the sons of Sem, according to their families, their tongues, their countries, their nations. Such are the families of the sons of Noah, according to their generations, their nations. And it is from them that emerged the nations which spread over the earth after the flood. All the earth had a single tongue and the same words. As they had left the

origin they found a plain in the country of Schinear, and they dwelt there. They said to one another: Come! Let us make bricks, and bake them in the fire. And brick served them as stone, and tar served as cement. Again they said: Come! Let us build ourselves a city and a tower whose summit touches the heavens, and let us make ourselves a name, so that we not be scattered over the face of all the earth.

I do not know just how to interpret this allusion to the substitution or the transmutation of materials, brick becoming stone and tar serving as mortar. That already resembles a translation, a translation of translation. But let us leave it and substitute a second translation for the first. It is that of [André] Chouraqui. It is recent and wants to be more literal, almost *verbum pro verbo*, as Cicero said should not be done in one of those first recommendations to the translator which can be read in his *Libellus de Optimo Genera Oratorum*. Here it is:

Here are the sons of Shem
for their clans, for their tongues,
in their lands, for their peoples.
Here are the clans of the sons of Noah for their exploits,
in their peoples:
from the latter divide the peoples on earth, after the flood.

And it is all the earth: a single lip, one speech.
And it is at their departure from the Orient: they find
    a canyon,
in the land of Shine'ar.
They settle there.
They say, each to his like:
"Come, let us brick some bricks.
Let us fire them in the fire."
The brick becomes for them stone, the tar, mortar.
They say:
"Come, let us build ourselves a city and a tower.
Its head: in the heavens.
Let us make ourselves a name,
that we not be scattered over the face of all the earth."

What happens to them? In other words, for what does God punish them in giving his name, or rather, since he gives it to nothing and to no one, in proclaiming his name, the proper name of "confusion" which will be his mark and his seal? Does he punish them for having wanted to build as high as the heavens? For having wanted to accede to the highest, up to the Most High? Perhaps for that too, no doubt, but incontestably for having wanted thus to *make a name for themselves*, to give themselves the name, to construct for and by themselves their own name, to gather themselves there ("that we not be scattered"), as in the unity of a place which is at once a tongue and a tower, the one as well as the other, the one as the other. He punishes them for having thus wanted to assure themselves, by themselves, a unique and universal genealogy. For the text of Genesis proceeds immediately, as if it were all a matter of the same design: raising a tower, constructing a city, making a name for oneself in a universal tongue which would also be an idiom, and gathering a filiation:

> They say:
> "Come, let us build ourselves a city and a tower.
> Its head: in the heavens.
> Let us make ourselves a name,
> that we not be scattered over the face of all the earth."
>
> YHWH descends to see the city and the tower
> that the sons of man have built.
> YHWH says:
> "Yes! A single people, a single lip for all:
> that is what they begin to do! . . .
> Come! Let us descend! Let us confound their lips,
> man will no longer understand the lip of his neighbor."

Then he disseminates the Sem, and dissemination is here deconstruction:

> YHWH disperses them from here over the face of all the earth.
> They cease to build the city.
> Over which he proclaims his name: Bavel, Confusion,
> for there, YHWH confounds the lip of all the earth,

and from there YHWH disperses them over the face of all
the earth.

Can we not, then, speak of a jealousy of God? Out of resentment against that unique name and lip of men, he imposes his
name, his name of father; and with this violent imposition he
opens the deconstruction of the tower, as of the universal language; he scatters the genealogical filiation. He breaks the lineage. He *at the same time* imposes and forbids translation. He
imposes it and forbids it, constrains, but as if to failure, the
children who henceforth *will bear* his name, the name that *he*
gives to the city. It is from a proper name of God, come from
God, descended from God or from the father (and it is indeed said
that YHWH, an unpronounceable name, *descends* toward the
tower) and from this *mark* that tongues are scattered, confounded
or multiplied, according to a descendance that in its very dispersion remains sealed by the only name that will have been the
strongest, by the only idiom that will have triumphed. Now, this
idiom bears within itself the mark of confusion, it improperly
means the improper, to wit: Bavel, confusion. Translation then
becomes necessary and impossible, like the effect of a struggle
for the appropriation of the name, necessary and forbidden in the
interval between two absolutely proper names. And the proper
name of God (given by God) is divided enough in the tongue,
already, to signify also, confusedly, "confusion." And the war
that he declares has first raged within his name: divided, bifid,
ambivalent, polysemic: God deconstructs. Himself. "And he war,"
one reads in *Finnegans Wake,* and we could follow this whole
story from the side of Shem and Shaun. The "he war" does not
only, in this place, tie together an incalculable number of phonic
and semantic threads, in the immediate context and throughout
this Babelian book; it says the declaration of war (in English) of
the One who says I am the one who am, and who thus was *(war)*;
it renders itself untranslatable in its very performance, *at least
in the fact* that it is enunciated in more than one language at a
time, at least English and German. If even an infinite translation
exhausted its semantic stock, it would still translate into *one*
language and would lose the multiplicity of "he war." Let us
leave for another time a less hastily interrupted reading of this

"he war,"[5] and let us note one of the limits of theories of translation: all too often they treat the passing from one language to another and do not sufficiently consider the possibility for languages to be implicated *more than two* in a text. How is a text written in several languages at a time to be translated? How is the effect of plurality to be "rendered"? And what of translating with several languages at a time, will that be called translating?

Babel: today we take it as a proper name. Indeed, but the proper name of what and of whom? At times that of a narrative text recounting a story (mythical, symbolic, allegorical; it matters little for the moment), a story in which the proper name, which is then no longer the title of the narrative, names a tower or a city but a tower or a city that receives its name from an event during which YHWH "proclaims his name." Now, this proper name, which already names at least three times and three different things, also has, this is the whole point of the story, as proper name the function of a common noun. This story recounts, among other things, the origin of the confusion of tongues, the irreducible multiplicity of idioms, the necessary and impossible task of translation, its necessity *as* impossibility. Now, in general one pays little attention to this fact: it is in translation that we most often read this *récit*. And in this translation, the proper name retains a singular destiny, since it is not translated in its appearance as proper name. Now, a proper name as such remains forever untranslatable, a fact that may lead one to conclude that it does not strictly belong, for the same reason as the other words, to the language, to the system of the language, be it translated or translating. And yet "Babel," an event in a single tongue, the one in which it appears so as to form a "text," also has a common meaning, a conceptual generality. That it be by way of a pun or a confused association matters little: "Babel" could be understood in one language as meaning "confusion." And from then on, just as Babel is at once proper name and common noun, confusion also becomes proper name and common noun, the one as the homonym of the other, the synonym as well, but not the equivalent, because there could be no question of confusing them in their value. It has for the translator no satisfactory solution. Recourse to apposition and capitalization ("Over which he proclaims his name: Bavel, Confusion") is not translating from one tongue into another. It comments, explains, paraphrases, but does not translate. At best it reproduces approximately and by dividing the equivocation into two words there where confusion gathered in potential, in all its potential, in the internal translation, if one can say that, which works the word in the so-called original tongue. For in the very tongue of the original *récit* there is a translation, a sort of transfer, that gives immediately (by some confusion) the semantic equivalent of the proper name which, by itself, as a pure proper name, it would not have. As a matter of fact, this intralinguistic translation operates immediately; it is not even an operation in the strict sense. Nevertheless, someone who speaks the language of Genesis could be attentive to the effect of the proper name in effacing the conceptual equivalent (like *pierre* [rock] in *Pierre* [Peter], and these are two absolutely heterogeneous values or functions); one would then be tempted to say *first* that a proper name, in the proper sense, does not properly belong to the language; it does not belong there, *although and because* its call makes the language possible (what would a language be without the possibility of calling a proper name?); consequently it can properly inscribe itself in a language only by allowing itself to be translated therein, in other words, *interpreted* by its semantic equivalent: from this moment it can no longer be taken as proper name. The noun *pierre* belongs to the French language, and its translation into a foreign language should in principle transport its meaning. This is not the case with *Pierre*, whose inclusion in the French language is not assured and is in any case not of the same type. "Peter" in this sense is not a *translation* of *Pierre*, any more than *Londres* is a translation of "London," and so forth. And *second*, anyone whose so-called mother tongue was the tongue of Genesis could indeed understand Babel as "confusion"; that person then effects a *confused* translation of the proper name by its common equivalent without having need for another word. It is as if there were two words there, two homonyms one of which has the value of proper name and the other that of common noun: between the two, a translation which one can evaluate quite diversely. Does it belong to the kind that Jakobson calls intralingual translation or rewording? I do not think so: "rewording" concerns the relations of transformation between common nouns and ordinary phrases. The essay "On Linguistic Aspects of Translation"[6] distinguishes three forms of translation. *Intralingual* translation interprets linguistic signs by means of other signs of the *same* language. This obviously presupposes that one can know in the final analysis how to determine rigorously the unity and identity of a language, the decidable form of its limits. There would then be what Jakobson neatly calls translation "proper," *interlingual* translation, which interprets linguistic signs by means of some other language—this appeals to the same presupposition as intralingual translation. Finally there would be intersemiotic translation or transmutation, which interprets linguistic signs by means of systems of nonlinguistic signs. For the two forms of translation which would not be translations "proper," Jakobson proposes a definitional equivalent and another word. The first he translates, so to speak, by another word: intralingual translation or *rewording*. The third likewise: *intersemiotic* translation or *transmutation*. In these two cases, the translation of "translation" is a definitional interpretation. But in the case of translation "proper," translation in the ordinary sense, interlinguistic and post-Babelian, Jakobson does not translate; he repeats the same word: "interlingual translation or translation proper." He supposes that it is not necessary to translate; everyone understands what that means because everyone has experienced it, everyone is expected to know what a language is, the relation of one language to another and especially identity or difference in fact of language. If there is a transparency that Babel would not have impaired, this is surely it, the experience of the multiplicity of tongues and the "proper" sense of the word *translation*. In relation to this word, when it is a question of translation "proper," the other uses of the word *translation* would be in a position of intralingual and inadequate translation, like metaphors, in short, like twists or turns of translation in the proper sense. There would thus be a translation in the proper sense and a translation in the figurative sense. And in order to translate the one into the other, within the same tongue or from one tongue to another, in the figurative or in the proper sense, one would engage upon a course that would quickly reveal how this reassuring tripartition can be problematic. Very quickly: at the very moment when pronouncing "Babel" we sense the impossibility of deciding whether this name belongs, properly and simply, to *one* tongue. And it matters that this undecidability is at work in a struggle for the proper name within a scene of genealogical indebtedness. In seeking to "make a name for themselves," to found at the same time a universal tongue and a unique genealogy, the Semites want to bring the world to reason, and this reason can signify simultaneously a colonial violence (since they would thus universalize their idiom) and a peaceful transparency of the human community. Inversely, when God imposes and opposes his name, he ruptures the rational transparency but interrupts also the colonial violence or the linguistic imperialism. He destines them to translation, he subjects them to the law of a translation both necessary and impossible; in a stroke with his translatable-untranslatable name he delivers a universal reason (it will no longer be subject to the rule of a particular nation), but he simultaneously limits its very universality: forbidden transparency, impossible univocity. Translation becomes law, duty and debt, but the debt one can no longer discharge. Such insolvency is found marked in the very name of Babel: which at once translates and does not translate itself, belongs without belonging to a language and indebts itself to itself for an insolvent debt, to itself as if other. Such would be the Babelian performance.

[. . . .]

—Translated by Joseph F. Graham

NOTES

1. Joseph F. Graham, ed. and trans., *Difference in Translation* (Ithaca, N.Y.: Cornell University Press, 1985), p. 206.

2. On the untranslatability of *récit*, see below, **"Living On: Borderlines,"** pp. 258–59.—Ed.

3. One of Derrida's most persistent questions concerns the gift, the possibility of a giving that is not also a taking back (see for example, below, **"At This Very Moment in This Work Here I Am,"** pp. 408–11). In this regard, he frequently recalls that a homonym of the German noun *Gift* is the adjective meaning poisonous.—Ed.

4. These translations are in turn translated here into English.—Ed.

5. See "Two Words for Joyce" [1987].—Ed.

6. In R. A. Brower, ed., *On Translation* (Cambridge, Mass.: Harvard University Press, 1959), pp. 232–39.—Ed.

ELEVEN

From "Living On: Border Lines" [1979]

("Survivre: Journal de bord" in *Parages* [1986])

One way to introduce this text is to translate part of the note with which Derrida presented its first publication in French following its "original" publication in English:

The first version of this text appeared in English in a work titled *Deconstruction and Criticism* (New York: Seabury Press, 1979). It is useful, perhaps, to say a few words about this work, or rather about the situation that explains, to a certain degree, its publication, composition, and form. Around 1975, people began to speak of a new school of literary criticisms or of philosophy that had formed at Yale (the "Yale group" or the "Yale school"). There would be much to say about the presumed reality, the diversity, or the overdetermined complexity of this phenomenon. I do not intend to get into these problems here; I only want to mention this circumstance: A publisher proposed to the supposed adherents of this "school" (my friends and colleagues Harold Bloom, Paul de Man, Geoffrey H. Hartman, J. Hillis Miller, and myself) to present what was called their "method," their project, or their axioms in a common volume and using an example of their choice. In short, an explanation of their own work! With varying degrees of conviction, no doubt, but a sufficiently shared one, we felt we had to accept the offer as a wager. So as to accentuate its character of a gamble or a wager, we then decided to adopt a very artificial rule for ourselves (it was especially so for me, obviously) which was to treat Shelley's great poem, *The Triumph of Life.**

Derrida takes up this wager in an altogether novel way. Once again, his text splits the page in two, this time horizontally: in the upper band, the main text pursues the complex senses of survival or living on of literature; in the lower band, a long running "note to the translator" for a text that was written to be translated. The note, called "Journal de bord" (shipboard journal, translated as "Border Lines") and dated like a journal, not only poses questions of translation but reflects on the institutional resistances to it and to deconstructive thinking. This resistance may be located in the complementary beliefs that a text (1) has identifiable limits or borders and (2) exists in a stable system of reference to other texts of "information" (its "context") which, ideally at least, can be fully represented, for example through a scholarly apparatus of notes. "Border Lines" challenges these two notions by overflowing at every opportunity the possibilities of complete reference. What is thus staged is the question of the relation between texts once their limits or borders can no longer be rigorously determined. As in **"The Double Session,"** Derrida shows how the writing we call "literary," that is, writing that is not on trial in the tribunal of truth, requires to be read *at once as referring* only to itself *and* as referring to another writing. It is a simulacrum, "reference without referent."

This doubled structure is displayed or deployed in a startling way in the upper text, "Living On." There Derrida reads two short narratives by Maurice Blanchot, *La Folie du jour* (The Madness of the Day) and *L'Arrêt de mort* (Death Sentence), as, in effect, "translations" of Shelley's *The Triumph of Life.* Although we cannot begin to summarize this reading here, the following excerpt, from the beginning of the text, can illustrate some of what is at stake for the institutions of reading when the borders of texts are no longer strictly determinable.

Derrida has written elsewhere extensively on Maurice Blanchot, whose *récits* he has described as having a very powerful effect on his own thinking about writing. Along with "Living On: Border Lines," these essays ("Pas," "The Law of Genre," "Title—to be specified") have been collected in the volume *Parages* [1986].

---

* *Parages* [1986], p. 118.

Living On: Border Lines

[. . . .]

If we are to approach a text, it must have an edge. The question of the text, as it has been elaborated and transformed in the last dozen or so years, has not merely "touched" "shore," *le bord* (scandalously tampering, changing, as in Mallarmé's declaration, *"On a touché au vers"*), all those boundaries that form the running border of what used to be called a text, of what we once thought this word could identify, i.e., the supposed end and beginning of a work, the unity of a corpus, the title, the margins, the signatures, the referential realm outside the frame, and so forth. What has happened, if it has happened, is a sort of overrun [*débordement*] that spoils all these boundaries and divisions and forces us to extend the accredited concept, the dominant notion

---

[. . . .] I wish to pose the question of the *bord*, the edge, the border, and the *bord de mer*, the shore. [These "Border Lines," in French, are entitled "Journal de bord"—usually translated "shipboard journal," but here also "journal on *bord*"] *(The Triumph of Life* was written in the sea, at its edge, between land and sea, but that doesn't matter.) The question of the borderline precedes, as it were, the determination of all the dividing lines that I have just mentioned: between a fantasy and a "reality," an event and a nonevent, a fiction and a reality, one corpus and another, and so forth. Here, from week to week in this pocket-calendar or these minutes [*procès-verbal*], I

of a "text," of what I still call a "text," for strategic reasons, in part—a "text" that is henceforth no longer a finished corpus of writing, some content enclosed in a book or its margins, but a differential network, a fabric of traces referring endlessly to something other than itself, to other differential traces. Thus the text overruns all the limits assigned to it so far (not submerging or drowning them in an undifferentiated homogeneity, but rather making them more complex, dividing and multiplying strokes and lines)—all the limits, everything that was to be set up in opposition to writing (speech, life, the world, the real, history, and what not, every field of reference—to body or mind, conscious or unconscious, politics, economics, and so forth). Whatever the (demonstrated) necessity of such an overrun, such a *débordement*, it still will have come as a shock, producing endless efforts to dam up, resist, rebuild the old partitions, to blame what could no longer be thought without confusion, to blame difference *as* wrongful confusion! All this has taken place in nonreading, with no work on what was thus being demonstrated, with no realization that it was never our wish to extend the reassuring notion of the text to a whole extratextual realm and to transform the world into a library by doing away with all boundaries, all framework, all sharp edges (all *arêtes:* this is the word that I am speaking of tonight), but that we sought rather to work out the theoretical and practical system of these margins, these borders, once more, from the ground up. I shall not go into detail. Documentation of all this is readily available to anyone committed to breaking down the various structures of resistance, his own resis-

---

shall perhaps endeavor to create an effect of *superimposing*, of superimprinting one text on the other. Now, each of the two "triumphs" writes (on *[sur]*) textural superimprinting. What about this "on," this "*sur*," and its surface? An effect of superimposing: one procession is superimposed on the other, accompanying it without accompanying it (Blanchot, *Celui qui ne m'accompagnait pas*). This operation would never be considered legitimate on the part of a teacher, who must give his references and tell what he's talking about, giving it its recognizable title. You can't give a course on Shelley without ever mentioning him, pretending to deal with Blanchot, and more than a

tance as such or as primarily the ramparts that bolster a system (be it theoretical, cultural, institutional, political, or whatever). What are the borderlines of a text? How do they come about? I shall not approach the question frontally, in the most general way. I prefer, within the limits that we have here, a more indirect, narrower channel, one that is more concrete as well: at the edge of the narrative, of the text *as* a narrative. The word is *récit*, a story, a narrative, and not *narration*, narration. The reworking of a textual problematic has affected this aspect of the text as narrative (the narrative of an event, the event of narrative, the narrative as the structure of an event) by placing it in the foreground.

(I note parenthetically that *The Triumph of Life*, which it is not my intention to discuss here, belongs in many ways to the category of the *récit*, in the disappearance or overrun that takes place the moment we wish to close its case after citing it, calling it forth, commanding it to appear.

1. *There is* the *récit* of double affirmation, as analyzed in "Pas" [in *Parages* (1986)], the "yes, yes" that must be cited, must recite itself to bring about the alliance [*alliance*, also "wedding band"] of affirmation with itself, to bring about its ring. It remains to be seen whether the double affirmation is *triumphant*, whether the triumph is affirmative or a paradoxical phase in the work of mourning.

2. *There is* the double narrative, the narrative of the vision enclosed in the general narrative carried on by the same narrator. The line that separates the enclosed narrative from the other—

---

few others. And your transitions have to be readable, that is, in accordance with criteria of readability very firmly established, and long since. At the beginning of *L'arrêt de mort*, the superimposing of the two "images," the image of Christ and, "behind the figure of Christ," Veronica, "the features of a woman's face—extremely beautiful, even magnificent"—this superimposing is readable "on the wall of [a doctor's] office" and on a "photograph." Inscription and reimprinting, reimpression, of light in both texts. *La folie du jour*. The course of the sun, day, year, anniversary, double revolution, the palindrome and the anagrammatic version or reversion of *écrit*, *récit*,

· ·

And then a Vision on my brain was rolled.

———————

· ·

—marks the upper edge of a space that will never be closed. What is the *topos* of the "I" who quotes himself in a narrative [of a dream, a vision, or a hallucination] within a narrative, including, in addition to all his ghosts, his *hallucinations of ghosts,* still other visions within visions [e.g., "a new Vision never seen before"]? What is his *topos* when he quotes, in the present, a past question formulated in another sort of present ["... 'Then, what is Life?' I said. ...."] and which he narrates as something that presented itself in a vision, and so on?

3. *There is* also the ironic, antithetical, underlying re-citation of the "triumphs of death" that adds another level of coding to the poem. What are we doing when, to practice a "genre," we quote a genre, represent it, stage it, expose its *generic law,* analyze it practically? Are we still practicing the genre? Does the "work" still belong to the genre it re-cites? But inversely, how could we make a genre work without referring to it [quasi-]quotationally, indicating at some point, "See, this is a work of such-and-such a genre"? Such an indication does not belong to the genre and makes the statement of belonging an ironical exercise. It interrupts the very belonging of which it is a necessary condition. I must abandon this question for the moment; it's capable

————————————————————————————

and *série.* The series [*écrit, récit, série,* etc.]. Note to the translators: How are you going to translate that, *récit* for example? Not as *nouvelle,* "novella," nor as "short story." Perhaps it will be better to leave the "French" word *récit.* It is already hard enough to understand, in Blanchot's text, in French. An essential question for the translator. The *sur,* "on," "super-," and so forth, that is my theme above, also designates the figure of a passage by *trans*-lation, the *trans-* of an *Übersetzung.* Version [version; also "translation into one's own language"], transference, and translation. *Übertragung.* The simultaneous transgression and reappropriation of a language

of disrupting more than one system of poetics, more than one literary pact.)

What is a narrative—this thing that we call a narrative? Does it take place? Where and when? What might the taking-place or the event of a narrative be?

I hasten to say that it is not my intention here, nor do I claim, nor do I have the means, to answer these questions. At most, in repeating them, I would like to begin a minute displacement, the most discreet of transformations: I suggest, for example, that we replace what might be called *the question of narrative* ("What is a narrative?") with *the demand for narrative.* When I say *demande* I mean something closer to the English "demand" than to a mere request: inquisitorial insistence, an order, a petition. To know (before we know) what narrative is, the narrativity of narrative, we should perhaps first recount, return to the scene of one origin of narrative, to the narrative of one origin of narrative (will that still be a narrative?), to that scene that mobilizes various forces, or if you prefer various agencies or "subjects," some of which *demand* the narrative of the other, seek to extort it from him, like a secret-less secret, something that they call the truth about what has taken place: "Tell us exactly what happened." The narrative must have begun with this demand, but will we still call the *mise en scène* [representation, staging] of this demand a narrative? And will we even still call it *mise en "scène,"* since that origin concerns the eyes [*touche aux yeux*] (as we shall see), the origin of visibility, the origin of origin, the birth of what, as we say in French, "sees the light of day" [*voit le*

[*langue*], its law, its economy? How will you translate *langue?* Let us suppose then that here, at the foot of the other text, I address a translatable message, in the style of a telegram, to the translators of every country. Who is to say in what language, *exactly* what language, if we assume that the translation has been prepared, the above text will appear? It is not untranslatable, but, without being opaque, it presents at every turn, I know, something to stop [*arrêter*] the translation: it forces the translator to transform the language into which he is translating or the "receiver medium," to deform the initial contract, itself in constant deformation, in the language of the

jour, is born] when the present leads to presence, presentation, or representation? "Oh, I see the daylight *[je vois le jour]*, oh God," says a voice in *La folie du jour*, a "narrative" *[récit"]* (?) by Maurice Blanchot. [. . . .]

What is judiciously called the question-of-narrative covers, with a certain modesty, a demand for narrative, a violent putting-to-the question, an instrument of torture working to wring the narrative out of one as if it were a terrible secret, in ways that can go from the most archaic police methods to refinements for making (and even letting) one talk that are unsurpassed in neutrality and politeness, that are most respectfully medical, psychiatric, and even psychoanalytic. For reasons that should be obvious by now, I shall not say that Blanchot offers a *representation*, a *mise en scène*, of this demand for narrative, in *La folie du jour*. it would be better to say that it is there to be read, "to the point of de*lire*ium," as it throws the reader off the track. For the same reasons, I do not know whether the text can be classified as being of the genre (Genette: the *mode* [mode; mood of a verb]) *"récit,"* a word that Blanchot has repeatedly insisted upon and contested, reclaimed and rejected, set down and (then) erased, and so forth. In addition to these general reasons there is a singular characteristic, involving precisely the (internal and external) *boundaries* or *edges* of this text. The boundary from which we believe we approach *La folie du jour*, its "first word" ("I"), opens with a paragraph that *affirms* a sort of triumph of life at the edge of death. The triumph must be excessive (in accordance with the "boundlessness" of hubris) and very close to what it triumphs

---

other. I anticipated this difficulty of translation, if only up to a certain point, but I did not calculate it or deliberately increase it. I just did nothing to avoid it. On the contrary, I shall try here, in this short steno-telegraphic band, for the greatest translatability possible. Such will be the proposed contract. For the problems that I wished to formalize above all have an irreducible relationship to the enigma, or in other words the *récit*, of translation. Above all, by making manifest the limits of the prevalent concept of translation (I do not say of translatability in general), we touch on multiple problems said to be of "method," of reading and teaching. The line that I seek to

over. This paragraph begins a narrative, it seems, but does not yet recount anything. The narrator introduces himself in that simplest of performances, an "I am," or more precisely an "I am neither ... nor ...," which immediately removes the performance from presence. The end of this paragraph notes especially the double excess of every triumph of life: i.e., the excessive double affirmation, *of* triumphant life, of death which triumphs *over* life.

> I am neither learned nor ignorant. I have known joys. That is saying too little: I am alive, and this life gives me the greatest pleasure. And what about death? When I die (perhaps any minute now), I will feel immense pleasure. I am not talking about the foretaste of death, which is stale and often disagreeable. Suffering dulls the senses. But this is the remarkable truth, which I am certain of: I feel boundless pleasure in living, and I will take boundless satisfaction in dying.

A number of signs make it possible to recognize a man in the first-person speaker. But in the *double* affirmation seen (remarked upon) in the syntax of triumph as *triomphe-de*, triumph *of* and triumph *over*, the narrator comes close to seeing a trait that is particularly feminine, a trait of feminine beauty, even.

> Men want to escape death, strange animals that they are. And some of them cry out "Die, die" because they want to escape life. "What a life. I'll kill myself. I'll give in." That is pitiful and strange; it is a mistake.

---

recognize within translatability, between two translations, one governed by the classical model of transportable univocality or of formalizable polysemia, and the other, which goes over into dissemination—this line also passes between the critical and the deconstructive. A politico-institutional problem of the university: it, like all teaching in its traditional form, and perhaps all teaching whatever, has as its ideal, with exhaustive translatability, the effacement of language [la langue]. The deconstruction of a pedagogical institution and all that it implies. What this institution cannot bear, is for anyone to tamper with [toucher à; also "touch," "change,"

Yet I have met people who have never told life to be quiet or told death to go away—almost always women, beautiful creatures.

Later, on the next-to-last page, we learn that this opening paragraph (the upper edge of *La folie . . .*) corresponds in its content and form, if not in its occurrence, to the beginning of the account *[récit]* that the narrator tries to take up *[aborder]* in response to the demands of his interrogators. This creates an exceedingly strange space: what appeared to be the beginning and the upper edge of a discourse *will have been* merely part of a narrative that forms a part of the discourse in that it *recounts* how an attempt was made—in vain!—to force a narrative out of the narrator. The starting edge will have been the quotation (at first not recognizable as such) of a narrative fragment that in turn will merely be quoting its quotation. For all these quotations, quotations of requotations with no original performance, there is no speech act not already the iteration of another, no circle and no quotation marks to reassure us about the identity, opposition, or distinction of speech events. The part is always greater than the whole, the edge *of* the set *[ensemble]* is a fold *[pli]* in the set (" 'Happy those for whom the fold/ Of . . .' "), but as *La folie du jour* unfolds, explains itself *[s'explique]* without ever giving up its "fold" to another discourse not already its own, it is better if I quote. If I quote, for example, these last two pages:

"concern himself with"] language, meaning *both* the *national* language *and*, paradoxically, an ideal of translatability that neutralizes this national language. Nationalism and universalism. What this institution cannot bear is a transformation that leaves intact neither of these two complementary poles. It can bear more readily the most apparently revolutionary ideological sorts of "content," if only that content does not touch the borders of language *[la langue]* and of all the juridico-political contracts that it guarantees. It is this "intolerable" something that concerns me here. It is related in an essential way to that which, as it is written above, brings out the limits of the

I had been asked, "Tell us exactly what happened." A story
[*Un récit*]? I began: I am neither learned nor ignorant. I have
known joys. That is saying too little. I told them the whole
story [*histoire*], and they listened with interest, it seems
to me, at least in the beginning. But the end was a surprise
to all of us. "That was the beginning," they said. "Now
get down to the facts." How so? The story [*récit*] was finished!

I was forced to realize that I was not capable of forming a
story out of these events. I had lost the thread of the narrative [*l'histoire*]: that happens in a good many illnesses. But
this explanation only made them more insistent. Then I
noticed for the first time that there were two of them and
that this departure from the traditional method, even though
it was explained by the fact that one of them was an eye
doctor, the other a specialist in mental illness, kept making
our conversation seem like an authoritarian interrogation
that was being supervised and guided by a strict set of rules.
Of course neither of them was the police chief. But because
there were two of them, there were three, and this third was
firmly convinced, I am sure, that a writer, a man who speaks
and argues with distinction, is always capable of recounting
facts that he remembers.

A story [*récit*]? No. No stories [*pas de récit*], never again.

By definition, there is no end to a discourse that would seek to
describe the invaginated structure of *La folie du jour*. Invagination is the inward refolding of *la gaine* [sheath, girdle], the in-

---

concept of translation on which the university is built, particularly
when it makes the teaching of language, even literatures, and even
"comparative literature," its principal theme. If *questions of method*
(here, a translators' note: I have published a text that is untranslatable, starting with its title, "Pas," and in "The Double Session,"
referring to "dissemination in the refolding [*repli*] of the *hymen*":
"*Pas de méthode* ["no method," but also a "methodical step"] for it:
no path comes back in its circle to a first step, none proceeds from
the simple to the complex, none leads from a beginning to an end.
['A book neither begins nor ends; at most it pretends to.' . . . 'Every

verted reapplication of the outer edge to the inside of a form where the outside then opens a pocket. Such an invagination is possible from the first trace on. This is why there is no "first" trace. We have just seen, on the basis of this example refined to the point of madness, how "the whole story [to which] they listened" is the one (the same but another at the same time) that, like *La folie du jour*, begins "I am neither learned nor ignorant. . . ." But this "whole story," which corresponds to the totality of the "book," is also only a part of the book, the narrative that is demanded, attempted, impossible, and so forth. Its end, which comes before the end, does not respond to the request of the authorities, the authorities who demand an *author*, an *I* capable of organizing a narrative sequence, of remembering and telling the truth: "exactly what happened," "recounting facts that he remembers," in other words saying "I" (I am the same as the one to whom these things happened, and so on, and thereby assuring the unity or identity of narratee or reader, and so on). Such is the demand for the story, for narrative, the demand that society, the law that governs literary and artistic works, medicine, the police, and so forth, claim to constitute. This demand for truth is itself recounted and swept along in the endless process of invagination. Because I cannot pursue this analysis here, I merely situate the place, the locus, in which *double invagination* comes about, the place where the invagination of the upper edge on its outer face (the supposed beginning of *La folie du jour*), which is folded back "inside" to form a pocket and an inner edge, comes to extend beyond (or encroach on) the invagination of the lower edge, on

---

method is a fiction.'] *Point de méthode* ["absolutely no method," but also "a point of method"]: that doesn't rule out a certain course to be followed" [*Dissemination*, p. 271]. The translators will not be able to translate this *pas* and this *point*. Will they have to indicate that this reminder is to be related to what is called the "unfinished" quality of Shelley's *Triumph* and the impossibility of fixing [*arrêter*] the opening and closing boundaries of *L'arrêt de mort*, all problems treated, in another mode, in the procession above? Will they relate this untranslatable *pas* to the double "knot" of double invagination, a central motif of that text, or, along with its entire semantic family,

its inner face (the supposed end of *La folie du jour*), which is folded back "inside" to form a pocket and an outer edge. Indeed the "middle" sequence ("I had been asked, 'Tell us exactly what happened.' A story? I began: I am neither learned nor ignorant. I have known joys. That is saying too little. I told them the whole story and they listened with interest, it seems to me, at least in the beginning. But the end was a surprise to all of us. 'That was the beginning,' they said. 'Now get down to the facts.' How so? The story was finished!"), this antepenultimate paragraph, recalls, subsumes, quotes without quotation marks the first sentences of *La folie du jour* (I am neither learned nor . . .), including in itself the entire book, including itself, but only after anticipating, by quoting it in advance, the question that will form the lower edge or the final boundary of *La folie du jour*—or *almost* final, to accentuate the dissymmetry of effects. The question "A story?", posed as a question in response to the demand (Do they demand a story, a *récit*, of me?) in the antepenultimate paragraph, will be taken up again in the final sequence ("A story? No. No stories, never again."), but again, just as in the previous instance, this repetition does not follow (chronologically or logically) what nevertheless seems to come before it in the first line, in the immediate linearity of reading. We cannot even speak here of a future perfect tense, if this still presumes a regular modification of the present into its instances of a present in the past, a present in the present, and a present in the future. In this requotation of the story [*ré-citation du récit*], intensified or reinforced here by the requotation of the *word* "*récit*," it is impossible to

---

to all the occurrences of "path," "past," "pass" in Shelley's *Triumph?*)— if the question of teaching (not only the teaching of literature and the humanities) runs throughout this book, if my participation is possible only with supplementary interpretation by the translators (active, interested, inscribed in a politico-institutional field of drives, and so forth), if we are not to pass over all these stakes and interests (what happens in this respect in the universities of the Western world, in the United States, at Yale, from department to department? How is one to step in? What is the key here for decoding? What am I doing here? What are they making me do? How are the boundaries

say which one quotes the other, and above all which one forms the border of the other. Each includes the other, comprehends the other, which is to say that neither comprehends the other. Each "story" (and each occurrence of the word "story," each "story" in the story) is part of the other, makes the other a part (of itself), each "story" is at once larger and smaller than itself, includes itself without including (or comprehending) itself, identifies itself with itself even as it remains utterly different from its homonym. Of course, at intervals ranging from two to forty paragraphs, this structure of *crisscross double invagination* ("I am neither learned nor [. . . .] A story? I began: I am neither learned nor [. . . .] The story was finished! [. . .] A story? No. No stories, never again.") never ceases to refold or superpose or *overemploy* itself in the meantime, and the description of this would be interminable. I must content myself for the moment with underscoring the supplementary aspect of this structure: the chiasma of this *double invagination* is always possible, because of what I have called elsewhere the iterability of the mark. Now, if we have just seen a strikingly complex example of this in the case of a *récit*, a story, using the word *"récit,"* reciting and requoting both its possibility and its impossibility, double invagination can come about in any text, whether it is narrative in form or not, whether it is of the genre of mode *"récit"* or not, whether it speaks of it or not. Nevertheless—and this is the aspect that interested me in the beginning—double invagination, wherever it comes about, has in itself the *structure of a narrative [récit] in deconstruction*. Here the narrative is irreducible. Even

---

of all these fields, titles, corpora, and so forth, laid out? Here I can only locate the necessity of all these questions), then we must pause to consider *[on devra s'arrêter sur]* translation. It brings the *arrêt* of everything, decides, suspends, and sets in motion . . . even in "my" language, within the presumed unity of what is called the corpus of a language. *9–16 January 1978*. What will remain unreadable for me, in any case, of this text, not to mention Shelley, of course, and everything that haunts his language *[langue]* and his writing. What will remain unreadable for me of this text, once it is translated, of course, still bearing my signature. But even in "my" language, to

before it "concerns" a text in narrative form, double invagination constitutes the story of stories, the narrative of narrative, the *narrative of deconstruction in deconstruction:* the apparently outer edge of an enclosure *[clôture]*, far from being simple, simply external and circular, in accordance with the philosophical representation of philosophy, makes no sign beyond itself, toward what is utterly *other*, without becoming double or dual, without making itself be "represented," refolded, superimposed, *re-marked* within the enclosure, at least in what the structure produces as an effect of interiority. But it is precisely this structure-effect that is being deconstructed here.

[. . . .]

---

which it does not belong in a simple way. One never writes either in one's own language or in a foreign language. Derive all the consequences of this: they involve each element, each term of the preceding sentence. [. . . .]

—*Translated by James Hulbert*

TWELVE

"Letter to a Japanese Friend"

("Lettre à un ami japonais" in *Psyché:*

Inventions de l'autre [1987])

This brief text, presented *in extenso,* needs little introduction. It addresses quite directly the question of translation in the guise of a long gloss on the word *deconstruction* as prolegomenon to its translation into Japanese. With the simple, descriptive title, however, Derrida also cites a certain tradition of the Western philosopher addressing himself to a question from the East, for example Malebranche's *Conversation between a Christian Philosopher and a Chinese Philosopher on the Existence and Nature of God,* or Heidegger's "Dialogue on Language Between a Japanese and an Inquirer" in *On the Way to Language.*

Letter to a Japanese Friend

10 July 1983

Dear Professor Izutsu,[1]

At our last meeting I promised you some schematic and preliminary reflections on the word "deconstruction." What we discussed were prolegomena to a possible translation of this word into Japanese, one which would at least try to avoid, if *possible,* a negative determination of its significations or connotations. The question would be therefore what deconstruction is not, or rather *ought* not to be. I underline these words "possible" and "ought." For if the difficulties of translation can be anticipated (and the question of deconstruction is also through and through *the* question of translation, and of the language of concepts, of the conceptual corpus of so-called Western metaphysics), one should not begin by naively believing that the word "deconstruction" corresponds in French to some clear and univocal signification. There is already in "my" language a serious *[sombre]* problem of translation between what here or there can be envisaged for the word and the usage itself, the reserves of the word. And it is already clear that even in French, things change from one context to another. More so in the German, English, and especially American contexts, where the *same* word is already attached to very different connotations, inflections, and emotional or affective values. Their analysis would be interesting and warrants a study of its own.

When I choose this word, or when it imposed itself upon me —I think it was in *Of Grammatology*—I little thought it would be credited with such a central role in the discourse that interested me at the time. Among other things I wished to translate and adapt to my own ends the Heideggerian word *Destruktion* or

Abbau. Each signified in this context an operation bearing on the structure or traditional architecture of the fundamental concepts of ontology or of Western metaphysics. But in French "destruction" too obviously implied an annihilation or a negative reduction much closer perhaps to Nietzschean "demolition" than to the Heideggerian interpretation or to the type of reading that I proposed. So I ruled that out. I remember having looked to see if the word "deconstruction" (which came to me it seemed quite spontaneously) was good French. I found it in the *Littré*: The grammatical, linguistic, or rhetorical senses *[portées]* were found bound up with a "mechanical" sense *[portée "machinique"].* This association appeared very fortunate and fortunately adapted to what I wanted at least to suggest. Perhaps I could cite some of the entries from the *Littré.* "*Déconstruction:* action of deconstructing. Grammatical term. Disarranging the construction of words in a sentence. 'Of deconstruction, common way of saying construction,' Lemare, *De la manière d'apprendre les langues,* chap. 17, in *Cours de langue Latine. Déconstruire.* 1. To disassemble the parts of a whole. To deconstruct a machine to transport it elsewhere. 2. Grammatical term . . . To deconstruct verse, rendering it, by the suppression of meter, similar to prose. Absolutely. ('In the system of prenotional sentences, one also starts with translation and one of its advantages is never needing to deconstruct,' Lemare, ibid., 3. *Se déconstruire* [to deconstruct itself] . . . to lose its construction. 'Modern scholarship has shown us that in a region of the timeless East, a language reaching its own state of perfection is deconstructed *[s'est déconstruite]* and altered from within itself according to the single law of change, natural to the human mind,' Villemain, *Préface du Dictionnaire de l'Académie.*"

Naturally it will be necessary to translate all of this into Japanese but that only postpones the problem. It goes without saying that if all the significations enumerated by the *Littré* interested me because of their affinity with what I "meant" *["voulais-dire"],* they concerned, metaphorically, so to say, only models or regions of meaning and not the totality of what deconstruction aspires to at its most ambitious. This is not limited to a linguistico-grammatical model, nor even a semantic model, let alone a mechanical model. These models themselves ought to be submitted to a deconstructive questioning. It is true then that these "models" have been behind a number of misunderstandings about the concept and word of "deconstruction" because of the temptation to reduce it to these models.

It must also be said that the word was rarely used and was largely unknown in France. It had to be reconstructed in some way, and its use value had been determined by the discourse that was then being attempted around and on the basis of *Of Grammatology*. It is to this use value that I am now going to try to give some precision and not some primitive meaning or etymology sheltered from or outside of any contextual strategy.

A few more words on the subject of "the context." At that time structuralism was dominant. "Deconstruction" seemed to be going in the same direction since the word signified a certain attention to structures (which themselves were neither simply ideas, nor forms, nor syntheses, nor systems). To deconstruct was also a structuralist gesture or in any case a gesture that assumed a certain need for the structuralist problematic. But it was also an antistructuralist gesture, and its fortune rests in part on this ambiguity. Structures were to be undone, decomposed, desedimented (all types of structures, linguistic, "logocentric," "phonocentric"—structuralism being especially at that time dominated by linguistic models and by a so-called structural linguistics that was also called Saussurian—socio-institutional, political, cultural, and above all and from the start philosophical). This is why, especially in the United States, the motif of deconstruction has been associated with "poststructuralism" (a word unknown in France until its "return" from the United States). But the undoing, decomposing, and desedimenting of structures, in a certain sense more historical than the structuralist movement it called into question, was not a negative operation. Rather than destroying, it was also necessary to understand how an "ensemble" was constituted and to reconstruct it to this end. However, the negative appearance was and remains much more difficult to efface than is suggested by the grammar of the word (de-), even though it can designate a genealogical restoration [*remonter*] rather than a demolition. That is why this word, at least on its own, has never appeared satisfactory to me (but what word is), and must always be girded by an entire discourse. It is difficult to effect it afterward because, in the work of deconstruction, I have had to, as I have to here, multiply the cautionary indicators and put aside all the traditional philosophical concepts, while reaffirming the necessity of returning to them, at least under erasure. Hence, this has been called, precipitously, a type of negative theology (this was neither true nor false but I shall not enter into the debate here).[2]

All the same, and in spite of appearances, deconstruction is neither an *analysis* nor a *critique* and its translation would have to take that into consideration. It is not an analysis in particular because the dismantling of a structure is not a regression toward a *simple element*, toward an *indissoluble origin*. These values, like that of analysis, are themselves philosophemes subject to deconstruction. No more is it a critique, in a general sense or in a Kantian sense. The instance of *krinein* or of *krisis* (decision, choice, judgment, discernment) is itself, as is all the apparatus of transcendental critique, one of the essential "themes" or "objects" of deconstruction.

I would say the same about *method.* Deconstruction is not a method and cannot be transformed into one. Especially if the technical and procedural significations of the words are stressed. It is true that in certain circles (university or cultural, especially in the United States) the technical and methodological "metaphor" that seems necessarily attached to the very word "deconstruction" has been able to seduce or lead astray. Hence the debate that has developed in these circles: Can deconstruction become a methodology for reading and for interpretation? Can it thus let itself be reappropriated and domesticated by academic institutions?

It is not enough to say that deconstruction could not be reduced to some methodological instrumentality or to a set of rules and transposable procedures. Nor will it do to claim that each deconstructive "event" remains singular or, in any case, as close as possible to something like an idiom or a signature. It must also be made clear that deconstruction is not even an *act* or an *operation.* Not only because there would be something "patient" or "passive" about it (as Blanchot says, more passive than passivity, than the passivity that is opposed to activity). Not only because it does not return to an individual or collective *subject* who would take the initiative and apply it to an object, a text, a theme, etc. Deconstruction takes place, it is an event that does not await the deliberation, consciousness, or organization of a subject, or even of modernity. *It deconstructs it-self. It can be deconstructed. [Ça se déconstruit.]* The "it" *[ça]* is not here an impersonal thing that is opposed to some egological subjectivity. *It is in deconstruction* (the *Littré* says, "to deconstruct it-self *[se déconstruire]* . . . to lose its construction"). And the "se" of "se déconstruire," which is not the reflexivity of an ego or of a consciousness, bears the whole enigma. I recognize, my dear friend, that in trying to make a word clearer so as to assist its translation, I am only thereby increasing the difficulties: "the impossible task of the translator" (Benjamin). This too is what is meant by "deconstructs."

If deconstruction takes place everywhere it *[ça]* takes place, where there is something (and is not therefore limited to meaning or to the text in the current and bookish sense of the word), we still have to think through what is happening in our world, in modernity, at the time when deconstruction is becoming a motif, with its word, its privileged themes, its mobile strategy, etc. I have no simple and formalizable response to this question. All my essays are attempts to have it out with this formidable question. They are modest symptoms of it, quite as much as tentative interpretations. I would not even dare to say, following a Heideggerian schema, that we are in an "epoch" of being-in-deconstruction, of a being-in-deconstruction that would manifest or dissimulate itself at one and the same time in other "epochs." This thought of "epochs" and especially that of a gathering of the destiny of being and of the unity of its destination or its dispersions *(Schicken, Geschick)* will never be very convincing.

To be very schematic I would say that the difficulty of *defining* and therefore also of *translating* the word "deconstruction" stems from the fact that all the predicates, all the defining concepts, all the lexical significations, and even the syntactic articulations, which seem at one moment to lend themselves to this definition or to that translation, are also deconstructed or deconstructible, directly or otherwise, etc. And that goes for the *word*, the very unity of the *word* deconstruction, as for every *word. Of Grammatology* questioned the unity "word" and all the privileges with which it was credited, especially in its *nominal* form. It is therefore only a discourse or rather a writing that can make up for the incapacity of the word to be equal to a "thought." All sentences of the type "deconstruction is X" or "deconstruction is not X" *a priori* miss the point, which is to say that they are at least false. As you know, one of the principal things at stake in what is called in my texts "deconstruction" is precisely the delimiting of ontology and above all of the third person present indicative: S *is* P.

The word "deconstruction," like all other words, acquires its value only from its inscription in a chain of possible substitutions, in what is too blithely called a "context." For me, for what I have tried and still try to write, the word has interest only within a certain context, where it replaces and lets itself be determined by such other words as "écriture," "trace," "differance," "supplement," "hymen," "pharmakon," "marge," "entame," "parergon," etc.[3] By definition, the list can never be closed, and I have cited only names, which is inadequate and done only for reasons of economy. In fact, I should have cited the sentences and the interlinking of sentences which in their turn determine these names in some of my texts.

What deconstruction is not? everything of course!

What is deconstruction? nothing of course!

I do not think, for all these reasons, that it is a *good word [un bon mot]*. It is certainly not elegant *[beau]*. It has definitely been of service in a highly determined situation. In order to know what has been imposed upon it in a chain of possible substitutions, despite its essential imperfection, this "highly determined situation" will need to be analyzed and deconstructed. This is difficult and I am not going to do it here.

One final word to conclude this letter, which is already too long. I do not believe that translation is a secondary and derived event in relation to an original language or text. And as "deconstruction" is a word, as I have just said, that is essentially replaceable in a chain of substitution, then that can also be done from one language to another. The chance, first of all the chance of (the) "deconstruction," would be that another word (the same word and an other) can be found in Japanese to say the same thing (the same and an other), to speak of deconstruction, and to lead elsewhere to its being written and transcribed, in a word which will also be more beautiful.

When I speak of this writing of the other which will be more beautiful, I clearly understand translation as involving the same risk and chance as the poem. How to translate

"poem"? a "poem"? . . .

With my best wishes,
Jacques Derrida

—Translated by David Wood and Andrew Benjamin

NOTES

1. Toshiko Izutsu is a well-known Japanese Islamologist.—ED.

2. Derrida enters into this question at length in "How to Avoid Speaking" [1987].

3. Derrida has often exploited the contradictory semantic possibilities of all these terms: "entame," for example, comes from a verb that means to incise, to cut or bite into, and thus also to begin something; "parergon" is that which is neither simply inside nor outside the work or "ergon," like the frame of a painting. Derrida takes the term as the title of his essay on Kant's *Third Critique* in *The Truth in Painting* [1978].—ED.

THIRTEEN

From "Restitutions of the Truth in Pointing" in

The Truth in Painting ("Restitutions: De la vérité en

pointure" in *La Vérité en peinture* [1978])

More than one language is put in play in this text and in more than one sense. First, it is a "polylogue" for an unspecified number of voices; second, its object is the altogether other "language" of painting, specifically the idiom of Van Gogh; third, it concerns an exchange (a "correspondence") between two apparently disparate points of view regarding a painting of Van Gogh's: that of the eminent American art historian Meyer Schapiro and that of the German thinker Martin Heidegger whose *Origin of the Work of Art* (1935) makes reference to one of Van Gogh's paintings of shoes.

Whose shoes are they? While Schapiro and Heidegger disagree over their attribution, the colloquy of Derrida and his interlocutors finds a secret correspondence beneath the overt disagreement: together, the two great professors attribute or restore the shoes to some owner, some subject (to Van Gogh himself or to a peasant). The gesture of restitution is essentially the same even though a great gulf divides the Heideggerian meditation on the origin of the work of art from Schapiro's historicism. From out of this gulf arise specters or ghosts of a recent German past, one that left mountains of abandoned shoes all over the European landscape. The discussants take up the notion of restitution (to the owner, to the artist, to the victims, to the past) with a certain detachment. Indeed, it is the *detachability* of the work from any context, all the ways in which the painted shoes are not tied up with or tied down to any subject, that impels this polylogue, for more than a hundred pages, in a back and forth movement, like laces crossing over the tongue of shoes. In the process, Derrida does not so much fill Van Gogh's shoes with his words as restore to words their condition of detachable things, abandoned, unlaced shoes. That condition lends itself to a range of tonal variations: from gay abandon to stark analysis to an almost sinister foreboding. No summary could do justice to all these crossings, but the following excerpts, from the first thirty-five pages, can give at least some notion of the polytonality of such a text.

"Restitutions" is the final essay of *The Truth in Painting*, a collection which brings together two other texts on the plastic arts (the works of Valerio Adami and Titus Carmel) as well as a long essay on Kant's *Third Critique* ("Parergon").

Restitutions of the Truth in Pointing [*pointure*]

for J. C. . . . . . sztejn

POINTURE (Latin *punctura*), sb. fem. Old synonym of prick. Term in printing, small iron blade with a point, used to fix the page to be printed on to the tympan. The hole which it makes in the paper. Term in shoemaking, glovemaking: number of stitches in a shoe or glove.

—Littré

I owe you the truth in painting, and I will tell it to you.

—Cézanne

But truth is so dear to me, and so is the *seeking to make true*, that indeed I believe, I believe I would still rather be a cobbler than a musician with colors.

—Van Gogh

——And yet. Who said—I can't remember—"there are no ghosts in Van Gogh's pictures"? Well, we've got a ghost story on our hands here all right. But we should wait until there are more than two of us before we start.

——Before we get going at the double [*pour appareiller*], you mean: we should wait until there are even more than three of us.

The first part of this "polylogue" (for *n*+I—female—voices) was published in no. 3 of the journal *Macula*, as part of a group of articles entitled *Martin Heidegger and the Shoes of Van Gogh*. In it, I take my pretext from an essay by Meyer Schapiro published in the same issue of *Macula* under the title "The Still Life as a Personal Object." This is a critique of Heidegger, or more precisely of what he says about Van Gogh's shoes in *The Origin of the Work of Art*. Schapiro's article, dedicated to the memory of Kurt Goldstein ("who was the first," says the author, "to draw my attention to this essay [*The Origin of the Work of Art*] presented in a lecture-course in 1935 and 1936"), first appeared in 1968, in *The Reach of Mind: Essays in Memory of Kurt Goldstein* (New York: Springer.].

TRANSLATORS' NOTE:—Translations from Heidegger take account of Derrida's French versions. The translators have however consulted the English translation of *The Origin of the Work of Art* by Albert Hofstadter, in Martin Heidegger, *Poetry, Language, Thought* (New York: Harper & Row, 1971).

——Here they are. I'll begin. What of shoes? What, shoes? Whose are the shoes? What are they made of? And even, who are they? Here they are, the questions, that's all.

——Are they going to remain there, put down, left lying about, abandoned [*délaissées*]? Like these apparently empty, unlaced [*délacées*] shoes, waiting with a certain detachment for someone to come, and to say, to come and say what has to be done to tie them together again?

——What I mean is, there will have been something like the pairing of a correspondence between Meyer Schapiro and Martin Heidegger. And that if we take the trouble to formalize a little, that correspondence would return to the questions I've just laid down.

——It would return to them. *Returning* will have great scope [*portée*] in this debate (and so will *scope*), if, that is, it's a matter of knowing to whom and to what certain shoes, and perhaps shoes in general, *return*. To whom and to what, in consequence, one would have to *restitute* them, render them, to discharge a debt.

——Why always say of painting that it renders, that it restitutes?

——To discharge a more or less ghostly debt, restitute the shoes, render them to their rightful owner; if it's a matter of knowing from where they *return*, from the city (Schapiro) or the fields (Heidegger), like rats, which I suddenly have an idea they look like (then who is these rats' Rat Man?), unless it is rather that they look like snares [*pièges à lacets*] lying in wait for the stroller in the middle of the museum (will he or she be able to avoid being in too much of a hurry and catching his or her feet in them?); if it's a question of knowing what revenue is still produced by their out-of-service dereliction, what surplus value is unleashed by the annulment of their use value: *outside* the picture, inside the *picture*, and, third, as a picture, or to put it very equivocally, *in their painting truth*; if it's a question of knowing

Old Shoes with Laces. National Vincent Van Gogh Museum, Amsterdam.

what ghost's step [*quel pas de revenant*], city dweller or peasant, still comes to haunt them ("the ghost of my other I," the other I of Vincent the signatory, as Schapiro suggests quoting Knut Hamsun—but Heidegger also does this, elsewhere); if it's a question of knowing whether the shoes in question are haunted by some ghost or are ghosting/returning [*la revenance*] itself (but then what are, who are in truth, and whose and what's, these things?). In short, what does it all come down to [*ça revient à quoi*]? To whom? To whom and to what are we to restitute, to reattach, to readjust precisely

——to what shoe size exactly, made to measure, adequately

——and where from? How? If at least it's a question of knowing, returning will be from long range [*d'une longue portée*].

What I'm saying is that there will have been a correspondence between Meyer Schapiro and Martin Heidegger.

One of them says in 1935: that pair comes back to, belongs to, amounts to the peasant, and even the peasant woman

——what makes him so sure that they are a *pair of* shoes? What is a pair?

——I don't know yet. In any case, Heidegger has no doubt about it; it's a pair-of-peasant-shoes (*ein Paar Bauernschuhe*). And *ça revient*, this indissociable whole, this paired thing, from the fields and to the peasant, man or even woman. Thus Heidegger does not answer one question, he is sure of the thing before any other question. So it seems. The other one, not agreeing at all, says after mature reflection, thirty-three years later, exhibiting the juridical exhibits (but without asking himself any questions beyond this and without asking any other question): no, there's been an error and a projection, if not deception and perjury, *ça revient*, this pair, from the city

——what makes him so sure that it's a *pair of* shoes? What is a pair, in this case? Or in the case of gloves and other things like that?

——I don't know yet. In any case, Schapiro has no doubts about this and lets none show. And according to him, *ça revient*, this pair, from the city, to some city dweller and even to a particular "man of the town and city," to the picture's signatory, to Vincent, bearer of the name Van Gogh as well as of the shoes which thus seem to complete/complement him, himself or his first name, just when he takes them back, with a "they're mine" ["*it's coming back to me*": *ça me revient*], these convex objects which he has pulled off his feet

——or these hollow objects from which he has withdrawn himself.

——It's only just beginning but already one has the impression that the pair in question, if it is a pair, might well not come back to anyone. The two things might then exasperate, even if they were not *made in order to* disappoint, the desire for attribution, for reattribution with surplus value, for restitution with all the profit of a retribution. Defying the *tribute,* they might well be made in order to remain-there.

———But what does *remain* mean in this case?

———Let us posit as an axiom that the desire for attribution is a desire for appropriation. In matters of art as it is everywhere else. To say: this (this painting or these shoes) is due to [*revient à*] X, comes down to [*revient à*] saying: it is due to me, via the detour of the "it is due to (a) me." Not only: it is properly due to such-and-such, man or woman, to the male or female wearer ("Die Bäuerin auf dem Acker *trägt* die Schuhe. . . . Die Bäuerin dagegen *trägt* einfach die Schuhe," says the one in 1935, "They are clearly pictures of the artist's *own* shoes, not the shoes of a peasant," replies the other in 1968, my emphasis), but it is properly due to *me,* via a short detour: the identification, among many other identifications, of Heidegger with the peasant and Schapiro with the city dweller, of the former with the rooted and the sedentary, the latter with the uprooted emigrant. A demonstration to be followed up, for let us have no doubt about this, in this restitution trial, it's also a question of the shoes, or even the clogs, and going only a little further back for the moment, of the feet of two illustrious Western professors, neither more nor less.

———It's certainly a question of feet and of many other things, always supposing that feet are something, and something identifiable with itself. Without even looking elsewhere or further back, *restitution* reestablishes in rights or property by placing the subject upright again, in its stance, in its institution. "The erect body," writes Schapiro.

———Let us then consider the shoes as an institute, a monument. There is nothing natural in this product. In the analysis of this example, Heidegger is interested in the product (*Zeug*). (As a convenient simplification, let us retain the translation of *Zeug* as "product." It is used in the (French) translation of *Holzwege,* for the translation of *The Origin of the Work of Art. Zeug,* as we must specify and henceforth remember, is doubtless a "product," an artifact, but also a utensil, a generally useful product, whence Heidegger's first question on "usefulness.") Speaking of this artifact, the one says, before even asking himself or posing any other question: this pair is due to the one (male or female). To the other, replies the other, proof in hand but without further ado, and the one does not amount to the same thing as [*ne revient pas à*] the other. But in the two attributions it does perhaps amount to the same thing via a short detour, does perhaps come down to a subject who says me, to an identification.

——And these shoes concern them [*les regardent:* literally, "look at them"]. They concern us. Their detachment is obvious. Unlaced, abandoned, detached from the subject (wearer, holder or owner, or even author-signatory) and detached/untied in themselves (the laces are untied)

——detached from one another even if they are a pair, but with a supplement of detachment on the hypothesis that they don't form a pair. For where do they both—I mean Schapiro on one side, Heidegger on the other—get their certainty that it's a question here of a pair of shoes? What is a pair in this case? Are you going to make my question disappear? Is it in order not to hear it that you're speeding up the exchange of these voices, of these unequal tirades? Your stanzas disappear more or less rapidly, simultaneously intercut and interlaced, held together at the very crossing point of their interruptions. Caesuras that are only apparent, you won't deny it, and a purely faked multiplicity. Your periods remain without enumerable origin, without destination, but they have authority in common. And you keep me at a distance, me and my request, measuredly, I'm being avoided like a catastrophe. But inevitably I insist: *what is a pair in this case?*

——detached in any case, they concern us, look at us, mouth agape, that is, mute, making or letting us chatter on, dumbstruck before those who make them speak (*"Dieses hat gesprochen,"* says one of the two great interlocutors) and who in reality are made to speak by them. They become as if sensitive to the comic aspect of the thing, sensitive to a point of imperturbably restrained hilarity. Faced with a procedure [*démarche*] that is so sure of itself, that cannot in its certainty be dismantled, the thing, pair or not, laughs.

———We should return to the thing itself. And I don't know yet where to start from. I don't know if it must be talked or written about. Producing a discourse, making a speech on the subject of it, on the subject of anything at all, is perhaps the first thing to avoid. I've been asked for a discourse. They've put a picture (but which one exactly?) and two texts under my nose. I've just read, for the first time, "The Still Life as a Personal Object: A Note on Heidegger and Van Gogh." And reread, once again, *Der Ursprung des Kunstwerkes.* I won't here write the chronicle of my previous readings. I'll retain from them only this, in order to get going. I have always been convinced of the strong necessity of Heidegger's questioning, even if it *repeats* here, in the worst as well as the best sense of the word, the traditional philosophy of art. And convinced of its necessity, perhaps, to the very extent that it does this. But each time I've seen the celebrated passage on "a famous picture by Van Gogh" as a moment of pathetic collapse, derisory, and symptomatic, significant.

———Significant of what?

———No hasty step here, no hurrying pace toward the answer. Hurrying along [*la précipitation du pas*]¹ is perhaps what no one has ever been able to avoid when faced with the provocation of this "famous picture." This collapse interests me. Schapiro also detects it in his own way (which is also that of a detective) and his analysis interests me thereby, even if it does not satisfy me. In order to answer the question of what such a collapse signifies, will we have to reduce it to a dispute over the attribution of the shoes? Will it be necessary, in painting or in reality, to fight over the shoes? Necessary to ask oneself only: who(se) are they? I hadn't thought of this but I now find myself imagining that, despite the apparent poverty of this quarrel over restitution or of this trafficking in shoes, a certain deal done might well make everything pass through it. In its enormity, the problem of the origin of the work of art might well pass through these lace holes, through the eyelets in the shoes (in a painting) by Van Gogh. Yes, why not? But on condition that this treatment, of course, should not be abandoned to the hands of Martin Heidegger or to the hands of Meyer Schapiro. I do say "not be abandoned," for we intend to make use of their hands, too, or even, what's more [*au reste*] of their feet.

The choice of the procedure to adopt is difficult. It slides around. What is certain is that there will have been correspondence between Heidegger and Schapiro. And that there is here something like a pairing-together in the difference of opinion, the enigma of a complementary fitting-together of the two sides, of one edge to the other. But I still don't know where to start from, whether I must speak or write about it, nor, above all, in what tone, following what code, with a view to what scene. And in what rhythm, that of the peasant or that of the city dweller, in the age of artisanal production or that of industrial technology? Neither these questions nor these scruples are outside the debate begun by Heidegger around the work of art.

But do I really want to undertake this procedure?

I shall begin by fixing a certainty that looks axiomatic. Settling myself in it as though in a place where things appear not to move, where things no longer slide around, I'll set off from there (very quickly), having blocked one of my feet in that place, one of my points, immobile and crouched before the starter's gun. This place which I begin by occupying slowly, before the race, can here only be a place of language.

Here it is. Questions about awkward gait (limping or shifty?), questions of the type: "Where to put one's feet?" "How is it going to work [*marcher*]?" "And what if it doesn't work?" "What happens when it doesn't work (or when you hang up your shoes or miss them with your feet)?" "When—and for what reason—it stops working?" "Who is walking?" "With whom?" "With what." "On whose feet?" "Who is pulling whose leg? [*qui fait marcher qui?*]" "Who is making what go? [*qui fait marcher quoi?*]" "What is making whom or what work?" etc., all these idiomatic figures of the question seem to me, right here, to be necessary.

Necessary: it's an attribute.

——So are the shoes. They're attributed to a subject, tied on to that subject by an operation the logico-grammatical equivalent of which is more or less relevant.

——*Necessary* remains an adjective which is still a little vague, loose, open, spreading. It would be better to say: question-idioms the form of which is very *fitting*. It fits. It adjusts, in a strict, tight, well-laced fashion, clinging tightly but flexibly, in vocabulary, letter, or figure to the very body of what you here wish to turn into an object, that is, feet. Both feet, that is of the first importance.

——But you don't say a pair of feet. You say a pair of shoes or gloves. What is a pair in this case, and where do they both get the idea that Van Gogh painted a pair? Nothing proves it.

[. . . .]

——I advance, then: what of shoes when it doesn't work/when they don't walk? When they are put on one side, remaining for a greater or lesser period, or even forever, out of use? What do they mean? What are they worth? More or less? And according to what economy? What does their surplus (or minus) value signal toward? What can they be exchanged for? In what sense (whom? what?) do they *faire marcher?* and make speak?

There's the subject, announced.

It returns slowly. But always too quickly—precipitate step/no hurry [*pas de précipitation*]—headfirst to occupy upright, instantaneously, the abandoned places; to invest and appropriate the out-of-use places as though they remained unoccupied only by accident, and not by structure.

The subject having been announced, let's leave the shoes here for a while. Something *happens*, something *takes place* when shoes are abandoned, empty, out of use for a while or forever, apparently detached from the feet, carried or carrying, untied in themselves if they have laces, the one always untied from the other but with this supplement of detachment on the hypothesis that they do not make a pair.

——Yes, let us suppose for example two (laced) right shoes or two left shoes, They no longer form a pair, but the whole thing squints or limps, I don't know, in strange, worrying, perhaps threatening and slightly diabolical fashion. I sometimes have this impression with some of Van Gogh's shoes and I wonder whether Schapiro and Heidegger aren't hastening to make them into a pair in order to reassure themselves. Prior to all reflection you reassure yourself with the pair.

——And then you know how to find your bearings in thought.[2]

——As soon as these abandoned shoes no longer have any strict relationship with a subject borne or bearing/wearing, they become the anonymous, lightened, voided support (but so much the heavier for being abandoned to its opaque inertia) of an absent subject whose name returns to haunt the open form.

——But precisely, it is never completely open. It retains a form, the form of the foot. Informed by the foot, it is a form, it describes the external surface or the envelope of what is called a "form," that is, and I quote Littré again, a "piece of wood in the shape [figure] of a foot which is used to assemble a shoe." This form or figure of the foot

——Schapiro will see the "face" [la figure] of Van Gogh in "his" shoes.

——This wooden "form" or figure of the foot replaces the foot, like a prothesis whose shoe remains ever informed. All these ghost-limbs come and go, go more or less well, don't always fit.

——So what is one doing when one attributes shoes? When one gives or restitutes them? What is one doing when one attributes a painting or when one identifies a signatory? And especially when one goes so far as to attribute painted shoes (in painting) to the presumed signatory of that painting? Or conversely when one contests his ownership of them?

——Perhaps this is where there will have been correspondence between Meyer Schapiro and Martin Heidegger. I've an interest in its having taken place. Apparently. But we don't yet know what this place is and what "to take place" signifies in this case, where, how, etc.

————The question's just been asked: what is one doing when one attributes (real) shoes to the presumed signatory of a painting which one presumes to represent these same shoes? Let's be more precise: *subject*-shoes (*support* destined to bear their wearer on the ground, of towns or fields, support which would here figure the first *substratum*, unless the wearer put them to a use other than that of walking, in which case the word "use" would, according to some, run the risk of perversion) but itself the subject of a canvas which in turn constitutes its subject or framed support. And it is this double *subject* (shoes in painting) that the two litigants want to see restituted to the true subject: the peasant man or woman on the one side, the city-dwelling painter on the other (a bit more of a subject through being the signatory of the picture supposed to represent his own shoes, or even himself in person: all the subjects are here as close as can be to themselves, apparently).

Where is the truth of this taking-place? *The Origin of the Work of Art* belongs to a great discourse on place and on truth. Through everything just announced, it can be seen to communicate (without its "author" 's knowing it?) with the question of fetishism, extended beyond its "political economy" or its "psychoanalysis" in the strict sense, or even beyond the simple and traditional opposition of the fetish with the thing itself.

Everything points to a desire to speak the truth about the fetish.

[. . . .]

————There are two types of object and the "form" of the shoe has another privilege: it combines in a system the two types of object defined by Freud: elongated, solid or firm on one surface, hollow or concave on the other. It turns inside out

————like a pair of gloves. Van Gogh painted a pair (?) of gloves (in January 1889, in Arles) and in the note which he devotes to it, Schapiro again seems to consider them to be "personal objects." He reappropriates them, hastens to pair them up, and even to pair them with the cypresses which appear in the same still life ("The choice of objects is odd, but we recognize in it Van Gogh's spirit. In other still lives he has introduced objects that *belong to him* (my emphasis—J.D.) in an intimate way—his hat and pipe and tobacco pouch. . . . His still lives are often personal subjects, little outer pieces of the self exposed with less personal but always significant things. Here the blue gloves, *joined like two hands* (my emphasis—J.D.) in a waiting passive mood, *are paired in diagonal symmetry* with a branch of cypress, a gesticulating tree that was deeply poetic to Van Gogh . . . the gloves and the branches *belong together . . .*" (my emphasis—J.D.).[3]

———I suggest that we don't yet risk dealing directly with this question of fetishism, with the reversibility of gloves, or with directionality in the pair. For the moment I'm interested in the correspondence between Meyer Schapiro and Martin Heidegger.

———We're marking time. We're not even sliding around, we're floundering, rather, with a slightly indecent complacency. To what are we to relate this word "correspondence" which keeps on returning? To this exchange of letters in 1965?

———I would be interested rather in a secret correspondence, obviously: obviously secret, encrypted in the ether of obviousness and truth, too obvious because in this case the cipher remains secret because it is not concealed.

In short, again entrusted to the purveyor of truth, this correspondence is a secret for no one. Its secret ought to be readable in black and white [*à lettre ouverte*]. The secret correspondence could be deciphered *right on the level of* the public correspondence. It does not take place anywhere else and is not inscribed elsewhere. Each of them says: I owe you the truth in painting and I will tell it to you. But the emphasis should be placed on the debt and on the *owe* [*doit: il doit* means "he must," "he ought," "he should," and also "he owes"], the truthless truth of truth. What do they both owe, and what must they discharge through this restitution of the shoes, the one striving to return them to the peasant woman, the other to the painter?

Yes, there was indeed that exchange of letters in 1965. Schap-

Still Life (basket with oranges and lemons, branches, gloves). Mellon Collection, Upperville, Virginia.

iro reveals it in "La nature morte," which is how one must translate into French "The Still Life," which you have just read. This "Dead Nature," the essay which bears this title, is a homage rendered, a present made to one dead, a gift dedicated to the memory of Kurt Goldstein, who had, during his lifetime, earned Schapiro's gratitude by this gesture at least: having given him *The Origin of the Work of Art"* to read ("It was Kurt Goldstein who first called my attention to this essay . . ."). In a certain way, Schapiro discharges a debt and a duty of friendship by dedicating his "Dead Nature" to his dead friend. This fact is far from being indifferent or extrinsic (we shall return to it), or at least the extrinsic always intervenes, like the *parergon*, within the scene. Remember these facts and dates. Meanwhile, I shall pick out a few of them drily. Having emigrated when very young, Schapiro teaches at Columbia (New York) where Goldstein, fleeing Nazi Germany in 1933 (having been imprisoned there, and then freed on condition of leaving the country) himself taught from 1936 to

1940. He arrived there after a painful stay of one year in Amsterdam, precisely. He wrote *The Structure of the Organism* there. These are the very years in which Heidegger was giving his lectures on *The Origin of the Work of Art* and his *Introduction to Metaphysics* course (the two texts in which he refers to Van Gogh).

This last act happens, then, in New York, Columbia University, where, unless I'm mistaken, Schapiro was already living and working when Goldstein arrived to teach from 1936 until his death, with a break during the war (Harvard and Boston from 1940 to 1945). This last act

———Is it the last?

———At the present date,[4] the last act is in New York, at this great university institution, Columbia, that has welcomed so many emigrant professors, but what a trip and what a story, for almost a century, for these shoes of Van Gogh's. They haven't moved, they haven't said anything, but how they've made people walk and talk! Goldstein, the aphasia-man, who died aphasic, said nothing about them. He simply indicated, pointed out Heidegger's text. But it all looks just as if Schapiro, from New York (where he also delivered Goldstein's funeral oration in 1965), was disputing possession of the shoes with Heidegger, was taking them back so as to restitute them, via Amsterdam and Paris (Van Gogh in Paris) to Van Gogh, but *at the same time [du même coup]* to Goldstein, who had drawn his attention to Heidegger's hijack. And Heidegger hangs onto them. And when both of them say, basically, "I owe you the truth" (for they both claim to be telling the truth, or even the truth of the truth—in painting and in shoes), they also say: I owe the shoes, I must return them to their rightful owner, to their proper belonging: to the peasant man or woman on the one side, to the city-dwelling painter and signatory of the painting on the other. But to whom in truth? And who is going to believe that this episode is merely a theoretical or philosophical dispute for the interpretation of a work or The Work of Art? Or even a quarrel between experts for the attribution of a picture or a model? In order to restitute them, Schapiro bitterly disputes possession of the shoes with Heidegger, with "Professor Heidegger," who is seen then, all in all, to have tried to put them on his own feet, by peasant-proxy, to put them *back* onto his man-of-the-soil feet, with the pathos of the "call of the earth," of the *Feldweg* or the *Holzwege* which, in 1935–36, was not foreign to what drove Goldstein to undertake his long march toward New York, via Amsterdam. There is much to discharge, to return, to restitute, if not to expiate in all this. It all looks as though Schapiro, not content with thanking a dead man for what he gave him to read, was offering to the memory of his colleague, fellow man and friend, nomad, émigré, city dweller,

——a detached part, a severed ear, but detached or severed from whom?

——the pair taken back, whisked away, or even snatched from the common enemy, or at any rate the common discourse of the common enemy. For Schapiro, too, and in the name of the truth, it is a matter of finding his feet again [*reprendre pied*], of taking back [*reprendre*] the shoes so as to put the right feet back in them. First of all by alleging that these shoes were those of a migrant and city dweller, "the artist, by that time a man of town and city," things later to get dangerously complicated by the fact that this migrant never stopped uttering the discourse of rural, artisanal, and peasant ideology. All these great professors will, as they say, have invested a lot in these shoes which are out of use in more ways than one. They've piled it on [*Ils en ont remis*]. *Remettre* would carry a lot of weight in this debate. The snares [*rets*] of these shoes are formed of these re- prefixes in *revenir* "to return" and *remettre*. *Remise des chaussures* ["giving the shoes back"; "putting the shoes back on"; "handing the shoes over"; "shoe shed"]. They are, they can always be detached (in all the senses we have listed), abandoned, *à la remise*. A temptation, inscribed from that moment on the very object, to put it back, to put the shoes back on one's feet, to hand them over to the subject, to the authentic wearer or owner reestablished in his rights and reinstated in his being-upright. The structure of the thing and the trial obliges you, then, always, to keep adding to it. The measure here is one of *supplementary retortion*.

———Which is what this incredible reconstitution is now doing. It's a delirious dramaturgy that projects in its turn: a collective hallucination. These shoes are hallucinogenic.

———Yes, I'm going rather too quickly here. Let's say that all this is going on into the bargain, and give me credit for the moment. Allow me a slight advance and let's say that I'm espousing what was, perhaps, on both sides, a delirium. There is persecution in this narrative, in this story of shoes to be identified, appropriated, and you know how many bodies, names, and anonymities, nameable and unnameable, this tale is made up of. We'll come back to it. What carries weight here, and what matters to me, is this correspondence between Meyer Schapiro and Martin Heidegger.

[. . . .]

———The literal correspondence, what you call the exchange of letters, is now (just about) a public phenomenon. Made public by Schapiro in his homage to the memory of Goldstein. This henceforth public exchange gave rise, apparently, to something like a disagreement. We could say that it resulted in a disagreement. At any rate, Schapiro who unveils and comments on this correspondence, thus hanging onto the last word, concludes on a disagreement. He claims to hold the truth of the shoes (of the picture) of Vincent (Van Gogh). And as he owes the truth, he restitutes it. He identifies (in all sense of this word) the painting and the shoes, assigns them their points or their proper size [*pointure*], names the work and attributes the subject of the work (the shoes) to the subject of the work, that is, to its true subject, the painter, Van Gogh. According to him, Heidegger gets both the painting and the shoes wrong. By attributing them to some peasant man or woman, he remains in error ("the error lies . . ."), in imaginary projection, the very thing against which he claimed to put us on our guard ("He has indeed 'imagined everything and projected it into the painting' "). According to Schapiro, Heidegger has put the shoes back onto (male or female) peasants' feet. He has, in advance, laced them, bound them on to peasant ankles, those of a subject whose identity, in the very contour of its absence, appears quite strict. Such, according to Schapiro, is the error, the imagination, the precipitate projection. It has many causes, Schapiro detects more than one of them, but let's leave that aside for the moment.

——But what's the cause of this so-called public correspondence?

——Like all causes, and everything on trial [*toute chose en procès*], the proximate cause is a sort of trap. Schapiro lays it for Heidegger before catching his own feet in it.

[. . . .]

So Schapiro, insouciant, lays a trap for Heidegger. He already suspects the "error," "projection," "imagination" in Heidegger's text pointed out to him by his friend and colleague Goldstein. The hearing having begun thus, he writes to Professor Heidegger (that's what he calls him when speaking of the colleague and correspondent, and simply Heidegger for the famous thinker, author of *The Origin of the Work of Art*): which picture exactly were you referring to? The "kind" reply from Professor H. ("In reply to my question, Professor Heidegger has kindly written me that the picture to which he referred is one that he saw in a show at Amsterdam in March 1930. This is clearly de la Faille's no. 255 [see figure 1].") closes on its author like a trap. You can hear the noise: clear. It's clear, "clearly," understood, the case has been heard, de la Faille 255, that can't come down/back to peasanthood: "They are the shoes of the artist, by that time a man of the town and city." Hearing over, sentence decided: all that's required is to complete or refine the account of this trial which, all in all, was rapidly expedited. The professor is caught. Schapiro, confirmed in his suspicion, can now reconstitute one of the possible mechanisms of the mistake, a mistake which is itself in the service of an instinctual and political pathos (the rural, peasant "ideology"): a sort of resoling carried out with the aid of the sole from another picture seen at the same exhibition in 1930. That was the first mistake, the first trap, before the one set for the professor by Schapiro to make up the pair and leave him no chance. This by way of reply to the question put to me a moment ago: all the causes of this trial will have been traps (as if figured in advance by the apparent stake of the debate: to whom is the trap due?), pitfalls or, if you prefer, snares [*des lacets*], traps with laces. *Old Boots with Laces*, this is the title given by the large catalog of the Tuileries exhibition (1971–72) (collection of the Vincent Van Gogh National Museum in Amsterdam) to the picture that Professor Schapiro claims to identify on the basis of Professor Heidegger's unwary reply, and which he reproduces under the title *Old Shoes*. I do not yet know how much is due to Van Gogh in the choice of this title. But as a certain essential indeterminacy forms part of our problem which is also the problem of the title and the discourse produced (for example by the author) *on the subject* of the picture, it is perhaps right to leave the thing some suspense. The authors of the catalog I just quoted took the de la Faille into account, the same de la Faille that is Schapiro's authority ("The titles given by Vincent in his correspondence, and commonly adopted, have been made more specific when they were not sufficiently explicit, whence some differences compared with either the titles usual in the past, or those of the new Catalogue Raisonné by J. Baart de la Faille . . ."). Whether named by Van Gogh or not, in a title or a letter, these laces (for tightening or slackening the grip, more or less strictly, on the bearing or borne subject) sketch out the very form of the trap. As fascinating as they are (by that very fact) negligible for the two professors who make not the slightest allusion to them. That's one of the causes: the lace. A thing whose name is, in French, also the name of a trap [*le lacet:* "snare"]. It does not stand only for what passes through the eyelets of shoes or corsets. Our voices, in this very place—

——I do indeed notice, now, that strange loop

——ready to strangle

——of the undone lace. The loop is open, more so still than the untied shoes, but after a sort of sketched-out knot

——it forms a circle at its end, an open circle, as though provisionally, ready to close, like pincers or a key ring. A *leash*. In the bottom right-hand corner where it faces, symmetrically, the signature "Vincent," *in red and underlined.* It occupies there a place very commonly reserved for the artist's signature. As though, on the other side, in the other corner, on the other edge, but symmetrically, (almost) on a level with it, it stood in place of the signature, as though it took the (empty, open) place of it . . .

——If the laces are loosened, the shoes are indeed detached from the feet and in themselves. But I return to my question: they are also detached, by this fact, one from the other, and nothing proves that they form a pair. If I understand aright, no title says "pair of shoes" for this picture. Whereas elsewhere, in a letter that Schapiro quotes moreover, Van Gogh speaks of another picture, specifying *"a pair of old shoes."* Is it not the possibility of this "unpairedness" (two shoes for the same foot, for example, are more the double of each other but this double simultaneously fudges both pair and identity, forbids complementarity, paralyzes directionality, causes things to squint toward the devil), is it not the logic of this false parity, rather than of this false identity, which constructs the trap? The more I look at this painting, the less it looks as though it could walk . . .

——Yes, but for that to be the case the "unpairedness" must remain a possibility which is, I shall say, a limit possibility, improbable. And what's more, even if Van Gogh had given a title to the picture, and entitled it "pair of . . . ," that would change nothing in the effect produced, whether or not it is sought after consciously. A title does not simply define the picture it's attached to or which it's detached from according to numerous and sometimes overdetermined modes. It can form part of the picture and play more than one role in it, provide more than one figure of rhetoric in it. "Pair-of-," for example, can induce one to think of parity, the "truth of the pair," while showing unpairedness, or the peerless [*le hors-pair*]. And then, another argument, the "unpairedness" can say and show parity, the truth of the pair, with much greater force. Just as, as we shall see, the out-of-use exhibits utility or idleness exposes the work.

——I find this pair, if I may say so, gauche. Through and through. Look at the details, the inside lateral surface: you'd think it was two left feet. Of different shoes. And the more I look at them, the more they look at me, the less they look like an old pair. More like an old couple. Is it the same thing? If one let oneself slip to the facility of the symbolism you were talking about just now, the obvious bisexuality of this plural thing would stem from the inside-out passivity, open like a glove, more offered, more undressed, of the left shoe (I specify: on the left of the picture, since unpairedness can also affect the layout of a "real" pair, the left shoe facing us from the left, and the right from the right, of the picture)

[. . . .]

——If, as Schapiro suggests, the signatory is the owner or, an important nuance, the wearer of the shoes, shall we say that the half-open circle of the lace calls for a reattachment: of the painting to the signature (to the sharpness, the *pointure,* that pierces the canvas), of the shoes to their owner, or even of Vincent to Van Gogh, in short a complement, a general reattachment as truth in painting?

——That's moving far too fast. Whatever proof you claim to have in hand, the signatory of a picture cannot be identified with the nameable owner of an essentially detachable object represented in the picture. It is impossible to proceed to such an identification without an incredible ingenuousness, incredible in so authorized an expert. An identificatory ingenuousness with respect to the structure of a picture, and even to that of an imitative representation in the simplest sense of a "copy." Identificatory ingenuousness with respect to the structure of a detachable object in general and with respect to the logic of its belonging in general. What interestedness can have motivated such a faux-pas, that's the question I was trying to ask a while ago with reference to the strange three-person restitution scene, all three of them great European university professors. Why suddenly this blindness, this putting-to-sleep, all of a sudden, of all critical vigilance? Why does lucidity remain very active, hypercritical, *around* this macula, but only on its edges? Why this hasty compulsion, driving the one to give as homage to the second, the dead one, a still life–dead nature snatched from (the no less hasty and compulsive interpretation of) the other, the third or the first as you wish, the fourth party as always remaining in exclusion? *Ça donne* the better to take back, *ça prend* as it gives,[5] as soon as *there are* these laces/snares

[. . . .]

And yet. *There is* homage. It gives. That's an *Es gibt*[6] that Heidegger will have given us, better than any other, to think about. The *Es gibt* "before" being, the literal [*à la lettre*] *Es gibt*, the *Sein* starting from (and returning to) the *Es gibt Sein*.

——But we haven't yet opened the file of this correspondence between Meyer Schapiro and Martin Heidegger. Let's take our time. In any case, wherever they come from or come back from, these shoes won't come back safe and sound [*à bon port*].

——Nor cheaply [*à bon marché*]. Despite the incredible bargaining, or because of the interminable outbidding of an analysis which is never finished tying together, this time

——They will have traveled a lot, traversed all sorts of towns and territories at war. Several world wars and mass deportations. We can take our time. They *are there*, made for waiting. For leading up the garden path. The irony of their patience is infinite, it can be taken as nil. So, we had got to this public correspondence and I was saying that, sealing a disagreement, this sealed exchange was holding, under seals, another correspondence. Secret, this one, although it can be read right off the other. A symbolic correspondence, in accord, a harmonic. In this communication between two illustrious professors who have both of them a communication to make on "a famous picture by Van Gogh"

——one of the two is a specialist. Painting, and even Van Gogh, is, so to speak, his thing, he wants to keep it, he wants it returned—

————what do we notice? Through the mutual esteem, the civility of a reciprocal legitimation which appears to button the most deadly thrusts, one can feel the effects of a common code, of an analogous (identical, identifiable) desire, a resemblance in assiduity [*empressement*] (which is also an eagerness [*empressement*] in the direction of identificatory resemblance), in short, a common interest, and even a common debt, a shared duty. They owe the truth in painting, the truth of painting and even painting as truth, or even as the truth of truth. (They must [*doivent*] speak the truth in painting. It is, of course, necessary to take into account the debt or duty—"I owe you"—but what does "speak" mean here? And speak *in painting*: truth spoken *itself*, as one says "in painting"? Or truth spoken about painting, in the domain of painting? Or truth spoken in painting, by the sole means of painting, no longer spoken but—"to speak" being only a manner of speaking, a figure—*painted*, truth silently painted, itself, in painting?) In order to do this, they both have an interest in *identifying*, in identifying the subject (bearer or borne) of these shoes, in tying up, tying back together *stricto sensu*, in their right sense, these objects which can't do anything about it—in identifying and reappropriating (for themselves), in using in their turn this strange out-of-use, this product productive of so much supplementary surplus value. At all costs its size, its *pointure* must be found, even if this "subject" is not the same one for both parties. They are in agreement, that's the contract of this tacit institution, to seek for one, or to pretend to seek for one, given that both are certain in advance that they have found it. Since it is a pair, first of all, and neither of them doubts this fact, there must be a subject. So that in this shoe market [*marché;* also, "a deal"], the contract, the institution, is first of all the parity between the shoes, this very singular dual relationship which fits together the two parts of a pair (identity and difference, total identity in the concept or in formal semantics, difference and non-overlap in the directionality of the traits). If there is a pair, then a contract is possible, you can look for the subject, hope is still permitted. A colloquy—and collocation—can take place, the dispute will be able to commence or commit. It will be possible to appropriate, expropriate, take, give, take back, offer, discharge, do homage or insult. Without which

——Why do you say that this correspondence is symbolic? Symbolic of what?

——Of the symbol. Of the *symbolon.* I said symbolic correspondence because of this prior, coded commitment, because of this colloquy contracted on the basis of a common interest (reattachment by a nexus, the annexation of the shoes or, and this is enough already, the mere formation of the statement "Whose are the shoes" or, what just about comes down [*revient*] to the same thing, in the infantry of this slightly military preparation, "Whose or what's are the feet" which are here the object of the professors' constant care). This implies a sort of reciprocal recognition (of the pair), a diplomatic exchange (double and reciprocal) or in any case the law of nations presupposed by a declaration of war. In order to commemorate the mutual commitment, the shoes are shared, each party keeps one piece of the *symbolon.*[7] And the same piece, or rather the similar and different piece of the same whole, the complementary piece. This is why the pair is the condition of the symbolic correspondence. There is no symbolic contract in the case of a double which does not form a pair. Which would not be one (selfsame) thing in two, but a two in identity.

——So, finally, this correspondence bears on what subject? On the subject of correspondence? On the subject of this parity of the pair?

——Ah, here we are. On what subject. The question "Whose are the feet?" to which they wanted to bring round [*faire revenir*] the question "Whose are the shoes?" assumes that the question "Of what" or "What are the feet?" has been resolved. Are they? Do they represent? Whom or what? With or without shoes? These shoes are more or less detached (in themselves, from each other and from the feet), and by that fact discharged: from a common task or function. *Both* because they are visibly detached and because—never forget the invisible ether of this trivial self-evidence—they are *painted* objects (out-of-work because they're in a work) and the "subject" of a picture. Nonfunctioning, defunct, they are detached, in this double sense, and again in an-

other double sense, that of being untied and that of the detach-
ment/secondment of an emissary: diplomatic representation, if
you like, by metonymy or synecdoche. And what is said of the
shoes can also be said, although the operation is more delicate
around the ankle, of the neck or the feet.

On what subject, then, this correspondence? On the subject of
the subject of reattachment. They're in a hurry to tie up the
thread with the subject. Detachment is intolerable. And the correspondence takes place on the subject of the true subject of the
subject of a "famous picture." Not only on the subject of the
subject of the picture, as they say, but of the subject (bearer or
borne) of the shoes which seem to form the capital subject of the
picture, of the feet of the subject whose feet, these shoes, and
then this picture itself seem here to be detached and as if adrift.
That makes a lot of things. And it's very complicated. The structure of detachment—and therefore of the subjectivity of these
different subjects—is different in each case. And we have to
make clear that the correspondence we're interested in aims to
efface all these differences. Among which I have not yet counted
the one which determines the (underlying) subjectivity of the
shoe in its fundamental surface, the sole. Nor the still (more or
less) fundamental subjectivity of the ground (on or without the
support of the canvas) along with this *pas de contact* (this *pas de
sujet*) which, rhythmically, raises the adhesion of a march/walk/
step. The *pas* is not present or absent. And yet it works [*marche*]
badly without a pair.

——But I'm very surprised. It was indeed Heidegger's text that
opened this debate. Now he leaves any problematic of subjectivity far behind him, doesn't he? Such a problematic in fact presupposes what is here, among other things, desedimented by him,
that is, the determination of the thing as *hypokeimenon*, support,
substratum, substance, etc.?

——That's one of the paradoxes of this exchange. Each discourse in it remains unequal, inadequate to itself. In *The Origin*,
the passage on "a famous picture by Van Gogh" belongs to a
chapter "Thing and Work." He is occupied in that chapter with
removing (but removal is not enough) the thing from the meta-

physical determinations that, according to Heidegger, have *set upon* it, covering it over and simultaneously assaulting it, doing it injury [*injure*] (*Überfall*), insulting [*insultant*], as the French translator has it, what is properly speaking the thing in the thing, the product in the product, the work in the work (*das Dinghafte des Dinges, das Zeughafte des Zeuges, das Werkhafte des Werkes*). These determinations of the *Überfall* go in pairs or couples. Among them is the determination of the thing as *underneath* (*hypokeimenon* or *hypostasis*) in opposition to the *symbebekota* which arise on top of it. This oppositional couple will be transformed, in Latin, into *subjectum* (*substantia*)/*accidens*. This is only one of the pairs of oppositions that *fall upon/attack* the thing. The other two are, according to Heidegger, that of *aisthēton/noēton* (sensible/intelligible) and that of *hylē/eidos-morphē* (matter/form-figure).

We must accompany for a while this Heideggerian procedure. It constitutes the context immediately *framing* the allusion to the "famous picture." And if Schapiro is right to reproach Heidegger for being so little attentive to the internal and external context of the picture as well as to the differential seriality of the eight shoe paintings, he ought himself to have avoided a rigorously corresponding, symmetrical, analogous precipitation: that of cutting out of Heidegger's long essay, without further precautions, twenty-odd lines, snatching them brutally from their frame which Schapiro doesn't want to know about, arresting their movement and then interpreting them with a tranquillity equal to that of Heidegger when he makes the "peasant's shoes" speak. Thus, getting ready to deal with shoes in painting and with *subjectum* in multiple senses, and with ground, background, support (the earth and the canvas, earth on the canvas, canvas on the earth, shoes on the earth, earth on and under the shoes, shod feet on the earth, the subject supposed to bear (or be borne by) the feet, the shoes, etc., the subject of the picture, its subject-object and its signatory subject, all this over again on a canvas with or without an underneath, etc.), in short, getting ready to deal with *being-underneath*, with ground and below ground, it is perhaps appropriate to mark a pause, before even beginning, around this *subjectum*.

[. . . .]

I think it's appropriate for [two] reasons. The question of the underneath as ground, earth, then as sole, shoes, sock—stocking —foot, etc., cannot be foreign to the "great question" of the thing as *hypokeimenon,* then as *subjectum.* And then, if it is accepted that the procedure of *The Origin* intends to lead back beyond, upstream of or to the eve of the constitution of the *subjectum* in the apprehension of the thing (as such, as product or as work), then asking it the question of the "subject," of the subject of this pair of shoes, would perhaps involve starting with a misapprehension, by an imaginary projective or erroneous reading. Unless Heidegger ignores (excludes? forecloses? denies? leaves implicit? unthought?) an *other* problematic of the subject, for example in a displacement or development of the value "fetish." Unless, therefore, this question of the *subjectum* is displaced *otherwise,* outside the problematic of truth and speech which governs *The Origin.* The least one can say is that Schapiro does not attempt to do this. He is caught in it and without even, apparently, having the least suspicion of this.

[. . . .]

——If, then, however, this "backward step" on the road of thought was supposed to go back behind any *"subjectum,"* how do we explain this naïve, impulsive, precritical attribution of the shoes in a painting to such a determined "subject," the peasant, or rather the peasant woman, this tight attribution and determination which direct this whole discourse on the picture and its "truth"? Would we all agree about calling this gesture naïve, impulsive, precritical, as I have just done?

——Yes, and on this precise point Schapiro's demonstration confirms what could very quickly be seen. But we still have to *demarcate* the place and function of this "attribution" in the text, trace the map of its effects in the long run of Heidegger's move, its apparent noncongruence with the dominant motifs of the essay: a climb back up behind the *subjectum,* indeed, but also a critique of representation, of expression, of reproduction, etc. We shall have to come back to this, and to the logic of the *Überfall.* On all these questions, and despite having a negative and punctual pertinence, Schapiro's determination seems to me to be soon exhausted. And its "impulsive or precritical naïveté" (I pick up these words) seems to me to be entirely symmetrical or complementary with the naïveté that he rightly denounces in Heidegger. The correspondence will forward these effects, right down to their details.

[. . . .]

Let's go back to before the allusion of the "famous picture," to the point where the chapter "Thing and Work" names "the *fundamental* Greek experience of the Being of beings in general." I emphasize *fundamental* (*Grunderfahrung*). The interpretation of the thing as *hypokeimenon* and then as *subjectum* does not only produce (itself as) a slight linguistic phenomenon. The transforming translation of *hypokeimenon* as *subjectum* corresponds, according to Heidegger, to another "mode of thought" and of being-there. It translates, transports, transfers (Heidegger emphasizes the passage implied in *über*) over and beyond the aforementioned *fundamental* Greek experience: "Roman thought takes over (*übernimmt*) the Greek words (*Wörter*) without the corresponding co-originary experience of what they say, without the Greek word (*Wort*). The absence-of-ground (*Bodenlosigkeit*) of Western thought opens with this translation."

The ground (of thought) comes then to be lacking when words lose speech [*la parole*]. The "same" words (*Wörter*) deprived of the speech (*Wort*) corresponding to the originarily Greek experience of the thing, the "same" words, which are therefore no longer exactly the same, the fantomatic doubles of themselves, their light simulacra, begin to walk above the void or in the void, *bodenlos*. Let's hang on for a long time to this difference between words and speech; it will help us in a moment, and again later, to understand, beyond the narrow debate on the attribution of these attributes, of these accidents that feet reputedly are, and that shoes are *a fortiori*, what the thing *says*. What one makes or lets it say, what it makes or allows to be said.

———Ought we to believe that there is some common topos between this deprivation of ground and the place of these shoes, their taking-place or their standing-in [*leur avoir-lieu ou leur tenir lieu*]? They do indeed have an air of being a bit up in the air, *whether* they appear to have no contact with the surface, as if in levitation above what nevertheless supports them (the one on the right, the most visibly "gauche" [left] of the two, seems a little lifted up, mobile, as if it were rising to take a step, while the other stuck more firmly to the ground), or *whether*, abandoned to their being-unlaced, they suspend all experience of the ground, since such experience presupposes walking, standing upright, and that a "subject" should be in full possession of his or her or its feet, or again *whether*, more radically, their status as represented object in the strict frame of a painted canvas, or even one hung on the wall of a museum, determines the *Bodenlosigkeit* itself, provokes or defines it, translates it, signifies it or, as you will, is it, *there*

——and the desire then to make them find their feet again on the ground of the fundamental experience

——no, no, or at least not so quickly. It's only a matter, for starters, of discovering a few cave-ins of the terrain, some abysses too in the field where advance so tranquilly

——Why no tranquillity? Why this persecution?

——the discourse of attribution, declarations of property, performances or investitures of the type: this is mine, these shoes or these feet to someone who says "me" and can thereby identify himself, belong to the domain of the nameable (common: the peasant man or woman, the man of the city; or proper: Vincent Van Gogh; and proper in both desires: Heidegger, Schapiro, who demand restitution). These abysses are not the "last word" and above all do not consist simply in this *Bodenlosigkeit* about which we've just been talking. At the very moment when Heidegger is denouncing translation into Latin words, at the moment when, at any rate, he declares Greek speech to be lost, he also makes use of a "metaphor." Of at least one metaphor, that of the foundation and the ground. The ground of the Greek experience is, he says, lacking in this "translation." What I have just too hastily called "metaphor" concentrates all the difficulties to come: does one speak "metaphorically" of the ground for just

A Pair of Boots. The Baltimore Museum of Art, The Cone Collection, Baltimore, Maryland.

anything? And of walking and shoes (clothing, the tool, the institution, even investiture) for thought, language, writing, painting and the rest.

What does Heidegger say? This: as soon as one no longer apprehends the things as the Greeks did, in other words as *hypokeimenon*, but instead as *substantia*, the ground falls away. But this ground is not the *hypokeimenon*, it's the originary and fundamental experience of the Greeks or of Greek speech which apprehends the things as being-underneath. This is the ground of the *hypokeimenon*. This (metaphorical?) doubling must be interrogated on its own account. And the underneath of the underneath leads to a thinking of the abyss, rather than of the *mise-en-abyme*, and the abyss would "here" be one of the places or nonplaces ready to bear the whole of this game [*un des lieux ou non-lieux prêts à tout porter de ce jeu*; also, "one of the off-the-peg, ready-made places or nonplaces of this game"].

———Which takes us far away from Schapiro's "Still Life . . ." and from what was a moment ago, if I remember rightly, called the offering to Goldstein of the severed ear.

———No, the offering of a pair (which perhaps never existed, which no one ever had) of things detached and tied back together again to make a present of them. A present [cadeau], as the [French] noun shows, in a chain. Has it gone away? What is it to go away [s'éloigner]? The é-loignement ent-fernt, he says, distances the distant [é-loigne le lointain] . . .[8]

———I'm not going away, I'm in the process, starting from here, of coming back to what the other says. For the thing is still more hidden away or wrapped up underneath its investiture than appears to be the case. At the very moment when he calls us back to the Greek ground and to the apprehension of the thing as hypokeimenon, Heidegger implies that this originary state still covers over something, falling upon or attacking it. The hypokeimenon, that underneath, hides another underneath. And so the Latin underneath (substantia-subjectum) causes to disappear, along with the Greek ground, the Greek underneath (hypokeimenon), but this latter still hides or veils (the figure of veiling, of veiling linen as over-under, will not take long to appear, and the hymen which will draw it into undecidability will not be unrelated to the sock, the socklet, or the stocking [le bas], between foot and shoe) a "more" originary thingliness. But as the "more" carries itself away, the thing no longer has the figure or value of an "underneath." Situated (or not) "under" the underneath, it would not only open an abyss, but would brusquely and discontinuously prescribe a change of direction, or rather a completely different topic.

———Perhaps that of this returning whose great scope, just now

———Perhaps. The topos of the abyss and a fortiori that of the mise-en-abyme could also hide, or in any case dampen a little the brusque and angular necessity of this other topics. And of this other pas. That's what interests me "underneath" this correspondence with respect to a "famous picture" of old unlaced walking shoes

——half-unlaced

——and when the question of its place is posed, if I can say that. How to take this correspondence and this transfer(ence), all these translations?

[. . . .]

—*Translated by Geoff Bennington and Ian Mcleod*

NOTES

1. "Pas" means step, but it is also the adverb of negation. Derrida will exploit throughout the text this double movement, advancing and negating, of the "pas." He has also written at length about Blanchot's "pas" in "Pas" (*Parages* [1986] and Freud's "pas de thèse" (see below, **"To Speculate—on 'Freud' "**).—ED.

2. A reference to Kant's 1786 article "Was heisst: sich in Denken orientiren," translated into French as *Qu'est-ce que s'orienter dans la pensée*, trans. A. Philonenko, 4th ed. (Paris: Vrin, 1978).—TRANS.

3. Meyer Schapiro, *Van Gogh* (New York: Abrams, 1950), p. 92.

4. I reproduce here the editorial note proposed by *Macula:* "Since that date, and at a time when it was already in galley proofs, the fiction which we publish here was so to speak acted out or narrated by Jacques Derrida at Columbia University (Seminar on Theory of Literature) at the invitation of Marie-Rose Logan and Edward W. Said. This session took place on 6 October 1977. Meyer Schapiro took part in the debate which followed. Editors' Note."

5. "Ça donne," it gives; "ça prend," it takes. The impersonal pronoun *ça* is also the French term for what Freud calls the "Es," in English the id.—ED.

6. The reference is to the Heideggerian "Es gibt Sein," literally "It gives Being," but in everyday usage "There is Being." For some commentary on this phrase, see below, **Envois**, p. **493ff.**—ED.

7. A *symbolon* is the token of a promise or commitment divided between the parties.—ED.

8. On Heidegger's use of *Entfernung*, see below, **Spurs**, pp. **358–59.**—ED.

Who are they trying to kid. What is being proposed to us. Flourishes? An anthology? by what
right. And the complete text is being dissimulated from us?
Not even an anthology. Some morsels of anthology. As an invitation, if possible, to rebind,
in any case to reread. Inside out and right side
out, while taking up again by all the ends.

Nevertheless, all these morsels cannot, naturally, be bound (together).

The object of the present work, as well as its
style, is the *morsel.*

Which is always detached . . .

—*Glas,* p. 118

PART FOUR

SEXUAL DIFFERENCE IN PHILOSOPHY

WITH THE term *logocentrism,* introduced in **Of Grammatology,** Derrida indicates in an economical manner the set of traits organizing the metaphysics of presence around a center (see above, pp. 34–53). By 1972, with the publication of **Margins of Philosophy, Dissemination,** and the lecture on Nietzsche eventually titled **Spurs,** the term has been expanded by the addition of a few letters, yielding the neologism or suitcase word: phallogocentrism. This expansion is in fact an explicitation of a basic article in the logocentric baggage that Derrida has been weighing and examining since his earliest writings: the privilege accorded to the phallus as a mark of presence. Derrida's orthographic invention signals an indissociability of the *phallo-* and the *logo-,* a continuity of phallus in logos, and thereby it indicates a certain sexual scene behind or before—but always within —the scene of philosophy.

Philosophy has always reasoned with and about sexual difference, although it has always seemed to do so slightly offstage, in the wings of its principal production. There, sexual difference has been brought to reason, which has also meant, almost without exception, that social, political, economic forms of the differentiation of the sexes have been grounded, and thus legitimated, in reason, by reason. Derrida's deconstruction of this scene proceeds, as it often does, by shifting focus from center stage to the margins so as to bring out the exclusions at work in the production of reason. Such a shift has several implications and consequences. First, it overturns the order of priority that treats the question of sexual difference as derivative of fundamental, ontological questions. Secondly and as a consequence, Derrida reserves no position of originary neutrality or neuterness from which to think sexual difference. Because there is difference at the origin, the phallogocentric privilege (which is the privilege of the one, the unitary origin, the Father) can constitute itself only through a reduction or effacement of this difference. Thus and thirdly, the reduction of sexual difference, which appears to occur far from the center of philosophic concern, would be made to appear as in fact indispensable to its centering.

It is, of course, quite arbitrary to isolate some "theme" of sexual difference (or, as in preceding sections, of literature or translation) in Jacques Derrida's writings. The movement of spacing or differencing is, rather, the very medium of this writing. Indeed, the thematization of sexual difference may be seen as part of the more general tendency to reduce that difference. It is precisely this tendency that Derrida's writing interrupts, but not without also demonstrating the necessity of such an interruption in the tradition of philosophical discourse about sexual difference or femininity. That necessity is confronted in a variety of texts where Derrida asks, in effect, What happens when philosophers speak of sexual difference or of women? Kant, Hegel, Nietzsche, Heidegger, and Levinas are cited to respond in the following selections.

Because such analyses are integral to the interruption of a phallogocentric construction of sexual differences, Derrida's writings have had a wide, and widely ambivalent, reception within recent feminism. This ambivalence can be easily traced to the fact that deconstruction does not accommodate any "-ism" (including "deconstructionism"). The reversal of the sexual opposition or the recentering of phallogocentrism must make way for a displacement or transgression of the limits that have constrained a repetition of phallogocentric structures. It is this work of displacement, at stake in all of Derrida's writings, that ceaselessly "de-isms" the seismic ground of thinking.

FOURTEEN

From *Glas* [1974]

One way to describe *Glas* is simply to invoke its volume: 100 cubic inches (10 × 10 × 1 in the original edition). On its large, squared pages, two wide columns face off in different type: smaller, denser on the left, larger, more spaced out on the right. Thumb through the pages and you will see a third type, the smallest of the three, cutting into the column at various points, forming inscribed incisions either along its outermost edge, or down the center (see illustration, p. 316). There are no notes, no chapter headings, no table of contents. Each column begins in what appears to be the middle of a sentence and ends, 283 pages further on, without any final punctuation.

What is going on here? Clearly many things at once, too many ever to allow anything but a very partial description. On every page, *Glas* demonstrates the borderless condition of texts, and their susceptibility to the most unexpected encounters. The Hegelian dialectic of Absolute Spirit, tracked relentlessly with the left hand, can thus be made to recognize something like its reverse image in the mirror of the writings of Jean Genet which are lovingly dissected with the right hand. The work of the negative which drives the dialectic toward an ever-higher synthesis on the left is constantly encroached upon by the glorification of the criminal underclass cited at length on the right. It is this double-columned movement up and down, rising and falling, not successively but always at the same time, that Derrida is tracing in its most paradoxical consequences for the dialectic of reason. The *glas* (death knell) is sounded on every page for the pretensions of the dialectic to totalize or absolutize pure spirit without any remainder in everything that pulls it down.

The pages included here are extracted from close to the center of the left-hand column. They concern specifically that moment in the

rationnel qui ne s'assemble qu'à lui-même dans sa réalité, est d'une part, en raison de cette immédiateté de son identité objective, le retour à la *vie (die Rückkehr zum Leben)*, mais elle a également relevé *(aufgehoben)* cette forme de son immédiateté et elle a son plus haut contraire en elle. » L'Idée, vie immédiate et naturelle, se relève, supprime et conserve, meurt en s'élevant à la vie spirituelle. La vie se développe donc dans la contradiction et la négativité, la métaphore entre les deux vies n'est que ce mouvement de la négativité relevante. « Le concept n'est pas seulement *âme (Seele)*, concept libre et subjectif qui est pour soi et possède de ce fait la *personnalité*, — le concept objectif, pratique, en et pour soi déterminé qui en tant que personne est une subjectivité impénétrable, atomique, mais qui, en même temps, n'est pas une individualité exclusive de toutes les autres mais pour soi une universalité et une connaissance, et

a dans son autre sa propre objectivité comme objet *(seine eigene Objektivität zum Gegenstande)*. Tout le reste est erreur, trouble, opinion *(Meinung)*, tendance, arbitraire et passage *(Vergänglichkeit)* ; seule l'Idée absolue est *être* (Sein), *vie* qui ne passe pas *(unvergangliches* Leben), vérité se connaissant, et elle est toute vérité. »

Même mouvement dans l'*Encyclopédie*, à la fin, quant au *Sa*. Le troisième terme revenant à l'immédiateté, ce retour à la simplicité s'opérant par la relève de la différence et de la médiation, la vie naturelle occupe à la fois la fin et le début. Dans leur sens ontologique, les métaphores sont toujours de la vie, elles rythment l'égalité imperturbable de la vie, de l'être, de la vérité, de la filiation : *physis*.

Le système hegelien commande donc qu'on le lise comme un livre de la vie. Les catégories de lecture doivent d'abord s'y plier. Parler de plusieurs états de la pensée hegelienne, d'un Hegel de jeunesse ou d'un Hegel achevé, c'est à la fois hegelien et anti-hegelien. Ainsi le livre de Bourgeois sur Hegel à Francfort applique à son sujet les catégories les plus préformationnelles de Hegel. Il oppose, certes, l' « avènement du hegelianisme de la maturité » au « hegelianisme naissant » mais précise que celui-ci « s'engage sur la voie du hegelianisme proprement dit, dont il formulera à Iéna l'intuition géniale en écrivant

96

Je n'ai pas le droit d'opérer ainsi, sélectionnons cependant, sectionnons dans les deux pages qui suivent pour joindre la cravate qui traîne (« ... polichinelle... la gloire... la fente adorable... mille précurseurs de Notre-Dame, ange annonciateur de cette vierge,

« Notre-Dame, ange annonciateur de cette vierge » : Notre-Dame n'est donc pas seulement un autre nom de la Vierge Marie, du Président, du Christ et de toute la Sainte Famille, il est aussi l'ange annonciateur de la vierge, comme un autre *prénom de la mère.*
Dans *Notre-Dame-des-Fleurs*, Divine aime Gabriel, surnommé l'Archange. Pour l'amener à l'amour, elle met un peu de son urine dans ce qu'elle lui donne à boire ou à manger. C'est ainsi qu'on s'attache les chiens, avait-elle entendu dire. Elle l'attire dans son grenier, y ménage une atmosphère funèbre (ténèbre, encens, glas) : « ... qu'un jour elle fît venir Gabriel là-haut. Les rideaux étant tirés, il se trouve dans une ténèbre d'autant plus massive qu'y moisissait depuis des années, comme un parfum d'encens glacé, l'essence subtile des pets éclos là. » Quand il la pénètre. Gabriel donne « à sa verge un frémissement comparable à celui d'un cheval qui s'indigne ». Il est vrai qu'en la pénétrant, à supposer qu'il porte quelque part le même prénom que cette putain de mère, il ne fait que retrouver sa forme et son lieu. Divine lui avait dit : « Je t'aime comme si tu étais dans mon ventre » ou encore : « Tu n'es pas mon ami, tu es moi-même. Mon cœur ou mon sexe. Une branche de moi.
« Et Gabriel, ému, mais souriant de fierté :
— Oh! macarelle. »

un jeune garçon blond (« Des filles blondes comme des garçons... » Je ne me lasserai pas de cette phrase, décidément, qui a la séduction de l'expression : « Un garde-française ») que j'observais dans les ensembles de gymnastique. Il dépendait des figures qu'il servait à tracer, et par cela n'était qu'un signe. ... en terre... nonne écartant son voile ... poème (ou fable) qui naquit de lui (miracle renouvelé d'Anne

—*Glas*, p. 96, courtesy Editions Galilée

Hegelian dialectic that negotiates with sexual difference, love, marriage, the family, the transition to the people, and eventually the state. Derrida has announced at the beginning (?) of *Glas* his choice to draw on the thread of the family as a guide to his reading of Hegel. The family is a first term in one of the syllogisms that Derrida situates as follows:

> In the major expositions of the *Encyclopedia* or the *[Element of the] Philosophy of Right,* the "objective spirit" is developed in three moments: abstract right *(Recht)*, morality *(Moralität)*, and *Sittlichkeit*—a term translated in various ways (ethics, ethical life, objective morality, *bonnes moeurs*) . . . Now, within *Sittlichkeit*, the third term and the moment of synthesis between right's formal objectivity and morality's abstract subjectivity, a syllogism in turn is developed.
>
> Its first term is the family.
>
> The second, civil or bourgeois society *(bürgerliche Gesellschaft)*.
>
> The third, the State or the constitution of the State *(Staatsverfassung)*.

Derrida then comments on what is at stake in the familial moment of the syllogistic series: "Its interpretation directly engages the whole Hegelian determination of right on one side, of politics on the other. Its place in the system's structure and development . . . is such that the displacements or the disimplications of which it will be the object could not have a simply local character" *(Glas,* pp. 4–5). That is, displacing the familial moment, the point at which sexual difference is determined in oppositional terms and then reduced, negated, *relieved (aufgehobene)* to permit passage to the next moment, has to shake up the whole structure. In effect, by reading this moment as the strangle-point of the vast dialectical architecture, Derrida "sexualizes" that structure throughout, disturbing the versions of innocence or neutrality that define it at its outset (the religion of flowers which is not-yet-sexual or guilty) and in its outcome (Absolute Spirit which is no-longer-sexual). Derrida writes that his choice itself is "far from innocent" because it engages Hegel's text there where unconscious motivations are at work, that remainder that continues to fall outside the totalizing circle of consciousness. One figure of the remainder is an unrelieved sexual difference.

"Before attempting an active interpretation, perhaps even a critical displacement," writes Derrida, "we must still patiently decipher this difficult and obscure text." It is to this work of patient deciphering that these pages are largely devoted, as Derrida follows Hegel's text step by step. Along the way, a detour is taken through Kant's discussion of sexual difference in his *Anthropology* in order to underscore the traits that distinguish it from Hegel's speculative dialectics.

[N.B.: *Glas* contains no footnotes that identify precisely the source of its numerous quotations. The translation respects this convention and does not add any translator's notes. The translator, John Leavey, has provided, however, a list specifying *Glas'* sources in a separate volume, *Glassary* (see bibliography, 1974). For the excerpt presented here, the quotations from Hegel are taken from *The First Philosophy of Spirit* (also called the *Jena Philosophy of Spirit*), *Philosophy of Nature, Lectures on the Philosophy of World History*, and *The Philosophy of Right*. The quotations from Kant are all from *Anthropology from a Practical Point of View*. In the edition of the translation, the excerpt is found on pp. 108–14 and 118–39, left column.]

[. . . .]

If we read Hegel from within, the problematic of *Sittlichkeit*, and then, in that, of the family, can henceforth be unfolded only in a philosophy of spirit. The absolute ethical totality having been defined "people-spirit" (*Volksgeist*), its genealogy must be traced. That is the task of the first philosophy of spirit (Jena). The three "powers" of consciousness (1. Memory, language. 2. The tool. 3. Possession, family.) constitute the spirit of a people at the term of their development. From an architectonic viewpoint, the third power, the family, marking the passage to *Sittlichkeit*, occupies at the same time the first phase, forms the first moment of ethical life, its most immediate and most natural moment. That will be confirmed, if such can be said, fifteen years later, in the *Philosophy of Right*.

In effect, right after it set out the third power, the Jena philosophy of spirit describes the *transition* from the family to the people. A transition in the strong and active sense of this word: self-destructive passage. The family, through marriage, possession, and education, annihilates or relieves itself, "sacrifices" itself, Hegel says. And consequently, in the course of a struggle for recognition, the family loses and reflects itself in another consciousness: the people. The family exists in the people only "relieved" (*aufgehobene*), destroyed, preserved, debased, degraded, raised.

What is consciousness, if its ultimate power is achieved by the family?

Consciousness is the Idea's or absolute being's return to self. Absolute being takes itself back, it is *sich zurücknehmend*, it retracts itself, contracts itself, reassumes and reassembles itself, surrounds and envelops itself with itself after its death in nature, after it lost itself, "fell," Hegel literally says, outside itself in(to) nature. The philosophy of nature is the system of this *fall* and this dissociation in(to) exteriority. The philosophy of spirit is the system of the relief of the idea that calls and thinks itself in the ideal element of universality.

The *transition* from nature to spirit is also a reversal. In its highest reaches, the transition is produced in the *organic,* after the mechanical, the chemical, and the physical. The transition signifying violent self-destruction and passage to the opposite, the relief of natural life in(to) spiritual life necessarily comes about through disease and death. So disease and death are the conditions of the spirit and of all its determinations, among others, the family.

Among others only?

The last chapters of the Jena *Philosophy of Nature*—more precisely the last sections of the last chapter—concern the "process of disease." Dissolution of natural life, disease works at the transition toward the spirit. The life of the spirit thus becomes the essence, the present truth of the past, the *Gewesenheit* of natural dissolution, of natural death. "With disease the animal transgresses (*überschreitet*) the limits of its nature; but animal disease is the becoming of the spirit." In the dissociation of the natural organization, the spirit reveals itself. It was working on biological life, like nature in general, with its negativity and manifests itself therein as such at the end; spirit will always have been nature's essence; nature is within spirit as its being-outside-self. In freeing itself from the natural limits that were imprisoning it, the spirit returns to itself but without ever having left itself. A procession of returning (home). The limit was within it; the spirit was chaining up, contracting, imprisoning itself *within itself.* It always repeats itself. The end of the analysis of animal disease: "*Nature exists in the spirit, as in what is its essence.*"

This joint will assure, in the circle of the *Encyclopedia,* the circle itself, the return to the philosophy of spirit. There again, after analyzing the genus animal and the sexual relationship, the last sections of the philosophy of nature treat of disease and death. Here the question would be to accomplish the teleology inaugurated by Aristotle, reawakened by Kant, the concept of internal finality having nearly been lost between them, in modern times. This internal finality is not conscious, as would be the position of an exterior end; it is of the order of "instinct (*Instinkt*)" and remains "unconscious." Instinct here is a determination of drive (*Trieb*).

The normal fulfillment of the biological process and, in it, of the generic process is death. Death is natural. And in the same stroke violent: no contradiction in that, no other contradiction than the contradiction internal to the process.

Genus designates the simple unity that remains (close) by itself in each singular subject, in each representative or example of itself. But as this simple universality is produced in judgment, in the originary separation (*Urteil*), it tends to go out of itself in order to escape morseling, division, and to find, meet itself again back home, as subjective universality. This process of reassembling, of regrouping, denies the natural universality that tends to lose itself and divide itself. Thus, the natural living one must die. The necessary differentiation of genus that determines itself in species provokes war. The species inflict on themselves a violent death. The genus naturally produces itself through its own violent self-destruction. Lamarck and Cuvier—cited at length— knew how to choose the criteria of specific differentiation: the teeth, claws, etc., the "weapons" by which the animal "establishes and preserves itself as a being-for-self, that is, differentiates itself."

Man, insofar as he is a living creature in nature, does not escape this war of species. This war is the negative face of the genus division. In its ordinary partition (*Urteil*), genus divides or multiplies itself into specific morsels only in order to reassemble itself (close) by itself. The bellicose and morseling operation of the generic process (*Gattungsprozess*) doubles itself with an affirmative reappropriation. Singularity rejoins, repairs, or reconciles itself with itself within the genus. The individual "continues itself" in another, feels and experiences itself in another. This begins with need and the "feeling of this lack." The lack is opened with the inadequation of the individual to the genus. The genus is in the individual as a gap, a tension (*Spannung*). Whence lack, need, drive: the movement to reduce the wound of the gap, to close the cut, to draw together its lips. In the same stroke, the drive tends to *accomplish* just what it strictly reduces, the gap of the individual to the genus, of genus to itself in the individual, the *Urteil*, the originary division and judgment. This operation that consists of filling in the gap, of uniting one to the other by carrying out the *Urteil* in the most pronounced way, is *copulation*. The word for copulation or coupling, for this general play of the copula, is *Begattung*, the operation of the genus (*Gattung*), the generic and generative operation. Just as what is rightly translated by sexual relationship (*Geschlechtsverhältnis*) also designates the relationship of genus, species, or race (family, lineage) or the sex relationship as the feminine or masculine gender (*Geschlecht*).

As is often the case, the section concerning the "sexual relationship" and copulation is augmented with an "appendix" by which precisely is abridged the classic *Encyclopedia of the Philosophical Sciences in Outline*. This addition (*Zusatz*) takes up again, almost literally, the end of the Jena *Philosophy of Nature*. In it Hegel treats of sexual difference. "The separation of the two sexes" presents a very singular structure of separation. In each sex the organic individuals form a totality. But they do not relate to those of the other sex as inorganic alterity. On each side they belong to the genus, "so that they exist only as *a single Geschlecht* (sex or gender)." "Their union is the effacement of the sexes, in which the simple genus has come into being (*Ihre Vereinigung ist das Verschwinden der Geschlechter, worin die einfache Gattung geworden ist*)." When two individuals of the same species copulate, "the nature of each goes throughout both, and both find themselves within the sphere of this generality." Each one is, as the party taking part, at once a part and a whole; this general structure overlaps them both, passes as bisexuality into each of them. What each one is in (it)self (a single species), each one actually posits as such in copulation. "The idea of nature here is actual in the male and female couple [pair, *Paare*]; up till now their identity and their being-for-self merely were for us only in our reflection, but they are now, in the infinite reflection of both sexes, experienced by themselves within themselves.

This feeling of generality is the highest to which the animal can be brought."

"Contradiction" inherent to the difference of sexes: both the generality of genus and the identity of individuals (its belonging to the genus) are "different" from their separate, particular (*besonderen*) individuality. "The individual is only one of the two individuals, and exists not as unity (*Einheit*), but only as singularity (*Einzelheit*)." Sexual difference opposes unity to singularity and thereby introduces contradiction into the genus or into the process of *Urteil*, into what produces and lets itself be constituted by this contradiction. Producing the contradiction, this process resolves the contradiction: the process of copulation aims at preserving, while annulling, this difference.

Copulation relieves the difference: *Aufhebung* is very precisely the relation of copulation to sexual difference.

The relief in general cannot be understood without sexual copulation, nor sexual copulation in general without the relief. In *general*: if one takes into account that the *Aufhebung* is described here in a strictly determinate (strangulated) moment of the becoming of the idea (the final moment of the philosophy of nature)—but also that this moment of life is re-marked at the term of the philosophy of spirit—then the *Aufhebung* of the sexual difference is, manifests, expresses, stricto sensu, the *Aufhebung* itself and in general.

Still in the appendix: "The activity of the animal consists in relieving this difference (*Die Tätigkeit des Tiers ist, diesen Unterschied aufzuheben*)." The process indeed has the form of a syllogism. And the "mediation or middle term" of the syllogism is the gap (*Spannung*), the inadequation between the individual and the genus, the necessity for the singular to look for "self-feeling" in the other.

What are the conditions of this relieving copulation? In describing what he calls the formation of sexual difference—or more precisely of the different sexes (*die Bildung der unterschiedenen Geschlechter*)—Hegel subjects to the most traditional, in any case Aristotelian, philosophical interpretation what he considers the assured acquisitions of the epoch's anatomical science. He found there the proof of a hierarchic-arranging dissymmetry.

The formation of the different sexes must be "different," differentiated. By reason of the "primordial identity of the formation," the sexual parts of the male and the female must certainly belong to the "same type," but in one or the other this or that part constitutes the "essential (*das Wesentliche*)." In the type's generality, all the parts are thus present in each sex, but one dominates here, the other there, in order to constitute the essence of the sex. The morphological type is bisexual in its underlying and microscopic structure. Within this structure, one element's prevailing provokes the hierarchy between the sexes.

But the difference is not so simple. To say that one element dominates here, the other there, is not enough: in the female the essence consists of indifference—rather the indifferent (*das Indifferente*); in the male the essence consists in the difference, the divided-in-two, rather, the opposition (*das Entzuweite, der Gegensatz*). Male and female are not opposed as two differents, two terms of the opposition, but as indifference and difference (opposition, division). The sexual difference is the difference between indifference and difference. But each time, in order to *relieve* itself, *difference* must be determined in—as *opposition*.

So difference is produced through the general identity of the anatomical type that goes on differentiating itself. In the lower animals, the difference is hardly marked at all. Certain locusts, for example the *Gryllus verruccivorus*, a kind of grasshopper, bear large testicles coming from vessels twisted into rolls like fascicles, testicles similar to large ovaries coming from egg ducts themselves rolled into fascicles. The same analogy between the testicles and the ovarian sacs of gadflies.

"The greatest difficulty": "discovering the female uterus in the male sexual parts." Unfortunately, people thought they recognized it in the testicle sac, in the scrotum, since the testicles seem precisely to be what corresponds to the ovaries. But instead, the prostate fulfils in man a function qualified to that of the uterus. In the man, the uterus lowers itself, falls to the state of a gland, in a kind of undifferentiated generality. Hegel refers here to Ackermann's *Darstellung der Lebenskräfte*. Ackermann has shown, on his hermaphrodite, the place of the uterus in the "former masculine formations." But this uterus is not only in (the) place of the prostate: the ejaculatory ducts also go through its substance and open at the *crista galli*, into the urethra. The lips of the vulva are moreover testicle sacs, and testicle formations filled the lips of the hermaphrodite. The medial line of the scrotum finally parts in the woman and forms the vagina. "In this way, the transformation (*Umbildung*) of one sex into the other is understandable. Just as in the man the uterus sinks down to a mere gland, so in the woman, the masculine testicle remains enclosed, enveloped (*eingeschlossen*) within the ovary."

An apparently anatomical description. But in its vocabulary and its syntax, the hierarchic evaluation mobilizes the object. The testicle "*bleibt eingeschlossen,*" remains enclosed, enveloped. The development, the bringing to light, the production has been insufficient, delayed, lagging behind [*en reste*]. From this teleological interpretation is drawn a very marked speculative conclusion: "On the other hand, the male testicle in the woman remains enclosed within the ovary, does not project into opposition (*tritt nicht heraus in den Gegensatz*), does not become for itself, does not become an active brain (*wird nicht für sich, zum tätigen Gehirn*), and the clitoris is inactive feeling in general."

"The clitoris is inactive feeling in general," "*der Kitzler ist das untätige Gefühl überhaupt,*" in general, absolutely, chiefly, above all, principally. Who and what says *überhaupt*?

This dissymmetry is not compensated for by the fall of the uterus in the man. What does not yet emerge in the woman is sexual activity. The sexual difference reproduces the hierarchical opposition of passivity to activity, of matter to form. Hegel always, expressly, determines Reason as Activity. The *Aufhebung*, the central concept of the sexual relation, articulates the most traditional phallocentrism with the Hegelian onto-theo-teleology.

Production, differentiation, opposition are bound to the value activity. That is the system of virility. The clitoris, which resembles the penis, is passive: "in the man on the contrary, we have there active sensibility (*haben wir dafür das tätige Gefühl*), the overflowing swelling of the heart (*das aufschwellende Herz*), the blood rushing into the *corpora cavernosa* and into the meshes of the spongy tissue of the urethra. To this rushing of blood in the man

who, we? magisterial we, we of *Sa*, we men? And what if it were always the same? And who-we-assists-us here

corresponds then in the woman the effusion of blood." The same abundance of blood fills and rises on the one side, pours out and is lost on the other. Swelling [*gonflement*] of the heart also says erection; *Aufschwellen* often signifies turgescence, intumescence.

Man's superiority costs him an inner division. In passively receiving, woman remains one (close) by herself; she works less but lets herself be worked (over) less by negativity. "The receiving [*Das Empfangen*: this is also the conceiving of childbirth] of the uterus, as simple behavior, as in the man, in this way, divided in two *(entzweit)* into the productive brain and the external heart (*in das produzierende Gehirn und das äusserliche Herz*). The man then, through this difference, is the active (*Der Mann ist also durch diesen Unterschied das Tätige*); but the woman is the receptacle (*das Empfangende*), because she remains in her undeveloped unity (*weil sie in ihrer unentwickelten Einheit bleibt*)."

Remaining enveloped in undifferentiated unity, woman keeps herself nearer the origin. Man is secondary, as the difference that causes passing into the opposition. Paradoxical consequences of all phallocentrism: the hardworking and determining male sex enjoys mastery only in losing it, in subjugating itself to the feminine slave. The phallocentric hierarchy is a feminism: man submits dialectically to Femininity and Truth, both capitalized, making man the *subject* of woman.

Subject and form: "*Coitus* must not be reduced to the ovary and the sperm as if the new formation were merely the assemblage of forms or parts of two partners, for the feminine certainly contains the material element, while the male contains the subjectivity. Conception is the contraction of the whole individual into the simple self-abandoning unity, into its representation (*in seine Vorstellung*). . . ." The seed is this simple representation itself, entirely reduced to one single "point," "as the name and the entire self." "Conception then is nothing but this: the opposed, this abstract representation become *a single one*."

This discourse on sexual difference belongs to the philosophy of nature. It concerns the natural life of differentiated animals. Silent about the lower animals and about the limit that determines them, this discourse excludes plants. There would be no sexual difference in plants, the first "*Potenz*" of the organic process. The Jena philosophy of nature stresses this. The tuber, for example, is undoubtedly divided (*entzweit sich*) into a "different *opposition* (*differenten* Gegensatz)" of masculine and feminine, but the difference remains "formal." This difference does not produce totalities, individual plants where some would be male and others female. "The difference between male plants and female plants is only a difference of parts on the same plant, not the formation of two individuals." Hegel notes in passing that in the cryptogam in general the sexual parts are assumed to be "infinitely small."

In this sense, the human female, who has not developed the difference or the opposition, remains closer to the plant. The clitoris nearer the cryptogam.

[. . . .]

We have yet to encounter the family. At least the human family, what, by a convenience more and more problematic, one would still be tempted to call the family *properly so called*: neither the infinite Holy Family, nor the natural cell of the finite living.

The analysis of the human family now seems accessible: on coming out of nature, when the spirit takes itself back, becomes an object for itself in consciousness. The first philosophy of spirit, at Jena, inscribes the first determination of the human family in a theory of consciousness. Thus its organizing concepts are those of *Potenz* and *Mitte*, power and middle term, milieu, center. The family is the third *Potenz*, the ultimate one, of consciousness. It achieves itself in *Sittlichkeit* and in the people-spirit.

As the spirit's return to (it)self, consciousness is the simple and immediate contrary of itself, is what it is conscious of, to wit its opposite. At once active and passive, identifying itself with its own proper opposite, consciousness separates itself from or by itself as from its object, but hems itself in as the strict unity of its own proper separation: "On the other hand (*das andre Mal*), consciousness is the contrary of this separation, the absolute being-one (*Einssein*) of the difference, the being-one of the existent difference and of the relieved difference." As such, as the two opposites *and* the movement of opposition, the differents *and* the difference, consciousness is *Mitte*, mediation, middle, medium.

Consequently, each "power" of consciousness will have the determination of a middle. And since consciousness is the relief of nature in(to) spirit, each of these middles guards within itself a natural relieved determination. Each corresponds every time to the idealization of a natural middle, and consciousness is the middle of ideality in general, then of universality in general. It is ether: absolutely welcoming transparency offering no resistance. Ether is not natural like air, but it is not purely spiritual. It is the middle in which the spirit relates to itself, repeats itself in going through nature like the wind.

Consciousness idealizes nature in denying it, produces itself *through* what it denies (or relieves). Through: the going through and the transgression leave in the ideal middle the analogical mark of the natural middle. There is thus a power and a middle corresponding to the air: memory and language; next, to the earth: labor and tool. In the case of the family, the third power, an essential supplementary complication: the middle through which my family produces itself is no longer *inorganic* like air or earth. It is no longer simply external to the ideal middle. More than one consequence will follow.

How does the family come to air and earth, that is, to language and memory, to labor and the tool?

Homogeneous and fluid, air allows showing through and resonating, seeing and hearing. Theoretico-phonic middle. The first power of consciousness is "pure theoretical existence." It determines and holds itself back as such in memory, that is, without solid assistance. The question is obviously that of the pure and living memory, a memory that would be purely evanescent without language, which furnishes it stable but still completely interior and spontaneous products. But because of this interiority and this spontaneity, language is a product that effaces itself in time. In time thoretical consciousness also disappears. It cannot *posit itself*, exist as theoretical consciousness. To do that, it must then go out of itself, pass yet into its opposite, deny its own proper theoreticity, its *air*. Theoretical consciousness cannot posit itself as theoretical consciousness except by becoming practical consciousness, through the earthly element. To the memory then is chained labor, to the linguistic product of memory the tool and the product of labor. Just as language was at once the effect and the organ of memory, the tool (*Werkzeug*) serves the labor from which it proceeds. In both cases, an activity gives rise to the production of a permanence, of an element of relative subsistence.

The family presupposes the two preceding powers, but it also goes through the *organic* element, desire and sexual difference. The permanent product is the child and family goods (*Familiengut*). Family property, proprietorship, finally raises inorganic nature (earth and air) to the ideality of a universal proprietorship guaranteed by juridical rationality. Then the ether again becomes absolute, and the family accomplishes itself by disappearing, by denying its singularity in the people-spirit.

Such is the general schema. Let us regard more closely the transition from the second to the ultimate *Potenz*, that is, the origin of the family.

In language, the invisible sonorous, evanescent milieu, theoretical consciousness effaces itself, denies itself, reduces itself to the punctual instant. So the theoretical freedom in that instant is negative and formal. As it is only a point, this freedom converts itself into its contrary. Its universality becomes pure singularity, its freedom caprice or hardheadedness (*Eigensinn*). The *proper sense* of this hardheaded freedom is death [*mort*]. In order to be sure to remain (close) by (it)self and not to release its hold on it, theoretical consciousness renounces everything. It wants to escape the death of the inorganic, to escape the earth, but it remains in the air and dies all the more (beautiful). The purity of life is death.

So practical consciousness is at once the negation and the posit(ion)ing of theoretical consciousness. This is played out in the passage from desire to labor.

Desire is theoretical, but as such is tortured by a contradiction that makes it practical.

In effect, theoretical consciousness (death) has only to do with the dead. In the opposition constituting theoretical consciousness, its object, its opposite is not a consciousness, but a thing—a dead thing—that itself does not oppose itself, does not of itself enter into relation. The dead thing is in the relation without, itself, relating-to. So theoretical consciousness has the form of a contradiction, the form of a relation that relates itself to something that is not related, that does not relate (itself) (*Widerspruch einer Beziehung auf ein absolut nicht Bezogenes*), that absolves itself of the relation.

This changes only with desire. Desire is related to a living thing, thus to something that relates (itself). So the negation of theoretical consciousness is first of all desire. Desire perforce implies just what it denies: theoretical consciousness, memory and language.

One might be tempted to conclude from this that desire is the proper(ty) of the speaking being. In fact Hegel does not refuse desire to the animal. So the passage from animal desire to human desire supposes theoretical consciousness and speaking [*parole*] as such. As such: for there is indeed also a theoretical attitude in the animal, if the theoretical is the relation to the dead thing. Nothing more theoretical in this regard than the animal. But neither the animal nor the theoretical can *posit itself as such.* According to a long-lived tradition, the animal would be incapable of both language and labor.

Hegel at least does not refuse desire to the animal. The animal even has the power to curb or inhibit its desire. Simply, in the animal the structure of inhibition is other. No doubt the tendency to annihilate the opposed object (desire) inhibits itself (*sich . . . hemmt*). The members of the opposition must be relieved (*als aufzuhebende*) and as such are they "posited." Desire itself is posited as "*ought-to-be* annihilated." Desire holds in check the destruction of what it desires, that is, of what it desires to consum(mat)e, destroy, annihilate. It wants to keep what it wants to lose. Desire is *of/for the Aufhebung.* Inhibition and relief are inseparable; the effect of ideality that always ensues also belongs to the structure of animal desire in general.

What then distinguishes animal desire from human desire? A question of time. The moments of the operation are dissociated and external in the animal *Aufhebung.* The annihilation and the preservation juxtapose themselves, hold themselves "separated in time (*in der Zeit auseinandergerückt*)." The consum(mat)ing and the suppression are not present at the same time, do not occupy the same present. So there is no *present Aufhebung* in the animal, *a fortiori* in inorganic nature. That is the very definition, and not just one predicate among others, of nature. In that sense, it is not absurd to say that there is no *Aufhebung* or dialectics of nature. At least the dialectics does not *present* itself there. The dialectics announces itself—already—according to the mode of the not-yet. Nothing more dialectical, however.

There is animality when consum(mat)ing and nonconsum(mat)ing follow one another but do not reassemble themselves. The animal as such (that is why it would have no history and would endlessly repeat itself), man as animal consum(mat)es, then does not consum(mat)e; destroys, then does not destroy; desires to destroy, then desires not to destroy; satiates itself, then stops itself; stops itself, then satiates itself; and begins again. This dissociation or this successiveness is precisely what human desire relieves. Inhibition, this time, inhabits the consum(mat)ing itself. Ideality, the effect of inhibition, *forms part* of the present of the consum(mat)ing. The *Aufhebung presently* produces itself there, in the heart of the enjoyment. "*Human* desire must be *ideal* (ideell) *in the relief itself* (im Aufheben selbst), it must be relieved (aufgehoben), and the object must equally, while (indem) it is relieved, remain (bleiben)."

So the *Aufhebung* relieves *itself* in present desire. Human desire: relief of the relief, relieving presence of the relief, relievance [relevance]. The truth of ideality presents itself there as such.

The *Aufhebung* is not some determinate thing, or a formal structure the undifferentiated generality of which applies itself to every moment. The *Aufhebung* is history, the becoming of its own proper presentation, of its own proper differentiating determination, and it is subject to the law, to the same law as what it is the law of: it first gives itself as immediate, then mediatizes itself by denying itself, and so on. That it is subject to the law of what it is the law of, this is what gives to the structure of the Hegelian system a very twisted form so difficult to grasp.

How does desire become labor? Why does desire remain in the animal whereas it cannot not posit itself in man's labor?

In animal desire—which constitutes the animal as such—ideality is not internal to consum(mat)ing, to satisfaction; ideality only succeeds desire. "The becoming actual of the relief, the stilling (*Stillung*) of desire, is [in the animal] an immediate be-coming-relieved, without ideality, without consciousness." (One could already conclude from this, against the so clear interest of this obscure humanism, that ideality, consciousness, the human-ity of desire, all that is the supplementary mediatization of ani-mal desire—neither more nor less.) Inasmuch as desire no longer has to do with a dead object and as the preserving ideality saves up desire, it is no longer a simply theoretical operation. Desire is already practical relation. Human desire is labor. In itself. This depends on inhibition in general structuring desire in the most interior and the most essential way. Room must be made for the generality of this structure; then one must ask whether some-thing like repression can figure a species of the genus *Hemmung* in this general structure, whether the logic of repression is com-patible with the general logic of inhibition and relief. If there were a decidable response to this question, it could not be said in a word.

So Hegel must simultaneously describe the emergence of hu-man desire and the emergence of the practical relation. There is no animal labor, and praxis is a "power" of consciousness. "The practical relation is a relation (*Beziehung*) of consciousness." This depends on annihilation of the object being, in its very simplicity, an operation that inhibits itself within itself and op-poses itself to itself (*ein in sich Gehemmtes und Entgegenge-setztes*). That is why desire is never satisfied, and there lies its "practical" structure itself. "Desire does not come to its satisfac-tion in its operation of annihilation." Its object stays, not because it escapes annihilation, keeps outside the range for annihilation, but because it stays *in* its annihilation. *Desire remains inasmuch as it does not remain*. Operation of *mourning*: idealizing con-sum(mat)ing. This relation is called labor. Practical conscious-ness *elaborates* in the place where it annihilates and holds to-gether the two opposites of the contradiction. In this sense labor is the middle (*Mitte*) of the opposition intrinsic to desire.

This middle in its turn posits itself, gives itself permanence. Without that, it would collapse into a pure negativity, would sink like a pure activity that of itself progressively removes itself. In order to posit itself, labor must then pass into its opposite, settle outside itself in the resistance of the middle. That is the origin of the *tool* (*Werkzeug*), the *object* (producer and product) *of labor.* "Labor is itself a thing (*Ding*). The *tool* is the existing rational middle, the existing universality, of the practical process."

What is such a thing (*Ding*)? What is the being-thing of that thing-there (*Ding*)? It's an existent universality because the *generality* of the implement prevents labor from being depleted in the singular acts of an empiric subjectivity. Without the tool's universal objectivity, labor would be a one-sided experience, would destroy and carry itself off into the ineffable multiplicity of deeds and gestures. So the tool guards labor from self-destruction, is the relieving ideality of *praxis,* is at once active and passive: the remain(s) of labor that enters tradition, practical history. But practical history as history of desire. Desire and labor disappear, with their objects, *as empiric individuals.* One desires, one consum(mat)es, one labors, it (*ça*) passes (away) and dies. As empiric individuals. So tradition (that is Hegel's word) is what resists this loss and constitutes the maintained ideality: not the finite and elaborated object, but the labor tool that can yet be of service, because of its generality structure. The tool is endowed with an ideal, reproducible, perfectible identity, gives rise to accumulation, and so on. So one cannot desire without desiring to produce tools, that is, production tools.

Now the most difficult step is to be taken: marriage.

Some lines—more elliptical than ever—close the analysis of the second "*Potenz*" (the tool) and must in sum explain the upsurge of the third (the family) in its first phase. So the question is accounting for the production of marriage by the tool.

As always, this movement has the form of a production by *posit(ion)ing*: objectification, contradiction, interiorization, subjectification, idealization, setting free, relief. Marriage: relief of the implement.

The implement is solid. Resistant thus to consum(mat)ing and assuring tradition, it acts at the same time as an outer constraint. Elaborative desire gives itself the tool, to be sure, but as an external thing and in a heteronomous relation. No longer does desire freely, spontaneously, from within, refrain from consum(mat)ing the other. Ideality still remains in a certain dissociable outside. The freedom of consciousness does not fully affirm itself in inhibitory reserve.

Marriage is the relief of this constraint, the interiorization of this exteriority, the consum(mat)ing of the implement. The labor of desire without instrument. The exteriority of the tool chain has just been defined: "The freedom of consciousness relieves this need, and inhibits the annihilating in enjoyment, through consciousness itself (*durch sich selbst*); that makes the two sexes into consciousness for one another, into beings and subsisters for one another . . . in such a way that in the being-for-self of the other, each is itself. . . ."

This is the first time the Jena philosophy of spirit touches on (and tampers with) sexual desire. The philosophy of nature treats of biological sexuality. As for desire, it had not yet been specified as sexual desire and therefore could as well be a matter of drinking and eating. So at the moment the *Aufhebung*, within enjoyment, inhibits, retains, and relieves pleasure in order not to destroy the other and so destroy itself as enjoyment; at the moment it limits in order to keep, denies in order to enjoy, as if through fear there were no need to reach, to yield to, a *too good* that would risk sweeping away what is given in its very own excess; at that furtive moment, very near and very far from itself, from its own proper present, hardly phenomenal, between night and day—the penumbra(l man) [*le pénombre*]—at that moment does Hegel determine desire as sexual desire. This secret of enjoyment that sacrifices itself, immolates itself to itself, say on the altar of enjoyment, in order not to destroy (itself), itself and the other, one in the other, one for the other—essential unenjoyment and im-potence—that is what Hegel calls love. The two sexes pass into each other, are one for and in the other—this constitutes the ideal, the ideality of the ideal.

This ideality has its "middle" in marriage. The inhibition freed in desire, the desire that "frees itself from its relationship with enjoyment," is love; and love's subsistence, its duration, its staying, its elementary middle is marriage. "And the sexual relationship comes to be that in which each one is one with the other in the being of the consciousness of each one, in other words, an ideal relation. Desire frees itself from its relationship with enjoyment; it becomes an immediate being-one (*Einssein*) of both in the absolute being for-(it)self of both, i.e., it becomes *love*; and the enjoyment is in this intuiting (*Anschauen*) of oneself in the being of the other consciousness. The relationship itself becomes in the same way the being of both and a relationship as durable (*bleibende*) as the being of both, that is, it becomes *marriage.*"

An appendix of the *Philosophy of Right* will distinguish marriage from concubinage by the "repression" of the natural impulse (there *Naturtrieb* is *zurückgedrängt*). Concubinage on the contrary satisfies the natural impulse.

We have again found the syllogistic deduction of love and marriage as the immediate unity of the family.

Duration, what remains (*bleibt*) of this moment that is to love what the implement is to labor, does not remain at peace. A new dialectical cycle starts up here, a new war begins to rage. The struggle to the death for recognition is inscribed here within the family syllogism. A difference between the Jena analysis and the much fuller one of the *Philosophy of Right*; the first comprehends, in the development concerning the child, an explanation of the struggle to the death for recognition and possession.

So marriage is the first moment of the family, its most natural and immediate moment. Marriage is monogamous: a constant implication declared later on in the *Philosophy of Right*: "Marriage, and essentially monogamy, is one of the absolute principles on which the *Sittlichkeit* of a community depends." Or again: "In essence marriage is *monogamy.*"

The free inclination of both sexes, marriage excludes any contract. Such an abstract juridical bond could in effect bind persons only to (dead) things, could not by right commit two living freedoms. In marriage there can be empiric determinations, "pathological" inclinations, but that is inessential.

Against marriage's essentiality no consideration of the empiric limitations of freedom can measure up. So Hegel never takes into consideration Kant's whole pragmatic anthropology, everything in it concerning conjugal agonistics, the struggle for mastery between husband and wife. Never does the philosophy of spirit state anything at all about the sex difference between the spouses. Nothing more logical: everything must happen as if the spouses were the same sex, were both bisexual or asexual. The *Aufhebung* has worked.

The war begins with the child. So all discourse on the inequality of the sexes in marriage would remain empiric, not pertinent, foreign to the essence of marriage. In "Characterization," the second part of his *Anthropology*, Kant analyzes the "Character of the Sexes" in and out of marriage. He does so in terms of the struggle for domination, the complex struggle wherein mastery passes from one sex to the other according to the domains and moments. Mastery is rarely where one expects to find it. The inequality of the sexes is the condition for a harmonious union. Equality of forces would render one sex unbearable to the other. So the progress of culture must favor inequality for the protection and propagation of the species. Bent to the teleology of nature, culture produces and accentuates the heterogeneity in the disproportion of the sexes. Man must be superior by his physical force and his courage, the woman by—I cite—her "natural talent [*Naturgabe*: natural gift] for mastering (*sich bemeistern*) man's inclination toward her." This strange superiority of the woman is not natural. It depends on the culture that thus privileges the woman, since in nature all superiority "is on the man's side." If, then, culture transforms the natural situation by providing some artificial superiority to the woman, a theory of culture—what Kant here calls anthropology—must have as its privileged, if not unique, object the status of femininity. Anthropology should be a theory of the woman. ". . . the peculiarly feminine proper(ty) (*weibliche Eigentümlichkeit*), more than the masculine sex, is a subject for study by the philosopher."

Culture does not limit itself to the simple revelation of an enveloped feminine specificity.

It grafts. The cultured woman's relative superiority is a graft of man: "In the state of brute nature (*Im rohen Naturzustande*) one can no more recognize [the specifically feminine characteristics] than those of crab apples or wild pears, which disclose their multiplicity (*Mannigfaltigkeit*) only through grafting (*Pfropfen*) or innoculation (*Inokulieren*)." Here the graft transforms only in order to display natural characteristics or properties, which explains why the relative superiority the graft confers on the woman seems to overturn the natural situation but consists only in knowing how to submit to man's inclination. "For culture does not introduce these peculiarly feminine characteristics," it only produces them, brings them to light, "only causes them to develop and become remarked under favorable circumstances."

Within this general anthropo-botany, Kant analyzes the war of the sexes in marriage. The woman has a taste for domestic war; the man flees it; he "loves domestic peace" and voluntarily submits to the woman's government. "The woman wants to dominate (*herrschen*), the man wants to be dominated (*beherrscht*) (particularly before marriage)." The consequence of culture, marriage frees the woman and enslaves the man; "the woman becomes free by marriage; the man loses his freedom thereby."

Simulacrum of reversal: the woman does not become the stronger, but culture makes her weakness a lever. The possibility of inverting the natural signs—femininity itself—prohibits analyzing an essence, a feminine nature. Femininity is the power to be other than what one is, to make a weapon of weakness, to remain secret. The woman has a secret (*Geheimnis*); the man is deprived of it. That is why he is easy to analyze (*Der Mann ist leicht zu erforschen*). Analysis of the woman is impossible; she does not reveal her secret, which does not prevent her, on the contrary, from regularly betraying that of others. Because she speaks: the reign of culture as the reign of the woman is also the field of speaking [*parole*]. Language never says anything but this perversion of nature by culture—by the woman. The feminine weapon is the tongue. She transforms the slave's weakness into mastery by the tongue but already, always, by that perversion of discourse that is chitchat, loquaciousness, verbosity, volubility (*Redseligkeit*). Thus does she triumph in the domestic war and love it, unlike the man who has something else to do outside. Accumulating all the rights, she triumphs in the war by ruse: sheltered behind her husband (the right of the stronger), she controls her master (the right of the weaker). The art of the lever.

Through this law of perversion that displaces the primitive hierarchy, the natural teleology continues to operate, realizes its normal, normalizing designs, through ruses and detours. The Kantian "description" doggedly restores its intention.

In effect the woman resembles a "folly" of nature, the human folly of nature. But by seducing the man, by leading him astray from his natural trajectory, she accomplishes in the final analysis the wise design of nature. The gap has been calculated for all time; the two sexes have been carefully and implacably ordained to this grand finality, without the subjects' understanding anything about it. That is why we cannot think feminine sexuality. Our categories, our aims, the forms of our consciousness are incapable of doing it, a bit like anthropomorphic metaphors in a discourse on God. In order to reach, to have access to, the "characteristic of the feminine sex," we must not regulate ourselves by the principle of our own proper finality, of "what we have devised ourselves as our end," but on "nature's end in the constitution of femininity." "Human folly" is a means with a view to this end that is "wisdom" when "the intention of nature" is considered. So the principle of the characteristic does not depend on "our own choice," but on a "higher intention": "preservation of the species," "the improvement of society and its refinement by femininity." According to what ways?

Having entrusted to the woman the "fruit of the womb" that allows the species to develop itself, nature has taken fright for the woman in which such a "pledge" was deposited; nature has preserved its daughter, sheltered her, has made her fearful and timid in the face of danger. She has been assured the man's protection. The woman's fear is nature's or life's fear for itself. Social refinement obeys the same finality. In order to favor that refinement, nature has made "the feminine sex the master (*Beherrscher*) of the masculine sex." This mastery has been assured by a moralization: not in the sense of the moral, of *Moralität*, but of mores, of *Sittsamkeit*, if not of *Sittlichkeit*. *Sittsamkeit* is decency, honesty, modesty, reserve. In the space of a few lines, one sees it opposed to morality (*Moralität*). With its ease and fluency of discourse and the games of mimicry, *Sittsamkeit* is even the mask of morality (the text would be made unreadable if *Sittsamkeit* were translated by morality), the ruse that enslaves man. Man is then, because of his "own magnanimity," "imperceptibly fettered by a child." Modesty, decency, reserve, *Sittsamkeit* indeed serves as veil or "cloak (*Kleid*)" to an invisible morality. The woman is on the side of *Sittlichkeit* or *Sittsamkeit*, which Kant places below morality. Hegel will reverse the relation of *Moralität* to *Sittlichkeit*. There a chiasm(us) is given that cannot be maintained in the limits of an "anthropology."

How does (feminine) perversion place itself at the service of the teleology hidden in marriage? And in what way does this teleological problem reproduce the chiasm(us)?

In the natural state, in the Kantian sense, the man's polygamy is nearly natural. The paradigmatic structure resembles the harem's. The man naturally desires the whole sex and not one woman; his dealings are only with exemplars of femininity. He does not love, he loves any woman, no matter whom. The woman is a kind of whore. *Conversely,* in the cultural state, the woman does not indulge the pleasure of the man outside of marriage, and of monogamous marriage; but she desires all men and so becomes, in act or intention, the whore. So the Kantian man never deals with anyone but the whore. And if this categorical pornographer were asked what he prefers, whore or virgin, he would respond virgin, knowing all the while full well that nature, which leads him to this, takes care to see to it that this comes down, at the limit, to the same thing. A situation that cannot be without relation to what Hegel will analyze as the beautiful soul and the unhappy consciousness.

In both cases, natural polygamy and historic monogamy, the place of the man always determines the concept. Monogamy is a man and a woman; polygamy is again a man and many women. The woman is never polygamous, neither in Kantian nature nor in Kantian society. So it appears: in truth the woman always has everything, both in monogamy and in polygamy. In the harem, for example, there is no true multiplicity and man loses every time, with every stroke. The women make war in order to restore the monogamous relationship and so that one among them has the whole man, at least potentially [*en puissance*]. With the result that they all have him, no one is deprived of him, and one among them also ends by reigning over him. Thus described, the harem belongs neither to nature nor to culture. Polygamy cannot be thought in this opposition. In nature there is no marriage; in true culture, it's monogamy. Kant qualifies as "barbaric" this unclassifiable phenomenon, this society that is no longer natural and not yet moral. Starting from this "perversion," one ought to interrogate the opposition of concepts from which polygamy escapes, that of the man about which Kant speaks, that of the woman about which he says nothing.

In the harem, the woman is no longer the "domestic animal" she had to be in nature; she begins to fight and use cunning to chain up the man's drive or captivate his desire. The harem is a prison, an enclosed precinct (*Zwinger*), but the woman already knows how to establish her mastery in it. The man no longer knows any repose there amid the busy competition of the women.

Such is the "barbaric constitution" of oriental polygamy, neither natural nor civil. In the monogamy of civil (bourgeois) society, as long as culture is not too developed, the man punishes the woman if she threatens to give him a rival. But when civilization (*Zivilisierung*) is refined to the point of decadence, when it permits "'gallantry" (the fact for a married woman of having lovers) and makes of it a fashion that makes jealousy rediculous, then the feminine characteristic "discloses itself." The gallant perversion reveals the true nature of the woman, her profound design: "with the favor of men but against them to lay claim to freedom and thereby, simultaneously, to take possession of the whole sex." This theft, this stealing (*Eroberung*) of the man by the woman is not simply condemned by Kant. In his analysis of the feminine perversion, the complex system of phallogocentrism can be read. But this system is always precarious and neutralizes itself, *contains* what contradicts it. Here, for example, Kant incessantly effaces the moralizing connotation that nonetheless seems so massive: he often specifies that one must not succumb to the illusions of consciousness or intention. In feminine perversion, in the cultural, symbolic, verbal ruses—all of this passes through the woman's tongue, Kant has to read the text of love in the tongue of the woman who herself knows how to bind virile energy—one must recognize a hidden natural process, a wisdom of nature. Kant's discourse, despite pronounced and ridiculous appearances, would not be, finally, the moral disqualification of a monstrosity.

But one must admit that this last proposition immediately reverses itself. If Kant does not maintain the discourse of antifeminine morals, it is because he moralizes through and through his recourse to nature, to the providential wisdom of her who keeps vigil over perversion. Nature is good, is a good woman, that is, in truth, by her productive force, her reason, her profound *logos* that dominates all the feminine chatterings, her imperturbable and always victorious logic, her educative resources, a father. The good woman is a father; the father is a good woman; and that is finally what speaks through the women, who intend to appropriate him.

Natural reserve: if, in bourgeois monogamous marriage, the woman wants to appropriate the whole sex, that is because the man (husband or father) is finite; he dies, often young, almost always before the woman, who remains, then, alone, young, widowed. And who will have had, thus, to prepare this mourning, who knows herself always threatened, in the state of lacking a man. She takes an interest, provisionally, in sex, on the maternal advice of nature. "Although this inclination is in ill repute, under the name of coquetry, it is not without a real justifiable basis. A young wife is always in danger of becoming a widow, and this leads her to distribute her charms to all men whose fortunes make them marriageable; so that, if this should occur, she would not be lacking in suitors."

This hidden teleology justifies all the dissymmetries and all the inequalities of development that Kant believes can be described under the title of sexual difference.

The woman wants to be a man, the man never wants to be a woman. "Whenever the refinement of luxury (*Luxus*) has reached a high point, the woman shows herself well-behaved (*sittsam*) only by compulsion (*Zwang*), and makes no secret in wishing that she might rather be a man, so that she could give larger and freer playing room (*Spielraum*) to her inclinations; no man, however, would want to be a woman." Kant does not enlarge on this last proposition, in the closing lines of the paragraph. It goes without saying that that's unheard of and will never be heard of. Even if by chance one believed one had come across such an aberration, what would it mean? What would it mean, for a man, to want to be a woman, seeing that the woman wants to be a man the more she cultivates herself? That would mean then, apart from the semblance of a detour, to want to be a man, to want to be—that is to say, to remain—a man.

Is it so simple? Does Kant say that the woman wants to be a

man? He says, more precisely, that she would like, in certain situations, to adorn herself with attributes of the man in order to realize her womanly designs: to be better able to have all men. She pretends to want to be a man or to be a man in order to "extend the playing room" of her inclinations. Everything is overturned: either the man who wants to be only a man wants to be a woman inasmuch as the woman wants to be a man; so he wants to be a woman in order to remain what he is. Or else the man who wants to be a woman only wants to be a woman since the woman wants to be a man only in order to reach her womanly designs. To wit, the man. And so on.

All this happens very quickly in the penumbra where desire itself binds itself, if something such as that exists.

In fact, even if she truly wanted to, which is not the case, the woman could never be a man. The masculine attributes with which she adorns herself are never anything but fake, signifiers without signification, fetishes. Are never anything but show [*montre*], but the watch [*montre*]. Badly adjusted [*réglée*] to the sun's movement. To illustrate that the woman can on no account appropriate the masculine attribute, for example or substitution, science, culture, the book, Kant denounces a kind of transvestism: "As for scholarly women, they use their *books* somewhat like a *watch*, that is, they wear the watch so it can be noticed they have one, although it is usually stopped or badly adjusted to the sun." The choice of paradigm once more confirms it: "characteristic genius" cannot be thought without the unconscious.

The endless dissymmetry between the sexes is accentuated before the taboo of virginity. The woman does not desire that the man be a virgin or continent before his marriage. She does not even ask herself any questions on this subject. For the man the question is "infinitely" important. Kant does not say that he requires virginity, or even that he desires it, but that for him the question is most serious. Perhaps he can love only virginity, perhaps he can never do so, perhaps his desire is born of the overlapping of virginity by its contrary. All this is played out in the gap of a sign that is almost nothing and necessarily describes itself in the subtlety of nuances and of wordplays: the man is patient (*duldend*), the woman tolerant (*geduldig*), and they do not suffer, do not behave in suffering (*dulden*) in the same way. The man is sensible (*empfindsam*), feeling, the woman impressionable (*empfindlich*), irritable, sensitive, touchy. The economy of the man tends to *acquiring*, that of the woman to *saving*. The man is jealous when he loves; the woman is jealous also when she does not love.

This cultural theory of the difference of sexes in marriage has no possible housing in the Hegelian philosophy of spirit. Love and marriage belong to the element of the freedom of consciousness and suppose the *Aufhebung* of sexual difference. The war described by pragmatic anthropology can take place in it, *in fact*, but only insofar as the partners are not *true* spouses, as the essence of marriage is not accomplished. In that case, one has gotten no further than the sexual life of empiric nature, before the emergence of *Sittlichkeit*. What Kant will have described would be in sum a structure of empiric, "pragmatic" accidents, a structure that does not come under the pure concept of marriage from which by vice and perversity it strays. Kant could not think, did not begin by thinking the concept marriage. This concept being posited, Hegel on the contrary wants to deduce its development and not its regression. Once more, Kant would remain no further along than this nondialectical conjunction of an empiricism and a formalism, a conjunction denounced in the article on natural law. Without proceeding from the essential unity of marriage, one accumulates and isolates without order the descriptive traits; one joins side by side empiric violence and contractual formalism.

The speculative dialectics of marriage must be thought: the being-one (*Einssein*) of the spouses, the consciousness of one in that of the other, such is the *medium*, the *middle* of exchange. The sexual opposition is relieved there. As means or mediation, this middle has two sides: the one by which the two spouses recognize one another and relieve their difference; the other, by which this consciousness must be, as middle, opposed to their own and must bear its relief.

That is the child. "It is the child in which they recognize themselves as one, as being in *one* consciousness, and precisely therein as relieved, and they intuit in the child this relief of themselves." They "produce" thus "their own death." In order to think this death, one must make the middle of consciousness intervene and must think childhood as consciousness. The natural child, as living animal, does not bear the death of its genitors. So the death of the parents *forms* the child's consciousness.

That is education. Empirico-formalism cannot think education because empirico-formalism cannot think the parents' necessary death in the child. Yet Kant speaks of the parents' death. One will say perhaps that this is still a matter of empiric death: the preference of the father for the daughter, of the mother for the son, above all for the most insolent, the most undisciplined son, these preferences are still explained by the possibility of widowhood. The child of the opposite sex would be the better support in old age. This derisively empiric explanation nevertheless covers the essential affect—mourning—that relates one of the parents to the child of the other sex after the death of the married partner. The mother loves the son according to the father's death; the father loves the daughter who succeeds the mother. By reason or way of the empiric, doesn't one thus go further than the Hegelian deduction of the parents' death, which seems rather undifferentiated and abstract from the sexual point of view? A chiasmus again: speculative dialectics thinks this death in its structural necessity, *thinks* it as it thinks the effacement of sexual difference that empiricism puts forward.

What is education? The death of the parents, the formation of the child's consciousness, the *Aufhebung* of its unconsciousness in(to) the form of ideality. "In education the *unconscious unity* of the child is relieved." One must not hurry to identify this idealizing relief with a "repression" of the "unconscious." But the question of such a translation cannot be avoided. Education (*Erziehung*) and culture (*Bildung*) violently delimit a matter by a form containing it. This violent form is ideal, passes through the instances of language and labor, of voice and tool. Like every formation, every imposition of form, it is on the male's side, here the father's, and since this violent form bears the parents' death, it imposes itself above all against the father. But the death of the father is only the real death of the mother, corresponds to the idealization of the father, in which the father is not simply annihilated. The relieving education interiorizes the father. Death being a relief, the parents, far from losing or disseminating themselves without return, "contemplate in the child's becoming their own relief." They guard in that becoming their own disappearance, reg(u)ard their child as their own death. And in reg(u)arding that disappearance, that death, they retard it, appropriate it; they maintain in the monumental presence of their seed—in the name— the living sign that they are dead, not that *they are dead*, but that *dead they are*, which is another thing. Ideality is death, to be sure, but to be dead—this is the whole question of dissemination—is that *to be* dead or to be *dead*? The ever so slight difference of stress, conceptually imperceptible, the inner fragility of each attribute produces the oscillation between the presence of being as death and the death of being as presence. As long as the parents are present to their death in the child's formation, as long as one keeps [*garde*] the sign or the seme of what is no longer, even were it the ashes consumed in the small morning of a penumbra(l man), the enjoyment remains, the enjoyment of just what is, even of what is dead as what is no longer. But if death is the being of what is no more, the no-more-being, death is nothing, in any case is no longer death. One's own proper death, when contemplated in the child, is the death that is de nied, the death that *is*, that is to say, denied. When one says "death is," one says "death is denied"; death is not insofar as one *posits* it. Such is the Hegelian *thesis*: philosophy, death's positing, its pose.

The child-relief of the loss. This loss, the labor of form on matter, the forming of unconsciousness, the economic process, production, exchange, dies away, is amortized. The *Aufhebung* is the dying away, the amortization, of death. That is the concept of economy in general in speculative dialectics.

Economy: the law of the family, of the family home, of possession. The economic act makes familiar, proper, one's own, intimate, private. The sense of property, of propriety, in general is collected in the *oikeios*. Whatever the exportation or the generalizing expropriation of the concept economy, that concept never breaks the umbilical cord attaching it to the family. Or rather yes, it always breaks the cord, but this rupture is the *deduction* of the family, belongs to the family process insofar as that process includes a cutting instance. The *Aufhebung*, the economic law of absolute reappropriation of absolute loss, is a family concept.

And thus political. The political opposes itself to the familial while accomplishing it. So the political economy is not one region of the general onto-logic; it is coextensive with it. All the more so since, in the Hegelian systematics, there is never any simply hierarchic relationships between genus and species: each part represents the whole, each region is capable of everything.

Thus ideality, the production of the *Aufhebung*, is an onto-economic "concept." The *eidos*, the general form of philosophy, is properly familial and produces itself as *oikos*: home, habitation, apartment, room, residence, temple, tomb, hive, assets, family, race, and so on. If a common seme is given therein, it is the guarding of the proper, of property, propriety, of one's own [*la garde du propre*]: this guarding retains, keeps back, inhibits, consigns the absolute loss or consum(mat)es it only in order better to reg(u)ard it returning to (it)self, even were it in the repetition of death. Spirit is the other name of this repetition.

Such is the cost of the child: "In education the *unconscious unity* of the child relieves itself (*hebt sich . . . auf*), articulates itself in (it)self (*gliedert sich in sich*), becomes *formed, cultured consciousness* (*gebildeten Bewusstsein*); the consciousness of the parents is its matter (*Materie*), at the cost of which (*auf deren Kosten*) it is formed; they (the parents) are for the child an unknown, obscure presentiment of itself; they relieve its simple, contracted (*gedrungen*) being-in-(it)self; what they give the child they lose; they die in it; for what they give it is their own consciousness."

If one cuts it off here, education could be a loss without return, a gift without a countergift, without exchange. But in truth exchange takes place. The other consciousness, the child's, in which the parents lose theirs, is their own proper consciousness. The other and one's own proper(ty) do not oppose each other, or rather yes, they do oppose each other, but the opposition is what permits, not what interrupts, the specular, imaginal, or speculative circulation of the proper, of one's own proper(ty). The proper, one's own proper(ty), posits itself in opposing itself in the other, in dis-tancing itself from itself. The unity of the specular and the speculative is remarked in the possibility for the parents to regard, to contemplate their own proper disappearance relieved in the mirror of the child, of the child in formation, as becoming-conscious; in the material unconscious they would see nothing, not even their own proper death, the death wherein they are guarded, not even death, then, or only death. *"Die Eltern schauen in seinem Werden ihr Aufgehobenwerden an"*: "the parents contemplate in the child's becoming their becoming-relieved."

The child's consciousness does not come to the world as to a material and inorganic exteriority. The world is already elaborated when education begins, is a culture penetrated, permeated, informed by the *"knowledge of his parents."* What first confronts the child as and in place of inorganic nature is inherited knowledge, already a certain ideality. So the child raises itself in(to) the "contradiction" between the real world and the ideal world. The process of education consists in relieving this contradiction. That is possible only with the disappearance (relieving) of the family itself, since the family is the place of this contradiction: it's the passage to the people-spirit.

Here intervenes the struggle to the death for recognition. It is most often known in the form given it by the *Phenomenology of Spirit*. Now previously three texts had treated of it: the *System of "Sittlichkeit"* (probably earlier, just a little bit; than the Jena *Philosophy of Spirit*), the Jena *Realphilosophie* (almost contemporaneous with the *Phenomenology of Spirit*), and the *Philosophy of Spirit*. This last one is the only one to explain this struggle within a problematics of the family.

The struggle in the family does not oppose, as is often believed, family heads. The text gives no indication of this. Once the family is constituted, as a power of consciousness, the struggle can break out only between consciousnesses, and not between empiric individuals. From this viewpoint, the gap narrows between the Jena text and that of the *Phenomenology*. If the *Phenomenology* takes up the family moment after the dialectic of master and slave, that is because in it the family is interrogated according to a very particular guiding thread: the passage from the ancient family and city to Roman law and formal morality. With the result, another architectonic phenomenon at first approach [*abord*] disconcerting, that in the *Phenomenology*, the moment of "morality" and of formal right follows that of the family, whereas the inverse is produced in the *Philosophy of Right*. In the *Phenomenology*, the Greek is inscribed in a general problematics of the history of the family. So there is no "evolution of Hegel's thought" there.

At the point where we are, the struggle to the death for recognition opposes consciousnesses, but consciousnesses that the family process has constituted as totalities. The individual who engages in war is an individual-family. The essence of consciousness cannot be understood without passing through the family "*Potenz.*" A phenomenology of spirit, that is, according to the subtitle, an "Experience of Consciousness," cannot be described without recognizing in it the onto-economic labor of the family. There is no pure consciousness, no transcendental ego into which the family kernel might be reduced. Here is situated the principle of a critique of transcendental consciousness as the formal *I think* (thinking is always said of a member of the family), but also a critique of concrete transcendental consciousness in the style of Husserlian phenomenology. Not only is there no monadic consciousness, no sphere to which the ego properly belongs, but it is impossible to "reduce" the family structure as a vulgar empirico-anthropological addition of transcendental intersubjectivity. Transcendental intersubjectivity would be abstract and formal—constituted and derived—if in it the family structure was not recognized as one of its essential structures, with all the powers Hegel implies therein: memory, language, desire, labor, marriage, the proprietorship of goods, education, and so on.

Consciousness does not relate to itself, does not reassemble itself as totality, does not become for itself—does not become conscious—except as, except in the family. "In the family, *the totality of consciousness* is the same thing as what becomes *for self*; the individual contemplates himself in the other." Consciousness posits itself for itself only through the detour of another consciousness that posits itself as the same and as other. So given there, standing up face to face, are two totalities. Singular totalities, since they also make two, are two: absolute, insoluble contradiction, impossible to live with. The relationship can only be violent. The two consciousnesses structurally need each other, but they can get themselves recognized only in abolishing, or at least in relieving, the singularity of the other—which excludes it. A pure singularity can recognize another singularity only in abolishing itself or in abolishing the other as singularity. The contradiction, although not explicit here in this form, opposes more precisely knowing (the *kennen* of *erkennen*), which can deal only with universal ideality, and the singularity of the totality "consciousness," being-in-family.

The struggle to the death that is triggered then between two stances seems, in its exterminating violence, more mercilessly concrete than it does in later texts. Nevertheless two conditions contain it, the concepts of which must indeed be carefully regulated.

1. Death, the "demonstration" that "is achieved only with death," destroys singularity, relentlessly hounds what in the other consciousness-family remains singular. This is not a matter of just death, but of the annihilation of the characteristics of singularity, of every mark of empiricalness. Is the name, for example, the stake that founders or the stake that saves itself in this war?

One will ask, what remains when all of the empiricalness is abolished? Nothing, nothing that may be present or existent. To be sure. But what is present, what *is* as such when there is only singularity? Nothing. One fights to the death, in any case, for nothing, such is no doubt the intention hidden in the shadow of the Hegelian discourse. By definition, this intention cannot be said as such, since discourse is precisely what makes the universal pass for something, gives the impression that the universal remains something, that something remains, when every singularity has been engulfed. Medusa's face watching over the Hegelian text in the penumbra(l man) that binds [*lie*] desire to death, that reads [*lit*] desire as the desire of, the desire for, death.

The question has not been answered: is the proper name of a family and of an individual *classed* in the family a pure singularity? No. Is it a pure ideality? No.

2. Second strict, conceptual condition: the death of singularity is always an *Aufhebung*. The so frequent translation of *Aufhebung* by *abolition* or *cancellation* effaces precisely this: that death abolishes the pure and simple abolition, death without ado, death without name. "It is absolutely necessary that the

totality which consciousness has reached in the family can recognize itself as the totality it is in another such totality of consciousness. In this recognition, each is for the other immediately an absolute singular *(ein absolut Einzelner)*; each posits itself *(setzt sich)* in the consciousness of the other, relieves *(hebt . . . auf)* the singularity of the other, or each posits the other in its consciousness as an absolute singularity of consciousness."

One consciousness can posit itself as such only in another consciousness: in order in it to see, to know itself, to get itself recognized. As soon as the other consciousness recognizes "my own," it goes out of its empiric singularity. I must incite it to this, and the radical going outside of empiric singularity has no other name but death. Putting to death implies here the whole chain of essential concepts (relief, posit(ion)ing as passage to the opposite, ideality as the product of negativity, and so on) of speculative dialectics.

The destruction of singularity must leave no remain(s), no empiric or singular remain(s). It must be total and infinite. If they should happen to desire to be loved, recognized by the other's consciousness, the subjects must accept to bear or suffer (here reciprocity is the rule) a wound, an infinite injury ("the injury *(Verletzung)* of any one of his singularities is therefore infinite"). The outrage, the offense, the violation *(Beleidigung)*, the collision *(Kollision)* ends only with death. As this collision, this violation is reciprocal *(gegenseitige)*, the project of mastery, of getting-oneself-recognized must in the same stroke engage infinite desire in a risk of absolute nonmastery: the subject must admit to itself that it no longer dominates its relation to the other. There it desires. It posits its desire only in risking death.

Total and real violence: to be sure language is implicated here, but in this affair mere words are worthless. The war is not conducted with volleys of signifiers, above all linguistic signifiers. With names perhaps, but is the proper name a linguistic signifier? Hegel insists on this: the struggle for recognition does not have its element in the tongue. The struggle is played out between bodies, to be sure, but also between economic forces, goods, real possessions, first of all the family's. The linguistic element implies an ideality that can be only the *effect* of the destruction of empiric singularities, an effect and not a middle of the struggle. In the *practical* war between singular forces, the injuries must bring about actual expropriations. They must wrest from the other the disposition of its own body, its language, must literally dislodge the other from its possessions. The field of the word does not suffice for this: "Language, explanations, promising are not this recognition, for language is only an ideal middle *(ideale Mitte)*; it vanishes as it appears; it is not a real recognition, one that remains *(bleibendes).*" The insistence is very marked: linguistic idealism, linguisticism, these can always upsurge again—the temptation is too strong—to sweeten or cicatrize the injury, to make one forget that the middle of the carnage is not ideal but "actual." "No one can prove this to the other through words, assurances, threats, or promises; for language is only the ideal existence of consciousness; here, on the contrary, actual opposites confront one another, i.e., absolutely opposed opposites that are absolutely for themselves; and their relation is strictly a practical one, it is itself actual; the middle of their recognition must itself be actual. *Hence they must injure one another.* The fact that each posits itself as exclusive totality in the singularity of its existence must become actual. The violation |*Beleidigung*: outrage, rape, abuse] is necessary."

Without this *Beleidigung* no consciousness, no desire, no relationship to the other could *posit itself.* But this breaking-in that comes to injure the other's proper(ty), the other's own, does not come down to a singular initiative, to the decision of a freedom. This breaking-in is engendered by a contradiction that inhabits the proper itself, one's own own. It is a matter here, since Hegel insists above all on the possession of things, rather than of one's own body proper, of a contradiction in the thing itself. It is contradictory that a thing *(Ding)* be some one's or some people's proper(ty), their own. "In particular each must be dislodged from its possession *(Besitze),* for in possession there lies the following contradiction: ..." An exterior thing, a thing, a universal reality of the earth, by essence exposed to all, cannot, without essential contradiction, stay in the power of a singularity. The contradiction must be resolved. It can be so only by the violent and total expropriation of the singularity. But if this injury were the redistribution of morsels of proprietorship, if a singular reappropriation followed, the same contradiction would persist. So the only end possible is to put to death singularity as such, the possession of proper(ty), of one's own, in general. What is said here of the body in general, of the thing of the earth, of everything that is exposed to the light, how is the exception of one's own body proper marked in this? As visibility and availability at least, the body proper is worked (over) by the same contradiction, the stake of the same struggle to the death.

Yet death does not resolve the contradiction. To say "on the contrary" would be too simple and one-sided. One must again speak of relief: the *Aufhebung* is indeed the contradiction of the contradiction and of the noncontradiction, the unity as well of this contradiction. Here, strictly, unity and contradiction are the same.

In effect I can make an attempt on others' life—in its singularity—only in risking my own. To posit oneself *(sich setzen)* as consciousness supposes exposure to death, engagement, pawning, putting in play *[en jeu]* or at pawn *[en gage]*. "When I go for his death, I expose myself to death *(setze ich mich selbst dem Tode aus)*, I put in play my own proper life *(wage ich mein eignes Leben)*." This putting (in play, at pawn) must, as every investment, amortize itself and produce a profit; it works at my recognition by or through the other, at the posit(ion)ing of my living consciousness, my living freedom, my living mastery. Now death being in the program, since I must *actually* risk it, I can always lose the profit of the operation: if I die, but just as well if I live. Life cannot endure in the incessant imminence of death. So I lose every time, with every blow, with every throw *[à tous les coups]*. The supreme contradiction that Hegel marks with less circumspection than he will in the *Phenomenology*.

[. . . .]

—*Translated by John P. Leavey, Jr., and Richard Rand*

FIFTEEN

From *Spurs: Nietzsche's Styles*

(*Éperons: Les Styles de Nietzsche* [1978])

First delivered as a lecture in 1972 with the title "The Question of Style" ("La Question du style"), *Spurs* proposes a reading of Nietzsche along the axis of "the woman question." It is one of Derrida's most important texts to take up this question, but also one of the most perplexing. Near the beginning, for example, one may read: "woman will be my subject." This assertion is then made to pass through the gauntlet of Nietzsche's warring styles which inscribe woman in many guises. When it comes out at the other end of the text, the assertion has been contradicted: "woman, then, will not have been my subject." What happens between these two statements erodes the ground from under woman (or sexual difference) as an essence or a Being that could enter into a stable opposition. Woman—*la* femme —has been differentiated.

One of the key passages from Nietzsche that Derrida reads between these two moments is a brief allegory from *Twilight of the Idols*, "How the 'Real World' at last Became a Myth: History of an Error." Nietzsche characterizes six stages in the history of the idea that a "real world" lies somewhere beyond the apparent world of phenomena. After the first, Platonic stage, this idea is taken up by Christianity which promises the real world in a life-after-death. At that point, Nietzsche notes, the idea *"becomes woman* [sie wird Weib]."* This notation (which Heidegger does not remark in his own reading of the same passage) acts as a kind of magnet pulling in the multifarious references to woman and women that Derrida has isolated in Nietzsche's texts, references that do not form any simple pattern but range from debasement to antifeminism to affirmation. It is woman as a figure of castration (the absence of the real world) that Derrida finds at work in the two versions of Nietzsche's condemnation of women, versions that are in fact inversions of each other: truth or lie, castrating or castrated. The rarest allusions are to that rarest of creatures, the affirmative woman "dissimulating, artist, dionysiac." This value of simulation or simulacrum beyond truth and lie recalls what Derrida has written elsewhere of the *pharmakon* and *hymen*, that is, to these other names that do not name an essence but an undecidable process of inscription. The styles and the spurs of the title both invoke pointed instruments with which to rend the castrating veil of femininized "truth" or with which to protect oneself from its castrating thrusts. But it is finally the irreducible plurality of Nietzsche's styles that interests Derrida. Only such a plurality can welcome the advent of an affirmative writing of the feminine, beyond the phallogocentric idea of "truth."

Pluralized in this way, Nietzsche's text can no longer be a simple object for hermeneutics, for the search for a single, essential meaning. *Spurs* also addresses the immense problem for interpretation posed by the plural, feminine text. Derrida writes that one has to accept the fact that one will never have done with the text's difference from itself. Not even Nietzsche could see clearly, in one blink of the eye, what he had spun out, somewhat like a spider lost in his own web. "There is loss, that can be affirmed, as soon as there is hymen . . . He was, he dreaded this castrated woman. He was, he dreaded this castrating woman. He was, he loved this affirmative women. All that at once, simultaneously or successively" (p. 372). Lost in his own text, "Nietzsche" cannot serve as the anchoring point of biographical reference for interpretation. The writing of Nietzsche's woman, the writing of the woman Nietzsche—"la femme (de) Nietzsche"? It is in the space of their difference, writes Derrida, that our interpretive readings risk losing anchor.

Spurs: Nietzsche's Styles

[. . . .]
Distances [1]

The question of style is always the examination, the weighing-in of a pointed object. Sometimes it is only a feather, a quill; but it may also be a stylet, or even a dagger. Objects with which one can, to be sure, launch a vicious attack on what philosophy calls matter or matrix so as to thrust a mark upon it, leave an imprint or a form upon it; but also so as to repel a menacing form, to keep it at a distance, to repress it and guard against it—while folding back or withdrawing, in flight, behind veils and sails [*voiles*].

Let us leave this elytron to float between the masculine and the feminine. Our tongue allows us such a pleasure, provided at least that we do not articulate.[2]

And as for veils and sails, while we're about it, Nietzsche will have exercised all the genres.

Thus the style would jut out, like a spur [*éperon*], for example the ram of a sailing ship, the *rostrum* or prong that surges ahead to meet the attack and cleave the opposing surface. Or yet again, still in a nautical sense, the point of rock that is also called a spur and that "breaks up the waves at the entrance to the harbor."

With its spur, then, style can *also* protect against the terrifying, blinding, mortal threat (of that) which *presents* itself, which obstinately makes itself seen: presence, the content, the thing itself, meaning, truth—unless this is *already* the abyss deflowered in all this unveiling of difference. *Already* [Déjà]:[3] the name of that which is effaced or subtracted beforehand, yet which leaves a mark, a subtracted signature on the very thing from which it withdraws—the here and now. It must be taken into account, which I will do; but the operation can be neither simple nor brought to a point in a single blow.

The French *éperon*, in Frankish or High German *sporo*, in Gaelic *spor*, becomes *spur* in English. In *Les mots anglais*, Mallarmé relates it to the verb *to spurn*: to disdain, rebuff, reject scornfully. One sees here not just a fascinating homonymy, but as well the operation of a historical and semantic necessity from one language to another: the English *spur* is the "same word" as the German *Spur*: trace, wake, indication, mark.

The spurring style, the long, oblong object, a weapon that parries as well as perforates; its oblong-foliated point drawing its apotropaic power from the cloth, webs, veils, and sails that are stretched taut, that fold or unfold around it, this style is also, don't forget, an umbrella.

For example, but it is not to be forgotten.[4]

So as to insist on that which imprints the mark of the styled spur on the question of woman (note that I did not say, as so many do, the *figure of woman*; that is what we will see stripped away here, carried off [*s'enlever*], the question of the figure being at once opened and closed by what is called woman); also so as to announce what will, from now on, regulate the play of the sails (for example, of a ship) around apotropaic anxiety; and so as to let an exchange finally appear between Nietzsche's style and Nietzsche's woman, here are a few lines from *Joyful Wisdom*:

> *Women and Their Effect in the Distance [ihre Wirkung in die Ferne].*
> Have I still ears? Am I only ear, and nothing else besides? [All of Nietzsche's questions, in particular when he questions woman, are coiled up in the labyrinth of an ear (. . .)] Here I stand in the midst of the surging of the breakers, [this is an untranslatable play on words: *Hier stehe ich inmitten des Brandes der Brandung. Brandung* is related to the conflagration expressed in *Brand* which itself also signifies the mark left by a burning branding iron. It is the seething surf, the waves rolling back over themselves as they crash against the rocky shoreline or break on the reefs, the cliffs, the *éperons*,] whose white flames fork up to my feet [so I too

am an *éperon*];—from all sides there is howling, threatening, crying, and screaming at me, while in the lowest depths the old earth shaker sings his aria [*seine Arie singt,* beware, Ariane is not far away] hollow like a roaring bull; he beats such an earth shaker's measure thereto, that even the hearts of these weathered rock-monsters tremble at the sound. Then, suddenly, as if born out of nothingness, there appears before the portal of this hellish labyrinth, only a few fathoms distant,—a great sailing ship [*Segelschiff*] gliding silently along like a ghost. Oh, this ghostly beauty! With what enchantment it seizes me! What? Has all the repose and silence in the world embarked here [*sich hier eingeschifft*]? Does my happiness itself sit in this quiet place, my happier ego, my second immortalized self? Still not dead, but also no longer living? As a ghost—like, calm, gazing, gliding, sweeping neutral being [*Mittelwesen*]? Similar to the ship, which, with its white sails, like an immense butterfly, passes over the dark sea! Yes! Passing *over* existence! [Über *das Dasein hinlaufen*!] That is it! That would be it!— It seems that the noise [*Lärm*] here has made me a visionary [*Phantasten*]! All great noise [*Lärm*] causes one to place happiness in the calm and in the distance [*Ferne*]. When a man is in the midst of his hubbub [*Lärm*], in the midst of the breakers [again *Brandung*] of his plots and plans [*Würfen und Entwürfen*], he there sees perhaps calm, enchanting beings glide past him, for whose happiness and retirement [*Zurückgezogenheit:* withdrawing in oneself] he longs—*they are women* [*es sind die Frauen*]. He almost thinks that there with the women dwells his better self [*sein besseres Selbst*]; that in these calm places even the loudest breakers [*Brandung*] become still as death [*Totenstille*], and life itself a dream of life [*über das Leben*]. [The preceding fragment, "We Artists!," which began with "When we love a woman," describes a movement that carries with it *simultaneously* the somnambulistic risk of death, the dream of death, sublimation, and the dissimulation of nature. The value of dissimulation cannot be dissociated from the relation of art to woman. (. . .)] [5] But still! But still! my noble enthusiast, there is also in the most beautiful sailing ship so much noise and bustling [*Lärm*], and alas, so much petty, pitiable bustling [*kleinen erbärmlichen Lärm*]! The enchantment and the most powerful effect of woman [*der Zauber und die mächtigste Wirkung der Frauen*], is, to use the language of philosophers, an effect at a distance [*eine Wirkung in die Ferne*], an *actio in distans*; there belongs thereto, however, primarily and above all—*distance!* [*dazu gehort aber, und vor allem*—Distanz!].[6]

Veils

What is the opening step of this *Dis-tanz*?[7] Nietzsche's writing already mimics it with an effect of style distributed *between* the Latin quotation *(actio in distans)* that parodies the language of the philosophers *and* the exclamation point, while the hyphen suspends the word *Distanz*. A pirouette or a play of silhouettes invites us to keep our distance from these many veils that make us dream of death.

Woman's seduction operates at a distance; distance is the element of her power. Yet one must keep one's distance from this song, this enchantment; one must keep at a distance from distance, not only, as one might think, to protect oneself from this fascination, but also in order to experience it. There must be distance (which is lacking) [Il faut *la distance (qui faut)*]; one must keep one's distance *(Distanz!)*, that's what we lack, that's what we fail to do. All this also sounds like the advice one man gives another: how to seduce without being seduced.

If it is necessary to keep one's distance from the feminine operation (from the *actio in distans*), which does not simply amount to approaching it, except at the risk of death *itself* [elle-même], it is perhaps because "woman" is not some thing, the determinable identity of a figure that appears in the distance, at a distance from other things, and which could be approached or left behind. Perhaps, as non-identity, non-figure, simulacrum, she is the *abyss* of distance, the distancing of distance, the division of spacing, distance itself, if it were still possible, which it is not, to say distance *itself* [elle-même]. Distance distances itself; the faraway furthers itself. Here we must have recourse to Heidegger's use of the word *Entfernung:* at once separation, removal, distance, and the distancing of distance, the distancing of the distant, de-distancing, the constituting destruction *(Ent-)* of the distant as such, the veiled enigma of proximation.

The spaced-out opening of this *Entfernung* gives rise to truth and there woman averts herself from herself, on her own [*la femme s'y écarte d'elle-même*].

There is no essence of woman because woman averts and averts herself from herself, on her own. Out of the depths, endless and unfathomable, she engulfs and enveils any essentiality, any identity, any properness. Blinded here, philosophical discourse founders—lets itself be hurled toward its ruin. There is no such thing as the truth of woman, but that is because this abyssal divergence of the truth, this non-truth is the "truth." Woman is a name of this non-truth of truth.

I will support this proposition with several texts, among many others.

On the one hand, Nietzsche assumes and takes up again, but in a way that will have to be qualified, this barely allegorical figure: truth as woman or as the movement of the veil of feminine modesty. The complicity (and not the unity) of woman, life, seduction, modesty, and all the effects of veiling *(Schleier, Enthüllung, Verhüllung)* is developed in a rarely quoted fragment. The formidable problem of that which unveils itself but once *(das enthüllt sich uns einmal).* I quote only the final lines:

> For ungodly, activity does not furnish us with the beautiful at all, or only does so once! I mean to say that the world is overfull of beautiful things, but it is nevertheless poor, very poor, in beautiful things. But perhaps this is the greatest charm [*Zauber*] of life: it puts a golden-embroidered veil [*golddurch-wirkter Schleier*] of lovely potentialities over itself, promising, resisting, modest, mocking, sympathetic, seductive. Yes, life is a woman!

But, on the other hand, the credulous and dogmatic philosopher who *believes* in this truth that is woman, who believes in truth just as he believes in woman, this philosopher has understood nothing. He has understood nothing of truth, nothing of woman. Because if woman *is* truth, *she* knows there there is no truth, that truth does not take place, and that no one has it, the truth. She is woman insofar as she, for her part, does not believe in truth, thus in what she is, in what she is believed to be, which therefore she is not.

In its maneuvers, distance strips the lady of her proper identity and unseats the philosopher-knight—unless, that is, he has not already received two spurs, two thrusts of style or dagger blows in an exchange that scrambles sexual identity:

[. . . .]

How can woman, who is herself truth, not believe in truth? And yet, how is it possible to be truth and still believe in it?

Beyond Good and Evil opens:

> Supposing truth to be a woman—what? is the suspicion not well-founded that all philosophers, when they have been dogmatists, have had little understanding of women [*sich schlecht auf Weiber verstanden*, have been misunderstanding as to women]? that the gruesome earnestness, the clumsy importunity with which they have been in the habit of approaching truth have been inept and improper means [*ungeschickte und unschickliche Mittel*] for winning a wench [*Frauenzimmer* is a term of contempt: an easy woman]?[8]

Truths

At this moment, Nietzsche causes the truth of woman, the truth of truth to veer off: "Certainly she has not let herself be won over—and today every kind of dogmatism stands sad and discouraged. *If it continues to stand at all!*"

Woman (truth) does not let herself be won over, taken (in).

In truth woman, truth does not let herself be taken (in)—by truth.[9]

That which will not be taken in (by) truth is—*feminine*, which one must not hasten to translate by femininity, woman's femininity, feminine sexuality, or by any other essentializing fetishes. These are precisely what, in their foolishness, the dogmatic philosopher, the impotent artist, or the inexperienced seducer believe they have won over.

This divergence of truth that carries it off and strips it of itself, that raises it between quotation marks (the screeching machination of a hooker, or crane [*grue*], its flight and claws),[10] everything in Nietzsche's writing that compels the suspension of "truth" between quotation marks—and, as a strict consequence, all the rest—which is thus going to *inscribe* the truth and, as a strict consequence, inscribe in general; all of this is, let us not even say the feminine, but the feminine "operation."

She writes (herself). Style comes back or comes down to her. Or rather: if style were the man (much as the penis, according to Freud, is the "normal prototype of the fetish"), then writing would be woman.

All these weapons circulate from hand to hand, passing from one opponent to the other, while the question remains of what I am doing here right now.

Must not these *apparently* feminist propositions be reconciled with the overwhelming corpus of Nietzsche's vehement antifeminism?

Their congruence—a word I will oppose here, by convention, to coherence—is very enigmatic, but strictly necessary. Such, in any case, would be the thesis of this presentation.

Woman, truth, is skepticism and veiling dissimulation: that is what we have to be able to think through. The *skepsis* of "truth" is as old as woman:

> I fear that women who have grown old [*altgewordene Frauen*] are more sceptical in the secret recesses of their hearts than any of the men; they believe in the superficiality of existence as in its essence, and all virtue and profoundity is to them only the disguising [*Verhüllung*] of this "truth," the very desirable disguising of a *pudendum*—an affair, therefore, of decency and modesty, and nothing more! (*Joyful Wisdom*, 64, *Sceptics*. Cf. also the conclusion especially of the introduction to *Joyful Wisdom*.)

"Truth" would be but a surface; it would only become profound, naked, and desirable by the effect of a veil—that falls over it. This truth is not suspended by quotation marks and it covers over the surface in a movement of modesty. But should that veil be suspended or be allowed to fall in a different way, there would be no more truth, or only "truth"—so written. *Le voile/tombe.*[11]

So why, then, this fear, this dread, this "modesty"?

Feminine distance abstracts truth from itself by *suspending* the relation to castration. It is suspended, like a stretched canvas, or broken off like a relation, but at the same time left hanging—in indecision. In the *épochē*.

Suspended relation to castration: not to the truth of castration, which woman does not believe in, nor to truth as castration, nor to truth-castration. Truth-castration, that's man's *business;* man busies himself with it because he has never come of age, he is never skeptical or secretive enough. In his credulousness and foolish innocence (which is always sexual, although it at times represents itself as expert mastery), he castrates himself and secretes the lure of truth-castration. (It is on this point that one should perhaps interrogate—unpack [*décapitonner*][12]—the metaphorical deployment of the veil, of the truth that speaks, of castration, and phallocentrism in the Lacanian discourse, for example.)

"Woman"—an epoch-making word[13]—does not believe either in the simple obverse of castration, anticastration. Much too clever for that, she knows (and we—who we?—should learn from her, or at least from her operation) that such a reversal would deprive her of any possible recourse to simulacra; it would, in truth, come down to the same thing and would land her back as surely as ever in the same old machine, in a phallogocentrism assisted by its crony: the reverse image of the pupil, the rowdy student, which is to say, the disciplined disciple of the master.

"Woman" needs the castration effect, because without it she would not be able to seduce or stir desire. But obviously she does not believe in it. "Woman" is what does not believe in it and plays with it. She takes aim and plays with it [*en joue*] as with a new concept or a new structure of belief meant to make one laugh. About man, from man—she knows and with a knowledge that no dogmatic or credulous philosophy will have been able to match—that castration *does not take place, has no place* [n'a pas lieu].

This formula is to be very carefully displaced. It marks first of all that the place of castration is not determinable: an undecidable mark or non-mark, a discreet margin the consequences of which are incalculable. (One of these, as I have observed elsewhere, amounts to the strict equivalence between the affirmation and the negation of castration, between castration and anticastration, between assumption and denegation of castration.[14] This is to be pursued later, under the heading of the *argument of the girdle* borrowed from Freud's text on fetishism.[15])

Adornments

If, on the contrary, it took place, castration will have been this syntax of the undecidable that guarantees all discourses pro and con by annuling them and equating them. It is the *coup pour rien*, the throw for nothing, the waste of time—which, nonetheless, is never attempted without some interest. Whence the extreme *"Skepsis des Weibes."*

Once she has rent the veil of modesty or truth in which she has been bound and held "in the greatest ignorance possible *in eroticis,"* a woman's skepticism knows no bounds. One has only to read "Von der weiblichen Keuschheit" ("On Female Chastity," *Joyful Wisdom*, 71): in "love and shame in contradiction," in the "proximity of God and animal," between the "enigma of this solution" and the "solution of this enigma," here "the ultimate philosophy and skepticism of the woman casts anchor." It is in this void that she casts her anchor *(die letzte Philosophie und Skepsis des Weibes an diesem Punkt ihre Anker wirft).*

"Woman" takes so little interest in truth, she believes in it so little that she is no longer concerned even by the truth as regards herself. It is "man" who believes that his discourse on woman or truth *concerns* woman—circumvents her. (This is the topographical question that I was attempting to sketch earlier—and that also kept slipping away as always—with regard to the undecidable contour of castration.) It is "man" who believes in the truth of woman, in woman-truth. And in truth, the feminist women who are the target of Nietzsche's constant sarcasm are men. Feminism is the operation by which woman wants to resemble man, the dogmatic philosopher, demanding truth, science, objectivity, that is, demanding the whole virile illusion, along with the castration effect that comes with it. Feminism wants castration—including that of woman. Gone is the style.

What Nietzsche clearly denounces in feminism is its lack of style: "Is it not the worst of taste when woman sets about becoming scientific *(wissenschaftlich)* in that fashion? Enlightenment *(Aufklären)* in this field has hitherto been the affair and the endowment of men *(Männer-Sache, Männer-Gabe)*—we remained 'amongst ourselves' *('unter sich')* in this" [*Beyond Good and Evil*, frag. 232; cf. also frag. 233].

It is true that elsewhere (frag. 206), but this is not in the least a contradiction, the mediocre man of science who creates nothing, who begets nothing, who is, in sum, content to mouth the rote words of science, whose eye is "like a reluctant smooth lake" that nevertheless at any moment can become the very keen eye "for what is base in those natures to whose heights he is unable to rise," this sterile man of science is compared to an old maid. Nietzsche, as is everywhere evident in his texts, is the thinker of pregnancy. He praises it in man no less than in woman. And because he was so easily moved to tears, because he sometimes spoke of his thought as of a woman pregnant with child, I often imagine him shedding tears over his swollen belly.[16]

> We remained 'amongst ourselves' in this; and whatever women write about 'woman,' we may in the end reserve a good suspicion as to whether woman really *wants* [Nietzsche's italics] or *can* want [*will* und wollen *kann*] enlightenment [*Aufklärung*] about herself . . . Unless a woman is looking for a new *adornment* for herself [*einen neuen* Putz *für sich*] in this way—self-adornment pertains to the eternal womanly, does it not?—she is trying to inspire fear of herself—perhaps she is seeking dominion [*Herrschaft*]. But she does not *want* truth [*Aber es will nicht Wahrheit*]: what is truth to a woman! From the very first nothing has been more alien, repugnant, inimical to woman than truth—her great art is the lie, her supreme concern is appearance [*Schein*] and beauty. (*Beyond Good and Evil*, frag. 232).

Simulation

The whole process of the feminine operation is spaced out within this apparent contradiction. Woman is twice the model, in a contradictory fashion: she is both praised and condemned for it. As writing does regularly and not by chance, woman plies the prosecutor's argument into the twisted *logic of the kettle*.[17] As a model of truth, she enjoys a seductive power that governs dogmatism, bewilders and keeps those credulous men, the philosophers, running all over the place. But inasmuch as she herself does not believe in truth, although she does find the truth that does not concern her to be in her interest, she is once again the model: this time the good model, or rather the bad model as good model. She plays at dissimulation, at adornment, deceit, artifice, artistic philosophy. She is a power of affirmation. If she continues to be condemned, it would be because she adopted the point of view of man in order to deny this affirmative power, to lie while still believing in the truth, and to reflect in a specular fashion the foolish dogmatism she provokes.

In its praise of simulation, of the "delight in dissimulation" [*die Lust an der Verstellung*], of histrionics, and of the "dangerous concept of 'artist'," *Joyful Wisdom* ranks both Jews and women among those expert simulators: artists. The association of the Jew and the woman is probably not insignificant. Nietzsche often gives them parallel treatment, which could send us back to the motif of castration and the simulacrum, or even the simulacrum of castration of which circumcision is the mark, the name of the mark. I quote from the end of this fragment (361) on "the histrionic capacity":

What good actor at present is *not*—a Jew? The Jew also, as a born literary man, as the actual ruler of the European press, exercises this power on the basis of his histrionic capacity: for the literary man is essentially an actor,—he plays the part of "expert," of "specialist."—Finally *women*. If we consider the whole history of women [that history which oscillates between histrionics and hysterics will come to be read a little later as a chapter in the history of truth], are they not *obliged* first of all, and above all to be actresses? If we listen to doctors who have hypnotized women [*Frauenzimmer*], or, finally, if we love them—and let ourselves be "hypnotized" by them,—what is always divulged thereby? That they "give themselves airs" ["give themselves for"], even when they—"give themselves" ... [*Daß sie "sich geben", selbst noch, wenn sie—sich geben* . . . once again the play here of both the quotation marks and the hyphens should be noted] Das Weib ist so artistisch, Woman is so artistic.[18]

To sharpen the terms of this category, one should recall as one listens to this equivocal praise, which is not that far from an indictment, that the concept of artist is always divided. There is the artist-histrion, the affirmative dissimulation, but there is also the artist-hysteric, the reactive dissimulation that belongs to the "modern artist." Nietzsche compares the latter precisely to "our little hysterics" and to "little hysterical women." In a parody of Aristotle, Nietzsche also heaps abuse on small women (*Joyful Wisdom*, frag. 75, "The Third Sex"). "And our artists are only too closely related to little hysterical women. But this is to speak against 'today' and not against the 'artist.' "

[. . . .]

Thus, the question of art, style, truth cannot be dissociated from the question of woman. But the question, What is woman? is suspended simply by the formulation of their common problematic. One can no longer *chercher la femme,* go looking for woman, or the femininity of woman or feminine sexuality. Or at least they cannot be found by any known mode of thought or learning—even if one cannot stop looking for them.

[. . . .]

Femina vita

History of an Error:[19] In each of its six sections, its six epochs, with the exception of the third one, a few words are underlined. In the second epoch, Nietzsche has underlined only the words *"sie wird Weib,"* it [the Idea] becomes woman.

Heidegger cites this section, reproduces its underlining, but his commentary avoids the woman, as always seems to be the case. All the elements of the text are analyzed, without exception, except for the becoming-woman of the idea (*sie wird Weib*). The phrase is abandoned, much as one would do in skipping over a concrete image in a philosophy book, or in tearing out an illustrated page or an allegorical representation in a serious book. All of which permits one to see without reading or to read without seeing.

By looking more closely at the *"sie wird Weib,"* we are not going *counter* to Heidegger, which is to say along the same path as his gesture. We are not going to do the contrary of what he does which would amount once again to the same thing. We are not going to pluck a mythological flower, this time to study it, to pick it up rather than let it drop.

Instead let us try to decipher this *inscription* of *woman:* Its necessity is surely neither that of a metaphorical or allegorical illustration without concept nor that of a pure concept without any fantasic design.

As the context clearly indicates, what becomes woman is the idea. The becoming-woman is a "process of the idea" (*Fortschritt der Idee*). The idea is a form of truth's self-presentation. So truth has not always been a woman. Woman is not always truth. They both have a history, they form a history—history itself perhaps, if history in the strict sense has always presented itself as such in the movement of truth—which philosophy cannot decipher on its own, being itself included therein. Before this progress in the history of the true-world, the idea was Platonic. And the *Umschreibung*, the transcription, the periphrasis, or the paraphrase of the Platonic utterance, in that inaugural moment of the idea, was, "Ich, Plato, *bin* die Wahrheit," "I, Plato, *am* the truth."

The second age, the age of the becoming-woman of the idea as the presence or representation of the truth, is therefore the moment when Plato can no longer say "I am the truth," when the philosopher is no longer the truth, when he is separated from it as from himself, when he no longer follows it, but only its traces, when he is exiled or allows the idea to be exiled. At this moment, history begins, all the trouble begins. At this point distance—woman—averts truth—the philosopher and bestows the idea. Which withdraws into the distance, becomes transcendent, inaccessible, seductive. It acts and shows the way from afar, *in die Ferne*. Its veils float in the distance, the dream of death begins: it is woman.

The true world—unattainable for now, but promised for the sage, the pious, the virtuous man ("for the sinner who repents").

(Progress of the idea: it becomes more subtle, insidious, incomprehensible—*it becomes woman* . . .)[20]

All the attributes, all the traits, all the attractions that Nietzsche saw in woman—seductive distance, captivating inaccessibility, the infinitely veiled promise, the transcendence that produces desire, the *Entfernung*—belong indeed to the history of truth as history of an error.

And then Nietzsche, as if in apposition or as if to explicate and analyze the "it becomes woman, adds *"sie wird christlich* . . ." and closes the parenthesis.

It is within the epoch of this parenthesis that one can attempt to draw this story's fabulous plot toward the motif of castration *in* the Nietzschean text, in other words, toward the enigma of the nonpresence of truth.

I will try to show that what is emblazoned in red letters by the *"it becomes woman . . . Christian"* is "she castrates (herself)":[21] she castrates because she is castrated, she plays out her castration in the epoch of a parenthesis, she feigns castration—both suffered and inflicted—in order to master the master from afar, to produce desire, and with the same stroke (it is here "the same thing"), to kill him.

A phase and a necessary periphrasis in the history of woman-truth, of woman as truth, of verification, and of feminization.

Let us turn the page of *Twilight of the Idols* to the one that follows the "History of an Error." Here opens the "Moral als Widernatur," "Morality as Anti-Nature" where Christianity is interpreted as *castratism (Kastratismus).* The extraction of a tooth, the plucking out of an eye are, says Nietzsche, Christian operations. They are acts of violence that belong to the Christian idea, to the idea become woman.

All the old monsters are agreed on this: *il faut tuer les passions* [It is necessary to kill passion]. The most famous formula for this is to be found in the New Testament, in that Sermon on the Mount, where, incidentally, things are by no means looked at *from a height.* There it is said, for example, with particular reference to sexuality: "If thy eye offend thee, pluck it out." Fortunately, no Christian acts in accordance with this precept. *Destroying* the passions and cravings, merely as a preventive measure against their stupidity and the unpleasant consequences of this stupidity— today this itself strikes us as merely another acute form of stupidity. We no longer admire dentists who "pluck out" [*ausreißen*] teeth so that they will not hurt any more.

Nietzsche opposes Christian extirpation or castration, at least that of the "early Church" (but we have not left the Church), to the spiritualization of passion. He seems to imply by this that no castration is at work in such a spiritualization—which is by no means obvious. I leave this problem open.

So the Church, the early Church, truth of the woman-idea, proceeds by ablation, extirpation, excision:

> The Church fights passion with excision [*Ausschneidung*, severance, castration] in every sense: its practice, its "cure," is *castratism*. It never asks: "How can one spiritualize, beautify, deify a craving?" It has at all times laid the stress of discipline on extirpation [*Ausrottung*] (of sensuality, of pride, of the lust to rule [*Herrschsucht*], of avarice [*Habsucht*], of vengefulness [*Rachsucht*]). But attack on the roots of passion means an attack on the roots of life: the practice of the church is *hostile to life* [*lebensfeindlich*].

Hostile to life, therefore hostile to woman who is life (*femina vita*): castration is an operation of woman against woman, no less than of each sex against itself and against the other.[22]

> The same means in the fight against a craving—castration, extirpation—is instinctively chosen by those who are too weak-willed, too degenerate, to be able to impose moderation on themselves . . . One should survey the whole history of the priests and philosophers, including the artists: the most poisonous things against the senses have been said not by the impotent, nor by the ascetics, but by the impossible ascetics, by those who really were in dire need of being ascetics . . . The spiritualization of sensuality is called *love*: it represents a great triumph over Christianity. Another

triumph is our spiritualization of *hostility.* It consists in a profound appreciation of the value of having enemies: in short, it means acting and thinking in the opposite way [*umgekehrt*] from that which has been the rule. The church always wanted the destruction of its enemies; we, we immoralists and Antichristians, find our advantage in this, that the church exists . . . The saint in whom God delights is the ideal eunuch.

Positions

The heterogeneity of the text makes it very plain: Nietzsche did not delude himself into thinking he knew what was going on with the effects called woman, truth, castration, or the *ontological* effects of presence or absence. Rather, he analyzed this very delusion. He was very careful to avoid the sort of precipitous denegation that would consist in erecting a simple discourse against castration and its system. Without a discreet parody, without a writing strategy, without a difference or divergence of pens, in a word, without style—the grand style—such a reversal comes down to the same thing in a noisy declaration of the antithesis.

Whence the heterogeneity of the text.

I will not try to treat here the large number of propositions concerning woman. Instead, I will attempt to formalize their rule and to reduce them to a finite number of typical and matrical propositions. Then I will indicate the essential limit of such a codification and the problem it entails for reading.

Three types of statement, then, three fundamental propositions which are also three positions of value, each stemming from a different place. After a certain kind of elaboration (which I can only indicate here), these positions of value might also take on the sense that psychoanalysis (for example) gives to the word *position.*

   1. Woman is condemned, debased, and despised as a figure or power of falsehood. The indictment is thus produced in the name of truth, of dogmatic metaphysics, of the credulous man who puts forward truth and the phallus as his own attributes. The—

phallogocentric—texts written from this reactive perspective are very numerous.

2. Woman is condemned and despised as a figure or power of truth, as a philosophical and Christian being, whether because she identifies herself with the truth, or because, at a distance from truth, she continues to play with it as with a fetish, to manipulate it to her advantage. Without believing in it, she remains, through guile and naïveté (and guile is always contaminated by naïveté), within the system and the economy of the truth, within the phallogocentric space. This trial is prosecuted from the point of view of the masked artist. The latter, however, still believes in woman's castration and he does not get beyond the inversion of the reactive and negative instance. Up to this point, woman is twice castration: truth and nontruth.

3. Beyond this double negation, woman is recognized, affirmed as a power of affirmation, dissimulation, as an artist, a dionysiac. She is not affirmed by man, but affirms herself, in herself and in man. In the sense I set out earlier, castration does not take place, has no place [*la castration n'a pas lieu*]. In its turn, antifeminism is reversed since it condemned woman only insofar as she was, she answered to man from the two reactive positions.

To form an exhaustive code out of these three types of statement, to try to reconstitute their systematic unity, one would have to be able to master the parodic heterogeneity of the style, of the styles, and to reduce them to the content of a thesis. It would also be necessary (but these two conditions are indissociable) that each value implicated in the three schemas be *decidable* within an oppositional couple, as if each term, for example woman, truth, castration, had a contrary.

But the graphics of the hymen or of the pharmakon inscribes the effect of castration within itself, even as it is not reducible to that effect.[23] At work everywhere, particularly in Nietzsche's text, this graphics irrevocably limits the pertinence of these hermeneutic or systematic questions. It always withholds a margin from the control of meaning or of the code.

This does not mean that one should passively take the side of the heterogeneous or the parodic (which would be to reduce them once again). Nor should one conclude that, because the master meaning, the unique and inviolate meaning, is unattainable, Nietzsche had an infinite mastery, an impregnable power, an impeccable manipulation of the trap, as if he had exercised a kind of infinite calculus, almost that if Leibniz's God. This time, however, it would be an infinite calculus of the undecidable in order to escape the hold of hermeneutics. Such a conclusion, in its very attempt to elude the snare, succumbs to it all the more surely. It makes of parody or the simulacrum an instrument of mastery in the service of truth or castration; it reconstitutes religion, the cult of Nietzsche for example, and serves the interest of a priesthood of parody interpreters [*prêtrise de l'interprète ès parodies, interprêtrise*].

No, parody always supposes somewhere a measure of naïveté, back to back with an unconscious, and the vertigo of nonmastery, a loss of consciousness. An absolutely calculated parody would be a confession or a table of the law.

One has to acknowledge, quite simply, that if the aphorisms on woman cannot be assimilated—first of all among themselves —to the rest, it is also because Nietzsche did not see his way too clearly there, nor could he take it all in with a blink of the eye, in a split second. This regular, rhythmic blindness takes place in the text. Nietzsche is a little lost there. There is loss, it can be affirmed, as soon as there is hymen.

Nietzsche is a little lost in the web of the text, like a spider overwhelmed by what has been produced around him—like a spider, I say, or like several spiders: Nietzsche's but also Lautréamont's, Mallarmé's, and those of Freud and Abraham.

He was, he dreaded this castrated woman.

He was, he dreaded this castrating woman.

He was, he loved this affirming woman.

All this at once, simultaneously or successively, depending on the places of his body and the positions of his history. He was dealing with so many women, within himself, outside of himself. Like another Council of Basel.

The Gaze of Oedipus

There is no one woman, no one truth in itself about woman in itself: that much he did say, along with the highly diverse typology, the horde of mothers, daughters, sisters, old maids, wives, governesses, prostitutes, virgins, grandmothers, big and little girls.

For this very reason, there is no one truth of Nietzsche or of his text. The phrase one reads in *Beyond Good and Evil*, "These are only—*my* truths," which underscores "*meine* Wahrheit sind," occurs precisely in a paragraph on women. *My* truths implies no doubt that these are not *truths* because they are multiple, variegated, contradictory. There is no one truth in itself, but what is more, even for me, even about me, the truth is plural. This passage is inserted between, on the one hand, the famous paragraph on "*der schreckliche Grundtext homo natura*" where Nietzsche appeals to the intrepid gaze of Oedipus *("unerschrocknen Oedipus-Augen")* with which to confront the decoys of the old metaphysical birdhandlers (*die Lockweisen alter metaphysischer Vogelfänger*), a wised-up Oedipus who no longer denies nor assumes their blinding accusation, and, on the other hand, the indictment of feminism, of "the eternal feminine," of "woman as such," Madame Roland, Madame de Staël, Monsieur George Sand, their "bad taste" (Nietzsche cites the Church's "taceat mulier in ecclesia," and Napoleon's "taceat mulier in polticis," and then adds, as a "true friend of women," "taceat mulier de muliere").[24]

There is thus no truth in itself of sexual difference in itself, of man or woman in itself; on the contrary, the whole of ontology, which is the effect of an inspection, appropriation, identification, and verification of identity, presupposes and conceals this undecidability.

Beyond the mythology of the signature, beyond the theology of the author, biographical desire gets inscribed in the text, leaves an irreducible, and irreducibly plural, mark there. Everyone's "granite stratum of spiritual fate" gives and receives these marks, form their matter. *L'érection tombe.*[25] The biographical text is fixed and stabilized for an uncertain duration; it constitutes for a long time the immovable stele, with all the dangers of this "monumental history" that were recognized beforehand by the *Untimely Meditations*. This granite is a system of

predetermined decision and answer to predetermined selected questions. In the case of every cardinal problem there speaks an unchangeable "das bin ich" ["this is I"]; about woman and philosophy, for example, a thinker cannot relearn [*umlernen*] but only learn fully [*auslernen*]—only discover all that is "firm and settled" with him on this subject ... Having just paid myself such a deal of pretty compliments [the spiritual fate has just been described as our stupidity] I may perhaps be more readily permitted to utter a few truths about 'woman as such': assuming it is now understood from the outset to how great an extent these are only—*my truths*.[26]

And in *Ecce Homo* ("Why I Write Such Good Books"), two sections (4 and 5) follow each other in which Nietzsche proposes successively that he has a "great number of possible styles," or that there is no such thing as "style in itself" because, as he says, he "knows women [or rather the female: *Weiblein*] well":

This knowledge is part of my Dionysian patrimony. Who knows? Maybe I am the first psychologist of the eternally feminine. Women all like me ... But that's an old story: save, of course the abortions among them [*verunglückten Weiblein*], the emancipated ones, those who lack the wherewithal to have children. Thank goodness I am not willing to let myself be torn to pieces! the perfect woman tears you to pieces when she loves you ...

From the moment the question of woman suspends the decidable opposition of the true and the non-true, from the moment it installs the epochal regime of quotation marks for all concepts belonging to this system of philosophical decidability, once it disqualifies the hermeneutic project that postulates a true meaning of a text and liberates reading from the horizon of the meaning of being or the truth of being, from the values of production of the product or the values of presence of the present—from that moment, what is unleashed is the question of style as a question of writing, the question of a spurring operation more powerful than any content, any thesis, or any meaning. The stylate spur [*éperon stylé*] traverses the veil, tears it not only in order to see or produce the thing itself, but to undo the self-opposition, the opposition folded upon itself of the veiled–unveiled, the truth as production, unveiling–dissimulation of the product made present. It neither raises nor lets fall the veil: it de-limits the veil's suspense—the epoch. But to de-limit, to undo, to come undone, when it is a matter of veils, is that not tanta-mount to unveiling once again? Or even to destroying a fetish? This question, *inasmuch as it is a question* (between *logos* and *theoria*, saying and seeing) remains, interminably.

[. . . .]

NOTES

1. There are two extant English versions of this text: a complete transla-tion by Barbara Harlow (University of Chicago Press, 1979) and an abridged translation by Ruben Berezdivin (in *The New Nietzsche: Contemporary Styles of Interpretation*, David B. Allison, ed., [New York: Dell, 1977]). The version presented here falls somewhere between a compilation of these other two versions and a new translation.—ED.

2. That is, provided that the word *voile* is not articulated in a sentence, it can float between its masculine form, which means "veil," and its femi-nine form, "sail."—ED.

3. On Derrida's use of this word as an abbreviated signature, see our introduction, p. **xxv**—ED

4. Derrida is pointing toward the final section of *Spurs*, not included here, where he reads a sentence from Nietzsche's unpublished fragments: "I have forgotten my umbrella." This section raises many questions about the interpretation of the Nietzschean text, the totality of which, Derrida sug-gests, might well be of the type of this isolated, enigmatic sentence.—ED.

5. *The Joyful Wisdom*, trans. Thomas Common (New York: Frederick Ungar, 1960), fragment 59.

6. Ibid, fragment 60.

7. *Tanz*, in German: dance—ED.

8. *Beyond Good and Evil*, trans. R. J. Hollingdale (Harmondsworth: Pen-guin, 1973).

9. This is only an approximate translation of Derrida's undecidable syn-tax in these two sentences: "La femme (la vérité) ne se laisse pas prendre. A la vérité la femme, la vérité ne se laisse pas prendre."—ED.

10. I.e., the lifting and suspending action of the quotation marks can lead one to think of the action of a crane, in French *une grue*, which also happens to be a slang term for prostitute.—ED.

11. This is a play on the word *tombe*, which is both the noun "tomb" and the third person present singular of "tomber," to fall. Thus the phrase could be translated as either "The veil falls" (it falls away or it is lowered into place) or "The veil/tomb."—ED.

12. A reference to Jacques Lacan's theory of the "point de capiton," literally a quilting stitch; see below, **"Le Facteur de la vérité,"** pp. **472–73.**—ED.

13. The expression "faire époque" that Derrida uses here revives the sense of the Greek, *epochē*, suspension.—ED.

14. See *Dissemination* [1972], p. 40, n. 39 and passim.

15. Derrida will develop his critique of the standard interpretation of fetishism in **Glas.** The argument of the girdle *(la gaine)* concerns a certain structure of restriction that reverses opposites.—ED.

16. "Mothers. Animals think differently from men with respect to the females; with them the female is regarded as the productive being [*als das produktive Wesen*]. There is no paternal love among them, but there is such a thing as love of the children of a beloved, and habituation to them. In the young, the females find gratification for their lust of dominion [*Herrschsucht*]; the young are a property [*Eigentum*], an occupation, something quite comprehensible to them, with which they can chatter: all this conjointly is maternal love,—it is to be compared to the love of the artist for his work. Pregnancy has made the female gentler, more expectant, more timid, more submissively inclined; and similarly intellectual pregnancy engenders the character of the contemplative, who are allied to woman in character:—they are the masculine mothers.—Among animals the masculine sex is regarded as the beautiful sex." (*Joyful Wisdom*, frag. 72) The characteristics of a woman are determined by the mother's image. They are designated and predestined from the moment of nursing: "From the mother [*Von der Mutter her*].—Everyone carries in himself an image of woman derived from the mother; by this he is determined to revere women generally, or to hold them in low esteem, or to be generally indifferent to them." (*Human, All Too Human*, I, trans. Walter Kaufman, in *The Portable Nietzsche* [New York: Viking, 1968], frag. 380).

17. This refers to the joke of the borrowed kettle that Freud first tells in *The Interpretation of Dreams*. In *Jokes and Their Relation to the Unconscious*, it serves as an example of the "mutual cancelling out by several thoughts, each of which is in itself valid" (*Standard Edition*, VIII, p. 205.) Derrida retells the joke often, for example, in **"Plato's Pharmacy"** (see above, pp. **135–36**).—ED.

18. On woman's mask as man's desire, see also fragment 405.

19. On this text, see above, p. **353**.—ED.

20. *Twilight of the Idols,* trans. Walter Kaufmann, in *The Portable Nietzsche* (New York: Viking, 1968).

21. *Elle (se) châtre:* the feminine pronoun *elle* refers first to the "idea," the idea that has become woman. One should also therefore translate: it castrates (itself). The fact that both translations can be correct may be seen as a castration effect, a withdrawal of truth of the sort Derrida is examining here.—ED.

22. As soon as sexual difference is determined as an opposition, the image of each term is inverted into the other. Thus the machinery of contra-

diction would be a proposition whose two x's are at once subject and predicate and whose copula is a mirror. While Nietzsche follows tradition by inscribing man in the system of activity (along with all the values that are associated with that system) and woman in the system of passivity, he also at times reverses the direction of the copula, or rather he explains the mechanism of reversal. *Human, All Too Human* (411) attributes understanding and mastery to the woman, sensitivity and passion to the man, whose intelligence is "in itself something passive" *(etwas Passives)*. Because desire is narcissistic, passivity loves itself as passivity in the other, projects it as "ideal," transfixes its partner in that passivity. In return, the partner loves its own activity. It actively renounces being the model of that activity and instead takes the other as model. The active—passive opposition speculates on its own homosexual effacement to infinity; it raises itself [*se relève*] in the structure of idealization or the desiring machine. "Women are often silently surprised at the great respect men pay to their character. When, therefore, in the choice of a pattern, men seek specially for a being of deep and strong character, and women for a being of intelligence, brilliancy, and presence of mind, it is plain that at the bottom men seek for the ideal man, and women for the ideal woman,—consequently not for the complement [*Ergänzung*] but for the completion [*Vollendung*] of their own excellence."

23. On the hymen and the pharmakon, see above, pp. **124–28** and pp. **185–87.**—ED.

24. *Jenseits* . . . 232 Cf. also 230 to 239. Whereas this might appear to contradict the statement: "The Perfect Woman.—The perfect woman [*das vollkommene Weib*] is a higher type of humanity than the perfect man, and also something much rarer. The natural history of animals furnishes grounds in support of this theory." (*Human All Too Human* [377]), it, on the contrary, confirms it.

25. "The erection falls" and "The erection tomb"; see above, note 11.—ED.

26. *Untimely Meditations*, trans. R. J. Hollingdale (Cambridge: Cambridge University Press, 1983), frag. 231.

SIXTEEN

"*Geschlecht:* Sexual Difference,

Ontological Difference"

(*"Geschlecht:* Différence sexuelle, différence

ontologique," in *Psyché: Inventions de l'autre* [1987])

The work of Martin Heidegger has, without a doubt, a preeminent importance for Derrida's thought. Explicit references to the German thinker are a constant feature of these writings, and everywhere Derrida supposes that the passage through the Heideggerian recasting of the philosophical legacy is an unavoidable one for whoever would continue to question that legacy. The relation to Heidegger evinced by these writings is not, for all that, a simple one, and Derrida can hardly be called a disciple of Heidegger or a Heideggerian. (It was, moreover, Heidegger himself who first ridiculed the notion that there was such a thing as a Heideggerian philosophy that could form disciples.) Instead, this relation could be characterized as a particularly stressed form of deconstruction. Derrida has pointed out on several occasions that the latter term was contrived in part as a translation of the use Heidegger makes of the two German words *Abbau* and *Destruktion* (see, for example, **"Letter to a Japanese Friend"**). But if he thus in some sense credits Heidegger with this notion, it is not in order to exempt the latter's texts from the pressures of deconstruction which, in effect, fold that operation back onto itself. The following text is a fine illustration of how Derrida reads both with and against Heidegger's text so as to locate certain points or layers where its deconstruction/*Destruktion* risks being stopped short.

The pressure point that is singled out here is sexual difference. As already clear in **Spurs,** where he noticed that Heidegger passes over Nietzsche's remark that "the idea became woman," Derrida is interested in the apparent lack of reference to sexual difference in Heidegger's thought. A passing reference in a text from 1928, however, leads him to question the place of the notion of *Geschlecht,* a word that, among other things, means sex in the sense of either masculine or feminine, within the distinction Heidegger makes of ontological from ontic difference. It is in the latter category that Heidegger seems to place sexual difference, that is, the category of determinate differences that can merely predicate *Dasein* which is itself neutral or neuter. But Derrida remarks that the reduction of sexual difference or its neutralization also occupies a privileged place in the existential analytic. From this indication, there emerges a sense of the neuter which is not simply negative (neither . . . nor) and which therefore does not imply an absence of sex. What is neutralized is sexual difference as a binary pair, a distinction between two, and no more than two, sexes. It is toward this possibility of thinking a sexuality in dispersion and multiplication, thus without the negativity always implied by the dialectic of a duality (and Hegel's or Kant's are but the most systematic versions of this dialectic; see **Glas**), that Derrida signals in the final pages.

Geschlecht:

Sexual Difference, Ontological Difference [1]

To Ruben Berezdivin

1928

Of sex, one can readily remark, yes, Heidegger speaks as little as possible, perhaps he has never spoken of it. Perhaps he has never said anything, by that name or the names under which we recognize it, about the "sexual-relation," "sexual-difference," or indeed about "man-and-woman." That silence, therefore, is easily remarked. Which means that the remark is somewhat facile. A few indications, concluding with "everything happens as if . . . ," and it would be satisfied. The dossier could then be closed, avoiding trouble if not risk: it is as if, in reading Heidegger, there were no sexual difference, and nothing of this aspect in man, which is to say in woman, to interrogate or suspect, nothing worthy of questioning, *fragwürdig*. It is as if, one might continue, sexual difference did not rise to the height of ontological difference: it would be on the whole as negligible, with regard to the question of the sense of being, as any other difference, a determinate distinction or an ontic predicate. Negligible for *thought*, of course, even if it is not at all negligible for science or philosophy. But insofar as it is opened up to the question of being, insofar as it has a relation to being, in that very reference, *Dasein* would not be sexed. Discourse on sexuality would thus be abandoned to the sciences or philosophies of life, to anthropology, sociology, biology, or perhaps even to religion or morality.

Sexual difference, we were saying or we heard ourselves saying, would not rise to the height of ontological difference. It changes nothing, apparently, to know that "rising to heights" should be out of the question, since the thought of difference gets on no such high horse; yet there is silence. One might even find this to be, precisely, haughty, arrogant, or provoking in a century when sexuality, commonplace of all babbling, has also become the currency of philosophic and scientific "knowledge," the inevitable *Kampfplatz* of ethics and politics. Not a word from Heidegger! One might judge this to be rather "grand style," this scene of stubborn mutism at the very center of the conversation, in the uninterrupted and distracted buzzing of the colloquium. In itself it has a waking and sobering value (but what exactly is everyone talking about around this silence?): Who, indeed, around or even long before him, has not chatted about sexuality as such, as it were, and by that name? All the philosophers in the tradition have done so, from Plato to Nietzsche, who for their part were irrepressible on the subject. Kant, Hegel, Husserl all reserved a place for it; they at least touched on it in their anthropology or in their philosophy of nature, and in fact everywhere.

Is it imprudent to trust Heidegger's manifest silence? Will this apparent fact later be disturbed in its nice philological assurance by some known or unedited passage when, while combing through the whole of Heidegger, some reading machine manages to hunt out the thing and snare it? Still, one must think of programing the machine, one must think, think of it and know how to do it. What will the index be? On which words will it rely? Only on names? And on which syntax, visible or invisible? Briefly, by which signs will you recognize his speaking or remaining silent about what you nonchalantly call sexual difference? What is it you are thinking beneath those words or through them?

What would be, in most cases, the sufficient basis for remarking today such an impressive silence? What measure would seem to suffice to allow that silence to appear as such, marked and marking? Undoubtedly this: Heidegger apparently said nothing about sexuality by name in those places where the best educated and endowed "modernity" would have fully expected it given its panoply of "everything-is-sexual-and-everything-is-political-and-reciprocally" (note in passing that the word "political" is rarely used, perhaps never, in Heidegger, another not quote insignificant matter). Even before the statistics were in, the matter would seem already settled. But there are good grounds to believe that the statistics here would only confirm the verdict: about what we glibly call sexuality Heidegger has remained silent. Transitive and significant silence (he has silenced sex) which belongs, as he says about a certain *Schweigen* ("*hier in der transitiven Bedeutung gesagt*"), to the path of a word [*parole*] he seems to interrupt. But what are the places of this interruption? Where is the silence working on that discourse? And what are the forms and determinable contours of that non-said?

You can bet that there's nothing immobile in these places where the arrows of the aforesaid panoply would pin things down with a name: omission, repression, denial, foreclosure, even the unthought.

But then, if the bet were lost, would not the trace of that silence merit the detour? It is not just anything he silences and the trace does not come from just anywhere. But why the bet? Because before predicting anything whatever about "sexuality," it may be verified, one must invoke chance, the aleatory, destiny.

Let it be, then, a so-called modern reading, an investigation armed with psychoanalysis, an enquiry authorized by all of anthropological culture. What does it seek? Where does it seek? Where may it deem it has the right to expect at least a sign, an allusion, however elliptical, a reference, to sexuality, the sexual relation, sexual difference? To begin with, in *Sein und Zeit*. Was not the existential analytic of *Dasein* near enough to a fundamental anthropology to have given rise to so many misunderstandings or mistakes regarding its supposed "*réalité-humaine*" or human reality as it was translated in France? Yet even in the analyses of being-in-the-world as being-with-others, or of care either in its self or as *Fürsorge*, it would be vain, it seems, to search even for the beginning of a discourse on desire and sexuality. One might conclude from this that sexual difference is not an essential trait, that it does not belong to the existential structure of *Dasein*. Being-there, being *there*, the *there* of being as such, bears no sexual mark. The same then goes for the reading of the sense of being, since, as *Sein und Zeit* clearly states (§ 2), *Dasein* remains in such a reading the exemplary being. Even were it admitted that all reference to sexuality isn't effaced or remains implied, this would only be to the degree that such a reference presupposes quite general structures (*In-der-Welt-sein als Mit- und Selbst-sein, Räumlichkeit, Befindlichkeit Rede, Sprache, Geworfenheit, Sorge, Zeitlichkeit, Sein zum Tode*). Yet sexuality would never be the guiding thread for a privileged access to these structures.

There the matter seems settled, it might be said. And yet! *Und dennoch!* (Heidegger uses this rhetorical turn more often than one would think: and yet, exclamation mark, next paragraph).

And yet the matter was so little or so ill understood that Heidegger had to explain himself right away. He was to do it in the margins of *Sein und Zeit*, if we may call marginal a course given at the University of Marburg an der Lahn in the summer semester 1928.[2] There he recalls certain "directive principles" on *"the problem of transcendence and the problem of SEIN UND ZEIT"* (§ 10). The existential analytic of *Dasein* can occur only within the perspective of a fundamental ontology. That is why it is not a matter of an "anthropology" or an "ethic." Such an analytic is only "preparatory," while the "metaphysics of *Dasein*" is not yet "at the center" of the enterprise, clearly suggesting that it is nevertheless on the program.

It is by the *name* of "*Dasein*" that I would here introduce the question of sexual difference.

Why name *Dasein* the being that constitutes the theme of this analytic? Why does *Dasein* give its "title" to this thematic? In *Sein und Zeit* Heidegger had justified the choice of that "exemplary being" for the *reading* of the sense of being: "Upon which being should one read off the sense of being. . . ?" In the end, the response leads to the "modes of being of a determinate being, *that* being which we the questioners ourselves are." If the choice of that exemplary being, in its "privilege," becomes the object of a justification (whatever may be its axiomatics and whatever one may think of them), Heidegger on the contrary seems to proceed by decree, at least in this passage, when it becomes a matter of *naming* that exemplary being, of giving it once and for all its terminological title: "That being which we ourselves are and which includes questioning as one of its possibilities of Being [*die Seinsmöglichkeit des Fragens*], we name being-there [we grasp it, arrest it, apprehend it 'terminologically,' *fassen wir terminologisch als Dasein*]." That "terminological" choice undoubtedly finds its profound justification in the whole enterprise and in the whole book by unfolding a *there* and a *being-there* which (nearly) no other predetermination should be able to command. But that does not remove the decisive, brutal, and elliptical appearance from this preliminary proposition, this declaration of name. On the contrary, it happens that in the Marburg course, the title of *Dasein*—its sense as well as its name—is more patiently qualified, explained, evaluated. Now, the first trait that Heidegger underlines is its *neutrality*. First directive principle: "For the being which constitutes the theme of this analytic, the title 'man' (*Mensch*) has not been chosen, but the neutral title '*das Dasein.*' "

At first glance the concept of neutrality seems quite general. It is a matter of reducing or subtracting, by means of that neutralization, every anthropological, ethical or metaphysical predetermination so as to keep nothing but a relation to itself, bare relation, to the Being of its being. This is the minimal relation to itself as relation to Being, the relation that the being which we are, as questioning, maintains with self and with its own proper essence. This relation to self is not a relation to an ego or to an individual, of course. Thus *Dasein* designates the being that, "in a determined sense," is not "indifferent" to its own essence, or to whom its own Being is not indifferent. Neutrality, therefore, is first of all the neutralization of everything but the naked trait of this relation to self, of this interest for its own Being (in the widest sense of the word "interest"). The latter implies an interest or a precomprehensive opening up for the sense of Being and for the questions thus ordained. And yet!

And yet this neutrality will be rendered explicit by a leap, without transition and in the very next item (second directive principle) in the direction of sexual neutrality, and even of a certain asexuality (*Geschlechtslosigkeit*) of being-there. The leap is surprising. If Heidegger wanted to offer examples of determinations to be left out of the analytic of *Dasein*, especially of anthropological traits to be neutralized, he had many to choose from. He begins with, and in fact never gets beyond, sexuality, more precisely sexual difference. It therefore holds a privilege and seems to belong in the first place—if one follows the statements in the logic of their connection—to that "factual concretion" that the analytic of *Dasein* should *begin* by neutralizing. If the neutrality of the title "*Dasein*" is essential, it is precisely because the interpretation of this being—which *we* are—is to be engaged *before* and *outside* of a concretion of that type. The *first* example of "concretion" would then be belonging to one or another of the two sexes. Heidegger doesn't doubt that they are two: "That neutrality means *also* [my emphasis—J.D.] that *Dasein* is neither of the two sexes [*keines von beiden Geschlechtern ist*]."

Much later, at any rate thirty years later, the word "*Geschlecht*" will be charged with all its polysemic richness: sex, genre, family, stock, race, lineage, generation. Heidegger will retrace in language, through irreplaceable path-openings (that is, inaccessible to common translation), through labyrinthine, seductive and disquieting ways, the imprint of paths that are often closed. Here they are still closed by the two. Two: that can not count anything but sexes, it seems, what are called sexes.

I have underlined the word *also* ("that neutrality means also . . ."). By its place in the logical and rhetorical chain, this "also" recalls that among the numerous meanings of that neutrality, Heidegger judges it necessary not so much to begin with sexual neutrality—which is why he also says "also"—but, nevertheless, *immediately after the only* general meaning that has marked neutrality up to this point in the passage, to wit the *human* character, the title "*Mensch*" for the theme of the analytic. That is the only meaning that up till then he has excluded or neutralized. Hence there is here a kind of precipitation or acceleration which can not itself be neutral or indifferent: among all the traits of man's humanity that are thus neutralized, along with anthropology, ethics, or metaphysics, the first that the very word "neutrality" makes one think of, the first that Heidegger thinks of in any case, is sexuality. The incitement cannot come merely from grammar, that's obvious. To pass from *Mensch*, indeed from *Mann*, to *Dasein*, is certainly to pass from the masculine to the neutral, while to think or to say *Dasein* and the *Da* of *Sein* on the basis of that transcendent which is *das Sein* ("*Sein ist das transcendens schlechthin*," *Sein und Zeit*, p. 28), is to pass into a certain neutrality. Furthermore, such neutrality derives from the nongeneric and nonspecific character of Being: "Being as fundamental theme of philosophy is not a genre of a being (*keine Gattung*) . . ." (ibid.). But once again, although sexual difference necessarily has a relation to saying, words, and language, still it cannot be reduced to a grammar. Heidegger designates, rather than describes, this neutrality as an existential structure of *Dasein*. But why does he all of a sudden insist on it with such haste? While in *Sein und Zeit* he had said nothing of asexuality (*Geschlechtslosigkeit*), it figures here at the forefront of the traits to be mentioned when recalling *Dasein*'s neutrality, or rather the neutrality of the title "*Dasein*." Why?

A first reason comes to mind. The very word *Neutralität* (neuter) induces a reference to binarity. If *Dasein* is neutral, and if it is not man (*Mensch*), the *first* consequence to draw from this is that it does not submit to that binary partition one most spontaneously thinks of in such a case, to wit "sexual difference." If "being-there" does not mean "man" (*Mensch*), a *fortiori* it designates neither "man" nor "woman." But if the consequence is so near common-sense, why recall it? Above all, why should one go to so much trouble in the continuation of the course to get rid of anything so clear and secure? Should one conclude that sexual difference does not depend so simply on all that which the analytic of *Dasein* can and must neutralize, to wit, metaphysics, ethics, and especially anthropology, or indeed any other domain of ontic knowledge, for example biology or zoology? Ought one to suspect that sexual difference cannot be reduced to an ethical or anthropological theme?

Heidegger's precautionary insistence lets one think, in any case, that these things are not a matter of course. Once anthropology (fundamental or not) has been neutralized and once it has been shown that anthropology cannot engage the question of being or be engaged with it as such, once it has been observed that *Dasein* is reducible neither to human-being, nor to the ego, nor to consciousness, nor to the unconscious, nor to the subject, nor to the individual, nor even to an *animal rationale*, one might have thought that the question of sexual different did not have a chance of measuring up to the question of the sense of being or of the ontological difference, that even its dismissal did not deserve privileged treatment. Yet unquestionably it is the contrary that happens. Heidegger has barely finished recalling *Dasein*'s neutrality, and then right away he has to clarify: neutrality also as to sexual difference. Perhaps he was responding to more or less explicit, naïve or sophisticated, questions on the part of his hearers, readers, students, or colleagues who were still held back, whether they liked it or not, within anthropological space: What about the sexual life of your *Dasein*? they might still have asked. And after having answered the question on that terrain by disqualifying it, in sum, after having recalled the asexuality of a being-there which is not an *anthropos*, Heidegger wishes to encounter another question, even perhaps a new objection. That is where the difficulties are going to begin to accumulate.

Whether one talks of neutrality or asexuality (*Neutralität, Geschlechtslosigkeit*), the words accentuate strongly a negativity which manifestly runs counter to what Heidegger thereby wishes to mark out. It is not a matter here of linguistic or grammatical signs at the surface of a meaning which, for its part, remains untouched. By means of such manifestly negative predicates, one must be able to read what Heidegger does not hesitate to call a "positivity" (*Positivität*), a richness, and even, in a heavily charged code, a power (*Mächtigkeit*). This clarification suggests that the asexual neutrality does not desexualize, on the contrary, its *ontological* negativity is not deployed with respect to *sexuality itself* (which it would instead liberate), but with respect to the marks of difference, or more precisely to *sexual duality*. There would be no *Geschlechtslosigkeit* except with respect to the "two"; asexuality would be determined as such only to the degree that sexuality is immediately understood as binarity or sexual division. "But such asexuality is not the indifference of an empty nothing (*die Indifferenz des leeren Nichtigen*), the feeble negativity of an indifferent ontic nothing. In its neutrality, *Dasein* is not just anyone no matter who, but the originary positivity (*ursprüngliche Positivität*) and power of essence [*être*] (*Mächtigkeit des Wesens*)."

If *Dasein* as such belongs to neither of the two sexes, that does not mean that its being is deprived of sex. On the contrary: here one must think of a predifferential, or rather a predual, sexuality —which does not necessarily mean unitary, homogeneous, or undifferentiated, as we shall see later. Then, beginning with that sexuality, more originary than the dyad, one may try to think at its source a "positivity" and a "power" that Heidegger is careful not to call sexual, fearing no doubt to reintroduce the binary logic that anthropology and metaphysics always assign to the concept of sexuality. But it would indeed be a matter here of the positive and powerful source of every possible "sexuality." The *Geschlechtslosigkeit* would not be more negative than *aletheia*. One might recall what Heidegger said regarding the *"Würdigung" des "Positiven" im "privativen" Wesen der Aletheia* (in *Platons Lehre von der Wahrheit*).

From this point, the course sketches a quite singular movement. It is very difficult to isolate in it the theme of sexual difference. I would be tempted to interpret this as follows: by a kind of strange and quite necessary displacement, it is sexual division itself that leads to negativity; so neutralization is *at once* the effect of this negativity and the effacement to which thought must subject it to allow an original positivity to become manifest. Far from constituting a positivity that the asexual neutrality of *Dasein* would annul, sexual binarity itself would be responsible, or rather would belong to a determination that is itself responsible, for this negativation. To radicalize or formalize too quickly the sense of this movement before retracing it more patiently, we could propose the following schema: it is sexual difference itself *as binarity*, it is the discriminative belonging to one or another sex, that destines or determines (to) a negativity that must then be accounted for. Going still further, one could even link sexual difference thus determined (one out of two), negativity, and a certain "impotence." When returning to the originality of *Dasein*, of this *Dasein* said to be sexually neutral, "originary positivity" and "power" can be recovered. In other words, despite appearances, the asexuality and neutrality that must first of all be subtracted from the binary sexual mark, in the analytic of *Dasein*, are in fact on the same side, on the side of *that* sexual difference—the binary—to which one might have thought them simply opposed. Would this interpretation be too violent?

The next three subparagraphs or items (§ 3, § 4, § 5) develop the motifs of neutrality, positivity, and originary power, the originary itself, without explicit reference to sexual difference. "Power" becomes that of an origin (*Ursprung, Urquell*), and moreover Heidegger will never directly associate the predicate "sexual" with the word "power," the first remaining all too easily associated with the whole system of sexual difference that may, without much risk of error, be said to be inseparable from every anthropology and every metaphysics. More than that, the adjective "sexual" (*sexual, sexuell, geschlechtlich*) is never used, at least to my knowledge, only the nouns *Geschlecht* or *Geschlechtlichkeit;* this is not without importance, since these nouns can more easily radiate toward other semantic zones. Later we will follow there some other paths of thought.

But without speaking of it directly, these three subparagraphs prepare the return to the thematic of *Geschlechtlichkeit*. First of all they efface all the negative signs attached to the word *neutrality*. The latter does not have the emptiness of an abstraction; neutrality rather leads back to the "power of the origin" which bears within itself the internal possibility of humanity in its concrete facuality. *Dasein*, in its neutrality, must not be confused with the existent. *Dasein* only exists in its factual concretion, to be sure, but this very existence has its originary source (*Urquell*) and internal possibility in *Dasein* as neutral. The analytic of this origin does not deal with the existent itself. Precisely because it precedes them, such an analytic cannot be confused with a philosophy of existence, with a wisdom (which could be established only within the "structure of metaphysics"), or with a sermonizing that would teach this or that "world view." It is therefore not at all a "philosophy of life." Which is to say that a discourse on sexuality of this order (wisdom, knowledge, metaphysics, philosophy of life or of existence) falls short of every requirement of an analytic of *Dasein* in its very neutrality. Has a discourse on sexuality ever come forward that did not belong to any of these registers?

It must be recalled that sexuality is not named in this last paragraph nor in the one that will treat (we will return to it) a certain "isolation" of *Dasein*. It is named in a paragraph in *Vom Wesen des Grundes* (the same year, 1928) which develops the same argument. The word occurs in quotation marks, in a parenthesis. The logic of the *a fortiori* raises the tone somewhat there. For in the end, if it is true that sexuality must be neutralized *a fortiori, erst recht*, why insist? Where is the risk of misunderstanding? Unless the matter is not at all obvious, and there is still a risk of mixing up once more the question of sexual difference with that of Being and the ontological difference? In that context, it is a matter of determining the ipseity of *Dasein*, its *Selbstheit* or being-a-self. *Dasein* exists only for its own sake [*à dessein de soi*] (*umwillen seiner*), if one can put it thus, but that means neither the for-itself of consciousness, nor egoism, nor solipsism. It is starting from *Selbstheit* that an alternative between "egoism" and "altruism" may arise and become manifest, as well as a difference between "being-I" and "being-you" (*Ich-sein/Dusein*). Always presupposed, ipseity is therefore also "neutral" with respect to being-me and being-you, "and with all the more reason with regard to 'sexuality' " (*und erst recht etwa gegen die "Geschlechtlichkeit" neutral*). The movement of this *a fortiori* is logically irreproachable on only one condition: It would be necessary that the said "sexuality (in quotation marks) be the assured predicate of whatever is made possible by or beginning with ipseity, here, for instance, the structures of "me" and "you," yet that it not belong to "sexuality," to the structure of ipseity, an ipseity not as yet determined as human being, me or you, conscious or unconscious subject, man or woman. Yet, if Heidegger insists and underlines ("with all the more reason"), it is because a suspicion has not yet been banished: What if "sexuality" already marked the most originary *Selbstheit*? If it were an ontological structure of ipseity? If the *Da* of *Dasein* were already "sexual"? What if sexual difference were already marked in the opening up to the question of the sense of Being and to the ontological difference? And what if neutralization, which does not happen all by itself, were a violent operation? "With all the more reason" may hide a more feeble reason. In any case, the quotation marks always signal some kind of citation. The current usage of the word "sexuality" is "mentioned" rather than "used," one might say in the language of speech act theory; it is cited to appear in court, warned if not accused. Above all, one must protect the analytic of *Dasein* from the risks of anthropology, of psychoanalysis, even of biology. Yet there still may be a door open for other words, or another usage and another reading of the word "*Geschlecht*," if not the word "sexuality." Perhaps another "sex," or rather another "*Geschlecht*," will come to be inscribed within ipseity, or will come to disturb the order of all its derivations, for example, that of a more originary *Selbstheit* making possible the emergence of the *ego* and of the *you*. Let us leave this question suspended.

Although this neutralization is implied in every ontological analysis of the *Dasein*, that does not mean that the "*Dasein* in man," as Heidegger often says, need be an "egoistic" singularity or an "ontically isolated individual." The point of departure in neutrality does not lead back to the isolation or insularity (*Isolierung*) of man, to his factual and existential solitude. And yet the point of departure in neutrality does indeed mean, Heidegger carefully observes, a certain original isolation of man: not, precisely, in the sense of factual existence, "as if the philosophizing being were the center of the world," but as the "*metaphysical isolation* of man." It is the analysis of this isolation which then brings out again the theme of sexual difference and of the dual partition within *Geschlechtlichkeit*. At the center of this new analysis, the very subtle differentiation of a certain lexicon already signals translation problems which are only going to get worse for us. It will always be impossible to consider them as either accidental or secondary. At a certain moment we will even be able to notice that the thought of *Geschlecht* and that of translation are essentially the same. The lexical hive brings together (or swarms) the series "dissociation," "distraction," "dissemination," "division," "dispersion." The *dis-* is supposed to translate, though only by means of transfers and displacements, the *zer-* of *Zerstreuung, Zerstreutheit, Zerstörung, Zersplitterung, Zerspaltung*. But an interior and supplementary frontier partitions yet again the lexicon: *dis-* and *zer-* often have a negative sense, yet sometimes also a neutral or nonnegative sense (I would hesitate here to say positive or affirmative).

Let us attempt to read, translate as literally as possible and interpret. *Dasein* in general hides, shelters in itself the internal possibility of a factual dispersion or dissemination (*faktische Zerstreuung*) in its own body (*Leiblichkeit*) and "thereby in sexuality" (*und damit in die Geschlechtlichkeit*). Every proper body of one's own [*corps propre*] is sexed, and there is no *Dasein* without its own body. But the linking proposed by Heidegger seems quite clear: the dispersing multiplicity is not primarily due to the sexuality of one's own body; it is its own body itself, the flesh, the *Leiblichkeit*, that draws *Dasein* originally into the dispersion and *in due course* [*par suite*] into sexual difference. This "in due course" (*damit*) insists in the interval of a few lines, as if *Dasein* were supposed to have or be a priori (as its "interior possibility") a body that *happens* to be sexual and affected by sexual division.

Here again, an insistence on Heidegger's part recalls that, like neutrality, dispersion (and all the meanings in *dis-* or *zer-*) must not be understood in a negative manner. The "metaphysical" neutrality of isolated man as *Dasein* is not an empty abstraction drawn from or in the sense of the ontic, it is not a *neither—nor*, but rather what is properly concrete in the origin, the "not yet" of factual dissemination, of dissociation, of being–dissociated or of factual dis-sociality: *faktische Zerstreutheit* here and not *Zerstreuung*. This dissociated being, unbound, or desocialized (for it goes together with the isolation of man as *Dasein*) is not a fall or an accident, a decline [*déchéance*] that has supervened. It is an originary structure of *Dasein* that affects it and the body, and *hence* sexual difference, with multiplicity and with lack-of-binding [*déliaison*], these two significations remaining distinct though gathered together in the analyses of dissemination (*Zerstreuung* or *Zerstreutheit*). Assigned to a body, *Dasein* is separated in its facticity, subjected to dispersion and parcelling out (*zersplittert*), and thereby (*ineins damit*) always disjunct, in disaccord, split up, divided (*zwiespältig*) by sexuality toward a determinate sex (*in eine bestimmte Geschlechtlichkeit*). These words, undoubtedly, have at first a negative resonance: dispersion, parcelling out, division, dissociation, *Zersplitterung, Zerspaltung*, quite like *Zerstörung* (demolition, destruction), as Heidegger explains; this resonance is linked with negative concepts from an ontic point of view, a fact that immediately entails a meaning of lesser value. "But something else is at issue here." What? Another meaning, marking the fold of a mani-fold "multiplication." We can read the characteristic sign (*Kennzeichnung*) by which such a multi-plication is recognizable in the isolation and factual singularity of *Dasein*. Heidegger distinguishes this multiplication (*Mannig-*

faltigung) from a simple multiplicity (*Mannigfaltigkeit*), from a diversity. One must also avoid the representation of a grand original being whose simplicity was suddenly dispersed (*zerspaltet*) into various singularities. It is rather a matter of elucidating the internal possibility of that multiplication for which *Dasein*'s own body represents an "organizing factor." The multiplicity in this case is not a simple formal plurality of determinations or of determinities (*Bestimmtheiten*); it belongs to Being itself. An "originary dissemination" (*ursprüngliche Streuung*) belongs already to the Being of *Dasein* in general, "according to its metaphysically neutral concept." This originary dissemination (*Streuung*) becomes, from an altogether determined point of view, *dispersion* (*Zerstreuung*): here a difficulty of translation forces me to distinguish somewhat arbitrarily between dissemination and dispersion, in order to mark out by a convention the subtle trait that distinguishes *Streuung* from *Zerstreuung*. The latter is the intensive determination of the former. It determines a structure of originary possibility, dissemination (*Streuung*), according to all the meanings of *Zerstreuung* (dissemination, dispersion, scattering, diffusion, dissipation, distraction). The word *Streuung* occurs but once, it seems, and it designates this originary possibility, this disseminality (if I may be allowed that word). Afterwards, the word is always *Zerstreuung*, which would add—but it isn't that simple—a mark of determination and negation, had not Heidegger warned us just a moment before against that value of negativity. Yet, even if not totally legitimate, it is hard to avoid a certain contamination by negativity, indeed by ethico-religious associations that would link that dispersion to a fall or to a corruption of the pure originary possibility (*Streuung*), which appears thus to be affected by a supplementary turn. It will indeed be necessary to elucidate also the possibility or fatality of that contamination. We will return to this later.

Some indications of this dispersion (*Zerstreuung*). First of all, *Dasein* never relates to *an* object, to a sole object. If it does, it is always in the mode of abstraction or abstention from other beings which always co-appear at the same time. This multiplication does not supervene because there is a plurality of objects; actually it is the converse that takes place. It is the originary disseminal structure, the dispersion of *Dasein*, that makes possible this multiplicity. And the same holds for *Dasein*'s relation to itself: it is dispersed, which is consistent with the "structure of historicity in the widest sense," to the extent that *Dasein* occurs as *Erstreckung*, a word the translation of which remains very risky. The word *extension* could all too easily be associated with *extensio*, which *Sein und Zeit* interprets as the "fundamental ontological determination of the world" according to Descartes (§ 18). Here something completely other is at issue. *Erstreckung* names a spacing which, "before" the determination of space as *extensio*, comes to extend or stretch out being-there, the *there* of Being, *between* birth and death. As an essential dimension of *Dasein*, the *Erstreckung* opens up the *between* that links it at once to its birth and to its death, the movement of suspense by which it itself *tends* and extends itself *between* birth and death, these two receiving their meaning only from that intervallic movement. *Dasein* affects itself with this movement, and that auto-affection belongs to the ontological structure of its historicity: "*Die Spezifische Bewegtheit des* erstreckten Sicherstreckens *nennen wir das* Geschehen *des Daseins*" (§ 72). The fifth chapter of *Sein und Zeit* links together precisely this intervallic tension and dispersion (*Zerstreuung*) (notably in § 75, p. 390). *Between* birth and death, the spacing of the *between* marks at once the distance and the relation, but the relation according to a kind of distension. This "between-two" as *relation* (*Bezug*) having a *link* [*trait*] with both birth and death belongs to the very Being of the *Dasein*, "before" any biological determination, for instance ("*Im Sein des Daseins liegt schon das 'Zwischen' mit Bezug auf Geburt und Tod,*" p. 374). The link thus enter-tained, inter-twined [*entre-tenu, entre-tendu*], held or drawn in, over or through the distance between [*entre*] birth and death, maintains itself *by* dispersion, dissociation, unbinding (*Zerstreuung, Unzusammenhang*, etc. Cf. p. 390 for example). That link, that between, *could not take place* without them. Yet to take them as negative forces would be to precipitate the interpretation, for instance to render it dialectical.

The *Erstreckung* is thus one of the determinate possibilities of essential dispersion (*Zerstreuung*). That "between" would be impossible without dispersion yet it constitutes only one of its structural dependents, to wit, temporality and historicity. Another dependent, another possibility—connected and essential—of originary dispersion is the originary spatiality of *Dasein*, its *Räumlichkeit*. The spatial or spacing dispersion is manifested, for instance, in language. Every language is first of all determined by spatial significations (*Raumbedeutungen*).³ The phenomenon of so-called spatializing metaphors is not at all accidental, nor within the scope of the rhetorical concept of "metaphor." It is not some exterior fatality. Its essential irreducibility cannot be elucidated outside of this existential analytic of *Dasein*, of its dispersion, its historicity, and its spatiality. The consequences therefore must be drawn, in particular for the very language of the existential analytic: all the words Heidegger uses necessarily refer back also to these *Raumbedeutungen*, beginning with the word *Zerstreuung* (dissemination, dispersion, distraction) which nevertheless names the origin of spacing at the moment when, as language, it submits to its laws.

The "transcendental dispersion" (as Heidegger still names it) thus belong to the essence of *Dasein* in its neutrality. "Metaphysical" essence, we are more precisely told in a course presented above all at that time as a metaphysical ontology of *Dasein*, whose analytic constitutes only a phase, undoubtedly preliminary. This must be taken into account in order to situate what is said here about sexual difference in particular. Transcendental dispersion is the possibility of every dissociation and parcelling out (*Zersplitterung, Zerspaltung*) into factual existence. It is itself "founded" on that originary character of *Dasein* that Heidegger then called *Geworfenheit*. One should be patient with that word, subtracting it from so many usages, current interpretations or translations (for instance dereliction, being-thrown). This should be done in anticipation of what the interpretation of sexual difference—which right away follows—retains in itself of that *Geworfenheit* and, "founded" on it, of transcendental dispersion. There is no dissemination that does not suppose such a "throw" [*jetée*], *Da* of *Dasein* as thrown [*jetée*]. Thrown "before" all the modes of throwing that will later determine it: project, subject, object, abject, trajectory, dejection; throw that *Dasein* cannot make its own in a project, in the sense of *throwing itself* like a subject master of the throw. *Dasein* is *geworfen:* this means that it is thrown before any project on its part, but this being-thrown is not yet *submitted* to the alternative of activity or passivity, this alternative being still too much in solidarity with the couple subject–object and hence with their opposition, one could even say with their objection. To interpret being-thrown as passivity could reinscribe it within the derivative problematic of subjecti(vi)ty (active or passive). What does "throw" mean before any of these syntaxes? And being-thrown even before the image of the fall, be it Platonic or Christian? There is a being-thrown of *Dasein* even "before" the appearance *appears*— in other words, "before" the advent for it there—of any thought of throwing amounting to an operation, activity, or initiative. And that being-thrown of *Dasein* is not a throw *in* space, in what is already a spatial element. The originary spatiality of *Dasein* depends on the throw.

It is at this point that the theme of sexual difference can reappear. The disseminal throw of being-there (understood still in its neutrality) is particularly manifest in the fact that *Dasein* is *Mitsein* with *Dasein*. As always in this context, Heidegger's first gesture is to observe an order of implication: sexual difference, or belonging to a genre, must be elucidated starting from being-with, in other words, from the disseminal throw, and not inversely. Being-with does not arise from some factitious connection; "it cannot be explained from some presumably originary generic being," by a being whose own body would be partitioned according to a sexual difference (*geschlechtlich gespaltenen leiblichen Wesen*). On the contrary, a certain generic drive of gathering together (*gattungshafte Zusammenstreben*), the union of genres (their unification, rapprochement, *Einigung*), has as "metaphysical presupposition" the dissemination of *Dasein* as such, *and thereby Mitsein*. The *Mit* of *Mitsein* is an existential, not a categorial, and the same holds for the adverbs of place (*Sein und Zeit*, § 26). What Heidegger calls here the fundamental metaphysical character of *Dasein* is not to be derived from any generic organization or from a community of living beings as such.

How does this question of *order* matter to a "situation" of sexual difference? Thanks to a prudent derivation that in turn becomes problematic for us, Heidegger can at least reinscribe the theme of sexuality, in rigorous fashion, within an ontological questioning and an existential analytic. As soon as one no longer pins one's hopes on a common *doxa* or a bio-anthropological science, both of which are sustained by a metaphysical preinterpretation, sexual difference remains to be thought. But the price of that prudence? Is it not to distance sexuality from every originary structure? To deduce it? Or in any case to derive it while thus confirming the most traditional philosophemes, repeating them with the force of a new rigor? And did not that derivation begin by a neutralization the negativity of which was laboriously denied? And once the neutralization is effected, does one not accede once again to an ontological or "transcendental" dispersion, to that *Zerstreuung* the negative value of which was so difficult to efface?

In this form these questions remain, undoubtedly, summary. But they could not be elaborated in a simple exchange with the passage in the course of Marburg which names sexuality. Whether it be a matter of neutralization, negativity, dispersion, or distraction (*Zerstreuung*), all of which are, if we follow Heidegger, indispensable motifs here for posing the question of sexuality, it is necessary to *return* to *Sein und Zeit*. Although sexuality is not named there, these motifs are treated in a more complex, more differentiated fashion, which does not mean, on the contrary, in an easier or more facile manner.

We must be content here to pose several preliminary indications. Resembling a methodical procedure in the course, neutralization is not unrelated to what in *Sein und Zeit* is called the "privative interpretation" (§ 11). One could even speak of a method, since Heidegger appeals to an ontology that is accomplished by or on the "way" of a privative interpretation. That way allows the "*a priori*'s to be brought out, and a note on the same page, crediting Husserl, says that it is well known that "a priorism is the method of every scientific philosophy that understands itself." In this context, it is a question, precisely, of psychology and biology. As sciences, they are founded on an ontology of being-there. This mode–of–being that is life is accessible, essentially, only through being-there. It is the ontology of life that requires a "privative interpretation": "life" being neither a pure *Vorhandensein* nor a *Dasein* (Heidegger says this without considering that the issue requires more than a mere affirmation: for him it seems to be obvious), it is accessible only by a negative operation of subtraction. One may very well wonder what is the being of a life which is *nothing but* life, which is neither this nor that, neither *Vorhandensein* nor *Dasein*. Heidegger never elaborated that ontology of life, but one can imagine all the difficulties it would have run into, since the "neither . . . nor" that conditions it excludes or overflows the basic structural (categorial or existential) concepts of the whole existential analytic. It is the whole problematic organization that is here in question, the one that subjects positive forms of knowledge to regional ontologies, and these to a fundamental ontology, which itself at that time was preliminarily opened up by the existential analytic of *Dasein*. It is no accident (once more, one might say, and show) if it is the mode of being of the *living*, the animated (hence also of the psychical) which raises and situates this enormous problem, or in any case gives it its most recognizable name. We cannot go into this matter here, but with the underlining of its all too often unnoticed necessity, it should at least be observed that the theme of sexual difference cannot be dissociated from it.

Let us for the moment keep to that "way of privation," the expression picked up again by Heidegger in § 12, and this time again to designate the *a priori* access to the ontological structure of the living. Once that remark is developed, Heidegger enlarges upon the question of those negative statements. Why do negative determinations impose themselves so often within this ontological characteristic? Not at all by "chance." It is because one must remove the originality of the phenomena from what has dissembled, disfigured, displaced, or covered them over, from the *Verstellungen* and *Verdeckungen*, from all those preinterpretations the negative effects of which must in their turn be annulled by the negative statements the veritable "sense" of which is truly "positive." This is a schema we recognized earlier. The negativity of the "characteristic" is therefore not any more fortuitous than the necessity of alterations or dissemblances which it attempts in some manner *methodically* to correct. *Verstellungen* and *Verdeckungen* are necessary movements in the very history of Being and its interpretation. They cannot be avoided, like contingent faults, any more than one can reduce inauthenticity (*Uneigentlichkeit*) to a fault or a sin into which one should not have fallen.

And yet. If Heidegger uses so easily the word *"negative"* when it is a matter of qualifying statements or a characteristic, he never uses it, it seems to me (or, more prudently, he uses it much less often and much less easily), to qualify the very thing that, in preinterpretations of Being, nevertheless makes necessary those methodical corrections which take a negative or neutralizing form. *Uneigentlichkeit, Verstellungen* and *Verdeckungen* are not of the order of negativity (the order of the false or of evil, of error, or of sin). And one can well understand why Heidegger carefully avoids speaking in this case of negativity. He thus avoids religious, ethical, indeed even dialectical schemas, claiming to go back further or "higher" than they.

It should then be said that no negative signification is ontologically attached to the "neuter" in general, particularly not to this transcendental dispersion (*Zerstreuung*) of *Dasein*. Thus, without speaking of negative value or of value in general (Heidegger's distrust of the value of value is well known), we must take into account the differential and hierarchical accentuation that regularly in *Sein und Zeit* comes to mark the neutral and dispersion. In certain contexts, dispersion marks the most general structure of *Dasein*. We saw this in the course, but it was already the case in *Sein und Zeit*, for example in § 12 (p. 56): "The *being-in-the-world* of *Dasein* is, with its facticity, always already dispersed (*zerstreut*) or even parcelled out (*zersplittert*) into determinate modes of *being-in*." Heidegger proposes a list of these modes and of their irreducible multiplicity. Yet elsewhere, dispersion and distraction (*Zerstreuung* in both senses) characterize the inauthentic ipseity of *Dasein*, that of *Man-selbst*, of that *One* which has been "distinguished" from the authentic and proper (*eigentlich*) ipseity (*Selbst*). As "anyone," *Dasein* is dispersed or distracted (*zerstreut*). The whole of that analysis is well known; we are only detaching from it that which concerns dispersion (cf. § 27), a concept one can again find at the center of the analysis of curiosity (*Neugier*, § 36). The latter, let us recall, is one of the three modes of falling (*Verfallen*) of *Dasein* in its everyday-being.

Later we shall have to return to the precautions Heidegger takes: falling, alienation (*Entfremdung*), and even downfall (*Absturz*) are not meant here as the theme of a "moralizing critique," a "philosophy of culture," a dogmatic religious account of the fall (*Fall*) from an "original condition" (of which we have neither ontic experience nor ontological interpretation) or of a "corruption of human nature." Much later, we will have to recall these precautions and their problematic character, when, in the "situation" of Trakl, Heidegger will interpret the decomposition and the de–essentialization (*Verwesung*), that is to say also a certain corruption, of the figure of man. It will still be a matter, even more explicitly this time, of a thought of *"Geschlecht"* or of the *Geschlecht*. I put it in quotation marks because the issue touches as much on the name as on what it names; and it is here as imprudent to separate them as to translate them. As we shall see, what is at stake is the inscription of *Geschlecht* and of the *Geschlecht* as inscription, stamp, and imprint.

Dispersion is thus marked *twice:* as general structure of *Dasein* and as mode of inauthenticity. One might say the same for the neutral: in the course, whenever it is a question of *Dasein*'s neutrality, there is no negative or pejorative index; yet "neutral," in *Sein und Zeit*, may also be used to characterize the "one," to wit, it is what becomes of the "who" within everyday ipseity: the "who," then, is the neutral (*Neutrum*), *"the one"* (§ 27).

This brief recourse to *Sein und Zeit* has perhaps allowed us better to understand the sense and necessity of that *order of implications* that Heidegger wants to preserve. Among other things, that order may also account for the predicates used by all discourse on sexuality. There is no properly sexual predicate; at least there is none that does not refer, for its sense, to the *general* structures of *Dasein*. So that to know what one is talking about, and how, when one names sexuality, one must indeed rely upon the very thing described by the analytic of *Dasein*. Inversely, so to speak, that disimplication allows the general sexuality or sexualization of discourse to be understood: sexual connotations can mark discourse, to the point of a complete takeover, only to the extent that they are homogeneous with what every discourse implies, for example the topology of those irreducible "spatial meanings" (*Raumbedeutungen*), but also all those other traits we have situated in passing. What would a "sexual" discourse or a discourse "on-sexuality" be that did not evoke farness [*éloignement*], the inside and the outside, dispersion and proximity, the here and the there, birth and death, the between-birth-and-death, being-with and discourse?

This order of implications opens up thinking to a sexual difference that would not yet be sexual duality, difference as dual. As we have already observed, what the course neutralized was less sexuality itself than the "generic" mark of sexual difference, belonging to one of *two* sexes. Hence, in leading back to dispersion and multiplication (*Zerstreuung, Mannigfaltigung*), may one not begin to think a sexual difference (without negativity, let us clarify) not sealed by a two? Not yet sealed or no longer sealed? But the "not yet" or "no longer" would still mean, already, a submission to the control and inspection of reason.

The withdrawal [*retrait*] of the dyad leads toward the other sexual difference. It may also prepare other questions. For instance, this one: How did difference get deposited in the two? Or again, if one insisted on consigning difference within dual opposition, how does multiplication get arrested in difference? And in sexual difference?

In the course, for the reasons given above, *Geschlecht* always names sexuality such as it is typed by *opposition* or by duality. Later (and sooner) matters will be different, and this opposition is called decomposition.

— *Translated by Ruben Bevezdivin*

NOTES

1. First and wholly preliminary part of an interpretation by which I wish to situate *Geschlecht* within Heidegger's path of thought. Within the path of his writings too, and the marked impression or inscription of the word *Geschlecht* will not be irrelevant. That word I leave here in its language for reasons that should become binding in the course of this very reading. And it is indeed a matter of "*Geschlecht*" (sex, race, family, generation, lineage, species, genre/genus) and not of *the Geschlecht:* one will not pass so easily toward the thing itself (the *Geschlecht*), beyond the mark of the word (*Ges-*

chlecht) in which, much later, Heidegger will remark the "imprint" of a blow or a stamp *(Schlag)*. This he will do in a text we shall not discuss here but toward which this reading will continue, by which in truth I know it is already magnetized: "Die Sprache im Gedicht, Eine Erörterung von Georg Trakls Gedicht" (1953) in *Unterwegs zur Sprache* (1959, pp. 36 ff.). [This text is taken up in "Heidegger's Hand: Geschlecht II" in *Psyché* (1987)—ED.]

2. *Metaphysische Anfangsgründe der Logik im Ausgang von Leibniz, Gesamt-Ausgabe*, volume 26.

3. Cf. also *Sein und Zeit*, p. 166.

SEVENTEEN

From "At This Very Moment in This Work Here I Am"

("En ce moment même dans cet ouvrage me voici,"

in *Psyché: Inventions de l'autre* [1987])

In an essay titled "Violence and Metaphysics" initially published in 1964 (reprinted in *Writing and Difference* [1967]), Derrida had first engaged at length with the thought of his contemporary, the French philosopher Emmanuel Levinas. He would later point out, for example in **Of Grammatology** (see above, p. 42) and "**Différance,**" that his formulations of notions such as the trace with which to delimit the metaphysics of presence had been worked out within close range of Levinas's sense of the trace of a past that has never been present, an absolute alterity. Yet, as he had always done with Heidegger, Derrida posed certain questions of Levinas that marked the limits of any convergence. In 1980, in a second essay on Levinas which was commissioned for a Festschrift and which is extracted below, these questions concern sexual difference.

The questions come mostly at the end of this polyvocal essay and are attributed to the feminine interlocutor who has been largely silent up until that point. The principal part of the essay elaborates a model of Levinas's writing as one that manages to inscribe or let be inscribed, beyond its representation or thematization, the altogether other which is nevertheless incommensurable with the language of presence, of being, of essence in which he is writing. Derrida is concerned to show how this achievement both constitutes the singularity of Levinas's work and yet, for the very reason that that work succeeds in bearing traces of the other, cannot be attributed to a single signature. Meanwhile, this whole development in the essay is represented as addressed to a feminine interlocutor. The latter feature is crucial to the essay because it recalls at every step the Saying of the other that overflows the present writing which Derrida is tracing through Levinas. In effect, as the first interlocutor remarks, she dictates that which he addresses or gives to her. We are led to relate this structure of address to the Levinasian notion of the trace, the Pro-noun *"il"* (both he and it) that "marks with its seal anything that may carry a name." When, therefore, the feminine interlocutor takes over the final pages, it is in order to ask about this masculine/neuter "il," whether it can in any sense comprehend *her* or *she*. What, she asks, is the relation Levinas proposes between *autrui* (others) as other sex, otherwise sexed, on the one hand, and *autrui* as the "altogether other, beyond or before sexual difference" on the other hand? It would appear, she says, that the former is understood as secondary and subordinate to the latter. She remarks that such a gesture of subordination has invariably meant, despite the distortion of logic required, situating a certain masculinity before the differentiation masculine/feminine. The consequences of this illogic are then played out as far as they will go: the Pro-noun of God which guards jealously its neutrality against any contamination by determined being, by sexual difference. (For an analysis of this figure of the jealous God and, in particular, of the final paragraphs of this essay, see above, my introduction, pp. **xxxi–xxv**.)

—He will have obligated [*Il aura obligé*].

At this very instant, you hear me, I have just said it. He will have obligated. If you hear me, already you are sensible to the strange event. Not that you have been visited, but as after the passing by of some singular visitor, you are no longer familiar with the place, those very places where nonetheless the little phrase—where does it come from? who pronounced it?—still leaves its resonance lingering [*égarée*].

As if from now on we didn't dwell there any longer, and to tell the truth, as if we had never been at home. But you aren't uneasy, what you feel—something unheard-of yet so very ancient—is not a malaise; and even if something is affecting you without having touched you, still you have been deprived of nothing. No negation ought to be able to measure up to what is happening so as to be able to describe it.

Notice you can still hear and understand yourself all alone, therefore, repeating the three words ("*il aura obligé*"); you have failed neither to hear its rumor nor understand its sense. You are no longer without them, without these words which are discreet, and thereby unlimited, overflowing with discretion. I myself no longer know where to stop them. What surrounds them? He will have obligated. The edges of phrase remain drowned in a fog. Nevertheless it seems quite plain and clearly set off in its authoritarian brevity, complete without appeal, without requiring any adjective or complement, not even any noun: he will have obligated. But precisely, nothing surrounds it sufficiently to assure us of its limits. The sentence is not evasive but its border lies concealed. About the phrase, the movement of which can't be resumed by any of the one, two, three words [*"il aura obligé"*] of one, two, three syllables, about it you can no longer say that nothing is happening at this very moment. But what then? The shore is lacking, the edges of a phrase belong to the night.

He will have obligated—distanced [*éloigné*] from all context.

That's right, distanced, which does not forbid, on the contrary, proximity. What they call a context and which comes to shut in the sense of a discourse, always more or less, is never simply absent, only more or less strict. But no cut *is* there, no utterance is ever cut from all context, the context is never annulled without remainder. One must therefore negotiate, deal with, transact with marginal effects [*les effets de bord*]. One must even negotiate what is nonnegotiable and which overflows all context.

Here at this very moment, when I am here trying to give you to understand, the border of a context is less narrow, less strictly determining than one is accustomed to believe. *"Il aura obligé"*: there you have a phrase that may appear to some terribly indeterminate. But the distance that is granted to us here would not be due so much to a certain quite apparent absence of an edge (*"il aura obligé"*, without a nameable subject, complement, attribute, or identifiable past or future on this page, in this work [*ouvrage*] at the moment when you hear yourself presently reading it), but rather because of a certain *inside* of what is said and of the saying of what is said *in* the phrase, and which, from within, if this may still be said, infinitely *overflows* at a stroke all possible context. And that at the very moment, in a work for example—but you don't yet know what I mean by that word, *work*—when the wholly other who will have visited this phrase negotiates the nonnegotiable with a context, negotiates his economy *as* that of the other.

He will have obligated.

You must find me enigmatic, a bit glib or perverse in cultivating the enigma every time I repeat this little phrase, always the same, and lacking context, becoming more and more obscure. No, and I say this without studying the effect, the possibility of this repetition is the very thing that interests me, interests you as well, even before we should happen to find it interesting, and

I should like slowly to move closer (to you, maybe, but by a proximity that binds [*lie*], he would say, to the first comer, to the unmatched other, before all contract, without any present being able to gather together a contact), slowly to bring myself closer to this, namely that I can no longer formalize since the event (*"il aura obligé"*) will have precisely defied within language [*la langue*] this power of formalization. He will have obligated to comprehend, let us say rather to receive, because affection, an affection more passive than passivity, is party to all this, he will have obligated to receive totally otherwise the little phrase. To my knowledge he has never pronounced it as such; this matters little. He will have obligated to "read" it totally otherwise. Now to make us (without making us) receive otherwise, and receive otherwise the otherwise, he has been unable to do otherwise than negotiate with the risk: in the same language, the language of the same, one may always ill receive what is thus otherwise said. Even before that fault, the risk contaminates its very proposition. What becomes of this fault then? And if it is inevitable, what sort of event is at issue? Where would it take place? ˙

He will have obligated. However distanced it may remain, there is certainly some context in that phrase.

You hear it resonate, at this very moment, in this work.

What I thus call—this work—is not, especially not, dominated by the name of Emmanuel Levinas.

It is rather meant to be given to him. Given according to his name, in his name as much as to his name. Therefore there are multiple chances, probabilities, you cannot avoid surrendering to them, so that the subject of the phrase, *"il aura obligé"*, might be Emmanuel Levinas.

Still it is not sure. And even if one could be sure of it, would one thereby have responded to the question, Who is the "He" (*"Il"*) in that phrase?

Following a strange title that resembles a cryptic quotation in its invisible quotation marks, the site of this phrase "princeps" doesn't allow you yet to know by what right *He* carries a capital. Perhaps not only as an *incipit,* and, in this hypothesis of another capital letter or of the capital letter of the Other, be attentive to all the consequences. It is drawn into the play of the irreplaceable *He* submitting itself to substitution, like an object, into the irreplaceable itself. He, without italics.

I wonder why I have to address myself to you to say that. And why after so many attempts, so many failures, here I am obligated to renounce the anonymous neutrality of a discourse proposed, in its form at least, to no matter whom, pretending self-mastery and mastery of its object in a formalization without remainder? I won't pronounce your name or inscribe it, but you are not anonymous at the moment when here I am telling you this, *sending it* to you like a letter, giving it to you to hear or to read, *giving* being infinitely more important to me than what it might transmit at the moment I receive the desire from you, at the moment when I let you dictate to me what I would like to give you of myself. Why? Why at this very moment?

Suppose that in giving to you—it little matters what—I wanted to give to him, him Emmanuel Levinas. Not render him anything, homage for example, not even render myself to him, but to give him something which escapes from the circle of restitution or of the *"rendez-vous"* ("Proximity," he writes, "doesn't enter into that common time of clocks that makes the rendez-vous possible. It is derangement."). I would like to do it faultlessly (*sans faute*), with a "faultlessness" [*"sans faute"*] that no longer belongs to the time or logic of the rendez-vous. Beyond any possible restitution, there would be need for my gesture to operate without debt, in absolute ingratitude. The trap is that I then pay homage, the only possible homage, to his work (*oeuvre*), to what his work says of the Work [*Oeuvre*]: "The Work thought to the end requires a radical generosity of the movement in which the Same goes toward the Other. Consequently, it requires an *ingratitude* from the other." He will have written this twice, in appearance literally identically, in *The Trace of the Other* and in *Signification and Sense*. But one cannot economize on this seriality, I will return to this.

Suppose then that I wished to *give* to him, to E. L., and beyond all restitution. I will have to do it in *conformance* with what he will have said of the Work in his work, in the Work of his work. I will still be caught in the circle of debt and restitution with which the nonnegotiable will have to be negotiated. I would be debating with myself, interminably, forever, and even before having known it, up to the point, perhaps, when I would affirm the absolutely anachronic dissymmetry of a debt without loan, acknowledgment, or possible restitution.

According to which he will have immemorially obligated even before calling himself by any name whatsoever or belonging to any genre whatsoever. The conformity of *conformance* is no longer thinkable within that logic of truth which dominates—without being able to command it—our language and the language of philosophy. If in order to give without restituting, I must still conform to what he says of the Work in his work, and to what he gives there as well as to a re-tracing of the giving; more precisely, if I must conform my gesture to what makes the Work in his Work, which is older than his work, and whose Saying according to his own terms is not reducible to the Said, there we are, engaged before all engagement, in an incredible logic, formal and nonformal. If I restitute, if I restitute without fault, I am at fault. And if I do not restitute, by *giving* beyond acknowledgment, I risk the fault. I leave for now in this word—fault—all the liberty of its registers, from crime to a fault of spelling. As to the proper name of what finds itself at issue here, as to the proper name of the other, that would, perhaps, return (or amount) to the same.

There you are, forewarned: it is the risk or chance of that fault that fascinates or obsesses me at this very moment, and what can happen to a faulty writing, to a faulty letter (the one I write you), what can remain of it, what the ineluctable possibility of such a fault gives to think about a text or a remainder. Ineluctable since the structure of "faultiness" is *a priori*, older even than any *a priori*. If anyone (He) tells you *from the start (d'abord):* "don't return to me what I give you," you are at fault even before he finishes talking. It suffices that you hear him, that you begin to understand and acknowledge. You have begun to receive his injunction, to give yourself to what he says, and the more you obey him in restituting nothing, the better you will disobey him and become deaf to what he addresses to you. All that might resemble a logical paradox or trap. But it is "anterior" to all logic. I spoke *wrongly* of a trap just now. It is only felt as a trap from the moment when one would pretend to escape from absolute dissymmetry through a will to mastery or coherence. It would be a way to acknowledge the gift in order to refuse it. Nothing is more difficult than to accept a gift. Now what I "want" to "do" here is to accept the gift, to affirm and reaffirm it as what I have received. Not from someone who would himself have had the initiative for it, but from someone who would have had the force to receive it and reaffirm it. And if it is thus that (in my turn) I give to you, it will no longer form a chain of restitutions, but another gift, the gift of the other. Is that possible? Will it have been possible? Shouldn't it have already taken place, before everything, so that the very question may emerge from it, which in advance renders the question obsolete?

The gift *is not.* One cannot ask, "what is the gift?"; yet it is only on that *condition* that there will have been, by this name or another, a gift.

Hence, suppose that beyond all restitution, in radical ingratitude (but notice, not just any ingratitude, not in the ingratitude that still belongs to the circle of acknowledgment and reciprocity), I desire (it desires in me, but the it (*le ça*) is not a neutral non-me), I desire to try to give to E. L. This or that? Such and such a thing? A discourse, a thought, a writing? No, that would still give rise to exchange, commerce, economic reappropriation. No, to give him the very giving of giving, a giving that might no longer even be an object or a present said, because every present remains within the economic sphere of the same, nor an impersonal infinitive (the "giving" [*le "donner"*] therefore must perforate the grammatical phenomenon dominated by the current interpretation of language), nor any operation or action sufficiently self-identical to return to the same. That "giving" must be neither a thing nor an act, it must somehow be someone (male or female), not *me:* nor him (*"he"*). Strange, isn't it, this excess that overflows language at every instant and yet requires it, sets it incessantly into motion at the very moment of traversing it? That traversal is not a transgression, the passage of a cutting limit; the very metaphor of overflowing [*débordement*] no longer fits insofar as it still implies some linearity.

Even before I attempt or desire to attempt it, suppose that the desire for that gift is evoked in me by the other, without however obligating me or at least before any obligation of constraint, of a contract, or gratitude, or acknowledgment of the debt: a duty without debt, a debt without contract. That should be able to do without him or happen with anyone: hence it demands, *at once,* this anonymity, this possibility of indefinitely equivalent substitution *and* the singularity, no, the absolute uniqueness of the proper name. Beyond any thing, beyond whatever might lead it astray or seduce it toward something else, beyond everything that could somehow or other return to me, such a gift should go right to the unique, to what his name will have *uniquely* named, to that uniqueness that his name will have given. This *right* does not derive from any right, from any jurisdiction transcendent to the gift itself; it is the right of what he calls, in a sense that perhaps you don't understand yet, because it disturbs language every time it visits it, *recitude* or *sincerity.*

Which his name will have *uniquely* named or given. But (but it would require saying *but* for every word) uniquely in another sense than that of the singularity that jealously guards its propriety or property as irreplaceable subject within the proper name of an author or proprietor, in the sufficiency of a self assured of its signature. Finally, suppose that in the wake of the gift I commit a fault, that I let a fault, as they say, slip by, that I don't write straight [*que je n'écrive pas droit*], that I fail to write as one must (but *one must* [*il faut*], *one must* understand otherwise the *one must*), or that I fail to give him, *to him,* a gift that is not *his.* I am not at this very moment thinking of a fault on his name, on his forename or patronym, but with such a default in the writing that in the end would constitute a fault of spelling, a bad treatment inflicted on this proper name, whether done consciously or expressly by me or not.

Since in that fault your body is at issue [*il y va*], and since, as I previously said, the gift I would make him comes from you who dictate it to me, your unease grows. In what could such a fault consist? Shall one ever be able to avoid it? Were it inevitable, and hence in the final account irreparable, why should reparation require claiming? And especially, above all, on this hypothesis, what would have taken place? I mean: What would happen (and about what? Or whom?)? What would be the proper place of this text, of this faulty body? Will it have properly taken place? Where should you and I, we, let it be?

——No, not let it be. Soon, we shall have to give it to eat, and drink, and you will listen to me.

[. . . .]

—— How, then, does he write? How does what he writes make a work (*ouvrage*), and make the Work [*Oeuvre*] in the work [*ouvrage*]? For instance, and most especially, what does he do when he writes in the present, in the grammatical form of the present, to say what cannot be nor ever will have been present, the *present said* only presenting itself in the name of a Saying that overflows it infinitely within and without, like a sort of absolute anachrony of the wholly other that, although incommensurably heterogeneous to the language of the present and the discourse of the same, nonetheless must leave a trace of it, always improbably but each time determinate, this one, and not another? How does he manage to inscribe or let the wholly other be inscribed within the language of being, of the present, or essence, of the same, of economy, etc., within its syntax and lexicon, under its law? How does he manage to give a place there to what remains absolutely foreign to that medium, absolutely unbound from that language, beyond being, the present, essence, the same, the economy, etc.? Mustn't one reverse the question, at least in appearance, and ask oneself whether that language is not *of itself unbound* and hence open to the wholly other, to its own beyond, in such a way that it is less a matter of exceeding that language than of treating it otherwise with its own possibilities? Treating it otherwise, in other words to calculate the transaction, negotiate the compromise that would leave the nonnegotiable intact, and to do this in such a way as to make the fault, which consists in inscribing the wholly other within the empire of the same, alter the same enough to absolve itself from itself. According to me that is his answer, and that *de facto* answer, if one may say so, that response in deed, at work rather in the series of strategic negotiations, that response does not respond to a problem or a question; it responds to the Other—for the Other —and approaches [*aborde*] writing in enjoining itself to that for-the-Other. It is by starting from the Other that writing thus gives a place and forms an event, for example this one: "*Il aura obligé.*"

It is that response, the responsibility of that response, that I

would like to interrogate in its turn. Interrogate, to be sure, is
not the word, and I don't yet know how to qualify what is
happening here between him, you and me, that doesn't belong to
the order of questions and responses. It would be rather his
responsibility—and what he says of responsibility—that inter-
rogates us beyond all the coded discourses on the subject.

Hence: What is he doing, how does he work [*oeuvre*] when,
under the false appearance of a present, in a more-than-present
[*plus-que-présent*], he will have written this, for example, where
I slowly read to you, at this very moment, listen:

> Responsibility for the other, going against intentionality
> and the will which intentionality does not succeed in dissi-
> mulating, signifies not the disclosure of a given and its
> reception, but the exposure of me to the other, prior to every
> decision. There is a claim laid on the Same by the other in
> the core of myself, the extreme tension of the command
> exercised by the Other in me over me, a traumatic hold of
> the other on the Same, which does not allow the Same time
> to await the other. [. . .] The subject in responsibility is
> alienated in the depths of its identity with an alienation
> that does not empty the Same of its identity, but constrains
> it to it, with an unimpeachable assignation, constrains it to
> it as no one else, where no one could replace it. The psyche,
> a uniqueness outside of concepts, is a seed of folly, already
> a psychosis. It is not an ego (*Moi*), but me (*moi*) under
> assignation. There is an assignation to an identity for the
> response of responsibility, where one cannot have oneself
> be replaced without fault. To this command continually put
> forth only a "here I am" [*me voici*] can answer, where the
> pronoun "I" is in the accusative, declined before any declen-
> sion, possessed by the other, sick,[2] identical. Here I am—an
> inspired saying, which is not a gift for the fine words or
> songs. There is constraint to give with full hands, and thus
> a constraint to corporeality. [. . .] It is the subjectivity of a
> man of flesh and blood, more passive in its extradition to
> the other than the passivity of effects in a causal chain, for
> it is beyond the unity of apperception of the *I think*, which
> is actuality itself. It is a being-torn-up-from-oneself-for-an-

other in the giving-to-the-other-of-the-bread-out-of-one's-own-mouth. This is not an anodyne formal relation, but all the gravity of the body extirpated from its *conatus essendi* in the possibility of giving. The identity of the subject is here brought out, not by resting upon itself, but by a restlessness that drives me outside of the nucleus of my substantiality.[3]

[....]

You have just heard the "present" of the "Here I am" freed for the other and declined before any declension. That "present" was already very complicated in its structure, one could say almost contaminated by that very thing from which it should have been rent. It is not the presumed signatory of the work, E. L., who says: "Here I am", me, presently. He *quotes* a "Here I am", he thematizes what is nonthematizable (to use that vocabulary to which he will have assigned a regular—and somewhat strange—conceptual function in his writings). But beyond the *Song of Songs* or *Poem of Poems*, the citation of whoever would say "Here I am" should serve to mark out *this* extradition when responsibility for the other gives me over to the other. No grammatical marking as such, no language or context would suffice to determine it. That present-quotation, which, as a quotation, seems to efface the present event of any irreplaceable "here I am," also comes *to say* that in "here I am" the self is no longer presented as a self-present subject, making itself present to itself (I-myself), it is declined before all declension, "in the accusative", and he

———He or she, if the interruption of the discourse is required. Isn't it "she" in the *Song of Songs?* And who would "she" be? Does it matter?

Nearly always with him, this is how he sets his work in the fabric: by interrupting the weaving of our language and then by weaving together the interruptions themselves, another language comes to disturb the first one. It doesn't inhabit it, but haunts it. Another text, the text of the other, arrives in silence with a more or less regular cadence, without ever appearing in its original language, to dislodge the language of translation, converting the version, and refolding it while folding it upon the very thing it

pretended to import. It disassimilates it. But then, that phrase
translated and quoted from the *Song of Songs* which, it should be
recalled, is already a response, and a response that is more or less
fictitious in its rhetoric, and what is more, a response meant in
turn to be *quoted*, transmitted, and communicated in indirect
discourse—this gives the accusative its greatest grammatical
plausibility (various translations render it more or less exactly:
"I opened to my beloved; / but my beloved had gone away, he
had disappeared. / I was outside myself when he spoke to me. . . .
I called him and he did not reply . . . They have taken away my
veil, the guards of the walls. / I implore you, daughters of Jerusa-
lem / If you find my beloved, / What will you say to him? . . . /
That I am sick of love.—" Or again, "I open myself to my darling
/ but my darling has slipped away, he has passed. / My being goes
out at his speaking: / I seek him and do not find him. / I call him:
he does not reply. . . . On me they take away my shawl, / the
guardians of the ramparts. / I appeal to you, daughters of Yer-
oushalaïm: if you find my darling, what will you declare to him?
/ —That sick of love, I . . ."), that phrase translated and quoted
(in a footnote, so as to open up and deport the principal text) is
torn from the mouth of a woman, so as to be given to the other.
Why doesn't he clarify that in this work?

——Doubtless because that remains in this context, and with
regard to his most urgent purpose, secondary. Here, at least, he
doesn't seem to answer that question. In the passage that quotes
the "here I am," which I have in turn read to you, the structure
of the utterances is complicated by the "astriction to giving."
What is quoted here is what no quotation should be able to
muffle; what is each time said only once, and henceforth exceeds
not the saying but the said in language. The phrase describes or
says what within the said interrupts it and at one stroke makes
it anachronistic with respect to the saying, negotiated between
the said and the saying and at the same time interrupting the
negotiation while forthwith negotiating interruption itself. Such
negotiation deals with a language, with the ordering of a grammar and a lexicon, with a system of normative constraints, which
tend to interdict what here *must be said [il faut dire]*, namely,
the astriction to giving and the extradition of subjectivity to the

other. The negotiation thematizes what forbids thematization, while during the very trajectory of that transaction it forces language into a contract with the stranger, with what it can only incorporate without assimilating. With a nearly illegible stroke the other stands the contaminating negotiation up [*fait faux-bond*], furtively marking the effraction with a saying unreduced to silence although no longer *said in language*. The grammatical utterance is there, but dislodged so as to leave room for (though not to establish residence in) a sort of agrammaticality of the gift assigned from the other: *I* in the accusative, etc. The interdictory language is interdicted but continues speaking; it can't help it, it can't avoid being continually and strangely interrupted and disconcerted by what traverses it with a single step, drawing it along while leaving it in place. Whence the essential function of a quotation, its unique setting to work, which consists in quoting the unquotable so as to lay stress on the language, citing it as a whole in order to summon *at once* as witness and as accused within its limits, (sur)rendered to a gift, as a gift to which language cannot open up on its own. It is not, then, simply a matter of transgression, a simple passage beyond language and its norms. It is not, then, a thought of the limit, at least not of that limit all too easily figured forth by the word *beyond* so necessary for the transaction. The passage beyond language requires language or rather a text as a place for the trace of a step that is not (present) elsewhere. That is why the movement of that trace, passing beyond language, is not classical nor does it render the *logos* either secondary or instrumental. *Logos* remains as indispensable as the fold folded onto the gift, just like the tongue (*langue*) of my mouth when I tear bread from it to give it to the other. It is also my body.

[. . . .]

Here now is another example. He speaks of "this book," even here, of the fabrication of "this work," of the "present work"; these expressions repeat themselves as with the above "at this moment," but this time interlaced with a series of "one musts." A "me" and "here I am" slide incessantly from the quotation to an interminable oscillation between "use" and "mention." This happens in the last two pages of *Otherwise than Being . . .* (chap-

ter VI: *Outside*). I select the following, not without some artificial abstraction: "Signification—one-for-the-other—relation with
alterity—has already been analyzed *in the present work* (my
italics, J.D.) as proximity, proximity as responsibility for the
Other [*autrui*], and responsibility for the Other—as substitution:
in its subjectivity, in its very bearing as separated substance, the
subject has shown itself as expiation-for-the-other, condition or
uncondition of hostage." I interrupt for an instant; *"in the present work"* the impresentable has therefore presented itself, a
relation with the Other [*Autre*] that defeats any gathering into
presence, to the point where no "work" can be rebound or shut
in upon its presence, nor plotted or enchained in order to form a
book. The present work makes a present of what can only be
given outside the book. And even outside the framework. "The
problem overflows the framework of this book." These are the
last words of the last chapter of *Totality and Infinity* (immediately before the *Conclusions*). But what overflows has just been
announced—it is the very announcement, messianic consciousness—on the internal border of that utterance, *on the frame* of
the book if not *in* it. And yet what is wrought and set to work in
the present work only makes a work outside the book. The
expression "in the present work" mimics the thesis and the code
of the university community; it is ironic. It has to be so as
discreetly as possible, for there would still be too great an assurance and too much glibness to break the code with a fracas.
Effraction does not ridicule; it indeed makes a present of the
"present work."

Let's continue: "This book interprets the *subject* as *hostage*,
and the subjectivity of the subject as substitution breaking with
the *essence* of being. The thesis exposes itself imprudently to the
reproach of utopianism, in the opinion that modern man takes
himself for a being among beings, while his modernity explodes
as an impossibility of staying at home. This book escapes the
reproach of utopianism—if utopianism be a reproach, if thought
can escape being utopian—by recalling that *what humanely took
place has never been able to remain shut in its place.*" "The
thesis" is therefore not posed; it is imprudently and defenselessly
exposed, and yet that very vulnerability is ("this weakness is
necessary," we will read a little later on) the provocation to

responsibility for the other; it leaves place for the other in a taking-place of *this* book where the *this here* no longer shuts in upon itself, upon its own subject. The same dehiscence that opened up the series of "at this moment" is there at work in "the present work," "this book," "the thesis," etc.. But the series is always complicated by the fact that the inextricable equivocation, contamination, soon it will be called "hypocrisy," is at once described and denounced in its necessity *by* "this book," by "the present work," by "the thesis," and *in* them, out of them, in them, but destined in them to an outside that no dialectic will be able to reappropriate into its book. Thus (I underline *it is necessary [il faut], it was necessary [il fallait]*):

> ... Each individual is virtually an elect, called forth to leave, in his turn—or without awaiting his turn—from the concept of the self, from his extension into the people, to respond to responsibility: *me*, that is to say, *here I am for the others*, called forth radically to lose his place—or his refuge within being, to enter within a ubiquity that is also a utopia. Here I am for the others—e-normous responsibility whose lack of measure is attenuated by hypocrisy from the moment it enters into my own ears, warned, as they are, of the *essence* of being, that is to say, of the way in which it carries on. Hypocrisy immediately denounced. But the norms to which the denunciation refers have been understood within the enormity of their sense, and in the full resonance of their utterance, true like an unbridled witness. *No less*, at any rate, *is necessary* for the little humanity that adorns the earth. .... There must be a de-regulation of essence by means of which essence may not solely find violence repugnant. This repugnance attests only to the phase of an inaugural or savage humanity, ready to forget its disgusts, to be invested as "essence of de-regulation," surrounding itself like all essence with honors and military virtues, inevitably jealous of its perseverance. For the little humanity that adorns the earth there must be a relaxing of essence to the second power: *in the just war made on war, to tremble—even shiver—every instant, because of that very justice.* There

must be this weakness. This relaxing virility, without cowardice, *was necessary* for the little cruelty that our hands repudiate. This is the sense, notably, which should have been suggested by the formulas repeated in *this book* (my italics, J. D.) about the passivity more passive than any passivity, the fission of the Self as far as myself, or about the consummation for the other without the act being able to be reborn from out of the ashes of that consummation.

I again interrupt: no Hegelian Phoenix after this consummation. *This book* is not only singular in not being put together like the others; its singularity has to do with *this* seriality here, absolute enchainment, rigorous yet with a rigor that knows how to relax itself as is necessary so as not to become totalitarian again, even *virile*, hence to free itself to the discretion of the other in the hiatus. It is in this seriality here and not another (the array in its homogeneous arrangement), in this seriality of derangement that one must hear each philosopheme deranged, dislocated, disarticulated, made inadequate and anterior to itself, absolutely anachronic to whatever is said about it, for example, "the passivity more passive than any passivity" and the whole "series" of analogous syntaxes, all the "formulas repeated in this book." Now you understand the necessity of this repetition. You thus approach the "he" ["*il*"] which occurs in this work and from which the "one must" ["*il faut*"] is said. Here are the last lines:

> *In this work* (my italics, J. D.) which does not seek to restore any ruined concept, the destitution and de-situation of the subject do not remain without meaning: following the death of a certain god inhabiting the hinter-worlds, the substitution of the hostage discovers the trace—unpronounceable writing—of what, always already past, always "he" ["*il*"] never enters any present and to whom no names designating beings, nor verbs where their *essence* resounds, are any longer appropriate, but who, Pro-noun *[Pro-nom]*, marks with his seal anything that can carry a name.

——Will it be said of "this work *[ouvrage]*" that it makes a work? From which moment? Of what? Of whom? Whatever the stages may be, the responsibility comes back to him, "he", to him, who *"undersigns"* every signature. Pro-noun without pronounceable name that "marks with its seal whatever can carry a name." This last phrase comes at the end of the book as if in place of a signature. Emmanuel Levinas recalls the preceding Pronoun that replaces and makes possible every nominal signature; by the same double stroke, he gives to it and withdraws from it his signature. Is it him, "he," that then is set to work? *Of him* that the work responds? Of him that one will have said, *"il aura obligé,"* "he will have obligated"? I do not think that between such a pro-noun and a name or the bearer of a name there is what one could call a difference or a distinction. This link between "he" and the bearer of a name is other. Each time different, never anonymous, *"he"* is (without sustaining it with any substantial presence) the bearer of the name. If I now transform the utterance, which came from I know not where and from which we took our point of departure (*"il aura obligé"*), by this one, "the work of Emmanuel Levinas will have obligated," would he subscribe to that? Would he accept my replacing "he" by Emmanuel Levinas in order to say (who) will have made the work in his work? Would it be a fault, as to "he" or as to him, E. L.?

——Now, I write at your dictation, "the work of E. L. will have obligated."

You have dictated it to me and yet what I write at this very moment, "the work of E. L. will have obligated," articulating together those common nouns and proper names, you don't yet know what that means. You don't know yet how *one must* read. You don't even know how, at this moment, *one must* hear this "one must" [il faut].

The work of E. L. *comprehends* an *other* manner to think obligation in the "one must," an *other* manner of thinking the work, and even of thinking thought. One must therefore read it otherwise, read there otherwise the "one must," and otherwise the otherwise.

The dislocation to which this work will have obligated is a dislocation without name; toward another thought of the name, a thought that is wholly other because it is open *to the name of the other*. Inaugural *and* immemorial dislocation, it will have taken place—another place, in the place of the other—only on the condition of another topic. An extravagant topic (u-topic, they will say, believing they know what takes place and what takes the place of) and absolutely other. But to hear the absolute of this "absolutely," one must have read the serial work that displaces, replaces, and substitutes this word "absolute." And to start with, the word "work." We endlessly get caught up in the network of quotation marks. We no longer know how to efface them, nor how to pile them up, one on top of the other. We no longer even know how to quote his "work" any longer, since it already quotes, under quotation marks, the whole language— French, Western, and even beyond—even if it is only from the moment and because of the fact that "he" must put in quotation marks, the pronominal signatory, the nameless signatory without authorial signature, "he" who undersigns every work, sets every work [*ouvrage*] to work [*met en oeuvre*], and "marks by his seal whatever can carry a name." If "he" is between quotation marks, nothing more can be said, about him, for him, from him, in his place or before him, that would not require a tightly knit, tied up and wrought [*ouvragée*] series, a whole fabric of quotation marks knitting a text without edge. A text exceeding language and yet in all rigor untranslatable from one tongue to another. Seriality irreducibly knots it to *a* language.

If you wish to talk of E. L.'s operation when he sets himself into "this work" [*ouvrage*], when he writes "at this moment," and if you ask, "What is he doing?" and "How does he do it?" then not only must you dis-locate the "he" who is no longer the subject of an operation, agent, producer, or worker, but you must right away clarify that the Work, as his work gives and gives again to be thought, is no longer of the technical or productive order of the operation (*poiein, facere, agere, tun, wirken, erzeugen*, or however it may be translated). You cannot therefore speak —pertinently—of the Work before what "his" work says of the Work, in its Saying and beyond its Said, because that gap remains irreducible. Nor is there any circle here, especially not a hermeneutic one, because the Work—according to his work—"is" precisely what breaks all circularity. There, near but infinitely distanced, the dislocation is to be found in the interior without inside of language which is yet opened out to the outside of the wholly other. The infinite law of quotation marks seems to suspend any reference, enclosing the work upon the borderless context which it gives to itself: yet behold here this law making absolute reference to the commandment of the wholly other, obligating beyond any delimitable context.

If, therefore, I now write "the work of E. L. will have obligated to an absolute dislocation," the obligation, as the work that teaches it, teaching also how one must teach, will have been without constraint, without contract, anterior to any engagement, to any nominal signature, which through the other responds for the other before any question or requisition, ab-solute thereby and ab-solving. "He" will have subtracted dissymmetrical responsibility from the circle, the circulation of the pact, the debt, acknowledgment, from synchronic reciprocity, I would even dare say from the annular alliance, from the *rounds [tour]*, from whatever makes a round from a finger and I dare say from a sex.

Can it be said? How difficult, probably impossible, to write or describe here what I seem on the verge of describing. Perhaps it is impossible to hold a discourse that holds itself at this moment, saying, explaining, constating (a constative discourse) E. L.'s work. There would have to be *[faudrait]* a writing that performs, but with a performative without present (who has ever defined such a performative?), one that would respond to his, a performative without a present event, a performative the essence of which cannot be resumed as to presence ("at this very moment," at this *present* moment I write this, I say *I*, presently; and it has been said that the simple utterance of an *I* was already performative), a performative heretofore never described, the performance of which must not, however, be experienced as a glib success, as an act of prowess. For at the same time it is the most quotidian exercise of a discourse with the other, the condition of the least virtuoso writing. Such a performance does not correspond to *[répond à]* the canonical description of a performative, perhaps. Well then, let the description be changed, or renounce here the word "performative"! What is pretty certain is that *that* performance derives nothing from the "constative" proposition, nor from any proposition at all; but inversely and dissymmetrically, every so-called constative proposition, every proposition in gen-

eral *presupposes* this structure before anything else, this responsibility of the trace (*per*forming or *per*formed).

For example, I wrote earlier: " 'he' will have withdrawn it
from the circle . . .". Now it would already be necessary—infinitely—that I take back and displace each written word in series.
Displacing being insufficient, I must rip away each word from
itself, *absolutely* rip it away from it-self (as, for example, in his
manner of writing "passivity more passive than passivity," an
expression that undetermines itself, can just as well pass into its
opposite, unless the ripping off stops somewhere, as if by a piece
of skin symbolically ripped off from the body and remaining,
behind the cut, adhered to it), I must absolutely detach it and
absolve it from itself while nevertheless leaving upon it a mark
of attachment (the expression "passivity more passive than passivity" does not become just any other expression, it does not
mean "activity more active than activity"); in order that two
annulments or two excesses not be equivalent, within indetermination, the ab-solving erasure must not be absolutely absolute.
I must therefore make each atom of an utterance appear faulty
and absolved; faulty in regard to what or whom? And why? When
I write, for example, " 'he' will have withdrawn it . . . etc.," the
very syntax of my phrase, according to the dominant norms that
interpret the French language, the "he" appears to be constituted
into an active subject, author and initiator of an operation. If "he"
were the simple pronoun of the signatory (and not the Pro-noun
marking with its seal whatever may carry a name . . .), it could
be thought that the signatory has the authority of an author, and
that "he" is the agent of the action that "will have withdrawn,"
etc. Now *it would have been necessary* to say, it must therefore
be said, that "he" has withdrawn nothing whatever, "he" has
made appear the possibility of that withdrawal, he has not *made*
it appear, he has *let* it appear, he has not let it *appear*, since what
he has let (not to be but to make a sign, and not a sign but an
enigma), what he has let produce itself as enigma, and to produce
itself is still too much, is not of the phenomenal order, he has
"let" "appear" the nonappearing as such (but the nonappearing
never disappears into its "as such," etc.) on the limit of the
beyond, a limit that is not a determinable, visible, or thinkable

line, and that has no definable edges, on the "limit," therefore, of the "beyond" of phenomena and of essence: that is to say (!) the "he" himself. That's it, the "he" himself, that is to say (!), the Other. "He" has said "He," even before "I" may say "I" and in order that, if that is possible, "I" may say "I."

That other "he," the "he" as wholly other, was only able to arrive at the end of my phrase (unless my phrase never arrived, indefinitely arrested on its own linguistic shore) by means of a series of words that are all faulty, and that I have, as it were, erased in passing, in measure, regularly, the one after the other, while leaving to them the force of their tracing, the wake of their tracement [tracement], the force (without force) of a trace that will have allowed passage for the other. I have written in marking them, in letting them be marked, by the other. That is why it is inexact to say that I have erased those words. In any case, I should not have erased them, I should have let them be drawn into a *series* (a stringed sequence of enlaced *erasures*), an interrupted series, a *series* of interlaced interruptions, a series of *hiatuses* (gaping mouth, mouth opened out to the cut-off word, or to the gift of the other and to the-bread-in-his-mouth) that I shall henceforth call, in order to formalize in economical fashion and so as not to dissociate what is not dissociable within this fabric, the *seriasure [sériature]*. That other "he" could have only arrived at the end of my phrase within the interminable mobility of this seriasure. He is not the subject-author-signer-proprietor of the work; it is a "he" without authority. It could just as well be said that he is the Pro-noun leaving its presignature sealed under the name of the author, for example, E. L., or conversely that E. L. is but a pronoun replacing the singular pronoun, the seal that comes before whatever can carry a name. From this point of view, E. L. would be the *personal* pronoun of "he." Without authority, he does not make a work, he is not the agent or creator of his work, yet if I say that he *lets* the work work (a word that remains to be drawn along), it must immediately be specified that this letting is not a simple passivity, not a letting of thought within the horizon of letting-be. This letting beyond essence, "more passive than passivity," hear it as the most provocative thought today. It is not provocative in the sense of the transgressive, and glibly shocking, exhibition. It is a thought also provoked, *first of all* provoked. Outside the law as law of the other. It is only provoked from its absolute exposure to the provocation of the other, exposure stretched out with all possible force in order not to reduce the *past anterior* of the other, so as not to turn inside out the surface of the self who, *in advance,* finds itself delivered to it body and soul.

"Past anterior" (in the past, in the present past), "first of all," "in advance": among the words or syntax whose setting in seriasure I have not yet sketched, there is the future anterior, which I shall have nonetheless used frequently, having no alternative recourse. For example, in the little phrase *"il aura obligé,"* or "the work of E. L. will have obligated" (Obligated to what? and who, in the first place? I have not yet said thou *[tu],* me, you *[vous],* us, them, they *[ils, elles],* it). The future anterior could turn out to be—and this resemblance is irreducible—the time of Hegelian teleology. Indeed, that is how the properly philosophical intelligence is usually administered, in accord with what I called above the dominant interpretation of language—in which the philosophical interpretation precisely consists. Yet *here indeed [ici même],* within *this* seriasure drawn along the *"il aura obligé,"* "he will have obligated," in *this* and not in another quite similar seriasure, but determining otherwise the same utterance, the future anterior, "here indeed," will have designated "within" language that which remains most irreducible to the economy of Hegelian teleology and to the dominant interpretation of language. From the moment when it is in accord with the "he" as Pro-noun of the wholly-other "always already past," it will have drawn us toward an eschatology without philosophical teleology, beyond it in any case, otherwise than it. It will have engulfed the future anterior in the bottomless bottom of a past anterior to any past, to all present past, toward that past of the trace that has never been present. Its future anteriority will have been *irreducible* to ontology. An ontology, moreover, made in order to attempt this impossible reduction. This reduction is the finality of ontological movement, its power but also its fatality of defeat: what it attempts to reduce is its own condition.

That future anteriority *there* would no longer decline a verb saying the action of a subject in an operation that would have been *present.* To say *"il aura obligé"*—in *this* work, taking into account what sets things to work within *this* seriasure—is not to designate, describe, define, show, etc., but, let us say, to *en-trace [entracer]*, otherwise said to perform within the in-ter(el)lacement *[entr(el)acement]* of a seriasure that obligation whose "he" will not have been the present subject but for which "I" hereby respond: Here I am, (I) come. *He* will not have been (a) present but he will have made a gift by not disappearing without leaving a trace. But leaving the trace is also to *leave* it, to aban-don it, not to insist upon it in a sign. It is to efface it. In the concept of trace is inscribed in advance the re-treat *[re-trait]* of effacement. The trace is inscribed in being effaced and leaving the traced wake of its effacement (etc.) in the *retreat*, or in what E. L. calls the "superimposition" ("The authentic trace, on the other hand, disturbs the order of the world. It comes 'superim-posed' . . . Whoever has left traces in effacing his traces did not mean to say or do anything by the traces he left."[4] The structure of superimposition thus described menaces by its very rigor, which is that of contamination, any *authenticity* assured of its trace ("the authentic trace") and any rigorous dissociation be-tween sign and trace ("The trace is not a sign like any other. But it also plays the role of a sign . . . Yet every sign, in this sense, is a trace," ibid.). The word "leave" in the locution "leave a trace" now seems to be charged with the whole enigma. It would no longer announce itself starting from anything other than the trace, and especially not from a letting-be. Unless letting-be be understood *otherwise*, following the sign the trace makes to it where it is allowed to be effaced.

What am I saying to you when I pronounce "leave me"? Or when you say "he has left me," or as in the *Song of Songs*, "he has slipped away, he has passed by"?

Otherwise said (the serial enchainment should no longer slip through a "that is to say" but instead it should be interrupted and retied at the border of the interruptions by an "otherwise said"), for this not-without-trace *[pas-sans-trace]*, the contami-nation between the "he" beyond language and the "he" within the economic immanence of language and its dominant interpre-tation, is not merely an evil or a "negative" contamination; rather it describes the very process of the trace insofar as it makes a work, in a work-making *[faire-oeuvre]* that must be grasped by means neither of work nor of making, but instead by means of what is said of the work in his work, by the saying of the said, by its inter(el)laced performance. There is no more a "negative" contamination than there is a simple beyond or a simple inside of language, on the one side and the other of some border.

Once again you find the logical paradoxy of *this* seriasure (but this one in its irreplaceable singularity counts for every other): one must, even though nobody constrains anybody, read his work, otherwise said, respond to it and even respond for it, not by means of what one understands by *work* according to the dominant interpretation of language, but according to what *his* work says, *in its manner*, of Work, about what it is, otherwise said, about what it *should (be)*, otherwise said about it should have (to be), as work at work in the work.

That is its dislocation: the work does not depart some utterance, or series of utterances; it re-marks in each atom of the said a marking effraction of the saying, a saying no longer a present infinitive, but already a past of the trace, a performance (of the) wholly other. And if you wish to have access to "his" work, you will have to have passed by what it will have said of the Work, namely, that it does not return to him. That is why you yourself must respond for it. It is in your hands, which can give it to him; I will even say more—dedicate it to him. At this moment, indeed:

> The Other can dispossess me of my work, take it or buy it, and thus control my very conduct. I am exposed to instigation. The work is dedicated to this foreign *Sinngebung* from its very origin in me . . . Willing escapes the will. The work is always, in a certain sense, an unsuccessful act *[acte manqué]*. I am not fully what I want to do. Whence an unlimited field of investigation for psychoanalysis or sociology that seizes the will in its apparition within the work, in its conduct or its products.[5]

The Work, such as it is at work, *wrought*, in the work of E. L., as one should read it if one must read "his" work, does not return —from the origin—to the Same; which does not imply that it *signifies* waste or pure loss within a *game*. Such a game would still, in its waste, be determined by economy. The gratuity of this work, what he still calls *liturgy,* "a losing investment" or "working without remuneration" *(Humanism of the Other Man),* resembles playing a game but is not a game; "it is ethics itself," beyond even thinking and the thinkable. For the liturgy of work should not even be *subordinated* to thinking. A work that is "subordinated to thinking" *(The Trace of the Other* and *Humanism of the Other Man),* still understood as economic calculation, would not make a Work.

What E. L.'s work will therefore have succeeded in doing—in the unsuccessful act it claims to be, like any work—is to have obligated us, before all contract of acknowledgment, to this dissymmetry which it has itself so violently and gently provoked: impossible to approach his work without first of all passing, already, by the re-treat of its inside, namely, the remarkable saying of the work. Not only what can be found said on this subject, but the inter(el)laced saying which comes to it from out of the other and never returns it to itself, and which comes (for example, exemplarily) from you (come), obligated female reader *[lectrice obligée].* You can still refuse to grant him that sense, or only lend yourself to that *Sinngebung* while still not approaching that singular ellipsis where nevertheless you are perhaps already caught.

——I knew. In listening I was nonetheless wondering whether I was comprehended myself, and how to stop that word: comprehended. And how the work knew me, whatever it knew of me. So be it: to begin by reading his work, giving it to him, in order to approach the Work, which itself does not begin with "his" work nor with whoever would pretend to say "my" work. Going toward the Other, coming from the Same so as not to return to it, the work does not come from there, but from the Other. And his work makes a work in the re-treat which re-marks this heteronomous movement. The re-treat is not unique, although it remarks the unique, but its seriasure is unique. Not his signature —the "he" undersigning and under seal—but his seriasure. So be it. Now if, in reading what he shall have had to give, I take account of the unique seriasure, I should, for example, ascertain that the word "work" no more than any other has no fixed sense outside of the mobile syntax of marks, outside of the contextual transformation. The variation is not arbitrary, the transformation is regulated in its irregularity and in its very disturbance. But how? By what? By whom? I shall give or take an example of it. More or perhaps another thing than an example, that of the "son" in *Totality and Infinity*, of the "unique" son or sons: "The son is not merely my work like a poem or an object." That is on page 254 of *Totalité et Infini* (Totality and Infinity p. 277), and I assume that the context is re-read. Although defined as beyond "my work," "the son" *here* seems rather to have the traits of what in other contexts, doubtless later on, is called, with a capital letter, the Work. Otherwise said, the word *work* has neither the same *sense* nor the same *reference* in the two contexts, without however there being any incoherence or contradiction among them. *They even have a wholly other link to sense and reference.*

"The son"—movement without return toward the other beyond the work—thus resembles what is called elsewhere and later on, the Work. Elsewhere and later on, I also read: "The link with the Other by means of the son . . ." *(Du Sacré au Saint)*.

Now, in the same paragraph of *Totality and Infinity* (and elsewhere) where it is nearly always "son" (and "paternity") that is said, a sentence talks of the "child" ("I don't have my child, I am my child. Paternity is a relation with the stranger who while being Other *[autrui]* . . . *is* me; a relationship of the ego with a self which is nevertheless not me."). Is it that "son" is another word for "child," a child who could be of one or the other sex? If so, whence comes that equivalence, and what does it mean? And why couldn't the "daughter" play an analogous role? Why should the son be more or better than the daughter, than me, the Work beyond "my work"? If there were no differences from this point of view, why should "son" better represent, in advance, this indifference? This unmarked indifference?

Around this question which I here abandon to its elliptical course, I interrogate the link, in E. L.'s Work, between sexual difference—the Other as the other sex, otherwise said as otherwise sexed—and the Other as wholly other, beyond or before sexual difference. To himself, his text marks its signature by a masculine "I–he," a strange matter as was elsewhere noted "in passing," a while back, by an other ("Let us observe in passing that *Totality and Infinity* pushes the respect for dissymmetry to the point where it seems to us impossible, essentially impossible, that it could have been written by a woman. The philosophical subject of it is man *[vir]*").[6] And on the same page that says "the son" lying beyond "my work," I can also read: "Neither knowledge nor power. In voluptuousness, the Other—the feminine— retires into its mystery. The relation with it (the Other) is a relation with its absence. . . ." His signature thus assumes the sexual mark, a remarkable phenomenon in the history of philosophical writing, if the latter has always been interested in occupying that position without re-marking upon it or assuming it, without signing its mark. But, as well as this, E. L.'s work seems to me to have always rendered secondary, derivative, and subordinate, alterity as sexual difference, the trait of sexual difference, to the alterity of a sexually non-marked wholly other. It is not woman or the feminine that he has rendered secondary, derivative, or subordinate, but sexual difference. Once sexual difference is subordinated, it is always the case that the wholly other, who is *not yet marked*, is *already* found to be marked by masculinity (he before he/she, son before son/daughter, father before father/ mother, etc.). An operation the logic of which has seemed to me as constant as it is illogical (last example to date, Freudian psychoanalysis and everything that returns to it), yet with an illogicality that will have made possible and thus marked all logic— from the moment it exists as such—with this prolegomenal "he." How can one mark as masculine the very thing said to be anterior, or even foreign, to sexual difference? My question will be clearer if I content myself with quoting. Not all of those passages where he affirms femininity as an "ontological category" ("The feminine figures among the categories of Being"), a gesture which always leaves me wondering whether it understands me to be *against* a tradition that would have refused me that ontological dignity, or whether better than ever it understands me to be *within* that very tradition, profoundly repeating it. But rather quoting these passages:

> Within Judaism woman will only have the destiny of a human being, whose femininity will solely count as an attribute . . . the femininity of the woman would know

neither how to deform nor how to absorb its human essence. In Hebrew 'woman' is called *Ichah*, because, the bible says, she comes from man, *Iche*. The doctors seize hold of this etymology in order to affirm the unique dignity of the Hebrew that expresses the very mystery of creation, woman derived quasi-grammatically from man. . . . "Flesh of my flesh and bone of my bones" signifies therefore an identity of nature between man and woman, an identity of destiny and dignity and also a subordination of sexual life to the personal link that is equality in itself. An idea more ancient than the principles on behalf of which modern woman fights for emancipation, yet the *truth* of all those principles in a sphere where the thesis that opposes itself to the image of an initial androgyny is supported as well, attached to the popular idea of the rib-side. That truth maintains a certain priority of the masculine; he remains the prototype of the human and determines eschatology. The differences of the masculine and the feminine are blotted out in those messianic times.[7]

Very recently:

The sense of the feminine will be found clarified by taking as a point of departure the human essence, the *Ichah* following the *Iche:* not the feminine following the masculine, but the partition—the dichotomy—between masculine and feminine following the human. . . . Beyond the personal relationship that establishes itself between these two beings issued from two creative acts, the particularity of the feminine is a secondary matter. It isn't woman who is secondary, it is the relation to woman *qua* woman that doesn't belong to the primordial human plan. What is primary are the tasks accomplished by man as a human being, and by woman as a human being. . . . The problem, in each of these lines we are commenting upon at this moment, consists in reconciling the humanity of men and women with the hypothesis of a spirituality of the masculine, the feminine being not his correlative but his corollary; feminine specificity or the difference of the sexes that it announces are not straight away situated at the height of the oppositions con-

stitutive of Spirit. Audacious question: How can the equality of the sexes proceed from a masculine property? . . .
There had to be a difference that would not compromise
equity, a sexual difference; and consequently, a certain pre-
eminence of man, a woman arrived later and *qua* woman as
an appendix to the human. Now we understand the lesson:
Humanity cannot be thought beginning from two entirely
different principles. There must be some *sameness* common to these *others:* woman has been chosen above man
but has come after him: *the very femininity of woman
consists in this initial afterwards [après coup].*[8]

Strange logic, that of the "audacious" question. It would be necessary to comment upon each step and verify that each time the
secondary status of sexual difference signifies the secondary status of the feminine (but why is this so?) and that the initial
status of the pre-differential is each time marked by the masculinity that should, however, have come only afterwards, like
every other sexual mark. It would be necessary to comment, but
I prefer, under the heading of a protocol, to underline the following: he is commenting himself and says that he is commenting;
it must be taken into account that this discourse is not literally
that of E. L. while holding discourse, he says that he is commenting upon the doctors *at this very moment* ("the lines we are
commenting upon at this moment," and further on, "I am not
taking sides; today, I comment"). But the distance of the commentary is not neutral. What he comments upon is consonant
with a whole network of affirmations which are his, or those of
him, "he." Furthermore, the position of commentator corresponds to a choice: to at least accompany and not displace, transform or even reverse what is written in the text that is com-
mented upon.

[. . . .]

I come then to my question. Since it *[elle]* is under-signed by
the Pro-noun He *[Il]* (before he/she, certainly, but it is not She),
could it be that in making sexual alterity secondary, far from
allowing itself to be approached from the Work, his, or the one
said to be, becomes a mastery, the mastery of sexual difference

posed as the origin of femininity? Hence mastery *of* femininity? The very thing that *ought not have been* mastered, and that one —therefore—has been unable to avoid mastering, or at least attempting to master? The very thing that ought not have been derived from an *archē* (neutral, and therefore, he says, masculine) in order to be subjected to it? The aneconomical, that ought not have been *economized*, situated in the house, *within* or *as* the law of the *oikos*? The secondary status of the sexual, and therefore, He says, of feminine difference, does it not thus come to stand for the wholly-other of this Saying of the wholly other within the seriasure here determined and within the idiom of this negotiation? Does it not show, on the inside of the work, a surfeit of un-said alterity? Or said, precisely as a secret or as a symptomatic mutism? Then things would become more complicated. The other as feminine (me), far from being derived or secondary, would become the other of the Saying of the wholly other, of this one in any case; and this last one *insofar* as it would have tried to dominate alterity, would risk, (at least to this extent) enclosing *itself* within the economy of the same.

Wholly otherwise said: made secondary by responsibility for the wholly other, sexual difference (and hence, He says, femininity) is retained, as other, within the economic zone of the same. Included in the same, it is by the same stroke excluded: enclosed within, foreclosed within the immanence of a crypt, incorporated in the Saying which says itself to the wholly other. To desexualize the link to the wholly-other (or equally well, the unconscious as a certain philosophical interpretation of psychoanalysis tends to do today), to make sexuality secondary with respect to a wholly-other that in itself would not be sexually marked ("beneath erotic alterity, the alterity of the one for the other; responsibility before eros"),[9] is always to make sexual difference secondary *as* femininity. Here I would situate his profound complicity with such an interpretation of psychoanalysis. This complicity, more profound than the abyss he wishes to put between his thinking and psychoanalysis, always gathers around one fundamental design: their common link to me, to the other as woman. That is what I would like to give them (first of all, to read).

Shall I abuse this hypothesis? The effect of secondarization, allegedly demanded by the wholly-other (as He), would become the cause, otherwise said the other of the wholly other, the other of a wholly other who is no longer sexually neutral but *posed* (outside the series within the seriasure) and suddenly determined as He. Then the Work, apparently signed by the Pro-noun He, would be dictated, aspired, and inspired by the desire to make She secondary, therefore *by* She *[Elle]*. She would then undersign the undersigned work from her place of derivable dependence or condition as last or first "Hostage." Not in the sense that undersigning would amount to confirming the signature, but countersigning the work, again not in the sense that countersigning would amount to redoubling the signature, according to the same or the contrary—but *otherwise than signing*.

The whole system of *this* seriasure would silently comment upon the absolute heteronomy in respect to She who would be the wholly other. *This* heteronomy was writing the text from its other side like a weaver its fabric *[ouvrage]*; yet it would be necessary here to undo a metaphor of weaving which has not imposed itself by chance: we know to what kind of interpretative investments it has given rise with regard to a feminine specificity which Freudian psychoanalysis *also regularly* derives.

I knew it. What I here suggest is not without violence, not even free of the redoubled violence of what he calls "traumatism," the nonsymbolizable wound that comes, before any other effraction, from the past anterior of the other. A terrifying wound, a wound *of life*, the only one that life opens up today. Violence faulty in regard to his name, his work, insofar as it inscribes his proper name in a way that is no longer that of property. For, in the end, the derivation of femininity is not a simple movement in the seriasure of his text. The feminine is also described there as a figure of the wholly other. And then, we have recognized that this work is one of the first and rare ones, in this history of philosophy to which it does not simply belong, not to feign effacing the sexual mark of his signature: hence, he would be the last one surprised by the fact that the other (of the whole system of his saying of the other) happens to be a woman and commands him from that place. Also, it is not a matter of reversing places and putting woman against him in the place of the wholly other as *archē*. If what I say remains false, falsifying, faulty, it is also to the extent that dissymmetry (I speak from my place as woman, and supposing that she be definable) can also reverse the perspectives, while leaving the schema intact.

It has been shown that ingratitude and contamination did not occur as an accidental evil. Its a sort of fatality of the Saying. It is to be negotiated. It would be worse without negotiation. Let's accept it: what I am writing at this very moment is faulty. Faulty up to a certain point, in touching, or so as not to touch, his name, or what he sets to work in his rigorously proper name in this unsuccessful act (as he says) within a work. If his proper name, E. L., is in the place of the Pronoun (He) which preseals everything that can carry a name, it isn't him, but Him, that my fault comes to wound in his body. Where, then, will my fault have taken bodily form? Where in His body will it have left a mark, in his own body, I mean? What is the body of a fault in this writing where the traces of the wholly other are exchanged, without circulating or ever becoming present? If I wished to destroy or annul my fault, I would have to know what is happening to the text being written at this very moment, where it can take place or what can remain of its remains.

In order to make my question better understood, I shall take a detour around what he tells us of the name of God, in the non-neutral commentary that he proposes.[10] According to the treatise *Chevouoth* (35a), it is forbidden to efface the names of God, even in the case when a copyist would have altered the form. The whole manuscript then has to be buried. Such a manuscript, E. L. says, "has to be placed into the earth like a dead body." But what does "placing in earth" mean? And what does a "dead body" mean, since it is not effaced or destroyed but "placed in the earth"? If one simply wanted to annihilate it—to keep [garder] it no longer—the whole thing would be burned, everything would be effaced without remains. The dys-graphy [dis-graphie] would be replaced, without remnant, by orthography. In inhuming it, on the contrary, the fault on the proper name is not destroyed, at bottom one keeps guard of it, as a fault, one keeps it at the bottom. It will slowly decompose, taking its time, in the course of a work of mourning in which, achieved successfully in spiritual interiorization, an idealization that certain psychoanalysts call introjection, or paralyzed in a melancholic pathology (incorporation), the other as other will be kept in guard, wounded, wounding, impossible utterance. The topic of such a faulty text remains highly improbable, like the taking-place of its remains in this theonymic cemetery.

If I now ask at this very moment where I should return my fault, it is because of a certain *analogy:* what he recalls about the names of God is something one would be tempted to say analogically for every proper name. He would be the Pro-noun *[Pro-nom]* or the First name *[Pré-nom]* of every name. Just as there is a resemblance between the face of God and the face of man (even if this resemblance is neither an "ontological mark" of the worker on his work nor "sign" or "effect" of God), in the same way there would be an analogy between all proper names and the names of God, which are, in their turn, analogous among themselves. Consequently, I transfer by analogy to the proper name of man or woman what is said of the names of God. And of the "fault" on the body of these names.

But things are more complicated. If, in *Totality and Infinity,* the analogy is kept, though not quite in a classical sense, between the face of God and the face of man, here on the contrary, in the commentary on the Talmudic texts, a whole movement is sketched in order to mark the necessity of interrupting that analogy, of "refusing to God any analogy with beings that are certainly unique, but who compose with other beings a world or a structure. To approach, through a proper name is to affirm a relation irreducible to the knowledge which thematizes or defines or synthesizes, and which, by that very fact, understands the correlate of that knowledge as being, as finite, and as immanent." Yet the analogy once interrupted is again resumed as an analogy between absolute heterogeneities by means of the enigma, the ambiguity of uncertain and precarious epiphany. Monotheistic humanity has a relation to this trace of a past that is absolutely anterior to any memory, to the ab-solute re-treat *[re-trait]* of the revealed name, to its very inaccessibility. "Square letters are a precarious dwelling whence the revealed Name already withdraws itself; effaceable letters at the mercy of the man who traces them or recopies them." Man, therefore, can be linked with this retreat, despite the infinite distance of the nonthematizable, with the precariousness and uncertainty of this revelation.

But this uncertain epiphany, on the verge of evanescence, is precisely that which *man alone can retain*. This is why he is the essential moment both of this transcendence and of its manifestation. That is why, through this ineffaceable revelation, he is called forth with an unparalleled straightforwardness.

But is that revelation precarious enough? Is the Name free enough in regard to the context where it lodges? Is it preserved in writing from all contamination by being or culture? Is it preserved from man, who has indeed a vocation to retain it, but who is capable of every abuse?

Paradox: the precariousness of the revelation is never precarious enough. But should it be? And if it were, wouldn't that be worse?

Once the analogy is resumed, as one resumes the interruptions and not the threads, it should be recalled, I should be able to transpose the discourse on the names of God to the discourse on human names, for example, where there is no longer an example, that of E. L.

And thus to the fault to which the one and the other expose themselves in body. The fault will always, already, have taken place: as soon as I thematize what, in his work, is borne beyond the thematizable and is put in a regular seriasure within which he cannot sign himself. Certainly, there is already contamination in his work, in that which he thematizes "at this very moment" of the nonthematizable. I am contaminating this irrepressible thematization in my turn, and not merely according to a common structural law, but just as much with a fault of my own that I will not seek to resolve or absolve within the general necessity. As a woman, for example, and in reversing the dissymmetry, I have added rape [*viol*] to it. I should have been even more unfaithful to him, more ungrateful, but was it not then in order to give myself up to what his work says of the Work: that it provokes ingratitude? Here to absolute ingratitude, the least foreseeable in his work itself?

I give and play ingratitude against jealousy. In everything I am talking about, jealousy is at stake. The thought of the trace as put in seriasure by E. L. thinks a singular relation of God (not contaminated by being) to jealousy. He, the one who has passed beyond all Being, must be exempt from any jealousy, from any desire for possession, for guarding, property, exclusivity, nonsubstitution, and so on. And the relation to Him must be pure of all jealous economy. But this without-jealousy [*sans-jalousie*] cannot not guard itself jealously; and insofar as it is a past absolutely held in reserve, it is the very possibility of all jealousy. Ellipsis of jealousy: seriasure is always a jalousie through which, seeing without seeing everything, and especially without being seen, before and beyond the phenomenon, the without-jealousy guards itself jealousy, in other words, loses itself, keeps-itself—loses-itself. By means of a series of regular traits and re-treats [*re-traits*]: the figure of jealousy, beyond the face. Never more jealousy, ever, never more zeal; is it possible?

If feminine difference presealed, perhaps and nearly illegibly, his work, if she became, in the depths of the same, the other of his other, will I then have deformed his name, to him, in writing, at this moment, in this work, here indeed, "she will have obligated" [*"elle aura obligé"*]?

———I no longer know if you are saying what his work says. Perhaps that comes back to the same. I no longer know if you are saying the contrary, or if you have already written something wholly other. I no longer hear your voice, I have difficulty distinguishing it from mine, from any other, your fault suddenly becomes illegible to me. Interrupt me.

[. . . .]

—*Translated by Ruben Berezdivin*

NOTES

1. The translator would like to thank Geoff Bennington for his generous advice on an earlier version of this translation.
2. "I am sick of love," *Song of Songs*, 5:8.
3. *Otherwise than Being, or Beyond Essence*, translated by Alphonso Lingis (The Hague: Martinus Nijhoff, 1981), pp. 141–42.
4. *Collected Philosophical Papers*, translated by Alphonso Lingis (The Hague: Martinus Nijhoff, 1987), p. 104.

5. *Totality and Infinity,* translated by Alphonso Lingis (The Hague: Martinus Nijhoff, 1979), pp. 227–28.

6. Jacques Derrida, "Violence and Metaphysics: Essay on the Thought of Emmanuel Levinas," in *Writing and Difference* (1967).

7. "Judaïsme et le féminin," in *Difficile liberté: Essais sur le judaïsme,* 2nd ed. (Paris: Albin Michel, 1976), p. 56–57.

8. "Et Dieu créa la femme," in *Du sacré au saint: Cinq nouvelles lectures talmudiques* (Paris: Editions de Minuit, 1977), pp. 132-42.

9. *Otherwise than Being,* p. 192, n. 27.

10. "Le nom de Dieu d'après quelques textes talmudiques," in *Du sacré au saint.*

EIGHTEEN

From "Choreographies" [1982]

In this written interview, Derrida responds to questions about sexual difference, femininity, and feminism. His replies summarize succinctly some of the major points of the texts included in this section. Specifically, Derrida reviews the two principal modes he has analyzed by which sexual difference is appropriated to phallogocentric ends: dialectical binarism or opposition (as assumed by Hegel and as parodied by Nietzsche), and neutralization of sexual difference through a movement of subordination to ontological difference (as performed to some extent by both Heidegger and Levinas). Derrida also comments on the use he has made of terms like *hymen* and *invagination* which, as the interviewer, Christie McDonald, remarks, "in their most widely recognized sense pertain to the woman's body." He situates his use in a strategy to resexualize philosophical or theoretical discourse which, as he has shown, tends on the contrary toward a strategy of neutralization. But terms such as these *imply* literally a folding that transforms or deforms the space within which differences, including sexual difference but also the various distinctions that have ordered sexual difference (originary or derived, ontological or ontic, etc.), have been positioned. Moreover, they cannot be appropriated by one of the sexes because, precisely, they render undecidable the line of cleavage between the two. Derrida concludes the interview by situating the frequent polyvocality of his texts (see above, **"Restitutions"** and **"At This Very Moment in This Work Here I am"**) within the dream of a "multiplicity of sexually marked voices," a dream that dares to put its weight in the balance with the preponderance of monological, monosexual discourse.

CHOREOGRAPHIES

Question I

CHRISTIE V. MCDONALD: Emma Goldman, a maverick feminist from the late nineteenth century, once said of the feminist movement: "If I can't dance I don't want to be part of your revolution." Jacques Derrida, you have written about the question of woman and what it is that constitutes "the feminine." In *Spurs/Eperons*, a text devoted to Nietzsche, style, and woman, you wrote, "that which will not be taken in (by) truth [truth?] is, in truth, feminine." And you warned that such a proposition should not be hastily mistaken for a "woman's femininity, for female sexuality, or for any other of those essentializing fetishes. These are precisely what, in their foolishness, the dogmatic philosopher, the impotent artist, or the inexperienced seducer believe they have won over."

What seems to be at play as you take up Heidegger's reading of Nietzsche is whether or not sexual difference is a "regional question in a larger order which would subordinate it first to the domain of general ontology, subsequently to that of a fundamental ontology and finally to the question of the truth [whose?] of being itself." You thereby question the status of the argument and at the same time the question itself. In this instance, if the question of sexual difference is not a regional one (in the sense of subsidiary), if indeed "it may no longer even be a question," as you suggest, how would you describe "woman's place"?

[. . . .]

DERRIDA: Perhaps woman does not have a history, not so much because of any notion of the "Eternal Feminine" but because all alone she can resist and step back from a certain history (precisely in order to dance) in which revolution, or at least the "concept" of revolution, is generally inscribed. That history is one of continuous progress, despite the revolutionary break— oriented in the case of the women's movement towards the reappropriation of woman's own essence, her own specific difference, oriented in short towards a notion of woman's "truth." Your "maverick feminist" showed herself ready to break with the most authorized, the most dogmatic form of consensus, one that claims (and this is the most serious aspect of it) to speak out in the name of revolution and history. Perhaps she was thinking of a completely other history: a history of paradoxical laws and nondialectical discontinuities, a history of absolutely heterogeneous pockets, irreducible particularities, of unheard of and incalculable sexual differences; a history of women who have— centuries ago—"gone further" by stepping back with their lone dance, or who are today inventing sexual idioms at a distance from the main forum of feminist activity with a kind of reserve that does not necessarily prevent them from subscribing to the movement and even, occasionally, from becoming a militant for it.

But I am speculating. It would be better to come back to your question. Having passed through several detours or stages, you wonder how I would describe what is called "woman's place"; the expression recalls, if I am not mistaken, "in the home" or "in the kitchen." Frankly, I do not know. I believe that I would not describe that place. In fact, I would be wary of such a description. Do you not fear that having once become committed to the path of this topography, we would inevitably find ourselves back "at home" or "in the kitchen"? Or under house arrest, *assignation à résidence* as they say in French penitentiary language, which would amount to the same thing? Why must there be a place for woman? And why only one, a single, completely essential place?

This is a question that you could translate ironically by saying that in my view *there is no one place for woman*. That was indeed clearly set forth during the 1972 Cerisy Colloquium devoted to Nietzsche in the lecture to which you referred entitled

Spurs/Eperons.[1] It is without a doubt risky to say that there is no place for woman, but this idea is not antifeminist, far from it; true, it is not feminist either. But it appears to me to be faithful in its way both to a certain assertion of women and to what is most affirmative and "dancing," as the maverick feminist says, in the displacement of women. Can one not say, in Nietzsche's language, that there is a "reactive" feminism, and that a certain historical necessity often puts this form of feminism in power in today's organized struggles? It is this kind of "reactive" feminism that Nietzsche mocks, and not woman or women. Perhaps one should not so much combat it head on—other interests would be at stake in such a move—as prevent its occupying the entire terrain. And why for that matter should one rush into answering a topological question (what is the place of woman [quelle est *la* place de *la* femme])? Or an economical question (because it all comes back to the *oikos* as home, *maison, chez-soi* [at home in this sense also means in French within the self], the law of the proper place, etc., in the preoccupation with a woman's place)? Why should a new "idea" of woman or a new step taken by her necessarily be subjected to the urgency of this topo-economical concern (essential, it is true, and ineradicably philosophical)? This step only constitutes a step on the condition that it challenge a certain idea of the locus [*lieu*] and the place [*place*] (the entire history of the West and of its metaphysics) and that it dance otherwise. This is very rare, if it is not impossible, and presents itself only in the form of the most unforeseeable and most innocent of chances. The most innocent of dances would thwart the *assignation à résidence,* escape those residences under surveillance; the dance changes place and above all changes places. In its wake they can no longer be recognized. The joyous disturbance of certain women's movements, and of some women in particular, has actually brought with it the chance for a certain risky turbulence in the assigning of places within our small European space (I am not speaking of a more ample upheaval en route to worldwide application). Is one then going to start all over again making maps, topographics, etc.? distributing sexual identity cards?

The most serious part of the difficulty is the necessity to bring the dance and its tempo into tune with the "revolution." The lack of place for [*l'atopie*] or the madness of the dance—this bit of luck can also compromise the political chances of feminism and serve as an alibi for deserting organized, patient, laborious "feminist" struggles when brought into contact with all the forms of resistance that a dance movement cannot dispel, even though the dance is not synonymous with either powerlessness or fragility. I will not insist on this point, but you can surely see the kind of impossible and necessary compromise that I am alluding to: an incessant, daily negotiation—individual or not—sometimes microscopic, sometimes punctuated by a poker-like gamble; always deprived of insurance, whether it be in private life or within institutions. Each man and each woman must commit his or her own singularity, the untranslatable factor of his or her life and death.

Nietzsche makes a scene before women, feminists in particular—a spectacle which is overdetermined, divided, apparently contradictory. This is just what has interested me; this scene has interested me because of all the paradigms that it exhibits and multiplies, and insofar as it often struggles, sometimes dances, always takes chances in a historical space whose essential traits, those of the matrix, have perhaps not changed since then in Europe (I mean specifically in Europe, and that perhaps makes all the difference although we cannot separate worldwide feminism from a certain fundamental europeanization of world culture; this is an enormous problem that I must leave aside here). In *Spurs/Eperons* I have tried to formalize the movements and typical moments of the scene that Nietzsche creates throughout a very broad and diverse body of texts. I have done this up to a certain limit, one that I also indicate, where the decision to formalize fails for reasons that are absolutely structural. Since these typical features are and must be unstable, sometimes contradictory, and finally "undecidable," any break in the movement of the reading would settle in a counter-meaning, in the meaning which becomes counter-meaning. This counter-meaning can be more or less naïve or complacent. One could cite countless examples of it. In the most perfunctory of cases, the simplification reverts to the isolation of Nietzsche's violently antifeminist statements (directed first against reactive, specular feminism as a figure both of the dogmatic philosopher and a certain relationship of man to truth), pulling them out (and possibly attributing them to me though that is of little importance) of the movement and system that I try to reconstitute. Some have reacted at times even more perfunctorily, unable to see beyond the end of phallic forms projecting into the text; beginning with style, the spur or the umbrella, they take no account of what I have said about the difference between style and writing or the bisexual complication of those and other forms. Generally speaking, this cannot be considered reading, and I will go so far as to say that it is to not read the syntax and punctuation of a given sentence when one arrests the text in a certain position, thus settling on a thesis, meaning or truth. This mistake of hermeneutics, this mistaking of hermeneutics—it is this that the final message [*envoi*] of "I forgot my umbrella" should challenge. But let us leave that. The truth value (that is, Woman as the major allegory of truth in Western discourse) and its correlative, Femininity (the essence or truth of Woman), are there to assuage such hermeneutic anxiety. These are the places that one should acknowledge, at least, that is, if one is interested in doing so; they are the foundations or anchorings of Western rationality (of what I have called "phallogocentrism" [as the complicity of Western metaphysics with a notion of male firstness]). Such recognition should not make of either the truth value or femininity an object of knowledge (at stake are the norms of knowledge and knowledge as norm); still less should it make of them a place to inhabit, a home. It should rather permit the invention of an other inscription, one very old and very new, a displacement of bodies and places that is quite different.

You recalled the expression "essentializing fetishes" (truth, femininity, the essentiality of woman or feminine sexuality as fetishes). It is difficult to improvise briefly here. But I will point out that one can avoid a trap by being precise abut the concept of fetishism and the context to which one refers, even if only to displace it. (On this point, I take the liberty of alluding to the discussions of fetishism and feminine sexuality in *Spurs, Glas* or **The Post Card,** specifically in "Le facteur de la vérité.") Another trap is more political and can only be avoided by taking account of the real conditions in which women's struggles develop on all fronts (economic, ideological, political). These conditions often require the preservation (within longer or shorter phases) of metaphysical presuppositions that one must (and knows already that one must) question in a later phase—or an other place—because they belong to the dominant system that one is deconstructing on a practical level. This multiplicity of places, moments, forms, and forces does not always mean giving way either to empiricism or to contradiction. How can one breathe without such punctuation and without the multiplicities of rhythm and steps? How can one dance, your "maverick feminist" might say?

[. . . .]

McDONALD: This raises an important question that should not be overlooked, although we haven't the space to develop it to any extent here: the complicated relationship of a practical politics to the kinds of analysis that we have been considering (specifically the "deconstructive" analysis implicit in your discussion). That this relationship cannot simply be translated into an opposition between the empirical and the nonempirical has been touched on in an entirely different context. Just how one is to deal with the interrelationship of these forces and necessities in the context of feminine struggles should be more fully explored on some other occasion. But let's go on to Heidegger's ontology.

[. . . .]

DERRIDA: To answer your question about Heidegger, and without being able to review here the itinerary of a reading in *Spurs/Eperons* clearly divided into two moments, I must limit myself to a piece of information, or rather to an open question. The question proceeds, so to speak, from the end; it proceeds from the point where the thought of the gift [*le don*] and that of of "propriation" disturb without simply reversing the order of ontology, the authority of the question, What is it?, the subordination of regional ontologies to one fundamental ontology. I am moving much too rapidly, but how can I do otherwise here? From this point, which is not a point, one wonders whether this extremely difficult, perhaps impossible idea of the gift can still maintain an essential relationship to sexual difference. One wonders whether sexual difference, femininity for example—however irreducible it may be—does not remain derived from and subordinated to either the question of destination or the thought of the gift (I say "thought" because one cannot say philosophy, theory, logic, structure, scene, or anything else; when one can no longer use any word of this sort, when one can say almost nothing else, one says "thought," but one could show that this too is excessive). I do not know. Must one think "difference" "before" sexual difference or taking off "from" it? Has this question, if not a meaning (we are at the origin of meaning here, and the origin cannot "have meaning") at least something of a chance of opening up anything at all, however im-pertinent it may appear?

[. . . .]

Question II

MCDONALD: The new sense of writing with which one associates the term deconstruction has emerged from the close readings that you have given to texts as divergent as those of Plato, Rousseau, Mallarmé, and others. It is one in which traditional binary pairing (as in the opposition of spirit to matter or man to woman) no longer functions by the privilege given to the first term over the second. In a series of interviews published under the title *Positions* in 1972, you spoke of a two-phase program (*phase* being understood as a structural rather than chronological term) necessary for the act of deconstruction.

In the first phase a reversal was to take place in which the opposed terms would be inverted. Thus woman, as a previously subordinate term, might become the dominant one in relation to man. Yet because such a scheme of reversal could only repeat the traditional scheme (in which the hierarchy of duality is always reconstituted), it alone could not effect any significant change. Change would only occur through the 'second' and more radical phase of deconstruction in which a "new" concept would be forged simultaneously. The motif of differance, as neither a simple "concept" nor a mere "word," had brought us the now familiar constellation of attendant terms: trace, supplement, pharmakon, and others. Among the others, two are marked sexually and in their most widely recognized sense pertain to the woman's body: *hymen* (the logic of which is developed in "The Double

Session") and *double invagination* (a leitmotif in "Living On:Borderlines").[3]

[. . . .]

It seems to me that while the extensive play on etymologies (in which unconscious motivations are traced through the transformations and historical excesses of usage) effects a displacement of these terms, it also poses a problem for those who would seek to define what is specifically feminine. That comes about not so much because these terms are either under- or overvalued as parts belonging to woman's body. It is rather that, in the economy of a movement of writing that is always elusive, one can never decide properly whether the particular term implies complicity with or a break from existent ideology.

[. . . .]

How can we change the representation of woman? Can we move from the rib where woman is wife ("She was called Woman because she was taken from man"—Genesis 2:23) to the womb where she is mother ("man is born of woman"—Job 14:13) without essential loss? Do we have in your view the beginning of phase two, a "new" concept of woman?

DERRIDA: No, I do not believe that we have one, if indeed it is possible to *have* such a thing or if such a thing could exist or show promise of existing. Personally, I am not sure that I feel the lack of it. Before having one that is new, are we certain of having had an old one? It is the word "concept" or "conception" that I would in turn question in its relationship to any essence which is rigorously or properly identifiable. This would bring us back to the preceding questions. The concept of the concept, along with the entire system that attends it, belongs to a prescriptive order. It is that order that a problematics of woman and a problematics of difference, as sexual difference, should disrupt along the way. Moreover, I am not sure that "phase two" marks a split with "phase one," a split the form of which would be a cut along an indivisible line. The relationship between these two phases doubtless has another structure. I spoke of two distinct phases for the sake of clarity, but the relationship of one phase to another is marked less by conceptual determinations (that is, where a new concept follows an archaic one) than by a transformation or general deformation of logic; such transformations or deformations mark the "logical" element or environment itself by moving, for example, beyond the "positional" (difference determined as opposition, whether or not dialectically). This movement is of great consequence for the discussion here, even if my formulation is apparently abstract and disembodied. One could, I think, demonstrate this: when sexual difference is determined by *opposition* in the dialectical sense (according to the Hegelian movement of speculative dialectics which remains so powerful even beyond Hegel's text), one appears to set off "the war between the sexes"; but one precipitates the end with victory going to the masculine sex. The determination of sexual difference in opposition is destined, designed, in truth, for truth; it is so in order to erase sexual difference. The dialectical opposition neutralizes or supersedes [Hegel's term *Aufhebung* carries with it both the sense of conserving and negating. No adequate translation of the term in English has yet been found] the difference. However, according to a surreptitious operation that must be flushed out, one insures phallocentric mastery under the cover of neutralization every time. These are now well known paradoxes. And such phallocentrism adorns itself now and then, here and there, with an appendix: a certain kind of feminism. In the same manner, phallocentrism and homosexuality can go, so to speak, hand in hand, and I take these terms, whether it is a question of feminine or masculine homosexuality, in a very broad and radical sense.

And what if the "wife" or the "mother"—whom you seem sure of being able to dissociate—were figures for this homosexual dialectics? I am referring now to your question on the "representation" of woman and such "loss" as might occur in the passage from man's rib to the womb of woman, the passage from the spouse, you say, to the mother. Why is it necessary to choose, and why only these two possibilities, these two "places," assuming that one can really dissociate them?

McDONALD: The irony of my initial use of the cliché "woman's place" which in the old saw is followed by "in the home" or "in the kitchen" leaves the whole wide world for other places for the same intent. As for the "place" of woman in *Genesis*, and

Job, as rib (spouse) or womb (mother), these are more basic functional differences. Nevertheless, within these two traditional roles, to choose one implies loss of the other. You are correct in observing that such a choice is not necessary; there could be juxtaposition, substitution or other possible combinations. But these biblical texts are not frivolous in seeing the functional distinction which also has distinguished "woman's place" in Western culture.

DERRIDA: Since you quote Genesis, I would like to evoke the marvelous reading that Levinas has proposed of it without being clear as to whether he assumes it as his own or what the actual status of the "commentary" that he devotes to it is.[4] There would, of course, be a certain *secondariness* of woman, *Ichah*. The man, *Iche*, would come first; he would be number one; he would be at the beginning. Secondariness, however, would not be that of woman or femininity, but the *division* between masculine and feminine. It is not feminine sexuality that would be second but only the relationship to sexual difference. At the origin, on this side of and therefore beyond any sexual mark, there was humanity in general, and this is what is important. Thus the possibility of ethics could be saved, if one takes ethics to mean that relationship to the other as other which accounts for no other determination or sexual characteristic in particular. What kind of an ethics would there be if belonging to one sex or another became its law or privilege? What if the universality of moral laws were modelled on or limited according to the sexes? What if their universality were not unconditional, without sexual condition in particular?

Whatever the force, seductiveness, or necessity of this reading, does it not risk restoring—in the name of ethics as that which is irreproachable—a classical interpretation, and thereby enriching what I would call its panoply in a manner surely as subtle as it is sublime? Once again, the classical interpretation gives a masculine sexual marking to what is presented either as a neutral originariness or, at least, as prior and superior to all sexual markings. Levinas indeed senses the risk factor involved in the erasure of sexual difference. He therefore maintains sexual difference: the human in general remains a sexual being. But he can only do so, it would seem, by placing (differentiated) sexuality beneath humanity which sustains itself at the level of the Spirit. That is, he simultaneously places, and this is what is important, masculinity [le masculin] in command and at the beginning (the arkhē), on a par with the Spirit. This gesture carries with it the most self-interested of contradictions; it has repeated itself, let us say, since "Adam and Eve," and persists—in analogous form—into "modernity," despite all the differences of style and treatment. Isn't that a feature of the "matrix," as we were saying before? or the "patrix" if you prefer, but it amounts to the same thing, does it not? Whatever the complexity of the itinerary and whatever the knots of rhetoric, don't you think that the movement of Freudian thought repeats this "logic"? Is it not also the risk that Heidegger runs? One should perhaps say, rather, the risk that is avoided because phallogocentrism is insurance against the return of what certainly has been feared as the most agonizing risk of all. Since I have named Heidegger in a context where the reference is quite rare and may even appear strange, I would like to dwell on this for a moment, if you don't mind, concerned that I will be both too lengthy and too brief.

Heidegger seems almost never to speak about sexuality or sexual difference.[5] And he seems almost never to speak about psychoanalysis, give or take an occasional negative allusion. This is neither negligence nor omission. The pauses coming from his silence on these questions punctuate or create the spacing out of a powerful discourse. And one of the strengths of this discourse may be stated (though I am going much too quickly and schematizing excessively) like this: it begins by denying itself all accepted forms of security, all the sedimented presuppositions of classical ontology, anthropology, the natural or human sciences, until it falls back this side of such values as the opposition between subject–object, conscious–unconscious, mind–body, and many others as well. The existential analytic of the Dasein opens the road, so to speak, leading to the question of being; the Dasein is neither the human being (a thought recalled earlier by Levinas) nor the subject, neither consciousness nor the self [le moi] (whether conscious or unconscious). These are all determinations that are derived from and occur after the Dasein. Now—and here is what I wanted to get to after this inadmissible acceleration—in a course given in 1928, Heidegger justifies to some degree the silence of *Sein und Zeit* on the question of sexuality [*Gesamtausgabe*, Band 26, No. 10, p. 171 ff.]. In a paragraph from the course devoted to the "Problem of the *Sein und Zeit*," Heidegger reminds us that the analytic of the *Dasein* is neither an anthropology, an ethics, nor a metaphysics. With respect to any definition, position, or evaluation of these fields, the *Dasein* is neuter. Heidegger insists upon and makes clear this original and essential "neutrality" of the *Dasein*: "That neutrality means also that the *Dasein* is neither of the two sexes. But such a-sexuality (*Geschlechtslosigkeit*) is not the indifference of an empty nothing, the feeble negativity of an indifferent ontic nothing. In its neutrality, *Dasein* is not just anyone no matter who *(Niemand und Jeder)*, but the originary positivity and power of being or of the essence, *Mächtigkeit des Wesens.*" One would have to read the analysis that follows very closely; I will try to do that another time in relation to some of his later texts. The analysis emphasizes the positive character, as it were, of this originary and powerful a-sexual neutrality which is not the neither–nor (*Weder–noch*) of ontic abstraction. It is originary and ontological. More precisely, the a-sexuality does not signify in this instance the absence of sexuality—one could call it the instinct, desire, or even the libido—but the absence of any mark belonging to one of the two sexes. Not that the *Dasein* does not ontically or in fact belong to a sex; not that it is deprived of sexuality; but the *Dasein* as *Dasein* does not carry with it the mark of this opposition (or alternative) between the two sexes. Insofar as these marks are opposable and binary, they are not existential structures. Nor do they allude in this respect to any primitive or subsequent bisexuality. Such an allusion would fall once again into anatomical, biological, or anthropological determinations, And the *Dasein*, in the structures and "power" that are originary to it, would come "prior" to these determinations. I am putting quotation marks around the word "prior" because it has no literal, chronological, historical, or logical meaning. Now, as of 1928, the analytic of the *Dasein* was the thought of ontological difference and the repetition of the question of being; it opened up a problematics that subjected all the concepts of traditional Western philosophy to a radical elucidation and interpretation. This gives an idea of what stakes were involved in a neutralization that fell back this side of both sexual difference and its binary marking, if not this side of sexuality itself. This would be the title of the enormous problem that in this context I must limit myself to merely naming: ontological difference and sexual difference.

And since your question evoked the "motif of difference," I would say that it has moved, by displacement, in the vicinity of this very obscure area. What is also being sought in this zone is the passage between ontological difference and sexual difference; it is a passage that may no longer be thought, punctuated, or opened up according to those polarities to which we have been referring for some time (originary–derived, ontological–ontic, ontology–anthropology, the thought of being–metaphysics or ethics, etc.). The constellation of terms that you have cited could perhaps be considered (for nothing is ever taken for granted or guaranteed in these matters) a kind of transformation of deformation of space; such a transformation would tend to extend beyond these poles and reinscribe them within it. Some of these terms, "hymen" or "invagination," you were saying, "pertain in their most widely recognized sense to the woman's body. . . ." Are you sure? I am grateful for your having used such a careful formulation. That these words signify "in their most widely recognized sense" had, of course, not escaped me, and the emphasis that I have put on resexualizing a philosophical or theoretical discourse, which has been too "neutralizing" in this respect, was dictated by those very reservations that I just mentioned concerning the strategy of neutralization (whether or not it is deliberate). Such resexualizing must be done without facileness of any kind and, above all, without regression in relation to what might justify, as we saw, the procedures—or necessary steps—of Levinas or Heidegger, for example. That being said, "hymen" and "invagination," at least in the context into which these words have been swept, no longer simply designate figures for the feminine body. They no longer do so, that is, assuming that one knows for certain what a feminine or masculine body is, and assuming that anatomy is in this instance the final recourse. What remains undecidable concerns not only but also the line of cleavage between the two sexes. As you recalled, such a movement reverts neither to words nor to concepts. And what remains of language within it cannot be abstracted from the "performativity" (which marks and is marked) that concerns us here, beginning—for the examples that you have chosen—with the texts of Mallarmé and Blanchot, and with the labor of reading or writing which evoked them and which they in turn evoked. One could say quite accurately that the hymen does not exist. Anything constituting the value of existence is foreign to the "hymen." And if there were hymen—and I am not saying if the hymen existed—property value would be no more appropriate to it for reasons that I have stressed in the texts to which you refer. How can one then attribute the existence of the hymen properly to woman? Not that it is any more the distinguishing feature of man or, for that matter, of the human creature. I would say the same for the term "invagination" which has, moreover, always been reinscribed in a chiasmus, one doubly folded, redoubled and inversed,[6] etc. From then on, is it not difficult to recognize in the movement of this term a "representation of woman"? Furthermore, I do not know if it is to a change in representation that we should entrust the future. As with all the questions that we are presently discussing, this one, and above all when it is put as a question of representation, seems at once too old and as yet to be born: a kind of old parchment crossed every which way, overloaded with hieroglyphs and still as virgin as the origin.

[....]

McDONALD: I would like to come back to the writing of the dance, the choreography that you mentioned a while back. If we do not yet have a "new" "concept" of woman, because the radicalization of the problem goes beyond the "thought" or the concept, what are our chances of "thinking 'difference' not so much before sexual difference, as you say, as taking off 'from' " it? What would you say is our chance and "who" are we sexually?

DERRIDA: At the approach of this shadowy area it has always seemed to me that the voice itself had to be divided in order to say that which is given to thought or speech. No monological discourse—and by that I mean here monosexual discourse—can dominate with a single voice, a single tone, the space of this half-light, even if the "proffered discourse" is then signed by a sexually marked patronymic. Thus, to limit myself to one account, and not to propose an example, I have felt the necessity for a chorus, for a choreographic text with polysexual signatures.[7] I felt this every time that a legitimacy of the neuter, the apparently least suspect sexual neutrality of "phallocentric or gynocentric" mastery, threatened to immobilize (in silence), colonize, stop, or unilateralize in a subtle or sublime manner what remains no doubt irreducibly dissymmetrical. More directly: a certain dissymmetry is no doubt the law both of sexual difference and the relationship to the other in general (I say this in opposition to a certain kind of violence within the language of "democratic" platitudes, in any case in opposition to a certain democratic ideology), yet the dissymmetry to which I refer is still let us not say symmetrical in turn (which might seem absurd), but doubly, unilaterally inordinate, like a kind of reciprocal, respective, and respectful excessiveness. This double dissymmetry perhaps goes beyond known or coded marks, beyond the grammar and spelling, shall we say (metaphorically), of sexuality. This indeed revives the following question: what if we were to reach, what if we were to approach here (for one does not arrive at this as one would at a determined location) the area of a relationship to the other where the code of sexual marks would no longer be discriminating? The relationship would not be a-sexual, far from it, but would be sexual otherwise: beyond the binary difference that governs the decorum of all codes, beyond the opposition feminine–masculine, beyond bi-sexuality as well, beyond homosexuality and heterosexuality, which come to the same thing. As I dream of saving the chance that this question offers I would like to believe in the multiplicity of sexually marked voices. I would like to believe in the masses, this indeterminable number of blended voices, this mobile of nonidentified sexual marks whose choreography can carry, divide, multiply the body of each "individual," whether he be classified as "man" or as "woman" according to the criteria of usage. Of course, it is not impossible that desire for a sexuality without number can still protect us, like a dream, from an implacable destiny which immures everything for life in the figure 2. And should this merciless closure arrest desire at the wall of opposition, we would struggle in vain: there will never be but two sexes, neither one more nor one less. Tragedy would leave this strange sense, a contingent one finally, that we must affirm and learn to love instead of dreaming of the innumerable. Yes, perhaps; why not? But where would the "dream" of the innumerable come from, if it is indeed a dream? Does the dream itself not prove that what is dreamt of must be there in order for it to provide the dream? Then too, I ask you, what kind of a dance would there be, or would there be one at all, if the sexes were not exchanged according to rhythms that vary considerably? In a quite rigorous sense; the exchange alone could not suffice either, however, because the desire to escape the combinatory itself, to invent incalculable choreographies, would remain.

— Translated by Christie V. McDonald

NOTES

1. See above.—ED.
2. See Rodolphe Gasché, "The Internal Border," and the response by Jacques Derrida, in *The Ear of the Other* [1982].
3. See above.—ED.
4. For the passage from Levinas and Derrida's longer commentary, see above, **"At This Very Moment in This Work Here I Am,"** pp. **431–32.**—ED.
5. Concerning Heidegger's "silence" on sexual differences, see above, **"Geschlecht,"** pp. **380–83.**—ED.
6. For "hymen," see above, **"The Double Session,"** pp. **124–28;** for "chiasmatic double invagination of the borders," see above, **"Living On : Borderlines,"** and "The Law of Genre," *Parages* [1986].—ED.
7. This is an allusion to "Pas" in *Parages* [1986], **"Restitutions"** (see above), **"At This Very Moment in This Work Here I Am"** (see above), and *Feu la cendre* [1987]. Derrida's most recent polyvocal text is in *Droit de regards* [1985].—ED.

JALOUSIE FIVE

I am seeking the right metaphor for the operation I am pursuing here. I would like to describe my gesture, the posture of my body behind this machine.

What it would be hardest for him to tolerate would be that I assure myself or others of the mastery of his text. [. . .]

No danger. We are very far from that; this right here, I repeat, is barely preliminary.

. . . a sort of dredging machine. From the hidden cabin (small, closed, glassed-in) of a crane, I manipulate some levers and (I saw this done at Saintes-Maries-de-la-Mer at Easter), from afar, I plunge a mouth of steel into the water. And I scrape the bottom, grab some stones and algae that I bring back up to the surface in order to set them down on the ground while the water quickly falls out of the mouth.

And I begin again to scrape, to scratch, to dredge the bottom of the sea.

I barely hear the noise of the water from the little room.

. . . some algae, some stones. . . . Detached.

—*Glas,* pp. 204–05

PART FIVE

TELE-TYPES (YES, YES)

I N THIS LAST section, we have grouped selections from several of Derrida's more recent works, in particular the collection titled **The Post Card: From Socrates to Freud and Beyond** [1980]. The latter work joins three essays on psychoanalysis and the psychoanalytic institution to a long introduction, **"Envois,"** that elaborates on what Derrida calls the postal principle. Abbreviated frequently as PP, the postal principle subsumes and displaces the pleasure principle which, as Freud writes in the first sentence of *Beyond the Pleasure Principle*, is assumed by the theory of psychoanalyis to regulate automatically "the course taken by mental events." Whereas the pleasure principle is conceived as regulating the "psychic apparatus" from within, as it were, Derrida's postal principle traverses the whole field of message transmission, of delegation and representation, in short, of *sending* within which the psychic apparatus of conscious representations and unconscious traces comes to be inscribed. It is not just Freud's description of the mental apparatus that is inscribed within the postal system, but his own position as inscriber of the letter sent as a legacy to the heirs of the psychoanalytic institution (a legacy, moreover, that that institution has had the greatest difficulty receiving). What is more, as the subtitle of *The Post Card* implies, Derrida sees the postal principle as traversing the history of Western metaphysics from Socrates to Freud and beyond. One of the most important stopovers on this routing of the message is Heidegger's notion of the sending of Being. As Alan Bass writes in the introduction to his translation of *The Post Card*:

An entire reading of this book could be organized around Heidegger's sentence [from *On Time and Being*], "A giving which gives only its gift, but in the giving holds itself back and withdraws, such a giving we call a sending. . . ." Recall that Heidegger is shifting his meditation of the relation between Being and time—or time and Being—via a shift of emphasis in the phrase *es gibt Sein*. In *The Post Card*, Derrida radicalizes this shift. The examination of *es gibt*—it gives, there is—in terms of *sending*, and the principles operative in any "sending system" (e.g., the postal system), reveals a certain indeterminacy intrinsic to the concept of *sending*.

The "sending system" of relays or posts between addressor and addressee (in French, *destinateur/destinataire*, words that retain the link to destiny and destination) cannot overcome this intrinsic indeterminacy because, as Derrida first put it in the essay on Lacan's seminar on "The Purloined Letter," "a letter can always not arrive at its destination. Its 'materiality' and 'topology' are due to its divisibility, its always possible partition. . . . Not that the letter never arrives at its destination, but it belongs to the structure of the letter to be capable, always, of not arriving. And without this threat . . . the circuit of the letter would not even have begun. But with this threat, the circuit can always not finish" (444).

This divisibility of the letter, as well as the necessary detachment of the sending, are the *material* conditions of what Derrida earlier called dissemination. The latter is working to displace the concept of signification which has always regulated the movement of signs, meanings, messages, letters in terms of a *circulation*. Since his earliest texts on Husserl's phenomenology of signification (see above, 8–28), Derrida has shown how only a persistent determination of signs as exclusively ideal (and therefore indivisible) can permit the notion of their circulation within, precisely, a closed circuit of meaning. The detachment of the sign would, according to this ideal schema, merely allow it to circle back to the place of its emission. In **Speech and Phenomena** and **Of Grammatology,** Derrida analyzes the ideality described by the privileged voice which hears-itself-speak in a circle of auto-affection. In the texts collected in *The Post Card*, this structure of circularity is described via that of a letter sent and received by the same in a trajectory Derrida analyzes in terms not only of auto-affection or the pleasure principle (*s'envoyer*, the reflexive form of the verb to send, when used in certain expressions, means to have it off with someone, to get laid), but as well of an attempted reversal or recuperation of dissemination that would allow one to inherit from oneself, to be one's own and only legitimate heir. Freud's recuperative speculations in *Beyond the Pleasure Principle* are read according to this impossible structure, but Derrida also places these speculations along the trajectory of the "letter" (in fact, a post card) posted twenty-five centuries earlier by Socrates and retransmitted by the heir, Plato. But it is precisely this order of inheritance and priority (Socrates before Plato, speech before writing, the pure idea before its material inscription or representation) that is put in question by the undecidability of *s'envoyer*. Who sends what to whom? Which inherits from the other? Is not this very structure of representation, delegation, and legacy conceived of as circulating only within the element of the Same, where the one is also always the other, in a homoerotic logic of the paternal bequest of itself to itself? The legacy of Platonic idealism, from Socrates to Freud and beyond, would be the ideal post card (indivisible, immaterial, purely intelligible) that still circulates in every theory of signification based on the model of the predicated subject: *S* is *P*, that is, Socrates is (the same as) Plato.

Derrida, bound no less than any other by the terms of the inheritance, does not suppose, as does Freud to an important extent, that it can be simply rejected. Such a belief is but the condition of a repetition and retransmittal, a reposting of the same letter. On the one hand, *s'envoyer* describes the structure of the most proper sense of desire, which is the drive of the proper toward proper-ness, toward self-appropriation. But, on the other hand (which is the hand of the other), the fact that this desire is impossible, that its condition of possibility as desire is its condition of impossibility (just as the possibility of the letter's not arriving at its destination is the condition of its sending) opens the way to a thinking of affirmation which is heir more to a Nietzschean than to a Platonic legacy. Saying yes to the other, to the dissemination of the desire of the proper, to the divisibility of its addresses requires an affirmation of the catastrophe that has befallen and continues to befall the unique, univocal, and unidirectional destination of Truth. It requires, that is, an affirmation of the other not as an accident that happens to the Same (to the self or to me), but as that which (the one who) sends me, addresses me (to) my self, which (who) dictates, therefore, what I can seem to address to the other. Derrida's thinking since *The Post Card* has been drawn more and more to examine the strangeness of the affirmative gesture, of the Yes (or the *oui, ja, si,* etc.) which, he shows, are at the very limits of language and its representation of the Same. As such, the Yes implies always a repetition, a (Yes) Yes. We close this volume with a recent text that explores this repetition of the Yes.

NINETEEN

From "Le Facteur de la vérité," in *The Post Card:*

From Socrates to Freud and Beyond

(La Carte postale: De Socrate à Freud

et au-delà [1980])

In a collection of interviews published under the title *Positions*, Derrida was asked by one of his interlocutors to specify "what relationship a problematic of writing seems to you to maintain to the problematic of the signifier such as Lacan has developed it, in which the signifier 'represents the subject for another signifier'."[1] The same interlocutor also wonders whether the "differences" that Derrida talks about are not just another name for what Lacan calls "the symbolic." Like many others at the time Derrida's writings first began to appear in France, this interviewer was attempting to understand them within the powerfully systematizing terms proposed by the psychoanalyst Jacques Lacan, as if to confirm thereby this system's comprehensive powers of explanation. Derrida responds only briefly in the interview to these questions by pointing out that dissemination escapes from and disorganizes the "order of the symbolic" as Lacan defines it. Subsequent to this exchange, however, Derrida added a long note which traces succinctly the limits of any rapprochement between Lacan's thinking and his own. He concludes the note with the mention of a work in progress on Lacan, particularly on his "Seminar on the *Purloined Letter*." Published first in

1975 and later collected in *The Post Card,* this essay, "Le Facteur de la vérité," constitutes Derrida's patient reply to those who are in a hurry to assimilate deconstruction to Lacanian psychoanalytic theory.

The first obstacle Derrida marks to such an assimilation is the supplementary framing of textual systems which psychoanalytic interpretation most often disregards. Once reframed by the psychoanalytic discourse, once the doubling operation of a textual supplement, which doubles any structure of meaning, is out of the picture, the text can appear to submit to a deciphering of its message. Jacques Lacan's seminar on Poe's short story, despite certain appearances to the contrary, remains within this hermeneutic model that treats a text as the vehicle of a truthful sense, here the truth of sense, the truth of truth. Derrida describes Lacan's reframing as a repeated truncation of a fourth term, producing thereby triangulated figures and tripartite structures within which the terms can circulate, exchange places, even as the structure itself remains firmly in place. Holding it in place is the phallus, which Lacan calls a transcendental signifier, but which Derrida shows to be actually functioning in Lacan's discourse as a signified, that is, a proper meaning. Lacan is illustrating his theory of the primacy of the signifier over the subjects who appear to manipulate it with Poe's story of a letter the contents of which are so unimportant to the intrigue that they need never be revealed to the reader. But this primacy of the letter or the signifier, inasmuch as it is serving to illustrate the truth of a psychoanalytic doctrine, constrains the letter always to return to the same place, its proper place. "This proper place . . . is the place of castration: woman as the unveiled site of the lack of a penis, as the truth of the phallus, that is castration."

As he had already done in **Spurs: Nietzsche's Styles,** Derrida points out that the complicity of these terms—woman, castration, truth— has had a long history, the history, precisely, of truth as presence. Lacanian psychoanalysis, far from delimiting the metaphysics of presence, reinscribes itself wholly within the tradition even as it powerfully renews that tradition's momentum. The theory of the symbolic as the place of castration, the place of, in Lacan's phrase, "le manque à sa place" (the missing-from-its-place, but also the lack-in-place-of . . .) can, paradoxically, function as the truth of a presence as soon as this lack itself has a proper place to which it always returns, i.e., the phallus. By rewriting Lacan's formula minus an acute accent, "le manque a sa place" (the lack has its place), Derrida shifts the accent in Lacan's discourse from the materiality of the signifier (which, in fact, Lacan would have finally disregarded) to the ideality of a signified, that which has its own place, which remains in its place no matter how many displacements are undergone by the signifier. It is this single and identical place of lack that finally differentiates Lacan's conceptualization of the symbolic from Derrida's understanding of dissemination. Or, as Derrida puts it in a formula that must be read more than once: "The difference which interests me here is that—a formula to be understood as one will—the lack does not have its place in dissemination" (**p. 467;** see **Spurs, p. 362,** for a comparable formula: "La castration n'a pas lieu").

The following excerpts from "Le Facteur de la vérité" are selected with a view toward at least two of the senses of the *facteur* in that title. On the one hand, factor, as in the element of something, here the factor of truth, which is not just one element among others, but the one that distributes all the others. Consistent with this sense, Derrida analyzes the truth system to which Lacan's discourse belongs or refers in terms that recall very closely the analyses of logocentrism and phonocentrism with which he began in **Speech and Phenomena** and **Of Grammatology.** On the other hand, a *facteur* in French is a mailman, and with this sense Derrida's analyses look ahead to the postal principle brought to the fore in **"Envois"** and **"To Speculate—on 'Freud'."**

[. . . .]

"Just so does the purloined letter, like an immense female body, stretch out across the minister's office when Dupin enters. But just so does he already *expect to find it* [my italics—J.D.], and has only, with his eyes veiled by green lenses, to undress that huge body.

"And that is why without needing any more than being able to listen in at the door of Professor Freud, he will go straight to the spot in which lies and lives what that body is designed to hide, in a gorgeous center caught in a glimpse, nay, to the very place seducers name the Castle Sant'Angelo in their innocent illusion of being certain that they can hold the city from there. Look! between the jambs of the fireplace there is the object already within reach of the hand the ravisher has but to extend . . ."[2]

The letter—place of the signifier—is found in the place where Dupin and the psychoanalyst expect to find it: on the immense body of a woman, between the "legs" of the fireplace. Such is its proper place, the terminus of its circular itinerary. It is returned to the sender, who is not the signer of the note, but the place where it began to *detach* itself from its possessor or feminine legatee. The Queen, seeking to reappropriate for herself that which, by virtue of the pact which subjects her to the King, i.e. by virtue of the Law, guaranteed her the disposition of a phallus of which she would otherwise be deprived, of which she has taken the risk of depriving herself, that she has taken the risk of dividing, that is, of multiplying—the Queen, then, undertakes to reform, to reclose the circle of the restricted economy, the circulatory pact. She wants the letter-fetish brought back to her and therefore begins by replacing, by exchanging one fetish for another: she emits—without really spending it, since there is an equivalence here—a quantity of money which is exchanged for the letter and assures its circular return. Dupin, as (the) analyst, is found *[se trouve]* on the circuit, in the circle of the restricted economy, in what I call elsewhere the stricture of the ring, which the Seminar analyzes as the truth of fiction. We will come back to this problem of economics.

This determination of the proper, of the law of the proper, of *economy*, therefore leads back to castration as truth, to the figure of woman as the figure of castration *and* of truth. Of castration as truth. Which above all does not mean, as one might tend to believe, to truth as essential dislocation and irreducible fragmentation. Castration-truth, on the contrary, is that which contracts itself (stricture of the ring) in order to bring the phallus, the signifier, the letter, or the fetish back into their *oikos*,[3] their familiar dwelling, their proper place. In this sense castration-truth is the opposite of fragmentation, the very antidote for fragmentation: that which is missing from its place has in castration a fixed, central place, freed from all substitution. Something is missing from its place, but the lack is never missing from it *[Quelque chose manque à sa place, mais le manque n'y manque jamais]*. The phallus, thanks to castration, always remains in its place, in the transcendental topology of which we were speaking above. In castration, the phallus is indivisible, and therefore indestructible, like the letter that *takes its place*. And this is why the motivated, never demonstrated presupposition of the materiality of the letter as *indivisibility* is indispensable for this restricted economy, this circulation of the proper.

The difference which interests me here is that—a formula to be understood as one will—the lack does not have its place in dissemination.

By determining the place of the lack, the topos of that which is lacking from its place, and in constituting it as a fixed center, Lacan is indeed proposing, at the same time as a truth-discourse, a discourse on the truth of the purloined letter as the truth of

The Purloined Letter. In question is a hermeneutic deciphering, despite any appearances or denegation. The link of Femininity and Truth is the ultimate signified of this deciphering.

[. . . .]

Point de Vue:[4] Truth in (the) Place of Female Sexuality

[. . . .]

Until now, our questions have led us to suspect that if there is something like a purloined letter, perhaps it has a supplementary trap: it may have no fixed location, not even that of a definable hole or assignable lack. The letter might not be found, or could always possibly not be found, or would be found less in the sealed writing whose "story" is recounted by the narrator and deciphered by the Seminar, less in the content of the story, than "in" the text which escapes, from a fourth side, the eyes both of Dupin and of the psychoanalyst. The remainder, what is left unclaimed, would be *The Purloined Letter*, i.e., the text bearing this title whose location, like the large letters once more become invisible, is not where one would expect to find it, in the framed content of the "real drama" or in the hidden and sealed interior of Poe's tale, but rather in and as the open, the very open, letter that is fiction. The latter, because it is written, at the very least implies a self-divesting fourth agency, which at the same time divests the letter of the text from whoever deciphers it, from the *facteur* of truth who puts the letter back into the circle of its own, proper itinerary: which is what the Seminar does in repeating Dupin's operation, for he, in accord with the circularity of the "proper itinerary" "has succeeded in returning the letter to its proper course" (S, p. 69), according to the desire *of* the Queen. To return the letter to its proper course, assuming that its trajectory is a line, is to correct a deviation, to rectify a departure, to recall, for the sake of the rule, i.e., the norm, an orientation, an authentic line. Dupin is adroit, knows his address, and knows the law. At the very moment one believes that by drawing triangles and circles, and by wielding the opposition imaginary/symbolic one grasps *The Purloined Letter*, at the very moment one reconstitutes the truth, the proper adequation, *The Purloined Letter* escapes through a too self-evident opening. As Baudelaire bluntly reminds us. The purloined letter is in the text: not only as an object whose proper itinerary is described, contained in the text, a signifier become the theme or signified of the text, but also as the text producing the effects of the frame. At the very moment when Dupin and the Seminar find it, when they determine its proper location and itinerary, when they believe that it is here or there as on a map, a place on a map as on the body of a woman, they no longer see the map itself: not the map that the text describes at one moment or another, but the map *[carte]* that the text "is," that is describes, "itself," as the deviation of the four *[l'écart du quatre]* with no promise of topos or truth. The remaining[5] structure of the letter is that—contrary to what the Seminar says in its last words ("what the 'purloined letter,' that is, the not delivered letter *[lettre en souffrance]* means is that a letter always arrives at its destination." S, p. 72)—a letter can always not arrive at its destination. Its "materiality" and "topology" are due to its divisibility, its always possible partition. It can always be fragmented without return, and the system of the symbolic, of castration, of the signifier, of the truth, of the contract, etc., always attempts to protect the letter from this fragmentation: this is the point of view of the King or the Queen, which arc the same here; they are bound by contract to reappropriate the bit. Not that the letter never arrives at its destination, but it belongs to the structure of the letter to be capable, always, of not arriving. And without this threat (breach of contract, division or multiplication, the separation without return from the phallus which was begun for a moment by the Queen, i.e., by every "subject"), the circuit of the letter would not even have begun. But with this threat, the circuit can always not finish. Here dissemination threatens the law of the signifier and of castration as the contract of truth. It broaches, breaches *[entame]* the unity of the signifier, that is, of the phallus.

At the moment when the Seminar, like Dupin, finds the letter where it is found *[se trouve]*, between the legs of woman, the deciphering of the enigma is anchored in truth. The sense of the tale, the meaning of the purloined letter ("what the 'purloined letter,' that is, the not delivered letter *[lettre en souffrance]*, means is that a letter always arrives at its destination") is uncovered. The deciphering (Dupin's, the Seminar's), uncovered via a meaning (the truth), as a hermeneutic process, itself arrives at its destination.

[. . . .]

We are not going to give an exposition of this system of the truth, which is the condition for a logic of the signifier. Moreover, it consists of what is *nonexposable* in the exposition. We will only attempt to recognize those characteristics of it which are pertinent to the Seminar, to its possibility and its limits.

First of all, what is at issue is an *emphasis [emphase]*, as could equally be said in English, on the authentic excellence of the spoken, of speech, and of the word: of *logos* as *phonē*. This emphasis must be explained, and its necessary link to the theory of the signifier, the letter, and the truth must be accounted for. It must be explained why the author of *The Agency of the Letter in the Unconscious* and of the Seminar on *The Purloined Letter* ceaselessly subordinates the letter, writing, and the text. For even when he repeats Freud on rebuses, hieroglyphics, engravings, etc., in the last analysis his recourse is always to a writing spiritualized *(relevé)* by the voice. This would be easy to show. One example, among many others: "A writing, like the dream itself, may be figurative, it is like language always articulated symbolically, that is, it is like language *phonematic*, and in fact phonetic, as soon as it may be read."[6] This *fact* has the stature of a *fact* only within the limits of the so-called phonetic systems of writing. At the very most, for there are nonphonetic elements in such systems. As for the nonphonetic field of writing, its factual enormity no longer has to be demonstrated. But small matter. What does count here, and even more than the relation of the *de facto* to the *de jure*, is the implied equivalence ("that is") between symbolic articulation and phonematicity. The symbolic occurs through the voice, and the law of the signifier takes place only within vocalizable letters. Why? And what relation does this phonematism (which cannot be attributed to Freud, and thus is lost in the unfolding of the return to Freud) maintain with a certain value of truth?

Both imports of the value of truth are represented in the Seminar, as we have seen. I. *Adequation*, in the circular return and proper course, from the origin to the end, from the signifier's place of detachment to its place of reattachment. This circuit of adequation guards and regards *[garde et regarde]* the circuit of the pact, of the contract, of sworn faith. It restores the pact in the face of what threatens it, as the symbolic order. And it is constituted at the moment when the *guardianship [la garde]* of the phallus is confided as guardianship *of the* lack. Confided by the King to the Queen, but thereby in an endless play of alternations. 2. *Veiling–unveiling* as the structure of the lack: castration, the *proper* site of the signifier, origin and destination of its letter, shows nothing in unveiling itself. Therefore, it veils itself in its unveiling. But this operation of the truth has a proper place: its contours *being [étant]* the place of the lack of Being *[manque à être]* on the basis of which the signifier detaches itself for its literal circuit. These two values of truth lean on and support each other *(s'étaient)*. They are indissociable. They need speech or the phonetization of the letter as soon as the phallus has to be *kept [gardé]*, has to return to its point of departure, has not to be disseminated en route. Now, for the signifier to be kept *[pour que le signifiant se garde]* in its letter and thus to make its return, it is necessary that in its letter it does not admit "partition," that one cannot say *some* letter *[de la lettre]*, but only a letter, letters, the letter (S, pp. 53 54). If it were divisible, it could always be lost en route. To protect against this possible loss the statement about the "materiality of the signifier," that is, about the signifier's indivisible singularity, is constructed. *This "materiality," deduced from an indivisibility found nowhere, in fact corresponds to an idealization.* Only the ideality of a letter resists destructive division. "Cut a letter in small pieces, and it remains the letter it is" (S, p. 53): since this cannot be said of empirical materiality, it must imply an ideality (the intangibility of a self-identity displacing itself without alteration). This alone permits the singularity of the letter to be maintained *[se garder]*. If this ideality is not the content of meaning, it must be either a certain ideality of the signifier (what is identifiable in its form to the extent that it can be distinguished from its empirical events and re-editions), or the *"point de capiton"*[7] which staples the signifier to the signified. The latter hypothesis conforms more closely to the system. This system is in fact the system of the ideality of the signifier. The idealism lodged within it is not a theoretical position of the analyst; it is a structural effect of *signification* in general, to whatever transformations or adjustments one subjects the space of *semiosis*. One can understand that Lacan finds this "materiality" "odd" ["*singulière*"]: he retains only its ideality. He considers the letter only at the point at which it is determined (no matter what he says) by its content of meaning, by the ideality of the message that it "vehiculates," by the speech whose meaning remains out of the reach of partition, so that it can circulate, intact, from its place of detachment to its place of reattachment, that is, to the same place. In fact, this letter does not only escape partition, it escapes movement, it does not change its place.

Aside from a phonematic limitation of the letter, this supposes an interpretation of *phonē* which also spares it divisibility. The voice occasions such an interpretation in and of itself: it has the phenomenal characteristics of spontaneity, of self-presence, of the circular return to itself. And the voice retains [*garde*] all the more in that one believes one can retain [*garder*] it without external accessory, without paper and without envelope: it finds itself [*se trouve*], it tells us, always available wherever it is found [*se trouve*]. This is why it is believed that the voice remains more than do writings: "May it but please heaven that writings remain, as is rather the case with spoken words" (S, p. 56). Things would be quite otherwise if one were attentive to the writing within the voice, that is, before the letter. For the same problem is reproduced concerning the voice, concerning what one might still call its "letter," if one wished to conserve the Lacanian definition of this concept (indivisible locality or materiality of the signifier). This vocal "letter" therefore also would be indivisible, always identical to itself, whatever the fragmentations of its body. It can be assured of this integrity only by virtue of its link to the ideality of a meaning, in the unity of a speech. We are always led back, from stage to stage, to the contract of contracts which guarantees the unity of the signifier with the signified through all the *"points de capiton,"* thanks to the "presence" (see below) of the *same* signifier (the phallus), of the "signifier of signifiers" beneath all the effects of the signified. This transcendental signifier is therefore also the signified of all signifieds, and this is what finds itself sheltered within the indivisibility of the (graphic or oral) letter. Sheltered from this threat, but also from the disseminating power that in *Of Grammatology* I proposed to call *Writing Before the Letter* (title of the first part): the privilege of "full speech" is examined there. The agency of the Lacanian letter is the *relève* of writing in the system of speech.[8]

"The drama" of the purloined letter begins at the moment—which is not a moment—when the letter *is retained [se garde]*. With the movement of the minister who acts in order to conserve it (for he could have torn it up, and this is indeed an ideality which then would have remained available and effective for a time),[9] certainly, but well before this, when the Queen wishes to retain it or refind it *[la garder ou la retrouver]:* as a double of the pact that binds her to the King, a threatening double, but one that in her guardianship *[sous sa garde]* cannot betray the "sworn faith." The Queen wishes to be able to play on two contracts. We cannot develop this analysis here; it is to be read elsewhere.

What counts here is that the indestructibility of the letter has to do with its elevation toward the ideality of a meaning. However little we know of its content, the content must be in relation to the original contract that it simultaneously signifies and subverts. And it is this knowledge, this memory, this (conscious or unconscious) retention which form its properness *[propriété]*, and ensure its proper course toward the proper place. Since its ultimate content is that of a pact binding two "singularities," it implies an irreplaceability and excludes, as uncontrollable threat and anxiety, all double simulacra. It is the effect of living and present speech which in the last analysis guarantees the indestructible and unforgettable singularity of the letter, the taking-place of a signifier which never is lost, goes astray, or is divided. The subject is very divided, but the phallus is not to be cut. Fragmentation is an accident which does not concern it. At least according to the certainty constructed by the symbolic. And by a discourse on the assumption of castration which edifies an ideal philosophy against fragmentation.[10]

In principle this is how the logic of the signifier is articulated with a phonocentric interpretation of the letter. The two values of the truth (adequation and movement of the veil) henceforth cannot be dissociated from the word, from present, living, authentic speech. The final word is that, when all is said and done, there is, at the origin or the end (proper course, circular destination), a word that is not feigned, a meaning that, through all imaginable fictional complications, does not trick, or that at that point tricks *truly*, again teaching us the truth of the lure. At this point, the truth permits the analyst to treat fictional characters as real and to resolve, at the depth of the Heideggerian meditation on truth, the problem of the literary text which sometimes led Freud (more naïvely, but more surely than Heidegger and Lacan) to confess his confusion. And we are still only dealing with a literature with characters! Let us cite the Seminar first. The suspicion that perhaps the author's purpose was not, as Baudelaire said, to state the true has just been awakened. Which, however, does not always amount to having a good time. Thus: "No doubt Poe is having a good time . . .

"But a suspicion occurs to us: might not this parade of erudition be destined to reveal to us the key words of our drama? Is not the magician repeating his trick before our eyes, without deceiving us this time about divulging his secret, but pressing his wager to the point of really explaining it to us without our seeing a thing? *That* would be the summit of the illusionist's art: through one of his fictive creations *truly to delude* us. And is it not such effects which justify our referring, without malice, to a number of imaginary heroes as real characters?

"As well, when we are open to hearing the way in which Martin Heidegger discloses to us in the word *aletheia* the play of truth, we rediscover a secret to which truth has always initiated her lovers, and through which they learn that it is in hiding that she offers herself to them *most truly*" (S, pp. 50–51).

Abyss effects are severely controlled here, a scientifically irreproachable precaution: this is science itself, or at least ideal science, and even the truth of the science of truth. From the statements I have just cited it does not follow that truth is a fiction, but that through fiction truth properly declares itself. Fiction manifests the truth: the manifestation that illustrates itself through evasion. *Dichtung* (poetic saying or fiction, this is both Goethe's and Freud's expression: just as for Heidegger, the issue is one of literary fiction as *Dichtung*) is the manifestation of the truth, its being-declared: "There is so little opposition between this *Dichtung* and *Wahrheit* in its nudity that the fact of the poetic operation rather should give us pause before the characteristic which is forgotten in all truth, that it declares itself in a structure of fiction."[11] Truth governs the fictional element of its manifestation, which permits it to be or to become what it is, to declare itself. Truth governs this element from its origin or its telos, which finally coordinates this concept of literary fiction with a highly classical interpretation of *mimesis:* a detour toward the truth, more truth in the fictive representation than in reality, increased fidelity, "superior realism." The preceding citation called for a note: "The suitability of this reminder for our subject would be sufficiently confirmed, if need be, by one of the numerous unpublished texts that Delay's opus provides us, enlightening them in the most appropriate way. Here from the *Unpublished Journal,* said to be from la Brevine where Gide lived in October 1894 (note on page 667 of his volume 2).

" 'The novel will prove that it can paint something other than reality—emotion and thought directly; it will show to what extent it can be deduced, *before the experience of things*—to what extent, that is, it can be composed—that it is a work of art. It will show that it can be a work of art, composed entirely out of its own elements, not out of a realism of petty and contingent facts, but a superior realism.' " There follows a reference to the mathematical triangle, and then: " 'It is necessary that in their relation itself each part of a work prove the truth of each other part, there is no need for any other proof. Nothing is more irritating than the testimony that M. de Goncourt gives for everything he asserts—he has seen! he has heard! as if proof via the real were necessary.' " Lacan concludes:

"It has to be said that no poet has ever thought otherwise . . . , but that no one follows through on this thought." And in the same article it is confirmed that it is a "person" who "bears" the "truth of fiction." This person is the "seductress" of the "young boy."[12]

Once one has distinguished, as does the entire philosophical tradition, between truth and reality, it immediately follows that the truth "declares itself in a structure of fiction."[13] Lacan insists a great deal on the opposition truth–reality, which he advances as a paradox. This opposition, which is as orthodox as can be, facilitates the passage of the truth through fiction: common sense always will have made the division between reality and fiction.

But once again, why would speech be the privileged element of this truth declared *as* fiction, in the mode or structure of fiction, of verified fiction, of what Gide calls "superior realism"?

As soon as the truth is determined as adequation (with an original contract: the acquitting of a debt) and as unveiling (of the lack on the basis of which the contract is contracted in order to reappropriate symbolically what has been detached), the guiding value is indeed that of propriation, and therefore of proximity, of presence, and of maintaining *[garde]:* the very value procured by the idealizing effect of speech. If one grants this demonstration, it will not be surprising to find it confirmed. If one does not, then how is one to explain the massive co-implication, in Lacanian discourse, of truth and speech, "present," "full" and "authentic" speech? And if it is taken into account, one better understands: 1. That fiction for Lacan is permeated by truth as something spoken and therefore as something nonreal. 2. That this leads to no longer reckoning, in the text, with everything that remains irreducible to speech, to the spoken word *[le dit],* and meaning *[vouloir-dire]:* that is, irreducible dis-regard, theft without return, destructibility, divisibility, the failure to reach a destination *(le manque à destination)* (which definitively rebels against the destination of the lack *[la destination du manque]:* an unverifiable nontruth).

When Lacan recalls "the passion for unveiling which has one object: the truth"[14] and recalls that the analyst "above all remains the master of the truth," it is always in order to link the truth to the power of speech. And to the power of communication as a contract (sworn faith) between two present things. Even if communication communicates nothing, it communicates to itself: and in this case better yet as communication, that is, truth. For example: "Even if it communicates nothing, the discourse represents the existence of communication; even if it denies the evidence, it affirms that speech constitutes truth; even if it is intended to deceive, the discourse speculates on faith in testimony."[15]

What is neither true nor false is reality. But as soon as speech is inaugurated, one is in the register of the unveiling of the truth as of its contract of properness *[propriété]:* presence, speech, testimony: "The ambiguity of the hysterical revelation of the past is due not so much to the vacillation of its content between the imaginary and the real, for it is situated in both. Nor is it because it is made up of lies. The reason is that it presents us with the birth of truth in speech and thereby brings us up against the reality of what is neither true nor false. At any rate, that is the most disquieting aspect of the problem.

"For it is present speech that bears witness to the truth of this revelation in present reality, and which grounds it in the name of that reality. Yet in that reality, only speech bears witness to that portion of the powers of the past that has been thrust aside at each crossroads where the event has made its choice."[16] Just before this passage there is a reference to Heidegger, which is not surprising; the reference resituates *Dasein* in the subject, which is more so.

As soon as "present speech" "bears witness" to the "truth of this revelation" beyond the true or the false, beyond what is truthful or lying in a given statement or symptom in their relation to a given content, the values of adequation or unveiling no longer even have to await their verification or achievement from the exterior of some object. They guarantee each other intrinsically. What counts is not whatever (true or false) is communicated, but "the existence of communication," the present revelation made within communication of the speech that bears witness to the truth. Whence the necessary relaying by the values of authenticity, plentitude, properness, etc. The truth, which is what must be refound *[retrouvé],* therefore is not an object beyond the subject, is not the adequation of speech to an object,[17] but the adequation of full speech to itself, its proper authenticity, the conformity of its act to its original essence. And the telos of this *Eigentlichkeit,* the proper aiming at this authenticity shows the "authentic way" of analysis, of the training analysis in particular. "But what in fact was this appeal from the subject beyond the void of his speech? It was an appeal to the very principle of truth, through which other appeals resulting from humbler needs will vacillate. But first and foremost it was the proper appeal of the void [appel propre du vide] . . ."[18]

From the proper appeal of the void to the achieving of full speech, the "realization" of full speech through the assumption of desire (of castration)—such, then, is the ideal process of analysis: "I have tackled the function of speech in analysis from its least rewarding angle, that of empty speech, where the subject seems to be talking in vain about someone who, even if he were his spitting image, can never become one with the assumption of his desire . . . If we now turn to the other extreme of the psychoanalytic experience—its history, it argumentation, the process of the treatment—we shall find that to the analysis of the here and now is to be opposed the value of anamnesis as the index and source of therapeutic progress; that to obsessional intrasubjectivity is to be opposed hysterical intersubjectivity; and that to the analysis of resistance is to be opposed symbolic interpretation. The realization of full speech begins here"[19]

Speech, here, is not full of something beyond itself which would be its object: but this is why all the more and all the better, it is full of itself, of its presence, its essence. This presence, as in the contract and the sworn faith, requires irreplaceable properness [propriété], inalienable singularity, living authenticity—so many values the system of which we have recognized elsewhere. The double, repetition, recording, and the mimeme in general are excluded from this system, along with the entire graphematic structure they imply; and they are excluded both in the name of direct interlocution and as inauthentic alienation. For example: "But precisely because it comes to him through an alienated form, even a retransmission of his own recorded discourse, be it from the mouth of his own doctor, cannot have the same effects as psychoanalytic interlocution."[20]

The disqualification of recording or repetition in the name of the act of living and present speech conforms to a well-known program. And is indispensable to the system. The system of "true speech," of "speech in act," cannot do without the condemnation, which stretches from Plato to a certain Freud, of the simulacrum of hypomnesis, hypomnesis condemned in the name of the truth, in the name of that which links *mnēmē, anamnesis, aletheia,* etc.

Materiality, the sensory and repetitive side of the recording, the paper letter, drawings in ink, can be divided or multiplied, destroyed or set adrift (since authentic originality is always already lost in them). The letter itself, in the Lacanian sense, as the site of the signifier and symbol of a sworn faith, and therefore of a true full and present speech, has as its property, its "singular," "odd" property in effect, "not to admit partition."

"Present speech," then, as "full speech": "I might as well be categorical: in psychoanalytic anamnesis, it is not a question of reality, but of truth, because the effect of full speech is to reorder past contingencies by conferring on them the sense of necessities to come, such as they are constituted by the little freedom through which the subject makes them present."[21]

Henceforth, a text, if it is living and animated, full and authentic, will be of value only by virtue of the speech it will have as its mission to transport. Therefore, there also will be full texts and empty texts. The former only "vehiculate" a full speech, that is, an authentically present truth which simultaneously unveils and is adequate to or identical with that which it speaks about. Which is itself, therefore ("the thing speaks of itself"), at the moment when it makes its return to the encircled hole and to the contract which constitute it. For example, as concerns Freud's text, which must be returned to, and be returned to itself as well (see above): "Not one of those two-dimensional, infinitely flat (as the mathematicians say) texts, which are only of fiduciary value in a constituted discourse, but a text that is the vehicle of a speech, in that speech constitutes a new emergence of the truth." Such a text, as present, inaugural, and constitutive speech, itself answers for itself if we question it, as is said in the *Phaedrus* of the *logos* which is its own father. It simultaneously gives the questions and the answers. Our activity of mobilizing "all the resources of our exegesis" is only in order "to make it [Freud's text] answer the questions that it puts to us, to treat it as a real speech, we should say, if we knew our own terms, in its transference value." Our "own terms": let us take this as the terms of the discourse which questions and answers, Freud's discourse.

"Of course, this supposes that we interpret it. In effect, is there a better critical method than the one which applies to the comprehension of a message the very principles of comprehension of which it is the vehicle? This is the most rational mode in which to experience its authenticity.

"Full speech, in effect, is defined by its identity with that which it speaks about."[22]

The exegete's full speech fills itself when it assumes and takes upon itself the "principles of comprehension" of the other's— here Freud's—message, to the extent that this message itself "vehiculates" a "full speech." The latter, since it is inaugural and "constitutes a new emergence of the truth," contracts only with itself: it speaks of itself by itself. This is what we are calling the *system* of speech, or the *system* of truth.

One cannot define the "hermeneutical circle," along with all the conceptual parts of its system, more rigorously or more faithfully. It includes all the circles that we are pointing out here, in their Platonic, Hegelian, and Heideggerian tradition, and in the most philosophical sense of responsibility:[23] to acquit oneself adequately of that which one owes (duty and debt).

[. . . .]

— *Translated by Alan Bass*

NOTES

1. *Positions* [1972], p. 80.

2. Jacques Lacan, "Seminar on *The Purloined Letter*," trans. by Jeffrey Mehlman, *Yale French Studies* (1972), no. 48, p. 66; hereafter abbreviated as S. References to other texts of Lacan will be either to the original French edition of *Ecrits* (Paris: Seuil, 1966) or to the partial translation by Alan Sheridan (New York: Norton, 1977). In the latter case, the title *Ecrits* will be followed by the indication *(tr.)*.—ED.

3. The Greek *oikos* means the house, the dwelling, and is also the root from which the word *economy* is derived.—TRANS.

4. *Point de* means both "point of" and "no, none at all." Thus, point of view/no view, blindness.—TRANS.

5. "*La structure restante de la lettre* . . ." For Derrida, writing is always that which is an excess remainder, *un reste*. Further, in French, mail delivered to a post office box is called *poste restante*, making the dead letter office the ultimate *poste restante*, literally "remaining mail." Thus, Derrida is

saying that Lacan's notion that the nondelivered letter, *la lettre en souf-france*, always arrives at its destination overlooks the structural possibility that a letter can always *remain* in the dead letter office, and that without this possibility of deviation and remaining—the entire postal system—there would be no delivery of letters to any address at all.—TRANS.

6. *"Situation de la psychanalyse en 1956," Ecrits*, p. 470.

7. *Capitonner* means to quilt; *point de capiton* is Lacan's term for the "quilted stitch" that links signifier to signified.—TRANS.

8. See above, **Of Grammatology** (pp. **42–46**); on this use of *relève*, see above, **"Différance,"** note **12.**—ED.

9. For a time only: until the moment when, unable to return a "material," divisible letter, a letter subject to partition, an effectively "odd" letter, he would have to release the hold over the Queen that only a destructible document could have assured him.

10. What we are analyzing here is the most rigorous philosophy of psychoanalysis today, more precisely the most rigorous Freudian philosophy, doubtless more rigorous than Freud's philosophy, and more scrupulous in its exchanges with the history of philosophy.

It would be impossible to exaggerate the import of the proposition about the indivisibility of the letter, or rather about the letter's self-identity that is inaccessible to fragmentation ("Cut a letter in small pieces, it remains the letter it is"), or of the proposition about the so-called "materiality of the signifier" (the letter) which does not bear partition. Where does this come from? A fragmented letter can purely and simply be destroyed, this happens (and if one considers that the unconscious effect here named letter is never lost, that repression maintains everything and never permits any degradation of insistence, this hypothesis—nothing is ever lost or goes astray—must still be aligned with *Beyond the Pleasure Principle*, or other letters must be produced, whether characters or messages).

11. *Ecrits*, p. 742.

12. *Ecrits*, p. 753.

13. For example: "Thus it is from elsewhere than the Reality with which it is concerned that the Truth takes its guarantee: it is from Speech *(la Parole)*. Just as it is from Speech that it receives the mark which institutes it in a structure of fiction.

"The primal word *(le dit premier)* decrees, legislates, aphorizes, is oracle, it confers upon the real other its obscure authority." *Ecrits*, p. 808.

14. "You have heard me, in order to situate its place in the investigation, refer with brotherly love to Descartes and to Hegel. These days, it is rather fashionable to 'surpass' the classical philosophers. I equally could have taken the admirable dialogue with Parmenides as my point of departure. For neither Socrates, nor Descartes, nor Marx, nor Freud can be 'surpassed' to the extent that they have conducted their investigations with that passion for unveiling which has a single object: the truth.

"As one of those, princes of the verb, and through whose fingers the strings of the mask of the Ego seem to slip by themselves, has written—I have named Max Jacob, poet, saint, and novelist—yes, as he has written in his *Dice Cup*, if I am not mistaken: the true is always new." *Ecrits*, p. 193. This is true, always. How not to subscribe to it?

15. "Empty and full speech in the psychoanalytic realization of the subject" in the Rome Report *(Function and Field of Speech . . .)*, *Ecrits* (tr.), p. 43—Trans.

16. Ibid., p. 47.—TRANS.

17. "True speech" is the speech authenticated by the other in faith sworn or given. The other makes speech adequate to itself—and no longer to the object—by sending back the message in inverted form, by making it true, by henceforth identifying the subject with itself, by "stating that it is the same." Adequation—as authentification—must pass through intersubjectivity. Speech "is therefore an act, and as such supposes a subject. But it is not enough to say that in this act the subject supposes another subject, for it is much rather that the subject is founded in this act as being the other, but in that paradoxical unity of the one and the other, by whose means, as has been shown above, the one depends upon the other in order to become identical to itself.

"Thus one can say that speech manifests itself not only as a communication in which the subject, in order to await that the other make his message true, is going to project the message in inverted form, but also as a communication in which this message transforms the subject by stating that it is the same. As is apparent in every given pledge, in which declarations like 'you are my wife' or 'you are my master' signify 'I am your husband,' 'I am your disciple.'

"Speech therefore appears all the more truly speech in that its truth is less founded in what is called adequation to the thing: true speech, thereby, is opposed paradoxically to true discourse, their truth being distinguished by the fact that the former constitutes the subjects' acknowledgment of their Beings in that they have an inter-est in them, while the latter is constituted by the knowledge of the real, to the extent that the subject aims for it in objects. But each of the truths distinguished here is changed by intersecting with the other in its path." *Ecrits*, p. 351 *(Variantes de la cure-type)*. In this intersecting, "true speech" always appears as more true than "true discourse," which always presupposes the order of true speech, the order of the intersubjective contract, of symbolic exchange, and therefore of the debt. "But true speech, in questioning true discourse about what it signifies, will find that signification always refers to signification, there being no thing that can be shown otherwise than with a sign, and henceforth will show true discourse to be doomed to error." *Ecrits*, p. 352. The ultimate adequation of the truth as true speech therefore has the form of making quits *(l'acquitte-ment)*, the "strange adequation . . . which finds its response in the symbolic debt for which the subject as subject of speech is responsible." *Ecrits* (tr.), p. 144. These are the final words of "The Freudian Thing." Adequation to the thing (true discourse) therefore has its foundation in the adequation of speech to itself (true speech), that is to the thing itself: in other words of *the*

Freudian thing to itself: "The thing speaks of itself" (*Ecrits* (tr.), p. 121), and it says: "I, the truth, speak." The thing is the truth: as cause, both of itself and of the things of which true discourse speaks. These propositions are less new, particularly in relation to the Rome Report, to *Variantes de la cure-type*, and to the texts of the same period, than their author says: "This is to introduce the effects of truth as cause at a quite different point, and to impose a revision of the process of causality—the first stage of which would seem to be to recognize the inherent nature of the heterogeneity of these effects.[5]" *Ecrits* (tr.), p. 127. (The footnote: "5. This rewritten paragraph antedates a line of thought that I have since explored further (1966)." *Ecrits* (tr.), p. 145.)

"True speech" (adequate to itself, conforming to its essence, destined to be quits of a debt which in the last analysis binds it only to itself) therefore permits the contract which permits the subject "to become identical to itself." Therefore it reconstitutes the ground of Cartesian certainty: the transformation of the truth into certainty, subjectification (the determination of the Being of beings as subject), and intersubjectification (the chain Descartes-Hegel-Husserl). This chain ceaselessly captures, in the *Ecrits*, Heideggerian motions which would appear, rigorously speaking, to be allergic to it, and would appear to have "destructive" effects on it. For the moment, let us abandon these kinds of questions—the most decisive ones—which Lacan's discourse never articulates.

18. *Ecrits* (tr.), p. 40.—TRANS.
19. Ibid. (tr.), pp. 45-46. TRANS.
20. Ibid. (tr.), p. 49.—TRANS.
21. Ibid. (tr.), p. 48.—TRANS.
22. *Ecrits*, p. 381.—TRANS.
23. This responsibility is defined immediately after, and on the basis of, the exchange of "full speech" with Freud, in its "true formative value": "For in question is nothing less than its adequation at the level of man at which he takes hold of it, no matter what he thinks—at which he is called upon to answer it, no matter what he wants—and for which he assumes responsibility, no matter what his opinion." *Ecrits*, p. 382. As concerns the "level of man," we do not have enough space to verify the essential link between metaphysics (several typical characteristics of which we are pointing out here) and humanism in this system. This link is more visible, if not looked upon more highly, in the conglomeration of statements about "animality," about the distinction between animal and human language, etc. This discourse on the animal (in general) is no doubt consistent with all the categories and oppositions, all the bi- or tri-partitions of the system. And it condenses no less the system's greatest obscurity. The treatment of animality, as of everything that finds itself in *submission* by virtue of a hierarchical opposition, has always, in the history of (humanist and phallogocentric) metaphysics, revealed obscurantist resistance. It is obviously of capital interest.

TWENTY

From "Envois," in *The Post Card*

(*La Carte postale* [1980])

You might read these *envois* as the preface to a book that I have not written. It would have treated that which proceeds from the *postes, postes* of every genre, to psychoanalysis. Less in order to attempt a psychoanalysis of the postal effect than to start from a singular event, Freudian psychoanalysis, and to refer to a history and a technology of the *courrier,* to some general theory of the *envoi* and of everything which by means of some telecommunication allegedly *destines* itself. . . . As for the "Envois" themselves, I do not know if their reading is bearable. You might consider them, if you really wish to, as the remainders of a recently destroyed correspondence.

These opening remarks are followed by the long text of "Envois," a "preface" which has gotten thoroughly out of hand and doubled the length of the book Derrida says he planned to write but did not. Getting out of hand is in fact the very condition of an *envoi,* which means a sending, a kickoff, a dispatch, a missive, or transmission; in short, it marks a passage out of hand and into a postal or telecommunications network from which the *envoi* may or may not emerge at its addressed destination. "Envois" indeed resembles the remains of a correspondence: a succession of dated fragments, a form of intimate address ("you, my love"), constant reference to sending and receiving letters or post cards of which the very ones we are reading seem to be part. No addressee or addressor is ever identified by his or her name, at least not a recognizable public name. These names would be but one of the things censored or cut out from the texts we are reading which are in fact punctuated by frequent gaps. Although the principal correspondent seems identifiable in almost every way with Jacques Derrida, the signatory of "Envois," at the same time nothing could be less certain than this sort of identification. In accordance with the postal principle, which these letters are both analyzing and submitting to, "identity" is but the spacing of a self-address, analogous therefore to the distance between addressor and addressee. There is no telling where that gap widens sufficiently to accommodate the conventions of a fictional first-person narrator.

The principal letter-writer has come across a post card which carries an illustration from a thirteenth-century manuscript. It shows Socrates writing at a table while Plato, standing immediately behind him, reaches over his shoulder as if to direct what his master is writing. For this correspondent, the image is uncannily reminiscent of his own "illustrations" of the structures of delegation, secondariness, and paternal legacy, structures largely inherited from the Platonic text. Profoundly fascinated by this image of an apparent reversal, since Socrates is supposed by a whole philosophical tradition to be, as Nietzsche puts it, "the one who does not write," the letter-writer pursues its implications on the back of countless copies of the post card, dispatched to "you," "you, my love." The letters shuttle between this apostrophe (the turning aside of discourse in a singular address) and the catastrophe (literally: an overturning) of destination which has already turned the address aside from itself. The singular address divides, fragments, goes astray, and, like a misdelivered post card, lays itself open to anyone's reading.

But the letter writer wonders: What is not already, like a post care, delivered up to public scrutiny, even to the police? Does not the postal principle (pp) lift the bar of the public–private (p–p) distinction? Indeed it does, and the letter-writer proposes to demonstrate this rule by publishing everything in this "intimate" correspondence that belongs or returns to the tropological (turning and turning aside) system of the post. The rest—represented by the blanks on the page—will have been saved from this destruction of singular address which is publication. However, since the postal system is first of all a system of *supports* for the messages it relays, this saving cannot take the form of preserving cards and letters. To save the singular address, the unreproducible "I love you," the letter-writer and his addressee will consign what remains to the flames. The only chance for the address is thus a radical forgetting, one that consumes even the traces of what has been forgotten.

[. . . .]

6 June 1977

[. . . .]

Do people (I am not speaking of "philosophers" or of those who read Plato) realize to what extent this old couple has invaded our most private domesticity, mixing themselves up in everything, taking their part of everything, and making us attend for centuries their colossal and indefatigable anaparalyses? The one in the other, the one in front of the other, the one after the other, the one behind the other?

[. . . .]

Be aware that everything in our bildopedic culture, in our politics of the encyclopedic, in our telecommunications of all genres, in our telematicometaphysical archives, in our library, for example the marvelous Bodleian, everything is constructed on the proto-colary charter of an axiom, that could be demonstrated, displayed on a large *carte*, a post card of course, since it is so simple, elementary, a brief, fearful stereotyping (above all say or think nothing that derails, that jams telecom.). The charter is the contract for the following, which quite stupidly one has to believe: Socrates comes *before* Plato, there is between them—and in general—an order of generations, an irreversible sequence of inheritance. Socrates is before, not in front of, but before Plato, therefore behind him, and the charter binds us to this order: this is how to orient one's thought, this is the left and this is the right, march. Socrates, he who does not write, as Nietzsche said

(how many times have I repeated to you that I also found him occasionally or even always somewhat *on the border* of being naïve; remember that photograph of him with his "good guy" side, at the beginning in any event, before the "evil," before the disaster?). He understood nothing about the initial catastrophe, or at least about this one, since he knew all about the others. Like everyone else he believed that Socrates did not write, that he came before Plato who more or less wrote at his dictation and therefore let him write by himself, as he says somewhere. From this point of view, N. believed Plato and overturned nothing at all. The entire "overturning" remained included in the program of this credulity. This is true *a fortiori*, and with an *a fortiori* different each time and ready to blow up otherwise, from Freud and from Heidegger.* Now, my post card, this morning when I am raving about it or delivering it *[quand je la délire ou la délivre]* in the state of jealousy that has always terrified me, my post card naïvely overturns everything. In any event, it allegorizes the catastrophic unknown of the order. Finally one begins no longer to understand what to come *[venir]*, to come before, to come after, to foresee *[prévenir]*, to come back *[revenir]* all mean —along with the difference of the generations, and then to inherit, to write one's will, to dictate, to speak, to take dictation, etc. One is finally going to be able to love oneself *[s'aimer]*

[. . . .]

Would like to address myself, in a straight line, directly, without *courrier*, only to you, but I do not arrive, and that is the worst of it. A tragedy, my love, of destination. Everything becomes a post card once more, legible for the other, even

---

*I must note it right here, on the morning of 22 August 1979, 10 A.M., while typing this page for the present publication, the telephone rings. The U.S. The American operator asks me if I accept a *"collect call"* from Martin (she says Martine or martini) Heidegger. I heard, as one often does in these situations which are very familiar to me, often having to call "collect" myself, voices that I thought I recognized on the other end of the intercontinental line, listening to me and watching my reaction. What will he do with the ghost or Geist of Martin? I cannot summarize here all the chemistry of the calculation that very quickly made me refuse *("It's a joke, I do not accept")* after having had the name of Martini Heidegger repeated several times, hoping that the author of the farce would finally name himself. Who pays, in sum, the addressee or the sender? who is to pay? This is a very difficult question, but this morning I thought that I should not pay, at least not otherwise than by adding this note of thanks. I know that I will be suspected of making it all up, since it is too good to be true. But what can I do? It is true, rigorously, from start to finish, the date, the time, the content, etc. Heidegger's name was already written, after "Freud," in the letter that I am in the course of transcribing on the typewriter. This is true, and moreover demonstrable, if one wishes to take the trouble of inquiring: there are witnesses and a postal archive of the thing. I call upon these witnesses (these waystations between Heidegger and myself) to make themselves known. All of this must not lead you to believe that no telephonic communication links me to Heidegger's ghost, as to more than one other. Quite the contrary, the network of my hookups, you have the proof of it here, is on the burdensome side, and more than one switchboard is necessary in order to digest the overload. It is simply, let me say for the ears of my correspondents of this morning (to whom I regret a bit, nevertheless, that I did not speak), that my private relation with Martin does not go through the same exchange.

if he understands nothing about it. And if he understands nothing, certain for the moment of the contrary, it might always arrive for you, for you too, to understand nothing, and therefore for me, and therefore not to arrive, I mean at its destination. I would like to arrive to'you, to arrive right up to you, my unique destiny, and I run I run and I fall all the time, from one stride to the next, for there will have been, so early, well before us

[. . . .]

9 June 1977

Plato wants to emit. Seed, artificially, technically. That devil of a *Socrates* holds the syringe. To sow the entire earth, to send the same fertile card to *everyone*. A *pancarte*, a pan-card, a billboard that we have on our backs and to which we can never really turn round. For example, poor Freud, Plato, via Socrates, via all the addressees who are found on the Western way, the relays, the porters, the readers, the copyists, the archivists, the guardians, the professors, the writers, the *facteurs* right?, Plato sticks him with his *pancarte* and Freud has it on his back, can no longer get rid of it. Result, result, for it is not so simple and as-I-show-in-my-book it is then Plato who is the inheritor, for Freud. Who pulls the same trick, somewhat, on Plato that Plato pulls on Socrates. This is what I call a catastrophe.

[. . . .]

you under stand, within every sign already, every mark or every trait, there is distancing, the post, what there has to be so that it is legible for another, another than you or me, everything is messed up in advance, cards on the table. The condition for it to arrive is that it ends up and even that it begins by not arriving. This is how it is to be read, and written, the *carte* of the adestination. Abject literature is on the way, and it spies on you, crouching within language, and as soon as you open your mouth it strips you of everything without even letting you enjoy getting underway again, completely naked, to the one you love, living, living, living, there, out of reach. The condition for me to renounce nothing and that my love comes back to me, and from me be it understood, is that you are there, over there, quite alive outside of me. Out of reach. And that you send me back

[. . . .]

Example: if one morning Socrates had spoken for Plato, if to Plato his addressee he had addressed some message, it is also that p. would have had to be able to receive, to await, to desire, in a word to have *called* in a certain way what S. will have said to him; and therefore what S., taking dictation, pretends to invent—writes, right? p. has sent himself a post card (caption + picture), he has sent it back to himself from himself, or he has even "sent" himself S. And we find ourselves, my beloved angel, on the itinerary. Incalculable consequences. Go figure out then if you, at this very moment, in your name

this is the catastrophe: when he writes, when he sends, when he makes his *(a)way*, S is p, finally is no longer totally other than p (finally I don't think so at all, S will have been totally other, but if *only* he had been totally other, truly totally other, nothing would have happened between them, and we would not be at this pass, sending ourselves their names and their ghosts like ping-pong balls). pp, pS, Sp, SS, the predicate speculates in order to send itself the subject

[. . . .]

3 September 1977

[. . . .]

All the precautions in the world are taken in vain, you can register your *envois* with a return receipt, crypt them, seal them, multiply coverings and envelopes, at the limit not even send your letter, still, in advance it is intercepted. It falls into anyone's hands, a poor post card, it ends up in the display case of a provincial bookseller who classifies his merchandise by name of city (I confess that I have often dug around in them, but only for you, searching for memories of our cities that would have transited into other memories, other histories, preferentially from before we were born, in the *belle époque*). Once intercepted — a second suffices — the message no longer has any chance of reaching any determinable person, in any *(determinable)* place whatever. This has to be accepted, and *j'accepte.* But I recognize that such a certainty is unbearable, for anyone. One can only deny this self-evidence, and, by their very function, those who deny it most energetically are the people charged with the carrying of the mail, the guardians of the letter, the archivists, the professors as well as the journalists, today the psychoanalysts. The philosophers, of course, who are all of that at once, and the literature people.

[. . . .]

Plato's dream: to make Socrates write, and to make him write what he wants, his last command, *his will. To make* him write what he wants by letting *(lassen)* him write what he wants. Thereby becoming Socrates and his father, therefore his own grandfather (PP), *and killing him.* He teaches him to write. *Socrates ist Thot* (demonstration of the PP). He teaches him to live. This is their contract. Socrates signs a contract or diplomatic document, the archive of diabolical duplicity. But equally constitutes Plato, who has already composed it, as secretary or minister, he the magister. And the one to the other they show themselves in public, they analyze each other uninterruptedly, *séance tenante,* in front of everyone, with tape recorder or secretary. What happens when there is a third party in front of the couch? Or another analyst who is providing himself a *tranche?* Obliquely, the book would also deal with Freud's correspondence (or Kafka's, since this is what you want), and with the last great correspondences (still hidden, forbidden), and it would also inscribe *Le facteur de la vérité* as an appendix, with the great reference to *Beyond* . . . , to the *Symposium,* and then above all to the *Philebus* on pleasure, which Freud never cites, it seems to me, although in a way he translates or transfers its entire program. As if via so many relays Socrates had sent him a post card, already a reproduction, a stereotype, an ensemble of logical constraints that Freud in turn comes to reproduce, ineluctably, without being too aware of it, in an incredible discourse on reproduction and on the repetition compulsion.

As soon as, in a second, the first stroke of a letter

divides itself, and must indeed support partition in order to identify itself, there are nothing but post cards, anonymous morsels
without fixed domicile, without legitimate addressee, letters open,
but like crypts. Our entire library, our entire encyclopedia, our
words, our pictures, our figures, our secrets, all an immense
house of post cards. A game of post cards (I recall at the moment
that the French translation of *Beyond* . . . makes Freud's pen put
a house of cards in the place where he literally says, I think, that
his edifice of "speculative" hypotheses could crumble in an instant, at any moment). There it is, to speculate on post cards, on
shares embossed with crowned heads.

[. . . .]

5 September 1977

[. . . .]

I am teaching
you pleasure, I am telling you the limit and the paradoxes of the
apeiron, and everything begins, like the post card, with reproduction. Sophie and her followers, Ernst, Heinele, myself and company dictate to Freud who dictates to Plato, who dictates to
Socrates who himself, reading the last one (for it is he who reads
me, you see him here, you see what is written on his card in the
place where he is scratching, it is for him that is written the very
thing that he is soon going to sign), again will have forwarded.
Postmark on the stamp, obliteration, no one is any longer heard
distinctly, all rights reserved, law is the rule, but you can always
run after the addressee as well as after the sender. Run in circles,
but I promise you that you will have to run faster and faster, at a
speed out of proportion to the speed of these old networks, or in
any event to their images. Finished, the post, or finally this one,
this epoch of the destinal and of the *envoi* (of the *Geschick* the
other old man would say: everything is played out in this, once
more, and we will not get around Freiburg, let it be said in
passing. *Geschick* is destiny, of course, and therefore everything
that touches on the destination as well as on destiny, and even
on "sort"—it means "sort," as you know, and there we are close
to the *fortune-telling book*. I also like that this word *Geschick*,
which everything ends up passing through, even the thinking of

the history of Being as dispensation, and even the gift of the *"es gibt Sein"* or *"es gibt Zeit,"* I like that this word also says address, not the address of the addressee, but the skill of whoever's turn it is, in order to pull off this or that, chance too somewhat, one dictionary says the *"chic"* — I'm not making it up! And *schicken* is to send, *envoyer*, to "expedite," to cause to leave or to arrive, etc. When Being is thought *on the basis of* the gift of the *es gibt* (sorry for the simplifying stenography, this is only a letter), the gift itself is given *on the basis of* "something," which is nothing, which is not something; it would be, hmmmm, like an *"envoi,"* destination, the destinality, sorry, of an *envoi* which, of course, does not send this or that, which sends nothing that is, nothing that is a "being," a "present." Nor to whoever, to any addressee as an identifiable and self-present subject. The post is an epoch of the post, this is not very clear, and how can I write you this in a letter, and in a love letter, for this is a love letter, you have no doubt, and I say to you "come," come back quick, and if you understand it it burns up the road, all the relays, it should not suffer any halt, if you are there —

P.S. I have again overloaded them with colors, look, I made up our couple, do you like it? Doubtless you will not be able to decipher the tatoo on *plato's* prosthesis, the wooden third leg, the phantom-member that he is warming up under *Socrates'* ass.

6 September 1977 I can't go on, I would like never to miss a pickup, and at least describe to you my impatience so that you hurry up a bit.

Okay, I've calmed down, and I will profit from it by clearing up, a bit, the story of the address, finally of the *Geschick*. This is very difficult, but everything is played out there. If what is called the post in the usual sense, in the strict sense if you wish, what everyone believes they understand under this heading (a same type of service, a technology which goes from the *courrier* of Greek or Oriental antiquity, along with the messenger who runs from one place to another, etc., up to the State monopoly, the airplane, the telex, the telegram, the different kinds of mailmen and delivery, etc.), if this post is only an epoch of the *envoi* in general — and along with its *tekhnē* it also implies a million things, for example identity, the possible identification of the emitters and the receivers, of the subjects of the post and of the poles of the message — , then to speak of post for *Geschick*, to say that every *envoi* is postal, *that the destinal posts itself*, is perhaps a "metaphoric" abuse, a restriction to its strict sense of a sense which does not permit itself to be narrowed into this sense. Doubtless this is what Martin would object. Although . . . For finally, one would have to be quite confident of the notion of "metaphor" and of its entire regime (more than he himself was, but there we would have to see . . . there is also what-I-call, citation, "the metaphoric catastrophe") in order to treat the figure of the post this way. The thing is very serious, it seems to me, for if there is first, so to speak, the *envoi*, the *Schicken* reassembling itself into *Geschick*, if the *envoi* derives from nothing, then the possibility of posts is always already there, in its very retreat *[retrait]*. As soon as *there is*, as soon as it gives *(es gibt)*, it destines, it tends (hold on, when I say "come" to you, I tend to you, I tender nothing, I tender you, yourself, I tend myself toward you, I await *[attends]* you, I say to you "hold," keep what I would like to give you, I don't know what, more than me doubtless, keep, come, halt, reassemble, hold us together, us and more than you or me, we are awaited *[attendus]* by this very thing, I know neither who nor what, and so much the better, this is the condition, by that very thing which destines us, drop it), as soon as there is, then, it destines and it tends (I will show this in the preface, if I write it one day, by rereading the play of *Geben*, *Schicken*, and *Reichen* in *Zeit und Sein*). If I take my "departure" from the destination and the destiny or destining of Being *(Das Schicken im Geschick des Seins)*, no one can dream of then *forbidding me to speak* of the "post," except on the condition of making of this word the element of an image, of a figure, of a trope, a post card of Being in some way. But to do it, I mean to accuse me, to forbid me, etc., one would have to be naïvely certain of knowing what a post card or the post is. If, on the contrary (but this is not simply the contrary), I think the postal and the post card on the basis of the destinal of Being, as I think the house (of Being) on the basis of Being, of language, and not the inverse, etc., then the post is no longer a simple metaphor, and is even, as the site of all transferences and all correspondences, the "proper" possibility of every possible rhetoric. Would this satisfy Martin? Yes and no. No, because he doubtless would see in the postal determination a premature (?) imposition of *tekhnē* and therefore of metaphysics (he would accuse me, you can see it from here, of constructing a metaphysics of the posts or of postality); and above all an imposition of the *position* precisely, of determining the *envoi* of Being as position, posture, thesis or theme (*Setzung, thesis,* etc.), a gesture that he alleges *to situate,* as well as technology, within the history of metaphysics and within which would be given to think a dissimulation and a retreat *[retrait]* of Being in its *envoi.* This is where things are the most difficult: because the very idea of the retreat (proper to destination), the idea of the halt, and the idea of the epoch in which Being holds itself back, suspends, withdraws, etc., all these ideas are immediately homogenous with postal discourse. To post is to send by "counting" with a halt, a relay, or a suspensive delay, the place of a mailman, the possibility of going astray and of forgetting (not of repression, which is a moment of keeping, but of forgetting). The *epokhē* and the *Ansichhalten* which essentially scan or set the beat of the "destiny" of Being, or its "appropriation" *(Ereignis),* is the place of the postal, this is where it comes to be and that it takes place (I would say *ereignet*), that it gives place and also lets come to be. This is serious because it upsets perhaps Heidegger's still "derivative" schema (perhaps), upsets by giving one to think that technology, the position, let us say even metaphysics do not overtake, do not come *to determine* and to dissimulate an *"envoi"* of Being (which would not yet be postal), but would belong to the "first" *envoi* — which obviously is never "first" in any order whatsoever, for example a chronological or logical order, nor even the order of *logos* (this is why one cannot replace, except for laughs, the formula "in the beginning was the logos" by "in the beginning was the post"). If the post (technology, position, "metaphysics") is announced at the "first" *envoi,* then there is no longer A metaphysics, etc. (I will try to say this one more time and otherwise), nor even AN *envoi,* but *envois* without destination. For to coordinate the different epochs, halts, determinations, in a word the entire history

of Being with a destination of Being is perhaps the most outland-
ish postal lure. There is not even the post or the *envoi,* there are
posts and *envois.* And this movement (which seems to me simultaneously very far from and very near to Heidegger's, but no
matter) avoids submerging all the differences, mutations, scan-
sions, structures of postal regimes into one and the same great
central post office. In a word (this is what I would like to articulate more rigorously if I write it one day in another form), as soon
as there is, there is differance (and this does not await language,
especially human language, and the language of Being, only the
mark and the divisible trait), and there is postal maneuvering,
relays, delay, anticipation, destination, telecommunicating network, the possibility, and therefore the fatal necessity of going
astray, etc. There is strophe (there is strophe in every sense,
apostrophe and catastrophe, address in turning the address [al-
ways toward you, my love], and my post card is strophes). But
this specification gives one the possibility of assimilating none
of the differences, the (technical, eco-political, phantasmatic etc.)
differentiation of the telecommunicative powers. By no longer
treating the posts as a metaphor of the *envoi* of Being, one can
account for what essentially and decisively occurs, everywhere,
and including language, thought, science, and everything that
conditions them, when the postal structure shifts, *Satz* if you
will, and posits or posts itself otherwise. This is why this history
of the posts, which I would like to write and to dedicate to you,
cannot be a history of the posts: primarily because it concerns
the very possibility of history, of all the concepts, too, of history,
of tradition, of the transmission or interruptions, goings astray,
etc. And then because such a "history of the posts" would be but
a minuscule *envoi* in the network that it allegedly would analyze
(there is no metapostal), only a card lost in a bag, that a strike, or
even a sorting accident, can always delay indefinitely, lose without return. This is why I will not write it, but I dedicate to you
what remains of this impossible project. The (eschatological,
apocalyptic) desire for this history of the posts worldwide is
perhaps only a way, a very infantile way, of crying over the
coming end of our "correspondence" — and of sending you one
more tear.

[. . . .]

10 September 1977

[. . . .]

They are dead and they travel through us in order to step up to the cashier, not them, their name, at every instant. At this very moment. How they resemble each other. Never forget that they have existed outside their names, truly. — How is that, you say. — Well, like you and me. — Not possible? — *Mais si, mais si.* And then every word must be franked in order to be addressed to whomever. Au-to-ma-tic-al-ly. Whatever I say, whatever I do, I must paste on myself a stamp with the effigy of this diabolical couple, these unforgettable comperes, these two patient impostors. A little engraving with this royal, basilical couple, sterile but infinite in its ideal progeniture. Cynically, without a cent, they have issued a universal stamp. A postal and fiscal stamp, by making themselves appear to advance funds. And on the stamp both are to be seen in the course, the one in front of the other, in the course, *en train,* of drawing a stamp and of signing the original. And they plaster themselves on the walls. An immense poster. This is a stamp. They have signed *our* I.O.U. and we can no longer not acknowledge it. Any more than our own children. This is what tradition is, the heritage that drives you crazy. People have not the slightest idea of this, they have no need to know that they are paying (automatic withdrawal) nor whom they are paying (the name or the thing: name is the thing) when they do anything whatsoever, make war or love, speculate on the energy crisis, construct socialism, write novels, open concentration camps for poets or homosexuals, buy bread or hijack a plane, have themselves elected by secret ballot, bury their own, criticize the media without rhyme or reason, say absolutely anything about chador or the ayatollah, dream of a great safari, found reviews, teach, or piss against a tree. They can even never have heard the name of p. and of S. (hey, I see them as very chirpy, suddenly). Via all kinds of cultural, that is postal, relays they pay their tax, and no need for that to be taxed with "platonism," and even if you have overturned platonism (look at them, turn the card, when they write upside down in the plane). Of course the tax goes only to the names, that is to no one (for the "living," notice, this is not absolutely, rigorously different), since the two pilots are no longer there, only subject, submitted, underlying their names, in effigy, their heads topped by their names. No more than Hegel, Freud or Heidegger, who themselves had to put themselves into the position of legatees, from the front or the back. Standing or lying, not a movement, not a step without them. I even would like to believe that those who liberate themselves better and more quickly, those at least who desire to pay the least and to "acquit" themselves most properly, are those who attempt to deal directly with them, as if this were possible, the patient philosophers, historians, archivists who are relentless over the issuing of the stamp, who always want to know more on this subject, dream of the original imprint. Me, for example. But naturally, the busier one gets liberating oneself, the more one pays. And the less one pays, the more one pays, such is the trap of this speculation. You will not be able to account for this currency. Impossible to return it, you pay everything and you pay nothing with this Visa or Mastercharge card. It is neither true nor false. The issuing of the stamp is simultaneously immense, it imposes and is imposed everywhere, conditions every other type, *timbre*, or tympan in general; and yet, you can barely see it, it is minuscule, infinitely divisible, composes itself with billions of other obliterating positions, impositions, or superimpositions. And we, my angel, we love each other posted on this network, at the toll booth one weekend return (fortunately we can love each other *[on peut s'aimer]*, in a car), crushed by taxes, in permanent insurrection against the "past," full of acknowledgments however, and virgin from debt, as at the first morning of the world.

[. . . .]

When I am creating correspondence (which is not the case here), I mean when I write several letters consecutively, I am terrified at the moment of putting the thing under seal. And if I were to make a mistake about the addressee, invert the addresses, or put several letters into the same envelope? This happens to me, and it is rare that I do no reopen certain letters, after having failed to identify them by holding them up to the light at the moment of throwing them into the box. My sorting *[tri]* and my postal traffic is this scene.

It precedes and follows the obsession of the pickup, the other one, the next one or the one that I missed. The obsessional moment occasionally lasts beyond the imaginable. Once the letter or the lot of letters is gone (I have finally unclenched my hand), I can remain planted in front of the box as if before an irreparable crime, tempted to await the following pickup in order to seduce the *facteur* and to take everything back, in order to verify at least one last time the adequation of addresses (I did this once, but it was somewhat different, in order to intercept my own mail which was going to be "forwarded" to a place that I did not want it to go, and where it would have arrived before me) and that there is indeed only one letter, the right one, per envelope. The situation is that of a confession without a crime (as if this were possible; *mais si, mais si!*), of an exhibit which becomes the cause of a crime. In any event, this confession before the mailbox does not await that one write, I mean "missives" in the impoverished sense, but already when one speaks, when one touches, when one comes. Not only is there always some post card, but even if you leave it virgin and without address, there are several at once, and in the same envelope

[. . . .]

The Postal Prospect is henceforth the site of the psych. and po problematic (the question of women, of psychoanalysis, and of politics, it brings them all together); the question of Power, as they still say, is first of all that of the post and telecommunications, as is well known. Then one must know: that the volume of mail is going to increase by 3% per year approximately, "spread unequally," says a principal Inspector of the P. and T., "over diverse objects of correspondence, with a higher percentage for the 'economic' mail and a levelling off for 'household' mail. This increase will be congruent with the development of informational systems which, in the years to come, will overwhelm not only the highly industrialized countries, but also the rest of the world." Suppose that I write a book, let us say "Plato and telecom.," it necessarily falls into the hands of Monsieur Brégou, principal Inspector of the Posts and Telecommunications, and he decides (because I quote him) to put it on sale, as they do sometimes, in all the post offices, the proceeds for the mailmen's benefit funds. The book is displayed in every branch, it wouldn't do badly. And then the translations. What's more, while increasing the sales (the price of one or two booklets of stamps) it would make Plato penetrate the hamlets. To increase the sales, on the publisher's advice I would criticize the publishing apparatuses and the media (which are also a postal agency) and would have a band placed around the book: the only writer to refuse such and such a show. I would be invited to be on it immediately, and at the last moment, to the surprise of everyone obviously, and I would accept on the condition of being permitted to improvise freely on the postal agency in the Iranian uprising (the revolutionary role of dis-tancing, the distancing of God or of the ayatollah telekommeiny giving interviews from the Parisian suburbs) provided that I nuance it a bit the next day in one of the dailies or weeklies. A very trivial remark, the relations between posts, police and media are called upon to transform themselves profoundly, as is the amorous message (which is more and more watched over, even if it has always been), by virtue of informatization, so be it. And therefore all the networks of the p.p. (psych. and pol). But will the relations between the police, the psychoanalytic institution, and letters be essentially affected? Inevitably, and it is beginning. Could Poe adapt *The Purloined Letter* to this? Is it capable of this adaptation? Here I would bet yes, but it would be very difficult. The end of a postal epoch is doubtless also the end of literature. What seems more probable to me is that in its actual state psychoanalysis, itself, cannot read *The Purloined Letter*, can only have itself or let itself be read by it, which is also very important for the progress of this institution. In any case, the past and present of the said institution are unthinkable outside a certain postal technology, as are the public or private, that is secret, correspondences which have marked its stages and crises, supposing a very determined type of postal rationality, of relations between the State monopoly and the secret of private messages, as of their unconscious effects. That the part of "private" mail tends toward zero does not only diminish the chances of the great correspondences (the last ones, those of Freud, of Kafka), it also transforms the entire field of analytic exertion — and in both the long and the short term, with all the imaginable and unimaginable conse-

quences for the "analytic situation," the "session," and the forms
of transference. The procedures of "routing" and of distribution,
the paths of transmission, concern the very support of the messages sufficiently not to be without effect on the content, and I
am not only speaking of the signified content. The "letter" disappears, others must be found, but this will be simultaneously
the unlimited empire of a postcardization that begins with the
trait itself, before what they call writing (even before mail as
sticks-messages and as *quippos*), *and* the decadence of the post
card in the "narrow" sense, the decadence which for barely more
than a century, but as one of the last phenomena, a sign of
acceleration toward the end, is part of the "classic" postal system, of the "posta," of the *station* in the mail's making its
(a)way, of the "document" to be transmitted, support and message. In everyday language the post, in the strict sense, is distinguished from every other telecommunication (telegraph or telephone, for example, telematics in general) by this characteristic:
the transport of the "document," of its material support. A rather
confused idea, but rather useful for constructing a consensus
around the banal notion of post—and we do need one. But it
suffices to analyze this notion of "document" or of material
support a bit for the difficulties to accumulate. (You have just
called from the station, you are settling down in the train, I feel
so calm suddenly. Several hours more and I am coming to get
you.) Now, a certain form of support is in the course of disappearing, and the unconscious will have to get used to this, and this is
already in progress. I was speaking to you just now of the progres-
sive disappearance of private mail and of my terror before the
"collective" envelope. I had not read Monsier Brégou at that
moment. I have just done so. Imagine our entire history, and the
most recent history, imagine it in Monsieur Brégou's "prospect":
"The development of informational systems, as much for the
post as for the users, certainly will permit the installation of new
modalities for the transmission of information. In the years to
come, exception made for the mail of private individuals ["exception made," which one, until when?], it can be thought that it
will no longer be writing that will be transported, but the perfo-
rated card, microfilm, or magnetic tape. The day will come that,
thanks to the 'telepost,' the fundamentals will be transmitted by

wire starting from the user's computer going to the receiving organs of the computer of the post office nearest [all the same] the residence of the addressee, who will be charged with the impression of the order or the bill [his distinction between the mail of individuals and the other supposes a bit quickly that the individuals, ourselves, we send on their way something entirely other than orders and bills: in fact these great technologues always really have a metaphysician's naïveté, it's part of the same thing]. It will remain for the postal employee only to place the envelope into distribution, which moreover will be able to encompass several correspondences emanating from different senders. The traditional process thereby will find itself upset for a major portion of the mail." Yes and no: for as long as it is not proven that into each of our so secret, so hermetically sealed letters several senders, that is several addressees have not already infiltrated themselves, the upset will not have been demonstrated. If our letters are upsetting, in return, perhaps it is that already we are several on the line, a crowd, right here, at least a consortium of senders and addressees, a real shareholders' company with limited responsibility, all of literature, and yet it is true, my unique one, that Monsieur Brégou is describing my terror itself, Terror itself. He insists, with all the satisfaction of a factory boss demonstrating the new machines he has just received. And he is waiting for others which will increase the returns, for the good of all, producers and consumers, workers and bosses: "At a time when rural civilization is giving way to an ever increasing urban concentration, the post will have to adapt itself to the needs of its clientele: a painful mutation, for example when the postal traffic of certain rural areas no longer justifies the maintenance of an office, while the lack of personnel makes itself felt painfully in the large agglomerations. To get to this point, perhaps it will be necessary to upset certain habits. Why not envisage an extension of the capacities of the post [here you are going to believe that I am inventing the words for the needs of my demonstration] which, *omnipresent* by means of its offices or its *'facteurs'* [I like the way he went at it with these quotation marks], could *treat all* [my emphasis] the operations placing the population in contact with the administration?" Hey! and even the contact between THE Population and THE Administration! Why not envisage omnipresence, says he. Of the offices and the *"facteurs."* I can't decide what is most striking here: the monstrosity of this future that the principal Inspector envisages, with a beatific and quite forward-looking insouciance (while he calmly converses with us about the worst of State and trans-State police, of generalized perforization: for example S. inanalysis with P. will be able to, and even will have to, because of the traffic jams, at the time of his session, send his tape or his cards of associations — free associations of course — to the said P., passing through Monsieur Brégou's omnipresent one. And in order to insure the autonomy of the psychoanalytic institution as concerns the State, the latter would name, at the proposal of the corps of certified analysts united in a General Assembly, and no matter what group they belong to, a Commission of wise men — they could be seven, for example — which would watch over all the transferences passing through the omnipresent one, so that confidentiality will be well maintained, out of the reach of all the police, even the secret police. Naturally, so that all this remains in conformity with the psychoanalytic vocation (how is it to be called otherwise?), with the spirit and the letter of Freud, six members of the Commission of the rights of psychoanalysis would be inanalysis, at least for a time, with the seventh, who in some fashion elected by general suffrage (it is a democracy that I am describing) would have to figure things out all by himself with the omnipresent one or with one of his *facteurs*, for example Monsieur Brégou) I don't know what terrifies me the most, the monstrousness of this prospective or on the contrary its ancestral antiquity, the very normality of the thing. In its essence, of course, in its *eidos* it is more than twenty-five centuries old.

[. . . .]

25 September 1977

[. . . .]

And you're right, the "correct," expert interpretation of S. and p. will change nothing. The icon is there, much more vast than science, the support of all our fantasies. In the beginning was their own fantasy, that was to engender everything, up to the work of Paris [the engraver whose work is reproduced on the post card. — ED.] According to *Plato* it was first *Socrates* who *will have written*, having made or let him write. There is there a *souffrance de la destination* (no, not a fate neurosis, although . . .) in which I have every right to recognize myself. I am suffering (but like everyone, no? me, I know it) from a real pathology of destination: I am always addressing myself to someone else (no, to someone else still!), but to whom? I absolve myself by remarking that this is due, before me, to the power, of no matter what sign, the "first" trait, the "first" mark, to be remarked, precisely, to be repeated, and therefore divided, turned away from whatever singular destination, and this by virtue of its very possibility, its very address. It is its address that makes it into a post card that multiplies, to the point of a crowd, my addressee, female. And by the same token, of course, my addressee, male. A normal pathology, of course, but for me this is the only *meurtrière:* one kills someone by addressing a letter to him that is not destined to him, and thereby declaring one's love or even one's hatred. And I kill you at every moment, but I love you. And you can no longer doubt it, even if I destroy everything with the most amorous patience (as do you, moreover), beginning with myself. *I'm destroying my own life,* I had said to him *[lui]* in English in the car. If I address myself, as it is said, always to someone else, and otherwise (right here, again), I can no longer address myself by myself. Only to myself, you will say, finally sending me all those cards, sending me *Socrates* and *Plato* just as they send themselves to each other. No, not even, no return, it does not come back to me. I even lose the identity of the, as they say, sender, the emitter. And yet no one better than I will have known how, or rather will have loved to destine, uniquely. This is the disaster on the basis of which I love you, uniquely. You, toward whom at this very moment, even forgetting your name I address myself.

[. . . .]

P.S. I forgot, you are completely right: one of the paradoxes of destination, is that if you wanted *to demonstrate,* for someone, that something never arrives at its destination, it's all over. The demonstration, once it had reached its end, would have proved what it was not supposed to demonstrate. But this is why, dear friend, I always say "a letter *can* always *not* arrive at its destination, etc." This is a chance.*

You know that I never say that I'm right and never demonstrate anything. They support this very badly, consequently they would like nothing to have happened, everything wiped off the map. Wait for me.

* P.S. Well, a chance, if you will, if you yourself can, and if you have it, the chance (*tukhē*, fortune, this is what I mean, good fortune, good fate: us). The mischance (the mis-address) of this chance is that in order *to be able* not to arrive, it must bear within itself a force and a structure, a straying of the destination, such that it *must* also not arrive in any way. Even in arriving (always to some "subject"), the letter takes itself away *from the arrival at arrival.* It arrives elsewhere, always several times. You can no longer take hold of it. It is the structure of the letter (as post card, in other words the fatal partition that it must support) which demands this, I have said it elsewhere, delivered to a *facteur* subject to the same law. The letter demands this, right here, and you too, you demand it.

[. . . .]

A day in May 1978

[. . . .]

I truly believe that I am singing someone who is dead and whom I did not know. I am not singing for the dead (this is the truth according to Genet), I am singing a death, *for* a dead man or woman already *[déjà].* Although since the gender and number remain inaccessible for me I can always play on the plural. And multiply the examples or working hypotheses, the hypotheses of mourning.

Thus I have lost my life writing in order to give this song a chance, unless it were in order to let it silence itself, by itself. You understand that whoever writes must indeed ask himself what it is asked of him to write, and then he writes under the dictation of some addressee, this is trivial. But "some addressee," I always leave the gender or number indeterminate, must indeed be the object of a choice of object, and chosen and seduced. "Some addressee" winds up then, to the extent that the approach, the approximation, the appropriation, the "introjection," all progress, no longer able to ask anything that has not already been whispered *[soufflé]* by me. Thereby everything is corrupted, there is only the mirror, no more image, they no longer see each other, no longer destine each other, nothing more. Do you think that this exhaustion is happening to us? We would have loved each other too much. But it is you I still love, the living one. Beyond everything, beyond your name, your name beyond your name.

[. . . .]

15 June 1978

[. . . .]

You are my only double, I suppose, I speculate, I postulate,

in sum everything that sets me on the march today, the entire postulate of my practical reason, all my heart, and I speculate on you, you are now the name, yourself, or the title of everything that I do not understand. That I never will be able to know, the other side of myself, eternally inaccessible, not unthinkable, at all *[du tout]*, but unknowable, unknown — and so lovable. As for you, my love, I can only postulate (for who else, with whom would I have dreamed this?) the immortality of the soul, liberty, the union of virtue and happiness, and that one day you might love me.

[. . . .]

9 October 1978

[. . . .]

from the very first *envoi:* no gift, gift step *[pas de don]*, without absolute forgetting (which also absolves you of the gift, *don*, and of the dose), forgetting of what you give, to whom, why and how, of what you remember about it or hope. A gift, if there is one, does not destine itself.

[....]

[....]

the end of my delirium around S and p. Prose begins here, starting with the expertise of the doctor who comes to teach me how to read the card. I had called him in for a consultation and here is his answer (he is writing to J.C., you recall that he had offered to take on this mission to the *Kunstgeschichte* specialist): "Dear Sir, your question can be answered quite simply. One has but to read the miniature verbally. Socrates is in the course of writing. Plato is beside him, but is not dictating. He is showing, with his index finger pointed toward Socrates: Here is the great man. With the left index finger he is drawing the attention of the spectators, who must be imagined more to the right toward the philosopher who is writing. Therefore he is rather subordinate, of lesser size and with a more modest headpiece. Please accept my kindest regards." He has to be believed, he is right. "Read verbally" must mean "literally." I am persuaded that he is literally right, and the entire context that one might imagine (and of which he himself has knowledge), the code which governs the gestures and positions in all this iconography, all of this, I have never doubted it, makes him right, and me too. It is I who should have read somewhat "verbally" and thereby unleashed literality. He reminds me a bit of Schapiro in his diagnosis. That being said, if I were given the time, I could demonstrate that nothing in my delirium is literally incompatible with his "very simple" answer, all that I'm doing is developing it a bit, and this is our history, and our difference. Moreover, the expert can be objective only in the extent (what an extent) to which his place is designated, assigned on the card, in the picture, and not facing it: a moment of the desire for objectivity, a tremor of the epistēmē whose origin regards you here in two persons. They are setting you, literally, and with a shake of the wand, on the way: know clearly, know clearly that, it must indeed be known, here is the truth of the picture, hold it close, the answer is very simple. Useless to lift up so many robes, it tears out the eyes.

[. . . .]

February 1979

I would still like to convince you. By publishing that which, concerning the post card, looks like a "post card" (let's say the brief sequence of a secret correspondence between Socrates and Freud conversing with each other at the bottom of the post card, about the support, the message, the inheritance, telecommunications, the *envoi*, etc.), we will finish off destruction. Of the holocaust there would remain only the most anonymous support without support, that which in any event never will have belonged to us, does not regard us. This would be like a purification of purification by fire. Not a single trace, an absolute camouflaging by means of too much evidence: cards on the table, they won't see anything else. They will throw themselves onto unintelligible remainders, come from who knows where in order to preface a book about Freud, about the Platonic inheritance, the era of the posts, the structure of the letter and other common goods or places. The secret of what we will have destroyed will be even more thoroughly destroyed or, amounting to the same thing, by all the evidence, with all its self-evidence more thoroughly preserved. Don't you think? Never will I have loved so much. And by means of the demonstration that only *is* [*est*] the post card, beyond everything that is, we will remain to be reborn. We will begin to love each other. I also like the cruelty of this scene, it still resembles, it resembles you. And then I would operate such that it would become absolutely i l l e g i b l e for you. You will recognize nothing yourself, you will feel nothing, and when you read even I will pass unnoticed. After this final murder we will be more alone than ever, I will continue to love you, living, beyond you.

[. . . .]

February 1979

I am reflecting upon a rather rigorous principle of destruction. What will we burn, what will we keep (in order to broil it better still)? The selection *[tri]*, if it is possible, will in truth be postal: I would cut out, in order to deliver it, everything that derives from the Postal Principle, in some way, in the narrow or wide sense (this is the difficulty, of course), everything that might preface, propose itself for a treatise on the posts (from Socrates to Freud and beyond, a *psychoanalysis of the post*, a *philosophy of the post*, the *of* signifying belonging or provenance, psychoanalysis or philosophy operating *since, on the basis of* the posts, I would almost say: on the basis of the nearest post office, etc.). And we burn the rest. Everything that from near or far touches on the post card (this one, in which one sees Socrates reading us, or writing all the others, and every post card in general), all of this we would keep, or finally would doom to loss by publishing it, we would hand it over to the antiques dealer or the auctioneer. The rest, if there is any that remains, is us, is for us, who do not belong to the card. We are the card, if you will, and as such, accountable, but they will seek in vain, they will never find us in it. In several places I will leave all kinds of references, names of persons and of places, authentifiable dates, identifiable events, they will rush in with eyes closed, finally believing to be there and to find us there when by means of a switch point I will send them elsewhere to see if we are there, with a stroke of the pen or the *grattoir* I will make everything derail, not at every instant, that would be too convenient, but occasionally and according to a rule that I will not ever give, even were I to know it one day. I would not work too hard composing the thing, it is a scrap copy of scrapped paths that I will leave in their hands. Certain people will take it into their mouths, in order to recognize the taste, occasionally in order to reject it immediately with a grimace, or in order to bite, or to swallow, in order to conceive, even, I mean a child.

[. . . .]

15 March 1979

The difficulty I would have in sorting out this *courrier* with the aim of publication is due, among other perils, to this one: you know that I do not believe in propriety, property, and above all not in the form that it takes according to the opposition public—

private (p–p, so be it). This opposition doesn't work, neither for psychoanalysis (especially with the tranche-ferential sectoring that is being lowered onto the capitals like a net that they themselves can no longer master: this is the fatality of the parallel police forces), nor for the post (the post card is neither private nor public), nor even for the police (they leave us, whatever the regime, only the choice between several police forces, and when a pp [public police] doesn't accost you in the street, another pp [private parallel police] plugs its microphones into your bed, seizes your mail, makes you spit it out in full ecstasy — and the secret circulates with full freedom, as secret you promise I swear, this is what I call a post card.)

[. . . .]

May 1979

It's the end of an epoch. The end of a race also or of a banquet that is dragging on until the small hours of morning (I no longer know to whom I was saying that "epoch" — and this is why I am interrogating myself on this subject — remains, because of the halt, a postal idea, contaminated in advance by *postal* differance, and therefore by the station, the thesis, the position, finally by the *Setzen* (by the *Gesetzheit des Sichsetzens* that he talks about in *Zeit und Sein*). The postal principle *does not happen to differance,* and even less to "Being," it destines them to itself from the very "first" *envoi.* Now there are also differences, there is only that, in postal differance; one can still, by means of a figure folded back over onto itself, name them "epochs" or subepochs. In the great epoch (the technology of which is marked by paper, pen, the envelope, the individual subject addressee, etc.) and which goes shall we say from Socrates to Freud and Heidegger, there are subepochs, for example the process of state monopolization, and then within this the invention of the postage stamp and the Berne convention, to use only such insufficient indices. Each epoch has its literature (which in *general* I hold to be essentially detective or epistolary literature, even if within it the detective or epistolary genre more or less strictly folds it back onto itself).

Here Freud and Heidegger, I conjoin them within me like the two great ghosts of the "great epoch." The two surviving grandfathers. They did not know each other, but according to me they form a couple, and in fact just because of that, this singular anachrony. They are bound to each other without reading each other and without corresponding. I have often spoken to you about this situation, and it is this picture that I would like to describe in *Le legs:* two thinkers whose glances never crossed and who, without ever receiving a word from one another, say the same. They are turned to the same side.

The master-thinkers are also masters of the post. Knowing well how to play with the *post restante.* Knowing how not to be there and how to be strong for not being there right away. Knowing how not to deliver on command, how to wait and to make wait, for as long as what there is that is strongest within one demands — and to the point of dying without mastering anything of the final destination. The post is always *en reste,* and always *restante.* It awaits the addressee who might always, *by chance,* not arrive.

And the postal principle is no longer a principle, nor a transcendental category; that which announces itself or sends itself under this heading (among other possible names, like you) no longer sufficiently belongs to the epoch of Being to submit itself to some transcendentalism, "beyond every genre." The post is but a little message, fold *(pli),* or just as well. A relay in order to mark that there is never anything but relays.

Nancy, do you remember Nancy?

In a word, this is what I am trying to explain to him. *Tekhnē* (and doubtless he would have considered the postal structure and everything that it governs as a *determination* (yes, precisely, your word), a metaphysical and technical determination of the *envoi* or of the destinality (*Geschick,* etc.) of Being; and he would have considered my entire insistence on the posts as a metaphysics corresponding to the technical era that I am describing, the end of a certain post, the dawn of another, etc.); now *tekhnē,* this is the entire — infinitesimal and decisive — differance, *does not arrive.* N o more than metaphysics, therefore, and than positionality; always, already it parasites that to which he says it happens, arrives, or that it succeeds in happening to *[arrive à arriver]*. This infinitesimal nuance changes everything in the relation between metaphysics and its doubles or its others.

Tekhnē does not happen to language or to the poem, to *Dichtung* or to the song, understand me: this can mean simultaneously that it does not succeed in touching them, getting into them, it leaves them virgin, not happening to arrive up to them *[n'arrivant pas à arriver jusqu'à eux]*, and yet it has to happen to them like an accident or an event because it inhabits them and occasions them.

[. . . .]

The entire history of postal *tekhnē* tends to rivet the destination to identity. To arrive, to happen would be to a subject, to happen to "me." Now a mark, whatever it may be, is coded in order to make an imprint, even if it is a perfume. Henceforth it divides itself, *it is valid several times in one time:* no more unique addressee. This is why, by virtue of this divisibility (the origin of reason, the mad origin of reason and of the principle of identity), *tekhnē* does not happen to language — which is why and what I sing to you.

[. . . .]

May 1979

What cannot be said above all must not be silenced, but written. Myself, I am a man of speech, I have never had anything to write. When I have something to say I say it or say it to myself, basta. You are the only one to understand why it really was necessary that I write exactly the opposite, as concerns axiomatics, of what I desire, what I know my desire to be, in other words you: living speech, presence itself, proximity, the proper, the guard, etc. I have necessarily written upside down — and in order to surrender to Necessity.

[. . . .]

End of June 1979

[. . . .]

I also thought that upon reading this sorted mail *[courier trié]* they could think that I alone am sending these letters to myself: as soon as they are sent off they get to me (I remain the first and last to read them) by means of the trajectory of a "combined" emitter–receiver. By means of this banal setup I would be the earpiece of what I tell myself. And, if you are following closely, *a priori* this gets to its destination, with all the sought-after effects. Or further, which amounts to the same, I find the best means to find myself *a priori*, in the course of awaiting or reaching myself, everywhere that it arrives, always here and there simultaneously, *fort und da*. So then it always arrives at its destination. Hey! this is a good definition of "ego" and of fantasy, at bottom. But there it is, I am speaking of something else, of you and of Necessity.

[. . . .]

30 July 1979

[. . . .]

if fire's due is impossible to delimit, by virtue of the lexicon and the "themes," it is not for the usual reason (give fire its due, light counter-fires in order to stop the progression of a blaze, avoid a holocaust). On the contrary, the necessity of everything *[du tout]* announces itself terribly, the fatality of saving everything from destruction: what is there, rigorously, in our letters that does not derive from the *forta:da*, from the vocabulary of going–coming, of the step, of the way or the away, of the near and the far, of all the frameworks in *tele-*, of the adestination, of the address and the maladdress, of everything that is passed and comes to pass between Socrates and Plato, Freud and Heidegger, of the "truth," of the *facteur*, *"du tout,"* of the transference, of the inheritance and of the geneaology, of the paradoxes of the nomination, of the king, of the queen and of their ministers, of the magister and of the ministries, of the private or public detectives? Is there a word, a letter, an atom of a message that rigorously speaking *should* not be withdrawn from the burning with the aim of publication?

To take an example, the most trivial and innocent example, when I write to you *"je vais mal,"* the phrase already derives from the thematics and the lexicon, in any event from the rhetoric of *going*, the *aller*, or the step, which form the subject of the three essays just as it belongs to the corpus of S/p. If i circumcise, and I will, it will have to bleed around the edges, and we will put in their hands, under their eyes, shards of our body, of what is most secret in our soul

[. . . .]

Perhaps they are going to find this writing too adroit, virtuosic in the art of turning away, perhaps perverse in that it can be approached from everywhere and nowhere, certainly abandoned to the other, but given over to itself, offered up to its own blows, up to the end reserving everything for itself. Why, they ask themselves, incessantly let the destination divide itself? You too, perhaps, my love, you too question yourself, but this perversion, first of all, I treat. It is not my own, it belongs to this writing that you, you alone, know me to be sick of. But the song of innocence, if you love me, you will let it come to you, it will arrive for you.

[. . . .]

8 August 1979

Who *will prove* that the sender is the same man, or woman? And the male or female addressee? Or that they are *not* identical? To themselves, male or female, first of all? They they do or do not form a couple? Or several couples? Or a crowd? Where would the principle of identification be? In the name? No, and then whoever wants to make a proof becomes a participant in our corpus. They would not prevent us from loving each other. And they would love us as one loves counterfeiters, imposters, *contre-facteurs* (this word has been looking for me for years): while believing that they are still dreaming of truth, authenticity, sincerity, and that out of what they burn they are paying homage to what they burn. One can only love that, the truth (ask Freud's uncle). Do you believe that one can love that, truly?

and you, you would have made me give birth

to the truth? Stretched out on my back, you know the scene well, I would have asked you, every night, "tell me the truth." And you, "but I have nothing to say to you myself." I wind up believing it. While waiting I talk and you listen, you understand more or less nothing, but this has not the slightest kind of importance

for this reason

Plato loved Socrates and his vengeance will last until the end of time.

but when the syngram has been published, he no longer will have anything to do with it, or with anyone — completely elsewhere —, the literary post will forward it by itself, q.e.d. This has given me the wish, *envie* (this is indeed the word), to publish under my name things that are inconceivable, and above all unlivable, for *me*, thus abusing the "editorial" credit that I have been laboriously accumulating for years, with this sole aim in mind. Will anyone let himself be fooled by such an intensely political demonstration? They are going to tell me again that I would not sign just anything: *prove it*

[. . . .]

— *Translated by Alan Bass*

TWENTY-ONE

From "To Speculate — on 'Freud'," in *The Post Card*

("Spéculer — sur 'Freud'," in *La Carte postale* [1980])

In a brief preface to his first published essay devoted to Freud, "Freud and the Scene of Writing" (in *Writing and Difference* [1967]), Derrida signaled several important ways in which deconstruction resembles psychoanalysis: both are concerned with the analysis of a repression that fails to prevent the return of the repressed in the form of symptoms; both bring out the enigma of presence as a duplication, an originary repetition; both discern the relation between consciousness or the "preconscious" and the *phōnē* or "verbal representation." And yet, writes Derrida, "despite the appearances, the deconstruction of logocentrism is not a psychoanalysis of philosophy." Because Freudian concepts belong to the history of metaphysics and are thus part of the logocentric repression, they cannot supply the conceptual tools for its deconstruction. This complicity of psychoanalysis and metaphysics has to be discerned at work behind Freud's persistence in seeking purely scientific or empirical grounds for the enterprise of psychoanalysis as a theory and a practice, as well as in his insistence on setting aside any consideration of the philosophical precedents of his own thought.

In "To Speculate — on 'Freud'," Derrida undertakes a long reading of Freud's *Beyond the Pleasure Principle,* a work whose "speculative" character has long divided the psychoanalytic institution. There, Freud sets out from the question of whether there is any evidence for a death drive, that is, a drive not governed by the pleasure principle and therefore unaccounted for by psychoanalysis which has understood the psychic mechanism as wholly under the sway of the latter principle. Derrida proposes to follow Freud step by step on his speculative voyage in order to remark the curious procedure of this text which consists in taking a step (beyond the pleasure principle) only to take it back in the next step. This cancelling cadence of the impossible step beyond is repeated in each of the seven chapters. Derrida calls this cadence that of "l'athèse," both the thesis and the "athesis," a posing and a suspending of the thesis of the death drive that compels its own repetition. The repetition compulsion, which Freud poses — and dismisses — as evidence of a death drive, is thus not only an *object* of this discourse, but its motive or driving force as well. The discourse on repetition repeats.

At stake in Freud's speculations is the institution of psychoanalysis both as a properly scientific (i.e., nonspeculative) science and as an original knowledge, not indebted to some antecedent discourse, for example philosophy. And since, unlike any other scientific discipline, psychoanalysis is bound up with the name of its founder, at stake, Derrida argues, is the properness of Freud's name. He relates the structure of a compulsive repetition to the structure of an impossible bequest of the name to itself, the name inheriting from itself. The scene of inheritance is brought out with particular complexity in Derrida's reading of the famous second chapter where Freud describes his observation and analysis of the *"fort/da"* game invented by a child who happened to be his grandson. This reading is excerpted at length below. (For further comments on "To Speculate — on 'Freud'," see above, my introduction, pp. **xxvi-xxviii.**)

To Speculate — on "Freud"

The title of this chapter, "Freud's Legacy," is a deliberately corrupt citation, which doubtless will have been recognized. The expression *legs de Freud*[1] is often encountered in the writings of Jacques Lacan and Wladimir Granoff. Naturally I leave the reader as judge of what is going on in this corruption.

This chapter was first published in the issue of *Etudes freudiennes* devoted to Nicolas Abraham. I had then prefaced it with this note:

> Extract of a seminar held in 1975 at *l'Ecole normale supérieure* under the heading *Life death*. Maria Torok, who became aware of this last year, told me that she was sensitive to certain intersections, convergences, affinities with some of the still unpublished works of Nicolas Abraham, among those which soon will appear in *L'Ecorce et le noyau* (*Anasemies* II, Aubier-Flammarion, coll. "La philosophie en effet"). This is what has encouraged me to publish this fragment here. Those who wish to delimit its import can also consider it as a reading of the second chapter of *Beyond the Pleasure Principle*. At this determined stage of the seminar, the question was to examine the (problematic and textual) specificity of *Beyond . . .*, of rebinding what is irreducible about a "speculation" with the economy of a scene of writing, which itself is inseparable from a scene of inheritance implicating both the Freuds and the psychoanalytic "movement." The session immediately preceding this one had specified the space of this investigation and the singularity of Freud's *speculative procedure [dé-*

marche]. This session had proposed some abbreviations, for example PP for pleasure principle, PR for reality principle.[2] Other fragments of the same seminar will appear soon in book form.

The "Same Roof" of the Autobiography

Nothing yet has contradicted or in any way contested the authority of a PP which always comes back *[revient]* to itself, modifies itself, delegates itself, represents itself without ever leaving itself *[se quitter]*. Doubtless, in this return to itself there may be, as we have demonstrated, the strict implication of a haunting by something *totally other*. The return never "acquits" the speculation of the PP. Doubtless it is never quits with it because it *takes place* within the PP it(him)self, and indebts it (him) at every *step [pas]*. And yet in Freud's discourse, let us say in the discourse of a certain speculator, on the subject of the PP which never quits itself, and therefore always speaks of it(him)self, nothing yet has contradicted the authority of the first principle. Perhaps it is that this PP cannot be contradicted. What is done without it (him), if anything is, will not *contradict*: first because it will not oppose itself to the PP (it will be done without him in him, with his own step without him), and then because it will be done without him by not saying anything, by stifling itself, inscribing itself in silence. As soon as it speaks it submits to the authority of the absolute master, the PP which (who) as such cannot be quiet. But which (who), by the same token, lets the other ventriloquate it (him): in silence then.

At the end of the first chapter the PP is thus confirmed in its absolute sovereignty. Whence the necessity of new problematics, of "fresh questions bearing upon our present problem."

Now, if one attempts to pay attention to the original modality of the "speculative," and to the singular *proceeding [démarche]* of this writing, its *pas de thèse*[3] which advances without advancing, without advancing itself, without ever advancing anything that it does not immediately take back, for the time of a detour, without ever positing anything that remains in its position, then one must recognize that the following chapter repeats, in place and in another place, the immobile *emplacement* of the *pas de thèse*. It repeats itself, it illustrates only the repetition of that very thing (the absolute authority of the PP) which finally will not let anything be done without it (him), except repetition itself. In any event, despite the richness and novelty of the content adduced in the second chapter, despite several marching orders and steps forward, not an inch of ground is gained; not one decision, not the slightest advance in the question which occupies the speculator, the question of the PP as absolute master. This chapter nonetheless is one of the most famous in *Beyond* . . . , the one often retained in the exoteric, and occasionally the esoteric, space of psychoanalysis as one of the most important, and even decisive, chapters of the essay. Notably because of the story of the spool and of the *fort/da*. And as the repetition compulsion *(Weiderholungszwang)* is put into communication with the death drive, and since in effect a repetition compulsion seems to dominate the scene of the spool, it is believed that this story can be reattached to the exhibition, that is, the demonstration, of the said death drive. This is due to not having read: the speculator retains *nothing* of this story about the *fort/da*, at least in the demonstration in view of a beyond of the PP. He alleges that he can still explain it thoroughly within the space of the PP and under its authority. And, in effect, he succeeds. It is indeed the story of the PP that he is telling us, a certain episode of its fabulous reign, to be sure an important moment of its (his) own genealogy, but still a moment of it(him)self.

I do not mean to say that this chapter is without interest, nor, above all, that the anecdote of the spool is without import. Quite to the contrary: it is simply that its import is perhaps not inscribed in the register of the *demonstration* whose most apparent and continuous thread is held in the question: are we correct, we psychoanalysts, to *believe* in the absolute domination of the PP? Where is this import inscribed, then? And in what place that could be both under the *mouvance*[4] of the PP, the graphics we pointed out the last time, and, simultaneously, the *mouvance* of the speculative writing of this essay, that which commits the essay to the stakes of this speculative writing?

Let us first extract a skeleton: the argumentative framework of the chapter. We observe that something repeats itself. And (has this ever been done?) the repetitive process must be identified not only in the content, the examples, and the material described and analyzed by Freud, but already, or again, in Freud's writing, in the *démarche* of his text, in what he does as much as in what he says, in his "acts," if you will, no less than in his "objects." (If Freud were his grandson, one would have to attend to repetition on the side of the gesture, and not only on the side of the *fort/da* of the spool, of the object. But let us not shuffle the cards; who said that Freud was his own grandson?) What repeats itself more obviously in this chapter is the speculator's indefatigable motion in order to reject, to set aside, to make disappear, to distance *(fort)*, to defer everything that appears to put the PP into question. He observes every time that something does not suffice, that something must be put off until further on, until later. Then he makes the hypothesis of the beyond come back *[revenir]* only to dismiss it again. This hypothesis comes back *[revient]* only as that which has not truly come back *[revenu]*, that which has only passed by in the specter of its presence.

Keeping, at first, to the argumentative framework, to the logical course of the demonstration, we observe that after having treated the example of traumatic neurosis, Freud renounces, abandons, resigns himself. He proposes to leave this obscure theme *(Ich mache nun den Vorschlag, das dunkle und düstere Thema der traumatischen Neurose zu verlassen ...). First dismissal.*

But after having treated "children's play," the anecdote of the spool and of the *fort/da*, Freud renounces, abandons, resigns himself again: "No certain decision *(keine sichere Entscheidung)* can be reached from the analysis of a single case like this".[5] *Second dismissal.* But what kind of singularity is this? Why is it important, and why does it lead to disqualification? Then, after another wave, another attempt to derive something from children's play, Freud renounces, abandons, resigns himself: "Nor shall we be helped in our hesitation between these two views by further considering children's play" (16). *Third dismissal.* Finally, the last words of the chapter. Freud has just invoked games and the imitative drives in art, an entire aesthetics oriented by the economic point of view. He concludes: "They are of no use for *our* purposes, since they presuppose the existence and dominance *[Herrschaft,* mastery] of the pleasure principle; they give no evidence of the operation [*Wirksamkeit*, being-at-work] of tendencies *beyond* the pleasure principle, that is, of tendencies more primitive *(ursprünglicher)* than it and independent of it" (17). *Fourth dismissal.* (Let us retain this code of mastery and of service or servitude; it will be less and less indifferent for us here. It can appear strange when in question are the relations between principles, and it is not *immediately* explained by the fact that a principle *(archē)* is both at the beginning and in command within language.)

This is the conclusion of the chapter. We have not advanced one step, only steps for nothing on the path of the manifest investigation. It repeats itself in place. And yet, in this foot-stamping, repetition insists, and if these determined repetitions, these contents, kinds, examples of repetition do not suffice to dethrone the PP, at least the repetitive form, the reproduction of the repetitive, reproductivity itself will have begun to work without saying anything, without saying anything other than itself silencing itself, somewhat in the way it is said on the last page that the death drives say nothing. They seem to accomplish their work without themselves being remarked, putting into their service the master himself who continues to speak out loud, the PP. In what can no longer even be called the "form" of the text, of a text without content, without thesis, without an object that is detachable from its detaching operation, in the *démarche* of *Beyond* . . . , this has come to pass in the same way, even before it is a question of the death drive in person. And even without one ever being able to speak of the death drive in person.

Such would be the de-monstration. Let us not abuse this facile play on words. The de-monstration makes its proof without showing [*montrer*], without offering any conclusion as evidence, without giving anything to carry away, without any available thesis. It proves according to another mode, but by marching to its *pas de démonstration*. It transforms, it transforms itself in its process rather than advancing the signifiable object of a discourse. It tends to fold into itself everything that it makes explicit, to bend it all to itself. The *pas de démonstration* is of that which remains in this *restance*.

Let us come back briefly to the content exhibited by this second chapter.

Among the new materials called upon at the end of the first chapter, among the questions that seem to resist the analytic explanation dominated by the PP, there are the so-called traumatic neuroses. The war has just given rise to great numbers of them. The explanation of the disorder by organic lesions has shown itself to be insufficient. The same syndrome (subjective ailments, for example melancholia or hypochondria, motor symptoms, enfeeblement and disturbance of mental capacities), is seen elsewhere, without any mechanical violence. In order to define the trauma, one must then distinguish between *fear (Furcht)* and *anxiety*. The first is provoked by the *presence* of a *known* and *determined* dangerous object; the second is related to an *unknown*, indeterminate danger; as a preparation for danger, anxiety is more a protection against trauma; linked to repression, it appears at first to be an effect, but later, in *Inhibition, Symptom and Anxiety* Freud will say, *a propos* of Little Hans, that anxiety produces repression. Neither fear (before a *determined* and *known* danger) nor anxiety (before an *unknown* and *indeterminate* danger) causes trauma; only fright *(Schreck)*—which actually puts one face to face with an *unknown* and *determined* danger for which one was not prepared, and against which anxiety could not protect—can do so.

Now what does one observe in the case of the fright that induces the so-called traumatic neuroses? For example that dreams—the most trustworthy method of investigating deep mental processes, Freud says at this point—have the tendency to reproduce the traumatic accident, the situation of fright. Here, Freud pirouettes curiously. Since it is granted, or if it is granted, that the predominant tendency of the dream is wish-fulfillment, how is one to understand what a dream reproducing a situation of violent unpleasure might be? Except by granting that in this case the function of the dream has been subject to an alteration that turns it away from its aim, or again by evoking "mysterious masochistic trends." At this point Freud drops these two hypotheses (but why?), to pick them up later, in chapter IV, at the moment of the most unrestrained speculation. He will admit then that certain dreams are the exception to the rule of wish fulfillment, which itself can be constituted only late, when all of psychic life has submitted itself to a PP whose beyond is then envisaged. He also will admit (in chapter IV) the operation of masochism, and even, contrary to what he had held previously, of a primary masochism. But for the moment, Freud drops these hypotheses, which, from the point of view of the rhetoric of the investigation, might appear unjustified. In an arbitrary and decisive style, he proposes to leave there the obscure theme of the traumatic neurosis, and to study the way the psychic apparatus works "in one of its earliest *normal* activities—I mean in children's play" (14).

Thus, he is in a hurry to get to this point, at the risk of abandoning an unsolved problem that he will have to come back to later, and especially at the risk of having the demonstration of a beyond of the PP not advance at all (which in effect will be the case). What is at stake in this haste, therefore, is something other, of another order. This *urgency* cannot be deciphered in the import of the demonstrative declaration, the manifest argumentation. The only justification for proceeding this way, in terms of classical logic or rhetoric, would be the following: one must first *come back [revenir]* to "normality" (but then why not begin with it?), and to the "earliest," most precocious normality in the child (but then why not begin with it?). When the normal and original processes will have been explored, the question of the traumatic neuroses will be taken up again. The problematic of the binding of energy then will have disengaged a more propitious space; the question of masochism also will be taken up again when the notions of topical agencies, of narcissism, and of the Ego will have been more fully elaborated.

Let us begin then with the "normal" and the "original": the child, the child in the typical and normal activity usually attributed to him, play. Apparently this is an activity entirely subject to the PP—and it will be shown that indeed it is, and entirely under the surveillance of a PP which (who) nevertheless permits it(him)self to be worked upon in silence by its (his) other —and as unaffected as possible by the second principle, the PR.

And then the argument of the spool. I am saying argument, the legendary argument, because I do not yet know what name to give it. It is neither a narrative, nor a story, nor a myth, nor a fiction. Nor is it the system of a theoretical demonstration. It is fragmentary, without conclusion, selective in what it gives to be read, more an argument in the sense of a schema made of dotted lines, or with ellipses everywhere.

And then what is given to be read here, this legend, is already too legendary, overburdened, obliterated. To give it a title is already to accredit the deposit or the consignment, that is, the investiture. As for the immense literature whose investment this legendary argument has attracted to itself, I would like to attempt a partial and naïve reading, as naïve and spontaneous as possible. As if I were interesting myself for the first time in the first time of the thing.

Initially, I remark this: this is the first time in this book that we have an apparently autobiographical, indeed domestic, piece. The appearance is veiled, of course, but all the more significant. Of the experience Freud says he has been the witness. The motivated witness. It took place in his family, but he says nothing about this. Moreover we know this just as we know that the motivated witness was none other than the child's grandfather. "I lived under the same roof as the child and his parents for some weeks . . ." (14). Even if an experiment[6] could ever be limited to observation, the conditions as they are defined were not those of an observation. The speculator was not in a situation to observe. This can be concluded in advance from what he himself says in order to accredit the seriousness of his discourse. The protocols of experimentation, including sufficient observation ("It was more than a mere fleeting observation, for I lived under the same roof as the child and his parents for some weeks . . ."), guarantee the observation only by making of the observer a participant. But what was his part? Can he determine it himself? The question of objectivity has not the slightest pertinence here—nor does any epistemological question in canonic form—for the primary and sole reason that the experiment and its account will pretend to nothing less than a genealogy of objectivity in general. How, then, can they be subject to the authority of the tribunal whose institution they repeat? But inversely, by what right is a tribunal forbidden to judge the conditions of its establishment? and, what is more, forbidden to judge the account, by a motivated witness, a participant, of the said establishment? Especially if the involved witness gives all the signs of a very singular concern: for example, that of producing the institutions of his desire, of grafting his own genealogy onto it, of making the tribunal and the juridical tradition his inheritance, his delegation as a "movement," his legacy, his *own*.[7] I will indeed refrain from insisting on the syntax of his *own*. Both so that you will not get lost right away, and because I suspect that he *himself* has a hard time recognizing *himself* among his own. Which would not be unrelated to the origin of objectivity. Or at least of this experiment, and the singular account we are given of it.

What is given is first filtered, selected, actively delimited. This discrimination is in *part* declared at the border. The speculator who does not yet say that he has truly begun to speculate (this will be on the fourth day, for there are seven chapters in this strangely composed book: we will come back to this), acknowledges this discrimination. He has not sought "to include the whole field covered by these phenomena." He has only retained the characteristics pertinent to the economic point of view. Economic: this might already be translated, if one plays a bit (play is not yet forbidden in this phase of the origin of everything, of the present, the object, language, work, seriousness, etc.), but not gratuitously, as point of view of the *oikos*, law of the *oikos*, of the proper as the domestico-familial and even, by the same token, as we will verify, as the domestico-funerary.[8] The grandfather speculator does not yet say that he has begun to speculate in broad daylight (the daylight will be for the fourth day, and yet), he will never say that he is the grandfather, but he knows that this is an open secret, *le secret de Polichinelle*. Secret for no one. The grandfather speculator justifies the accounts he is giving, and the discrimination he operates in them, in broad daylight. The justification is precisely the economic point of view. Which until now has been neglected by the "different theories of children's play," and which also constitutes the privileged point of view for *Beyond. . .*, for what he who here holds or renders the accounts is doing, to wit, writing. "These theories attempt to discover the motives which lead children to play, but they fail to bring into the foreground the *economic* motive, the consideration of the yield of pleasure *(Lustgewinn)* involved. Without wishing to include the whole field covered by these phenomena, I have been able, through a chance opportunity which presented itself, to throw some light upon the first game invented by himself *(das erste selbstgeschaffene Spiel)* that was played by a little boy of one and a half. It was more than a mere fleeting observation, for I lived under the same roof as the child and his parents for some weeks, and it was some time before I discovered the meaning of the puzzling activity which he constantly repeated" (14; sl. mod.).

He has profited from an opportunity, a chance, he says. About the possibility of this chance he says nothing. From the immense discourse which might inundate us here, but which is held back, let us retain only this: the opportune chance has as its propitious terrain neither the family (the narrow family, the small family in its nucleus of two generations: Freud would not have invoked the opportune chance if he had observed one of his nearest, son, daughter, wife, brother or sister, mother or father), nor the nonfamily (several weeks under the same roof is a familial experience). The field of the experiment is therefore of the type: family vacationcy.[9] A supplement of generation always finds here reason to employ or deploy its desire.

From the first paragraph of the account on, a single trait to characterize the object of the observation, the action of the game: repetition, repeated repetition *(andauernd wiederholte Tun)*. That is all. The other characteristic ("puzzling," *rätselhafte*) describes nothing, is void, but with a vacancy that calls out, and calls for, like every enigma, a narrative. It envelopes the narrative with its vacancy.

It will be said: yes, there is another descriptive trait in this first paragraph. The game, of which the repetition of repetition consists, is a *selbstgeschaffene* game, one which the child has produced or permitted to be produced by itself, spontaneously, and it is the first of this type. But none of all this (spontaneity, autoproduction, the originality of the first time) contributes any descriptive content that does not amount to the self-engendering of the repetition of itself. Hetero-tautology (definition of the Hegelian speculative) of repeated repetition, of self-repetition. In its pure form, this is what play will consist of.

It gives time. There is time.

The grandfather (who is more or less clandestinely the) speculator (already not yet) repeats the repetition of repetition. A repetition between pleasure and unpleasure, of a pleasure and an unpleasure whose (agreeable–disagreeable) content, however, is not added to repetition. It is not an additive but an internal determination, the object of an analytic predication. It is the possibility of this analytic predication which slowly will develop the hypothesis of a "drive" more original than the PP and independent of it (him). The PP will be overflowed, and is so in advance, by the speculation in which it (he) engages, and by its (his) own (intestine, proper, domestic, familial, sepulchral) repetition.

Now—fold back (reapply) what the grandfather, who still is hiding from himself that he is the grandfather, says here without hiding it from himself, reapply what he has said, by repeating it, about the repetition of the grandson, the eldest of his grandsons, Ernst. We will come back to this in detail. Fold back what he says his grandson is doing, with all the seriousness appropriate to an eldest grandson called Ernst *(the importance of being earnest)*,[10] but not Ernst Freud, because the "movement" of this genealogy passes through the daughter, the daughter wife who perpetuates the race only by risking the name, (I leave it to you to follow this factor[11] up to and including all of those women about whom it is difficult to know whether they have maintained the movement without the name or lost the movement in order to maintain, in that they have maintained, the name;[12] I leave it to you to follow this up suggesting only that you not forget, in the question of the analytic "movement" as the genealogy of the son-in-law, Judaic law), fold back, then, what he says his grandson is doing seriously on what he himself is doing by saying this, by writing *Beyond...*, by playing so seriously (by speculating) at writing *Beyond...*. For the speculative heterotautology of the thing is that the beyond is *lodged* (more or less comfortably for this *vacance*) in the repetition of the repetition of the PP.

Fold back: *he* (the grandson *of* his grandfather, the grandfather *of* his grandson) compulsively repeats repetition without it ever advancing anywhere, not one step. He repeats an operation which consists in distancing, in pretending (*for a time*, for time: thereby writing and doing something that is not being talked about, and which must give good returns) to distance pleasure, the object or principle of pleasure, the object and/or the PP, here represented by the spool which is supposed to represent the mother (and/or, as we will see, supposed to represent the father, in the place of the son-in-law, the father as son-in-law, the other family name), in order to bring it (him) back indefatigably. It (he) pretends to distance the PP in order to bring it (him) back ceaselessly, in order to observe that itself it (himself he) brings itself (himself) back (for it (he) has in it(him)self the principial force of its (his) own economic return, to the house, his home, near it(him)self despite all the difference), and then to conclude: it (he) is still there, I am always there. *Da.* The PP maintains all its (his) authority, it (he) has never absented it(him)self.

One can see that the description to follow of the *fort/da* (on the side of the grandson of the house) and the description of the speculative game, so painstaking and so repetitive also, of the grandfather writing *Beyond* . . . overlap down to their details. It is the same application. I have just said: one can see that they overlap. Rigorously speaking, it is not an overlapping that is in question, nor a parallelism, nor an analogy, nor a coincidence. The necessity that binds the two descriptions is of another kind: we would have difficulty naming it; but of course this is the principal stake for me in the selective and motivated reading that I am repeating here. Who causes (himself) to come back *[revenir]*, who makes who come back *[revenir]* according to this double *fort/da* which conjugates, the same genealogical (and conjugal) writing, the narrated *and* the narrating of this narrative (the game of the "serious" grandson with the spool and the serious specu-lation of the grandfather with the PP)?

This simple question in suspense permits us to glimpse the following: the description of Ernst's serious game, of the eldest grandson of the grandfather of psychoanalysis, *can no longer be read solely* as a theoretical argument, as a strictly theoretical speculation that tends to *conclude* with the repetition compul-sion *or* the death drive *or* simply with the internal limit of the PP (for you know that Freud, no matter what has been said in order vehemently to affirm or contest it, *never concludes on this point*), but can also be read, according to the supplementary necessity of a *parergon*,[13] as an autobiography of Freud. Not simply an autobiography confiding his life to his own more or less testamentary writing, but a more or less living description of his own writing, of his way of writing what he writes, most notably *Beyond* . . . . In question is not only a folding back or a tautological reversal, as if the grandson, by offering him a mirror of his writing, were in advance dictating to him what (and where) he had to lay out on paper; as if Freud were writing what his descendence (in sum holding the first pen, the one that always passes from one hand to another) prescribed that he write; as if Freud were making a return to Freud through the connivance of a grandson who dictates from his spool and regularly brings it back, with all the seriousness of a grandson certain of a privileged contract with the grandfather. It is not only a question of this tautological mirror. The autobiography *of the writing* posits and deposits (deposes) simultaneously, in the same movement, the psychoanalytic movement. It performs, and bets on that which gave its occasional chance. Which amounts *[revenant]* to saying in sum, (but who is speaking here?), I bet that this double *fort/da* cooperates, that this cooperation cooperates with initiating the psychoanalytic cause, with setting in motion the psychoanalytic "movement," even being it, even *being* it, in its being *itself*, in other words, in the singular structure of its tradition, I will say in the proper name of this "science," this "movement," this "theoretical practice" which maintains a relation to its history like none other. A relation to the history of its writing and the writing of its history also. If, in the unheard-of event of this cooperation, the unanalyzed remainder of an unconscious remains, if this remainder is at work, and from its alterity constructs the autobiography of this testamentary writing, then I wager that it will be transmitted blindly by the entire movement of the return to Freud.[14] The remainder which in silence works upon the scene of this cooperation is doubtless illegible (now or forever, such is a *restance* in the sense in which I take it), but it defines the sole urgency of what remains to be done, is truly its only interest. Interest of a supplementary repetition? interest of a genetic transformation, of a renewal effectively displacing the essential? This alternative is lame, it is in advance made to limp by the *démarche* one can read here, in the bizarre document which concerns us.

I have never wanted to abuse the abyss, nor, above all, the *mise "en abyme."*[15] I do not believe in it very much, I am wary of the confidence that it inspires fundamentally, I believe it too representative either to go far enough or not to avoid the very thing toward which it allegedly rushes. I have attempted to explain myself on this question elsewhere. Onto what does a certain appearance of *mise "en abyme"* open—and close—here? This appearance is not immediately apparent, but it has had to play a more or less secret role in the fascination exerted on the reader by the small story of the spool, this anecdote that could have been taken as banal, impoverished, truncated, told in passing, and without the slightest import for the ongoing debate, if one is to believe the relater of the story himself. The story that is related, however, seems to put into *"abyme"* the writing of the relation (let us say the history, *Historie,* of the relation, and even the history, *Geschichte,* of the relater relating it). Therefore the related is related to the relating. The site of the legible, like the origin of writing, is carried away with itself. Nothing is any longer inscribable, and nothing is more inscribable *[rien n'est plus inscriptible].* The notion of the repetition *"en abyme"* of Freud's writing has a relation of structural *mimesis* with the relation between the PP and "its" death drive. The latter, once again, is not opposed to the former, but hollows it out with a testamentary writing *"en abyme"* originally, at the origin of the origin.

Such will have been the "movement," in the irreducible novelty of its repetition, in the absolutely singular event of its double relation.

If one wished to simplify the question, it could become, for example: how can an autobiographical writing, in the abyss of an unterminated self-analysis, give to a worldwide institution *its* birth? The birth of whom? of what? and how does the interruption or the limit of the self-analysis, cooperating with the *mise "en abyme"* rather than obstructing it, reproduce its mark in the institutional movement, the possibility of this remark from then on never ceasing to make little ones, multiplying the progeniture with its cleavages, conflicts, divisions, alliances, marriages, and regroupings?

Thus does an autobiography speculate, but instead of simplifying the question, one would have to take the process in reverse, and recharge its apparent premise: what is autobiography if everything that follows from it, and out of which we have just made a long sentence, is then possible? We do not yet know, and must not pretend to know. Even less as concerns a self-analysis. He who called himself the first, and therefore the only, one to have attempted, if not to have defined it, did not himself know, and this must be taken into account.

To go forward in my reading, I now need an essential possibility whose chance, if it can be put thus, will have been momentous: it is that every autobiographical speculation, to the extent that it constitutes a legacy and the institution of a movement without limit, must take into account, in its very performance, the mortality of the legatees. As soon as there is mortality, death can in principle overtake one at every instant. The speculator then can survive the legatee, and this possibility is inscribed in the structure of the legacy, and even within this limit of self-analysis the system of which supports the writing somewhat like a grid. The precocious death, and therefore the mutism of the legatee who can do nothing about it: this is one of the possibilities of that which dictates and causes to write. Even the one who apparently will not have written, Socrates,[16] or whose writing is supposed to double discourse, or above all listening, Freud and several others. One then gives oneself one's own movement, one inherits from oneself for all time, the provisions are sufficient so that the ghost at least can always step up to the cashier. He will only have to pronounce a name guaranteeing a signature. One thinks.

This has happened to Freud, and to several others, but it does not suffice that the event occupy the world theater for its possibility to be illustrative of it.

And what follows is not only an example.

Conjoint Interpretations

There is a mute daughter. And more than another daughter who will have used the paternal credit in an abundant discourse of inheritance, it is she who will have said, perhaps, this is why it is up to your father to speak. Not only my father, but your father. This is Sophie, the daughter of Freud and mother of Ernst whose death soon will toll in the text. Very softly, in a strange note added afterward.

I am taking up my account exactly at the point at which I left it off, without skipping over anything. Freud sets the stage, and in his fashion defines the apparently principal character. He insists upon the normality of the child. This is the condition for justifiable experimentation. The child is a paradigm. He is therefore not at all precocious in his intellectual development. He is on good terms with everyone.

Particularly with his mother.

Following the schema defined above, I leave it to you to relate —to refold or to reapply—the content of the narrative to the scene of its writing, and to do so here for example, but elsewhere too, and this is only an example, by exchanging the places of the narrator and of the principal character, or principal couple, Ernst-Sophie, the third character (the father—the spouse—the son-in-law) never being far off, and occasionally even too close. In a classical narrative, the narrator, who allegedly observes, is not the author, granted. If it were not different in this case, taking into account that it does not present itself as a literary fiction, then we would have to, will have to reelaborate the distinction between the narrator's *I* and the author's *I* by adapting the distinction to a new "metapsychological" topic.

Thus he is apparently on good terms with everyone, especially his mother, since (or despite the fact that) he did not cry in her absence. She occasionally left him for hours. Why didn't he cry? Freud simultaneously seems to congratulate himself for the child's not crying and to be surprised, even sorry, about it. Is this child fundamentally as normal as Freud himself imagines him to be? For in the very same sentence in which he attributes his grandson's excellent personality to the fact that he did not cry for his daughter (his mother) during such long absences, he adds "although" or "and yet." He was very attached to her, not only had she herself breast-fed him, she had cared for him with help from no one. But this small anomaly is quickly erased, and Freud leaves his "although" without consequences. Everything is fine, excellent child, *but.* Here is the *but:* this excellent child had a disturbing habit. One does not immediately get over Freud's imperturbable conclusion at the end of his fabulous description of the disturbing habit: "I eventually realized that it was a game." Here is the description, and I will interrupt my translation at moments.

"The child was not at all precocious in his intellectual development. At the age of one and a half he could say only a few comprehensible words; he could also make use of a number of sounds which expressed a meaning [*bedeutungsvolle Laute*, phonemes charged with meaning] intelligible to those around him. He was, however, on good terms with his parents and their one servant-girl, and tributes were paid to his being a 'good [*anständig*, easy, reasonable] boy.' He did not disturb his parents at night, he conscientiously obeyed orders not to touch certain things or go into certain rooms, and above all [*vor allem anderen*, before all else] he never cried when his mother left him for hours, although he was greatly attached to this mother, who had not only fed him herself but had also looked after him without any outside help" (p. 14).[17]

I interrupt my reading for a moment. The picture painted is apparently without a shadow, without a "but." There is indeed an "although" and a "however," but these are counterweights, internal compensations used to describe the balance: he was not at all precocious, even a bit slow, *but* he was on good terms with his parents; he did not cry when his mother left him, *but* he was attached to her, and for good reason. Am I alone in already hearing a restrained accusation? The excuse itself has left an archive within grammar: "however," "although." Freud cannot prevent himself from excusing his daughter's son. What, then, is he reproaching him for? But is he reproaching him for what he excuses him for, or for what excuses him? the secret fault for which he excuses him, or precisely that which excuses him for his fault? and with whom would the prosecutor be identified in the mobile syntax of this trial?

The big "but" will arise immediately afterward and this time as a shadow in the picture, although the word *but* itself is not there. It is translated as "however" *(nun)*: now, still it happens that, nonetheless it remains that, it must be said however, and nevertheless, fancy that, "This good little boy, however, had an occasional disturbing habit . . ."

What (despite everything) is satisfactory about this excellent child, that is, his normality, his calm, his ability to bear the absence of the beloved daughter (mother)[18] without fear or tears —all of this makes some cost foreseeable. Everything is very constructed, very propped up, dominated by a system of rules and compensations, by an economy which in an instant will appear in the form of a disturbing habit. Which permits him to bear what his "good habits" might cost him. The child too is speculating. How does he pay (himself) for accepting the order not to touch certain things? How does the PP negotiate between good and bad habits? The grandfather, the father of the daughter and mother, actively selects the traits of the description. I see him rushing and worried, like a dramatist or director who has a part in the play. Staging it, he has to act with *dispatch [il se dépêche]*: to control everything, have everything in order, before going off to change for his part. This is translated by a peremptory authoritarianism, unexplained decisions, interrupted speeches, unanswered questions. The elements of the *mise en scène* have been put in place: an original normality in relation to the good breast, an economic principle requiring that the withdrawal of the breast (so well dominated, so well withdrawn from its withdrawal) be overpaid by a supplementary pleasure, and also requiring that a bad habit reimburse, eventually with profit, good habits, for example the orders not to touch certain things. . . . The *mise en scène* hastens on, the actor-dramatist-producer will have done everything himself, he also knocks the three or four times,[19] the curtain is about to rise. But we do not know if it rises on the scene or in the scene. Before the entrance of any character, there is a curtained bed. All the comings and goings, essentially, will have to pass before the curtain.

I myself will not open this curtain—I leave this to you—onto all the others, the words and things (curtains, canvases, veils, hymens, umbrellas, etc.) with which I have concerned myself for so long.[20] One could attempt to relate all these fabrics to one another, according to the same law. I have neither the time nor the taste for this task, which can be accomplished by itself or done without.

Rather, here is Freud's curtain along with the strings pulled by the grandfather.

"This good little boy, however, had an occasional disturbing habit of taking any small objects he could get hold of and throwing them away from him into a corner, under the bed, and so on, so that hunting for his toys (*Spielzeuge*, playthings) and picking them up [*zusammensuchen*, to search in order to bring together, to reassemble] was often not easy work" (14).[21]

The work is for the parents, but also for the child who expects it from them. And the work consists of reassembling, of searching in order to bring together, of reuniting to order to *give back.* This is what the grandfather calls work, an often difficult work. In return, he will call play the dispersion which sends far away (the operation of distantiation), and will call playthings the collection of manipulated objects. The entire process is itself divided; there is a division which is not the division of labor, but the division between play and work: the child *plays* at throwing away his "toys," and the parents *work* at reassembling them, which is often not easy. As if in this phase of the operation the parents were not playing and the child were not working. He is completely excused from working. Who would dream of accusing him of this? But the work is not always easy, and one heaves a little sigh. Why does he disperse, why does he send far away everything he has at hand, and who and what?

The spool has not yet made its appearance. In a sense, it will be only an example of the process Freud has just described. But it will be an exemplary example, yielding a supplementary and decisive "observation" for the interpretation. In the exemplary example the child throws away and brings back to himself, disperses and reassembles, gives and takes back by himself: he reassembles the reassembling *and* the dispersion, the multiplicity of agents, work and play, into a single agent, apparently, and into a single object. This is what the grandfather will understand as "a game," at the moment when all the strings are brought back together, held in one hand, dispensing with the parents, with their work or play which consisted in straightening up the room.

The spool has not yet made its appearance. Until now *Spielzeug* has designated only an aggregate, the set of toys, the unity of a multiplicity that can be scattered, that the parents' work at reassembling, precisely, and that the grandfather here reassembles in one word. This collective unity is the apparatus of a game that can *dislocate* itself: can change its place and fragment or disperse itself. The word for things as a set, in this theory of the set, is *Zeug,* the instrument, the tool, the product, the "thing," and, according to the same semantic transition as in French or in English, the penis. I am not commenting on what Freud says, I am not saying that Freud is saying: by dispersing his objects or playthings into the distance the child not only separates himself from his mother (as will be said further on, and even from his father), but also, and primarily, from the supplementary complex constituted by the maternal breast and his own penis, allowing the parents, but not for long, to reassemble, to cooperate in order to reassemble, to reassemble themselves, but not for long, in order to reassemble what he wants to dissociate, send away, separate, but not for long. If he separates himself from his *Spielzeug* as if from himself and with the aim of allowing himself to be reassembled, it is that he himself is also an aggregate whose reassemblage can yield an entire combinatorial of sets. All those who play or work at reassembling are participants. I am not saying that Freud says this. But he will say, in one of the two footnotes I have mentioned, that it is indeed himself or his image that the child "plays" at making appear–disappear also. He is part of his *Spielzeug.*

The spool has not yet made its appearance. Here it is, again preceded by an interpretive anticipation: "As he did this [throwing away his entire *Spielzeug*] he gave vent to a loud, long-drawn-out 'o-o-o-o,' accompanied by an expression of interest and satisfaction, which according to the common judgment [22] of his mother and the writer of the present account [the daughter and the father, the mother and the grandfather are here conjoined in the same speculation] was not a mere interjection but represented the German word *'fort'* [gone, far away]. I eventually realized that it was a game and that the only use he made of any of his toys [*Spielsachen*] was to play 'gone' [*fortsein*] with them" (14–15).

Freud's intervention (I am not saying the grandfather's intervention, but the intervention of whoever recounts what the observer experienced, whoever finally realized that "it was a game":

there are at least three instances of the same "subject," the narrator-speculator, the observer, the grandfather, the latter never being openly identified with the two others by the two others, etc.)—Freud's intervention deserves to give us pause. He recounts that as an observer he has also interpreted. And has named. Now, what does he call a game, rather than work, the work itself consisting of reassembling? Well, paradoxically, he calls a game the operation that consists in not playing with one's toys: he did not employ them, he did not use *(benütze)* his toys, he says, he did not make them useful, *utensiles,* except by playing at their being gone. The "game" thus consists in not playing with one's toys, but in making them useful for another function, to wit, being-gone. Such would be the deviation or *teleological* finality of this game. But a teleology, a finality of distantiation with its sights set on what, on whom? For what and for whom, this utilization of that which is usually given as gratuitous or useless, that is, play? What does this nongratuitousness yield? And for whom? Perhaps not a single profit, nor even any profit at all, and perhaps not for a single speculative agency. There is the teleology of the interpreted operation and there is the teleology of the interpretation. And the interpreters are many: the grandfather, the said observer, the speculator, and the father of psychoanalysis, here the narrator, and then, and then, conjoined to each of these instances, she whose judgment would have concurred, in coinciding fashion *(übereinstimmenden Urteil)* to the extent of being covered by it, with the father's interpretation.

This coincidence which conjoins the father and the daughter in the interpretation of the o-o-o-o as *fort* is odd for more than one reason. It is difficult to imagine the scene in detail, or even to accredit its existence and everything recounted within it. But it remains that Freud reports it: the mother and the observer are somehow reassembled in order to make the *same* judgment on the meaning of what their son and grandson articulated before them, even for them. Try to figure out where the induction of such an identity, such an identification of point of view, comes from. But we can be sure that wherever it does come from, it has come round and has bound the three characters in what must more than ever be called the "same" speculation. They have secretly named the "same" thing. In what language? Freud asks himself no questions about the language into which he translates the o/a. To grant it a semantic content bound to a determined language (a given opposition of German words) and from there a semantic content which surpasses language (the interpretation of the child's behavior), is an operation impossible without multiple and complex theoretical protocols. One might suspect that the o/a is not limited to a simple formal opposition of values the content of which could vary without being problematical. If this variation is *limited* (which is what must be concluded from the fact—if, at least, one is interested in it—that the father, the daughter, and the mother find themselves reunited in the same semantic reading), then one can put forward the following hypothesis: there is some proper noun beneath all this, whether one takes the proper noun in the figurative sense (any signified whose signifier cannot vary or be translated into another signifier without a loss of signification induces a proper noun effect), or in the so-called literal, "proper" sense. I leave these hypotheses open, but what seems certain to me is the necessity of formulating hypotheses on the conjoining interpretations of o-o-o-o, that is, o/a, in whatever language (be it natural, universal, or formal), the interpretations conjoining the father and the daughter, the grandfather and the mother.

And the grandson and the son: for the two preceding generations have sought to be together, have been, says one of the generations, conscious of being together in order to understand in their common verdict what their child intended to have them understand, and intended that they understand together. There is nothing hypothetical or audacious about saying this; it is an analytical reading of what Freud's text says explicitly. But we know now what a tautology can bring back by gushing over.

And what if this were what the son, I mean the grandson, were after, what if this superimposing coincidence in the judgment *(Urteil)* were what he believed without knowing it, without wanting it? The father is absent. He is far away. That is, since one must always specify, one of the two fathers, the father of a little boy so serious that his play consists in not playing with his toys but in distancing them, playing only at their distantiation.

In order to make his play useful for himself. As for the father of Sophie and of psychoanalysis, he is still there. Who is speculating?

The spool still has not yet made its appearance. Here it is. To send it off, the child was not lacking in *address*.[23]

It follows immediately. "One day I made an observation which confirmed my view. The child had a wooden spool[24] *(Holzspule)* with a piece of string *(Bindfaden)* tied round it. It never occurred to him to pull it along the floor behind him, for instance, and play at its being a carriage, but rather he held the spool by the string and with great address *(Geschick)* threw it over the edge of his little curtained bed (or veiled bed, *verhängten Bettchens*), so that it disappeared into it, at the same time uttering his expressive *(bedeutungsvolle,* meaningful) 'o-o-o-o.' He then pulled the spool out of the bed again by the string and hailed its appearance with a joyful 'Da' *(there)*. This, then, was the complete game *(komplette Spiel)*—disappearance and return *(Verschwinden und Wiederkommen)*. As a rule one only witnessed its first act, which was repeated untiringly as a game in itself, though there is no doubt that the greater pleasure was attached to the second act."

And with this word a call for something. A call for a footnote that I will read presently.

"This, then," says Freud, "was the complete game." Which immediately implies: this, then, is the complete observation, and the complete interpretation of this game. Nothing is missing, the game is saturable and saturated. If the completion were obvious and certain, would Freud insist upon it, remark upon it as if he quickly had to close, conclude, enframe? One suspects an incompletion (in the object, or in its description) all the more in that: (1) this is the scene of an interminable repeated supplementation, as if it never finished completing itself, etc; and (2) there is something like an axiom of incompletion in the structure of the scene of writing. This is due at very least to the position of the speculator as a motivated observer. Even if completion were possible, it could neither appear for such an "observer" nor be declared as such by him.

But these are generalities. They designate only the formal conditions of a determined incompletion, the signifying absence of a particularly pertinent given trait.. Which may be on the side of the scene described, or on the side of the description, or in the unconscious which binds the one to the other, their unconscious that is shared, inherited, telecommunicated according to the same teleology.

It speculates on the return, it is completed in coming back: the greater pleasure, he says, although this spectacle is less directly seen, is the *Wiederkommen*, the re-turn. And yet, that which thereby again becomes a revenant must, for the game to be complete, be thrown away again, indefatigably. It speculates on the basis of the return, on the departure of that which owes it to itself to return. On what has come back from leaving or just left again *[A ce qui revient de partir ou vient de repartir]*.

It is complete, he says.

And yet: he regrets that it does not roll along as it should roll along. As it should have rolled along if he, himself, had been holding the string.

Or all the strings. How would he, himself, have played with the kind of yo-yo that is thrown in front of or beneath oneself, and which returns as if by itself, on its own, by rolling itself up anew? Which comes back as if by itself, if it has been sent off correctly? One must know how to throw it in order *to make* it return by itself, in other words in order *to let* it return. How would the speculator himself have played? How would he have rolled the thing, made it roll, let it roll? How would he have manipulated this lasso? Of what would his address have consisted?

He seems surprised, adding to this surprise a confident regret that the good little boy never seemed to have the idea of pulling the spool behind him and playing at its being a carriage: or rather at its being a wagon *(Wagen)*, a train. It is as if one could wager *(wagen* again) that the speculator (whose contrary preference, that is, railway phobia, *Eisenbahn*, is well enough known to put us on the track) would himself have played choo-choo with one of these "small objects" *(kleinen Gegenstände)*. Here then is the first problem, the first perplexity of the father of the object or the grandfather of the subject, of the father of the daughter (mother: Ernst's object) or the grandfather of the little boy (Ernst as the "subject" of the *fort/da*): but why doesn't he play train or carriage? Wouldn't that be more normal? And why doesn't he play carriage by pulling the thing behind him? For the thing is a vehicle in convoy.[25] If he had been playing in his grandson's place (and therefore playing with his daughter, since the spool replaces her, as he will say in the next paragraph, or at least, following its/his thread, is but a trait or train leading to her, in order to come just to depart from her again), the (grand)father would have played carriage [I must be pardoned all these parentheses, the (grand)father or the daughter (mother), they are necessary in order to mark the syntax in erasure of the genealogical scene, the occupation of all the places and the ultimate mainspring of what I began by calling the athesis of *Beyond* . . .]: and since the game is serious, this would have been more serious, says he, quite seriously. Too bad that the idea never occurred to him (for instance!) to pull the spool behind him on the floor, and thus to play carriage with it: *Es fiel ihm nie ein, sie zum Beispiel am Boden hinter sich herzuziehen, also Wagen mit ihr zu spielen, sondern es warf. . . .* This would have been more serious, but the idea never occurred to Ernst. Instead of playing on the floor *(am Boden)*, he insisted on putting the bed into the game, into play, on playing with the thing over the bed, and also in the bed. Not in the bed as the place where the child himself would be, for contrary to what the text and the translation have often led many to believe (and one would have to ask why), it appears he is not in the bed at the moment when he throws the spool. He throws it from outside the bed over its edge, over the veils or curtains that surround its edge *(Rand)*, from the other side, which quite simply might be into the sheets. And in any event, it is from "out of the bed" *(zog . . . aus dem Bett heraus)* that he pulls back the vehicle in order to make it come back: *da*. The bed, then, is *fort*, which perhaps contravenes all desire; but perhaps not *fort* enough for the (grand)father who might have wished that Ernst had played more seriously on the floor *(am Boden)* without bothering himself with the bed. But for both of them, the distancing of the bed is worked upon by this *da* which divides and shares it: too much or not enough. For the one or for the other.

What is to play train, for the (grand)father? To speculate: it would be never to throw the thing (but does the child ever throw it without its being attached to a string?), that is, to keep it at a distance continuously, but always at the same distance, the length of the string remaining constant, making (letting) the thing displace itself at the same time, and in the same rhythm, as oneself. This trained train does not even have to come back *[revenir]*, it does not really leave. It has barely come to leave when it is going to come back.

It is going. This is what would suit and go for the (grand)father-speculator. Which enables him to be certain of the measure of the thing only by depriving himself of an extra pleasure, the very pleasure that he describes as the principal one for Ernst, to wit, the second act, the return. He deprives himself of this pleasure in order to spare himself the pain or the risk of the bet. And in order not to put the desired bed into play.

To play carriage also indeed would be "to pull" the invested object "behind him" *(hinter sich herzuziehen)*, to keep the locomotive well in hand and to see the thing only by turning around. One does not have it before one. As does Eurydice or the analyst. For the speculator (the analyst) is obviously the first analysand. The analysand-locomotive for whom the law of listening is substituted for the law of looking.

It is not for us to judge the normality of the child's choice, and we know about it only according to what the ascendant reports. But we might find the ascendant's inclination[76] strange. Everything occurs around a bed and has never occurred except around a bed surrounded with veils or curtains: what is called a "skirted crib." If the child were indeed outside the bed but near it, occupied with it, which his grandfather seems to reproach him for, then these curtains, these veils, this cloth, this "skirt" that hides the bars, form the inner chamber of the *fort/da*, the double screen which divides it inside itself, dividing its internal and its external aspects, but dividing it only by reassembling it with itself, sticking it to itself doubly, *fort:da* I am calling this, once more, and necessarily, the *hymen*[27] of the *fort:da*. The veil of this "skirt" is the interest of the bed and the *fort:da* of all these generations. I will not venture saying: it is Sophie. How could Ernst have seriously played carriage using a veiled bed, all the while pulling the vehicle behind him? One asks oneself. Perhaps quite simply it was his *duty* not to do anything with the object (obstacle, screen, mediation) named bed, or edge of the bed, or limen or hymen, his duty to stay off to one side completely, and thereby to leave the place free, or to stay inside completely (as is often believed), which would have set loose less laborious identifications. But in order to have the *Spielzeug* or "small object" behind onself, with or without bed, in order to have the toy represent the daughter (mother) or the father [the son-in-law, as will be envisaged further on, and the (grand)father's syntax easily skips the parenthesis of a generation with a step to the side], one must have ideas. Follow the comings and goings of all these *fils* (strings, sons). The grandfather regrets that his grandson did not have them, these (wise or foolish) ideas of a game without a bed, unless it be the idea of a bed without a curtain, which does not mean without hymen. He regrets that his grandson has not had them, but he himself has not failed to have them. He even considers them natural ideas, and this is what would better complete the description, if not the game. By the same token, if one might say, he regrets that his grandson has indeed had the ideas that he has had for himself. For if he has had them for himself, it is indeed that his grandson has not failed to have them for him also.

(This entire syntax is made possible by the graphics of the margin or the hymen, of the border and the step, such as was remarked elsewhere. I will not exploit it here.)

For, in the end, was this bed with so necessary and so undecidable a border a couch? Not yet, despite all the Orphism of a speculation. And yet.

What the grand(father-)speculator calls the complete game, thus, would be the game in its two phases, in the duality, the redoubled duality of its phases: disappearance/re-turn, absence/re-presentation. And what binds the game to itself is the *re-* of the return, the additional turn of repetition and re-appearance. He insists upon the fact that the greatest quantity of pleasure is in the second phase, in the *re-*turn which orients the whole, and without which nothing would come. *Revenance*, that is, returning, orders the entire teleology. Which permits one to anticipate that this operation, in its so-called complete unity, will be entirely handed over to the authority of the PP. Far from being checked by repetition, the PP also seeks to recall itself in the repetition of appearing, of presence, of representation, and, as we shall see, via a repetition that is mastered, that verifies and confirms the mastery in which it consists (which is also that of the PP). The mastery of the PP would be none other than mastery in general: there is not a *Herrschaft* of the PP, there is *Herrschaft* which is distanced from itself only in order to reappropriate itself: a tauto-teleology which nevertheless makes or lets the other return in its domestic specter. Which thus can be foreseen. What will return *[reviendra]*, in having already come, not in order to contradict the PP, nor to oppose itself to the PP, but to mine the PP as its proper stranger, to hollow it into an abyss from the vantage of an origin more original than it and independent of it, older than it within it, will not be, under the name of the death drive or the repetition compulsion, an *other master* or a *counter-master*, but something other than mastery, something completely other. In order to be something completely other, it will have to not oppose itself, will have to not enter into a dialectical relation with the master (life, the PP *as* life, the living PP, the PP alive). It will have to not engage a dialectic of master and slave, for example. This nonmastery equally will have to not enter into a dialectical relation with death, for example, in order to become, as in speculative idealism, the "true master."

I am indeed saying the PP as mastery in general. At the point where we are now, the allegedly "complete game" no longer concerns any given object in its determination, for example the spool or what it supplements. In question is the *re-* in general, the returned or the returning *[le revenu ou le revenant]*—to return *[revenir]* in general. In question is the repetition of the couple disappearance–reappearance, not only reappearance as a moment of the couple, but the reappearance of the couple which must return. One must make return the repetition of that which returns and must do so on the basis of its returning. Which, therefore, is no longer simply this or that, such and such an object which must depart/return, or which departs-in-order-to-return, but is departure–returning itself, in other words, the presentation of itself of representation, the return to-itself of returning. No longer an object which would re-present itself, but representation, the return of itself of the return, the return to itself of the return. This is the source of the greatest pleasure, and the accomplishment of the "complete game," he says: that is, that the re-turning re-turns, that the re-turn is not only of an object but of itself, or that it is its own object, that what causes to return itself returns to itself. This is indeed what happens, and happens without the object itself re-become the subject of the *fort/da,* the disappearance–reappearance of itself, the object reappropriated from itself: the reappearance, one can say in French, of one's own "bobine" [see note 24], with all the strings in hand. This is how we fall upon the first of the two footnotes. It is called for by the "second act" to which "the greater pleasure" is unquestionably attached. What does the note say? That the child plays the utility of the *fort/da* with something that is no longer an object–object, a supplementary spool supplementing something else, but with a supplementary spool of the supplementary spool, with his own *"bobine"* with himself as object–subject within the mirror/without the mirror. Thus: "A further observation subsequently confirmed this interpretation fully. One day the child's mother had been away for several hours and on her return *(Wiederkommen)* was met with the words, 'Baby o-o-o-o!' which was at first incomprehensible. It soon turned out, however *(Es ergab sich aber bald),* that during this long period of solitude *(Alleinsein),* the child had found a method of making *himself* disappear *(verschwinden zu lassen).* He had discovered his reflection in a full-length mirror which did not quite reach to the ground, so that by crouching down he could make his mirror-image *fort* [gone away] (15, n. 1).

This time, one no longer knows at what moment it came to pass, led one to think *(Es ergab sich . . .),* or for whom. For the grandfather-observer still present in the absence of his daughter (mother)? Upon the return of the latter, and conjointly again? Did the "observer" still need her to be there in order to reassure himself of this conjunction? Does he not make her return himself without needing her to be there in order to have her at his side? And what if the child knew this without needing to have this knowledge?

Therefore he is playing at giving himself the force of his disappearance, of his *"fort"* in the absence of his mother, in his own absence. A capitalized pleasure which does without what it needs, an ideal capitalization, capitalization itself: by idealization. One provides oneself (and dispenses with) the head of what one needs by doing without it in order to have it. A capitalized pleasure: the child identifies himself with the mother since he disappears as she does, and makes her return with himself, by making himself return without making anything but himself, her in himself, return. All the while remaining, as close as possible, at the side of the PP which (who) never absents itself (himself) and thus provides (for himself) the greatest pleasure. And the enjoyment is coupled. He makes himself disappear, he masters himself symbolically, he plays with the dummy, the dead man, as if with himself, and he makes himself reappear henceforth without a mirror, in his disappearance itself, maintaining himself like his mother at the other end of the line. He speaks *to himself* telephonically, he calls himself, recalls himself, "spontaneously" affects himself with his presence–absence in the presence–absence of his mother. He makes himself *re-*. Always according to the law of the PP. In the grand speculation of a PP which (who) never seems to be absent itself-(himself) from itself-(himself). Or from anyone else. The telephonic or telescripted recall provides the "movement" by contracting itself, by signing a contract with itself.

Let us mark a pause after this first footnote.

For in having been played out for all ages, all of this has just begun.

"La Séance continue"
(Return to Sender, the Telegram, and the Generation of
the Sons-in-Law)

The serious play of the *fort/da* couples absence and presence in the *re-* of returning *[revenir]*. It overlaps them, it institutes repetition as their relation, relating them the one and the other, the one to the other, the one over or under the other. Thereby it plays with itself *usefully*, as if with its own object. Thus is confirmed the abyssal "overlapping" that I proposed above: of the object or the content of *Beyond. . .* , of what Freud is supposedly writing, describing, analyzing, questioning, treating, etc., and, on the other hand, the system of his writing gestures, the scene of writing that he is playing or that plays itself. With him, without him, by him, or all at once. This is the same "complete game" of the *fort/da*. Freud does with (without) the object of his text exactly what Ernst does with (without) his spool. And if the game is called complete on one side and the other, we have to envisage an eminently symbolic completion which itself would be formed by these two completions, and which therefore would be incomplete in each of its pieces and consequently would be completely incomplete when the two incompletions, related and joined the one to the other, start to multiply themselves, supplementing each other without completing each other. Let us admit that Freud is writing. He writes that he is writing, he describes what he is describing, but this is also what he is doing, he does what he is describing, to wit, what Ernst is doing: *fort/da* with his spool *[bobine]*. And each time that one says *to do*, one must specify: *to allow* to do *(lassen)*. Freud does not do *fort/da*, indefatigably, with the object that the PP is. He does it with himself, he recalls himself. Following a detour of the *télé*,[28] this time an entire network. Just as Ernst, in recalling the object (mother, thing, whatever) to himself, immediately comes *himself* to recall *himself* in an immediately supplementary operation, so the speculating grandfather, in describing or recalling this or that, recalls *himself*. And thereby makes what is called his text, enters into a contract with himself in order to hold onto all the strings, the sons *[fils]* of the descendance. No less than of the ascendance. An *incontestable* ascendance. The incontestable is also that which needs no witness. And which, nevertheless, cannot not be granted its rights: no countertestimony appears to have any weight before this teleological auto-institution. The net *[filet]* is in place, and one pulls on a string *[fil]* only by getting one's hand, foot, or the rest, caught. It is a lasso or a lace.[29] Freud has not positioned it. Let us say that he has known how to go about things, to get caught in it *[s'y prendre]*. But nothing has been said yet, nothing is known about this knowledge, for he himself has been caught in advance by the catching. He could not have or foresee this knowledge entirely, such was the condition for the overlapping.

Initially this is imprinted in an absolutely formal and general way. In a kind of *a priori*. The scene of the *fort/da*, whatever its exemplary content, is always in the process of describing in advance, as a deferred overlapping, the scene of its own description. The writing of a *fort/da* is always a *fort/da,* and the PP and *its* death drive are to be sought in the exhausting of this abyss. It is an abyss of more than one generation, as is also said of computers. And is so, as I said, in an absolutely formal and general way, in a kind of *a priori,* but the *a priori* of an aftereffect. In effect, once the objects can substitute for each other to the point of laying bare the substitutive structure itself, the formal structure yields itself to reading: what is going on no longer concerns a distancing rendering this or that absent, and then a rapprochement rendering this or that into presence; what is going on concerns rather the distancing of the distant and the nearness of the near, the absence of the absent or the presence of the present. But the distancing is not distant, nor the nearness near, nor the absence absent or the presence present. The *fortsein* of which Freud is speaking is not any more *fort* than *Dasein* is *da.* Whence it follows (for this is not immediately the same thing), that by virtue of the *Entfernung* and the *pas* in question elsewhere, the *fort* is not any more distant than the *da* is here. An overlap without equivalence: *fort:da.*

Freud recalls himself. His memories and himself. As Ernst does with the glass and without the glass. But his speculative writing also recalls itself, something else and itself. And specularity above all is not, as is often believed, simply reappropriation. No more than the *da.*

The speculator himself recalls himself. He describes what he is doing. Without doing so *explicitly,* of course, and everything I am describing here can do without a thoroughly auto-analytic calculation, whence the interest and necessity of the thing. It speculates without the calculation itself analyzing itself, and from one generation to another.

He recalls *himself.* Who and what? Who? himself, of course. But we cannot know if this "himself" can say "myself"; and, even if it did say "myself," which me then would come to speak. The *fort:da* already would suffice to deprive us of any certainty on this subject. This is why, if a recourse, and a massive recourse, to the autobiographical is necessary here, the recourse must be of a new kind. This text is autobiographical, but in a completely different way than has been believed up to now. First of all, the autobiographical does not overlap the auto-analytical without limit. Next, it demands a reconsideration of the entire *topos* of the *autos*. Finally, far from entrusting us to our familiar knowledge of what autobiography means, it institutes, with its own strange contract, a new theoretical and practical charter for any possible autobiography.

Beyond. . ., therefore, is not an *example* of what is allegedly already known under the name of autobiography. It writes autobiography, and one cannot conclude from the fact that in it an "author" recounts a bit of his life that the document is without value as truth, science, or philosophy. A "domain" is opened in which the inscription, as it is said, of a subject in his text (so many notions to be reelaborated) is also the condition for the pertinence and performance of a text, of what the text "is worth" beyond what is called an empirical subjectivity, supposing that such a thing exists as soon as it speaks, writes, and substitutes one object for another, substitutes and adds itself as an object to another, in a word, as soon as it *supplements*. The notion of truth is quite incapable of accounting for this performance.

The autobiographical, then, is not a previously opened space within which the speculating grandfather tells a story, a given story about what has happened to him in his life. What he recounts is autobiography. The *fort:da* in question here, as a particular story, is an autobiography which instructs: every autobiography is the departure/return of a *fort/da*, for example this one. Which one? The *fort/da* of Ernst? Of his mother conjoined with his grandfather in the reading of his own *fort/da*? Of *her* father, in other words of *his* grandfather? Of the great speculator? Of the father of psychoanalysis? Of the author of *Beyond. . .*? But how can one accede to the latter without a spectral analysis of all the others?

Elliptically, lacking more time, I will say that the graphics, the autobiographics of *Beyond. . .*, of the word *beyond* (*jenseits* in general, the step beyond in general), imprints a prescription upon the *fort:da*, that of the overlapping by means of which proximity distances itself in *abyme (Ent-fernung)*. The death drive is *there*, in the PP, that activates itself with a *fort:da*.

Freud, it will be said, recalls himself. Who? What? Trivially, first of all, he recalls himself, he remembers himself. He tells himself and tells us an incident which remains in his memory, in his conscious memory. The remembrance of a scene, which is really multiple, consisting as it does of repetitions, a scene that happened to another, to two others (one male, one female), but who are his daughter and his grandson. His eldest grandson, let us not forget, but who does not bear the name of the maternal grandfather. He says that he has been the regular, durable, trustworthy "observer" of this scene. He will have been a particularly motivated, present, intervening observer. Under a roof which although not necessarily his, nor simply a roof in common, nevertheless belongs to *his own*, almost, with an almost that perhaps prevents the economy of the operation from closing itself and therefore conditions the operation. Under what headings can one say that in recalling what happens (on) to the subject (of) Ernst he is recalling himself, recalling that it happened to him? Under several interlaced, serial headings, in the "same" chain of writing.

First, he recalls to himself that Ernst recalls (to himself) his mother: he recalls Sophie. He recalls to himself that Ernst recalls his daughter to himself in recalling his mother to himself. The equivocal syntax of the possessive here is not merely an artifact of grammar. Ernst and his grandfather are in a genealogical situation such that the most possessive of the two can always be relayed by the other. Whence the possibility immediately opened by this scene of a permutation both of places and of what indeed must be understood as genitives: the mother of the one is not only the daughter of the other, she is also his mother; the daughter of the one is not only the mother of the other, she is also his daughter, etc. Even at the moment when the scene, if this can be said, took place, and even before Freud undertook to relate it, he was in a situation to identify himself, as is all too readily said, with his grandson, and, playing both colors, to recall his mother in recalling his daughter. This identification between the grandfather and the grandson is attested to as an ordinary privilege, but, and we will soon have more than one proof of this, it could be particularly spectacular for the forebear of psychoanalysis.

I have just said: "Already even at the moment when the scene, if this can be said, took place." And I add a *fortiori* at the moment of desiring to write about it, or of sending oneself a letter about it, so that the letter makes its return after having instituted its postal relay, which is the very thing that makes it possible for a letter *not* to arrive at its destination, and that makes this possibility-of-never-arriving divide the structure of the letter from the outset. Because (for example) there would be neither postal relay nor analytic movement if the place of the letter were not divisible and if a letter always arrived at its destination. I am adding *a fortiori*, but let it be understood that the *a fortiori* was prescribed in the supplementary graphics of the overlapped taking place of what too hastily would be called the primary scene.

The *a fortiori* of the *a priori* makes itself (a bit more) legible in the second note of which I spoke above. It was written afterward, and recalls that Sophie is dead: the daughter (mother) recalled by the child died soon after. Was in a completely different way recalled elsewhere. Before translating this supplementary note, it must be situated in the itinerary. It follows the first note only by a page, but in the interval a page has been turned. Freud has already concluded that no certain decision can be reached from the analysis of so singular a case. Such is his conclusion after a paragraph full of peripateias, a paragraph which begins by confirming the rights of the PP: this is the moment when the interpretation *(Deutung)* of the game explains how the child compensates himself, indemnifies himself, reimburses himself for his pain (the disappearance of the mother) by playing at dis-reappearance. But Freud immediately distances, sends off, this interpretation insofar as it has recourse to the PP. For if the mother's departure is necessarily disagreeable, how can it be explained according to the PP that the child reproduces it, and even *more often* in its disagreeable phase (distancing) than in its agreeable one (return)? It is here that Freud is obliged, curiously, to modify and to complete the previous description. He must, and in effect does, say that one phase of the game is more insistent and frequent than the other: the completion is unbalanced, and Freud had not mentioned it. Above all, he tells us now that the "first act," the distancing, the *Fortgehen*, was in fact independent: it "was staged as a game in itself" *("fur sich allein als Spiel inszeniert wurde")*. Distancing, departure, is therefore a complete game, a game quasi-complete unto itself in the great complete game. We were correct, even more correct than we said, not to take the allegation of completion as coin of the realm. Thus, it is because distancing is itself an independent and more insistent game that the explanation by the PP must once more *fortgehen,* go away, distance itself in speculative rhetoric. And this is why no decision can be reached from the analysis of such a case.

But after this paragraph Freud does not simply renounce the PP. He tries it twice more, after the final resigned suspension of it in this chapter. 1. He tries to see in the active assumption of a passive situation (since the child is unable to affect his mother's displacement) a satisfaction (and therefore a pleasure), but a satisfaction of a "drive for mastery" *(Bemächtigungstrieb),* which Freud curiously suggests would be "independent" of whether the memory was pleasurable or not. Thus would be announced a certain beyond of the PP. But why would such a drive (which appears in other texts by Freud, but which plays a strangely erased role here) be foreign to the PP? Why could it not be juxtaposed with a PP that is so often designated, at least metaphorically, as mastery *(Herrschaft)?* What is the difference between a principle and a drive? Let us leave these questions for a while. 2. After this try, Freud again attempts "another interpretation," another recourse to the PP. It is a question of seeing it function *negatively.* There would be pleasure in making disappear; the sending away that distances the object would be satisfying because there would be a (secondary) interest in its disappearance. What interest? Here, the grandfather gives two curiously associated or coupled examples: the sending away of his daughter (mother) by his grandson and/or the sending away of his son-in-law (father), who here—a significant fact and context—makes his first appearance in the analysis. The son-in-law–father appears only to be sent away, and only at the moment when the grandfather attempts a negative interpretation of the PP according to which the grandson sends his father off to war in order not to be "disturbed in his exclusive possession of his mother." This is the sentence that calls for the note on Sophie's death. Before translating this paragraph on the two negative functionings of the PP, note included, I am extracting a notation from the preceding paragraph. I have extracted it only because it did appear dissociable to me, like a parasite from its immediate context. Perhaps it is best read as an epigraph for what is to follow. In the preceding paragraph it resonates like a sound come from elsewhere, that nothing in the preceding sentence calls for, and that nothing in the following sentence develops: a kind of assertive murmur that peremptorily answers an inaudible question. Here it is then, to be read without premises or consequences: "It is of course naturally indifferent *(natürlich gleichgültig)* from the point of view of judging the affective nature of the game whether the child invented it himself or made it his own on some outside suggestion *(Anregung)*." (15).[30] Oh? Why? Naturally indifferent? Really! Why? What is a suggestion in this case? What are its byways? From whence would it come? That the child made his own, appropriated *(zu eigen gemach)*, the desire of someone else, man or woman, or the desire of the two others conjoined, or that inversely he gave occasion to the appropriation of his own game (since the appropriation can take place in both senses, either hypothesis being excluded)—all this is "naturally indifferent"? Really! And even if it were so for the "affective evaluation," which therefore would remain the same in both cases, would this be equivalent for the subject or subjects to whom the affect is related? What is incontestable is that all these questions have been deferred, distanced, dissociated.

I now translate the attempt at another interpretation, concerning the negative strength of the PP. In it, the successive sending away of the mother and the father is pleasurable and calls for a note: "But still another interpretation may be attempted. Throwing away *(Wegwerfen)* the object so that it was 'gone' *(fort)* might satisfy an impulse of the child's, which was suppressed in his actual life, to revenge himself on his mother for going away from him. In that case it would have a defiant meaning: 'All right, then, go away! I don't need you. I'm sending you away myself.' A year later, the same boy whom I had observed at his first game used to take a toy, if he was angry with it, and throw it on the floor, exclaiming: 'Go to the war! [*Geh in K(r)ieg!*, the r in parentheses taking into account the actual and reconstituted pronunciation of the child]. He had heard at that time that his absent father was 'at the war,' and was far from regretting his absence; on the contrary he gave the clearest indications that he had no desire to be disturbed in his exclusive possession of his mother" (16). Call for a note on Sophie's death. Before coming to it, I emphasize the certainty with which Freud differentiates between, if it can be put thus, the double sending away. In both cases, the daughter [mother] is desired. In the first case, the satisfaction of the sending away is secondary (vengeance, spite); in the second it is primary. "Stay where you are, as far away as possible," signifies (according to the PP) "I prefer that you come back" in the case of the mother, and "I prefer that you do not come back" in the case of the father. This, at least, is the grandfather's reading, his reading of the indications which, he says, do not deceive, "the clearest indications" *(die deutlichsten Anzeichen).* If they do not deceive, actually, one might still ask whom they do not deceive, and concerning whom. In any event, concerning a daughter (mother) who should stay where she is, daughter, mother. Wife, perhaps, but not divided, or divided between *the two Freuds [les deux Freud]* in their "exclusive possession," divided between her father and her offspring at the moment when the latter distances the parasite of his own name, the name of the father as the name of the son-in-law.

The name which is also borne by his other brother, the rival. Who was born in the interval, shortly before the death of the daughter (mother). Here, finally, is the second note, the supplementary note written afterward. The date of its inscription will be important for us: "When this child was five and three-quarters, his mother died. Now that she was really *fort* ('o-o-o') [only three times on this single occasion], the little boy showed no signs of grief. It is true that in the interval a second child had been born and had roused him to violent jealousy" (16).

This cadence might lead one to believe that a dead woman is more easily preserved: jealousy is appeased, and idealization interiorizes the object outside the rival's grasp. Sophie, then, daughter there, mother here, is dead, taken from and returned to every "exclusive possession." Freud can have the desire to recall (her) (to himself) and to undertake all the necessary work for her mourning. In order to speak of this one could mobilize the entire analysis of *Mourning and Melancholia* (published several years before, three at most) and the entire descendance of this essay. I will not do so here.

In the most crushing psychobiographical style, there has been no failure to associate the problematic of the death drive with Sophie's death. One of the aims has been to reduce the psychoanalytic significance of this so ill-received "speculation" to a more or less reactive episode. Several years later, will not Freud himself say that he had somewhat "detached" himself from *Beyond*. . . ? But he had also foreseen the suspicion, and the haste with which he counteracts it is not designed to dispel it. Sophie dies in 1920, the very year in which her father publishes *Beyond* . . . On July 18, 1920, he writes to Eitingon: "The '*Beyond*' is finally finished. You will be able to certify that it was half finished when Sophie was alive and flourishing."[31] He knows in fact, and says to Eitingon, that "many people will shake their heads over it *[Beyond* . . .]."[32] Jones recalls this request to bear witness and wonders about Freud's insistence upon his "unruffled conscience over it *[Beyond]*": is there not here some "inner denial"?[33] Schur, who can hardly be suspected of wanting to save *Beyond* . . . from such an empirico-biographical reduction (he is among those who would seek to exclude *Beyond* . . . from the corpus), nevertheless affirms that the supposition of a link between the event and the work is "unfounded." However, he specifies that the term "death drive" appears "shortly after the deaths of Anton von Freund and Sophie."[34]

For us, there is no question of accrediting such an empiricobiographical connection between the "speculation" of *Beyond* . . . and the death of Sophie. No question of accrediting even the hypothesis of this connection. The passage we are seeking is otherwise, and more labyrinthine, of another labyrinth and another crypt. However, one must begin by acknowledging this: for his part, Freud admits that the hypothesis of such a connection has a meaning to the extent to which he envisages and anticipates it, in order to defend himself against it. It is this anticipation and this defense that have meaning for us, and this is where we start to seek. On 18 December 1923 Freud writes to Wittels, the author of a *Sigmund Freud, His Personality, His Teaching, and His School:* "I certainly would have stressed the connection between the death of the daughter and the Concepts of the *Jenseits* in any analytic study on someone else. Yet still it is wrong. The *Jenseits* was written in 1919, when my daughter was young and blooming, she died in 1920. In September 1919 I left the manuscript of the little book with some friends in Berlin for their perusal, it lacked then only the part on mortality or immortality of the protozoa. *Probability is not always the truth."*[35]

Freud therefore admits a *probability.* But what *truth* could be in question here? Where is the truth of a *fort:da* from which everything derives/drifts away *(dérive),* including the concept of truth?

I will confine myself to "overlapping" Freud's work after Sophie's definitive *Fortgehen* with the work of his grandson as *Beyond . . .* will have reported it.

1. The irreparable wound *as* a narcissistic injury. All the letters of this period speak of the feeling of an "irreparable narcissistic injury" (letter to Ferenczi, 4 February 1920, less than two weeks after Sophie's death).[36]

2. But once she is *fort,* Sophie can indeed stay where she is. It is a "loss to be forgotten" (to Jones, 8 February). She is dead "as if she had never been" (27 January, to Pfister, less than a week after Sophie's death). "As if she had never been" can be understood according to several intonations, but it must be taken into account that one intonation always traverses the other. And also that the "daughter" is not mentioned in the phrase: "snatched away from glowing health, from her busy life as a capable mother and loving wife, in four or five days, as if she had never been."[37] Therefore the work goes on, everything continues, *fort-geht* one might say. *La séance continue.*[38] This is literally, and in French in the text, what he writes to Ferenczi in order to inform him of his mourning: "My wife is quite overwhelmed. I think: *La séance continue.* But it was a little much for one week."[39] What week? Watch the numbers. We had pointed out the strange and artificial composition of *Beyond . . .* in *seven* chapters. Here, Sophie, who was called "the Sunday child" by her parents, is snatched away in "four or five days," although "we had been worried about her for two days," starting with the arrival of the alarming news, on the very day of von Freund's burial. This is the same week, then, as the death of von Freund, which we know, at least via the story of the ring [requested by the widow of the man who was to have been a member of the "Committee" of seven, where he was replaced by Eitingon, to whom Freud gave the ring that he himself wore][40] was yet another wound in what I will call Freud's alliance. The "Sunday child" is dead in a week

after seven years of marriage. Seven years—is this not enough for a son-in-law? The "inconsolable husband," as we soon will see, will have to pay for this. For the moment the *"séance"* continues: "Please don't worry about me. Apart from feeling rather more tired I am the same. The death, painful as it is, does not affect my attitude toward life. For years I was prepared for the loss of our sons; now it is our daughter . . . . 'The unvaried, still returning hour of duty' [Schiller], and 'the dear lovely habit of living' [Goethe] will do their bit toward letting everything go on as before" (to Ferenczi, 4 February 1920, less than two weeks later).[41] On 27 May, to Eitingon: "I am now correcting and completing 'Beyond,' that is, of the pleasure principle, and am once again in a productive phase . . . . All merely [a matter of] mood, as long as it lasts."[42]

3. Third "overlapping" characteristic: ambivalence concerning the father, the father of Ernst, that is, the son-in-law of the grandfather, and the husband of Sophie. The battle for the "exclusive possession" of the daughter (mother) rages on all sides, and two days after her decease *(Fortgehen)*, Freud writes to Pfister: "Sophie leaves behind two boys, one aged six and the other thirteen months [the one Ernst would have been jealous of, as of his father], and an inconsolable husband [indeed] who will have to pay dearly for the happiness of these seven years . . . I do as much work as I can, and am grateful for the distraction. The loss of a child seems to be a grave blow to one's narcissism; as for mourning, that will no doubt come later . . ."[43] The work of mourning no doubt comes later, but the work on *Beyond* . . . was not interrupted for a single day. This letter is situated between Sophie's death and cremation. If the work is a "distraction," it is that he is not just working on just anything. This interval between the death and the cremation (a form of *Fortgehen* which can only have quite singular effects on a work of mourning) is marked by a *story about trains and even of children's trains*, an anecdote imprinted on all of Freud's letters of this week. No train to go to the deceased, she who is already gone *(fort)*, before going up in ashes. A letter to Binswanger first alludes to von Freund's death: "We buried him on 22 January. The same night we received a disquieting telegram from our son-in-law Halberstadt in Hamburg. My daughter Sophie, aged 26, mother of two

boys, was stricken with the grippe; on 25 January she died, after a four days' illness. At that time our railroads were shut down, and we could not even go there. Now my deeply distressed wife is preparing for the trip, but the new unrest in Germany makes it doubtful that this intention can be carried out. Since then a heavy oppression has been weighing on all of us, which also affects my capacity for work. Neither of us has got over the monstrous fact of children dying before their parents. Next summer—this will answer your friendly invitation—we want to be together somewhere with the two orphans and the inconsolable husband whom we have loved like a son for seven years. If this is possible!"[44] Is it possible? And in the letter to Pfister I have already cited in order to point out the allusion to the "seven years" and to the "distraction" of work, the problem of the train to the deceased is posed again, placed in a differentiated network: ". . . as if she had never been. We had been worried about her for two days, but were still hopeful [will she come back?]. From a distance it is so difficult to judge. The distance still remains. We could not, as we wished to, go to her at once when the first alarming news came, because there were no trains, not even a children's train. The undisguised brutality of our time weighs heavily on us. Our poor Sunday child is to be cremated tomorrow. Not till the day after tomorrow will our daughter Mathilde and her husband, thanks to an unexpected concatenation of circumstances, be able to set off for Hamburg in an Entente train. At least our son-in-law was not alone. Two of our sons who were in Berlin are already with him . . ." ("Children from starving Austria were sent abroad by an international children's aid association," notes Schur.)[45]

The "inconsolable husband who will have to pay dearly for the happiness of these seven years" will not have remained alone with the deceased. Freud is represented by his own, despite the suspension of the trains, by another daughter and two sons, bearers of the name (recall his *preferred* game—the train kept at a constant distance).

The classical institution of a science should have been able to do without the Freuds' name. Or at least should have made of its forgetting the condition and proof of its transmission, its proper inheritance. This is what Freud believed or affected to believe, half believed, as in the classical model of science, the model which he fundamentally will have never renounced *playing* at for psycholanalysis. Two weeks before Sophie's death, he writes to Jones. Havelock Ellis has just maintained that Freud is a great artist, and not a scientist. Keeping to the same categories, the same oppositions, the very ones that we are putting to the test here, Freud makes a rejoinder. In it, the great speculator in sum declares himself ready to pay for science with his own, proper name, to pay the insurance premium with his own name. "This [what Ellis says] is all wrong. I am sure in a few decades my name will be wiped away and our results will last"[46] (February 12, 1920). To pay for (the) science (of) with his proper name. To pay, as I said, the insurance premium with his own name. And to be able to say "we" ("our discoveries") while signing by himself. It is as if he did not know, already, that in paying for science with his proper name, it is also the science of his proper name that he is paying for, that he pays himself with a postal money order sent to himself. For this operation it suffices (!) to produce the necessary postal relay. The science of his proper name: a science which for once is essentially inseparable, as a science, from something like a proper name *[nom propre]*, as an effect of a proper name which the science allegedly accounts for (in return) by making its accounts *to it*. But the science of his proper name *[nom propre]* is also that which remains to be done, as the necessary return to the origin of and the condition for such a science. Now, the speculation will have consisted—perhaps—in allegedly paying in advance, paying as dearly as necessary, the charges for such a return to sender. This is a calculation without foundation, for the abyssal devaluation or surplus value ruin it, and ruin even its structure. And yet there must have been a way to bind his name, the name of his own (for this cannot be done alone), to this ruin, a way to speculate on the ruin of his name (new life, new science) which preserves what it loses. No one any longer has to be there in order to preserve, but it preserves itself in the name which for itself preserves it. Who? What? It remains to be had/seen *[Reste à s'avoir]*.

4. Let us continue to analyze the "overlapping" structure of the *Fortgehen*. Freud, in his name, recalls his daughter (his "favorite" daughter, let us not forget, the one whose image pre-

served in a medallion around his wrist he will show to a female patient: from his hand, held by a kind of band, she will have followed, preceded, accompanied the entire movement), and recalls his grandson. Within the *fort:da*, identification in every sense passes through the relay of the structural identification with the grandson. This privileged identification once more will be paid for by an event that is exemplary for more than one reason. In itself this event implies Ernst's younger brother, the very one who exasperated, like another son-in-law, the jealousy of the older brother, a jealousy very comprehensible to and well understood by the grandfather. The "exclusive possession" of the daughter (mother) is at stake. This exemplary event indeed confirms that in its "overlapping" the *fort:da* leads autobiographical specularity into an autothanatography that is in advance expropriated into heterography. In 1923, the year in which he warns Wittels against any probabilistic speculation on the relation between *Beyond* . . . and Sophie's death, what happens? The cancer of the mouth reveals its malign and fatal character. First of the thirty-three operations. Freud had already asked Deutsch to help him "disappear from the world with decency" when the time came. In 1918 he already thought that he was going to die (in February 1918, as you know he had always believed), but then recalled (himself to) his mother: "My mother will be eighty-three this year, and is now rather shaky. Sometimes I think I shall feel a little freer when she dies, because the idea of her having to be told of my death is something from which one shrinks back."[47] All speculation, as we said above, implies the terrifying possibility of this *usteron proteron*[48] of the generations. When the face without face, name without name, of the mother returns, in the end, one has what I called in *Glas* the logic of obsequence. The mother buries all her own. She assists whoever calls herself her mother and follows all burials.

In 1923, then, first operation on the mouth. On the grandfather's mouth, yes, but also, almost at the same time, on Heinerle's (Heinz Rudolph) mouth, Sophie's second son, Ernst's younger brother. Tonsils. He is the preferred grandson, the preferred son of the preferred daughter. His grandfather considered him, says Jones, "the most intelligent child he had ever encountered." (He did not think as much of Ernst, the older brother.)

They talk together about their operation, as if it were the same, of their mouth, as if it were the same, the mouth eating itself and speaking through what it eats: " 'I can already eat crusts. Can you too?' "[49]

Following the operation, and then weakened by miliary tuberculosis, less resistant than his grandfather, Heinerle dies. On 19 June 1923: Freud is seen to cry. For the only time. The following month he confides to Ferenczi that he feels depressed for the first time in his life. Several years later, in 1926, Binswanger loses his elder son, and on this occasion Freud tells Binswanger what Heinerle had been for him: he who had taken the place of children and grandchildren. Thus he lives the death of his entire filiation: "This is also the secret of my indifference—it was called courage—toward the danger to my own life."[50] The following year: "I have survived the Committee that was to have been my successor. Perhaps I shall survive the International Association. It is to be hoped that psychoanalysis will survive me. But it all gives a somber end to one's life" (to Ferenczi, 20 March 1924).[51] That he hoped for this survival of psychoanalysis is probable, but *in his name,* survival on the condition of his name: by virtue of which he says that he *survives* it as the place of the proper name.

He also confides to Marie Bonaparte, 2 November, 1925: since the death of the one who took the place of filiation for him, who was a kind of universal legatee, and bearer of the name according to the affect (the community's filiation assured by the woman, here by the "favorite" daughter; and in certain Jewish communities the second grandson must bear the first name of the maternal grandfather; everything could be settled by a Judaic law), he no longer succeeds in attaching himself to anyone.[52] Only the previous ties are maintained. No more ties, no more contracts, no more alliances, no more vows to attach him to any future, to any descendance. And when the ties are only from the past, they have passed. But Marie Bonaparte, who is part of the old alliance, receives the confidence, the act of this confidence which in a way renews the engagement by declaring it past. Of this, as of a certain effect of inheritance, she will remain the depository. If I insist upon the confession to Marie Bonaparte, it is in order to have it forwarded. By the *facteur de la vérité* (mailman, factor of truth) into the family scene on the side of the French branch, at the moment when one believes that a testament is unsealed. Who then will not enter into "exclusive possession," as one enters into a dance or trance? One of the elements of the drama: several families bear the same name without always knowing it. And there are *other* names in the *same* family. (Here, I interrupt this development. If one is willing to read its consequences, including its appendix in *Le facteur de la vérité,* one will perceive, perhaps, a contribution to a decrypting still to come of the French analytic movement.)[53]

The condition of filiation: its mourning or, rather, as I named it elsewhere, its mid-mourning. In 1923 Heinerle, the place holder of filiation, is gone *(fort),* the pains in the mouth remain, terrible and threatening. He is more than half sure of what they hold in store for him. He writes to Felix Deutsch: "A comprehensible indifference to most of the trivialities of life shows me that the working through of the mourning is going on in the depths. Among these trivialities I count science itself."[54] As if the name, in effect, was to be forgotten, and this time along *with* science. But even if he more than half believed it, this time or the preceding one, when he linked science to the loss of the name, will we believe it? No more this time than the preceding one.

Of this *fort:da* as the work of mid-mourning and of speculation operating on itself, as the great scene of the legacy, the abyss of legitimation and delegation, there would still be, to the point of no longer being countable, other sons, strings *[fils].* Let us limit ourselves here to the work of mid-mourning (introjection and/or incorporation, mid-mourning here being represented by the bar between *and and/or or,* which for structural reasons seems to me as necessary as it is necessarily impure),[55] to the work of mid-mourning in the relationship to oneself *as grandson and as younger brother of the grandson.* It is with the younger brother of the grandson, the place holder of all filiation, that death seems irremmediable, descendance wiped out, and for the first time *cried over,* the depression insurmountable (for a time), new alliances forbidden. But in order to understand, in order to attempt to understand the closure of alliances to his future, perhaps one has to pull on other strings, sons of the past. For example, let us name Julius. Freud's younger brother, who occupied Heinerle's place in relation to Ernst. He died at the age of eight months. Freud at that time was two. Ernst was one and a half when the *fort:da* was observed.[56] Says Jones: "Before the newcomer's birth the infant Freud had had sole access to his mother's love and milk, and he had to learn from the experience how strong the jealousy of a young child can be. In a letter to Fliess (1897) he admits the evil wishes he had against his rival and adds that their fulfillment in his death had aroused self-reproaches, a tendency that had remained ever since. In the light of this confession it is astonishing that Freud should write twenty years later how almost impossible it is for a child to be jealous of a newcomer if he is *only fifteen months old* when the latter arrives."[57]

It repeats (itself) and overlaps. But how to separate this graphics from that of the legacy? Between the two, however, there is no relation of causality or condition of possibility. Repetition legates itself, the legacy repeats itself.

If the guilt is overlapped with the one whose death he lived as his own death, *to wit* the death of the other, of Ernst's younger brother as of his younger brother, Julius, one holds several (only) of the strings in the lace of murderous, mournful, jealous, and guilty identifications which entrap speculation, infinitely. But since the lace constrains speculation, it also constrains it with its rigorous stricture. The legacy and jealousy of a repetition (already jealous of itself) are not accidents which overtake the *fort:da;* rather they more or less strictly pull its strings. And assign it to an auto-biothanato-hetero-graphic scene of writing.

This scene of writing does not recount something, the content of an event which would be called the *fort:da.* This remains unrepresentable, but produces, there producing itself, the scene of writing.

[. . . .]

—*Translated by Alan Bass*

NOTES

1. The bilingual pun—legs, legacy—is at work throughout. It is related to Derrida's analysis of the rhetoric of *Beyond* . . . , Freud's repeated gesture

of taking another *step* forward that goes nowhere, the rhetoric of the athesis. *Step* in French is *pas*, which is also the most common word of negation. This fits extremely well with the idea of steps for nothing, the "legwork" of the legacy. I have indicated the play on *pas* in brackets throughout.—TRANS.

2. These abbreviations, when pronounced in French, could be mistaken for *pépé*, a common child's name for grandfather, and *père*, father. Derrida lets this possible confusion play throughout the text.—ED.

3. To continue note 1, I have also indicated the play on *démarche* throughout. The best English equivalent is procedure, but this loses the play on *marche*, from *marcher* (to walk, to work, as in *ça marche*) and on *de-* as a prefix of negation. To put it elliptically, the *athesis* depends upon a *démarche*, or as Derrida puts it here, a *pas de thèse*: a *no*-thesis that is as formally organized as any ballet step.—TRANS.

4. *Mouvance* refers both to the relation of dependence between two fiefs, and to the state of being in movement. The former meaning relates to everything that Derrida has to say about the *dominance* of the PP, the prince and the satellites in the "society" of the drives. The latter meaning relates to Derrida's use of noun-verbs suspended between the active and the passive, as in *différance, restance, revenance*. In fact, as a description of the relation between fiefs, *mouvance* has either an active or a passive sense also.— TRANS.

5. *Beyond the Pleasure Principle*, in *The Complete Psychological Works of Sigmund Freud*, James Strachey, ed. and trans. (London: Hogarth Press, 1953–1974), vol 18, p. 16, all further page references will be given in the text.—ED.

6. Experiment in French is *expérience*, and has the cognate double meaning.—TRANS.

7. "His own" here are *les siens*, which has the sense of one's closest relations. This is the syntax that is referred to in the next sentence.—TRANS.

8. *Oikos*, home, is the Greek root of *economy*.—ED.

9. *Vacance* in French is both vacation and the state of vacancy. Derrida is punning on the fact that Freud observed Ernst while on vacation with a grandson who is also somewhat outside the family, in that he has a different last name. And of course vacation is the time when the family is *away (fort)*. —TRANS.

10. In English in the original.—TRANS.

11. Factor is *facteur*, which is also the mailman, as in *le facteur de la vérité*.—TRANS.

12. The allusion is to Freud's other daughter, Anna, who became a psychoanalyst and whose (considerable) authority in the psychoanalytic movement was challenged by Jacques Lacan.—ED.

13. That which borders a work *(ergon)*, e.g., a picture's frame or a statue's pedestal. This is the title of Derrida's essay on Kant's *Third Critique* in *The Truth in Painting* [1978].—ED.

14. An allusion to the Lacanian school which proposes to "return to Freud."—ED.

15. *En abyme* is the heraldic term for infinite reflection, e.g., the shield in the shield in the shield ... Derrida has used this term frequently. The appearance of *mise en abyme* here is the overlap between what Freud says and what Freud does in *Beyond* ... —TRANS.

16. On Socrates's delegation of writing to his inheritor, see above, **"Envois."**—ED.

17. Strachey's translation sometimes does not convey the nuances of the German original which are particularly important in this chapter. I will give a few instances of these discrepancies. All references to the German text are to the *Gesammelte Werke*, vol. 13 (London: Imago, 1940), and will be given as *GW* and a page number. Thus Strachey has translated Freud's *"wenn die Mütter es für Stunden verliess"* (*GW*, 13) as "when his mother left him for a *few* hours."—TRANS.

18. Derrida will indicate Sophie's place in this scene as that of the *fille (mère)*, daughter (mother); but a *fille mère* is also an unwed mother. This latter designation would seem to correspond to the effacement of Freud's son-in-law and Ernst's father, Halberstadt.—ED.

19. Referring to the traditional knocks that precede the raising of the curtain in French theater.—TRANS.

20. On these curtains and "jalousies," see above, my introduction, pp. **xxxvii-xxxviii.**—ED.

21. The last three words are *"keine leichte Arbeit"* (*GW*, 13) which Strachey has given as "quite a business."—TRANS.

22. Freud's phrase (*GW*, 13) is *"übereinstimmenden Urteil,"* which Strachey has given as "were agreed in thinking."—TRANS.

23. *GW*, 13. The pun on *address* exists in German as well *(Geschick)*, and is crucial to Derrida's analysis of this passage.—TRANS.

24. *GW*, 13. I have consistently modified Strachey's "reel" to read "spool" *(Spule)*. The "spool" in French is *bobine*, which has an additional slang sense of "face" or "head." This play on *bobine* will be indicated in the text. —TRANS.

25. To indicate the impossibility of translating Derrida's sentence here, and the long commentary to which it could give rise, I will simply cite it: *"Car la chose est un véhicule en translation."*—TRANS.

26. *"la pente de l'ascendant."* An elaborate play on words, since *pente* also has the sense of a cloth that goes over the canopy of a bed. *Ascendant*, of course, is the opposite of descendant, but has a resonance of *ascent*, again relating it to *pente* ("inclination" in both senses).—TRANS.

27. *Hymen* is irreducibly both virginity and consummation (marriage), related here to the *conjoined* interpretations of the father and the daughter, grandfather and mother, of what takes place around the bed. See also **"The Double Session,"** above.—TRANS.

28. *Télé* is the French equivalent of the American expression *TV*—the English "telly" is almost perfect here—as well as the prefix to "telecommunication," communication at a distance, from the Greek *tēle* (distant, *loin*, *fort*). "Network" at the end of this sentence translates *chaîne*, which has the

sense of chain and of network, as in a television or radio station, one of the télé-'s byways or detours.—TRANS.

29. Concerning the double stricture of the *lace* in relation to the *fort:da*, I must refer to **Glas** [1974] and to **"Restitutions of the Truth in Pointing"** [see above].

30. *GW*, 13. Freud's phrase is *"fur die affektive Einschätzung dieses Spieles,"* which Strachey mistakenly gives as "judging the *effective* nature of the game." (Perhaps an uncorrected typographical error?)—TRANS.

31. Cited in Max Schur, *Freud: Living and Dying* (New York: International Universities Press, 1972), p. 329.—TRANS.

32. Cited in Ernest Jones, *The Life and Work of Sigmund Freud*, vol. 3 (New York: Basic Books, 1957), p. 40. Hereafter I will refer to Jones 1 and Jones 3 to distinguish between the volumes of this work.—TRANS.

33. Jones 3, p. 40.—TRANS.

34. Schur, pp. 328–29.—TRANS.

35. Cited in Jones 3, p. 41; Freud's emphasis.—TRANS.

36. Cited in Schur, p. 331.—TRANS.

37. Ibid., p. 330.—TRANS.

38. *La séance continue* means "the session proceeds, continues," in the sense of parliamentary procedure, but also the resonance of an analytic session.—TRANS.

39. Cited in Jones 3, p. 19.—TRANS.

40. Anton von Freund was a wealthy Hungarian supporter of psychoanalysis who donated several funds for analytic publications and instruction. The "Committee" was the official, secret group that was formed around Freud after the break with Jung. Freud presented each member with a Greek intaglio ring. Communication was by circular letter. The original 1913 members were Jones, Ferenczi, Rank, Abraham, Sachs, and Freud.—TRANS.

41. Cited in Schur, p. 331.—TRANS.

42. Ibid.—TRANS.

43. Ibid., p. 330.—TRANS.

44. Ibid., p. 329.—TRANS.

45. Ibid.—TRANS.

46. Cited in Jones 3, p. 21.—TRANS.

47. Cited in Schur, pp. 314–15.—TRANS.

48. The *usteron proteron* is the "preceding falsehood" on which a fallacious argument is based. Freud used the term in his theoretical explanation of hysteria in *The Project for a Scientific Psychology* (1895).—TRANS.

49. Cited in Jones 3, p. 92.—TRANS.

50. Cited in Schur, p. 360.—TRANS.

51. Cited in Jones 3, p. 66.—TRANS.

52. Ibid., p. 92.—TRANS.

53. See the complete text of **"Le facteur de la vérité"** [1980] where Derrida considers Marie Bonaparte's more "classical" psychoanalytic reading of the Poe story, as well as Lacan's peremptory dismissal of it.—ED.

54. Cited in Jones 3, p. 91.—TRANS.

55. See "Fors: The Anglish Words of Nicolas Abraham and Maria Torok" [1976]. On mid-mourning *(demi-deuil)*, see "Ja, ou le faux-bond" [1977].

56. The original edition of *La carte postale* read that Freud was one and a half when Julius died, i.e., the age of Ernst when the *fort:da* was observed. This was corrected in discussion with Derrida.—TRANS.

57. Jones 1, pp. 7–8.—TRANS.

TWENTY-TWO

From "Ulysses Gramophone: Hear Say Yes in Joyce"

("Ulysse gramophone: Ouï-dire de Joyce," in *Ulysse*

gramophone: Deux mots pour Joyce [1987])

"What right do we have to select or interrupt a quotation from *Ulysses?*" asks Derrida in this essay first presented as the introductory lecture to the Ninth International James Joyce Symposium. "This is both legitimate and illegitimate, to be made legitimate like an illegitimate child" (p. 45). Our *Reader* closes with a legitimate–illegitimate set of quotations of Derrida quoting *Ulysses,* setting his signature beside and beneath that of Joyce, but also beside and beneath that of Molly Bloom whose final "yes I said yes I will Yes," as Derrida notes, "occupies the place of the signature at the bottom right of the text" (p. 54). In so doing, this legitimate–illegitimate collection of excerpts and interrupted quotations (or jealous blinds that conceal more than they reveal) ends on the note of a double affirmation—yes, yes—which forms one of the most persistent threads of Derrida's meditation here. But only one among others, although perhaps the easiest to lift out of the pattern Derrida weaves through Joyce's warp.

Pattern, however, is not the best word because it hides too neatly the series of apparently chance encounters that Derrida is also recounting and reflecting upon. Many of these encounters are place names—Tokyo, Ohio, Ithaca—all of which Leopold Bloom stumbles upon in the course of his day and all of which the lecturer had visited while preparing his lecture. These crossing paths, not just geographical but also "in the chance form of letters, telegrams, of newspapers called *The Telegraph*, for example, long-distance writing, and also of post cards" (32), lead Derrida to wonder at what point the aleatory itself is already on the vast Joycean program whose system would resemble a central post office or telephone switchboard. In *Ulysses*, in fact, there is mention of a main switchboard—a "trunk line"—operated by Elijah, which just happens to be Derrida's Hebrew name, which in French is written Elie, which resonates with the name of Bloom's ad agency Helys, which contains an anagram of "yes," as does also Ulysses, as does (almost) Joyce, as does, if one switches languages, Elijah or, in yet another tongue, Derrida, and so on . . . The reader is hereby referred to the complete text of "Ulysses Gramophone" in which one will also find, for instance, the peripatetic narrator telling his audience of Joyce experts about the brand of yogurt, discovered in Ohio, called *Yes* that advertises itself with the slogan: "Bet You Can't Say No to Yes," or the books for commercial travelers displayed side by side in the newsstand of a Tokyo hotel with the titles *16 Ways to Avoid Saying No* and *Never Take Yes for an Answer.*

No legitimating agency can authorize the excision of most of this programmatological narrative. On the other hand, we have retained here Derrida's question to the gathering of scholars concerning the nature of an institution that would promote expertise in the matter of Joyce's works. If indeed the Joycean text puts the aleatory on the program, the chance encounter of letters and languages, then is not expertise or mastery a forever receding horizon? And must one not then imagine Joyce having had a really good laugh in anticipation of the spectacle of a meeting of "Joyce specialists"? To be sure, but there are in turn two ways of hearing this laughter and of responding to it: as a reactive, derisive, ironic laugh that echos the accents of mastery, that reminds one of an indebtedness one can never liquidate and that therefore prevents one from hearing and responding "without resentment and without jealousy," as Derrida writes in another essay on Joyce;[1] or as an affirmative laughter, a joyce-ful wisdom that bids one hear the "yes" before anything else.

It is the latter tone that resonates here, but not only here. In all of Derrida's writings, this laughter is to be heard, even or especially there where the most serious, deadly stakes are in play. Future Derrida *Readers* and readers should not forget to listen for it.

[. . . .]

If I am not mistaken, the first phone call sounds with Bloom's words: "Better phone him up first" in the sequence entitled "AND IT WAS THE FEAST OF THE PASSOVER."[1] A little before, he had somewhat mechanically, like a record, repeated this prayer, the most serious of all prayers for a Jew, the one that should never be allowed to become mechanical, to be gramophoned: *Shema Israel Adonai Elohanu.* If, more or less legitimately (for everything and nothing is legitimate when we lift out segments as examples of narrative metonymy), we cut out this element from the most obvious thread of the narrative, then we can speak of the telephonic *Shema Israel* between God, who is infinitely removed (a long-distance call, a collect call from or to the "collector of prepuces"), and Israel. *Shema Israel* means, as you know, call to Israel, listen Israel, hello Israel, to the address of the name of Israel, a person-to-person call.[2] The "Better phone him up first" scene takes place in the offices of *The Telegraph* (and not *The Tetragram*) newspaper and Bloom has just paused to watch a kind of typewriter, or rather a composing machine, a typographic matrix: "He stayed in his walk to watch a typesetter neatly distributing type." And as he first of all reads it backwards ("Reads it backwards first"), composing the name of Patrick Dignam, the name of the father, Patrick, from right to left, he remembers his own father reading the hagadah in the same direction. In the same paragraph, around the name of Patrick, you can follow the whole series of fathers, the twelve sons of Jacob, et cetera, and the word "practice" crops up twice to scan this patristic and perfectly paternal litany ("Quickly he does it. Must require some practice that." And twelve lines lower, "How quickly he does that job. Practice makes perfect"). Almost immediately after this we read, "Better phone him up first": *"plutôt un coup de téléphone pour commencer,"* the French translation says. Let's say: a phone call, rather, to begin with. In the beginning, there must have been some phone call.

Before the act or the word, the telephone. In the beginning was the telephone. There would be much to say about the apparently random figures that this *coup* de *téléphone*[3] plays on; we hear it resonate unceasingly. And it sets off within itself this *yes* toward which we slowly, moving in circles around it, return. There are several modalities or tonalities of the telephonic *yes,* but one of them, without saying anything else, amounts to marking, simply, that one is *there,* present, listening, on the other end of the line, ready to respond but not for the moment responding anything other than the preparation to respond (hello, yes: I'm listening, I can hear that you are there, ready to speak just when I am ready to speak to you). In the beginning the telephone, yes, in the beginning of the *coup de téléphone*

[. . . .]

Telephonic spacing is particularly superimprinted in the scene entitled "A DISTANT VOICE." The scene crosses all the lines in our network, the paradoxes of competence and institution, represented here in the shape of the professor, and, in every sense of the word, the *repetition* of the "yes" between eyes and ears. All these telephonic threads can be drawn from one paragraph:

> A DISTANT VOICE
> ——I'll answer it, the professor said going. . . .
> ——Hello? *Evening Telegraph* here . . . Hello? . . . Who's there? . . . Yes . . . Yes . . . Yes . . .
> The professor came to the inner door.
> ——Bloom is at the telephone, he said. (*U,* 137–38)

Bloom-is-at-the-telephone. In this way, the professor defines a particular situation at a certain moment in the novel, no doubt, but as is always the case in the stereophony of a text that gives several levels to each statement, always allowing for metonymic extracts—and I am not the only reader of Joyce to indulge in this

pursuit, at once legitimate and abusive, authorized and illegitimate—the professor is also naming the permanent essence of
Bloom. It can be read by means of this particular paradigm: *he is
at the telephone,* he is always there, he belongs to the telephone,
he is both riveted and destined there. His being is a being-at-the-
telephone. He is hooked up to a multiplicity of voices and answering machines. His being-there is a being-at-the-telephone, a
being for the telephone, in the way that Heidegger speaks of a
being for death of *Dasein*. And I am not playing with words when
I say this: Heideggerian *Dasein* is also a being-called, it is always,
as we are informed in *Sein und Zeit*, and as my friend Sam Weber
reminded me,[4] a *Dasein* that accedes to itself only on the basis
of the Call *(der Ruf)*, a call which has come from afar, which
does not necessarily use words, and which, in a certain way, does
not say anything. The whole of chapter 57 of *Sein und Zeit* on
the subject of *der Ruf*, down to the last detail, could be adjusted
to this analysis, drawing, for example, on phrases like the following: *Der Angerufene ist eben dieses Dasein; aufgerufen zu seinem eigensten Seinkönnen (Sich-vorweg . . .) Und aufgerufen ist
das Dasein durch den Anruf aus dem Verfallen in das Mann. . . .*
The called one is precisely *this Dasein;* convoked, provoked,
interpellated toward its possibility of being the most proper (before itself). And in this way the *Dasein* is hailed by this call,
called out to, called out of the collapse into the "One". Unfortunately, we do not have the time to enter further into this analysis, within or beyond the jargon of *Eigentlichkeit*, which this
university [Frankfurt] may well remember.

    ——Bloom is at the telephone, he said.
    ——Tell him to go to hell, the editor said promptly. X is
Burke's public house, see? (*U*, 138)

Bloom is at the telephone, hooked up to a powerful network
to which I shall return in a moment. He belongs in his essence
to a polytelephonic structure. But he is at the telephone in the
sense that one also *waits* on the telephone. When the professor
says, "Bloom is at the telephone," and I shall shortly say, "Joyce
is at the telephone," he is saying: he is waiting for someone to
respond to him, waiting for an answer, which the editor, who
decides the future of the text, its safekeeping or its truth, does

not want to give—and who at this point sends him to hell, into the depths, in the *Verfallen*, the hell of censured books.[5] Bloom is waiting for an answer, for someone to say, "hello, yes," that is, for someone to say, "Yes, yes," beginning with the telephonic *yes* indicating that there is indeed another voice, if not an answering machine, on the other end of the line. When, at the end of the book, Molly says, "yes, yes," she is answering a request, but a request that she requests. She is at the telephone, even when she is in bed, asking, and waiting to be asked, on the telephone (since she is alone) to say, "yes, yes." And the fact that she asks "with my eyes" does not prevent this demand from being made by telephone; on the contrary: "well as well him as another and then I asked him with my eyes to ask again yes and then he asked me would I yes to say yes my mountain flower and first I put my arms around him yes and drew him down to me so he could feel my breasts all perfume yes and his heart was going like mad and yes I said yes I will Yes" (*U*, 704).

The final "Yes," the last word, the eschatology of the book, gives itself up only to *reading*, since it distinguishes itself from the others by an inaudible capital letter, an inaudible, only visible remains, the literal incorporation of the *yes* in the eye of the language, of the *yes* in the *eyes*. Language of eyes, of ayes. *Langue d'oeil.*[6]

We still do not know what *yes* means and how this small word, if it is one, operates in language and in what we glibly refer to as speech acts. We do not know whether this word shares anything at all with any other word in any language, even with the word *no*, which is most certainly not symmetrical to it. We do not know if a grammatical, semantic, linguistic, rhetorical, or philosophical concept exists that is capable of this event marked *yes*. Let us leave that aside for the moment. Let us, and this is not merely a fiction, act *as if* this did not prevent us, on the contrary, from hearing what the word *yes* governs. We will move on to the difficult questions later, if we have time.

Yes on the telephone can be crossed, in one and the same occurrence, by a variety of intonations whose differential qualities are potentialized on long stereophonic waves. They may appear to be limited to interjection, to the mechanical quasi signal that indicates either the mere presence of the interlocutory

Dasein at the other end of the line (Hello, yes?), or the passive docility of a secretary or a subordinate who, like some archiving machine, is ready to record orders *(yes sir)* or who is satisfied with purely informative answers *(yes, sir; no, sir)*. Here is just one example among many. I have deliberately chosen the section where a typewriter and the trade name H. E. L. Y.'S lead us to the last piece of furniture in this vestibule or this techno-telecom-munication preamble, to a certain gramophone, at the same time as they connect us to the network of the prophet Elijah. So here we are, though of course I have sectioned and selected, filtering the noise on the line:

> Miss Dunne hid the Capel street library copy of *The Woman in White* far back in her drawer and rolled a sheet of gaudy notepaper into her typewriter.
>
> Too much mystery business in it. Is he in love with that one, Marion? Change it and get another by Mary Cecil Haye.
>
> The disk shot down the groove, wobbled a while, ceased and ogled them: six.
>
> Miss Dunne clicked at the keyboard:
>
> ——16 June 1904. [almost eighty years.]
>
> Five tallwhitehatted sandwichmen between Monypeny's corner and the slab where Wolfe Tone's statue was not, eeled themselves turning H. E. L. Y.'S and plodded back as they had come. . . .
>
> The telephone rang rudely by her ear.
>
> ——Hello. Yes, sir. No, sir. Yes, sir. I'll ring them up after five. Only those two, sir, for Belfast and Liverpool. All right, sir. Then I can go after six if you're not back. A quarter after. Yes, sir. Twentyseven and six. I'll tell him. Yes: one, seven, six.
>
> She scribbled three figures on an envelope.
>
> ——Mr Boylan! Hello! That gentleman from *Sport* was in looking for you. Mr Lenehan, yes. He said he'll be in the Ormond at four. No, sir. Yes, sir. I'll ring them up after five.
> (*U*, 228–29)

It is not by accident that the repetition of *yes* can be seen to assume mechanical, servile forms, often bending the woman to her master, even if any answer to the other as a singular other must, it seems, escape those forms. In order for the *yes* of affirmation, assent, consent, alliance, of engagement, signature, or gift to have the value it has, it must carry the repetition within itself. It must *a priori* and immediately confirm its promise and promise its confirmation. This essential repetition lets itself be haunted by an intrinsic threat, by an internal telephone which acts like a parasite, like its mimetic, mechanical double, its incessant parody. We shall return to this fatality. But we can already hear a gramophony which records writing in the liveliest voice. *A priori* it reproduces it, in the absence of all intentional presence of the affirmer. Such gramophony responds, of course, to the dream of a reproduction which *preserves* as its truth the living *yes*, archived in the form of the most living voice. But by the very same token, it gives way to the possibility of parody, of a *yes* technique that persecutes the most spontaneous, the most giving desire of the *yes.* To meet *(répondre à)* its destination, this *yes* must reaffirm itself immediately. Such is the condition of a signed commitment. The *yes* can only speak *itself* if it promises itself its own memory. [*Le oui ne peut* se *dire que s'il se promet la mémoire de soi.*] The affirmation of the *yes* is the affirmation of memory. *Yes* must preserve itself, and thus reiterate itself, archive its voice in order to give it once again to be heard and understood.

This is what I call the gramophone effect. *Yes* gramophones itself and, *a priori*, telegramophones itself.

The desire for memory and the mourning of the word *yes* set in motion the anamnesic machine. And its hypermnesic overacceleration. The machine reproduces the quick *[le vif]*, it doubles it with its automaton.

[....]

I was telling you about my travel experiences, my round trip, and about a few phone calls. If I am telling stories, it is to put off speaking about serious things and because I am too intimidated. Nothing intimidates me more than a community of experts in Joycean matters. Why? I wanted first of all to speak to you about this, to speak to you about authority and intimidation. The page that I am going to read was written on the plane to Oxford, Ohio, a few days before my trip to Tokyo. I had decided at that time to put before you the question of competence, of legitimacy, and of the Joycean institution. Who has a recognized right to speak of Joyce, to write on Joyce, and who does this well? What do competence and performance consist of here?

When I agreed to speak before you, before the most intimidating assembly in the world, before the greatest concentration of knowledge on such a polymathic work, I was primarily aware of the honor that was being paid me. I wondered by what claim I had managed to make people think I deserved it, if only to a minor degree. I do not intend to answer this question here. But I know, as you do, that I do not belong to your large, impressive family. I prefer the word family to that of foundation or institute. Someone answering, yes, in Joyce's name, to Joyce's name, has succeeded in linking the future of an institution to the singular adventure of a proper name and a signature, a *signed* proper name, for writing out one's name is not yet signing. In a plane, if you write out your name on the identity card which you hand in on arrival in Tokyo, you have not yet signed. You sign when the gesture whereby, in a certain place, preferably at the end of a card or a book, you inscribe your name again, takes on the sense of a *yes*, this is my name, I certify this, and, yes, yes, I will be able to attest to this again, I will remember later, I promise, that it is indeed I who signed. A signature is always a *yes, yes,* the *synthetic* performative of a promise and a memory that conditions every commitment. We shall return to this obligatory departure point of all discourse, following a circle which is also that of the *yes*, of the "so be it"—of the amen and the hymen.

I did not feel worthy of honor that had been bestowed on me, far from it, but I must have been nourishing some obscure desire to be part of this mighty family which tends to sum up all others, including their hidden narratives of bastardy, legitimation, and illegitimacy. If I have accepted, it is mainly because I suspected some perverse challenge in a legitimation so generously offered. You know better than I that the worried concern regarding familial legitimation is what makes *Ulysses*, as well as *Finnegans Wake*, vibrate. I was thinking, in the plane, of the challenge and the trap: Experts, I said to myself, with the lucidity and experience that a long acquaintance with Joyce confers on them, ought to know better than most to what extent, beneath the simulacrum of a few signs of complicity, of references or quotations in each of my books, Joyce remains a stranger to me, as if I did not know him. They realize that incompetence is the profound truth of my relationship to this work which I know finally only indirectly, through hearsay, through rumors, through what people say, second hand exegeses, always partial readings. For these experts, I said to myself, the time has come for the deception to be exposed, and how better to expose or denounce it than at the opening of a large symposium?

So, in order to defend myself against this hypothesis, which was almost a certainty, I asked myself: but in the end what does competence come down to in the case of Joyce? And what can a Joycean institution or family, a Joycean international be? I do not know how far we can speak of the modernity of Joyce, but if this exists, beyond the apparatus for postal and programophonic technologies, it consists in the fact that the declared project of keeping generations of university scholars at work for centuries of babelian edification must itself have been drawn up using a technological model and the division of university labor that could not be that of former centuries. The scheme of bending vast communities of readers and writers to this law, of detaining them by means of an interminable transferential chain of translation and tradition, can equally well be attributed to Plato and Shakespeare, to Dante and Vico, without mentioning Hegel or other finite divinities. But none of these was able to calculate, as well as Joyce did, his move, by regulating it on certain types of world research institutions prepared to use not only means of transport, of communication, or organizational programming that allow an accelerated capitalization, a crazy accumulation of interest in terms of knowledge blocked in Joyce's name, even as he lets you all sign in his name as Molly would say ("I could often have written out a fine cheque for myself and write his name on it" *U*, 702), but also modes of archivization and consultation of data unheard of for all the grandfathers whom I have just named, omitting Homer.

Hence the intimidation: Joyce experts are the representatives as well as the effects of the most powerful project for programming the totality of research in the onto-logico-encyclopedic field for centuries, all the while commemorating its own, proper signature. A Joyce scholar has the right to dispose of the totality of competence in the encyclopedic field of the *universitas*. He has at his command the computer of all memory, he plays with the entire archive of culture—at least of what is called Western culture, and of that which in this culture returns to itself according to the Ulyssean circle of the encyclopedia; and this is why one can always at least dream of writing *on* Joyce and not *in* Joyce from the fantasy of some Far Eastern capital, without, in my case, having too many illusions about it.

The effects of this preprogramming, which you know better than I, are admirable and terrifying, and sometimes intolerably violent. One of them has the following form: nothing can be invented *on the subject* of Joyce. Everything we can say about *Ulysses*, for example, has already been anticipated there, including, as we have seen, the scene about academic competence and the ingenuousness of metadiscourse. We are caught in this net. All the gestures by which we might attempt to take the initiative are already announced in an overpotentialized text that will remind you, at a given moment, that you are captive in a network of language, writing, knowledge, and *even narration*. That is one of the things I wanted to demonstrate earlier, in recounting all these stories, which were moreover true. [. . . .] We have verified that all this had its narrative paradigm and was *already* recounted in *Ulysses*. Everything that happened to me, including the narrative that I would attempt to make of it, was already predicted and pre-narrated in its dated singularity, prescribed in a sequence of knowledge and narration, within *Ulysses*, to say nothing of *Finnegans Wake*, by a hypermnesic machine capable of storing in an immense epic work, along with the memory of the West and virtually all the languages in the world *up to and including traces of the future*. Yes, everything has already happened to us with *Ulysses* and has been signed in advance by Joyce.

It remains to be seen what happens to this signature in these conditions, and this is one of my questions.

This situation is one of reversal, stemming from the paradox of the *yes*. Moreover, the question of the *yes* is always linked to that of the *doxa*, to what is opined in opinion. So this is the

paradox: just when the work of such a signature starts operating
—some might say subjugating, at any rate relaunching *for itself*,
so that there might be a return—the most competent and reliable production and reproduction machine, it simultaneously
ruins its model. Or, at least, it threatens its model with ruin.
Joyce laid stakes on the modern university, but he challenges it
to reconstitute itself after him. He marks its essential limits.
Basically, there can be no Joycean competence, in the certain and
strict sense of the concept of competence, with the criteria of
evaluation and legitimation that are attached to it. There can be
no Joycean foundation, no Joycean family; there can be no Joycean legitimacy. What is the relation between this situation, the
paradox of the *yes*, or the structure of a signature?

The classical concept of competence supposes that one can
rigorously disassociate knowledge (in its act or in its position)
from the event that one is dealing with, and especially from the
ambiguity of written or oral marks—let's call them gramophon-
ies. Competence implies that a metadiscourse is possible, neutral
and univocal with regard to a field of objectivity, whether or not
it has the structure of a text. Performances ruled by this competence must in principle lend themselves to translation with
nothing left over on the subject of the corpus that is itself translatable. Above all they should not be essentially of a narrative
type. In principle, one doesn't tell stories in the university; one
does history, one recounts in order to know and to explain; one
speaks about narrations or epic poems, but events and histories
(stories) must not be produced there under the heading of insti-
tutionalizable knowledge. Now with the event signed by Joyce, a
double bind has become at least explicit (for we have been caught
in it since Babel and Homer and everything else that follows): on
the one hand, we must write, we must sign, we must bring about
new events with untranslatable marks—and this is the frantic
call, the distress of a signature that is asking for a *yes* from the
other, the pleading injunction for a counter-signature; but on the
other hand, the singular novelty of every other *yes*, of every other
signature, finds itself already phonoprogrammed in the Joycean
corpus.

I do not notice the effects of the challenge of this double bind on myself alone, in the terrified desire I might have to belong to a family of Joycean representatives among whom I will always remain an illegitimate son; I also notice these effects on you.

On the one hand, you are legitimately assured of possessing, or being in the process of constructing a supercompetence, which would measure up to a corpus that includes virtually all the corpuses treated in the university (sciences, technical domains, religion, philosophy, literature, and, co-extensive to all this, languages). With regard to this hyperbolic competence, nothing is transcendent. Everything is *internal,* mental telephony; everything can be integrated into the domesticity of this programmo-telephonic encyclopedia.

But, on the other hand, one must realize at the same time, and *you do realize this,* that the signature and the *yes* that occupy you are capable—it is their destination—of destroying the very root of this competence, of this legitimacy, of its domestic interiority, capable of deconstructing the university institution, with its internal or interdepartmental divisions, as well as its contract with the extra-university world.

Hence the mixture of assurance and distress that one can sense in "Joyce scholars." From one point of view, they are as crafty as Ulysses, knowing, as did Joyce, that they know more, that they always have one more trick up their sleeve. Whether it is a question of totalizing resumption or of subatomistic micrology (what I call "divisibility of the letter"), one can do no better; everything can be integrated in the "this is my body" of the corpus. But, from another point of view, this hypermnesic interiorization can never be closed on itself. For reasons that have to do with the structure of the corpus, the project, and the signature, there can be no assurance of any principle of truth or legitimacy.

Given that nothing new can take you by surprise from the inside, you also have the feeling that something might eventually happen to you from an unforseeable outside. And you have guests.

You are awaiting the passage or the second coming of Elijah. And, as in all good Jewish families, you always have a place set for him. Waiting for Elijah, even if his coming is already gramophoned in *Ulysses,* you are prepared to recognize, without too many illusions, I think, the external competence of writers, philosophers, psychoanalysts, linguists. You even ask them to open your colloquia.

[. . . .]

When you call on incompetents, like me, or on allegedly external competences, knowing full well that these do not exist, is it not both because you want to humiliate them and because you are awaiting from these guests not only some news, some good news, come at last to deliver you from the hypermnesic interiority in which you go round in circles like hallucinators in a nightmare, but also, paradoxically, a legitimacy? For you are at once very sure and very unsure of your rights, and even of your community, of the homogeneity of your practices, your methods, your styles. You cannot rely on the least consensus, on the least axiomatic concordat among you. Basically, you do not exist, you are not founded to exist as a foundation, and this is what Joyce's signature gives you to read. So you call on strangers to come and tell you, as I am doing in reply to your invitation: You exist, you intimidate me, I recognize you, I recognize your paternal and grandpaternal authority, recognize me and give me a diploma in Joycean studies.

Of course you do not believe a word of what I am saying to you at the moment. And even if it were true, and even if, yes, it is true, you would not believe me if I told you that I am also called Elijah: no, this name is not inscribed on my official documents, but it was given to me on my seventh day. Moreover, Elijah is the name of the prophet present at *all* circumcisions. He is the patron, if we can put it like this, of circumcisions. The chair on which their newborn baby boy is held is called "Elijah's chair."

[. . . .]

So where are we going with the alliance of this Joycean community? What will become of it at this pace of accumulation and commemoration in one or two centuries, taking into account new technologies for archiving and storing information? Finally, Elijah is not me, nor some stranger come to say this thing to you, the news from outside, even the apocalypse of Joycean studies, that is, the truth, the final revelation (and you know that Elijah was always associated with an apocalyptic discourse). No, Elijah is you: you are the Elijah of *Ulysses*, who is presented as a large telephone exchange ("HELLO THERE, CENTRAL!" *U*, 149), the marshalling yard, the network through which all information must transit. We can imagine that there will soon be a giant computer of Joycean studies ("operating all this trunk line. . . . Book through to eternity junction" *U*, 473). It would capitalize all publications, coordinate and teleprogram all communication, colloquia, theses, papers, and would draw up an index in all languages. We would be able to consult it any time by satellite or by "sunphone," day and night, taking advantage of the reliability of an answering machine. "Hello, yes, yes, what are you asking for? Oh, for all the occurrences of the word *yes* in *Ulysses?* Yes." It would remain to be seen if the basic language of this computer would be English and if its patent would be American, given the overwhelming and significant majority of Americans in the trust of the Joyce Foundation. It would also remain to be seen if we could consult this computer on the word *yes*, and if the *yes*, in particular, the one involved in consulting operations, can be counted, calculated, numbered. A circle will shortly lead me back to this question.

In any case, the figure of Elijah, whether it be that of the prophet or the circumciser, of polymathic competence, or of telematic mastery, is only a synecdoche of Ulyssean narration, at once smaller and greater than the whole.

We should, then, get rid of a double illusion and a double intimidation. (1) No truth can come from outside the Joycean community, that is, without the experience, the cunning, and the knowledge amassed by overtrained readers. But (2) inversely, or symmetrically, there is no model for "Joycean" competence, no interiority and no closure possible for the concept of such a competence. There is no absolute criterion for measuring the relevance of a discourse on the subject of a text signed "Joyce." The very concept of competence finds itself shaken by this event. For we must write, write in one language, while we respond to the *yes* and countersign in another language. The very discourse of competence (that of neutral, metalinguistic knowledge immune from all untranslatable writing, etc.) is thus incompetent,

the least pertinent there is on the subject of Joyce, who, moreover, also finds himself in the same situation whenever he speaks
of his "work".

Instead of pursuing these generalities, and bearing in mind
time passing, I return to the *yes* in *Ulysses*. For a very long time,
the question of the *yes* has mobilized or traversed everything
that I have been trying to think, write, teach, or read. To cite
only the example of readings, I had devoted seminars and texts
to the *yes*, to the double *yes* in Nietzsche's *Zarathustra* ("Thus
spake Zarathustra," Mulligan moreover says—*U*, 29), the *yes*,
yes of the hymen, which is still the best example, the *yes* of the
great midday affirmation, and then the ambiguity of the double
yes: one of them comes down to the Christian assumption of
one's burden, the *Ja, Ja* of the donkey overloaded as Christ was
with memory and responsibility; and the other *yes, yes* that is
light, airy, dancing, solar is also a *yes* of reaffirmation, of promise, and of oath, a *yes* to the eternal recurrence.[7] The difference
between the two *yes*es, or rather between the two repetitions of
the *yes*, remains unstable, subtle, sublime. One repetition haunts
the other. For Nietzsche, who, like Joyce, anticipated that one
day professorships would be set up to study his *Zarathustra*, the
yes always finds its chance with a certain kind of woman. In the
same way, in Blanchot's *La folie du jour*, the quasi-narrator attributes the power to say *yes* to women, to the beauty of women,
beautiful insofar as they say *yes*: "*J'ai pourtant rencontré des
êtres qui n'ont jamais dit à la vie, tais-toi, et jamais à la mort,
va-t-en. Presque toujours des femmes, de belles créatures*" (Yet I
have met people who have never said to life, "Quiet!", who have
never said to death, "Go away!" Almost always women, beautiful creatures.)

The *yes* then, would be of woman—and not just of the mother,
the flesh, the earth, as is so often said of Molly's *yes*es in the
majority of readings devoted to her: "Penelope, bed, flesh, earth,
monologue," said Gilbert, and many others after him and even
before him, and here Joyce is no more competent than anyone
else. This is not false, it is even the truth of a certain truth, but
it is not all, and it is not so simple. The law of gender *[genre]*[8]
seems to me to be largely overdetermined and infinitely more
complicated, whether we are speaking of sexual or grammatical

gender, or again of rhetorical technique. To call this a monologue is to display a somnambulistic carelessness. So I wanted to listen again to Molly's *yes*es. But could one do this without making them resonate with all the *yes*es that prepare the way for them, correspond to them, and keep them hanging on the other end of the line throughout the whole book? So, last summer in Nice I read *Ulysses* again, first in French, then in English, pencil in hand, counting the *oui*'s and then the *yes*es and sketching out a typology of them. As you can imagine, I dreamt of hooking up to the Joyce Foundation computer, and the result is not the same from one language to the other.

Molly is not Elijah *(Elie)*, is not *Moelie* (for you know that the Moy'l is the circumciser), and Molly is not Joyce, but even so: her *yes* circumnavigates and circumscribes, encircling the last chapter of *Ulysses*, since it is at once her first and her last word, her send-off *[envoi]* and her closing cadence *[chute]:* "Yes because he never did" and finally "and yes I said yes I will Yes" (*U*, 704). The last, eschatological "Yes" occupies the place of the signature at the bottom right of the text. Even if one distinguishes, as one must, Molly's "yes" from that of *Ulysses*, in which she is but a figure and a moment, even if one distinguishes, as one also must do, these two signatures (that of Molly and that of *Ulysses*) from that of Joyce, even so they read each other and call out to *[s'appellent]* each other. They call to each other precisely through a *yes*, which always inaugurates a scene of call and request: it confirms and countersigns. Affirmation demands *a priori* confirmation, repetition, the safekeeping, and the memory of the *yes*. A certain narrativity is to be found at the simple core *[coeur simple]* of the simplest *yes:* "I asked him with my eyes to ask again yes and then he asked me would I yes to say yes" (*U*, 704), and so on. A *yes* never comes alone, and one is never alone in saying *yes*. Nor do we laugh alone, as Freud says, and we shall come back to this. And Freud also stresses that the unconscious never says *no*.

But in what way does the Joycean signature imply what we will curiously refer to here as the question of *yes*? There is a question of the *yes*, a request of the *yes*, and perhaps, for it is never certain, an unconditional, inaugural affirmation of the *yes* that cannot necessarily be distinguished from the question or the request. Joyce's signature, or at least the one that interests me here, though I will never claim to exhaust the phenomenon, cannot be summarized by the affixing of his seal in the form of the patronymic name and the play of signifiers, as they say, in which to reinscribe the name "Joyce." The inductions to which these associations and society parlor games have for a long time been giving rise are easy, tedious, and naively jubilatory. And even if they are not entirely irrelevant, they begin by confusing a signature with a simple mention, apposition, or manipulation of the name as conferred by one's civil status. However, neither in its juridical phenomenon, as I have just suggested, nor in the essential complexity of its structure, does a signature amount to the mere mention of a proper name. Nor can the proper name itself, which a signature does not merely spell out or mention, be reduced to the legal patronym. The latter risks setting up a screen or mirror toward which psychoanalysts, in a hurry to conclude, would rush headlong like dazzled birds. I have tried to show this for Genet, Ponge, and Blanchot.[9] As for the scene of the patronym, the opening pages of *Ulysses* should suffice to educate the reader.

Who is signing? Who is signing *what* in Joyce's name? The answer cannot be in the form of a key or a clinical category that could be pulled out of a hat whenever a colloquium required. Nevertheless, as a modest foreword, which might be of interest only to me, I thought it possible to examine this question of signature through that of the *yes* which it always implies and insofar as it espouses *[se conjoint]* here, it marries, *[se marie]* another question: Who is laughing and how does one laugh *with* Joyce, in a singular way *in* Joyce, and since *Ulysses?*

[. . . .]

But why laugh and why laughter? No doubt, everything has already been said on laughter in Joyce, on parody, satire, derision, humor, irony, mockery. And on his Homeric laughter and his Rabelaisian laughter. It remains perhaps to think of laughter, precisely, as a remains. What does laughter want to say? What does laughter want? *[Qu'est-ce que ça veut dire, le rire? Qu'est-ce que ça veut rire?]* Once one recognizes that, in principle, in *Ulysses* the virtual totality of experience, of meaning, of history, of the symbolic, of language, and of writing, the great cycle and the great encyclopedia of cultures, scenes, and affects, in sum, the sum total of all sum totals tends to unfold itself and reconstitute itself by playing out all its possible combinations, while writing seeks to occupy virtually all the spaces, well, the totalizing hermeneutic that makes up the task of a worldwide and eternal institution of Joyce studies will find itself confronted with what I hesitate to call a dominant affect, a *Stimmung* or a *pathos*, a tone that re-traverses all the others and that nevertheless is not part of the series of the others since it *re-marks* all of them, adds itself to them without allowing itself to be added in or totalized, in the manner of a remains that is at once quasi-transcendental and supplementary. And it is this *yes–laughter [oui–rire]* that overmarks not only the totality of the writing, but all the qualities, modalities, genres of laughter whose differences might be classified into some sort of typology.

[. . . .]

With a certain ear, with a certain hearing, I can hear a reactive, even a negative, *yes–laughter [oui–rire]* resonate. It takes joy in hypermnesic mastery and in spinning spiderwebs that defy all other possible mastery, as impregnable as an alpha and omega-programophone in which all histories, all stories, discourses, knowledge, all the signatures to come that Joycean and a few other institutions might address, would be prescribed, computed in advance outside the scope of any effective computer, understood in advance, captive, predicted, partialized, metonymized, exhausted, like subjects, whether they know it or not. And science, consciousness [*conscience*] cannot fix the situation, on the contrary. It just allows its supplementary calculation to be put to the service of the master signature. It may laugh at Joyce, but it thereby indebts itself once again to him. As is said in *Ulysses*, "*Was Du verlachst wirst Du noch dienen.*/Brood of mockers" (*U,* 197).

There is a James Joyce whom one can hear laughing at this omnipotence, at this great *tour joué:* a trick played and a grand tour completed. I am speaking of the tricks and tours of Ulysses, the trickster, the cunning one *[le retors]*, and of the great tour he completes when on his return *[retour,]* he has come back from everything, from all his illusions. This is triumphal, jubilatory laughter, certainly, but it is also, since jubilation always betrays some kind of mourning, the laughter of resigned lucidity. For omnipotence remains phantasmatic, it opens and defines the dimensions of phantasm. Joyce cannot *not know this*. He cannot, for example, not know that the book of all books, *Ulysses* or *Finnegans Wake*, is still fairly inconsequential among the millions and millions of other works in the Library of Congress.

[. . . .]

Even in its resignation to phantasm, this *yes-laughter [oui-rire]* reaffirms the control of a subjectivity that draws everything together as it draws itself together, or as it delegates itself to the word, in what is merely a vast dress rehearsal *[répétition]*, during the sun's movement, one day from east to west. It heaps abuse on others and on itself, sometimes sadistically, sardonically: it is the cynicism of a sneering grin, of sarcasm, and of mocking laughter: *brood of mockers*. It heaps a burden on itself and loads itself down, gaining weight and growing pregnant with the whole of memory; it assumes the resumption, the exhaustion, the parousia. It is not contradictory to state, regarding this *yes-laughter*, that it is that of Nietzsche's Christian donkey, the one who cries *Ja, ja*, or even of the Judeo-Christian beast that wants to make the Greek laugh once he has been circumcised of his own laughter: absolute knowledge as the truth of religion, memory, guilt, literature of burden *[littérature de somme]*—as we say, "beast of burden"—and literature that summons one to appear before the law *[littérature de sommation]*, the moment of the debt. A, E, I, O, U, *I owe you*: This *I* constitutes itself in the debt itself; it only comes into its own, there where it was, on the basis of the debt.[10]

[. . . .]

This yes-laughter of encircling reappropriation, of all-powerful Odyssean recapitulation, accompanies the installation of a structure virtually capable of impregnating in advance its patented signature, even that of Molly, with all the countersignatures to come, even after the death of the artist as an old man, who moves off with only the empty shell, the accident of a substance. The machine of filiation—legitimate or illegitimate—functions well and is ready for anything, ready to domesticate, circumcise, circumvent everything; it lends itself to the encyclopedic reappropriation of absolute knowledge which gathers itself up close to itself, as Life of the Logos, that is, also in the truth of natural death. We are here in Frankfurt to bear witness to this in commemoration.

But the eschatological tone of this yes-laughter also seems to me to be worked over or traversed—I prefer to say *haunted*—joyously ventriloquized by a completely different music, by the vowels of a completely different song. I can hear it too, very close to the other one, as the yes-laughter of a gift without debt, the light almost amnesic, affirmation, of a gift or an abandoned event, which in classical language is called "the work," a lost signature without a proper name that only shows and names the cycle of reappropriation and domestication of all the paraphs in order to delimit their phantasm, to contrive the break-in necessary for the coming of the other, an other whom one can always call Elijah, if Elijah is the name of the unforeseeable other for whom a place must be kept, and no longer Elijah, head of the megaprogramotelephonic network, Elijah, the great switchboard operator, but the other Elijah: Elijah, the other. But there we are, this is a homonym: Elijah can always be one and the other at the same time, we cannot invite the one without the risk of the other turning up. But this is a risk that must forever be run. I return then, in this final movement, to the risk or the chance of this contamination of one yes-laughter by the other, of the parasiting of one Elijah, that is to say of one me, by the other.

Why have I linked the question of laughter, of a laughter which *remains* as the fundamental and quasi-transcendental tonality, to that of the "yes"?

In order to ask oneself what happens with *Ulysses*, or with the arrival of whatever, whomever—of Elijah for example—it is necessary to try to think the singularity of the event, and therefore the uniqueness of the signature, or rather of an irreplaceable mark that cannot necessarily be reduced to the phenomenon of copyright, legible in the patronym after circumcision. It is necessary to try to think circumcision, if you like, beginning with a possibility of the mark, that of a trait that precedes and provides its figure. Now if laughter is a fundamental or abyssal tonality in

Ulysses, if its analysis is not exhausted by any of the forms of knowledge available precisely because it laughs at knowledge and from knowledge, then laughter bursts out in the event of signature itself. And there is no signature without *yes.* If the signature does not amount to the manipulation or the mention of a name, it supposes the irreversible commitment of the person confirming, who *says* or *does* yes, the token of some mark left behind. Before asking oneself who is doing the signing, whether Joyce is or Molly is, or what is the status of the difference between the author's signature and that of a figure or a fiction signed by an author; before conversing about sexual difference as duality and expressing one's conviction of the "onesidedly womanly woman" (and here I am quoting Frank Budgen and others after him) of Molly's character, the beautiful plant, the herb or *pharmakon,* [11] or of the "onesidedly masculine" character of James Joyce; before taking into consideration what Joyce says about the non-stop monologue as "the indispensable countersign to Bloom's passport to eternity" (and once again, the competence of Joyce in letters and conversations does not seem to me to enjoy any privilege); before manipulating clinical categories and a psychoanalytical knowledge that are largely derivative in view of the possibilities we are talking about here, it is necessary to ask oneself what a signature is: It requires a *yes* more "ancient" than the question "what is?" since the latter presupposes it; it is thus "older" than knowledge. It is necessary to ask for what reason the *yes* always comes about as a *yes, yes.* I say the *yes* and not the word "yes," for there can be a *yes* without the word, which is precisely our problem.

One ought, then, to have preceded all of this with a long, knowledgeable, and thoughtful meditation on the meaning, the function, the presupposition above all of the *yes:* before language, in language, but also in an experience of the plurality of languages that perhaps no longer belongs to linguistics in the strict sense. The expansion toward a pragmatics seems to me to be necessary but inadequate so long as it does not open itself up to a thinking of the trace, of writing, in a sense that I have tried to explain elsewhere and which I cannot go into here.

What is it that is spoken, written, what occurs *[advient]* with *yes?*

Yes can be implied without the word being said or written. This explains, for example, the multiplication of *yes*es everywhere in the French version when it is assumed that a *yes* is marked by English sentences from which the word *yes* is in fact absent. But at the limit, given that *yes* is co-extensive with every statement, there is a great temptation, in French but first of all in English, to double up everything with a kind of continuous *yes*, even to double up the *yes*es articulated simply to mark the rhythm, intakes of breath in the form of pauses or murmured interjections, as sometimes happens in *Ulysses*. This *yes* comes —from me to me, from me to the other in me, from the other to me—to confirm the primary telephonic "Hello": yes, that's right, that's what I'm saying, I am, in fact, speaking, yes, there we are, I'm speaking, yes, yes you can hear me, I can hear you, yes, we are in the process of speaking, there is language, you are receiving me, it's like this, it takes place, happens, is written, is marked, yes, yes.

But let's set out again from the *yes phenomenon*, the manifest *yes* patently marked as a *word*, spoken, written, or phonogramed. Such a word says but says nothing in itself, if by saying we mean designating, showing, describing some thing to be found outside language, outside marking *[hors marque]*. Its only references are other marks, which are also marks of the other. Given that *yes* does not say, show, name anything that is beyond marking, some would be tempted to conclude that *yes* says nothing: an empty word, barely an adverb, since all adverbs, in which grammatical category *yes* is situated in our languages, have a richer, more determined semantic charge than the *yes* they always presuppose. In short, *yes* would be transcendental adverbiality, the ineffaceable supplement to any verb: in the beginning was the adverb, yes, but as an interjection, still very close to the inarticulated cry, a preconceptual vocalization, the perfume of a discourse.

But can one sign with a perfume? Just as we can replace *yes* neither by a thing which it would be supposed to describe (it describes nothing, states nothing, even if it is a sort of performative implied in all statements: yes, I am stating, it is stated, etc.), nor even by the thing it is supposed to approve or affirm, likewise one cannot replace the *yes* by the names of the concepts supposed to describe this act or operation, if indeed this is an act or operation. The concept of activity or of actuality does not seem to me apt to account for a *yes*. And this quasi-act cannot be replaced by *approval, affirmation, confirmation, acquiescence, consent*. The word *affirmative* used by the military to avoid all kinds of technical risks, does not replace the *yes;* it supposes it once again: yes, I am saying *affirmative.*

What does this *yes* lead us to think, this *yes* that names, describes, designates nothing, and that has no reference outside marking (and not outside language, for *yes* can get by without words, or at least the word *yes*)? In its radically nonconstative or nondescriptive dimension, even if it is saying "yes" to a description or a narration, *yes* is *par excellence* and through and through a performative. But this characterization seems to me inadequate. First because a performative must be a *sentence* and one which is sufficiently endowed with meaning by itself, in a given conventional context, if it is to bring about a determined event. Now I believe, yes, that—to put it in a classical philosophical code—*yes* is the transcendental condition of all performative dimensions. A promise, an oath, an order, a commitment always implies a *yes, I sign.* The *I* of *I sign* says *yes* and says *yes* to itself, even if it signs a simulacrum. Any event brought about by a performative mark, any writing in the widest sense of the word involves a *yes,* whether or not it is phenomenalized, that is, verbalized or adverbalized as such. Molly says *yes,* she remembers *yes,* the *yes* that she spoke with her eyes to ask for *yes* with her eyes, et cetera.

We are in an area which is *not yet* the space where the big questions of the origin of negation, affirmation or denegation can and must be deployed. Nor are we even in the space where Joyce was able to reverse *"Ich bin der Geist, der stets verneint"* by saying that Molly is the flesh that always says *yes.* The *yes* we are talking about now is "anterior" to all these reversing alternatives, to all these dialectics. They suppose it and envelop it. Before the *Ich* in *Ich bin* affirms or negates, it poses itself or pre-poses itself: not as *ego,* as the conscious or unconscious self, as masculine or feminine subject, spirit or flesh, but as a pre-performative force that, for example, in the form of the "I" marks that "I" as addressing itself to some other, however undetermined he or she is: "Yes-I," or "Yes-I-say-to-the-other," even if *I* says *no* and even if *I* addresses itself without speaking. The minimal, primary *yes*, the telephonic "hello" or tap [*coup*] through a prison wall, marks, before meaning or signifying: *I-here*, listen answer, there is some mark, there is some other. Negativities may ensue, but even if they completely take over, this *yes* can no longer be erased.

I have had to yield to the rhetorical necessity of translating this minimal and undetermined, almost virgin, address into words, into words such as "I," "I am," "language," at a point where the position of the *I*, of being, and of language still remains derivative with regard to this *yes*. This is the whole problem for anyone wishing to speak on the subject of the *yes*. A metalanguage will always be impossible here insofar as it will itself suppose the event of the *yes* which it will be unable to comprehend. The situation will be the same for any accountancy or computation, for any calculation aiming to regulate a series of *yes*es according to the principle of reason and its machines. *Yes* marks that there is address to the other. This address is not necessarily a dialogue or an interlocution, since it supposes neither voice nor symmetry, but the haste, in advance, of a response that is already asking. For if there is some other, if there is some *yes*, then the other no longer lets itself be produced by the same or by the self. *Yes*, the condition of any signature and any performative, addresses itself to some other that it does not constitute, and to whom it can only begin by *asking*, in response to a request that is always anterior, *to ask him/her* to say *yes*. Time appears only with this singular anachrony. These commitments may remain fictitious, fallacious, and always reversible, and the address may remain invisible or undetermined; this does not change anything in the necessity of the structure. *A priori* it breaks off all possible monologue. Nothing is less a monologue than Molly's "monologue," even if, within certain conventional limits, we have the right to consider it as deriving from the genre or type known as the "monologue." But a discourse comprised between two *Yes*es of different quality, two *Yes*es with capital letters, and therefore two gramophoned *Yes*es, could not be a monologue, but at the very most a soliloquy.

But we can see why the appearance of a monologue imposes itself here, precisely because of the *yes, yes*. The *yes* says nothing and asks only for another *yes*, the *yes* of an other, which, as we will shortly see, is analytically—or by *a priori* synthesis—implied in the first *yes*. The latter only situates itself, advances itself, marks itself in the call for its confirmation, in the *yes, yes*. It begins with the *yes, yes*, with the second *yes*, with the other *yes*, but as this is still only a *yes* that *recalls*, (and Molly is remembering, is recalling to herself *[se rappelle]* from the other *yes*), we might always be tempted to call this anamnesis monologic. And tautological. The *yes* says nothing but the *yes*, another *yes* that resembles it even if it says *yes* to the advent of an altogether other *yes*. It appears monotautological or specular, or imaginary, because it opens up the position of the *I*, which is itself the condition of all performativity. Austin reminds us that the performative grammar *par excellence* is that of a sentence in the first person of the present indicative: yes, I promise, I accept, I refuse, I order, I do, I will, and so on. "He promises" is not an explicit performative and cannot be so unless an *I* is understood, as, for example, in "I swear to you that he promises."

[. . . .]

The self-positioning in the *yes* or the *Ay* is, however, neither tautological nor narcissistic; and it is not egological even if it commences the movement of circular reappropriation, the odyssey that can give rise to all these determined modalities. It holds open the circle that it commences. In the same way, it is not yet performative, not yet transcendental, although it remains presupposed in any performativity, *a priori* in any constative theoricity, in any knowledge, in any transcendentality. For the same reason, it is preontological, if ontology expresses what is or the being of what is. The discourse on being supposes the responsibility of the *yes:* yes what is said is said, I am responding, or the interpellation of being is responded to, and so on. Still in telegraphic style, I will situate the possibility of the *yes* and of the *yes-laughter [oui-rire]* in that place where transcendental egology, the ontoencyclopedia, the great speculative logic, fundamental ontology, and the thought of being open onto a thought of the gift and of sending which they presuppose but cannot contain.

[. . . .]

The self-affirmation of the *yes* can address itself to the other only by recalling itself to itself *[se rappelant à soi]*, in saying to itself *yes, yes.* The circle of this universal presupposition, fairly comic in itself, is like a dispatch *[envoi]* to oneself, a sending back *[renvoi]* of self to self which *both never leaves itself and never arrives* at itself. Molly says to herself (apparently talking to herself), reminds herself, that she says *yes* in asking the other to ask her to say *yes*, and she starts or finishes by saying *yes* to the other in herself, but she does so in order to say to the other that she will say *yes* if the other asks her, yes, to say *yes.* This sending back and forth *[envois et renvois]* always mimics the situation of questions and answers in scholastics. And the scene of "sending oneself to oneself, getting it off with oneself" is repeated many times in *Ulysses* in its literally postal form.[12] And it is always marked with scorn, like the phantasm and failure themselves. The circle does not close.

[. . . .]

So it is a matter of self-sending *[s'envoyer]*, and in the end of sending oneself someone who says *yes* without needing, in order to say it, what the French idiom or *argot* babelizes under the terms of *s'envoyer*: to get it off with oneself or someone. Self-sending barely allows itself a detour via the virgin mother when the father imagines sending himself, getting off on, the seed of a consubstantial son: "a mystical estate, an apostolic succession, from only begetter to only begotten" (*U*, 207). It is one of the passages on "*Amor matris*, subjective and objective genitive," which "may be the only true thing in life. Paternity may be a legal fiction" (*U*, 207).

[Another] example precedes it slightly and comes immediately after *Was Du verlachst*: "He Who Himself begot, middler the Holy Ghost, and Himself sent Himself, Agenbuyer, between Himself and others, Who . . ." (*U*, 197). Two pages later:

——Telegram! he said. Wonderful inspiration! Telegram! A papal bull!

He sat on a corner of the unlit desk, reading aloud joyfully:

——*the sentimentalist is he who would enjoy without*

incurring the immense debtorship of the thing done. Signed:
Dedalus. (*U*, 199)

To be more and more aphoristic and telegraphic, I will say in
conclusion that the Ulyssean circle of self-sending commands a
reactive yes-laughter, the manipulatory operation of hypermnesic reappropriation, whenever the phantasm of a signature wins
out, a signature gathering the dispatch together near itself. But
when (and it is only a question of rhythm) the circle opens,
reappropriation is renounced, the specular gathering together of
the dispatch lets itself be joyfully dispersed in a multiplicity of
unique yet innumerable dispatches, then the other *yes* laughs,
the other, yes, laughs.

But here's the thing: The relationship of one *yes* to the Other,
of one *yes* to the other, and of one *yes* to the other *yes*, must be
such that the contamination of the two *yes*es remains inevitable.
And not only as a threat: but also as a chance. With or without
words, taken as a minimal event, a *yes* demands *a priori* its own
repetition, its own memorizing, demands that a *yes to* the *yes*
inhabit the arrival of the first *yes*, which is therefore never simply originary. We cannot say *yes* without promising to confirm it
and to remember it, to keep it safe, countersigned in another *yes*;
we cannot say *yes* without promise and memory, without the
promise of memory. Molly remembers, recalls herself to herself.
This memory of a promise begins the circle of appropriation,
bringing with it all the risks of technical repetition, of automa-
tized archives, of gramophony, of simulacrum, of wandering deprived of address and destination. A *yes* must entrust itself to
memory. Having come already from the other, in the dissymmetry of the demand, and from the other of whom it is requested to
request a *yes*, the *yes* entrusts itself to the memory of the other,
of the *yes* of the other and of the other yes. All the risks already
crowd around from the first breath of *yes*. And the first breath
hangs on the breath of the other, already, always a second breath.
It remains there out of sound and out of sight, linked up in
advance to some "gramophone in the grave."

We cannot separate the twin *yes*es, and yet they remain completely other. Like Shem and Shaun, like writing and the post.
Such a coupling seems to me to ensure not so much the signature

of *Ulysses* but the *vibration* of an event which *succeeds only in/ by asking.* A differential vibration of several tonalities, several qualities of yes-laughter which do not allow themselves to be stabilized in the indivisible simplicity of one sole dispatch, of self to self, or of one sole consigning, but which call for the counter-signature of the other, for a *yes* which would resonate in a completely other writing, an other language, an other idiosyncrasy, stamped with an other *timbre.*

[. . . .]

—Translated by Tina Kendall and Shari Benstock

NOTES

1. *Ulysses* (London: Penguin, 1968), p. 124. All further references to this edition will be indicated by *U*, followed by the page number.—ED.

2. Elsewhere, in the brothel, it is the circumcised who say the "Shema Israel," and once again the dead sea, the *Lacus Morte*, shows up: "THE CIRCUMCISED: (In a dark guttural chant as they cast dead fruit upon him, no flowers) Shema Israel Adonai Elohena Adonai Echad" (*U*, 496).

And since we are talking about *Ulysses*, the dead one, the gramophone, and soon laughter, here is *Remembrance of Things Past:* "He stopped laughing; I should have liked to recognize my friend, but, like Ulysses in the Odyssey when he rushes forward to embrace his dead mother, like the spiritualist who tries in vain to elicit from a ghost an answer which will reveal its identity, like the visitor at an exhibition of electricity who cannot believe that the voice which the gramophone restores unaltered to life is not a voice spontaneously emitted by a human being, I was obliged to give up the attempt." Earlier we read: "The familiar voice seemed to be emitted by a gramophone more perfect than any I had ever heard." *The Past Recaptured*, Andreas Mayor, trans. (New York: Vintage Books, 1971), pp. 188–89.

3. Derrida calls attention here to the word *coup* in the expression *coup de téléphone,* telephone call, and thus to the resonance with figures of chance and randomness (*coup de dés,* throw of the dice; *coup de chance,* stroke of luck) as well as the arbitrary imposition of an order or a law (e.g., *coup d'état*). The word *coup* has been given a large field of play throughout Derrida's writing; cf., in particular, *Glas* and *Dissemination.*—ED.

4. See Samuel Weber, "The Debts of Deconstruction and Other, Related Assumptions" in William Kerrigan and Joseph H. Smith, eds., *Taking Chances: Derrida, Psychoanalysis, and Literature* (Baltimore: The Johns Hopkins University Press, 1984), pp. 59 ff.—ED.

5. In the French *Bibliothèque Nationale,* certain materials considered scandalous are shelved in an area called *l'enfer* (hell).—ED.

6. Literally, language of the eye, but one hears and sees as well *langue d'oïl*, the medieval northern language from which modern French derives for the most part. The latter was distinguished from the southern language—*langue d'oc*—by the different words for yes: *oïl (oui)* and *oc*. Earlier in the essay, Derrida noted that Italian was also sometimes called the "langue de *si.*"—ED.

7. On Nietzsche and affirmation see especially *The Ear of the Other* [1982]; also **Spurs,** above.—ED.

8. "The Law of Genre" is the title of one of Derrida's essays (in *Parages*) on the Blanchot text mentioned here, *La folie du jour;* see as well **"Living On,"** above.—ED.

9. Derrida has written on Genet's signature in *Glas*, on Ponge's signature in *Signsponge*, and on Blanchot in *Parages.*—ED.

10. This passage is making oblique reference to Freud's famous formula: *Wo Es war, soll Ich werden,* which is usually translated as "Where Id was, there shall Ego be."—TRANS.

11. On this word, see above, **"Plato's Pharmacy,"** pp. 185–87.—ED.

12. Literally, *s'envoyer* would mean to send oneself something. But this form of the verb is used colloquially in the expressions: *s'envoyer quelqu'un* (literally to send oneself someone), to make it with someone, to have it off with someone, to get laid; *s'envoyer en l'air* (literally, to send oneself into the air), also to have it off, get some, or get laid. The only point at which colloquial English might be seen to approach such a use would be in expressions like "You send me," "That really sends me."—ED.

All the examples are thus cut out and cut across
each other. Look at the holes, if you can.
—*Glas,* p. 210

Bibliography of Works by Jacques Derrida

The following bibliography lists, by date of publication in France, all the major texts Derrida has published as of 1990. Essays first published separately and later reprinted as book chapters or in a collection are generally listed under the latter date. The French entry is followed by reference to the American edition of the English translation, if available. In the rare cases in which a translation was published before the French edition, this order is reversed and the entry is listed by date of publication of the translation. The titles of works included or excerpted in *A Derrida Reader* are printed in boldface.

This bibliography is extensive, but not exhaustive. It does not list absolutely everything Derrida has so far published and it does not give a history of the publication of each text, many of which have appeared in several different forms and places. For more complete information, readers are directed to "A Jacques Derrida Bibliography: 1962–1990" by Albert Leventure, forthcoming in *Textual Practice* (vol. 5, no. 1 [Spring 1991]). I was fortunate in being able to consult Leventure's bibliography in manuscript while compiling this list and acknowledge gratefully the thoroughness of his research.

Derrida's work is being translated into English at a considerable pace. Many of the untranslated titles listed here may have been translated by the time this bibliography appears. Although I was not always able to anticipate forthcoming publications, I have noted texts that will be translated for two important volumes of Derrida's writings currently in preparation, both edited by Deborah Esch and Thomas Keenan: *Institutions of Philosophy* (Harvard University Press) and *Negotiations: Writings* (University of Minnesota Press).

1962: "Introduction à *L'Origine de la géométrie* par Edmund Husserl." Paris: Presses Universitaires de France. *Edmund Husserl's "Origin of Geometry": An Introduction.* Translated with an introduction and afterword by John P. Leavey, Jr. Lincoln: University of Nebraska Press, 1989 (rev. ed.). [Derrida's presentation of his own translation of Husserl's text.]

1967: *La Voix et le phènomène: Introduction au problème du signe dans la phénoménologie de Husserl.* Paris: Presses Universitaires de France. **Speech and Phenomena and Other Essays on Husserl's Theory of Signs.** Edited and translated with an introduction by David B. Allison. Evanston, Ill.: Northwestern University Press, 1973.

De la grammatologie. Paris: Editions de Minuit. **Of Grammatology.** Translated with an introduction by Gayatri Chakravorty Spivak. Baltimore, Md.: The Johns Hopkins University Press, 1976.

L'écriture et la différence. Paris: Editions du Seuil. *Writing and Difference.* Translated with an introduction by Alan Bass. Chicago: University of Chicago Press, 1978. [This collection contains essays on formalist literary criticism ("Force and Signification"), on Foucault's *History of Madness* ("Cogito and the History of Madness"), on the poet Edmond Jabès ("Edmond Jabès and the Question of the Book," and "Ellipsis"), on Emmanuel Levinas ("Violence and Metaphysics"), on the French interpretation of Hegel's *Phenomenology of Mind* (" 'Genesis and Structure' and Phenomenology"), on Antonin Artaud ("La parole soufflée" and "The Theater of Cruelty and the Closure of Representation"), on Freud's "metaphor" of writing ("Freud and the Scene of Writing"), on Georges Bataille's reading of Hegel ("From Restricted to General Economy: An Hegelianism without Reserve"), and on the structuralism of Claude Lévi-Strauss ("Structure, Sign, and Play in the Discourse of the Human Sciences").

1972: *La dissémination.* Paris: Editions du Seuil. Dissemination. Translated with an introduction by Barbara Johnson. Chicago: University of Chicago Press, 1981. [Beside **"Plato's Pharmacy"** and **"The Double Session,"** this collection contains two other long essays: "Hors livre," on the genre of the preface, with particular reference to Hegel, and "Dissemination," on *Nombres* by Philippe Sollers.]

Marges de la philosophie. Paris: Editions de Minuit. Margins of Philosophy. Translated by Alan Bass. Chicago: University of Chicago Press, 1982. [Beside **"Tympan," "Différance,"** and **"Signature Event Context,"** this collection contains: *"Ousia* and *Grammē:* Note on a Note from *Being and Time,"* "The Pit and the Pyramid: Introduction to Hegel's Semiology," "The Ends of Man" (on Sartrean humanism and the anthropological interpretation of Hegel, Husserl, and Heidegger), "The Linguistic Circle of Geneva," "Form and Meaning: A Note on the Phenomenology of Language," "The Supplement of Copula: Philosophy before Linguistics" (on Emile Benveniste's linguistic categories), "White Mythology: Metaphor in the Text of Philosophy" (on Aristotelian rhetoric), and "Qual Quelle: Valéry's Sources."]

Positions. Paris: Editions de Minuit. Translated by Alan Bass. Chi-

cago: University of Chicago Press, 1981. [A series of three interviews, the first Derrida ever gave. His interlocutors are members
of the *Tel Quel* group (Henri Ronse, Julia Kristeva, Jean-Louis
Houdebine, and Guy Scarpetta). He is interrogated about, among
other things, his relation to semiology, Marxism, and Lacanian
psychoanalysis.]

1974: *Glas.* Paris: Editions Galilée. [Reprinted, in two volumes, by Denoël/
Gonthier, 1981.] **Glas.** Translated by John P. Leavey, Jr., and Richard Rand. Lincoln: University of Nebraska Press, 1986. [A companion volume to the translation, *Glassary* (also University of Nebraska Press, 1986), contains a very useful index, concordance, and
list of references.]

1975: "Economimesis." In *Mimesis: Des articulations.* Edited by Sylviane
Agacinski et al. Paris: Aubier–Flammarion, 1975. "Economimesis." Translated by Richard Klein. *Diacritics*, vol. 11, no. 2 (1981),
pp. 3–25. [On Kant's *Critique of Judgment*.]

1976: *L'Archéologie du frivole: Lire Condillac.* Paris: Denoël/Gonthier. *The
Archeology of the Frivolous: Reading Condillac.* Translated with
an introduction by John P. Leavey, Jr. Pittsburgh, Pa.: Duquesne
University Press, 1980; reprinted, Lincoln: University of Nebraska
Press, 1987. [Derrida's essay prefaces a new edition of Condillac's
Essai sur l'origine des connaissances humaines, which had long
been unavailable in French.]
"Entre crochets: Entretien avec Jacques Derrida, 1ère partie." *Digraphe* no. 8, pp. 97–114. [Translation forthcoming in *Negotia-
tions*; a long written "interview" that ranges widely and in which
Derrida discusses *Glas* in particular; see below, Part II, "Ja, ou le
faux-bond," 1977.]
"Fors: Les mots anglés de Nicolas Abraham et Maria Torok." Foreword to Nicolas Abraham and Maria Torok, *Cryptonomie: Le Ver-
bier de l'Homme aux loups.* Paris: Aubier–Flammarion. "Fors: The
Anglish Words of Nicolas Abraham and Maria Torok." Translated
by Barbara Johnson as foreword to Nicolas Abraham and Maria
Torok, *The Wolf Man's Magic Word: A Cryptonomy.* Translated
(except for Derrida's foreword) with an introduction by Nicholas
Rand. Minneapolis: University of Minnesota Press, 1986.
"Où commence et comment finit un corps enseignant." In *Politiques
de la philosophie: Châtelet, Derrida, Foucault, Lyotard, Serres.*
Edited by Dominique Grisoni. Paris: Grasset, pp. 60–89. [Trans-
lation forthcoming in *Institutions.*]

1977: "L'âge de Hegel." In *Qui a peur de la philosophie*, edited by GREPH
[Groupe de recherches sur l'enseignement de la philosophie]. Paris:
Aubier–Flammarion, pp. 73–107. "The Age of Hegel." Translated
by Susan Winnett. *Glyph Textual Studies I*, 1986. [The "mani-

festo" of the GREPH, of which Derrida was founding member and long-time president; the French volume contains another brief essay by Derrida, "La Philosophie et ses classes," pp. 445–50.]

"Ja, ou le faux-bond: Entretien avec Jacques Derrida, 2ème partie." *Digraphe*, no. 11, pp. 83–121. [Translation forthcoming in *Negotiations*; see above, "Entre crochets," 1986.]

Limited Inc abc. . . . Baltimore, Md.: The Johns Hopkins University Press. [The French text was published as a supplement to its English translation, by Samuel Weber, which appeared first in *Glyph* 2. (On this debate with the American philosopher John Searle, see above our presentation of **"Signature Event Context,"** p. **81.**) The English translation has been reprinted, along with "Signature Event Context" and a new afterword, "Toward an Ethic of Discussion," also translated by Samuel Weber, in *Limited Inc*, edited by Gerald Graff. Evanston, Ill.: Northwestern University Press, 1988. French edition, under the same title: Paris: Galilée, 1990.]

"Scribble (pouvoir/écrire)." Preface to Bishop Warburton's *The Divine Legation of Moses Demonstrated: Essay on the Hieroglyphs of the Egyptians.* Paris: Aubier–Flammarion, pp. 7–43. "Scribble (writing–power)." Abridged translation by Cary Plotkin. *Yale French Studies*, 58 (1979), pp. 116–47.

1978: *Eperons: Les styles de Nietzsche.* Introduction by Stefano Agosti. Paris: Aubier–Flammarion. **Spurs: Nietzsche's Styles.** Translated by Barbara Harlow. Chicago: University of Chicago Press, 1979. [The American edition is bilingual.]

La Vérité en peinture. Paris: Aubier–Flammarion. **The Truth in Painting.** Translated by Geoff Bennington and Ian McLeod. Chicago: University of Chicago Press, 1987. [A collection of Derrida's writings on painting and aesthetics; beside **"Restitutions of the Truth in Pointing,"** it contains a preface ("Passe-Partout"), a long essay on Kant's *Critique of Judgment* ("Parergon"), catalogue texts for the painter Valerio Adami ("+R (Into the Bargain)"), and the artist Gérard Titus-Carmel ("Cartouches").]

1979: "Me—Psychoanalysis: An Introduction to the Translation of 'The Shell and the Kernel' by Nicolas Abraham." Translated by Richard Klein. *Diacritics*, vol. 9, no. 1, pp. 4–12. [The French text, "Moi—la psychanalyse," is included in *Psyché*, 1987.]

"Philosophie des Etats Généraux." In *Etats Généraux de la philosophie.* Paris: Flammarion, 1979. [The opening address delivered to the Estates General of Philosophy convened in 1979 by a group of philosophers to address the curtailment of the teaching of philosophy in French lycées and universities; translation forthcoming in *Institutions.*]

"Living On: Borderlines." Translated by James Hulbert. In *Decon-*

struction and Criticism. Edited by Harold Bloom et al. New York: Seabury Press. "Survivre: Journal de bord" first published in *Parages* (1986).

1980: *La Carte postale: de Socrate à Freud et au-delà.* Paris: Aubier–Flammarion. **The Post Card: From Socrates to Freud and Beyond.** Translated with an introduction by Alan Bass. Chicago: University of Chicago Press, 1987. [Beside **"Envois,"** **"To Speculate—on 'Freud',"** and **"Le Facteur de la vérité,"** this volume contains a short essay on transference in psychoanalysis, "Du tout."]

"Ocelle comme pas un." Preface to *L'enfant au chien-assis,* by Jos Joliet. Paris: Editions Galilée. [Untranslated.]

1982: **"Choreographies: An Interview with Jacques Derrida."** Edited and translated by Christie V. McDonald. *Diacritics,* vol. 12, no. 2 (Summer), pp. 66–76. [No published French version.]

"Coup d'envoi." In *Extraits d'un rapport pour le Collège International de Philosophie.* [Part of Derrida's contribution to the report commissioned by the Minister of Education, which became the founding document of the Collège International de Philosophie; this institution was established in 1983 with Derrida as its first president; translation forthcoming in *Institutions.*]

L'Oreille de l'autre: Otobiographies, transferts, traductions: Textes et débats avec Jacques Derrida. Edited by Claude Lévesque and Christie V. McDonald. Montréal: VLB Editions. *The Ear of the Other: Otobiography, Transference, Translation: Texts and Discussions with Jacques Derrida.* Edited by Christie V. McDonald. Translated by Peggy Kamuf and Avital Ronell. Lincoln: University of Nebraska Press, 1988 (rev. ed.). [Contains an essay on Nietzsche, "Otobiographies: The Teaching of Nietzsche and the Politics of the Proper Name," and two roundtable discussions, on the topics of autobiography and translation, with participants at a colloquium in Montreal in 1979; the French text of the essay was published separately by Editions Galilée in 1984 as *Otobiographies: L'enseignement de Nietzsche et la politique du nom propre.*]

1983: *D'un ton apocalyptique adopté naguère en philosophie.* Paris: Editions Galilée. "Of an Apocalyptic Tone Recently Adopted in Philosophy." Translated by John P. Leavey, Jr. *The Oxford Literary Review,* vol. 6, no. 2 (1984), pp. 3–37. [This is the text of Derrida's lecture presented at the colloquium devoted to his work held at Cerisy-la-Salle in 1980. It was first printed in the volume of the proceedings from that colloquium: *Les fins de l'homme: À partir du travail de Jacques Derrida.* Edited by Philippe Lacoue-Labarthe and Jean-Luc Nancy. Paris: Editions Galilée, 1981. This volume also contains interesting exchanges between Derrida and the other participants.]

"La langue et le discours de la méthode." *Recherches sur la philosophie et la langage,* no. 3, pp. 35–51. [Untranslated.]

"My Chances/*Mes chances:* A Rendez-Vous with Some Epicurean Stereophonies." Translated by Irene E. Harvey and Avital Ronell. In *Taking Chances: Derrida, Psychoanalysis, and Literature.* Edited by Joseph H. Smith and William Kerrigan. Baltimore: The Johns Hopkins University Press, 1984, pp. 1–32. "Mes chances: au rendez-vous de quelques stéréophonies épicuriennes" in *Cahiers Confrontation* no. 19 (1988). [An essay on the relations between psychoanalysis and telepathy; the volume of essays is integrally translated in the French journal.]

"The Principle of Reason: The University in the Eyes of Its Pupils." Translated by Catherine Porter and Edward P. Morris. *Diacritics,* vol. 13, no. 3, pp. 3–20. "Les pupilles de l'Université: Le principe de raison et l'idée de l'université." *Cahiers du Collège International de Philosophie,* no. 2 (1986), pp. 7–34.

"The Time of a Thesis: Punctuations." Translated by Kathleen McLaughlin. In *Philosophy in France Today.* Edited by Alan Montefiore. Cambridge: Cambridge University Press, 1983, pp. 34–50. [The text of Derrida's presentation at his thesis defense, June 1980; French version in *Du Droit à la philosophie* (1990).]

1984: "Bonnes volontés de puissance (une réponse à Hans-Georg Gadamer)." *Revue Internationale de Philosophie,* vol. 38, no. 151, pp. 341–43. "Three Questions to Hans-Georg Gadamer." In *Dialogue and Deconstruction: The Gadamer–Derrida Encounter.* Edited and translated by Diane P. Michelfelder and Richard E. Palmer. Albany: State University of New York Press, 1989. The same volume includes another text by Derrida, "Interpreting Signatures (Nietzsche/Heidegger): Two Questions." [A brief "encounter" with the leading spokesman of Heideggerian hermeneutics.]

"Languages and Institutions of Philosophy." Translated by Sylvia Söderlind et al. *Recherches Sémiotiques/Semiotic Inquiry,* vol. 4, no. 2, pp. 91–154. "Les langages et les institutions de la philosophie." *Texte: Revue de critique et de théorie littéraire,* no. 4, pp. 9–39.

"*Mochlos,* ou le conflit des facultés." *Philosophie,* no. 2, pp. 21–53. [English translation forthcoming in *Institutions.*]

"No Apocalypse, Not Now (full speed ahead, seven missiles, seven missives)." Translated by Catherine Porter and Philip Lewis. *Diacritics,* vol. 14, no. 2, pp. 20–31. The French text, "No Apocalypse, Not Now (à toute vitesse, sept missiles, sept missives)," is included in *Psyché;* see 1987. [The text of Derrida's lecture to a colloquium on "nuclear criticism."]

Signéponge/Signsponge. Bilingual edition. Translated by Richard Rand. New York: Columbia University Press. [On the poet Francis Ponge.

The complete French text of *Signéponge* was also published in 1988 by Editions du Seuil.]

"Voice II. . . ." Translated by Verena Andermatt Conley. *Boundary 2*, vol XII, no. 2, pp. 68–93. [Letter response to Conley's questions about "masculine"/"feminine" voice; a bilingual text.]

1985: A reading of the photo-novel *Droit de regards* by Marie-Françoise Plissart. Paris: Editions de Minuit. "Right of Inspection." Translated by David Wills. *Art & Text*, no. 32 (Autumn 1989), pp. 19–97.

"Le langage." In *Douze leçons de philosophie*. Edited by Christian Delacampagne. Paris: Editions de la Découverte, pp. 14–26. [A telephone "interview" and practical lesson in "speech acts"; translation forthcoming in *Negotiations*.]

"Popularités: Du droit à la philosophie du droit." Foreword to *Les Sauvages dans la cité: Auto-émancipation du peuple et instruction des prolétaires au XIXe siècle*. Paris: Champ Vallon, pp. 12–19. [On "popular" philosophy, with reference to Kant; translation forthcoming in *Institutions*.]

"Préjugés: Devant la loi." In *La faculté de juger*. Paris: Editions de Minuit, pp. 87–139. "Before the Law." Abridged translation by Avital Ronell. In *Kafka and the Contemporary Critical Performance: Centenary Readings*. Edited by Alan Udoff. Bloomington: Indiana University Press, 1987, pp. 128–49. [The text of Derrida's lecture, on a short story of Kafka's, presented at the Cerisy-la-Salle colloquium on the work of Jean-François Lyotard.]

"Des Tours de Babel." Translated by Joseph F. Graham. In *Difference in Translation*. Edited by Joseph F. Graham. Ithaca, N.Y.: Cornell University Press, pp. 165–248. [A bilingual edition. The French text is reprinted in *Psyche*; see 1987.]

1986: "Antinomies de la discipline philosophique: Lettre préface." In *La Grève des philosophes: Ecole et philosophie*. Paris: Osiris. [On certain antinomies, with reference to Kant, in the teaching of philosophy in the current university; translation forthcoming in *Institutions*.]

"But, beyond. . . ." Translated by Peggy Kamuf. *Critical Inquiry*, vol. 13 (Autumn), pp. 155–70. [No French edition; in the form of an open letter, Derrida replies to criticism of "Racism's Last Word" (see *Psyché*, 1987).]

"Declarations of Independence." Translated by Tom Keenan and Tom Pepper. *New Political Science*, no. 15 (Summer), pp. 7–15. [From a 1976 lecture at the University of Virginia on the American Declaration of Independence. The French text is included in *Otobiographies*; see entry for *L'Oreille de l'autre*, 1982.]

"Forcener le subjectile." In *Dessins et portraits d'Antonin Artaud*.

Edited by Jacques Derrida and Paule Thévenin. Paris: Gallimard. [English translation forthcoming.]

Mémoires for Paul de Man. Translated by Cecile Lindsay, Jonathan Culler, Eduardo Cadava, and Peggy Kamuf. New York: Columbia University Press (1st ed., 1986; revised and augmented edition, 1989.) [The text of three commemorative lectures written for Paul de Man after the latter's death in 1983; revised edition includes "Like the Sound of the Sea Deep Within a Shell" (first published 1988), which addresses the discovery, in 1987, of articles de Man wrote between 1940 and 1942 for a collaborationist newspaper in Brussels; see also "Biodegradables," 1989. The French edition, *Mémoires pour Paul de Man,* was published by Editions Galilée in 1988.]

Parages. Paris: Editions Galilée. [Collection of Derrida's essays on the *récits* of Maurice Blanchot. Includes, beside **"Living On: Border Lines"** (see 1979), "Pas," "Title (to be specified)," and "The Law of Genre." While "Pas" has yet to appear in English translation, "Title (to be specified)" has been translated by Tom Conley (*Sub-Stance* 31, 1981, pp. 5–22) and "The Law of Genre" by Avital Ronell (*Glyph* 7, 1980, pp. 176–232; reprinted in *Critical Inquiry,* vol. 7, no. 1, Autumn 1980, pp. 55–81).]

Schibboleth, pour Paul Celan. Paris: Editions Galilée. "Shibboleth." Translated by Joshua Wilner. In *Midrash and Literature.* Edited by Geoffrey Hartman and Sanford Budick. New Haven: Yale University Press, 1986, pp. 307–47.

1987: *De l'esprit: Heidegger et la question.* Paris: Editions Galilée. *Of Spirit: Heidegger and the Question.* Translated by Geoffrey Bennington and Rachel Bowlby. Chicago: University of Chicago Press, 1989.

"Chôra." In *Poikilia: Etudes offertes à Jean-Pierre Vernant.* Paris: Editions de l'EHESS, pp. 265–96. [Translation forthcoming; on the *chôra* mentioned in Plato's *Timaeus.* This text became the basis of Derrida's collaboration with the architect Peter Eisenman; see below, "Pourquoi Peter Eisenman. . . ."]

Feu la cendre. Paris: "Bibliothèque des voix," editions des femmes. [Polyphonic text in which Derrida mediates on the *cendres*—ashes, cinders—scattered throughout his other texts; accompanied by cassette recording of Derrida and the actress Carole Bouquet reading the text; not translated into English.]

Psyché: Inventions de l'autre. Paris: Galilée. A collection of 25 essays, most of which are listed here unless they appeared first in translation.

"Admiration de Nelson Mandela, ou les lois de la réflexion." "The Laws of Reflection: Nelson Mandela, in Admiration." Translated by Mary Ann Caws and Isabelle Lorenz. In *For Nelson Mandela.* Edited by Jacques Derrida and Mustapha Tlili. New

York: Seaver Books, 1987. [The latter volume is a translation of the book of essays offered to Nelson Mandela published first in Paris (Gallimard) in 1986.]

"L'aphorisme à contretemps." [Untranslated; on *Romeo and Juliette*.]

"Cinquante-deux aphorismes pour un avant-propos." "Fifty-Two Aphorisms for a Foreword." Translated by Andrew Benjamin. In *Proceedings of the Symposium on Deconstruction in Art and Architecture*. London: Academy Editions, 1988.

"Comment ne pas parler: Dénégations." "How To Avoid Speaking: Denials." Translated by Ken Frieden. In *Languages of the Unsayable: The Play of Negativity in Literature and Literary Theory*. Edited by Sanford Budick and Wolfgang Iser. New York: Columbia University Press, 1989, pp. 3–70. [On negative theology, particularly Master Eckhart.]

"Le dernier mot du racisme." "Racism's Last Word." Translated by Peggy Kamuf. *Critical Inquiry*, vol. 12 (1985), pp. 290–99. [Text commissioned by the Association of Artists of the World Against Apartheid for the catalogue of an itinerant exhibit of art works that will continue to be shown around the world until *apartheid* is abolished in South Africa. For some polemic concerning this text, see above, "But beyond . . . ," 1986.]

"Désistance." Preface to *Typography*, by Philippe Lacoue-Labarthe. Translated by Christopher Fynsk. Cambridge, Mass.: Harvard University Press, 1989.

"Des Tours de Babel." See 1985.

"En ce moment même dans cet ouvrage me voici." **"At This Very Moment in This Work Here I Am."** Translated by Ruben Berezdivin. In *Re-Reading Levinas*. Edited by Robert Bernasconi and Simon Critchley (forthcoming).

"Envoi." "Sending: On Representation." Abridged translation by Peter and Mary Ann Caws. *Social Research*, vol. 49, no. 2 (Summer 1982), pp. 294–326.

"Géopsychanalyse—et 'the rest of the world'." [The text of the opening lecture to a colloquium on psychoanalysis in Latin America; translation forthcoming in *Negotiations*.]

"*Geschlecht*: Différence sexuelle, différence ontologique." **"Geschlecht: Sexual Difference, Ontological Difference."** Translated by Ruben Berezdivin. *Research in Phenonomenology*, vol. 13 (1983), pp. 65–83.

"Une idée de Flaubert: La lettre de Platon." "An Idea of Flaubert: 'Plato's Letter'." Translated by Peter Starr. *MLN*, vol. 99 (Sept. 1984), pp. 748–68.

"Lettre à un ami japonais." **"Letter to a Japanese Friend."** Translated by David Wood and Andrew Benjamin. In *Derrida and Différance*. Edited by David Wood and Robert Bernasconi. Evanston Ill.: Northwestern University Press, 1988, pp. 1–5.

"La main de Heidegger: (*Geschlecht* II)." "*Geschlecht* II: Heidegger's Hand." Translated by John P. Leavey, Jr. In *Deconstruction and Philosophy: The Texts of Jacques Derrida.* Edited by John Sallis. Chicago: University of Chicago Press, 1987, pp. 161–96.

"Moi—la psychanalyse." See 1978.

"Les Morts de Roland Barthes." "The Deaths of Roland Barthes." Translated by Pascale-Anne Brault and Michael Nass. In *Continental Philosophy I: Philosophy and Non-Philosophy Since Merleau-Ponty.* Edited by Hugh J. Silverman. New York and London: Routledge, 1988, pp. 259–97. [Essay first published in a memorial issue of the review *Poétique.*]

"No Apocalypse, Not Now (à toute vitesse, sept missiles, sept missives)." See 1984.

"Nombre de oui." "A Number of Yes." Translated by Brian Holmes. *Qui Parle,* vol. 2, no. 2 (Fall 1988), pp. 120–33. [Originally published in a memorial volume for Michel de Certeau.]

"Point de folie—maintenant l'architecture." English translation (same title) by Kate Linker. In Bernard Tschumi, *La Case vide.* London: Architectural Association, Folio VIII. [On the architectural plans of Bernard Tschumi for the Parc de la Villette in Paris; Derrida collaborated with the American architect Peter Eisenman for this project.]

"Pourquoi Peter Eisenman écrit de si bons livres." "Why Peter Eisenman Writes Such Good Books." Translated by Sarah Whiting. In *Architecture and Urbanism* [Tokyo], August, 1988, pp. 113–24. [On the collaboration with architect Eisenman for the design of a garden at the Parc de la Villette; see above, "Point de folie . . . ," 1986, and "Chôra," 1987.]

"Psyché: Invention de l'autre." **"Psyche: Inventions of the Other."** Translated by Catherine Porter. In *Reading de Man Reading.* Edited by Wlad Godzich and Lindsay Waters. Minneapolis: University of Minnesota Press, 1989.

"Le retrait de la métaphore." "The *Retrait* of Metaphor." Translated by F. Gasdner et al. *Enclitic,* vol. 2, no. 2, pp. 5–33. [A supplement to "The White Mythology" (*Marges,* 1972); on Heidegger and metaphor.]

"Télépathie." "Telepathy." Translated by Nicholas Royle. *The Oxford Literary Review,* vol. 10, nos. 1–2 (1988), pp. 3–41. [A "postscript" to **"Envois"** in *The Post Card.*]

Ulysse Gramophone: Deux mots pour Joyce. Paris: Editions Galilée. [The translations of the two essays on Joyce have been published separately: "Two Words for Joyce." Translated by Geoff Bennington. In *Post-Structuralist Joyce: Essays from the French.* Edited by Derek Attridge and Daniel Ferrer. Cambridge: Cambridge University Press, 1984, pp. 145–58. And **"Ulysses Gramophone: Hear Say Yes in Joyce."** Translated by Tina Kendall and Shari Benstock. In *James Joyce: The Augmented Ninth.* Edited by Bernard Benstock. Syracuse, N.Y.: Syracuse University Press, 1988, pp. 27–75.]

1988: **"Che cos'è la poesia."** In *Poesia* (Milan), vol. 1, no. 11, pp. 5–10. Translated by Peggy Kamuf in *A Derrida Reader.* New York: Columbia University Press, 1991.

"Interview with Jacques Derrida (by Jean-Luc Nancy)." Translated by Peter T. Connor. *Topoi,* vol. 7, no. 2, pp. 113–121. [The longer French version of this interview is titled " 'Il faut bien manger', ou le calcul du sujet," *Cahiers Confrontation* 20 (1989), pp. 91–114.]

"The Politics of Friendship." Translated by Gabriel Motzkin. *The Journal of Philosophy,* vol. 85, no. 11, pp. 632–45. [No published French text.]

1989: "Biodegradables: Seven Diary Fragments." Translated by Peggy Kamuf. *Critical Inquiry,* vol. 15, no. 4, pp. 812–73. [Derrida's response to a number of critical replies to the essay "Like the Sound of the Sea . . ." on Paul de Man's wartime journalism (see *Mémoires,* 1986); no published French text.]

"Rhétorique de la drogue." *Autrement,* no. 106. [Derrida responds to questions for a special issue of this review titled *L'Esprit des drogues;* untranslated.]

"Toward an Ethic of Discussion." Translated by Samuel Weber. In *Limited Inc.* [An afterword to the debate with John Searle; see above, 1977.]

1990: *Du Droit à la philosophie.* Paris: Galilée. [A collection of essays, many of which are listed above, on the institution and teaching of philosophy.]

Mémoires d'aveugle, L'autoportrait et autres ruines. Paris: Reúnion des Musées Nationaux. [The text for an exhibition of drawings at the Louvre.]

Le Problème de la genèse dans la philosophie de Husserl. Presses Universitaires de France. [The first publication of Derrida's master's thesis from 1954.]

"Some Statements and Truisms about Neologisms, Newisms, Postisms, Parasitisms, and Other Small Seismisms." Translated by Anne Tomiche. In *The States of "Theory."* Edited by David Carrol. New York: Columbia University Press, pp. 63–94.

Beside the written interviews included in the above list, Derrida has given a number of informal interviews for publication, some of which have been translated into English. Once again, this list is not exhaustive.

1983: "Derrida l'insoumis." *Le Nouvel observateur*, September 9, pp. 62–67; interview with Catherine David. "Interview with Derrida." Translated by David Allison et al. In *Derrida and Différance*. Edited by David Wood and Robert Bernasconi. Evanston, Ill.: Northwestern University Press, 1988, pp. 71–82.

1984: "Deconstruction and the Other." In *Dialogues with Contemporary Continental Thinkers: The Phenomenological Heritage*. Edited by Richard Kearney. Manchester: Manchester University Press, pp. 105–26.

"Women in the Beehive: A Seminar with Jacques Derrida." *subjects/objects* (Spring). Reprinted in *Men in Feminism*. Edited by Alice Jardine and Paul Smith. New York and London: Methuen, 1987, pp. 189–203.

1987: "Deconstruction in America." An interview with James Creech, Peggy Kamuf, and Jane Todd. Translated by James Creech. In *Critical Exchange*, no. 17 (Winter), pp. 1–33.

Interview with Imre Salusinszky. In *Criticism in Society*. Edited by Imre Salusinszky. New York and London: Methuen, 1987, pp. 9–24.

"Some Questions and Responses." In *The Linguistics of Writing: Arguments Between Language and Literature*. Edited by Nigel Fabb, Derek Attridge, Alan Durant, and Colin MacCabe. Manchester: Manchester University Press, 1987, pp. 252–64.

1989: "Jacques Derrida in Conversation with Christopher Norris." *Architectural Design*, vol. 58, nos. 1–2, pp. 6–11.

Selected Works on Jacques Derrida

and Deconstruction

The principle of selection for the following list is availability to readers of English and French. I have listed only a handful of the hundreds of separate essays in journals or collections; otherwise the entries are restricted to monographs, anthologies, and special issues of journals.

Arac, Jonathan, Wlad Godzich, and W. Martin, eds. *The Yale Critics: Deconstruction in America*. Minneapolis: University of Minnesota Press, 1983.

L'Arc, no. 54 (1973). "Jacques Derrida" (in French).

Bennington, Geoffrey. "Deconstruction and the Philosophers (The Very Idea)." *Oxford Literary Review*, vol. 10, nos. 1–2 (1988).

Berman, Art. *From the New Criticism to Deconstruction: The Reception of Structuralism and Post-Structuralism*. Urbana and Chicago: University of Illinois Press, 1988.

Brunette, Peter and David Wills. *Screenplay: Derrida and Film Theory*. Princeton: Princeton University Press, 1989.

Caputo, John D. *Radical Hermeneutics: Deconstruction and the Hermeneutic Project*. Bloomington: Indiana University Press, 1987.

Carroll, David. *Paraesthetics: Foucault, Lyotard, Derrida*. New York and London: Methuen, 1987.

Culler, Jonathan. "Jacques Derrida." In John Sturrock, ed., *Structuralism and Since: From Lévi-Strauss to Derrida*. Oxford: Oxford University Press, 1979.

——*On Deconstruction: Theory and Criticism After Structuralism*. Ithaca, N.Y.: Cornell University Press, 1982.

Dasenbrock, Reed Way, ed. *Redrawing the Lines: Analytic Philosophy, Deconstruction, and Literary Theory*. Minneapolis: University of Minnesota Press, 1989.

Diacritics, vol. 15, no. 4 (Winter 1985). "Marx after Derrida."

Ecarts: Quatre essais à propos de Derrida. Paris: Fayard, 1983.

Fish, Stanley. "With the Compliments of the Author: Reflections on Austin and Derrida." *Critical Inquiry*, vol. 8, no. 4 (1982).

Frow, J. "Foucault and Derrida." *Raritan*, vol. 5, no. 1 (1985).

Gasché, Rodolphe. "Deconstruction as Criticism." *Glyph* 6 (1979).

—— *The Tain of the Mirror: Derrida and the Philosophy of Reflection.* Cambridge, Mass.: Harvard University Press, 1986.

Genre, vol. 17, nos. 1–2 (Spring–Summer 1984). "Deconstruction at Yale."

Giovannangeli, D. *Ecriture et répétition: Approche de Derrida.* Paris: Union Générale d'Editions, 1979.

Hartman, Geoffrey. *Saving the Text: Literature/Derrida/Philosophy.* Baltimore, Md.: The Johns Hopkins University Press, 1981.

Harvey, Irene E. *Derrida and the Economy of Difference.* Bloomington: Indiana University Press, 1986.

Johnson, Barbara. "Introduction" to *Dissemination*, translated by Barbara Johnson. Chicago, Ill.: University of Chicago Press, 1981.

The Journal of the British Society for Phenomenology, vol. 17, no. 3 (October 1986). "The Philosophy of Jacques Derrida."

Kerrigan, William and Joseph H. Smith, eds. *Taking Chances: Derrida, Psychoanalysis, and Literature.* Baltimore: The Johns Hopkins University Press, 1984.

Klein, Richard. "Prolegomenon to Derrida." *Diacritics*, vol. 2, no. 4 (1972).

Kofman, Sarah. *Lectures de Derrida.* Paris: Galilée, 1984.

Krupnick, Mark, ed. *Displacement: Derrida and After.* Bloomington: Indiana University Press, 1983.

Lacoue-Labarthe, Philippe and Jean-Luc Nancy, eds. *Les fins de l'homme: À partir du travail de Jacques Derrida.* Paris: Galilée, 1981.

Leavey, John P., Jr. *Glassary.* Lincoln: University of Nebraska Press, 1986.

Laruelle, Jean-François. *Les Philosophies de la différence.* Paris: Presses Universitaires de France, 1986.

Leitch, Vincent B. *Deconstructive Criticism: An Advanced Introduction.* New York: Columbia University Press, 1983.

Llewelyn, John. *Derrida on the Threshold of Sense.* London: Macmillan, 1986.

Maclean, Ian. "Un dialogue de sourds? Some Implications of the Austin–Searle–Derrida Debate." *Paragraph* 5 (March 1985).

Melville, Stephen W. *Philosophy Beside Itself: On Deconstruction and Modernism.* Minneapolis: University Of Minnesota Press, 1986.

Michelfelder, Diane P. and Richard E. Palmer, eds. *Dialogue and Deconstruction: The Gadamer–Derrida Encounter.* Albany: State University of New York Press, 1989.

Muller, John P. and William J. Richardson, eds. *The Purloined Poe: Lacan, Derrida, and Psychoanalytic Reading.* Baltimore, Md.: The Johns Hopkins University Press, 1988.

Norris, Christopher. *Deconstruction: Theory and Practice.* London and New York: Methuen, 1982.

—— *Derrida.* Cambridge, Mass.: Harvard University Press, 1987.

The Oxford Literary Review, vol. 3, no. 2 (1978). "Derrida."

Research in Phenomenology, no. 8 (1978). "Reading(s) of Jacques Derrida." [Contains "A Derrida Bibliography" by John P. Leavey, Jr., and David Allison.]

Rapaport, Herman. *Heidegger and Derrida: Reflections on Time and Language.* Lincoln: University of Nebraska Press, 1989.

Ray, William. *Literary Meaning: From Phenomenology to Deconstruction.* Oxford: Basil Blackwell, 1984.

La Revue philosophique de la France et de l'Etranger, Special Issue "Derrida," April–June, 1990.

Rorty, Richard. "Philosophy as a Kind of Writing: An Essay on Derrida." *New Literary History,* vol. 10, no. 1 (1978).

Ryan, Michael. *Marxism and Deconstruction: A Critical Articulation.* Baltimore, Md.: The Johns Hopkins University Press, 1982.

Staten, Henry. *Wittgenstein and Derrida.* Lincoln: University of Nebraska Press, 1984.

Taylor, Mark. *Erring: A Postmodern A/theology.* Chicago, Ill.: University of Chicago Press, 1984.

Sallis, John, ed. *Deconstruction and Philosophy: The Texts of Jacques Derrida.* Chicago, Ill.: University of Chicago Press, 1987.

Silverman, Hugh J., ed. *Continental Philosophy II: Derrida and Deconstruction.* London and New York: Routledge, 1984.

Silverman, Hugh J. and Don Ihde, eds. *Hermeneutics and Deconstruction.* Albany: State University of New York Press, 1985.

Sub-stance, no. 7 (Fall 1973). "Literature . . . and Philosophy? The Dissemination of Derrida."

Ulmer, Gregory L. *Applied Grammatology: Post(e)-Pedagogy from Jacques Derrida to Joseph Beuys.* Baltimore, Md.: The Johns Hopkins University Press, 1985.

——"Sounding the Unconscious." In John P. Leavey, Jr., *Glassary.* Lincoln: University of Nebraska Press, 1986.

Weber, Samuel. *Institution and Interpretation.* Minneapolis: University of Minnesota Press, 1987.

Wood, David. *The Deconstruction of Time.* Atlantic Highlands, N.J.: The Humanities Press, 1989.

——"An Introduction to Derrida." *Radical Philosophy,* no. 21 (1979), pp. 18–28.

Wood, David and Robert Bernasconi. *Derrida and "Différance."* Evanston, Ill.: Northwestern University Press, 1988.

Index of Works by Jacques Derrida

Boldface page numbers indicate selections in this volume.

Index

This index contains more than one "fictional" entry (e.g., presence, inscription, unconscious [!]). The reader is advised, in those cases, to consider page references as indicating some sample locations.